A
FOREST
ON
MANY
STEMS

A FOREST ON MANY STEMS

ESSAYS
ON THE
POET'S NOVEL

EDITED BY
LAYNIE BROWNE

NIGHTBOAT BOOKS
NEW YORK

Copyright © 2021 by Nightboat Books
Introduction and editing by Laynie Browne
All rights reserved
Printed in the United States
ISBN: 978-1-64362-025-1
Cover art by: Noah Saterstrom
Design & typesetting: adam b. bohannon & Kit Schluter
Text set in Adobe Text Pro & Gotham

Cataloging-in-publication data is available from the Library of Congress
Nightboat Books
New York
www.nightboat.org

Then from a great disturbance
The most delicate message accumulates
But you must know why you write a novel, said Vodonoy
It's not to displace anything
It has context and metronome
By insisting on a comprehension of every word I am free to
    signify place though not represent it
So I must oppose the opposition of poetry to prose

—Lyn Hejinian, from *Oxota*

CONTENTS

V. Portrait / Documentary / Representation / Palimpsest

VI. Metamorphic / Distance / Aural Address / Wandering

ALPHABETICAL CONTENTS

Introduction
The Poet's Novel: A Form of Refusal

LAYNIE BROWNE

Molière famously writes, "Everything that is not prose is verse, and every-thing that is not verse is prose." His wit points to the absurdity of drawing absolute lines between genres. I approach this anthology with a similar in-tent and ultimate refusal to separate texts into categories. Is there such a thing as a poet's novel? Lyn Hejinian writes in *Oxota: A Short Russian Novel*, "So I must oppose the opposition of poetry to prose" (93). What I propose with this collection is to bring focus to many works which resist label or category, and to draw attention to a form about which little has been artic-ulated. Some of these works have been overlooked because they are hybrid, cross-genre texts, or simply because they are uniquely and utterly without precedent. Many illuminate the poetry, or encourage the work of the poet which follows. Rilke writes in a letter regarding his *Notebooks of Malte Lau-rids Brigge*, "My new book whose firm, close-grained prose is like a school and an advance that had to come so as to enable me, sometime later to write all the others . . ." (49). Regardless of what has enabled them, the primary reason for this collection is the works themselves, by whatever names one wishes to call them. The books discussed in this collection are incompara-ble, extraordinary works of innovative prose by poets.

The poet's novel is both a refusal to choose one form over another, and an adamant acceptance of the possibility of a singular form forged by dual impulses. The appeal of the poet's novel is the liberty not to choose. This collection's epigram, "Context & Metronome" taken from Hejinian's *Oxo-ta*, illustrates such resistance: the texts discussed successfully meld *context*, which suggests borders, history and narrative, with *metronome*, which sug-gests musicality, register, formal restraints and adherence to a set of careful-ly chosen processes that may or may not be disclosed to a reader.

The texts represented in this book are the result of writers who are not content to reside in the known, who in the face of limitation of one form will create another. The leap from one textual behavior to another suggests an emphasis on process, and an impulse against completion in favor of detour, fracture, digression, displacement and discontinuity. Rosmarie Waldrop writes in the introduction to her novel *The Hanky of Pippin's Daughter*, "My novel would have to stake its progress on not knowing where it was going" (xi). Instead of bringing expectations to the text a reader is pressed to listen. As Nicole Brossard writes in her introduction to *Blue Books*, "Everything I intuited, though I hadn't the words to express it, vigorously drove me towards poetry but also towards fiction, into that disturbing zone where the unimaginable and the unthinkable find, if not an explanation, then at least a haven compatible with the vertigo at their source" (9-10).

If there is such a thing as a poet's novel, how to explore some of the various forms it may take? What are the qualities of prose that tend to be classified as those of a poet's novel? Why do poets turn to prose? And within the oeuvre of any given writer (one who writes both poetry and prose) what is the relationship between the two forms? What purposes does prose fill that poetry perhaps does not? I began asking these questions when I noted that certain novels are indispensible to poets. Of these, there are various categories and one is novels *not* written by poets, but which behave nonetheless in some manner like poems. A few that come to mind are Virginia Woolf's, *The Waves*, Proust's *In Search of Lost Time*, Melville's *Moby Dick,* Djuna Barnes' *Nightwood* and Clarice Lispector's *Agua Viva*. Then there is the category of novels written by poets that are in some ways are indistinguishable from poems. In this second category I place the texts in this collection.

What does it mean for a novel to behave like a poem? Some departures from normative narrative prose include parataxis, collage, repetition, cut-up, appropriation, re-framing and associative and sound based momentum. If one can count upon a conventional novel not to leave a reader stranded, a poet's novel is less accommodating. Narrative becomes a looming question or an undomesticated animal, in the sense that there is no expectation for neatness, action, linear movement, or conclusion. Plot, along with expectations of probability and closure, is not held aloft as ideal. One does not know what an animal climbing in through one's window and under the bed, will do.

Why are poets enamored with texts that climb through windows and behave in peculiar manners enacting inscrutable designs? It may be that we desire the company of such texts because we cannot understand or justify their behavior. This makes them, like persons, compelling. The poet's novel stands up and yells something inappropriate during a public lecture. It might also remain in its seat quietly, yet describe the impulse to scream at various moments, whether or not it does so. Perhaps the poet's novel spends three hundred pages contemplating whether to scream. The inner life thus described is not a series of events. The poet's novel seeks to translate invisible gestures that occur all day, every day, akin to music, bodily breaking apart sensation, perception, and attempts to make sense of the myriad non-sensical happenings which surround us. And yet the opposite is also true. The poet's novel may be composed of the found, may have no wish to represent interior or even impressionistic or non-rational sense. In its refusal to participate in conventions the poet's novel sometimes depicts a *novel* realism, in which attempts are not made to provide a clear entrance or passage through the text. Such indeterminacy strongly encourages a reader to actively engage with language.

So potent are some of these works that they are best imbibed slowly. As Abigail Lang aptly notes in her essay on *The Great Fire of London,* one of Roubaud's aims is to create a work which avoids ending. He achieves this aim by providing multiple provisory endings. Thus, the reader is required to suspend a predetermined sequential progression. And this brings us to another way to describe the poet's novel. Along with suspension of conventional notions of plot, narrative, conflict and conclusion, a poet's novel has an entirely different relation to time. While most conventional novels tend to move forward in time, toward some impending action, the poet's novel has no such concern. Often the poet's novel instead illustrates how time behaves in the mind—not chronologically and not at all in an orderly manner. Repetition is a common device in poet's prose, as is a text that instead of propelling the reader forward, continually sends the reader back to question what comes before. Alice Notley writes, "Poetry tends to abolish time and present experience as dense and compressed. Prose is society's enabler, it collaborates with it in its linearity. A poem sends you back into itself repeatedly, a story leads you on."

How to describe the language of a poet's novel? It is impossible to generalize as the works discussed here are so various, yet the quality of attention to language is essential. A text may be written at the level of the book, chapter, paragraph, sentence, phrase, word, phoneme, or even the individual letter. Both the texture of language chosen, and the length of the units of composition are connected to the mobility or method of rhythm and movement in the text. In all of the texts discussed here attention to language is heightened and foregrounded to the extent that language itself, the medium in which the form is pronounced, becomes visible as material. This is not true in many conventional novels, in which language can be transparent to the extent that a reader may forget it entirely. Of course, one could argue that all writers pay attention to language, but perhaps with varying intent. Is the intent for language to carry an idea, a plot, a character? The question becomes to what degree does language itself becomes focal point, object of investigation, character, syntactical setting? To what extent is language aware of itself, as perceptual process?

In considering the poet's novel it is also useful to consider the poetic sentence (which may take the liberty to call a chapter, a paragraph or a monosyllabic utterance a *sentence*). And yet, regardless of length, it becomes pertinent here to note, as Silliman does in *The New Sentence* that ". . .the sentence is the hinge unit of any literary product" (78). Prose poems such as Stein's *Tender Buttons* undoubtedly inform the poet's prose of many of the writers in this collection in that it offers startling possibilities for narrative. Where else may we understand a handkerchief as, "A winning of all the blessings, a sample not a sample because there is no worry" (24). In Stein we are permitted to look for the narrative in each word, and the narrative implied between individual words: we are liberated from a dictated mode of creating meaning. Within each sentence, time is sealed, creating potential expansiveness and contractility. One can converse within or inhabit a poem, but a novel proceeding sentence by poetic sentence is generally more capacious. In Stein's *How To Write* we find a wide array of ways to consider the sentence. Among them: "What is the difference between a sentence and words. A sentence has been ample" (118). Ample does not necessarily imply great size, but the quality of space which allows for a concept to unfold and which may invoke process over product. A novel, even a poet's novel, can give one the sense of a roof over one's head. For that reason alone it is not surprising that so many poets have succumbed to this contradictory form.

In a profusion of recent innovative novels by poets, one may consider the sentence as that movable unit of composition that allows causal residence, an abode, a location. These works are characterized by the use of the sentence as an unorthodox, multi-valent dwelling. One may become happily lost in the strikingly original connective tissue or abrupt sentences in Peter Waterhouse's poem / novel *Language, Death, Night, Outside*, in which each word is a potential transit. Or one may meander in the languid sentences in Bolaño's *Antwerp*. He writes, "The images set off down the road and yet they never get anywhere, they're simply lost, says the voice—and the hunchback asks himself, hopeless for who?" (18). With the intent of a poet, the sentence becomes a place to reside, to question, and in itself, a form to untangle. Each sentence may intuit an intricate world, a tiny novel or prose poem. This density and unabashed celebration of language as a material is a refuge from the whirlwind of novels in which one is propelled by story to come to the end of things. Desire to know what happens, instead of being a catalytic force turning pages, becomes a journey within each sentence, thus suspended more slowly. An elaborate poetic sentence is like the concentration of deliberate stillness in which much interior movement takes place. To see the movement one has to do more than read. One has to peer into the sentence, look through its many windows. This is the concentration necessitated in reading a poet's novel, a world we might miss entirely if we do not stop to ask, where is the window? Where is the door? Which word or words or pause become transit? May I climb onto the roof and gaze through the chinks that need patching? Thus the reader becomes at once acrobat, astute upon ladders, a tree-climbing, parachuting visitor. How to arrive, how to enter, wondering always about vantage, and a carefulness in approach? Waterhouse writes, "What did not express itself, was silent over there, but sounded here, seen from the railroad embankment, like the text of an invitation, like speaking to, pulling toward, saving a place for" (115).

I have arranged this collection with the intent to illustrate various engines or mobilizing aspects of the poet's novel. For ease of locating authors an alternate alphabetical table of contents is also included. Each section is named in an attempt to reflect the complexity of the works. Texts are grouped into the sections according to one dominant impulse in the piece so that readers can begin to consider various approaches to the form. I'll say a brief word about each section here. The first section: *The Verse Novel*, reflects the oldest form of the poet's novel, which persists to this day and consists of works entirely in verse, such as Browning's *Aurora Leigh*, as well as works which move fluidly between verse and prose such as Notley's *Culture of One*. The second section, *Genre Mash-ups*, is perhaps the most various as it includes texts which begin with a specific sub-genre of fiction, such as in Berrigan's *Clear the Range*, which uses a cowboy pulp novel as found material, or Spicer's Detective Novel *The Tower of Babel*. In this section, texts work to disrupt, celebrate, parody, cut-up or reinvent genre. The third section is *Interior Lyric / Displacement / Cartographic Time*. In this section the lyric is informed by elements such as a focus on intricate structure, as in Christensen's *Azorno*, and in mapping relation of interior to geography as in Creeley's *The Island*. The fourth section, *Prose Poem / Concatenation / Novel Borders*, includes texts that extend the impulse of the prose poem, as in Adán's *The Cardboard House*, in which each section could read as an individual prose poem and yet the entire book also reads like a novel. The fifth section *Portrait / Documentary / Representation / Palimpsest* is also quite various. It includes Thalia Field's operatic novel *Ululu*, a wildly inventive archetypal portrait, as well as NourbeSe Philip's time traveling interrogation of silence in *Looking For Livingstone*. The fifth section: *Metamorphic / Distance / Aural Address / Wandering* includes epistolary impulse in Mackey's *From a Broken Bottle Traces of Perfume Still Emanate* as well as the lexical wanderings of W.G. Sebald in *Rings of Saturn*. Wandering suggests a rejection of closure. A multiplicity of meanings is created by various techniques such as alexia or "word blindness" incorporated as a method by Scalapino in *The Dihedrons Gazelle-Dihedrals Zoom,* or the use of individual words as transits in Waterhouse. The final section, *Identification / Dissolution / Polemic / Bildungsroman* contains novels by Pamela Lu, Juliana Spahr, Renee Gladman and others, in which identity is sought not as endpoint or static frame, but as defining process and an exploration of relationships forged between language and cultural architectures.

On omissions, if I had included every poet's novel I wished to include here, the length of this book would deem it unprintable. Further, my interests are too various for a neat and orderly assemblage or even an argument for why some texts and not others. I can only say, these works in particular, the works in themselves, are the reason for this book. Because many of these works do not fit neatly into categories, many have not received the attention they deserve. I hope that this anthology can serve as a corrective. This collection represents a particular and incomplete vision to which I hope others will add. In the process of selecting texts, I did devise a few criteria that provided defining boundaries. For the most part, the writers represented in this collection are identified primarily as poets. I did not include memoir, or creative non-fiction prose. Although new and wonderful novels by poets keep appearing I did not consider any texts published later than 2011. As an editor I aspire to create a commons for scholarship, artistic expression, debate, and a proliferation of new writing. I am indebted to the contributors of this book for crucial work in bringing this particular list of texts to light.

These essays are written by poets, and the approaches taken are as diverse as the poets themselves. From Laura Moriarty we have an impressive complete catalogue and analysis of "light" in Keith Waldrop's, *Light While There Is Light.* From Norma Cole we have a series of letters written to poet Stacy Doris on Emmanuel Hocquard's *AEREA dans les forêts de Manhattan.* Brandon Brown considers the oeuvre of Kevin Killian's reviews as a type of "epic" or sprawling expansive novel. Contributors to this text are fantastic writers who bring what poets uniquely may bring: acute insights, surprising approach and creative vision. They come to these challenging texts with the dual perspective of writer and reader. My hope is that the essays in this collection provide insight into the relationship between poetry and prose, motivations for the movement between the two forms, and above all entrances to these remarkable texts. The title of this book is taken from Leslie Scalapino's volume *The Dihedrons Gazelle-dihedrals Zoom.* In keeping with her visionary originality, generosity and prolific body of work, *A Forest on Many Stems* suggests a collective organic space infused with optimism. This anthology is an attempt to raise a common abode for enlivening conversations between writers and texts which are sustaining sources of creative growth. One could argue that poets will always court the uncategorizable, respond to the uniqueness of the present, and resist predictability. The power to change form is one of the most irresistible freedoms. Often an initial invisibility is akin to a form of triumph.

WORKS CITED

Bolaño, Roberto, *Antwerp*, Trans. Natasha Wimmer. New York: New Directions, 2010. Print.

Brossard, Nicole, *The Blue Books*, Toronto: Coach House Books, 2003. Print.

Hejinian, Lyn. *Oxota*, Great Barrington, Mass: The Figures, 1991. Print.

Molière, *Le Bourgeois Gentilhomme*, Act II, sc. iv. 2008.

Notley, Alice, "A Conversation with Alice Notley on the Poet's Novel" Interview with Laynie Browne: *Jacket* 2. 15 Mar. 2013. Web.

Rilke, Rainer Maria, Selected Letters 1902-1926. Trans. R.F.C. Hull. London: Quartet Books, 1988. Print.

Silliman, Ron, *The New Sentence*, New York: Roof Books, 1989. Print.

Stein, Gertrude, *How to Write*, Paris: Plain Editions. 1931. New York: Dover Books, 1975. Print.

Stein, Gertude, *Tender Buttons*, New York: Claire Marie, 1914, Gertrude Stein, *Writings 1932—1946* (New York: Library of America, 1998). Los Angeles: Sun & Moon, 1990. Print.

Waterhouse, Peter, *Language Death Night Outside*, trans. Rosmarie Waldrop. Providence, RI: Burning Deck. 2009. Print.

Waldrop, Rosmarie, *The Hanky of Pippin's Daughter* in *Two Novels by Rosmarie Waldrop*. Evanston: Northwestern University Press: 2001. Print.

I

VERSE NOVEL

Poetry tells me I'm dead; prose pretends I'm not
—ALICE NOTLEY, *Culture of One*

"You Cannot Count That You Should Weep For This Account"
Aurora Leigh And The Problem Of Math

ANNE BOYER

The decade in which Elizabeth Barrett Browning wrote *Aurora Leigh* was a decade of revolution and reaction, of common tragedy and of friendships intensified by vital literary and political possibility. In 1846, Elizabeth Barrett Browning wrote to Robert Browning that she wanted to create a "completely modern" novel-poem but was still searching for its subject. In 1847, the Brownings moved to Florence, and the American philosopher Margaret Fuller, also visiting Italy, fell in love with the revolutionary Count Ossoli. In 1848, the revolutions flare across Europe, and the new baby Ossoli-Fuller is born and sent to the countryside so Fuller could help the revolutionary cause. In 1850, Barrett Browning and Fuller became close friends. Barrett Browning suffered her fourth miscarriage. Fuller and the Count and the baby and Fuller's book on revolutions soon drown in a ship-wreck of the coast of Fire Island, a ship-wreck foretold by Fuller herself—"my life proceeds as regularly as the fates of a Greek tragedy, and I can but accept the pages as they turn."

It is not until 1856 that the "completely modern" novel-poem, *Aurora Leigh*, is published, and in it, we find its eponymous heroine looking exactly like Margaret Fuller and Margaret Fuller now looking like the epic "female genius" Aurora Leigh. This wasn't the first time the Fuller appeared posthumously as a character in the works of her friends. In 1852 she appeared as Zenobia, the spirited feminist at the Fourierist commune in Nathaniel Hawthorne's satiric *Blythsdale Romance*. Yet before Aurora Leigh was made into Margaret Fuller, of Margaret Fuller into Zenobia, Margaret Fuller was making herself into Germaine de Staël's "female genius" Corrine. Before Margaret Fuller was Corrine, Corrine was made from who wrote her—Germaine de Staël herself. Included in all of this—Elizabeth Barrett Browning as Aurora Leigh, too, as also Margaret Fuller as also Corrine as also Germaine de Staël as Corrine and everyone as Germaine de Staël—there is George Sand, who is also all of them, who Barrett Browning describes as "True genius, but true woman." Before Barrett Browning, Fuller, de Staël, Corrine, or Sand, is the Sibyl. This is the Sibyl's story:

An old woman came to the King with nine books. When she asked
the king to buy them, he refused: she went away and burned three of
them. Next the old woman came to the King with six books. When she
asked the King to buy these six for the same price she had asked for
the nine, he refused. She burned three more. When the old woman
returned with the last three books, she asked the same price she had
asked for the nine and had asked for the six. Intrigued by these books
which diminished in number but remained constant in value, the King
bought the remaining three, and when he opened them, he found the
old woman had written in these books the destiny of the state.

It is no accident that any work drawing from the character of the "American Sibyl" Margaret Fuller, who drew herself from the Sibyline character of
Corrine, would be written in the nine books of the Sibyl. "There were seasons," wrote Fuller's friends, " when she seemed borne irresistibly on to the
verge of prophecy, and fully embodied one's notion of a sibyl." It is also no
accident that these women "female geniuses" had a particularly Sibyline relationship to the future and the state. These were times in which revolution
made the west feel as foundational as early Rome, and the relation of these
early feminist writers to the erupting nationalisms and workers' struggles
were, in essence, almost always the Sibyl's "I told you so."
The nine books of the state are also not accidentally the number of
months involved in human gestation, and *Aurora Leigh*'s structure reflects
a highly intentional feminized calculation. The poem, however, is as often
about that which eludes calculation as that which can be precisely calculated. For the epic problem of *Aurora Leigh,* or one of them, is that she lives
in a time of math. Like many of her female intellectual peers of the Euro-American mid-19th century, *Aurora Leigh* is in love with, and in despair
of, and in conflict with a phalanstery-building Fourierest: "Romney Leigh,
who lives by diagrams / And crosses out the spontaneities / of his individual, personal life, / With formal universals." Even the "non-fictional" Fuller, while sympathetic to Fourier's aims, offers this critique, which in many
ways resembles a more subtle version of Aurora's: "Educated in an age of
gross materialism, Fourier is tainted by its faults; in attempts to reorganize
society, he commits the error of making soul the result of health of body,
instead of body the clothing of soul."
The problem Aurora faces is a problem of her era: what is a feminist poet
to do when in impossible love with a programmatic utopian, who thinks
the only thinking which can change the world is the thinking through of
systems in which the masses are materials to be moved? Aurora fears if she

would agree to marry such a man, she will be reduced to her materiality only: "he might cut / my body into coins to give away." She is a person who would like to retain an individual feeling in a time of systems; a person who would like to retain this newfound feminist-personhood in a time when nations formed and ambitious men had only dreams of what they could make new.

"All men," Aurora tells us, "are possible heroes: every age, / Heroic in proportions, double-faced, / Looks backward and before." *Aurora Leigh* is an epic poem, but because what Barrett Browning wanted to write was a "completely modern" epic, it is also must take the form popular, often feminized form of the "parlor" novel. The challenge of Barrett Browning's aspiration for a "completely modern" novel-poem is this: the times she was writing about were not in themselves yet entirely modern. In *Aurora Leigh*, what Browning calls the "double vision" of the poet involves perceiving a contradiction—looking two directions at once. Here, romanticism and a nascent modernism agitate each other at their edges.

Aurora's political life is her personal life.

Aurora knows that she is a poet, but Romney Leigh believes that women, for what he believes to be their inability to engage in systematic analysis, are incapable of sufficiently comprehending the world to either change it or make poetry of it:

> Your quick-breathed hearts,
> so sympathetic to the personal pang
> close on each separate knife stroke, yielding up
> a whole life at each wound . . . you gather up
> a few such cases, and when strong, sometimes
> will write of factories and of slaves, as if
> your father was a negro, and your son
> a spinner in the mills.

He continues:

> You cannot count
> That you should weep for this account, not you!
> You weep for what you know . . .
> You could as soon weep for the rule of three,
> Or compound fractions. Therefore, this same world,
> Uncomprehended by you, must remain
> Uninfluenced by you—Women as you are,

mere women, personal and passionate ... .
We get no Christ from you,—and verily
We shall not get a poet

As Romney indicts Aurora and all women that "cannot count" for "weeping for this account," so Aurora indicts Romney—that he is blind to the ways of poetry and to all which is non-material and incalculable: "Your Fouriers failed," she tells him, "because not poets enough to understand."

This debate between Romney and Aurora, that is between the programmatic male revolutionaries and the feminist thinkers, is not original to *Aurora Leigh*. Note its first articulation in de Staëls *Literature and its Relation to Social Institutions*. De Staël writes of the men of the French revolution:

These men thought they could simplify their calculations by omitting suffering, feeling, and imagination; they made no conception of the nature of general truths ... Calculation is neither good nor useful unless it recognizes all exceptions and regularizes all differences. If a single case is allowed to escape, the result will be false, just as the slightest numerical error makes the solution of a problem impossible.

Or as Aurora tells Romney: "I hold you will not compass your poor ends / of barley feeding and material ease, / without a poet's individualism / to work your universal."

In the invocation of *Aurora Leigh*, no muse is asked to sing: no hero appears. This is an epic, but in the place of bard and muse and hero is the individual woman who writes:

Of writing many books there is no end;
And I who have written much in prose and verse
For others' use will write now for mine, —

What Aurora writes is because of Aurora, and about Aurora, and for Aurora:

as when you paint your portrait for a friend
who keeps it in a drawer and looks at it
long after he has ceased to love you, just
to hold together what he was and is.

What does it mean for a woman to write an epic for herself as if painting a self-portrait for a male friend who has ceased to love her but who uses her self-produced image as an instrument of selfhood? These first eight lines announce *Aurora Leigh*'s epic content as a kind of multiplication: the hero of this epic does not speak, "of all the cities he saw, the minds he grasped, The suffering deep in his heart at sea," but instead of the contradictory and proliferating "female" self.

Aurora is a woman who lacks women ("I felt a mother-want about the world") and disappoints men ("I Aurora Leigh, was born / to make my father sadder"). Aurora is a woman who also makes herself "not overjoyous, truly," and so in this singular lack and double disappointment, Aurora is all things at once: the bard, the muse, the hero, and the reader—one who is as distant as a man who looks at an image of a woman he has ceased to love "to hold together what he is and was." Although the anti-invocation of *Aurora Leigh* would suggest that this is a poem intended to be intensely private, this very sense of privacy is the public content itself. Aurora performs the subjective, the individual, the private, but this is performance is an argument of example, for with *Aurora Leigh*, the epic expands and multiplies to include the questions of the contemporary:

> this live, throbbing age,
> that brawls, cheats, maddens, calculates, aspires,
> and spends more passion more heroic heat
> betwixt the mirrors of its drawing-rooms
> than Roland with his knights

Although *Aurora Leigh* is known as a "female epic," this is not, in fact, its primary nature— *Aurora Leigh* is not, first, a female epic, but a 19th century one. That is, any epic of the nineteenth century must also be the epic of the women question, and the question of work, and the question of the class struggle, and the question of romantic love and its relation to the marketplace and to gender, and so such content, of women's lives and work and market and love must be also in the form invented to tell such women's lives: the novel. In its form, *Aurora Leigh* is a similarly kind of wrestling between idealism and materialism, the feminine and the masculine, the individual and the collective, and the class struggle and the struggle of women.

Aurora Leigh is a form which had to invent itself to tell its story: it is an epic form which wrestles with the novel form which wrestles with the form of memoir and the memoir's wrestling with the elegy. In the end, nothing is resolve—not form, nor plot. Romney relents, now blind, and a "failed" leftist, who confesses "we talk by aggregates / and think by systems" and promises Aurora:

Fewer programmes, we who have no prescience.
Fewer systems, we who are held and do not hold.
Less mapping out of the masses, to be saved,
By nations or by sexes.

Aurora, for her part, who had always willfully resisted love, decides "Art is much, but love is more" and marries him.

In her attempt to be a poet whose "sole work is to represent the age / their age, not Charlemagne's," Barrett Browning has met the obstacle of the modern: her contemporary. For the "modernity" in which Barrett Browning writes is one caught in the contradictions of its period's reaching toward modernism: the one between its women, which seeks to expand romantic ideology to the female subject, and the male materialist reaction to Romanticism (and to "the feminine"). This poem novel, assembled in the teeming contradictions of mid-19th century Europe, is as if a machine made of the new, running on the fuel of the old. But its Romanticism, so importantly, is a counter-romanticism of the feminists, just as its modernism is also a counter-modernism of class struggle, and its form is a counter-form (no novel, no poem, no epic). It is a book about impossible fusion, that between women and men, genius and women, poetry and politics, individual sentiment and systematic analysis. Further, it is a book about the impossible fusions of form: it must make, at every turn, a claim for poetry as it veers frequently away from the poetic to the novelistic. It must make epic that which in its very nature resists all claims to the epic: the personal, the feminine, the romantic, the private. It must make a claim against romantic love all the while it tells the story of a romantic love. In this, the book remains as much of a told-you-so to the future, in which all these contradictions swell, to the state the book of Sibyl: for what is the problem of Aurora Leigh but the problem of feminist arithmetic: how can society make a new tomorrow from calculation when we have omitted half the numbers from our math?

Cane in the Classroom
Jean Toomer's Classic

JULIE PATTON

Some texts resonate so deeply within us that we never forget their haunting spaces. So we read them again and again, to ourselves and to others. This is what I do with Jean Toomer's *Cane*. Published in 1923, Cane is a seed-book at the root of modern American poetics, memorable for its striking language and rich, sensual imagery, and its alternation of prose vignettes and poems.

> Oracular
> Redolent of fermenting syrup,
> Purple of the dusk,
> Deep-rooted cane.

These lines from *Cane* describe intimate connections between a people and nature. People the color of caramel, oak leaves, gold glowing and deep purple ripened plums and pitch, immersed in their environment in a manner reminiscent of Hale Woodruff's *Cotton Pickers* (1941). This intermingling of ground and figure in *Cane* invites us to explore the relationship between humans and their environment, between language and place. Sugar cane forms the background of Toomer's text. His characters are steeped in cane, their lives tied to the slow motion grind of it, and rage at the boiling point:

> The scent of cane came from the copper pan and drenched forest and the hill that sloped to the factory town, beneath its fragrance. It drenched the men in circle seated around the stove. Some of them chewed at the white stalks, but there is no need for them to, if all they wanted was to taste the cane.

Everyone breathes this air; it colors the speech, thickens the tongue, and extends the southern drawl.

Toomer's lush stream of consciousness pulls us into a time and place that surges with the rhythm of a people trying to get a foothold. In this sense, *Cane* echoes the African diaspora: "The dixie pike has grown from a goat path in Africa." But Toomer focuses on another mass odyssey, that of black people to the big cities of the north. The reader is awash in this critical moment, the south-to-north migration of a group so held in limbo that contemporary African-American literature still holds this pattern between its teeth. The seasons and internal rhythms of the agrarian past come through in the work of Toni Morrison, Alice Walker, Zora Neale Hurston and Jamaica Kincaid. On the other hand, prose writers such as James Baldwin, Paul Beatty, Walter Mosely, and Ann Petry foreground urban conditions. *Cane* plays with this dichotomy. The north frames a largely male domain while the American south is conflated with nature and the fecundity of women.

> And when the wind is in the south, the soil of my homeland falls like a fertile shower upon the lean streets of the city.

In *Cane*, city and country, poetry and prose, male and female, dawn and dusk, black and white *appear to be* a space apart; but Toomer makes it clear that each informs or resonates the other. Some of my Harlem and South Bronx public school students trace a similarly alternating pattern. I can tell which ones hopscotch between South Carolina and Manhattan, Mexico or Puerto Rico and the Bronx: traces of these places show up in their vocabularies.

I read *Cane* to my students to provoke the creative writing impulse in them, but I have another motive as well. Like Toomer, I view writing as a potential nature preserve for endangered voices. Toomer wanted to articulate a future for a world facing extinction. Decrying the devastation of nature and some aspects of folk culture tied to land, he scored his memories of it into *Cane* as if the pages were another kind of earth, a field of view for preserving that world. Yet *Cane* is not a nostalgic lament for the segregated, sharecropper South, with its painfully oppressive conditions; it is an affirmation of the historical, cultural, and spiritual significance of a nation at a pivotal point in its history, faced with escalating industrialization.

> Red soil and sweet-gum tree
> So scant of grass
> So prolifigate of pines
> Now just before an epoch's sun declines.

In the Toomer poem "Song of the Son," the "son of the soil" returns to remind "a song-lit race of slaves" about the roots he fears they'll lose in city streets:

Though late, O soil, it is not too late yet
To catch thy plaintive soul, leaving soon gone . . .

Cane's characters live in close contact with the land because they are tied to it, yoked to the earth they sweat over and till. The enforced cutting of cane in the sharecropper South left a deep mark, another incision branding the skin of the so-called children of *Cane*. In this book, plum-dark women held forth against a blood-burning moon, people and earth change shapes in the dark. Life in *Cane* is not romantic or idealized. It is often oppressive, violent, and terrifying. People disappear under the cover of a darkness Toomer refuses to cloak his own identity in, as he insists on blurring the color lines, or "passing" in a world that *Cane*'s dusk-colored Karintha would never be allowed access to: "Her skin is like dusk on the eastern horizon."

The blurring of borders in *Cane* echoes the dreamy edges that poetry encourages: a migration of meaning, as in this poem by Michael Spann, a Harlem fourth grader, writing in response to hearing passages from *Cane*:

I find the chains of my ancestors and the underground railroad
A stair of broken wood-stack of stairs . . .
This is how they got out.
A big clear hit sky. There is no moon or stars. It is black out.
We light candles. As you come from the doctor it gets dark.
It's time to go home.
You sing and count plump sheep to go to sleep and have a red wobbled
    dream.

Like Elegba, the Yoruba trickster god, Toomer is always at a crossroads. He is the writer as nomad, searching for a deeper, more oneiric place of being, outside the identifying labels attached to an uprooted people. He is hell-bent on making a place out of a non-place, enclosing a space to be. He backtracks over the same words, the same scene, as if digging deeper to make a receptive space for others to live in as well.

People tend to read black literature for its sociological content and ignore its aesthetic achievement. Experts argue about which texts constitute an *authentic black experience* for children, and which authors should represent African American and which should not. Rich legacies are oversimplified, homogenized into sound-bytes everyone can chew on. (One such "expert" once informed me that the writing of many of my Harlem students wasn't "black enough.") I wrote about some related concerns in my teaching diary:

Hic sunt leones ("here there are lions") was the designation used by Renaissance cartographers to indicate unknown and unmapped corners of the world—the vanishing point they directed their imaginations toward. The contemporary "Inner city" conjures up a similarly forbidding terrain, with high walls and monsters sitting at the portals. Graffitied walls are presumed to be the disembodied voice of a culture echoing the fragmentation and dissolution of a community. I know first hand how language can carve up the city streets, dismember one's sense of home. I can recall when another designation first skirted the edges of the place I called home. The word *ghetto* hovered about our heads for years before finally settling down on them. I remember asking my mother what they called the turf she inhabited as youth. She said, "Oh, they just called it 'the neighborhood.'"

But language can enable us to re-site ourselves, renew and enrich our lives. Imaginative writing provides tools to reroute our lives in a different landscape of meaning and address.

In my workshops with young children, I read aloud to them, walking around the classroom, bearing down on specific words to instill a dreamy and mysterious atmosphere, going on Gaston Bachelard's assumption that "the best training for poets is achieved through reverie, which puts us in sympathy with words and substances."

ORATORS. Born one an I'll die one . . . Been shaping words t fit my soul. Never told y that before, did I? Thought I couldn't talk. I'll tell y. I've been shaping words; ah, but sometimes theyre beautiful an golden an have a taste that makes them fine t roll over with y tongue.

Past/oral? No. I read parts of *Cane* to my elementary school students for a variety of reasons: to steep them in listening, to call attention to Toomer's imaginative use of language, or simply to fill the room with startling images. Of course I skip over the earthier passages, but it doesn't matter, since I am not emphasizing narrative.

I jump-start one imaginative writing exercise by using my voice to highlight a vocabulary that will sensitize my students to their surroundings, seizing details in the passage that emphasize the fact that the city (in our case, New York) is also land.

Through the cement floor her strong roots sink down. They spread under the asphalt streets. Dreaming, the streets roll over on their bellies, and suck their glossy health from them. Her strong roots sink down and spread under the river and disappear in blood lines that waver south. Her roots shoot down.

In reading *Cane* aloud, I project certain words the way a painter dabs on color. *Boll weevils, dew, knolls, dusk, cotton-stalks,* and *pines* dot the landscape. *Cane* is perfectly scored for ear, and I read it as a background text before giving an imaginative writing exercise that focuses on the associations and meaning inherent in sound. We start with familiar *clouds, flower, rain, tree, pigeon,* etc. then move on to *mountain, forest, river,* (things that are absent from the city). I don't explain much, I simply urge my students to *listen* to each word, to *see* what it is trying to tell them, and to *notice* the shape and feel of the word in their mouths. Some words have a music, an inner mystery or depth that attracts the students, and they fall into mysterious words, contemplating them. I emphasize the idea that the world speaks and inscribes us in myriad ways. The children count the ways—trees "tell us" the seasons, deer and birds leave tracks we can trace, rivers babble, and rain rains.

Contemplating a certain word as both noun and verb introduces students to the idea that houses *house* us, clouds *cloud,* and rain definitely *rains,* and this prepares them for a writing process that underscores a particular word's journey; otherwise students often end up with static poems instead of complex, shifting ones. I read *Cane* beforehand to establish groundwork for this sense of movement. In any case, the students approach the assignment with the imperative of listening to a given word and thinking about what it does or about its impact on their lives. *Cloud, dusk, fern, rose,* or *snow.*

When I was a child, the "doing" words in my reader, *Skip Along,* were particularly inspiring. *Run, skip, hop.* There was something compelling about the fact that we were bombarded with "doing" words while anchored to our seats. *Come here . . . See my . . . Look up* always pointed to the outside world. The interplay between those commands and my own imagination made me leap, and I eagerly anticipated going outside to do all the thrilling things watercolor children and lithographed animals were engaged in all day long. But, as a visiting writer, I don't bring in childhood readers, I bring in literature that tumbles from my own shelves, even grown-up books such as *Cane.* I trust that the hop, skip, and jump of my students' minds can help span the distance.

In poetry, one can situate one unlikely thing next to another. Art accommodates the deviating paths, twists, and turns real life can't. The analogical curves and spirals of poetry counter the linear thinking that rules the classroom. In this sense, language is both a way of creating space and extending its margins.

Writing and reading go hand in hand, just as listening and spinning once did. I go from classroom to classroom. The ancient storyteller went from village to village. In my imaginative writing workshops, I observe similar relationship between work rhythms and stories. The students spin their own "yarns" before or after my delivery of *Cane*. Walter Benjamin said that storytelling was never a job for the voice alone; hands pick up the rhythm, lace, thread, or pound it into the work. To me, writing is a recovery of lost gestures. In my urban classrooms, the rhythm of the sewing needle is replaced by the rhythm of the pen, and "when the rhythm of work has seized [them]. [they] listen to the tales in such a way that the gift of retelling them comes to [them] all by itself" (Benjamin).

The joy of reading *Cane* to children is ultimately about the art of repeating stories. Call and response—the dialogue continues as contemporary urban culture bears witness and testifies to the intimacy of the human voice and human gestures. Thousands of schoolchildren have opened their ears to the fresh cadence of writers in the schools, such as June Jordan, Kurt Lampkin, Victor Hernández Cruz, Bernadette Mayer, Ron Padgett, Pedro Pietri, Grace Paley, Abiodun Oyewole, Wayne Providence, Janice Lowe, and others performing work that shores up distant voices in a new landscape of meaning. In *Cane*, many of my students hear speech rhythms that are akin to their own. Somewhere, inside the words, there's a pine-torched night punctuated by cries, yells, and whimpers that recall the voices of holy rollers or a wailing blues song. My reading of *Cane* emphasizes this sense of echo.

> Their voices rise . . . the pine trees are guitars,
> Strumming, pine needles fall like sheets of rain . . .
> Their voices rise . . . the chorus of cane

The alternation of prose and poetry and the persistent references to pine knots in *Cane* echo the culture of harvesting rituals:

> O Negro slaves, dark purple ripened plums
> Squeezed and bursting in the pine-wood air
> Pour O pour that parting soul in song,
> O pour it in the sawdust glow of night,
> Into the velvet pine-smoke air to night
> And let the valley carry it along

The lyrical patterns of *Cane* reverberate in African American music and poetry. In it we still hear the chant connecting distant bodies and continents, the relationship between body and speech in African work rhythms. And today's percussion-based rap is the banished talking drum beating an ancient meter and rhythm into a new language.

WORKS CITED

Bachelard, Gaston. *The Poetics of Space*. Maria Jolas, trans. Boston: Beacon, 1969.

Benjamin, Walter. *Illuminations*. Harry Zahn. New York: Schocken, 1969.

Toomer, Jean. *Cane*. New York: Liveright, 1975.

This essay was initially published in the book *Sing the Sun up: Creative Writing Ideas from African American Literature* edited by Lorenzo Thomas. Reprinted by permission of Teachers & Writers Collaborative.

The Monster in the Rotunda
Anne Carson's *Autobiography of Red*

SASHA STEENSEN

As soon as the word 'genre' is sounded . . . a limit is drawn . . . one must not cross a line of
demarcation, one must not risk impurity, anomaly, or monstrosity.

JACQUES DERRIDA

I was drawn to the Geryon story because of his monstrosity.

ANNE CARSON

The poet writing a novel crosses, as Derrida writes, the "line of demarcation" (205). She enters into new territory, but brings her poetic sensibilities
with her. Notice how quickly impurity becomes monstrosity. The hybrid is
a monster—something made impure by the mixing of two (or more) otherwise "pure" things. As readers, when genres are mixed, or even when writers generally associated with one genre stray into another, our interpretive
options are multiplied, and sometimes even confused. We might reach back
in search of some "pure" genre to situate the text at hand. There is, of course,
no such purity. But if there were, the original, the pure genre, would be
poetry. Poetry, after all, predates literacy; it existed before genres existed.

This is a decidedly western place to begin, but this essay addresses the
classicist poet Anne Carson, so we might as well begin with Plato. All poems, according to Plato, were "narrative" poems in which past, present or
future events were conveyed; thus Plato's three categories, often taken to be
the first generic delineations, emerged as a way to distinguish who was doing the narration. Poems in which characters were the only speakers were
dramatic poems ("supplied by comedy and tragedy"); the "opposite style,
in which my poet is the only speaker," Plato notes, was best illustrated by
the dithyrambic poem, and if both the poet and characters spoke, then we
were in the midst of an epic poem. But where was the lyric poem?[1] Thought
and emotion are not events, and so for many centuries, what we now call
the lyric poem escaped genre's grasp.

But Plato's omission goes beyond the fact that lyric poems are not, in
the strict sense of the word, narratives. Nor can we attribute this omission
to Plato's fear that the lyric poet's favorite subject—desire—might corrupt
the populace. After all, tragedians, comic poets, and epic poets concerned

themselves with this topic as well, and they were granted a place in Plato's taxonomy. It was *how* the lyric poet handled this subject that made her all the more dangerous (79). For Plato, poetry in which "the poet everywhere appears and never conceals himself... becomes simple narration." The poem narrated by the poet (rather than by a character) is a poem in which the poet is always present, never hidden, resulting in a narration that is simple, uncomplicated. But the lyric poet is always concealed, and her poem always complicated, by the lack intrinsic in language itself. In *Eros the Bittersweet,* Anne Carson writes,

> Writing about desire, the archaic poets made triangles with their words. Or, to put it less sharply, they represent situations that ought to involve two factors (lover, beloved) in terms of three (lover, beloved, and the space between them, however realized)... There is something essential to Eros here. The lyric poets caught its outline with sudden sharpness, and left that in the writing. (77)

Composing as they were in the period of early literacy when the newly adopted Phoenician alphabet was undergoing rapid transformation, Greek lyric poets were uniquely positioned to see the "edges of the units of language and the edges of those units called 'reader' and 'writer'" (ETB, 108). These edges must have reminded them of the edges between lover and beloved. This kind of awareness exceeds narration, and creates a third space that keeps reader and writer, lover and beloved, at a distance from one another. Carson calls this space Eros. By way of his or her "tactics of triangulation," the lyric poet points to Eros, perhaps even touches it (ETB, 79). This volatile space threatens Plato's polis, and so for many centuries, the lyric poet is happily banished to an island outside of genre.

The novel, too, will have to wait for its generic marker, but the novel and the lyric poem have something else in common as well. Carson tells us that the early Greek and Roman novelists "play out as dilemmas of plot and character all those facets of erotic contradiction and difficulty that were first brought to light in lyric poetry" (ETB, 79). If the difference between the archaic lyric poem and the early novels is not necessarily a difference of subject matter, nor is it simply a matter of metrics or lineation (or the lack thereof), is it then the insertion of "plot and character" into Eros's drama that differentiates the novel from the lyric poem? Can we say that lyric poems are without characters? Are there no lyric poems in which the speaker is at some distance from the author? And what about plot? In the early 1600's, Spaniard Francisco Cascales made the radical observation that the lyric poem has for its plot not an event, but a thought (Gennett, 30). Even if the lyric poem can be said to have a plot, thoughts are not as easily plotted as events. The lyric poem replaces Plato's "simple narration" with authorial self-reflection and a particular attention to the opaque nature of language itself, something less prevalent in the novel, the epic poem, or the dramatic poem.

What happens to this thought-plot when the lyric poet writes a novel? What shape does it take, and how does it keep and exceed this shape? There are as many (and more) answers to these questions as there are essays in this book, but Anne Carson likens her novel in verse to a building with a central room and several entrance and exit points. It is, as she says in a *Paris Review* interview, "the archaic lyric rotunda," and without interruption or prompting from the interviewer, she goes on to say, "I was drawn to the Geryon story because of his monstrosity." The plot, then, of this "Novel in Verse" is monstrosity, not just as a subject, but as a thought process. It takes the shape of a round, central room which cannot be viewed in its entirety. The corridors leading to and from this room provide a vantage point from which to glimpse Stesichoros's original lyric poem. It is tempting to view the forty-seven chapters which constitute Carson's imaginative remaking of the Geryon story as the rotunda, and the other material—the "proemium," Stesichoros's translated fragments, the testimonia, the syllogism, and the interview—as ancillary. But in the *Paris Review* interview, Carson is clear that she sees Stesichoros's original ancient poem *as* the inaccessible center. The other "angles" that she creates, including the "Romance" that makes up the majority of the book, are impassable thresholds that prompt the reader to consider not just who is telling the story, but how the story is told.

How the story is told depends, for the poet, on the nature of the story. Because so much of Stesichoros's poem has been lost, there is, in Carson's words, "no adequate representation of it I can give" (Interview). For the poet, "adequate representation" is an oxymoron. In *Economy of the Unlost*, Carson tells us that the poet " . . . feels a lack. He is provoked by a perception of absence within what others regard as a full and satisfactory present" (Carson, *Nox*). That which history has obscured is magnetic; it beckons the poet toward its ever-present absence. In turn, the poet searches for a form that might give shape to the particular lack she faces. Often this form is monstrous. Geryon is a monster—a red creature with wings. Stesichoros was drawn to him, and so is Carson. Each responded to his monstrosity unconventionally. In her proemium, "Red Meat: What Difference Did Stesichoros Make?" Carson writes:

If Stesichoros had been a more conventional poet he might have taken the point of view of Herakles and framed a thrilling account of the victory of culture over monstrosity. But instead the extant fragments of Stesichoros's poem offer a tantalizing cross section of scenes, both proud and pitiful, from Geryon's own experience . . . But that is enough proemium. You can answer for yourself 'What difference did Stesichoros make?' by considering his masterpiece . . . the fragments of the *Geryoneis* itself read as if Stesichoros had composed a substantial narrative poem then ripped it to pieces and buried the pieces in a box with some song lyrics and lecture notes and scraps of meat . . . Here. Shake" (6-7).

Stesichoros, faced with this monstrous story, unconventionally takes up the monster's point of view. Carson, faced with the inaccessibility of Stesichoros's text, responds unconventionally by multiplying access points rather than privileging one over the other and smoothing over the fissures. The poet, "provoked by a perception of absence," is not content with a story whose plot is merely a linear retelling of fully available event. "There were," Carson tells us in the proemium, "many different ways to tell a story like this" (5).

It seems prudent, before going any further, to take a walk around Carson's rotunda. The center remains always at a distance, visible, but somewhat obscured. As we circle this absent center, hugging the walls, we find seven alcoves, seven different vantage points from which to consider the question, "What Difference Did Stesichoros make?" Even before we set foot in this strange building, the façade—the title—alerts us that this book resists categorization. It is an autobiography of both a color and a character, but it is not an autobiography of Carson, so in the strict sense of the word, it is not an autobiography at all. Though it suggests hybridity, its subtitle "A Novel in Verse," seems simple enough. It draws a line; it demarcates, and we feel situated, at least momentarily. But, as we enter into the text, our expectations are frustrated. We must enter and exit several alcoves before anything that resembles a "novel" appears. Our first alcove, which must also serve as an entrance, is the "proemium," a short essay that offers some answers to the question it poses in its subtitle—"What Difference Did Stesichoros Make?" We learn of the poet's unique relationship to adjectives; we learn that he offended Helen of Troy, prompting her to blind him; we learn that he earns his sight back by writing a palinode. But perhaps most importantly, we are reminded of our interpretative roles as readers. The reader is told to answer the subtitle's question "for yourself" (6). In order to do so, we must take the metaphorical box that holds

Stesichoros's extant fragments in our hands. Since we cannot literally hold the fragments, this "box" is Carson's book, which we hold in more ways than one. "Here," she writes, "Shake," and with that we turn the page, stepping into the next alcove, "Red Meat: Fragments of Stesichoros."

These fragments are Carson's own experimental translations of Stesichoros's *Geryoneis*. Ian Rae, who compares Carson's translations to Andrew Miller's, observes that Carson includes anachronisms, omits large portions of text, and replaces Miller's heroic diction with a more contemporary, less elevated diction. Rae argues, "Carson combines glimpses of ancient and modern narratives in a style that foreshadows the perspectival shifts of the concluding interview" (236). Extending this observation, these "perspectival shifts" characterize not just the concluding interview, but the other sections as well, and the book as a whole. Each alcove we enter provides us with yet another perspective from which to view the circular middle room. After the proemium and Carson's translations, we likely feel prepared, and even anxious, to enter the "novel," but Carson postpones yet again. We must first make our way through three more alcoves, appendices A, B, and C. Because we are unaccustomed to finding an appendix at the beginning of a book, we find ourselves asking, what does it mean if three appendices precede the "meat" of the book? In the case of *Autobiography of Red,* these appendices have the effect of reinforcing the importance of the previous "Red Meat" sections, undermining our tendency to see them as prefatory. The appendices are not modifying or commenting on the "novel," but rather, they are commenting on Carson's meditations on Stesichoros and his text. In this way, she places Stesichoros's *Geryoneis*, much of which is missing, in the center, in the middle room of the rotunda.

What do these appendices, themselves crucial components of this book, add to the information we have already received? In Appendix A, "Testimonia on the Question of the Stesichoros's Blinding by Helen," we learn that the ancient poet incorporated both "blasphemy" and apology in his work (15). The lesson of the palinode—"saying the opposite of what you said before"— is a lesson that exceeds the genre of the palinode itself (15). It is a lesson Carson surely learns and employs, both in *Autobiography of Red* and across her oeuvre. In the case of *Autobiography of Red,* Carson employs this poetic palinode to bring divergent genres into collision with one another. By doing so, she demonstrates the ways in which the "lines of demarcation" are not lines at all, but permeable boundaries. Appendix B consists of only three translated lines from Stesichoros's palinode, one of which reads, "No it is not the true story" (17). This reinforces not just Stesichoros's willingness to retract a statement, but also Carson's insistence in the proemium

THE MONSTER IN THE ROTUNDA • 21

that there are "many different ways to tell a story like this" (5). Appendix C, "Clearing up the Question of Stesichoros's Blinding By Helen," is a disjunctive syllogism with 20 premises, or it might be more accurate to argue that this appendix takes the form of 21 partial disjunctive syllogisms. Whatever the case might be, the syllogisms, to use Carson's own words regarding Stesichoros's fragments, "withhold as much as they tell" (6). The final premise—"If Stesichoros was a blind man either we will lie or if not not—" reminds us that this text, whatever it might be—autobiography, novel, poem—is concerned with truth (and lies) and story telling, among other things, and so now, surely, we can enter the largest alcove, the section of the text that most closely resembles a "novel" (20).

But is it a "novel" in the strict sense of the word? Carson's title page for this section further complicates the generic tangle that the previous five sections created. The title page reads "Autobiography of Red: A Romance." In *Eros the Bittersweet,* Carson tells us "Our terms 'novel' and 'romance' do not reflect an ancient name for the genre" (78). She notes that these are prose works of "erotic sufferings" in which "it is generically required that love be painful" (ETB, 78). These are the first Greek novels, and as you will remember, these novelists learn the drama of "erotic contradiction" from the archaic lyric poets (ETB, 79). By choosing to replace the subtitle "A Novel in Verse" with "A Romance," Carson reminds us that the early novel and the lyric poem were not as far apart as we might assume, but she is also preparing us for the story of Geryon and Herakles as *she* tells it—the story of a tragic homosexual love triangle between the red monster Geryon, the testosterone ridden Herakles and Herakles's boyfriend, Ancash.

Lest we assume that this section, with its fully developed characters and relatively linear plot, is the primary story of the book, the shift in subtitle reminds us of the previous five sections. It seems that the "Novel in Verse" might apply not to Carson's (relatively) lengthy retelling of Geryon's story in this sixth section, but to the different stories we encounter across all seven sections of the book. By offering an additional subtitle for this sixth section, we are urged to resist the tendency to let this longer, plot-driven section dominate the book as a whole. It is simply another alcove, albeit a consuming one, from which to view Stesichoros and his text, however inaccessible both might be.

The language Carson uses to articulate her attraction to Stesichoros is telling. We will recall that she was drawn to Stesichoros's unconventionality. It is Stesichoros's "tantalizing cross section of scenes, both proud and pitiful" that attract Carson and that come to serve as a model for her *Autobiography of Red* (6). Not unlike Stesichoros's "cross section of scenes," Carson's multiple vantage points allow for the fact that there are "many different ways to tell a story like this" (5). But if this sixth section is simply another alcove, what vantage point(s) does it offer, and what particular elements of the story does it concern itself with? In many ways, this section provides a dramatization of Carson's scholarly concerns in *Eros the Bittersweet*. We watch as Geryon struggles, almost simultaneously, with unrequited love and with the failures of representation. Geryon is acutely aware of the ways in which "the words we read and the words we write never say exactly what we mean. The people we love are never just as we desire them. The two *symbola* never perfectly match. Eros is in between" (109).

At the same time, Carson praises Stesichoros for resisting the heroic "point of view" and providing an alternative to the all too familiar "account of the victory of culture over monstrosity" (6). Carson, too, is in search of such an alternative, and, in this sixth section of *Autobiography of Red*, she glimpses it. While most of Carson's characters attempt to dominate and neutralize Geryon's monstrosity—he is abused by his brother, ignored by his father, and rejected by his lover—Geryon, precisely because of his "monstrous" nature, finds himself uniquely situated to detect the lack at the center of all desire. Carson writes:

> The word *each* blew towards him and came apart on the wind. Geryon had always had this trouble: a word like *each,* when he stared into it, would disassemble itself into separate letters and go. A space for its meaning remained there but blank (Carson, AOR 26).

Just like the early Greek novels, which were the offspring of the archaic lyric poem, this Romance takes as its subject, lack. It may be Geryon's "trouble," but as an artist, it becomes an asset. "Who is the real subject of most love poems?" Carson asks, "Not the beloved. It is that hole" (ETB, 30). The lyric poets, the early novelists, Carson, and Geryon alert us to these Eros-shaped holes. However painful this awareness might be, it is instructive. The monster becomes culture's teacher. Or, more accurately, the monster reassumes the role of culture's teacher. Etymologically, the English word "monster" is linked to the Latin words "monstrum," meaning "that which teaches" and "monstrare," which means, "to show." Both Latin words stem from the word "monere"—to warn. The theme of teaching or guiding is thus implicit in the etymology. In short, monstrosity is instructive. It is that which teaches just as it is that which frightens and destabilizes us. Destabilization is a powerful tool. Hybridity is monstrous.

Geryon makes objects not unlike Carson's monstrous text, all of which are part of his "autobiography." These include: a tomato with hair crafted from a ten dollar bill; a list of facts and assumptions about himself—"Some say Geryon had six hands six feet some say wings"; a series of questions; and finally, working in his preferred medium, Geryon produces a collection of photographs (37). These photographs become the final chapters of Carson's Romance, but not as visual objects. Rather, they appear as linguistic descriptions followed by associated observations and memories. For example, Chapter XLIII, "Photographs: I am a Beast," begins with the line "It is a photograph of a guinea pig lying on her right side on a plate" (139). What follows this line is a description of a meal of guinea pig that Geryon shared with Herakles and Ancash. The final lines of this chapter reflect what the absent photograph must depict—"In the cooling left eye of the guinea pig/ they all stand reflected/ pulling out their chairs and shaking hands. The eye empties" (140). The photograph is not provided; it is described. The description is of absence, and in the second-to-last photograph chapter of the book, "Photographs: #1748," this absence is fully present—"It is a photograph he never took, no one here took it" (145). After this, no more photographs appear; the lack that has been the subject of this Romance is finally allowed its space, but in the meantime, so many other uncategorizable spaces have been created, and together they form a monstrous body. Just as the poet searches for the form that most closely approximates her expression, Geryon's autobiography must be monstrous.

The reader having passed through a building, monstrous in its layout— the alcoves like limbs, the faceless head at the center—feels prepared to exit the rotunda, but there is one more alcove—the interview—that must be traversed. Like the appendices earlier, this interview serves to remind us that each section of the book is crucial to its overall architecture. Even more importantly, though, if we hold that Stesichoros's fragmented poem is, in fact, at the center of this building, the interview gives us one final glimpse of that partial text. By questioning Stesichoros, primarily about his temporary blindness, the interviewer reveals a way of seeing. Because all fragmented texts include a "space where a thought would be," Stesichoros's fragments, as well as his life, provide us with an opportunity to see what is missing (Interview). Furthermore, the interview postpones the conclusion. Such postponement is inherent, Carson says, in the relationship between the writer and the reader, the lover and the beloved. She writes:

> The intention to consummate desire puts the lovers at odds with the novelist, whose novel will end unless he can subvert their aim. There is something paradoxical in the relations between a novelist and his lovers. As a writer he knows their story must end and wants it to end.

So, too, as readers we know the novel must end and want it to end. "But not yet!" say the readers to the writer. "But not yet!" says the writer to his hero and heroine. "But not yet!" says the beloved to the lover. And so the reach of desire continues. (ETB, 81)

Carson extends this reach in the last few lines of the interview, when Stesichoros remarks, "So glad you didn't ask about the little red dog," to which the interviewer answers, "Next time" (149). For many years, I interpreted this non-ending as a two-pronged invitation—to go back into Carson's text and to seek further contact with Stesichoros's work. But in 2013, Carson published *Red Doc>* , her sequel to *Autobiography of Red*. While this text takes up the characters from Carson's "Romance," none of the forms are repurposed. In *Red Doc>*, desire continues its reach, finding yet another form. But that is another essay, one that must be, for the time being, postponed.

NOTE

1. Dithyrambic poetry, it should be noted, differs from lyric poetry in that its main purpose was to honor the gods, specifically Dionysus. While dithyrambs were thought to have a single speaker, choruses often performed them. More importantly, despite the often ecstatic state of the speaker, the focus was not on the poet's or speaker's emotions, but on the god being praised.

WORKS CITED

Carson, Anne. *Autobiography of Red*. New York: Alfred A. Knoff, Inc., 1998.

Carson, Anne. *Economy of the Unlost*. Princeton: Princeton University Press, 2002.

Carson, Anne. *Eros the Bittersweet*. Champaign: Dalkey Archive Press, 2000.

Carson, Anne. Interview by Will Aitken, "The Art of Poetry," *Paris Review*, No. 88, 2004.

Carson, Anne. *Nox*. New York: New Directions, 2010. Not paginated.

Derrida, Jaques. "The Law of Genre," *Glyph: Textual Studies*, 7, 1980, 202-32.

Gennett, Gerard. *The Architext: An Introduction*, trans. Jane E. Lewin, Quantam Books, Berkeley: University of California Press, 1979, 30.

Plato, *The Republic*, Book III, Classics Archive (ed Daniel C Stevenson), 1994-2000, classics@classics.mit.edu

Rae, Ian. *From Cohen to Carson: The Poet's Novel in Canada*. Montreal: McGill-Queen's University Press, 2008.

Muse X: Lyn Hejinian's *Oxota*
A Short Russian Novel

JULIE CARR

Genres are not to be mixed. I will not mix genres.

—JACQUES DERRIDA "THE LAW OF GENRE" (1980)

Within this injunction / promise / prediction lies a broader demand for order, clarity, and accommodation, for established norms, rules, and codes, and for obedience. And yet Derrida will go on to suggest that the "law of genre" always holds within it its own perversion, its own betrayal: "What if there were, lodged within the heart of the law itself, a law of impurity or a principle of contamination?" he writes. "And suppose the condition for the possibility of the law were the *a priori* of a counter-law, an axiom of impossibility that would confound its sense, order, and reason?" (57).

Derrida locates this ever-present transgression in the propensity of genres to announce themselves, either directly (as in the subtitle "A short Russian Novel"), or indirectly, as when a text does something genre-specific (a poem justifies left, or a novel foreshadows). Such moments of genre-performance, argues Derrida, are the moments when the genre stops *being itself* in order to *speak about itself.* Just when most stridently announcing its adherence to the "law," the genre breaks out of its natural or total adherence to that law, and thus creates a fissure. "Making genre its mark, a text demarcates itself" (65).

This argument feels very particular to its moment; all the surprise attacks of deconstruction might, in 2016, inspire a smile, rather than a gasp. Nonetheless, it resonates quite immediately with an idea we now have about gender—that term that always seems so close to genre, and not only because of orthography—an idea that's been part of academic understandings of gender at least since Judith Butler's *Gender Trouble,* and part of some cultural understandings of gender for much longer (for behind *Paris is Burning*, Cindy Sherman, Riot grrrl, and straight-edge boys in plaid and Carhartt, we had Oscar Wilde's carnations and cloaks, Baudelaire's prostitute performing the "barbaric elegance . . . of her own invention" (Baudelaire, 430). "What is called gender identity is a performative accomplishment compelled by social sanction and taboo. In its very character as performative resides the possibility of contesting its reified status," wrote Butler (Butler, 520). In the performative status of genre too (of all genre at all times) lies the possibility of its own transgression. Or, as Victorianist Dino Felluga puts it, "the self-conscious remarking of genre within a text not only ensures the interpretation of texts but also ensures the performative instability of generic form" (Felluga, 390).

In this essay I'm interested in tracing the interplay between the performance and transgression of genre and the performance and transgression of gender in three texts from three different periods, the Victorian, the Modernist, and the Post-Modern, and to reveal how all three lean on figures of androgyny as muse, a muse I'll call "Muse X," for the transgressions they seek and perform.

Derrida introduces the theme of "gender" by way of a parenthetical aside early in his essay when he is attempting to broaden the concept of "genre" to mean something like "category." But as we move toward the end of the essay, we see that "gender" has been his true theme all along:

> The question of the literary genre is not a formal one: it covers the motif of the law in general, of generation in the natural and symbolic senses, of birth in the natural and symbolic senses, of the generation of difference, sexual difference between the feminine and masculine genre/gender, of the hymen between the two, of relations between the two, of an identity and difference between the feminine and the masculine. (74)

Reading Blanchot's *La Folie du jour*, Derrida argues that the real thrust of this strange mixed-genre work is not to say something about the permeability of literary genres, but rather to say something about the permeability of genders, to make a case for the neutral, trans, or mixed gender of the narrator/protagonist: "'I,' then, can keep alive the chance of being a fe-male or of changing sex" (76). The mixing of genres is, then, an opportunity or metaphor for the blending or mixing of genders. Perhaps Derrida indicates much more broadly that formal experiment makes possible an expansion at the ground floor of social organization.

Let me move back now to the middle of nineteenth-century England where the "law of gender" was particularly strangling to women, where laws around women's ability to own property, hold custody of their children, pursue education or career were beginning to face a long and urgent process of contestation.

Elizabeth Barrett Browning published her "poem-novel" *Aurora Leigh* in 1856 at the beginning of the women-lead effort toward marriage reform.[1] Until the Married Women's Property Acts of the 1870s and early eighties, a married woman in Britain, under common law, could not own or will personal property.[2] All that a woman owned prior to marriage was forfeited to her husband; all her subsequent earnings were also legally his. This legal reality was, as many have argued, consistent with an ideology in which a married woman's identity was subsumed into the identity of the husband. As the often-quoted late-eighteenth-century saying puts it, "In law husband and wife are one person, and the husband is that person" (quoted in Holcombe, 18).

Barrett Browning was extremely active in the effort to reform these laws. In fact, the petition for the first Married Women's Property Act (1870) was sometimes referred to as "the petition of Elizabeth Barrett Browning, Anna Jameson, Mary Howitt, Mrs. Gaskell" (the other three women were important activists for feminist causes) (Leighton, 103). While *Aurora Leigh* in some senses offers us a traditional "marriage plot," it presents this plot with full awareness that the denouement of such narratives were problematic for women. As much as the poem can be read as reinforcing Victorian marriage ideology, it must also be read as leveling a serious critique against the Victorian "law of gender."

The novel opens with Aurora, a recently orphaned young woman who must leave Italy to live with her paternal aunt in England. She is literary and ambitious, a poet, and yet these qualities are significantly squelched by her strict and conventional aunt who believes women should (as Aurora satirically puts it), "keep quiet by the fire / And never say 'no' when the world says 'ay,'" that they are best put to use to "fatten household sinners" (I:436-440).

Aurora meets Romney Leigh, her cousin and the heir to her father's fortune (which will become "hers" too if she marries him). Romney, a young man with socialist leanings, mocks Aurora's poetry, arguing that she cannot in fact write great works because of her gender. Women, argues Romney, cannot really be poets because they tend to focus on the details of life rather than on broad generalities: "You generalize / Oh, nothing, - not even grief! Your quick-breathed hearts, / So sympathetic to the personal pang / . . . The human race / To you means, such a child, or such a man, / You saw one morning waiting in the cold" (II: 184-191).

Here we have a familiar dichotomy. Women feel too much to be useful to a general public. Their strength lies in their attention to particulars, to subjective experiences, to "the dust of the actual" (II: 482). But general matters, matters of politics, philosophy, and morals, what Aurora calls "universals," belong to the male. (But Romney doesn't find Aurora entirely useless. On the contrary, he finds her marriageable. His proposal elicits only scorn from Aurora who, recognizing his hypocrisy, retorts with great sarcasm "Anything does for a wife" [II: 367].)

> "Woman as you are," continues Romney,
> Mere woman, personal and passionate,
> You give us doating mothers, and perfect wives,
> Sublime Madonnas, and enduring saints!
> We get no Christ from you—and verily
> We should not get a poet in my mind. (II: 220-5)

What's behind this slide from Christ to poet? Is it simply that Christ in his martyrdom takes on universal suffering, something that poets are supposedly attuned to? That is, it seems, how Romney sees it.

But Christ is Western culture's dominant symbol for the fusion of just the opposing qualities that Romney (and the culture at large) has so deftly gendered. As Murray Krieger writes, "Through the mysteries of Christ's double—and doubly paradoxical—status as man and as God, the worldly body can contain the undying spirit, as worldly history can contain the eschatological or the Old Testament can contain the New" (6-7). At once human and divine, at once time-bound individual and timeless figure for universal compassion and love, Christ joins these gendered categories in one body. Romney's claim "We get no Christ from you" becomes a challenge for Aurora, for Browning, to discover precisely how we might locate Christ in the body of a woman, or in the body of a woman's text. And though it can be said that Browning produces a Christ-figure in the body of the martyred character Marian, to me it's the text's form, the genre-blending text itself, that best becomes that androgynous typological transgression.

One of the most often quoted passages in *Aurura Leigh* reveals how Browning imagines just this blending of universal truths and concrete particulars in generic terms.

> The critics say that epics have died out
> With Agamemnon and the goat-nursed gods.
> I'll not believe it, I could never deem
> . . .
> That Homer's heroes measured twelve feet high.
> They were but men: - his Helen's hair turned grey
> And Hector's infant whimpered at a plume
> As yours last Friday at a turkey-cock.
> . . .

> But poets should
> Exert a double vision; should have eyes
> To see near things as comprehensively
> As if afar they took their point of sight,
> And distant things as intimately deep
> As if they touched them. Let us strive for this. (V:185-190)

The domestic novel (a feminized form) thus meets the epic poem (gendered male) through the doubled vision of the new poet: she who can see "near things" as deeply as "distant." This "double vision" is, then, Christ's vision, for by virtue of his double ontology, Christ finds intimacy with universal and individual suffering alike.

The marriage plot allows Browning to present two ways of life, two ways of seeing, to mark their differences and then to reunite them only when the domination of one over the other is undone. At their reunion, Romney's been beaten down by disappointments and failure while Aurora has succeeded wildly in her ambitions. Further, Romney's been maimed; he becomes marriageable only after fire has destroyed his sight. Only after this blinding is "double vision" possible, for Patriarchy's violence demands a violent undoing. And while the marriage of Romney and Aurora is not quite the making of a mixed or neutrally gendered person, while it can't fairly be read as a total rejection of patriarchal ideologies, my point is that the mixed-gendered "person" *is* figured, formally, in the text itself: mixed genre becomes the mixed gender that Browning cannot quite articulate narratively. As it "marries" domestic and localized material with epic form, the text itself achieves the "double vision" of an un-gendered Christ.

Let me now turn to a more recent "mixed genre" text that features more concretely a crucial figure of androgyny: William Carlos Williams' *Paterson*. The debate between genres and their propensities, or between genders and theirs, is offered quite early on in *Paterson* through the figure of Marcia Nardi. But we can look to the opening of Book I to see that Williams is alert to the same tension—between the general / universal and the particular / subjective—as *Aurora Leigh*. "To make a start / out of particulars / And make them general" begins Williams (3). This is Browning's "double vision" seemingly achieved: the poet instructs himself to generalize only after "particulars" have been seen or expressed—the two poles already wed. And yet the marriage between particulars and generalities (things and ideas) proves a bit rockier than that. Trouble is announced through the inclusion of the difficult, unhappy voice of Marcia Nardi.

Nardi's letters to the doctor ("Paterson" in the text), rendered in prose, complain about the breakdown of their friendship. She feels ignored, tossed aside, disregarded. She's distraught, lonely, and broke. But when their personal relationship is not taking center stage, Nardi describes another point of contention in their attitudes toward writing. Nardi accuses the doctor of writing a literature "disconnected from life" (87), one that cares about other people only "theoretically—which doesn't mean a God damned thing" (82).

Nardi advocates instead for literature grounded in what Aurora would call the "dust of the actual," the particulars of real life. Indeed, Williams is concerned with this too—drawing on history, news, personal letters, and other detritus of the real throughout *Paterson*. And yet, in giving Nardi such a dominant position, in highlighting her prose letters, rather than her poems (which Williams also had access to), Williams genders genre: poetry, the genre of abstraction and idealization, of general ideas and universal themes, belongs to "Paterson," to the male voice. Prose, the genre of detail, of fact, of messy and subjective material realities, belongs to Nardi, the book's central female.

And yet Williams, like Browning before him, seeks to unite these voices. One could say that *Paterson* achieves just that, bringing genders and genres together between the covers of a single volume. But Williams also *figures* this meeting or blending of genres / genders in a body, his Muse X:

There is a woman in our town
walks rapidly, flat bellied

In worn slacks upon the street
. . .
Neither short
nor tall, nor old nor young
her
    face would attract no

adolescent. Grey eyes looked
straight before her.
    Her

                hair
was gathered simply behind the
ears under a shapeless hat.

Her
    hips were narrow, her
                    legs
thin and straight. She stopped

me in my tracks—until I saw
her
    disappear in the crowd.
 . . . .
she was dressed in male attire,
as much as to say to hell

with you.
 . . .
have you read anything I have written?
It is all for you (218)

This androgynous muse, this woman in male dress who says "to hell with you" to patriarchy— answers the problem of gender that is also a problem of genre (or vice versa). She fascinates because her defiance points forward to the political freedom of women, and by extension of all people—but also because in her androgynous form she unites not only genders, but also the two opposing efforts of Williams' writing: the first being to touch the actual, the other being to imagine the possible. That is why she is at once desirable and distant, at once a real woman with erotic appeal and an ideal muse figure (neither short nor tall, young nor old: in other words, an abstraction) for whom Williams writes.

There is much more to say about how *Paterson* (and also *Aurora Leigh*) works through these desires. In a longer essay I'd say something about how Williams abandons this androgynous muse and replaces her with his "son" (Ginsberg). But I'll turn now to my final text, Lyn Hejinian's *Oxota: A Short Russian Novel* (1991) in order to see how a writer from our time manages to thematize the blending of genres and genders as a means toward dissolving the damaging oppositions articulated by cousin Romney, these oppositions that continue to exert control over our writings and our identities.

First, one should say that from *Aurora Leigh* to *Oxota* the poem-novel has come a very long way. Though Hejinian includes characters, scenes, and events, the links between them are never particularly clear or sustained. As Jacob Edmund has written, "*Oxota*'s sentences do not appear to relate to one another in a linear way . . . narrative fragments appear everywhere . . .

while never taking the form of a coherent whole" (Edmund, 89). Marjorie Perloff reads the book's style as result of competing aesthetic urges, writing "But how, we might ask, do we reconcile the poetics of the language movement with the demands of narrative?"

But these stylistic difficulties of the text also reveal, I think, the ways in which Hejinian attempts to disturb the gendered binaries of political history and domestic life, of the general with the particular, of the ideal with the real. One could say, in fact, that *Oxota*—set in Russia in and around glasnost, but seeming to take place almost entirely within the kitchens and living rooms of friends—realizes, more successfully than *Paterson*, the marriage of the political and the daily, the historical and the intimate. Indeed, Hejinian announces her rejection of the oppositions facing Browning at the start of Book 3:

> So I must oppose the opposition of poetry to prose
> Just as we can only momentarily oppose control to
> discontinuity, sex to organization, disorientation to domestic
>   time and space, and glasnost (information) to the hunt (93)

And earlier:

> The mere mood of our words was producing content
> The sheer detail was required
> Sleep is an orientation
> There's no need to distinguish a poem from prose (79)

Exposing the lie at the structure of genre law, Hejinian refuses to hierarchize Aurora's double vision. The "moods" and "details" so present throughout *Oxota* are not distinct or outside of the capital H history (glasnost) that frames the book and might be considered its "general" subject-matter.

And yet, as any reader of this vast and deeply disjunctive text will experience, our readerly expectations around prose and poetry are not so easily dissuaded. No matter what pleasure we might find in passages like this: "Take a naked doll and a spoon, a lifted city / A great pastiche / You're wrong / I was straightening the blanket around where I sat, while Vasya turned up the tape machine," for most of us they will be very different pleasures than the ones we discover in so-called "realist" novels where events and commentary on such events organize around causalities.

If Hejinian is, then, transgressing genre by refusing to satisfy readerly expectations, how is this tied to a theory of gender? In her 1991 interview "Comments for Manual Brito" Hejinian writes:

> There tends to be some confusion or misconception, inherent maybe
> to Western thinking, which assumes a separation between, for exam-
> ple, form and content, verb and noun, process and condition, progress
> and stasis. But in fact these pairs and their parts constitute a dynamic,
> a momentum, a force. Quantities are change, not categories, . . . By
> the way, this can be said for gender, too—man and woman. Being a
> woman isn't a state so much as it's an impetus, with certain momen-
> tum, occurring at various velocities and in various directions . . . Or
> one could speak about literary form, which isn't form at all but force.
> (*Inquiry*, 182)

While the oppositions Hejinian lists here (states vs. forces) can't be
mapped directly onto those we've been discussing (generalities vs. particu-
larities), we can see that for Hejinian oppositions or binaries are inherently
problematic, perhaps most of all when they become gendered. Gender law,
like genre law, provides us only with false choices. We must write as we live,
dynamically.

The androgynous figure doesn't play as strong a role in *Oxota* as it does
in Hejinian's later work, *A Border Comedy*, where she writes (just one of
many examples) of "changing sexes / in changing dreams" where "A breast
appeared, off me, but incompletely / On the man I am / A woman / I or she
/ All of this being 'gender by degrees'" (*Border*, 17). *Oxota* (like its model,
Pushkin's *Eugene Onegin*) is more frequently concerned with loosening the
boundaries between art and life and between History and the domestic, between universal themes and seemingly trivial detail (gendered categories all,
as we've seen). Indeed, while the series of poems that make up Book Two
are given titles suggesting such themes: Truth, Nature, Passion, Suffering,
Death, the poems themselves discuss their themes only briefly and obliquely,
offering up fractured details of daily life rather than treatises. Here, by way of
example, is the opening of "Chapter Seventy-Seven: Suffering":

> A stench left from cooking fish lay frenzied, felt inert
> Or a yellow rose frustrated in the Summer Garden
> Mayakovsky said that horses never commit suicide because they don't
>   know how to   talk—they could never explain their suffering
>
> Each night has wiped a suffering diagonally—in such conditions each
>   voice and face   becomes distorted
>
> From a neighboring building an infant has been crying for five hours (88)

None of these statements could really be said to apply generally to the "universal" theme of suffering; instead they give us instances of such: a stench, a frustrated bloom, a crying baby. The poem exemplifies precisely the accusation that Romney leveled against Aurora: "You generalize / Oh, nothing, - not even grief! / . . . .The human race / To you means, such a child, or such a man, / You saw one morning waiting in the cold." One could say that Hejinian's poems stand defiantly on the side of "such a child, or such a man," arguing, however, that there is no "human race," but only humans, no generalized pain, but only instances of it, just as there are instances of, but no general, redemption:

Chapter Eighty: Redemption

Two rams, which ram redeemed
One ram wasted, one ram waiting (91)

But Hejinian does not only perform gender / genre blending through pointedly drawing together universals and particulars; androgyny or gender-neutral identity also surfaces directly, and when it does it's significantly tied to questions of genre. Here is "Chapter 141: The Genders of Everyday Life" in its entirety:

We have split for many occasions
Arkadii!
Ho!
I disagree with you, I said
And I agree, he said—you're right!
About postmodernism
A city of genres
Take a naked doll and a spoon, a lifted city
A great pastiche
You're wrong
I was straightening the blanket around where I sat, while Vasya turned
   up the tape
            machine
An unfinished conspiracy
Love and they are odd—a mounting context
We love the sexes of conditions we never leave.

You will notice that this is the same chapter I quoted from above. But now that we have the title and final lines, we might see how it does more than simply trouble narrative with parataxis and disjunction. We can read this poem now as playfully but significantly exploring the problem of gender division that is at once a problem of genre division.

"We have split for many occasions" begins the poem, and, guided by the title, we read this splitting as, in part, the splitting and dividing of genders (suggesting here the splitting and dividing of cells within the womb). Indeed the "I" (assumed female) and the "he" are not in much accord, they can't even agree to disagree! The city they argue within, which Hejinian calls "a city of genres" is also, clearly, a city of genders: the naked doll and the spoon both obliquely indicate the female, while Arkadi performs a typically "masculine" task, adjusting a machine. The two characters cannot be said to have transgressed their gendered roles, indeed while "he" fiddles with technology, she toys with a feminized object of domestic comfort—a blanket. In fact, in the poem's final line Hejinian remarks on the adherence to "gender law" going on here: "We love the sexes of conditions we never leave." However, let's remember Derrida and Butler: only when the "conditions" of gender (or genre) are recognized as such, when such conditions are labeled and performed, can we find "the possibility of contesting [their] reified status."

Indeed, a little while later in *Oxota* we get "a face from which a pronoun is missing," and then the following: "I am not I, said a chalk on the wall / Dickface, said a paint on the door close to cozy / I adore you, my cunt, said Dimitri in English" (192). Here the human is conflated with written or painted surfaces, surfaces who speak, at once rejecting or announcing (exaggeratedly, performatively) their compliance with gendered terms or norms. Dimitri speaking English reminds us that a "cunt" is only language; gendered identities are just languages we try on and try out. And while it might seem perverse to read this passage as an instant of gender transgression, I can't not take the face with its missing pronoun as the Muse X behind this work. If the political thrust of this "poem—novel" is to resist the oppressive forces of oppositions ("I must oppose the opposition") to break down, just for starters, the Cold War legacy that made enemies of otherness, then these passages and others reveal how Hejinian must include the dissolving of gendered binaries in her task. In that we have for so long believed (even if subtly) in the myths that gender our genres, *Oxota*, like the other texts we have been looking at, must in blending genre, blend gender.

"The future calls for perverse crossings" writes Dino Felluga (384). And while here he means the crossings of genres and periods for literary study, we know that the same is true for gender, as the violence at the center of normative gender compliance becomes more and more evident before our eyes. And conversely, just as gender, when aware of its own construction, becomes not a "state," but an attitude, a performance—genre too must be understood as never natural or total, but always partial, performative, and political. "Instability marks the site of historical and cultural change" (389), says Felluga. As we find ourselves in a "city of genders" that Barrett Browning could only have dreamed of, "a boundary is not that at which something stops but, as the Greeks recognized, that from which something begins" (Hejinian, Border, 18).

NOTES

1. The material in this paragraph is repurposed from my book *Surface Tension: Ruptural Time and the Poetics of Desire in Late Victorian Poetry*, 122-23.
2. For a more detailed description of these laws and their origins see Lee Holcombe 18-36, and Mary Poovey 70-72.

WORKS CITED

Baudelaire, Charles. "The Painter of Modern Life." *Selected Writings on Art & Artists*. P.E. Charvet, trans. Cambridge: Cambridge University Press, 1972.

Browning, Elizabeth Barrett. *Auora Leigh*. New York: W.W. Norton, 1996.

Butler, Judith. "Performative Acts and Gender Constitution: An Essay on Phenomenology and Feminist Theory." *Theater Journal 40 (4)*, 1988: 519-531.

Carr, Julie. *Surface Tension: Ruptural Time and the Poetics of Desire in Late Victorian Poetry*. Champaign; London; Dublin: Dalkey Archive, 2013.

Derrida, Jacques. "The Law of Genre"

Edmund, Jacob. Bridging Poetic and Cold War Divides in Lyn Hejinain's *Oxota* and Vikram Seth's *Golden Gate*

Felluga, Dino. "Novel Poetry: Transgressing the Law of Genre." *Victorian Poetry*, Vol. 41, No. 4, *Whither Victorian Poetry*? (Winter, 2003): 490-499.

Hejinian, Lyn. *A Border Comedy*. New York: Granary Books, 2001.

—. *The Language of Inquiry*. Berkeley: University of California Press, 2000.

—. *Oxota: A Short Russian Novel*. Great Barrington, MA: The Figures, 1991.

Holcombe, Lee. *Wives and Property: Reform of the Married Women's Property Law in Nineteenth-Century England*. Toronto; Buffalo: University of Toronto Press, 1983.

Krieger, Murray. *A Reopening of Closure*. New York: Columbia University Press, 1989.

Leighton, Angela. *Victorian Women Poets: Writing Against the Heart.*
    Richmond: University of Virginia Press, 1992
Perloff, Marjorie. "How Russian Is it?: Lyn Hejinian's *Oxota.*"
Poovey, Mary. *Uneven Developments: The Ideological Work of Gender in
    Mid-Victorian England.* Chicago: University of Chicago Press, 1988.
Williams, William Carlos. *Paterson.* NY: New Directions, 1992.

Down in the Dump
The Abject in Alice Notley's *Culture of One*

LAURA HINTON

The Dark could not perceive its own form
. . . Did the dark want to know itself?

—NOTLEY, *CULTURE OF ONE*

Culture of One is a "poet's novel" about a woman who lives in the local dump, a garbage heap that exists on the marginal outskirts of an unnamed desert Southwest town. As poet Alice Notley has commented on this 2011 work in a recent interview, *Culture of One* may stand as "a book of poems"; but it also "has character, plot, dialogue, and all the trappings of a novel" (Browne, paragraph 6). In this essay, I want to explore those "trappings" and their possible meaning—or the destruction of meaning: a violence initiated by the work's multiple generic identities or lack thereof. That "lack" in *Culture of One* is tied to the figure of the dump, and the lady who resides in the shadows of society's refuse. The female character who "inhabits" (a bit like a ghost) the strangely strewn if beautiful language constructing this dump, and this poet's novel, is our guide into the lost representation of "the abject." Julia Kristeva has used this term for the psychic state of horror and its visceral response to that which lies outside subjects, objects, and the "desire for meaning"—through "opposition to 'I'" (Kristeva, 2). The abject is perhaps the darkest trajectory of human experience, trying to "know itself."

The abject exists as a *de facto* psychic dump in Kristevan theory, an expression of the inexpressible, or that condition society would deny or repress. It encodes the multiplicity of a psychoanalytic—and I would argue also linguist—space, when one faces that which is unintelligible or "improper" according to rules of social decorum; it is that which lies outside delineated cultural bounds. Abjection arises when one confronts the abject repudiation of a given society. Our Lady of the Dump, named Marie, lives in and amidst the abject figured by her garbage-littered ground. No one can be "the abject"; for it exists, as Kristeva notes, at the other side of knowledge or identification of "self." Marie, who is without either "self" or the conventionally "proper" objects of culture—like property—utilizes the refuse at hand and creates her own "culture of one." The site of this

DOWN IN THE DUMP • 39

detritus rejected by all others is abjectly "improper / unclean," in Kristevan terminology. And the woman who maintains a "home" there exists "at the border of my condition as a living being" (Kristeva, 3).

Marie, the dump, and some of the other figures populating this book may be abjectly desolate and disturbing to many readers. And so may be Notley's refusal to cohere to any disciplinary genre, since the "poet's novel" itself represents an "improper" invasion of genre, making it difficult to categorize or critique as a text. As a discursive text, *Culture of One* certainly defies most traditional literary constructs and bounds. And yet, like the case of the diseased Ruby—one of the characters who inhabits this desert landscape, and also does not, because she is "dead"—the text of *Culture of One* is "awesome and ugly" at once (74). Marie and her dump are located "down" in the gutter, perhaps, of social form and hierarchy. But by taking up the outsider stance this abject space represents, Marie experiments with the unrepresentable. Both Marie and her dumpsite open up a space of fecundity and creative growth—as Marie utilizes rejected non-objects to create a multi-media artist's canvas. The abject Marie and her squalid vacant landscape suggest that poetic language itself is an abject linguistic landscape and that the poet's novel is made from such found (non-)objects.

As opposed to some of Notley's prose-poem works, like *Désamère* or *Songs and Stories of the Ghouls*—which she herself states "are [works] in prose and observe the rules of prose fiction" (Browne, paragraph 6), *Culture of One* may be more of what Kenneth Patchen called (in his own experiments with prose poetry) an "antinovel'" (Patchen quoted in Deville, 87). Notley's book is a "novel that is not a novel," to borrow that phrase from Leslie Scalapino as she reflects upon her own poet's fiction;[1] it is a seemingly jumbled mix of both semi-referential and completely non-referential prose and poetry paragraphs, which also engages enjambed free-verse lines. Almost like the rejected pieces of former objects strewn around in patchwork disorder at a small-town dump, Notley's prose paragraphs and poetry passages—which are both and neither—loosely are held together by faint or partial appearances of socially down-and-out characters, as well as a few spirits or ghosts. These "characters" are not fleshed out; instead, they pop up, temporarily appear, and then disappear through the chapter-like sequences that are more aptly described as broken "segments."[2] These "segments" do not pretend conventional coherence, one to the other. They do not attempt to form cause-effect logical relationships nor to breed "proper" plot transitions. Things "happen" in this book. But these are the "activities" of the abject: the making of a work of art out of garbage, the burning of Marie's shack by "mean girls," the listening to a dead wife's voice.

If narrative-style "voice" does permeate this fiction—giving it some of the effects of novelistic point of view—that perspective is shattered by the poet-"narrator's" lack of individualism as she merges with other figures and her own identity is thwarted (seemingly happily so). Reflecting upon this book's "problems" with character, plot and narrative or poetic voice, one might say that *Culture of One* is a poet's novel almost without the conventions of either poetry or novels.

But a novel-style plot along with some characterization does exist in *Culture of One*. At best we might call the plot episodic—or fractured. Yet blurts of "activity" amongst the "characters," and blurred moments of description, are all offered within and around a completely unromanticized setting that portrays the smallness of a desert town, inhabited mostly by unsavory derelicts who make *Culture of One* such a fascinating, strangely authentic anthropological study. Parts of plot, like pieces of characterization, act as do societal and literary artifact and debris. They function like the "debris" of prior novel forms that refuse to be buried in this poet's novel—but cannot be pieced together "properly," only *re*-"plotted."

While the odds and ends and heads and tails of poetic imagery through description of people and objects may aptly conjure the world surrounding Marie's desert-dump spatial referent, these parts and particles of an existing external "world" engage with a poetic aporia lacking causal logic, transitional statements and the usual novelistic descriptions that (rather falsely, I might add) provide images: substitute images that stand as visual referents, but images that allow a reader to at least *pretend* to view the world as object. Not all sentence passages follow the wilderness of Lang Po parataxis. We can imagine Marie walking to the Buy-Rite supermarket, for instance; or we can note the use of subordination (and a brief suggestion of causality) in the following passage concerning Ruby, her daughter:

> Ruby lay cushioned, dead. She got sick and died, like
> everyone. (20)

And yet there is an absurdity at the heart of these sentences placed together, an irreverent tip-of-the-hat to "classic prose." The body of the dead Ruby emerges—or is shed—out of the blue, so to speak. We have no context for this event or series of events—as statements. We then read that Ruby's partner, Leroy, hears Ruby talking to him from her deceased, (non-)person state. In the case of the passage above, the "description" of the dead Ruby "cushioned" in her coffin immediately devolves into a meditation upon the character of the strange Leroy, who usually likes to tell "lies" (20).

Another feature of *Culture of One* as a "novel" text is the use of its "chapter headings." But these are actually word phrases that rarely offer relevant information to the passage they announce. These "headings" do not label or describe the content to follow. Instead, they are linguistically innovative, funny, sometimes even gorgeous phrases, like "Stop Pop" or "Tangled Jade." And they do sometimes obliquely introduce a character or a concept (as in "Then I became Mercy" (9) or "The Codex" (29)). The "headings" frame the formlessness that typifies the book's sequences, its "patchwork" of lyric text and prose passages. These "headings" refuse to bind together "novelistic" themes. Instead, they invite openings to their own interpretation, and to that of the text passages that follow. And they have the effect of *pausing* sequential logic typical to the novelistic text. As they open up white space between sequences of text on the page, they *destroy* what might be traditionally novelistic "prose" in this language, by literally stopping the reader's march in quest of progressive linear meaning. Alternatively, they open up a decided space of unknowability as well as contemplation. Like the desert-scape and "city" described below, these headings are "nothing"—except as part of a flowing and continuous text running away from—and suspending—"meaning":

Oh city when nothing will exist . . .
. . . Your towers once grew like wildflowers . . . . (37)
. . . .
Doesn't yet know what they mean. I think we'd better
Call on the Devil now; we're doomed, the girls say. (61)

The segments themselves are both separate and distinct as well as "complete" and full as integral units. They reveal some gorgeous poetry. And they might initiate a piece of story, or a motif, as in references to "the girls" who are "doomed" (the "mean girls") in the passage cited above (from "Someone Put You Out," on the destruction by local "mean-girl teens" of Marie's dump-house (61). The segments might also dismantle the beginning of any potential story or motif entirely. They usually do both. They never fit together like a jigsaw puzzle to reveal a completed picture or visualized form of "reality," usually the mission of more conventional novelistic writing or even lyric poetry. Rather, the segments are "mere" passages of *writing,* in the Barthesian sense of *l'écriture.*[3] They retain their separations and interstices both. They are blank to meaning. But their destruction of *narrative* "meaning," as they juxtapose and rub against one another, also offers the possibility of generating the unrepresentable abject.

Clearly, the novel "trappings" of *Culture of One* are problematic. They make us ask: what is a *poet's* novel? Does it exist? Yet this book is neither "just" poetry or prose. Nor is it a prose poem—although it contains prose-poetry passages. I am suggesting, rather, that *Culture of One* performs or *acts like* the classic prose poem, whose legacy goes back to the work of Charles Baudelaire. That function of the prose-poem, according to Michel Deville, is "to redefine the parameters governing our expectations of what a poem . . . should look and sound like" (Deville, 2). Like the prose poem and other unconventional "inter-genre" writings, to use the term coined by Ron Silliman in his Introduction to *The American Tree* (2), *Culture of One* subverts features of both poetry and prose—and even the notion of generic boundaries themselves. Taking Notley at her word, however, that *Culture of One* is "my most novel-like book" (Browne, paragraph 6), I turn to discussion of the features of classic prose narrative, which typify the novel tradition. It is helpful to note that Viktor Shklovsky's analysis of prose fiction is not so much predicated upon "character, plot, dialogue," to recall Notley's words, but upon certain shared "devices" (in Russian, *"priem"*). These "devices" create what Shklovsky suggests are subliminally expected patterns in prose fiction.

The "devices" that form those patterns include—in classic formations of novel plot—tautologies and parallelisms, for example. These are the repeating patterns that generate what Shklovsky calls a "norm" in the writing style, a "norm," in turn, however, repeatedly disrupted. This process of establishing a "norm" followed by the disruption of that expected pattern is what Shkolvsky has importantly termed "defamiliarization" (*ostranenie*, sometimes translated as "strangeness" (Shkolvsky, 27-33)). "Deceleration" is one artistic device that Shklovsky says literally "decelerates" or slows down any expected "norm" or anticipated resolution in fiction. He explains that "deceleration" operates on the level of the typical prose fiction plot,[4] to mark that plot with "a web of sounds [and] movements," all *in addition to* plot "ideas" (Shklovsky, 45). Applying this concept from Shklovsky to *Culture of One*, I would say that what is so abjectly "dark" in this book's sketchy suggestion of plot are the ways in which its "web of sounds, movements" involve the "idea" of the garbage pit as both site and situation for the "normally" inexpressible abject. The "dump" site bears the repeated if unbidden quest for unexpected psychic knowledge through Marie's artistic exploration of human detritus and rejected shards from the culture she herself has flown. In the absence of fictional tautologies or the regularized patterns typifying fictional prose, the garbage pit "dump" is the repeating leitmotif. Reversing any concept of "norm" or motif, this book enacts a kind of totalizing "defamiliarization," in which a dump formalizes a symbolic "dump" upon which it linguistically sits. This poet's novel is itself composed out of *linguistic* debris and shards, forming scattered paradigms missing their (formerly) functional parts.

It is in this abandoned landscape that a "culture of one" emerges and is born. Marie's bizarre but beautiful, empty and depleted world that this book so strangely, astonishingly, celebrates is the "deviation of the norm" that Shklovsky suggests is the groundwork for fictional plots. As he remarks, "deviation from the norm may . . . become the point of departure and yardstick for other deviations" (Shklovsky, 33). Notley's poet's novel, however, undermines and excavates that groundwork remaining in typical prose fictional plots in general. And it does so by rejecting the binarism suggested in that distinction Shklovsky makes between "norm" and "deviation" to begin with. If *Culture of One* mangles—through its poetry / prose—a symbolic junk heap that once represented the "norm" of society, this book insists that poetry and prose belong together in their jumbled inconstant failed unities. Prose *is* poetry; poetry *is* prose. That separation is arbitrary, however long honored by conventional society and its literary traditions. Notley's work screws this binary logic, inverts and spills it out—like a garbage truck emptying its contents so that the garbage lover, like an artist, can pick through the contents, recontextualize objects, rename them. Recognized orders of literary language break down in this "poet's novel"—a phrase which I am forced to treat as an oxymoron in this case. And language's supposedly communicational aspects are part of the "truck's" emptying process. Call it the abject at work in the realm of literary language. *Culture of One* presents this *new* literary language *itself* as the abject, and revitalizes the radiant horror of the literary, linguistic dystopia.

Like the abject, *Culture of One* reproduces the severed ties between subject and object. In this shadowy landscape surrounding the dumpsite, the personae of the town exist and don't exist. Many of them do manage, however, to reveal some disturbing and contradictory character traits. If the abject, as Kristeva writes, is "homologous" to "the jettisoned object" that gives the subject meaning and yet that also "draws me toward the place where meaning collapses" (Kristeva, 2), every "character" spun inside the fiction of *Culture of One* "exists"—but only as that shattered, rejected, (non-) subject.

Interestingly, according to Kristeva, the abject of "the improper / unclean" may originate as a feeling that arises from "loathing an item of food, a piece of filth, waste, or dung . . . food loathing is perhaps the most elementary and most archaic form of abjection" (Kristeva, 2). One of Marie's first introductions within the text of *Culture of One* comes in a segment entitled "Old Food." As with all "chapter-like" segments, this piece is not actually *about* the subject of "old food." But while "Old Food" does not describe literal food debris and fecund rot, it *does* describe habits of human deceit and the emotional boundary crossings of "proper" social functioning, which unfold amidst the social scene of the characters swirling around Marie. Just because she lives at the dump, Leroy, we are told in "Old Food," makes up his "lies" about her and details of her daily life, like her diet:

> Marie lived in a gully at the dump on the outskirts of town, in a palm-frond shack, with her dogs . . . She walks to the Buy Rite . . . . She enters the Buy-Rite. Leroy, the liar, sells her food then tells lies to everyone about her . . . .
> . . . . One lie, that she cooked lizards and ate them. (12-13)

Leroy's "lies" are like the spasms Kristeva associates with the experience of the abject. They trigger socially nauseating reversals of the socially "proper" that are then critiqued, implicitly, by the poet-narrator. Marie's *lack* of proper abode and diet is not just socially criticized in the figure of Leroy but internalized in the poet's novel, just as are new formations of the abject (non-)"subject." As Kristeva explains, this "subject" is ontologically "homeless," negating "my-self." Kriseva writes:

> . . . I spit *myself out* . . . within the same motion through which "I" claim to establish *myself* . . . The corpse (or cadaver: *cadere*, to fall) . . . is cesspool, and death." (Kristeva, 3)

The eviscerated "self," and its "my-self" rejection, is again suggested in the "Old Food" segment when Marie becomes the woman who trespasses the land of the dead. She is "A woman [who] stands in a dreamed cemetery where her daughter lies" (12). The evocation of Ruby in her grave associates Marie, her mother, as substitute "death." We read:

> Okay, Marie is dead. She inhabits texture of everything. An angel
>
> before you. You've got to make a life, you can't die. (12)

Not only is the topic of Marie's abject state of (non-being) "death" and the dead-daughter's buried abject corpse repeatedly called forth through these ghostly passages; but so, too, are remnants of either diseased, badly

shaped, or eviscerated human body parts—exemplified in the segment entitled "Overmodeled Skull." Again, this "title" is not descriptive. And the passage that follows does not mention a skull at all. But the titled segment goes
on to reflect upon the abjection associated with a reading of female sexual
parts: a woman's "crotch" that "still has power, with its tremendous frightening / slit . . . ." And this reading reverberates against another phrase, the
"soft world, full of murders / committed for one by others" (9). "Cellulite" is
another segment named for human body parts viewed as rejected, unpleas-
ant (in this case, one that conventions of socialized female beauty revile). In
this segment, we are told of "The pretty cell of your womb," showing "the
light of Eve Love," who is the local heroin addict. Like Eve Love's addiction,
the poet's novel's own abject forms repeat their "compulsions" to "destroy
yourself," a process which the narrator admits, "I serve" (21).

By "living" in the dump at that Kristevan "border . . . as a living being,"
Marie is a *female* "dump." She is down in the dump and she is "death"; she
is lied about and / or terrorized by local figures—like the "mean" or "cruel girls," those insular small-town angry teens who walk around with their
hairdos full of "resin and beeswax and rootlets / on their helmet heads, and
huge ears shaped like butterflies" (34). Yet even if vilified and harassed by
other abject figures, Marie is never dissuaded to vacate the vacancy of her
abject surroundings. Instead, ironically, she is "building this culture out of
will / and language and garbage" (29). From the time we are introduced to
Marie, it is hard not to notice that our Lady of the Dump is also the town
artist plying her (non-) trade:

> Marie made things in the gully: she made her life . . . she wrote things
> down on paper discarded in the dump . . . she made figures out of
> wood . . . . (10)

In other words, Marie takes it upon herself to remodel society's debris
and fashion its uselessness into something interesting and provocative. Her
process of "re"-making and "re"-inventing is her own culture-making ideal,
however unobjectified her "products" are or might become. Out of rot and
nothingness, Marie's own fecundity and creativity is inaugurated.

The fictional artist within the fiction, Marie, indeed, is sympathetically
aligned with the poet-narrator. "Marie's next priority," we are told in the
book, is working on "The codex." The "codex" is a parallel manuscript to
that of the one the poet-narrator is composing in *Culture of One*. As found
object, it exists as some writer-artist's forsaken manuscript discovered on
top of Marie's dung heap. This abject (non-)object is retrieved by Marie; its

rejected (unpublished, unread) status becomes fodder for Marie's (pretend) "usefulness." Salvaging it from the dump encourages her creative exploration. The codex is described winningly as

> a true dump
> manuscript, a book of pages of any paper, cardboard
> covers, with text and illustrations in ink, crayon, the occasional blood,
> and other pigments exactly at hand—char-black rubbed leaf, there
> aren't often petals out here (29)

Reading such passages, one can almost experience the fumes emitting from "the codex" and feel the abject dampness of this abandoned yet embodied text. Its figure for human refuse and the creative potential in abjection is strangely blended with the body of the artist: Marie herself—and the (missing) body in this book of the poet-author.

Marie becomes like a codex scribe and a writer both. She is *distinct* from the poet-narrator and *like* her at once—even blended *with* her (again, on the level of the body, in the "blood and other pigments"). Marie fuses / is confused with (and by) the poet-narrator throughout *Culture of One*, just as Marie is fused within the meta-frame of the book as dump, and as artist's lair. The book works on all levels of "author" and "poet's workshop," "plot setting" and "language landscape." Marie quite literally "models" for the poet-narrator what to do. This fact is asserted in one of the early segments also named for an abject human-body part, called "Skull," in which we are never certain who is speaking—the poet-narrator-Marie, or all of these personae combined:

> I took a skull and transformed it. It looks like
> a different one . . . .
>   . . .
> Then I know I'm the beautiful monster I've made . . . . (11)

If the "I" in this passage is Marie *and* the poet-narrator, the "I" must be a multiple construct of (non-)being, whose state of abjection is continuously rejecting or "expelling," in that Kristevan term, "*myself*" (ironically a term Kristeva places in the first-person singular in her theory). The writer behind and amidst *Culture of One*, like Marie, is not only a scribbler of the abject (on paper scraps), but is a figure of the genre-destroying—also creating / re-creating—multi-media artist. Marie is making a hybrid text out of the codex and other dump elements. She literally sculpts other art objects out of her found materials. Working with the "media" available at hand, Marie "wrote things down on paper discarded in the dump and she made figures out of wood and rocks and cord . . . and whatever" (10). A sculptor and writer of / upon scraps, and a rejected-manuscript "codex" redactor, Marie and the poet-narrator reshape the available field of reading / writing / visual-art bounds.

Marie plays the role of the classical anthropological *bricoleur*, inventing and re-inventing "culture" continuously, out of the shards of what might be others' rubble heap. "Where does culture come from?" the poet-narrator asks—then answers her own question: "It comes from the materials you do it with." (10). "Culture, and the poet's novel, is that arbitrary series of linguistic activities and other utterance-like performances that humanity generates, however abject their effect or role. "Culture" is this engagement "of one," in applied continuous flow. "Culture" does not invent the world and remain static; it constantly is being re-made out of its own salvage. And art is that which pieces together cultural images of other images, and that someone "calls" art, however arbitrarily:

> When she made the shark out of rotting wood, I guess it was just a fish. A carp, probably; but she called it a shark. (10)

The cultural-artistic activity that takes place in Marie's dump represents what the larger framing device of the book itself is in the process of activating. These are the other characters, besides Marie, who are generated in the scrap heap that is this poet's novel. Figures like Leroy or dead Ruby are not the psychologically interior characters of conventional fiction, but stand as remnants of the abject hybrid landscape that was once literary formalism. Character figures carry only random "personality" traits. Leroy, for example, is first depicted in an action; he "drove to the casinos to play keno, boring keno" (making Leroy boring too?). A little later he is described as having "dark hair / making a peninsular shape down on his forehead; wavy hair; / he wore glasses" even though he has "never read a word in his life" (19). Leroy is a figure of radical paradoxes. It is not unexpected, then, when we learn he undergoes at least one dramatic, rather immediate change, from performing as the town liar—"Leroy had been lying so / much he couldn't think straight"—to performing as the town prophet, who speaks only truth by talking to the dead. Following a snake bite and the death of Ruby: "(. . .) The shock of the bite—and the trauma of Ruby's death—make Leroy tell the truth. Though it sounds / more than ever like lies" because he says he "talk[s]" to her [Ruby] . . . I see her in the afterlife (36-37).

"Truth" occurs through the surreal risen Ruby, filtered through her (non-)existence. Hence, if Leroy is the man who once spreads rumors that Marie is "some sort of witch or crazy person," he also understands that what Marie is doing is

inventing the world, and they / were in competition ... (19)

Leroy, like Marie—or other even more mysterious figures like the Eve Love who is "Marie's reprobate daughter, or is she?" (13)—relays the charged reflection of a traditional character barely surviving the novel's representational mirror. Notley's "characters" are not fleshed out and "whole." They are like cartoon stick figures—and yet credible as actors / people who fill the vacancies in the society of this desert community / dumpsite. What could be more authentically "real" in contemporary U.S. society than those frequent visits to the local Buy Rite by Marie? Leroy, the liar-turned-psychic-soothsayer, Marie as Our Lady of the Dump, the dead Ruby, Eve Love, the mean girls, the Satanic girl (with whom the mean girls associate in "a graduated back / way—up from gullies, and creosote bushes" (56)) all stand in stark contrast to other figures who are not characterological personae at all, but might best be described as collective, community energies of the beatific and moral good. These are goddess figures with stage names, who are even more difficult to differentiate, one from the other. Like Marie, they are usually associated with the witness figure of the poet-narrator herself. These goddess figures pose, however, "Not a clear image" (3).

The figure of Mercy is one of them, with her "thousand arms," a spiritual guide who is "Really completely healing" (58). Mercy is modeled upon the East Asian Buddhist "bodhisattva," called in China Guanyin, short for Guanshiyin. She is both goddess of compassion and mother figure; she embraces suffering humanity with her compassionate arms, and also traditionally has offered women the promise of fertility.[5] The poet-narrator identifies with Mercy's creative, generative powers:

I became Mercy with her one thousand arms; they were all I was. All over my front and from my back
. . .
... The arms were the space of me: what was my face

Yet another Asian goddess spirit who presents herself in *Culture of One* is Tara, who comes from ancient Hindu tradition (her name "Tara" comes from Sanskrit). Tara is a goddess of wisdom who is viewed in a range of colors. In the segment entitled "A Tale of Mercy," the voice of Mercy seems to compete with—and yet also become the same as—her divine sister Tara:

> Oh, around the 6th century the concept of Tara was elaborated
> In the north of India, from where it passed to Java and Tibet. I'm
> Older than that . . .
>
> . . . I touch myself and lose my social presentation of
> clothes and hair, becoming crystalline, plasmatic . . . . (35)

The poet-narrator, too, is repeatedly associated with Tara, just as she is with Mercy (like she is Marie). In "Once Again," the poet-narrator tells of walking

> . . . into the body of grey Tara, the lotus cloud, encompassing
> the elementary school and the desert and mountains behind. This is
> a fully bloomed grey lotus. I don't have to know anything, any
>
> more. Nonetheless there are words in the grain of the cloud (31)

The lotus image has long been connected to the goddess of Mercy. If Marie is the local "madwoman," a woman living on a dunghill, this passage/segment continues to tell us that the abject is in and of us all: "We are connected to the same lotus" (31).

Is that the voice of Mercy or Marie? Or the voice of the poet-narrator? Undifferentiated identities and the multiple "vocals" in this poet's novel lack the social structure to be "peopled," maintaining the strange presence of the abject in its stead. "Dumped" together, Marie who is Tara who is Mercy who is the authorial-voice of this poet's novel is also "Mary"—as in "Virgin Mary." Our Lady of the Dump is, after all, a spiritualized apparition like a Virgin Mary sighting in *Culture of One.* "She" is both the artist who makes these books of radical "strangeness" possible, and spiritual irony itself. Contained in the likely identities of a possible historic "Virgin" Mary is, after all, the abjection of Christ's mother in Christian theology and iconography.

For the "Virgin" Mary's ideality is socially concealed in the abjection of her truer condition. Not only is she a weeping "Pieta" of art, holding the corpse of her child; but, as recent scholarship about the "Virgin Mary" of tradition suggests, this female figure of the divine *as she has been worshipped* is a derivative of the Egyptian goddess Isis and other widely revered historical female deities of the Mediterranean Basin (hence, the manifestation of so many "Black Madonnas" in churches and shrines around Christianized Europe). Furthermore, any historical mother of a "Jesus of Nazareth" figure would have likely been a temple "prostitute," implied even in Mary's name, which in its original Hebrew implies a girl who would be socially reared for purposes of the so-called Sacred Marriage. This pagan ritual of sexual ceremony, intended by desert people to encourage the fertility of crops and livestock, was widely practiced throughout Mesopotamia-influenced northern Palestine (the location of Nazareth) and other pre- and post-Hellenic cultures of the region.

Is "Marie"—or Mary—the abject version of an abject "Virgin," whose ideal iconic image in the history of Christianity and its art undermines Biblical insistence on monotheism? Middle-Eastern religious scholarship suggests that these sexual rites celebrating pagan goddesses were commonplace among the Hebrew-Jewish tribes and non-Jews alike, and that they inevitably threatened monotheism's invention at its roots.[6] "Marie" (an English / Italian variant on the Latin "Maria," from the Hebrew for "Miryam") is the working-girl signifier of religious-institutionalism's rejection of the abject "*im*proper." Marie's / Mary's job is to excavate the roots of society's ambitions and false ideals, and reveal within its loftiest and most revered forms the existence of—the artistic-linguistic *performance* of—the abject. The woman living in the dump in *Culture of One*, hence, stays there as a highly subversive agent of monotheistic culture. She is an agent that undermines the grand fictions upon which much of Western culture is built. Like her nemesis Leroy, curiously, Marie's figure "lies"—and also speaks the truth. In this fiction of a cultural fiction, and in the context of the hybrid poet's novel, a (non-)genre, many secrets that "lie" within American latter-day civilization are revealed. Marie's "culture" is not just of "one," but exists on the fringes of nowhere and everywhere. Leroy may be "counterfeit like all kings" ("king," in essence, only of the Buy-Rite store). But this poet's novel and its queen of the garbage castle "isn't counterfeit" at all. Instead, she "came into this world to master it in her own way / . . . changed your thoughts . . . ." (29). Marie and her abject "culture" represent a darker truth.

NOTES

1. Leslie Scalapino uses this phrase to describe her prose-poetry work, *The Return of Painting* in its "Appendix," published in the collection *Trilogy* (Northpoint Press, 1990).

2. Traditional novel chapters or traditional lyric poems as units in a conventional poetry collection do not exist in this text.

3. See Roland Barthes's discussion of "*l'écriture,*" which is loosely translated as "writing," in *Writing Degree Zero*. Translated by Annette Lavers and Colin Smith. Jonathan Cape, 1967.

4. For example, Shklovsky writes, "deceleration" occurs in "the device of a belated rescue . . . widely used in legends and in adventure novels," in which the "fate of the hero, caught, it seems, in a hopeless predicament," is "unexpectedly resolved" (33, 35). Or another type of deceleration is the device of "framing." Examples of this latter type occur in *A Thousand and One Nights*, "in which amidst the most terrifying torments, at death's door, the characters relate or . . . hear out . . . all sort of fables" (42).

5. The Mercy goddess probably emerged from the Mahayana Buddhists, and her name in Sanskrit (first recorded version in the 5th Century) is Avalokitasvara. In Daoist belief, she is a figure not only of unconditional love and compassion, champion of the sick and poor, but also a fertility goddess who can grant good fortune linked to the birth of children.

6. For one such discussion of the pagan goddess that "Mary" might have named and represented, see Michael Jordon, *The Historical Mary: Revealing the Pagan Identity of the Virgin Mother* (Ulysses Press, 2003).

WORKS CITED

Browne, Laynie. "A Conversation with Alice Notley on the Poet's Novel." *Jacket2*, March 15, 2013.

Deville, Michel. *American Prose Poem: Poetic Form and the Boundaries of Genre.* UP Florida, 1998.

Kristeva, Julia. *The Powers of Horror: An Essay on Abjection*. Translated by Leon S. Roudiez. Columbia UP, 1982.

Notley, Alice. *Culture of One.* Penguin Poets, 2011.

Shklovsky, Viktor. *Theory of Prose.* Translated by Benjamin Sher. Dalkey Archive Press, 1990.

Silliman, Ron, editor. *The American Tree.* National Poetry Foundation, 1986.

This article was originally published in the *Journal of Foreign Languages and Cultures,* 3, 1 (June 2019).

II

GENRE MASH-UPS

Composite, Cut-Ups, Review, Sci Fi, Writer as Detective

The images set off down the road and yet they never get anywhere, they're simply lost, it's hopeless, says the voice—and the hunchback asks himself, hopeless for who?
—ROBERTO BOLAÑO, *Antwerp*

The Cornucopia is Mapped
with a Slipping Venn-Diagram and a Möbius Strip
William Carlos Williams and his *The Great American Novel*

SARAH VAP

William Carlos Williams called his anti-greatamericannovel *The Great American Novel*.

Williams wrote his *The Great American Novel* in 1923.

Williams sutured things together to make his *The Great American Novel*.

He sutured in the stuff of popular magazines, he sutured in the stuff of his letters with Ezra Pound, he sutured in a past-due bill, he sutured in advertisements from newspapers, he sutured in the reviews of other peoples' Great American Novels, he sutured in details from case notes of his patients and he sutured in the stuff from history and ethnography books.

"No ideas but in things." Williams coined this phrase—it became one of the great white Modernist dictums. And so it follows that his *The Great American Novel* is full of things.

Williams was not only a writer, he was also a physician. As we see in the novel, he sutured together women after he gave them hysterectomies. I imagine he imagined suturing together those women at the same time that he sutured together the bits and pieces of America, as he understood it, into his *The Great American Novel*.

He was a family doctor for primarily the working class of Rutherford, NJ. He delivered the babies. He fixed the bones. He sent dying people to specialists, or eased them toward death himself. He sutured this and he sutured that just as.

Williams sutured together his *The Great American Novel* from the entire trove of words available to him in America and yet—all the while he wrote his *The Great American Novel*, he searched for one, single word: the perfect word. *Le mot juste* . . . A search at the heart of his novel that is also antithetical to the idea of a novel.

But not only must the word be perfect . . . . ."That's all very fine about *le mot juste* but first the word must be free." (171) The word he searches for across his *The Great American Novel* must be perfect *and* free.

We're never to understand, reading his *The Great American Novel*, how or what a free word is. And, as far as I can tell, he fails, surely purposefully, across the entirety of his *The Great American Novel* to find *le mot juste*, to find the free word.

And what are we to make of that?

He speaks of free words in his *Autobiography*, as well.

I was permitted by my medical badge to follow the poor, defeated body into those gulfs and grottos. And the astonishing thing is that at such times and in such places—foul as they may be with the stinking ischio-rectal abcesses of our comings and goings—just there, in all its greatest beauty, may for a moment be *freed* to fly for a moment guiltily about the room. (Emphasis mine.)

But what is *it* that flies free guiltily for a moment in the stink of the comings and goings of the bodies? Is it that holy grail, his *le mot juste*? He continues:

In illness, in the permission I as a physician have had to be present at deaths and births, at the tormented battles between daughter and diabolic mother, shattered by a gone brain—just there—for a split second—from one side or the other, it has fluttered before me for a moment, a phrase which I quickly write down on anything at hand, any piece of paper I can grab. (289).

No—not a word, but a phrase. In *Autobiography*, the momentarily-freed language, freed only in the most-liminal instants between life and death, is *the phrase*.

In his *The Great American Novel*, he searches for a single (perfect, free) word. In his *Autobiography*, he searches for a single (freed) phrase. Which makes us wonder: why is he writing a novel? Or an autobiography?

And thinking further on *freedom* and *America*—they are like bees and honey, like "wish" and "wash," *non*?

They are purposefully invoked together both in his *The Great American Novel* and in his *Autobiography*, but nothing is simple, and everything slips, in the Venn-Diagrams of Williams' "things" and "ideas." No ideas but in things.

In the very first line of his *The Great American Novel*, Williams writes: "If there is progress then there is a novel." This anti-greatamericannovel, then, seems to exist in the spaces between a single word (*le mot juste*), the phrase (flying about the birth and death room for but an instant), and progress (interminable). But his particular *The Great American Novel* achieves none of them.

I have to think this is the point. This non-achievement isn't an accident: this is his purpose.

Progress . . . progression, that most-American violence, becomes equivalent to the accumulation of words that is the novel. Williams undoes the novel, undoes America, undoes progress, undoes freedom, even as he writes his *The Great American Novel*. And this is not a criticism of the book on my part—I'm not interested in his achieving any of those things. This isn't an accident on his part: this interesting and relentless fail is the purpose of this poet's novel.

Williams circles the unfound, perfect, free word with his circular language and circular sutures and circular naming of "things," and then calls all that failure-to-find and circularity his *The Great American Novel*.

As someone who lived in the same small town in New Jersey his entire life, Williams is billed as the *most American*, and even most provincial, of American poets.

Yet Williams also attended schools in Geneva, Paris, and Germany.

Yet Williams traveled widely in Europe.

He spent weekends with his friends Man Ray and Mina Loy and Marcel Duchamp and Marianne Moore in New York City.

He had his affairs. He had his cars. He had his parents from other countries who spoke other languages.

Williams is paradoxical—and especially his American-ness.

Williams wanted to modernize American poetry by imbuing it with the speech of contemporary America.

In his *The Great American Novel* Williams was trying to be funny, and his title proves this. His Quixotic search for the single perfect word proves this.

Nonetheless, Williams took his *The Great American Novel* seriously. At least, he took its failure seriously. Its purpose was to fail. Its purpose was to undermine the values that would make possible a belief in something called a Great American Novel.

In Williams' take on it, there is no plot in *The Great American Novel*. There is an accumulation of things and people and, in them, his ideas. There are no transformations or transcendences in his novel. There are no problems solved, and at the end, the reader arrives nowhere. Williams undoes all expectations about a novel, and especially, an American novel, and extra-especially, a Great American Novel. The arrival nowhere, the circularity, the non-transcendence, the non-revelation, the no moral to the story, the lack of developed characters, the tone of "meh" . . . . All are part of the effort to undo the ideas he wants to undo.

In his *Autobiography* Williams calls his *The Great American Novel* "a satire on the novel form in which a little (female) Ford car falls more or less in love with a Mack truck." That love affair takes up but a moment of his *The Great American Novel*. His plot summary is, itself, satire, feint, and failure.

I think Williams' *The Great American Novel* was a serious effort to show a failing endeavor, a failing set of values, and a non-novel-mind. His *The Great American Novel* enacted the failing endeavor that is any mindset, or person, or industry that might seriously attempt a greatamericannovel.

A failing The-ness. A failing Great-ness. A failing American-ness. A failing Novel-ness.

Williams shows an ongoing concern with immigrants and Native Americans in his *The Great American Novel*. What kind of concern it is, exactly, is hard to decipher. But his *The Great American Novel* is full of references to, and information about, and descriptions of, poor people, immigrant people, female people, and people of color.

Williams describes actual women in *The Great American Novel*. Women who ask for hysterectomies. Women who are wide and strong. Women who are naked girls.

He observes vulnerable people, he describes vulnerable people, but I'm never really sure how he feels about them. If he cares about them. I am never sure what he understands or intends about the implications of such descriptions. If he's critical of the plights he describes. If he's critical of the people. What sorts of intentions are behind his inclusions. How these things matter.

Ezra Pound approved of the novel, according to their letters. In a letter from Williams to Pound, dated Sept. 11, 1922, he writes: "I am overwhelmed by your approval of my NOVEL." (Williams' emphasis.) This same letter opens with the unsettling, upsetting, inscrutable "If I yank negroid morons and continue to do so it is only in defeat—knowing that I cannot run on air."

Or his next letter to Pound, November 22 of the same year, Williams writes: "God knows I should like to sit down quietly in contemplation before a few undiseased and naked cunts for a few months—sit down that is until I should recuperate from my last ten years vigil."

Certainly Williams saw all kinds of people. Certainly Williams had access to frail or intimate parts of people's bodies. Had access to people whose bodies were breaking, whose lives were difficult. He had access to cunts. Williams' people slip into *things*. His female patients, his lovers?: *a few undiseased and naked cunts*.

"Somehow a word must be found," says the narrator / writer of his *The Great American Novel*. "Only words and words. He ate another bunch of grapes. More words. And never THE word."

The book suggests its failure throughout. The book suggests grandiosity throughout.

"I feel sincerely that all they say of me is true, that I am truly a great man and a great poet." (167), says the narrator / writer of his *The Great American Novel*. The author of Williams' *The Great American Novel*, then, is a *poet*—and no, not just that, but a *GREAT POET*—who, a few pages later, admits that he doesn't even know what a novel is. "What then is a novel?" He asks. Immediately he answers his own question:

Un novello, pretty, pretty Baby. It is a thing of fixed form. It is pure English. Yes, she is of Massachusetts stock. Her great grandfather was thrown out of the Quaker church for joining the Continental army. Hates the English. Her life is a novel—almost too sensational. The story of Miss Li—so well told.

And so here we have a definition of the novel within his *The Great American Novel*, written, as we know, by a narrator who refers to himself as a Great Poet.

So, let's try to unpack this Great Poet-narrator's definition of novel!

- *Novello* in Italian meant *new* until sometime in the sixteenth century, when it began to mean *new story*—and then this new story progressed until it meant in Italian what it now means in English: a novel.
- Novel, which in English can also still mean new.
- Remember, Pound's famous (white) Modernist dictum was: "Make it new." So, according to the definition Williams gives, the novel is also new—like a baby. A pretty, pretty Baby.
- This novel, this newness is, however, the kind of newness that is stationary, according to Williams' definition: "It is a thing of fixed form." Which is: impossible, contradictory, counter-intuitive, a koan.

But it gets even more impossible. Let's keep parsing Williams' Great Poet-narrator's definition.

- *Un novello* is Italian, which is also "pure English."
- The novel, (a masculine noun in Italian), is also a female of Massachusetts stock.

- Which might also intimate: American. The novel is a female American.

I'll keep going, but trying to follow the syntax becomes extremely difficult.

- The novella, the pretty Baby, the fixed form—they are all, or one of them is, pure English. They are all, or one of them is, a "she" of Massachusetts stock. They all, or one of them, hate(s) the English.
- They are pure English: but they hate the English.
- They all hate themselves, newly. Newly, but in a predictable way, in a fixed form!
- They all, or one of them, (continuing with his definition), have a life that *is a novel*.
- The novel has a life that is novel? Or, the "she" has a life that is novel?

The syntax, by the end of the definition, is incredibly slippery, multiple, refuses clarity. Each thing points to many possible other things. No ideas but in things—but with shifting and slippery things, we get shifting and slippery ideas.

The definition of "novel," as it is given to us by the Great Poet-narrator / writer of William's *The Great American Novel*, and as it is understood through the series "things," (people) is: ?

I can't stop!—I'll keep trying to parse this definition of novel.

- The novel is Miss Li, or, the "she" is Miss Li.
- Miss Li, we could understand, is *well told*.

The surname Li "is a pinyin or Wade-Giles romanization of several distinct Chinese surnames that are written with different characters in Chinese. Li is the most common among them, shared by 93 million people in China, and more than 100 million worldwide. Languages using the Latin alphabet do not distinguish among the different Chinese surnames, rendering them all as Li." (Wikipedia).

- Miss Li might be *one particular person*, who happens to be well told. Or,
- Miss Li might be an *idea* of "Chinese, female." Or,
- She might be an *idea* of the "melting pot" of "America." Or,
- She might be an *idea* of "novel."

So, how does his *The Great American Novel* proceed after this slippery, contradictory, and specifically *poetic* definition "novel"?

The line immediately following the Great Poet narrator/writer's definition of novel in his *The Great American Novel*: "*Qu'avez-vous vu?*" French for: what did you see?

Line immediately following "*Qu'avez-vous vu?*": "Speak of old Sun Bow pacing his mesa instead of Felipe Segundo in the barren halls of El Escorial— or asleep in his hard bed at one corner of the griddle."

- A directive: Speak. Who speaks? A novel? A greatamericannovel speaks of old Sun Bow pacing his mesa?
- And whatever or whoever is being told to speak, they are also being told they should NOT speak of Felipe Segundo, the European king in his palace. Felipe Segundo, that
- European King who used the vast wealth he stole from the New World to fund the imperial Catholic Church back in Europe—he should not be spoken of. Instead: old Sun Bow should be spoken of.
- Sun Bow is important to this anti-greatamericannovel, the European kings are not.

And here, I also have to ask—:

- Is he saying that his *The Great American Novel* should speak of *old Sun Bow* either pacing his mesa, or (old Sun Bow) asleep in his hard bed at one corner of the griddle? OR,
- Is Williams saying that his *The Great American Novel* should *not speak* of *Felipe Segundo* in the barren halls of El Escorial or (Felipe Segundo) asleep in the hard bed at one corner of the griddle.

Yes, he is.

All these slippery variations of syntax and "definition" and reference are being purposefully used by Williams. He's not a careless writer who doesn't use punctuation well. He's being multiple, he's being ambivalent, he's being circular.

And to what end?

The syntax of Williams' *The Great American Novel* is a functional möbius strip made of "things."

The things of Williams' *The Great American Novel* can be tracked only via something like a 4-D and slippery Venn-diagram.

As we have seen, people are often the "things" of his *The Great American Novel*. And Williams' people usually aren't the primarily European and Mediterranean peoples and gods and heroes and mythological references that are found in his friend Ezra Pound's poetry.

There is some effort to de-center the greatamericannovel from its history of whiteness, its history of European-ness. The people focused on in Williams' *The Great American Novel* are, as he sees it, American peoples.

People must then hold the "ideas" of his *The Great American Novel*, because, if we follow his dictum, Williams has no ideas but in things. But can we, then, articulate the ideas that must follow?

Next line after Sun Bow: "My mother would have a little Negro boy come with a brush and sit at her feet and brush her legs by the hour."

Next line after the little black boy brushing her feet by the hour: "Expressionism is to express skillfully the seething reactions of the contemporary European consciousness. Cornucopia. In at the small end and—blui! Kandinsky."

Wait—what?

People of America are represented, yes, thing-like, and as perceived by his own European consciousness. And Williams knows it. Yet the list of people ends with this naming of one (European, theoretical, abstract, high-art, white, masculine) individual person: Kandinsky.

And what does that image mean? Expressionism into the "small end" of the "cornucopia"— blued, is his Kandinsky? Is this passage following his definition of the novel an image of the horn of plenty: Is this his image of America?

Who knows!!

But we could say that, perhaps, Williams understands that he has a primarily male and a white European consciousness, even though he is billed as the *most American* of modernist poets.

We could say that Williams also understands that America is made up of Chinese women, of Native Americans, of black children, of women of Massachusetts stock, of English, of individuals like the specifically named (maybe) Sun Bow and Miss Li.

In his *The Great American Novel*, Williams, I could say, does not endeavor to *only* tell the story of European Consciousness. I could say that, despite that wish, he understands he is able, finally, to do nothing else.

And I could say that Williams does endeavor to include people who are not white, European-descent men. He makes some kind of an effort to present the cornucopia!

And I could say that his *The Great American Novel*, to this end, does also fail.

And I could say that his *The Great American Novel*, despite his efforts, and as he knew it would, and as he intended it to do, but self-critically, *only* tells the story of a white man of European descent.

And I could say that Williams wanted his *The Great American Novel* (functionally, conceptually) to fail. Even as satire. Which it does. Which it should.

This failure, for me, succeeds as a project if it is a purposeful, useful, functional, deeply truthful, and poetic failure of a novel.

Failure in purpose. Failure in language. Failure in America. Failure in particular American *ideas*. Failure of *le mot juste*.

And poetry, just like Great Poet-narrator of an anti-greatamericannovel, loves to endeavor toward failures of such sorts.

Williams and I, neither of us believe enough in this American idea of white male intellectual glory to believe in a Great American Novel. Bah. At least, I think he doesn't believe in it. But the Mobius strip of his *The Great American Novel* turns and turns. And the Venn-diagrams of his "Cornucopia" of things slips and slips. And the ideas, usefully, rightly, are still failing.

Friendship as Method in Ashbery & Schuyler's *A Nest of Ninnies*

GEOFFREY G. O'BRIEN

When a poet elects to write a novel the resulting text raises two related questions: why inhabit this other genre and why abandon one's genre-identity at all? The text may or may not answer these questions, but it is charged with them for the reader who knows the author's work in verse; the internal compositional choices as to structure, content, and diction will seem doubly full, standing as instances of what the poet values in prose and of why she would "abandon" poetry to produce it. There is also the reasonable assumption that the poet who crosses over into prose fiction will bring with her, intentionally or involuntarily, many of the habits and capacities of verse—lyric attunement to situation, a productively estranging vocabulary, a care for the insides of sentences that rivals attention to the fictive insides of characters. But what happens when, instead of a Poet's Novel, we encounter a Poets' Novel, when the apostrophe of possession moves along with the genre and the text becomes the collaborative construction of two poets rather than univocal lyric utterance and singular narration? This is the question John Ashbery and James Schuyler's *A Nest of Ninnies* poses: as a poets' novel, it's an example of both genre and procedure, at once inviting questions about the turn from verse to prose fiction and disabling easy answers about lyric charge and poetic sensibility since the novel was not made by a poet's mind, or even by minds, but by the method of writing running between them.

The particular collaborative procedure by which most of the novel was written—alternating sentences while in each other's company—discourages plotting and turns the space of prose composition into a formal conversation between two poet-friends as well as a transpersonal meditation on the vernacular and commodity culture in which they were raised. It is no accident then that most of this novel's prose is in quotation marks. The novel's longstanding predilection for reporting speech, and with that speech a set of master codes for social relations, here becomes a figure for the two poets' procedural conversation which is itself the sign of their embodied friendship. If the novel is typically produced and consumed alone, then this "novel" (Ashbery himself uses these scare quotes to insist they didn't write

Ninnies for public consumption but as a mutual entertainment) would at least be literally dialogic in its production, only possible for the most part when the poets formed a first person plural: "It seemed we needed to be in each other's presence to write it" (6).

There are many singular plurals in *Ninnies* besides its co-authorship and the friendship that collaboration denotes: the singular / plural of the title itself and the fact that it is also the title of another, much older book; the suburbs and the nuclear family structure to which the title here in part refers; the way in which the characters' constant use of quotation nearly makes French and English constitute a single language; even the printing off of multiple characters named "Memmo." But perhaps the quietest form is the novel itself, co-tenanted by both traditional fictional materials and verse effects like disjunction and citation. The novel is typically read as a satire of "America and her tragic suburbs" (79), but it is equally a parody of the fiction form itself that sends its prose elements towards the condition of poetry: made overwhelmingly of dialogue, its characters' utterances are for the most part unresponsive to each other, more intercut monologues "apropos of nothing" (18) than a representation of plausible conversation; its chaptering is as reasonless or anti-conceptual as a strophe, simply happening after a certain duration of sentence-making, marking disruptions of time and place rather than a developing narrative. Fiction's traditional "[w]ork doesn't get done," instead "one abandons it" (134), much like the method by which this fiction was written: each author abandoning the ongoingness to his partner, turn by turn, and the chapters proceeding by a serial abandonment of scene and issue. But this internal reference to the work of writing the novel is also a "version of Valéry's dictum" (134) that poems are never finished, only abandoned, suggesting that there is a way in which a collaborative prose fiction that abandons the usual work of the genre—"the lack not only of sex but even of much of a plot" (6)—verges on becoming a poem.

However, *Ninnies* is not a poem, it is only somewhat like a poem: written by poets, unconcerned with conventional narrative trajectory, and studded with estranging, low-frequency words like *caprine, rutilant, commensals, farandole,* and *foehn* that disrupt a fictional world and call us back to the material qualities of the sign. It would be more accurate then to say that *Ninnies* is less a novel or a poem than the record of a compositional procedure by which, as Ashbery puts it in the Preface, he and Schuyler had "ambled along, addressing each other through our ninny characters . . . simply to entertain ourselves" (7). These ninnies are borrowed from Robert Armin's 1608 satire, *A Nest of Ninnies,* which Ashbery refers to as "an Elizabethan *sottiserie*" (7), but this novel is as much parody as satire. A parody is literally a song that runs alongside something else and here that song is the method by which two poets address each other via the types and residues of "the 1930s world of our childhoods" (7). The novel's dialogue, its reported speech, also reports on an actual conversation between Ashbery and Schuyler in which they speak their poetic friendship alongside the genre of prose and the structuring language of family, nesting in its empty idioms and absurd positions "where children play among the ruins of the language" (188) until the familiar (in every sense) is also un-.

In pedantically distinguishing between parody and satire, I'm leaving room for this literary friendship between two queer men to function as both more and less than an antagonistic alternative to the heteronormative family structures the book comically over-represents. The compositional procedure by which that representation happens may be a metonym for an embodied friendship between Ashbery and Schuyler, but it happens as much alongside (and in the voices of) the family model as it does against it—this is, after all, the world of "our childhoods." It is hard to disentangle moments satirizing the suburban family nest from moments of unrepentant nostalgia for its sheltering function and apertures onto cultures high, low, and middlebrow. Perhaps this is why the family unit in *Ninnies* is lampooned primarily via its functioning all too well. At the novel's beginning, a brother and sister live together as though man and wife (it isn't till page 20 that the relationship between Alice Bush and her brother Marshall is clarified); though adults, neither Fabia nor Victor Bridgewater has as yet escaped the nest of their parents' home, nor can the much older Irving Kelso leave his mother. The love of family, which is supposed to school children in love-relations and then graduate them into families of their own, here seems to be too strong, keeping adult kids from becoming people who would have somewhere and someone else to go to. While this hypostasis of the familial bond is surely one of the jokes that the novel starts as early as its title, it is worth remarking that these over-persistent family ties also look a great deal like friendship, an optional relation between persons rather than the imposed relation of the nuclear. Even as the family unit is rendered morbidly vigorous by the co-authors, it also begins to approximate their own mutuality—friendship and family are parodies of each other rather than the terms of an opposition.

Family is as hard to abandon as writing (either Valéry's poem *or Ninnies'* authorial "turns") is easy to, a contrast the novel establishes fairly early on:

> Victor leaned wearily against the sink. "I don't know why I'm never able to bring anything to a successful completion. I intended to leave

home today and wrote Mother a letter yesterday saying I was. But it got so cold during the night that I decided to wait till this morning, and the mail came before I was out of the house. It hardly seems worthwhile to go through with it now."

While the letter can be dashed off and casually mailed, the son cannot bring its declarations "to a successful completion," cannot make narrative good on writing's promises by following through on what Mother has been told. If we look at this passage as procedure rather than as satire of family's fatal gravity, not being able to bring things to completion becomes the definition of the "successful" or at least the successive. Whether Ashbery or Schuyler wrote "Victor leaned wearily against the sink" (my money is on Ashbery given the sentence's echoes of Ashbery's opening sentence of the novel, "Alice was tired."), each ensuing sentence becomes one of two authors' reactions to the other, a tennis match that also produces the illusion of topical and subjective continuity called "Victor Bridgewater." The "But" that begins the paragraph's fourth sentence is as much a sign of the poets' reactions to each other as it is an indication of a logic internal to Victor's brief story. Successive incompletions are the formal method by which the novel produces speech and event, constantly leaving sentences without arriving at narrative satisfaction; the method divorces cumulative writing from plot's destiny.

When the adult children are finally able to leave their familial nests they do so by entering into matrimonial engagements that are indistinct from small business—an antiques partnership between Victor and the Frenchwoman Nadia Tosti (and her sister Claire) or the Italian restaurant opened by Alice Bush and the Giorgio (cf. de Chirico) she acquired while abroad. This belated and instantaneous transfer from family of origin to marriage as going concern is obviously more satire than parody, literalizing what we already half-know, that the nuclear family is a productive economic arrangement in addition to whatever else it may be and sponsor. Yet even here, late in the novel, when the pairings-off come fast and furious (the inveterate bachelor Irving Kelso will also find a mate in Claire Tosti) and come with business plans, it is still hard to see this as only a critique of heterocapitalism or a satire of the enduring applicability of the nineteenth century's fictional "marriage market"; the very tidiness and explicitness of the matchmaking satire also render the characters modular and their interactions and affiliations then become recombinative. It is as much a villanelle or sestina of proper names as it is a tidying up of narrative's loose ends and assertion of the relation of eros to property. This liability of putative persons to recombination is one more way the novel admits that its characters, despite their distinct proper names, have always been the fungible sources from whose mouths comes the invariant, alternating speech of the poets' game, a song from the nest.

Long before we arrive at these false resolutions, *Ninnies* has been thinking about the unsuccessful completions by which narrative transmits itself: chapters. But in this novel we cannot think chapter on its own, as a formal division, because its way of happening is intimately tied to another prose resource: dialogue. Here are the opening sentences of Chapters 2–9:

"What are you going to do today, Fabia," Victor asked.
"Miss Alice Bush," Irvin Kelso said . . . .
"I'm disappointed," Fabia said.
"I'm sorry," Fabia said . . . .
"Snowdrops," Mrs. Bridgewater said . . .
"It's wonderful what white paint will do for a place," Victor said.
"I have just spoken to the concierge," Dr. Bridgewater said.
"It's hard to believe it wasn't built to look that way," Alice said . . . .

Not only does there seem to be a rule developing that chapters must begin with dialogue (this will begin to fray in Chapter 10, for an interesting reason we will consider later), but there's a second quiet constant, the nearly invariant verb for expressing past speech: "said." That invariance might remind us of the virtuosic and relentless use of forms of the verb *to flow* in Ashbery's "Into the Dusk-Charged Air," but here the unchanging verb denies its characters idiosyncrasy. They all possess and are possessed by the same power of speech, or the names may change but the saying remains the same. When we imagine that some of these sentences must be Ashbery's and some Schuyler's, the persistence of this flat, inexpressive verb of expression becomes even more charged—it is a dictional ground on which the two poets can meet or a playful cascade of reactions to each other, a game in which the authors see how long they can occupy the loud position of chapter's opening with a formal shadow-rule that gives the lie to differences in character and thus to speech itself. The ubiquitous *said* is at once a sign of the characters' exchangeability and impersonality and of the good transpersonality of the writing itself.

Using "said" over and over in the pattern-apprehensible position of a chapter's first sentence, in a place where fiction's form most resembles a verse capacity to mark repetition, is not the only reason dialogue reliably occurs there. As I mentioned above, each of these moments of dialogue also marks a jump through time and space—at first from house to house in a suburb of Connecticut (Ch.2) and then into New York City (Ch.3), further afield to Florida (Ch.4), and eventually to France and Italy (Ch. 8 and 9). The violation of time from chapter to chapter is insignificant, traditional, and the violation of place-continuity only slightly less so, but that these disruptions or leaps are routinely effected by dialogue is crucial. Opening with dialogue denies in each case a prefatory narration that would situate us in the new context about to unfold and possibly even explain how and why the fiction had gotten to this new time and place or what had happened in the backformed and fictive interval between one chapter's close and the next's inception; instead, initially unsituated speech. What this does is associate dialogue with something other than its embedding in situation—it becomes not only a formal position within a logic of chaptering, but a sign, and an instance, of the fictive leap itself rather than the new context leaped to. As such, initial dialogue further asserts itself as a record of the poets' own leaps of execution, since of course whoever wrote the last sentence of the prior chapter is not the author of this opening moment of reported speech. Character-speech at chapter's opening marks the invisible passage in authorship between Ashbery and Schuyler as much as it marks a motion through unsupplied fictional time and space.

In Chapter 10, something else happens:

> Mrs. Bridgewater averted her gaze from the flotsam, then looked hastily back, lest she step off the quay and into it. (111)

While this opening breaks the string of quotation marks and *said*s to which we've grown accustomed at chapter's beginning, it is not the only new formal development that occurs here. If we look hastily back at the last sentence of Chapter 9 (in fact the entire last paragraph bears consideration), we find a new character has been introduced into the narration:

> Before Victor could ask the question that leaped to his lips, Claire and Nadia came down the stairs. They were dressed in Austrian walking outfits and singing the "Swing Duet" from *Véronique*. The sight of Victor halted them mid-trill. Just at that moment, another thunderbolt erupted from the chimney, plunging the hotel in darkness. And there we must leave them for a while. (110)

The transpersonal and thus doubly unattributed narration of Ashbery and Schuyler suddenly acquires a name: "we." It's the first appearance of the overpopulated narrator in the novel (now nearly two-thirds of the way through) and, as with so many other moments and strategies in *Ninnies*, it is both conventional and not. We are used to the *we* of narration signifying a moment of direct address to an abstracted audience of readers, and there is no reason to doubt that that version is in play here, but beyond the first person plural of narrator and readers the *we* here also refers to the group of two generating the narration, the smallest first person plural there is, and one in which there is not yet room for any readers. As a description of the novel's composition and that composition's division into sentence-turns and optional chapter-divisions, this last sentence suddenly and explicitly asserts what every other sentence and moment of dialogue has been saturated with: the presence of two authors "singing a 'Swing Duet'" of procedure ("we must leave") and plunging spaces into narrative darkness so they can be left for new ones. It is retroactively less of a surprise then that Chapter 10 breaks with the dialogic opening Chapters 2 through 9 established right after this *we* of narration directly expresses itself—suddenly the "ninnies" no longer need to be the exclusive and indirect method by which Ashbery and Schuyler are "addressing each other." The characters are not merely left in the dark hotel by the narration and chaptering, but are abandoned as the primary site of authorial play and conversation. In a text without narrative necessity, "we must leave" can refer to little else but the productive exigency of procedure.

Once the singular plural of authorship has announced itself, its mentions pile up: "How the controversial work of art was finally removed . . . need not concern our readers" (120); "At the sight of our friends, she threw up her arms in dismay" (125-26); "We shall never know, since Fabia remained silent" (151). The characters of the novel and their speech have played host to a set of poets' decisions, a constant responsiveness about what colloquialisms, clichés, maxims, and actual poetry can be folded into the novel's materials. Both idiom and quotation cast reported speech and its character source as themselves the retransmission of another source, in this case two poets' traded reactions. This is what all the citationality in the novel ultimately refers to—the side song of procedure in which speech functions primarily as the cumulative materials of collage, the constructivism of poetry nesting in another genre.

Now that that collaborative principle has emerged as the principal character, the diction of narration begins to change as well, increasingly studding the text with arcane vocabulary more appropriate to a metrical or lyrical context than the informatic field of a satire. Those words I quoted above—*caprine, rutilant, commensals, farandole,* and *foehn*—all appear in the last third of the book, after the appearance of this "we," with *foehn* standing as the novel's very last word. In some ways the novel turns out to have been a deliberately unwitting, exquisite-corpselike passage from the zero-degree factual narration of "Alice was tired," with which the novel opens, to the running polylingual anapests and alliteration of "in the teeth of the freshening foehn" with which the "novel" closes. The emphasis on rare signifiers and their rhythmic properties attends the emergence of this compound poet-narrator who has been an absent, silent presence all along.

In fact, we could say that this "we" was heretofore the Chapter 13 of the novel, which doesn't exist (the novel goes straight from Chapter to 12 to Chapter 14 like a good elevator). That missing chapter or missing name for a chapter is at once a culturally-approved, idiomatic gap in sequence (a disjunction like chaptering become a disjunction *in* chaptering), a pet fear (*triskaidekaphobia*) of the odd, a polite euphemism, and an attack on linear sequence. As a conventional attack on the convention of sequence, it's emblematic of *Ninnies*, affectionately celebrating and making use of the very objects of its satire (family, novel, parlance) until they have a second life as parody, one sung by two singers, sentence by sentence. All the meanings of chapter 13 present absence ultimately refer to the decisions of its co-authors and are just like a pair of chairs discussed late in the novel—though "perfectly traditional," their "designs . . . are full of occult meaning" (166).

WORK CITED

Ashbery, John and Schuyler, James. *A Nest of Ninnies* (Vermont: Z Press, 1983).

A Greater Greatness
Max Brand's *Twenty Notches*
becomes Ted Berrigan's *Clear the Range*

EDMUND BERRIGAN

First Encounters

Clear the Range, with a bright yellow and white colored cover, always stood out in the bookcase. It was written by my father, Ted Berrigan, and there is also a large, crudely-drawn black and white picture of a cross-eyed cowboy with a handle bar mustache. The cover is a collaboration between Berrigan and the artist George Schneeman. The book attracted my attention as a teenager, but I couldn't quite understand what was going on in it, and was unable to bring myself to read it.

A few years later I took the copy with me to college. Reading it as a student of poetry, I was determined to get through it. The language was wild and interesting, but the plot was still incomprehensible. I treated it like a book of poems and read random passages from it. One in particular always stayed with me:

No man would make a fence. For his own part The Sleeper had no conscience. He had some peculiar charm that was connected to this, some mysterious power and attraction which made a snake point invariably at his eye. This power was sufficiently accurate to allow at least two or three good inches to a line.

Suppose, then, that he had been a quarter of an inch greater, the little tiger! In that case he'd shrink; he'd be pestered by a howling cloud of boy-wasps. He would have been drinking, free of charge, in the bar. He'd lie in a corner, with a sack over his face, and a pool of red flies all around. For nothing was easier than to drive air through the heart of the enemy.[1]

It seemed like advice, though I didn't understand how to follow it. Yet the passage felt complete, like a mysterious prose poem. Reading it now, the quality of pronouncement is absolute and profound, the representation of wildlife is fantastic and vivid, and each turn is unexpected. The concluding sentence is stunning as a self-reflection. None of it seems to make narrative sense, but the remark about adding "two or three good inches to a line" sounds writerly—a sly remark indicating that the confusion in the details is intentional.

Process And *Twenty Notches*

Though first published in 1977 by Adventures in Poetry/Coach House South, *Clear the Range* was begun in the mid-sixties. According to Ron Padgett, the book

> was inspired by a similar project that I was doing, called "Motor Maids Across The Continent", which in turn was inspired by the cross-out procedure that Kenneth Koch showed me one afternoon at his office at Columbia probably in the spring of 1964. Before that, Ted had never done a cross-out of found material, not to my knowledge, at least.[2]

The found text used by Berrigan for *Clear the Range* is Max Brand's *Twenty Notches*, a pulp western novel originally published in six parts in *Western Story Magazine* in 1932.[3] The plot revolves around a thief and tramp named "the Sleeper" (lowercase t), who sets out on a quest to acquire a famous gun—one with twenty notches on it, representing kills. The gun is believed to be magical, in that it can't miss.

Brand, whose real name was Frederick Schiller Faust, had a classical education, which remained a reference point for him as he wrote over a hundred western novels and short stories. At one point while living in Italy, he hired a tutor so that he could learn to read Homer in Greek. The influence of his classical education and his study of Greek mythology are present in *Twenty Notches*.[3]

> the Sleeper stood up and almost laughed in the darkness. So Perseus, with winged heels and the magic sword, might have stood beside the Gorgon.[4]

The harshness and violence that occurred in America's push west are part of the national mythology, and a continuing subject in artistic and entertainment culture. The mythos of the gun fighter in America resonates to this day, as gun violence and gun rights issues continue to be prominent in the news. *Twenty Notches* is a traditional western, with gun fights, card games, a helpless heroine, valuable horses, and black and white standards of justice. Violence is a mediating force. When the Sleeper acquires the loaded revolver early on in *Twenty Notches*, he quells his fear with the reflection: "did he not carry six deaths in one holster?"[4]

Berrigan plows through that mythology, literally crossing it out so that what remains is just a sculpted resemblance. While the structure of the story remains somewhat intact, the interactions and manners of the characters become entirely unpredictable. A comparison of the two books reveals that Berrigan rearranged the order of the chapters he used, weaving chapters that appear at the end of *Twenty Notches*, into the beginning of *Clear the Range*. Berrigan's chapters, generally 2-4 pages, also do not directly mimic the chapter structuring of *Twenty Notches,* as two chapters in *Clear the Range* may be constructed from one in *Twenty Notches*.

Crossing out may have been a new method for Berrigan, but he had recently used cut up in his breakthrough poem sequence *The Sonnets*, composed in 1963. He remarked in a famous reading of *The Sonnets* at 80 Langton Street in San Francisco in 1981, that it was the writing of that book which had enabled him to become the poet he was.[5] The cut-up method had helped transform him from a writer of sentimental verse[6] to the writer of an important work of post-modern poetry. Berrigan's reordering of chapters in *Clear the Range* is a technical idea that comes right out of *the Sonnets*, which includes poems where the lines of the original structure have been rearranged, and certain lines reoccur throughout the sequence. The 60s was an important time for experimentation in Berrigan's work, though doubts about the quality of *Clear the Range* would keep him from finishing and publishing it for over a decade.[*]

Berrigan's editing choices can be tracked in a comparison of the two books. In *Twenty Notches*, the Sleeper finds the house of his antagonist: Trot Enderby. Enderby is the famed owner of the gun with twenty notches, which the Sleeper hopes to steal. In their initial encounter, Enderby offers the Sleeper food in exchange for work, then leaves him in his front yard, watched by a couple of guard dogs. The Sleeper evades them, and heads to the front door to pick the lock:

> Then from his pocket he took a sliver of steel and worked it into the keyhole. It was so simple that the Sleeper smiled a little; the wards of that old fashioned lock were to his touch like an open, sunlit road, and presently the door gave before him.[4]

The Sleeper (with a capitol T[**]) in *Clear the Range* inhabits a more abstract landscape. Rather than the house full of normal objects, there is "nothing in the house except a door." Berrigan has removed most of the

physical reference to the situation and replaces it with an oblique rendering
of the scene.

> Then from his pocket he took a sliver. It was so simple The Sleeper
> smiled little. The wards of fashion were like an open, sunlit road.

The excising of the selected text has radically altered the dimensions of
the encounter. Instead of stepping into the house, The Sleeper steps into
"the slowness behind him."

Berrigan replaces the linear structure of *Twenty Notches* with a collection
of chapters where time and place are constantly shifting. The length of the
form, and sculptural quality of Berrigan's method have combined to create
an interior landscape full of spectacular moments, rather than cohesive narrative. The method also leaves a double impression of the original narrative
and the sculptor's path through it. *Clear the Range* is a poem carved out of
prose, and resembles both.

Cole Younger, the Sleeper, and Greatness

A result of the liberties taken with structure in *Clear the Range* is that the
narrative story remains somewhat incoherent, but a constant element in
the book is the interaction between The Sleeper and his antagonist, Cole
Younger.*** In the opening of the book, the tramps are passing near the
house of Cole Younger. The Sleeper is convinced by an older tramp that
Cole Younger, as a killer of twenty men, is worth pursuing. The Sleeper is
curious, and heads out to find him, only to become trapped by his guard
dogs. After a short time, he comes to admire his captor:

> ... the longer he remained in this unroofed torture chamber, the
> more mysterious appeared the power of Cole Younger. Besides there
> are strange things to be learned in this world. What is too marvelous,
> that can be true. There are certain fatal superstitions that are current
> among the knights of the road. The Sleeper knew them. He believed
> them.

The Sleeper makes up his mind "that he would never leave Cole Younger." He deifies him and reveres him, noting at one point that "He looked
more formed than Eve."

> It seemed to The Sleeper that there might well be some peculiar un-
> canny power. Now, he called It, "Cole Younger."

The ground has been set for their relationship, and for the rest of the book Cole Younger and The Sleeper are constantly circling and confronting each other, with the location and timeframe always shifting. Every chapter is a reimagining of their encounter, an endless sizing up. The aim of the contest is greatness. The need for greatness is never explained, except that "greatness fills the mind of man more than anything in the world" and one of the signs of greatness is the ability to "Clear the Range". Cole Younger has this greatness and is capable of mythic acts.

" . . . here's a needle. I found it in a haystack," says Cole Younger.

The Sleeper is in awe of him, to the point where they are attracted to each other. "I wanted you before, but I want you ten times more now," Cole Younger proclaims to The Sleeper. Berrigan plays with the implied sexual tension and connection between the two, as well as the protagonist's name.

The Sleeper began to dream. The central core of that dream was himself. Only Cole Younger could keep The Sleeper awake.

Cole Younger does not appear at all in *Twenty Notches*. Berrigan has changed the name of several of the characters from that book to Cole Younger. It lends a bizarre consistency to the story, but also has the effect of the two characters being introduced to each other several times throughout the book. After the initial encounter, the circumstances of their subsequent encounters vary wildly. In an early chapter in a hotel/saloon, The Sleeper looks across a crowded room and suddenly sees "the flaming grin of Cole Younger." In a later chapter, The Sleeper is sitting with "a letter in his pocket addressed to a Mr. Cole Younger . . . Somewhere in the future he was to meet Cole Younger." The two characters have interacted in the majority of the chapters before that point, and there is no clear indication of a temporal shift. When the Sleeper finally sees him enter the room, he bawls. In yet another encounter, the multiplicity of Cole Younger, the killer of twenty men, shows when his face has "turned into twenty dead men."

The Sleeper often seems to be gaining the upper hand in the contest. Cole Younger suddenly passes away, but he gets back up a paragraph later and keeps talking. In another instance "The Sleeper destroyed Cole Younger. Then he destroyed science." And finally, towards the end of chapter 23, The Sleeper shoots Cole Younger. Or he seems to:

"Cole Younger . . . fired both guns into the floor. Automatically he sat down. Thump! It looked cheap. Red burst out of the side of his head, he raised his wound to heaven and died! He was wounded, or rather, he was not wounded."

Cole Younger staggers to the door, is led back by Evil, and proceeds to dry The Sleeper's boots with his hair. Younger again heads towards the door. A mule comments in the background. The Sleeper has a revelation. "It was the center of a mind he had looked into, but only a head he had touched." Cole Younger seems to have survived the encounter.

Clearing the Range and Cole Younger's Daughter

The Sleeper aspires to "be the first man to actually Clear the Range." In chapter 8 he comes across a game of poker between two men, Drengk and Bonney. "Something is happening," exclaims Drengk. "Somebody's dream is happening," replies Bonney. Dreaming is a strong touch point for *Clear the Range*, an obvious association for The Sleeper. It also offers a frame of reference for a reader's ability to interpret the strange time leaps and abstractions that the methodology of the book has created.

The Sleeper realizes that killing Drengk and Bonney "would clear the first stage of the range." The parallel encounter in *Twenty Notches* occurs towards the end of the book, as part of an elaborate escape. Berrigan has moved it up, stepping up the action between two chapters, where the main focus is the shooting of a rabbit—the Sleeper's first use of the gun with twenty notches. The range refers to the field of adversaries, and those two are dispatched.

Between chapters 14 and 15, while The Sleeper and Cole Younger are talking, The Sleeper launches into a story about a time ten years prior, when The Sleeper and Cole Younger were trying to connect. He tells the story in the third person, as if they were not the characters in question. The Sleeper tells Cole Younger that Cole Younger announces to him to "Clear the Range." Cole Younger later goes on to advise: "If a door is not opened at once, it never will be." "What do you mean?" says The Sleeper. "I have told you more than words," says Cole Younger.

A transformation is required to Clear the Range, something more than murder. The Sleeper launches into his own analysis of The Sleeper and of Cole Younger. He observes that The Sleeper's "eyes were dull . . . more like the eyes of an ox than of a gunfighter hoping to 'Clear the Range'". The Sleeper was "a great machine. Only a great man can aspire to the greater greatness of a machine!" By the end of the story, The Sleeper has "made his three big tries to Clear the Range, lost all his money and one leg." Physical deformity has occurred but is never mentioned again, nor is Clearing the Range.

As the conflict between The Sleeper and Cole Younger continues, a new character emerges: Cole Younger's daughter. In *Twenty Notches*, she is Evelyn, the daughter of Morice, a one-legged old rancher, and a love interest for the Sleeper. She is a prize to be won, romantically attached to one of the antagonists, and a perfect companion for the Sleeper—one he falls for at first sight. The end result in that heroic story is predictable.

Berrigan transforms her into Cole Younger's daughter, and her role is more mysterious than waiting around to be chosen by either the hero or the villain. She comes "springing lightly from of the ground" in chapter seven, and immediately kisses the Sleeper, as Cole Younger conducts their courtship. She then appears intermittently, a constant draw, until the conclusion. He sees her rustle "her half-wings in the darkness." He asks her for "all," and she gives it. Rather than follow a delicate romantic story, Berrigan replaces delicacy with abstraction and vulgarity.

> The Sleeper could feel the good vibrations, light quick chattering against the steel chamber of his body. The heart of The Sleeper was touched. What young man can resist such beauty in distress. He went to the girl quickly. Before she could so much as open her mouth to speak, The Sleeper fucked her, monstrously.
>
> The strange manners of the courtship continue. The touch of her hand is like ice. She tells him that he is "true and good." "I stab you with words," she tells him a short while later. The Sleeper regrets his actions, and considers himself a scoundrel.
>
> He tried to conjure up a vision of the gentle. It refused to rise!

Cole Younger's daughter tells him a story about her past in Mexico. An American trader came, and stole her. But he was shot and killed by her father, Cole Younger. The Sleeper faints at the telling, and then suddenly he is in the story, escorting her to the border. When they reach "the foot of the terrible mountains," she grabs him and takes him "into a new life." The Sleeper is recounting this story to Cole Younger, and draws a gun on him, aiming it at his heart. He demands that Cole Younger speak. He speaks the closing line of the book: "Sleeper, that girl was not my daughter!" The last line offers a dramatic revelation, and it feels like an ending, but nothing else is explained by this reveal. The book doesn't end as much as it freezes.

Ideas And Devices

"A string flowed from Cole Younger's lips, then stopped halfway at his hips."

Clear the Range was a staging ground that Berrigan filled with rhymes, quick references to musicians and poets such as the Beach Boys, Bob Dylan, and Allen Ginsberg, and other literary devices. Berrigan's use of capitalization reflects his a playful approach, as he transforms dramatic concepts into proper nouns (Murder, Civil War Veterans, Life and Death, Fear, Time, Nature). *Clear the Range* is also a collection of dramatic and funny one-liners (Love saved his hand. He thought of pneumonia.), allowing Berrigan's sense of humor a free reign. This includes a number of sexual jokes, with references to five-legged thoroughbreds, and characters who are "gay as a cricket."

Berrigan also lets his exuberance for certain phrases show through, with certain usages of language echoing in his later poems. "Get the Money," described by Padgett as Ted's favorite Damon Runyan-ism, and a reflection of Berrigan's economic life as a poet, appears multiple times.[8] Berrigan's amused usage of the word angst ("I've never heard of angst") would be boiled down during Berrigan's period of short poems in the early 70s:

Angst
I had angst.[9]

The use of the word "ripped" is a key to Berrigan's take on inspiration as a physical experience. It is used in the first line of chapter 6, "Ice ripped his ears," and appears again in his final encounter with Cole Younger's daughter: "the childish slenderness of her round wrists ripped The Sleeper totally out of his mind." This sense of the word would culminate for Berrigan in his poem "Matinee", a translation of the short poem, "Mattina", by Giuseppe Ungaretti:

Matinee
Morning (ripped out of my mind again).[9]

The wording of Ungaretti's original poem is "M'illumino d'imenso," which Andrew Frisardi roughly translated as "I turn luminous in the immensity of spaces."[10]

Being "ripped out of his mind" is a fitting description for the mode employed for *Clear the Range*—a sense that any event or moment is not only inspiring, but completely redefines reality in its perception.

"Never be born, Never be died," was also a key phrase for Berrigan. The Sleeper says it to himself at one point, shortly before Cole Younger will die and then continue living. It is an apt description of how the characters in this book are affected by mortality, and implies that living is a state beyond the structure of meaning that is applied to it. The phrase would also appear in one of Berrigan's later poems "Christmas Card (for Barry & Carla)" from *A Certain Slant of Sunlight*. In an essay on that book, Alice Notley noted that the phrase "was remembered by Berrigan for years from a tiny pamphlet by a Japanese artist/poet . . . " whose name is not recalled.[7] It is interesting that this phrase remained important for Berrigan two decades later, towards the end of his life.

Ending

"Now the face of Cole Younger darkened. He stood up and said again: The End."

There's a recurring usage of "The End" and variations on the phrase. The words first appear in chapter 2, and are repeated throughout by different characters. "That's all" and "It's the Finish" appear with a similar finality, as if the pronouncement of those words was a stunning revelation that would cease time. After each finale, the action continues, until finally "The End" are the last words of the book, closing the structure.

NOTES

1 Berrigan, Ted, *Clear the Range*. Adventures in Poetry/Coach House South, 1977. All quotations from here on without reference are from *Clear the Range*.

2 From an email from Ron Padgett dated 7-28-13. In a follow-up email Padgett noted that parts of "Motor Maids Across the Continent" have been published in the poetry magazine *Sal Mimeo*, published by Larry Fagin, who co-published *Clear the Range* with Coach House Editions.

3 Tuska, Jon, "Frederick Faust". maxbrandonline.com, 2008

4 Brand, Max, *Twenty Notches*. Ace Books, 1977

5 *80 Langston Street Residence Program, 1981.*

6 Berrigan Ted, *The Sonnets*. Penguin, 2000

7 Notley, Alice, *Coming After*. The University of Michigan Press, 2005

8 Padgett, Ron, *Ted*. The Figures, 1993

9 Berrigan, Ted, *The Collected Poems of Ted Berrigan*. Ed. Anselm Berrigan, Edmund Berrigan, and Alice Notley. University of California Press, 2005

10 Ungaretti, Giuseppe, *Selected Poems*. Translator Andrew Frisardi. Carcanet, 2003

WORKS CITED

80 Langston Street Residence Program, 1981.

Berrigan, Ted, *Clear the Range*. Adventures in Poetry/Coach House South, 1977.

Berrigan, Ted, *The Collected Poems of Ted Berrigan*. Ed. Anselm Berrigan, Edmund Berrigan, and Alice Notley. University of California Press, 2005

Berrigan Ted, *The Sonnets*. Penguin, 2000

Brand, Max, *Twenty Notches*. Ace Books, 1977

Notley, Alice, *Coming After*. The University of Michigan Press, 2005

Padgett, Ron, *Ted*. The Figures, 1993

Tuska, Jon, "Frederick Faust". maxbrandonline.com, 2008

Ungaretti, Giuseppe, *Selected Poems*. Translator Andrew Frisardi. Carcanet, 2003

Lying in Wait
On Roberto Bolaño's *Antwerp* as a Poet's Novel

JOSHUA MARIE WILKINSON

What poems lack is characters who lie in wait for the reader.

ROBERTO BOLAÑO IN ANTWERP

About half way through the fifth and final book of Roberto Bolaño's novel pentalogy *2666*, two characters in World War II Cologne called Reiter and Ingeborg meet and begin to spend "many hours together, sometimes talking about the most random things" (774). They have sex and talk, get sick, hallucinate some, and fall in love: "They talked about books, about poetry (Ingeborg asked Reiter why he didn't write poetry and he answered that all poetry, of any style, was contained or could be contained in fiction)" (774).

What could it mean for poetry to be "contained in fiction?" That somehow they could become indistinguishable? Or does Reiter mean that fiction can do whatever poetry can do because it can go one step further by subsuming poetry itself? Maybe this idea offers a clue as to how to think about the poet's novel in general, and, more specifically, Bolaño's first and most peculiar little novel, *Antwerp*.

Here is Roberto Bolaño in a late interview:

> Nicanor Parra says that the best novels are written in meter. And Harold Bloom says that the best poetry of the twentieth century is written in prose. I agree with both. But on the other hand I find it difficult to consider myself an active poet. My understanding is that an active poet is someone who writes poems. I sent my most recent ones to you and I'm afraid they're terrible, although of course, out of kindness and consideration, you lied. I don't know. There's something about poetry. (Maristain, 67)

Who knows if *Antwerp* is a poet's novel, exactly. It seems clear, at least from the confession above, that—though he published several collections of poetry in his lifetime and beyond—Bolaño didn't think much of his poems, and even hesitated to call himself a poet at all. That Bolaño happens to "agree with both" Parra and Bloom here is our good fortune, as his novels are poetic and poetry-obsessed in the best ways possible, even if they were not composed in meter. It's well known that Bolaño is a writer's writer: the characters from his best-known books are often poets, literary critics, novelists, journalists, writers of other stripes, or, of course, detectives.

• • •

Surely somebody has said it more elegantly elsewhere in these pages, so I'll put it bluntly: any fictional prose out of keeping with popular mainstream markets is often derided, dismissed, or simply ignored. To cite a recent example, last week, when *The New York Times* asks Anna Quindlen, "What kinds of stories are you drawn to? Any you steer clear of?" Her reply is: "I think 'experimental fiction' is a synonym for 'Give me a break'" (Quindlen).

Now, I should tell you that I don't know who Anna Quindlen is. (Apparently she authored a book called *Lots of Candles, Plenty of Cake*, which sounds good!) That she puts "experimental fiction" in quotes is telling. More telling, perhaps, is that the editors decided to use this quote as the subheading to introduce the author's interview in the *Sunday Book Review*, arguably one of the paper's most prominent spots.

Here's David Foster Wallace, also from an interview, published posthumously:

> I think *avant-garde* fiction has *already* gone the way of poetry. And it's become involuted and forgotten the reader. Put it this way, there are a few really good poets who suffered because of the desiccation and involution of poetry, but for the most part I think American poetry has gotten what it's deserved. And, uh, it'll come awake again when poets start speaking to people who have to pay the rent, and fuck the same woman for thirty years. That's off the record: that's really nasty (Lipsky, 91).

This is transcribed from an audio conversation, and it's kind of nice to read Wallace without his skeining explanations and contextualizing—without, in short, his footnotes. I realize I'm a bit off topic, but I think the way that Quindlen and Wallace figure "experimental" and "avant-garde" fiction (respectively) is familiar to poets already. I hasten to say, yes, we get it. Or at least: this is basically what I *assumed* you were thinking.

But look at how quickly Wallace leaps to *poetry* in order to ground his claim about avant-garde fiction. The off-the-cuff dismissal of Quindlen (i.e., "Give me a break") and the active derision of Wallace (i.e., "American poetry has gotten what it's deserved") I think capture two overlapping sentiments about literary writing disparaged from within, not from without.

What fascinates me is of course the *literary* writer (here Quindlen, there Wallace) just ventriloquizing market capitalism. Writer, behave! Serve the marketplace! Make a cultural object worthy of millions! But millions of what, dollars? slavering shareholders? queuing customers?

Somewhere between these terrible pits of self-indulgence (poetry, on the one side) and ignominious experimentation (avant-garde fiction on the other) lives, wheezing in its own prosaic juices: the poet's novel. Bastard of one, foster child to another, or just an orphan tapping absently at the door of whichever genre might be at home.

Perhaps genre is merely a construct we inflate in order to throw certain poisoned darts at, darts like Maggie Nelson's *Bluets* or *Dictee* by Theresa Hak Kyung Cha or *The Activist* by Renee Gladman or Bhanu Kapil's *Humanimal*.

But why blow up the balloon at all? Why not just read the works themselves? Who cares what category they're placed in? Nelson herself says, "I don't mind if anyone calls my work 'lyric essay'; I don't care much about classification, as it comes after the fact of the writing" (from *Black Warrior Review* online). I agree with Nelson—that classification comes after the fact—but perhaps we talk about genre because context is useful to foreground a piece of writing's radicality, provocation, divergence from norms, and obliteration of dominant assumptions about what a work of literature is and does, what it looks like and what it says—and how or what it can be said to mean.

Perhaps the discussion of literary genre is a foil for norms and conventions. That writers like Gertrude Stein and Virginia Woolf, Etel Adnan and Renata Adler, Eileen Myles, Alice Notley, and Anne Carson have written some of the most ineradicable and tricky to categorize works should hardly come as a surprise—to say nothing of the genre-breaking work—years after the fact—that has helped us to re-imagine what remains of Sappho's fragments, Sei Shōnagon's *Pillow Book*, and especially Emily Dickinson's fascicles, as theorized by Susan Howe or Virginia Jackson.

All this is to say, the project of working within and between genres for a writer is a fraught and fertile terrain—whether "it comes after the fact" or one is consciously writing a *novel* that, to its author even, remains "unintelligible" as *Antwerp* seemed to Bolaño, or so he put in his introduction to the book. One goal perhaps is to find a form that suits the work, not vice versa.

Here is Adam Phillips, from a recent interview in *Bomb*: "there are large parts of ourselves that don't fit into the available forms, or for which new forms must be found" (*Bomb* online). Phillips is talking about our lives—

with respect to our identities, our psyches, sexualities, practices, and our relationships—but I think it works for literary writing as well. A large part of our creative practices don't "fit into the available forms" either, and writers like Roberto Bolaño and Maggie Nelson demonstrate how to renovate or create a form from within *and* without, respectively.

• • •

Which brings us, finally, to Roberto Bolaño's *Antwerp*.

In some ways, I don't care if there is such a thing as a poet's novel. It would seem that there are writers that call themselves poets; some of those poets write what they call novels.

The thing about the poet's novel, whatever it might be, is that—at least in the case of *Antwerp*—it's concerned with the novel and the poem simultaneously, which is to say, it's not playing *neither/nor* or even *either/or*—instead it ventures to become *both novel and poem*: something excessive, undeterminable, and outside the ken or logic of dominant cultural reading practices. Even, perhaps especially, if its author wants to call it a novel, which Bolaño called *Antwerp*.

• • •

Roberto Bolaño's *Antwerp* was written between 1980-1982 and first published in Spain in 2002 as *Amberes*. Natasha Wimmer's translation into English arrived in 2010 from New Directions. According to Bolaño's introduction to *Antwerp*:

> In those days, if memory serves, I lived exposed to the elements, without my papers, the way other people live in castles. I never brought this novel to any publishing house, of course. They would've slammed the door in my face and I'd have lost the copy. I didn't even make what's technically termed a clean copy. The original manuscript has more pages: the text tended to multiply itself, spreading like a sickness . . . I worked at night. During the day I wrote and read. I never slept. (ix)

In a way, what difference does it make that Bolaño called it a "*novel*"? Surely the language—the writing—of the thing is what fascinates us, or should. Yet knowing that Bolaño himself thought of the book *as* a novel seems important for thinking of it as *distinct* from his lesser-known poems, and from his more "entertaining" novels (to use Bolaño's word) like *The Savage Detectives* and *2666*, which are hardly mainstream fiction in form.

Here's how Bolaño framed *Antwerp* in a conversation with Mónica Maristain, a year before he died:

> The only novel that doesn't embarrass me is *Amberes*, maybe because it continues to be unintelligible. The bad reviews it has received are badges of honor from actual combat, not skirmishes with simulated fire. The rest of my "work" is not bad. They're entertaining novels. Time will tell if they're anything more. (Maristain, 117)

Maybe Bolaño is being coy here about *Antwerp* being his "only novel that doesn't embarrass" him, but that he allows that it may be so "because it continues to be unintelligible" is a curious statement. Unintelligible to whom? to its author? its readers? To its critics? That he calls his other novels merely "entertaining" is important: clearly Bolaño himself thought that he was doing something different in *Antwerp*. An early sentence from the book reads: "The language of others is unintelligible to me" (7), thus mirroring back the writing itself to its author, about which more later.

• • •

Antwerp has all the elements of a genre novel (crime thriller) *par excellence*: a placid beachside resort on the Mediterranean; a bunch of teenagers partying wildly; a grisly murder; and detectives in pursuit of the killer, where just about anybody in the book seems to be a viable suspect. Even some of the language isn't too far off from an Agatha Christie paperback. Here is a scene from the middle of *Antwerp*:

> From here I watch an old cop approach the body with hesitant steps. A cold breeze is blowing, raising goose bumps. The cop kneels by the body: with a dejected gesture, he covers his eyes with his left hand. A flock of starlings rise. They circle over the policeman's head and then disappear. The policeman goes through the dead man's pockets and piles what he finds on a white handkerchief that he's spread out on the grass. (43)

Pretty classic: a narrator watching a cop's procedure with a dead body, replete with the narrator's perspectival coloring. The cop is "old" and his steps are "hesitant"; his gesture is a "dejected" one. It seems to be a neutral

description of events unfolding in the present tense, but upon closer examination, we can see the cop's features filled in by a subjective hand, an interested party just far enough beyond the scene to feign omniscience, and just
close enough to give us the juicy report. We lean in, going: then what? and
now what? It's straight out of film noir, and the details are shrewdly opaque
(here he "piles what he finds") and now detailed (there "a white handkerchief that he's spread out on the grass") to exacerbate the mystery and the
forward motion of the plot.

Yet—to play a little *compare and contrast*—here are the opening sentences of *Antwerp*:

> The kid heads toward the house. Alley of larches. The Fronde. Neck-
> lace of tears. Love is a mix of sentimentality and sex (Burroughs). The
> mansion is just a façade—dismantled, to be erected in Atlanta. 1959.
> Everything looks worn. Not a recent phenomenon. From a long time
> back, everything wrecked. And the Spaniards imitate the way you
> talk. The South American lilt. An alley of palms. Everything slow and
> asthmatic. Bored biologists watch the rain from the windows of their
> corporations. It's no good singing *with feeling*. My darling, wherever
> you are: it's too late, forget the gesture that never came. "It was just a
> façade." The kid walks toward the house. (3)

Not only does it *not* read like the crime novel bit from above (and they
are separated by forty pages), it reads much more like a prose poem: the
leaps in meanings, the heavy fragmentation modulated by periods, and
the lack of a unified perspective, to name just a few things possible to say
about it.

There are repeated resonances, which disturb us towards meaning: that
virtually the same sentence (though not quite) opens and closes the page;
that "façades" are mentioned twice and appearances ("just a façade" and
"Everything looks worn") loom large. But there is a tenor here as well, an
emotional resonance that surfaces through the accumulation of subtle and
not-so-subtle images: "Necklace of tears," the Burroughs quote, and words
like "dismantled," "worn," "wrecked," "imitate," "slow and asthmatic,"
"Bored," and phrases like "too late," "It's no good," etc. Even if we don't
know who these biologists are, of course, their boredom to "watch the rain
from the windows of their corporations" seems to fit the "slow and asthmatic" qualities of everything else described. In other words, no matter how un-
plot-like the language is, the emotional feeling of the piece is pretty unified.
We might simply call it a somber mood.

One of the fascinating things about *Antwerp* is how it oscillates carefully between language that resembles a prose poem and passages that seem pulled from a detective novel. Because it's set up with the oblique leaps of a mind in the act of imagining and describing, remembering and listening, there is a certain defamiliarizing quality of the noirish parts. They seem cut out of another movie and transcribed directly in somehow. Oscillating between these modes—I'll argue—is hardly an accident, and it's what I mean by re-imagining a genre from *within* that very genre itself. In other words, Bolaño is trafficking in the tropes of noir fiction—and all his later works of fiction do as well—but for now he's not satisfied unless he can transform the genre significantly into something more "unintelligible."

The other wonderfully salient feature of *Antwerp* is that the text itself is obsessed with writing, with its own formation, with its own performance and renovation of genre, and with its own authorship. Yes, it's a meta-novel, and in the best possible disappearing horizon kind of way.

In parts, the central characters are obsessed with writing, especially through the articulated frustration of what they cannot write: "The man sits at one of the cafes in the hypothetical ghetto. He writes postcards because breathing prevents him from writing the poems he'd like to write. I mean: free poems, no extra tax" (4). The text works to privilege poetry especially, and often by denigrating it: "I'm alone, all the literary shit gradually falling by the wayside—poetry journals, limited editions, the whole dreary joke behind me now" (10). Poetry is the butt of the "dreary joke" often enough, but it's usually slashed at because the "writers" have failed to produce any worthy of its name.

Other parts of the novel want to foreground the difficulty of naming, the work of writing figured as an impossibility itself: "I can't string two words together. I can't express myself coherently or write what I want. I should probably give up everything and go away, isn't that what Teresa of Avila did? (Applause and laughter.)" (12).

Often enough "the writer"—and we can't ever be certain of who's speaking in any of these passages—appeals to one genre because of an apparent failure in another: "He spends the evenings sitting outdoors at the bar of the riding school where he works, trying to write, but he can't. Nothing comes out, as they say in common parlance. The man realizes that he's finished. All he writes are short crime stories" (15). The suggestion of course is that if one "can't write" one must *resort to* some fair to middling genre. In other words, if a form fails you: choose an easier form—which is precisely the opposite of what *Antwerp* itself does. Put differently, the book stages the failure of high genre (poetry) and low genre (crime novels) only to combine them into something altogether new and out of keeping with the author's other works. Here is a longer scene where genre writing is again figured, and again associated with a kind of failure by a character to *maintain* one's writing *in a genre*:

> With oily steps, four or five waiters approach the shack where they sleep. One of them used to write poetry, but that was a long time ago. The author said: "I can't be pessimistic or optimistic, everything is determined by the beat of hope that manifests itself in what we call reality." I can't be a science fiction writer because my innocence is mostly gone and I'm not crazy yet . . . Words that no one speaks, that no one is required to speak . . . Hands in the process of geometric fragmentation: writing that's stolen away just as love, friendship, and the recurring backyards of nightmares are stolen away . . . Sometimes I get the sense that it's all 'internal' . . . Maybe that's why I lived alone and did nothing for three years . . . (52, with Bolaño's ellipses)

Finally, we cut to scenes where the bodies of the murdered kids are discovered, and those in charge are forced to deal with them. But what's fascinating is that "the author" is a full character without access to certain parts of the story that he himself is telling. It's a parody of writing, but it also seems invested un-ironically in the limit of what we can say about atrocities, however fictitious in a crime noir:

> The brakes squealed and the cops got out. There's something obscene about this, said the medic when nobody was listening. I'll probably never come back to the clearing in the woods, not with flowers, not with the net, not with a fucking book to spend the afternoon. His mouth opened but the author couldn't hear a thing. He thought about the silence and then he thought "there's no such thing," "horses," "waning August moon." Someone applauded from the void. I said I guessed this was happiness. (64)

This isn't the only appearance of "the author" in the book and this isn't the only appearance of somebody's "applause" either, as a sarcastic joke—as a way to demonstrate another perspective outside the work, and as a way to laud and demean the reader both—overlooking, judging, valuing, etc.

In a chapter called "The Redhead," after a long description of the woman the chapter refers to, he writes, "It may seem strange but I never wanted to sleep with her. Someone applauds from a dark corner" (47). Later still he takes it a step further—the author encountering his own overheard applause now: "And did I do everything? did I kiss her when she'd stopped expecting kisses? (Miles from here people are applauding, and that's why I feel such despair.)"

The applause in these instances—and there are others throughout—figure the audience and the reader, but they figure them *for the author* as a self-conscious device to shut the author down, for the author to provoke the opposite of what he might have wanted to feel or do.

At times *Antwerp* presents the writer as somebody morphing into his characters: "The writer is a dirty man, with his shirt sleeves rolled up and his short hair wet with sweat, hauling barrels of garbage. He's also a waiter who watches himself filming as he walks along a deserted beach, on his way back to the hotel" (69). This fusion of sorts ("He's also a waiter" and thereby works at the resort where the murders occurred) can only be realized in *Antwerp* as a self-conscious one, as he "watches himself filming as he walks . . ." The sense here is that "the writer" can fuse with his characters— here as an onlooker, there as the potential murderer—but not without the *further* distance of someone with a recording device of his own, watching "himself filming as he walks . . ."

Bolaño, apparently liking the threads that meta-writing allows him to follow, goes even one step further with "the author" here:

> Doubly afraid of himself because he couldn't help falling in love once a year at least. Then a succession of port-a-potties, cheap reprints, kids puking, while a retarded girl dances on the silent terrace. All writing on the edge hides a white mask. That's all. There's always a fucking mask. The rest: poor Bolaño writing at a pit stop. (66)

The sense in *Antwerp* is that the loop is endless, the horizon is an infinite vanishing point, and Bolaño and "Bolaño" and "the writer" and "the author" (all four, at least) can write themselves into the work all they want, but that only *increases* the distance, never laying bare the reality of the situation, never betraying the "real story," to say nothing of catching the murderer. Thus, it swerves further and further away from the whodunit, and formally looks more and more—over the course of the novel—like a poem of oblique emotional connections.

As a result, by the time we return, at book's end, to the failures of the work to body forth—for the mystery to have been solved, for the restoration of order, for the writer to have *become* the triumphant detective, as, say, a Chandler novel might figure him—instead we get the charge of that failure as the activating force of creativity: "Of what is lost, irretrievably lost, all I wish to recover is the daily availability of my writing, lines capable of grasping me by the hair and lifting me up when I'm at the end of my strength" (78). In other words, precisely where the writing fails as a good murder mystery, it succeeds in reviving the text. Whatever writing is "lost, irretrievably lost" is "recovered" or recuperated for us otherwise, precisely because it has failed its appropriate genres.

Just as the writers in the book fall short at poetry, at science fiction, at writing, *Antwerp* as a poem fails. And as a novel it falls short too, after all: it's too poetic. The author himself has failed to become "intelligible," and the book we close thereby succeeds with the force and spirit of something altogether stranger than either genre on its own could muster.

Near the end, we encounter the only mention of the book's namesake: "'Every word is useless, every sentence, every phone conversation' . . . 'She said she wanted to be alone' . . . I wanted to be alone too. In Antwerp or Barcelona. The moon. Animals fleeing. Highway accident. Fear" (68, with Bolaño's ellipses). "Antwerp" here is just another *elsewhere* surrounded by gestures of failed communication. And like the stalled tale of *Antwerp* itself, it signals a seemingly arbitrary place: one at which we fail to arrive.

Of course, arrival is not the point; the point, perhaps instead, is to signal some distant beacon in order to ensure one's failure to arrive, thereby locating oneself a far cry from the light it throws. And perhaps it has little to do with the Belgian city itself and the *most* to do with that "or" between "Antwerp" and "Barcelona"—a potential distance, an articulated arbitrariness, a place on which the mind fixates, seemingly at random, to tell itself the story of its own stalled present, only to swerve away from it as ineluctably as it appeared. As in a poem.

WORKS CITED

Bolaño, Roberto. *Antwerp*. New York: New Directions, 2002. *2666*. New York: Picador, 2008.

Lipsky, David. *Although of Course You End Up Becoming Yourself: A Road Trip with David Foster Wallace*. New York: Broadway Books, 2010.

Maristain, Mónica. *Roberto Bolaño: The Last Interview & Other Conversations*. Brooklyn, NY: Melville House Publishing, 2009.

Nelson, Maggie. "An Interview with Maggie Nelson . . . " Tuscaloosa, AL: *Black Warrior Review*. July 2012.

Phillips, Adam. Interview by Sameer Padania. New York: *Bomb*, No 113, 2010.

Quindlen, Anna. "By the Book" [interview] in the New York Times Sunday Book Review, April 18, 2013.

Obituary of the Many: Gail Scott[*]

CARLA HARRYMAN

Introduction

The writing and form of *The Obituary* does not so much shift between poetry and prose as it interleaves them such that the text might seem to sound
like poetry and behave like a novel, or visa versa—depending on how one
listens to this text, which does ask one to tune one's ear to its language with
a somewhat musical attitude. Gail Scott does consider it a novel as do I;
although one that reimagines the novel for the twenty-first century. It is a
novel of prose experiment meeting avant, language-centered poetry in the
context of the Quebecois, experimental feminist milieu that has nourished
Scott's writing since 1980.

    The Obituary draws from critical and psychoanalytic theory of earlier pe-
riods, particularly Walter Benjamin's theory of history and the theory of the
phantom in Nicolas Abraham's and Maria Torok's *The Shell and the Kernel*
and *The Wolf man's Magic Word: A Cryptonymy*. In this essay, I focus on the
writings of Abraham and Torok. Taken together, the two works by Abraham and Torok attempt a mid-century psychoanalytic revision of Freud.
The Obituary is not a mirror or proof of theory, but a creative work that
makes something of it related to and other from theory.

• • •

Obituary of the Many: A Reading
    These Wars on the Radio
    Are Keeping Us from Our Own

In pale Mile-End, behind the night sheds, little pink clouds come
tippling tippling down. And huge yellow maple leaves, not cold
enough to turn red, tumbling, tumbling on regrowing November
grass, to lie like yellow hands. From the kitchen radio, the ack-ack-
swat of the most sophisticated of bombs weigh up to two tons from
the most fantastically shaped planes . . .

> Oh X
> do you remember
> when Afghan spelt dope
> embroidered vests, vast
> windswept steppes
> with tanned shaggy fashion models
> standing slant on them?

*

I'm that Face on the 3rd. She looks out, barely visible behind those grey ventians in upper Triplex window. This former resident of madam B's in the town of S-D has a reputation for hating children. I also liking cats. Enough not to have one. That overconfident ground-floor Potter with chocolate Lab named Latte feigning shock when I told her that. She's from The Outters, so instead of the friendly tangled back courtyards we used to have, now looking down from Settler-Nun flats onto North America's biggest crop: lawn. Hours get spent artfully arranging plastic lawn sets shaped like dinosaurs in it . . . (5-6)

I note in this opening scene language as an enactment of perceptions and events, with the narration moving through time and space on horizontal and vertical pathways. We begin at the local scene of the climate changing Mile-End of Francophone Montreal where the war of the present elsewhere is broadcast via radio. The prose then cuts into this present scene a mock poetic reverie of an earlier time when the narrator possessed a more innocent identification with the pleasures of global trade. Through such analeptic tactics Scott's phrasings draw attention to language as a plastic/poetic medium within prose. It is a language, porous and multi-voiced, that gathers to the novelistic scene a concatenated image of global political violence and local pettiness. Present in this local are the hauntings of body parts envisioned as falling leaves sutured to the radio's discourse of bombs. Such poetic tactics within Scott's narrative repeatedly bring the spatially distant wars of the present and the temporally distant genocides of the past into the local scene.

The stylization of the prose voice is formed by elisions of sound and grammar with stress, increasingly, on present participle, which leaves action suspended. Also, here we note an initial introduction to our composite character: the narrator refers to herself as both subject and object and in first and third person. Turning from our lyric-tragic reading of the first paragraph, we will note the narrative wit of a fanciful iteration in the plural, which offers the reader some clues about how to read the text: *"Hey! Stay put [Face] while we go to get th' story! Yes, we disburse."* (23)

The composite narrator of *The Obituary* in the figures of Rosine, the fly on the wall, the Bottom Historian, and the non/narrative text itself does disburse, seeking a means to paste the story together out of shards of remaining evidence and a plot borrowed from Alfred Hitchcock's *Dial M for Murder*. The main scene of this dispersion is the Mile-End apartment, where I/th' fly flits voyeuristically to interior building walls; Rosine in her writing office and bedroom time-space travels in thought; and the Bottom Historian reports "omnisciently" from the basement. There also appears the face, or Face, which Rosine has identified as an apparition of herself; though we may also come to view Face as something entombed within Rosine or within the building.

The composite narrator, situated as much in narrative representation as nonnarrative language, periodically acknowledges that the reader may be looking for the story as well. With tongue-in-cheek, the narrative informs our reader again and again story is about to be found, reassuring her that its acerbic "extra Dia-Jeesis" will release a satisfying elixir of tale-told by book's end; though this tease, or eventuality, of plot is complicated by the language of excess that is severed from or sutured to plot. Here the fly presents itself as figure of the extra-diagetic text informing the reader:

> We phantoms in th' extra Dia-Jeesis. Unrelated to love's object, therefore getting' to keep th' one sense unconnected to it. (81)[1]

In a footnote, the Bottom Historian explains that the sense the fly is referring to is "the sixth sense, of course," something we associate with both intuition and gothic modes. As a figure of keen intuition, the fly in this example becomes an iteration of and a figure for a psychoanalytic trope *and* a comic element in a gothic-noir scenario. This figure of the narrative telling acts both as a prosthetic extension of the omniscient narrative voice and as a phantom of the narration detached from the love plot.

One is reminded of this being a novel through its deployment of voice as character, its recursive strategies, and its return to and intensification of certain constants upon which we rely to understand its historical and psychological dimensions as consequential to its characters. One such constant is that aspect of Rosine that seems to be lying on her bed as if part dead, in the melancholic sense, until the end of the novel. Through this trope, mournfulness and melancholy appear as the novel's underlying emotional and affective modes. In Rosine's habitus, story moves at a dirge-like pace as if a slow current flowing below the hyper-mobile linguistic landscape of the non/narrative events of *The Obituary*. The stillness of melancholic time, the retardation of the mourning process, and the slowness of reading time required of a non/narrative work of such linguistic eventfulness and density conspire to prolong "denouement" far beyond its common deferrals. Closing in on the novel's literal end, we are yet informed by the Bottom Historian:

> Here it behooves I/~~Basement~~ Bottom Historian, to surface. *Encore*. For purpose of resetting intrigue on path to dénoument. Even if believing, with all lucid spirits, that to plot is to parody remembrance. (115)

Will the story, given this anxiety of parody stay covered up, sealed within attempts to find it? Will linguistic heterogeneity successfully obstruct the pathways via which the writing subject or storyteller seeks the tale? This question becomes a comic node of plot suspense itself.

My summary of *The Obituary* interleaves psychoanalytic concepts and the meandering, digressive stream of Scott's story line. It begins with the lonely figure of Rosine, who suffers from a recent break-up and from her mother Veera's death, an event in the mid-past of the narrative. Our melancholy heroine emotionally conflates loss of lover with loss of mother. The confusion of the lost object leaves her psychically stuck or stalled. Rosine's psychic impasse is aligned with her seeming to have disappeared, while her disappearance is simultaneously figural and literal: she has both disappeared into herself and shut herself away in her room. Her analyst, however, is ironically concerned with the Rosine whose actual whereabouts have become unknown. In each of these versions of disappearance is a gap in the narration of the tale.

We know from the novel's epigraph that the narrator and/or narrative is haunted by phantoms "or the gaps left within us by the secrets of others." The epigraph is taken from Nicholas Abraham and Maria Torok's incomplete theory of the transgenerational phantom, a theory which both enlarges upon and contests "Freudian theories of psychopathology, since here symptoms do not spring from the individual's life experiences but from someone else's psychic conflicts, traumas, or secrets." (Rand: 166).[2] One aspect of this incompleteness is related to a conception of language through which the words of the transgenerational phantom circulate in society and become deformed political instruments. In this aspect, their theory moves toward a revolution in psychoanalysis in which the psychopathology of the phantom may result in a theory of the political unconscious. Yet, Abraham and Torok also criticize Freudian theory for its departures from the clinical space, the space of transaction between individuals. They view psychoanalytic theory as having hardened, theoretically and clinically around concepts and evidence that prematurely foreclose diagnosis and hence treatment. However, the path from clinic to society remains an open question in Abraham and Torok's work.

This open question is taken up by Scott as a prompt for constructing instances in which the reader can observe the possible ways in which commonplace idiom performs as linguistic untruth that encrypts reality in buried histories of political violence. But the novel is not only a text that fictionally fills in the missing clinical evidence with the fabric of narrative. Scott exploits both gothic lore and psychoanalytic constructs of the phantom, bringing these to bear on the novel as a form that is able to hold within it many forms and genres, from critical theory to the ghost story. With the tongue-in-cheek of a surrealist, Scott uses the popular trope of the gothic to poke at rigid values and assumptions about identity, class, and readerships that continue to press against and challenge psychoanalytic frameworks.

Abraham and Torok explain the religious or mythological narrative of the phantom as a universal invention: this is the ghost that cannot rest due to suffering, shaming, and repression by their family or society. The hallucinated phantom is "meant to objectify...the gap produced in us by the concealment of some part of a love object's life." (171) This "metapsychological fact" that circulates within the gothic is also an object for Scott, but in her work it might be thought to be a figure for the restructuring of value. Scott mocks the ways in which, in conventional narrative, division between the secular and the spectral are pre-assigned to figures in a rigid class system of type. What may have been repressed for instance is the content or quality of mind, thought, or action of subjects who are conventionally only represented as objects or types in narrative. One example of this is the ghostly young cop, who appears against type, with his thoughts straying to André Breton's *Nadja* as he haunts the hallway of Rosine's apartment.

Against such comic-critical deployments of the phantasm is set its tragic aspect in the figure of Veera, the mother Rosine grieves. Veera is an assimilated Metis whose narrative of assimilation is suppressed (therefore she is *not* Metis)[3] by her father, who knows but does not speak (under survival-determined conditions perhaps) his knowledge of Cree origin in the family. For causes we might construe but that remain unstated, Rosine becomes host to the gap left by her grandfather's repression. This haunting is of "the thing" that gets worked out in the narrative's plot. It is important that this narrative of Rosine's mourning process, enabled by her discovery of what the grandfather didn't tell about genealogy, is born through a silence that acts upon each family member such that their performance of personhood and gender is shaped around the silence. There is no one unaffected by the fact that what is apparent is yet unseen and not voiced.

Simultaneous to the forward movement of plot, or Rosine's seeking of a way to introject loss, the narrative is shifting among the voices of the text overwriting the centrality of any given voice and the singular story of grievable loss as if undertaking a task (a proper burial or unearthing of truth?) related to something huge that the singular grief is contingent upon but which yet exists beyond the grief of the individual.

At first we may come to the conclusion that the grieving character is not successfully processing her grief. She has symptoms of paranoia, such as hallucinations that weave themselves into normal or naturalistic recollection, projection, and modes of contemplation or intellectual reflection. She stays in her room—though she also time-space travels around the city and to the provinces like a ghost herself, narrating her part as motile cell of story from the inside of her room or "crypt;" but the language that is the medium of the introjecting (processing) of grief slowly releases its "elixir." Though the heterogeneous language of the phantom from which this elixir must emit cannot be processed without an "accident." This event of fortune happens at a visit to the dentist, who supplies a missing piece of the puzzle via X-ray of the skull, which is mongoloid and hence likely Aboriginal. The event of this accident supports Abraham's observation that one's capacity to introject and thereby process the trauma of another who inhabits one's own psyche is typically limited due to a lack of "sufficient material to construct the phantom." (175) The discovery of genetic type as an accidental occurrence points both to the kind of gap in evidence that frustrates Abraham's pursuit of his theory and to the potential arbitrariness and constructedness of any plot. The plot therefore does not complete the text but, rather, returns us to the non/narrative dimension of the work, one that is, in part, shaped by the uncertainties or instabilities produced by and productive of silence, or the affects of silences.

• • •

Within artistic genres, silence is associated with negative spaces in visual art and poetry and with the stop or pause of music. Silence may be perceived as an absence in an otherwise sound-filled chamber (the flute goes mute) or outside space. In plotted narrative, silence is the site of the secret and its discovery. In psychoanalytic theory silence is associated with a myriad of concepts including Abraham and Torok's Crypt, which renders the lost object inaccessible to the language of psychic processing or introjection. Silence in a psycho-social dynamic may encourage noise about X that covers up anxiety about Y. In politics silence may be associated with the privilege of power to hold knowledge close and to cover-up or lie. Historical narration is formed by the impossibility of telling everything, by the surprise appearance that changes expectations or the course of events, by what is excluded for its apparent insignificance or political antagonism to a dominant perspective, and by revision.

But silence can also show itself as a sign of respect for another; it is a medium of meditative space or of the thoughtful relationship to the present from which a new thing can arise. It can also be a feature of political or communal barricade whereby those who are protecting themselves have temporarily removed themselves from conflict or threat. When people go inside to protect themselves from threat, the "outside" may not be privy to the word and deeds that occur within the communal interior. Silence is therefore multi-directional and inconstant. The languages of such diverse modes of silence, from the aesthetic stop or pause to the unspeakable word of the crypt, from the buried narrative of historical denial to the inaccessibility of the protected site, are strong features of the topography of Scott's novel.

In the introduction to his English translation, Nicholas T. Rand discusses Abraham and Torok's *The Shell and the Kernel* as a work exploring renewals of psychoanalysis. (1) He points to the authors' departures from Freud as he emphasizes their insistence "on the particularity of any individual's life story, the specificity of texts, and the singularity of historical situations." This attentiveness to particularity puts pressure on Freudian constructs, which "need to be abandoned or revamped if inconsistent with the actual life experience of patients or the facts of a text." A person ought not to be analyzed "in the light of predetermined ideas, such as theories of repressed incestuous wishes or fear of the castrating father, as such analysis "run the risk of condemning the person's genuine suffering to eternal silence." *The Obituaries* perspective on suffering, in part, corresponds to this critique. The role that sexuality and libidinal drive plays in Scott's text is one in which repression and its corresponding silences occur within the phantom's (singular) and phantoms' (plural) transmissions, but the text itself is able to express and present sexuality, desire, and somatic experiences of pleasure *and* pleasure's miserable variations with a sense of glee, even as glee is sometimes accompanied by shame; as, for instance, in a reverie on a bus which prompts the day-dreaming Rosine to almost touch the breasts of a stranger.

Shame is the companion of the semi-living, the specter of which appears in the body that lies akimbo on Rosine's bed, a body that may be her own or that of Veera—the dying maternal body projected onto "self." This body of indeterminate status and identity is a palimpsest of erotic and deathward desire, written over by Rosine's longing for X's "extra-large" cunt, sex sprees in cars, and the revenge of plastic sex toys set out on the apartment balcony in plain view as a protest against the dinosaur furniture that territorializes the *crop* of lawn in the apartment courtyard. The language of sexual repression everywhere has a "crack" that can open to the eros of "crop," sabotaging the conscious value for property.

The binary of silence and unrepressed language or knowledge is woven into a fabric of binaries that are marked by their instability. The interleaving of life and death in its psychological and fictive dimensions is one such binary that mingles in a third dimension of non/narration in which aspects of a thinking subject's inquiry can materialize, but not in their totality. Another fuzzy binarism is that of the "amasses" and their complement, the "amassee," represented in the figure of the landlord.

A feature of the landlord or amassee's suffering is her incapacity to observe surroundings in a meaningful manner and a lack of interest in or curiosity about the buried histories of her dwelling: she stands as an object of judgment, a figure for capitalism's process of erasing the visible signs of its material history and the struggles that give form to its violence. The landlord's obsessive complaining about trivial things, including the lesbian residents in her building, corresponds with her lack of curiosity as a feature in the capitalist landscape of erased material history. The association of repression with acquisitiveness is a familiar psychoanalytic trope, and one that is queered in the now-you-see-it now-you-don't humor related to Rosine's tortured love life. Our narrator *qua* composite character becomes the counterpoint to and mediums of the curiosity so lacking in the landlord. The language of Rosine, the fly, the Bottom Historian's fascination with historical *matter* fuses the unrepressed knowledge of the present to the past:

> #4995 [stands] directly over buried pylons of former magnificent Crystal Palace, built for agricultural + commercial exposition purposes. Where ca. 1885, mid rows of faces on iron beds erupting like plastic bubbles into fetid putrid pus, lying Shale Pit Workers! Of neighborouing Saint-John-Baptist, dying in smallpox epidemy, raging in our filth . . ." (13)

This compressed semi-archival and semi-fictional account of the "Shale Pit Workers" is one of many examples in which the material aspects of history are revealed as cover and burial of that upon which we the living owe our own material circumstance. The collective aspect of living within more than one historical moment is one of the profound gaps in or silences of contemporary cosmopolitan life. The question of the repression of that which historically gives life is complicated; Scott calls forth the ideological aspects of our forgetting at a moment in which psychoanalytic theories and ideology critique themselves have become subject to competitive theories that have sought to replace them and/or superseded them.

One of the unanswered questions of Scott's novel has to do with the ways language factors into suppression of history, collective knowledge, and personal or interpersonal experience. Rand persistently points to two threads of Abraham and Torok's essay collection: one thread leads to their critique of hardened theoretical terminology and the other, which is more unresolved, leads to the potential of the theory of the phantom to be brought to bear on what we might call "the political unconscious."[4]

The transposition of the psychological dimension onto collective event and trauma is at the heart of Scott's *Obituary*. It is the thing that haunts the narrative of life and death and which actual obituaries are largely designed to ignore or underplay. The melancholy of the novel is the product of collective trauma while the mourning process is a function of personal and familial loss. When Rosine at the end of the novel has processed and purged her grief, we are not left with resolution but with the irresolute noise of the text's last one word sentence, "Eeeeeeenglish?"

This senseful nonsense, in which a cultural dominant, the English language, is transformed to sonic screech, echoes other nonsensical events of the text. One such event entails Rosine's having borrowed or stolen the landlord's Book of Genocides. The pun is obvious, but what Rosine does with the book is arbitrary and without explanation. One by one, she tears its pages throughout several chapters of the novel, releasing and letting them fall in the manner of the prematurely hand-like leaves falling from the trees in the opening scene. To these falling pages accrue a litany or dirge of proper names—Somalia, East Timor, Eritrea—that might draw shivers up the reader's spine. The fact that these elsewheres such as the bombed Afghanistan *acking* through the radio noise in Rosine's backyard are so present on home turf yet away from the scene of slaughter, returns us to the "no one" unaffected by the fact that what is apparent is yet unseen and not (sufficiently) voiced.

Who speaks that which ought to be or can be spoken is clearly all to the point. One of the significant silences of this work is the silence that accommodates the space of others whose voices may or may not be addressed or that may or may not choose to participate in Scott's text. Yet there are several instances in the novel in which absent voices are enabled via the lingua franca of western theoretical text, here entwined in the language of Walter Benjamin, Nicolas Abraham, Maria Torok, and Nicholas Rand:

> The past + its objects, as saying great Walter B. Solely graspable to present as fragment or flash of illumination at moment of extreme contradiction. Implying any flickering planetary molecule [+ its shadow, memory]. Animate or inanimate. Capable of impacting any other. Which, when understood, fully. Will restore to rightful status the discerning Indigenous peoples. Who knowing nothing happening in any one planetary domain or moment. Ever definitely lost to any other.
> (116)

• • •

The text's difficulty begins with the writing subject's reading of the world comprised of many worlds. The anxiety about what is inaccessible in these worlds is an anxiety related to what one is affected by in material reality but can't discern. The apartment building, which Scott sometimes refers to as the true character of the novel, with its buried history—its Crystal Palace past where Settler Nuns treated Shale Pit workers for smallpox—stands as a figure for discernment within the material world. The writing subject, who reads the apartment building as both historical artifact and living environment, is explicit about her anxiety that the persisting burial of material history under the ever new of late commodity culture in the twenty-first century global city endangers our capacity to project hopeful utopian desire. An advocacy for change that would make use of rather than tear down the existing built world, a world made by the invisible laboring many, is in *The Obituary* perceived to be on the wane in the cosmopolitan zone. This is one of the sources of the book's melancholy, I think. It is a melancholy that cannot be covered by the individual's encounter with trauma. This is a melancholy that is turned inside out, into the social dimension. It's effects on *The Obituary's* narration is to slow down the story line. The melancholic aspect slows down the narrative of mourning such that the novel seems to some more like a new form of poetry.

NOTES

*The essay presented in *The Poet's Novel* is an abridged version of a longer performative work that was first presented as a keynote lecture for*The Crypt(ic)*, the 2014 Comparative Literature and Society-Annual Graduate Student Conference, Columbia University, New York. A second version of the talk was presented at the University of Auckland and can be found at this site: http://www.nzepc.auckland.ac.nz/features/harryman-watten/

1 Rand, Nicholas T.: Editors Note to "Notes on the Phantom: A complement to Freud's *Metasychology*," by Nicholas Abraham in *The Shell and the Kernel* by Maria Torok and Nicholas Abraham. Chicago, 1994.

2 To be Metis one would have to identify and be recognized as Metis.

3 The "political unconscious," of Abraham and Torok, which is a concept arising from clinical practices differs significantly from that of political theorist Frederic Jameson's well-known discussion in *The Political Unconscious*.

WORKS CITED

Scott, Gail. *The Obituary*. Callicoon, New York: Nightboat, 2012.

Torok, Maria and Abraham, Nicolas. Ed., trans., and intro. Nicholas T. Rand. *The Shell and the Kernel*, Chicago: University of Chicago, 1994.

Kevin Killian's Epic Poem of Happiness

BRANDON BROWN

In 2017, Essay Press published *Selected Amazon Reviews, Volume 3,* written by Kevin Killian and edited by Dia Felix. The new selection by Felix follows previous editions by Hooke Press (2006) and Push Press (2011), both chapbooks published by small Bay Area presses. Together, the three books collect 120 or so of the 2,638 reviews Killian published on Amazon in his lifetime.

Years ago, I overheard a friend describe Killian's Amazon reviews as his *Maximus Poems,* the truth of which filled me with delight and wonder. The contrast of Olson's high modernist epic of heroic self-aggrandizement and celebration of colonial adventure with Killian's vulnerable, satiric, aphoristic pieces about ordinary commodities, small press poets, and popular culture stars suggests a tender hyperbole. But, with a little reflection, the comparison is actually quite apt. It provides insight into what Killian's reviews are like as *literature.* Like Robert Duncan's *Structure of Rime,* Rachel Blau DuPlessis's *Drafts,* or the *Fast and Furious* film series, the Amazon reviews constitute an epic work which has amassed over many years and remains an open-ended artwork, collecting discrete units into a sound, if unwieldy, paradoxical, and perverse, edifice.

Michael Myers defines epic literature in *The Bedford Introduction to Literature:* "A lengthy narrative poem, ordinarily concerning a serious subject containing details of heroic deeds and events significant to a culture of a nation" (Meyer, 2128). Georg Lukács writes about the epic's inextricable relationship to other forms, like the novel, in *Theory of the Novel:* "Artistic genres now cut across one another, with a complexity that cannot be disentangled" (Lukács, 41). Both of these attempts to define and contextualize the epic in literature recall Killian's Amazon reviews. Together they constitute a lengthy work involving narrative, digression, fiction, memoir, truth and lies. Perpendicular with the quotidian and the sublime, the individual reviews themselves take the glamor of ordinary life seriously and organize Killian's artistic heroes into a pantheon. Their obsession with the things (and images, and sounds) that we use to populate our everyday make them fully a song of contemporary culture, if not exactly Myers's "nationhood."

Consider the classic example of epic, the poems of Homer. *Iliad* tells the story of the Mycenaean warlord Agamemnon, who convenes an armada of mercenaries to sail to Troy and attempt to kidnap the wife of his brother, who has herself been kidnapped by Paris, prince of Troy. The version which was eventually written down and transmitted to us is over 15,000 lines long. Of course, it existed in other "editions": semi-improvised each time a professional performer of epic (the rhapsode) opened their mouth to sing. Like the accumulating comments on an ecstatically negative social media thread, other stories were woven by rhapsodes into this central narrative. Long digressions sing the stories of the Gods and their cloudy hijinks, as well as the communities of warriors integrating and disintegrating quickly on the fields outside the citadel of Troy. Special epithets are reserved for the appurtenances of their martial costume and kitchen tools.

Of course there are plenty of "serious subjects" and "details of heroic deeds," seeing as the whole poem is about sex, violence, and family. And while the events of the Trojan War took place hundreds of years before the poet named Homer was presumed to exist, those events still contributed to a broad sense of what it meant to be Greek. Not just in the way that it reinforces the terrifying traffic in women, misogyny, and xenophobia the average Greek would have considered ordinary, but even for the administration of anybody's daily life. The poem tells you how to react if you have accidentally stabbed a god, but also how to prepare a lamb for a group of ravenous military assholes.

The popularity of ancient epic is legible not only in the centrality of its narrative stories for ancient Mediterraneans. Its formal qualities are preserved in literary forms quite different from Homer's. The meter of epic, dactylic hexameter, was so closely identified with the Homeric works that later poets could use the meter as a way of signaling to readers that their poems just got *extremely serious.* This same dynamic permitted poets to use the meter ironically. Like Courbet's great canvasses, which situate the work of working class proles and rural farmers on the scale of world history and myth, poets who used dactylic hexameter to describe something banal transformed epic's grave prosody by letting a little air in and giving their scant lyrics the very rhythm of gravitas.

Kevin Killian's literary and artistic output had astonishing range. His works span known genres and found new ones. He wrote in historically legible forms like the *collection of poems* and the *novel.* But his oeuvre also includes short stories, criticism, biography, memoir, plays, essays, photography, and his relentless cry in the vast desert of corporate retail web space: the epic collection of Amazon reviews.

As in Killian's books, the narrator of the Amazon reviews is semi-reliable, semi-knowable at best. Their speaker is not always or not exactly Killian, necessarily. This semi-reliable or semi-veritable narrator is typical of Killian's poetry and fiction. In his 1997 poetry book *Argento Series,* Killian writes through Italian horror director Dario Argento's work—with all its campy blood, guts, screams, and excessively gory death scenes—as a way to address the unspeakable horror of the AIDS crisis. In that book's follow-up, *Action Kylie,* Australian pop singer Kylie Minogue is not simply a Beatrice, but a mirror for Kevin Killian himself, off of whom glittering light refracts and bends in unpredictable directions.

These spectacular screens enable Killian to offer himself in different iterations for his readers. But as this writing is also intensely concerned with questions of narrative itself, the language of the foil brings about a tension between the "authentic" voice of a narrator and the staged language of a fictional character. The effect is an uncanny splitting of the subject, throwing the real "Kevin Killian" into question. It's this splitting that is the theme of "Who Is Kevin Killian?" in 1996's collection of stories, *Little Men.*

"Who Is Kevin Killian?" is staged as an interview between Kevin Killian and an unnamed interlocutor. The conceit is that "Kevin Killian" has taken a truth serum and must answer the interviewer's questions without dissimulating. But instead of responding with a series of answers that provide insight and clues to the hard identity of "Kevin Killian," "Kevin" evades, deflects, digresses, compliments the interviewer's outfit, and finally seduces the interviewer him or herself into forgetting to follow the question to its end. But we can still ask, can't we? Who *is* "Kevin Killian?"

One answer to this question was temporarily offered on his Amazon profile page—a new platform for writers of epic to describe themselves—which has since disappeared. Killian wrote, "What do I like to read, listen to, or watch? People who love me know that the best way to satisfy me is with some 'one handed' reading material, or with something avant-garde, I don't really care." The juxtaposition of pornography and avant-garde literature is a classic gesture of New Narrative writing. As Killian himself describes in a talk on 1980's gay poetry, activism, and AIDS, "We (New Narrative writers) wanted to infuse the stories of our lives with the rigors of theoretical discourse. We wanted to bring the body back to writing, by any means necessary, and so we employed everything from the lamps of biology to the badlands of porn to get it there" (Unpublished essay).

Just as Amazon "hall of fame" reviewer Kevin Killian claims to "not care" whether he is jerking off reading porn or engaging with a difficult new avant garde work, the reviews confirm a deeply elusive narrator. For instance, in Killian's January 4, 2007 review of "14K Ruby and Diamond 'Dynasty' Necklace'," he writes,

As an American boy growing up in France, I became mesmerized by an enchanting painting of an ancestor that hung never very far from the hearth. (Killian, *Selected Amazon Reviews, Vol. 2,* unpaginated)

Killian did not grow up in France. He grew up on Long Island. Did that suburban home come equipped with a proper "hearth?" I doubt it. But who cares? For this epic work, unlike that of *Iliad,* the veracity of the hero's upbringing is irrelevant. The many Kevin Killians that stage as author of these reviews occasionally contradict each other's possibly reality. You can grow up in Long Island and you can grow up French nobility; rarely can you do both. The attentive reader will note that "Kevin Killian" is a gay man, a loyal husband married to a woman, a father to several children, a childless husband, an uncle, a helpful neighbor, an international flaneur, an office worker in San Francisco, etc. Some of these Kevin Killians participated in reality.

Epic is usually site-specific. For centuries, *Iliad* and *Odyssey* existed as fluid collections of formulas loosely arranged around a common story which would find different specific forms based on which rhapsode was on stage. Later epics took the form of a book. Most of them, like *Maximus Poems,* take the form of very big books. Killian's Amazon reviews, of course, are inscribed into Amazon.com, a website, a space where others gather to buy objects and, if spurred to write a review of these objects, make their own public songs. Given a comment box and time, Amazon users yearn to tell their tales. One way some of us give form to the totality of our lives in the present is by praising or blaming commodities. "I bought a car stereo," this literature announces as a way to tell the story of a life. "Let me tell you about it."

Killian's epic doesn't solve the crisis of an all-encompassing ideological imperative to buy nor the crises of plenitude and loss which such an imperative brings about. However, as an epic poem, the Amazon reviews give a very particular shape to our collective desire to sing our stories through the objects we populate our lives with. This desire, thwarted as it often is, frequently causes the most morbid depression. Killian's poem, on the other hand, concerns itself with human happiness.

The epic is familiar with happiness. Lukacs describes the epic as the literary genre which, by taking up the heaviness and density of totality, brings about a lightness he associates explicitly with happiness. He writes,

Epic creates distances, but in the sphere of the epic (which is the sphere of life) distance means happiness and lightness, a loosening of the bonds that tie men [sic] and objects to the ground, a lifting of the heaviness, the dullness, which are integral to life and which are dispersed only in scattered happy moments. (Lukacs, 57)

When I think about the tension between my hatred for the dilapidated form of capitalism in the present which causes vast human immiseration, and my love for the beings and objects which appear through, because of, and despite that immiseration, it is a humiliating and depressing thought. A heavy and immobilizing thought. The proximity of these beings and objects easily drifts into feelings at once oppressive and irreparable.

It's this depression that Killian's epic work combats, by giving us a way to formalize our experience of the "scattered happy moments" of a life in and through what we love and despise. In other words, what we desire, with desire's simultaneous plethora and lack. By loosening the grave bonds of objects and their value, the Amazon reviews permit these objects to appear in a new, auratic glow. Spotlight bending in sex-drenched air off Kylie's exhausted forehead. Consider, for instance, the 2009 review for Advil, titled "Feels So Good."

> Ordinarily I agree with James Koenig's reviews 1000 per cent. Not for nothing is he one of Amazon's top 100 reviewers. And yet, when he tells us we might as well just get the generic version of ibuprofen, as well as brand name Advil, I demur sharply.
>
> Other reviewers recommend Advil for its ease of use, but I'm here to tell you the main reason to buy it is that it is tasty and sweet, rather like a cherry. If common sense and doctors warnings didn't preclude it, I would be popping Advils all day just to get that delicious taste in my mouth, like a kid in a candy store.
>
> First week of January I had an industrial accident at my office when a large box of heavy paper stock tumbled down onto my foot from a great height. Rushed to the hospital, I found myself weak and faint, and when the doctor told me that I should be having an Advil every four hours for the next three months, to reduce swelling and to heal the fracture, I perked up considerably. Now in front of me as I type, is a king size dispenser of Advil, used to be an oversized Pez dispenser in black and gold, wearing Tim Lincecum's uniform, which some friends had bought me on a trip to the SF Giants stadium here. Now it dispenses Advil and I find myself looking at the clock wishing it was four hours later already. I'm hooked I guess, and a little piece of me wishes I could return to the days of youth when I needed nothing, no poppy or mandragora as Shakespeare says, but in the meantime I do enjoy a nice Advil every four hours, and as a side benefit, its healing atoms have sped the recovery of my swollen foot inside its sturdy surgical boot. (Killian, *Selected Amazon Reviews, Vol. 2,* unpaginated)

On a literal level, "Feels so Good" dispenses advice on reducing and managing bodily pain. Bur it also contains another story. Many stories. To me, "Feels So Good" contains all of life. It brings us into the contemporary office and its discontents. It bears witness to a pervasive tedium which makes any interruption, even and especially the pharmaceutical, a desirable rupture. It speaks to addiction and the bittersweet dark mirror of pharmaceutical pleasure.

You don't need to consult the elusive and difficult literary theory of Georg Lukacs to understand Killian's epic work as one concerned primarily with human happiness. In his own description, Killian locates the genesis of the work in a surfeit of such. Having suffered a drastic health scare in late 2001, he was given various drugs which would "stop me from doing this or that." Like smoking cigarettes, one of the worst and best of the things the Gods delivered to human beings. These medications proved so effective in producing a state of durable happiness that Killian felt his career as a writer might be over. Don't writers need to suffer to write? Yet, when his friend Arnold Kemp gave him a book for his birthday that year, Killian wrote his first review on Amazon—the first writing as his recovery commenced.

From there, dozens, hundreds, thousands of reviews. After the inception of this epic work, Killian published a book of stories, a novel, new books of poetry. He wrote new plays and had gallery shows of his photographs of scantily dressed men. The world historical catastrophe in which all of these works were made hasn't lessened or lightened—far from it—but Killian's epic work lightens the burden of *enduring* it.

WORKS CITED

Killian, Kevin. *Argento Series.* San Francisco: Krupskaya, 2001.

Killian, Kevin. *Action Kylie.* Oakland: In Girum Imus Nocte et Consumimur Igni, 2008.

Killian, Kevin. *Little Men.* Lingo Books, 1996.

Killian, Kevin. *Selected Amazon Reviews Volume 1.* Oakland: Hooke Press, 2006.

Killian, Kevin. *Selected Amazon Reviews Volume 2.* San Francisco: Push Press, 2011. Unpaginated.

Killian, Kevin. *Selected Amazon Reviews Volume 3.* Essay Press, 2017.

Lukacs, Georg. *The Theory of the Novel.* Cambridge: MIT Press, 1977.

Myers, Michael, ed. *The Bedford Introduction to Literature.* Bedford/St. Martin's, 2016.

Dark Light
Paradox & Subversion in Laura Moriarty's *Ultravioleta*

BRENT CUNNINGHAM

As with most phrases, the term "poet's novel" signifies along a spectrum. At the more sociological end it can mean a novel written by someone whose primary identity is as a poet, regardless of the aesthetics of the text itself. In this essay I will be concerned with the other end of that spectrum, where the phrase implies a set of aesthetic principles at odds with fiction proper.

I'll be delving into one work in particular, Laura Moriarty's *Ultravioleta*. It so happens that *Ultravioleta* is very much a "poet's novel" in the first, sociological sense. Moriarty has published over a dozen books of poetry, has taught poetry, and in her book *A Tonalist* (and elsewhere) foregrounds the dynamics of poetry's social infrastructure. But the formal arrangement of *Ultravioleta* is also an extreme example of the "poet's novel" in the other sense, where a work sets out to subvert fiction's paradigm at the most fundamental level. It is a text that writes generic resistance directly into its plot, its characters, its sense of narrative time. In its universe, where paper ships are propelled by the engines of thinking and writing, the problem of literary form's production neatly literalizes into the book's content.

Before travelling too far *there*, however, it is worth sketching the basic literary conventions *Ultravioleta* sets itself against, if only so we don't mistake genre—and, in particular, the genre of fiction—for some kind of immaterial abstraction. To suggest a metaphor Moriarty probably didn't intend with her title, ultraviolet light (the "poet's novel") does not depend on visible light (the conventional novel) to exist, yet conceptions about one kind of light do alter and inform conceptions of the other.

In the May/June 2013, issue of *Poets & Writers* magazine there is an article by Benjamin Percy called "Writing with Urgency" that can act as our exemplar. In it Percy lays out six steps to building a good story, steps familiar to anyone who has read other "how to write fiction" articles. Even within the same issue there are other articles rehearsing strikingly similar precepts, and chances are that Percy himself has no feelings of ownership over these rules, which are presented as universally effective techniques—just part of the skill set every experienced writer needs to learn and follow. They are as follows: establish a clear goal, create a sense of human urgency, create obstacles that ramp up the tension, create lower-order goals, create some sort of ticking clock, and delay gratification by withholding information.

Ultravioleta violates all six steps flagrantly. Moreover it knowingly—as a matter of the novel's ecology and material—sets out to rigorously, if often ambiguously, interrogate the premises and history behind the formulation of such conventions. For instance the following passage can—with only a slight contortion of the mind—be read as a rebuttal to Percy. It utilizes the digressive form that runs throughout the book, then ends with some relatively direct thoughts on the subject of withholding information (Percy's step #6):

> Humans, especially those who are Martians, believe that the answers will allow them to get their edge again, the edge they imagine themselves to have had and lost. Nahid is beginning to suspect that even the questions are wrong. She suspects that the I actually measure distance in the personal and idiosyncratic ways that they eat and sleep and live. She figures that they agree to these human interpretations of their measurements because they agree to everything. What they can't or won't do is supply a straight answer to a simple question. It is evident that withholding information creates suspense, frustration and nostalgia—sometimes anger. She perceives that an I can get pretty fat in a setup as sweet as that. There are limits to how long such a situation can be maintained, but, she notes to herself, they can be fiddled with. (132)

True to form, this "argument" against straight answers then gives way to more speculation, more digression, more anti-narrative. But the basic terms of Moriarty's resistance to fiction's methodologies are clear: the personal and idiosyncratic over the professional and systematic, for example, as well as the connection of "withholding information" with manipulation and privilege. Much of *Ultravioleta* could be read, similarly, as a meta-argument over issues of literary form. This impression is only reinforced by the thinness of the plot.

Let's take a moment to describe that plot. In *Ultravioleta*, a variety of space travelers—some clones, some humans, some robots, some aliens who are called "I," and a number of hybrids of the above—travel around time and space, think, talk, have a dinner, and eventually get on board a paper ship called Ultravioleta. A couple of the main characters may or may not plummet into the center of Europa, after which the I's may or may not go extinct.

The main reason the plot in *Ultravioleta* doesn't possess Percy's "sense of human urgency," or even much in the way of specificity, is not because it lacks traditional tensions and complexities (and hence can be easily summarized). Rather, it is because the book's language systematically undercuts the reader's trust that any of the depicted events are actually happening. In the world of *Ultravioleta* everything "seems," everything is conditioned by this or that character's "belief," everything occurs "as if." "The library explodes," announces a typical paragraph in *Ultravioleta*, then immediately follows this urgent turn of events with an equally typical negation—or possible negation—of that event's reality: "Cap reels back but it is all in Ada's mind" (140).

This fluidity between the real and mental accounts for the plot's lack of "lower-order goals" nested inside of higher-order goals, as Percy admonishes. But it isn't just the plot that destabilizes fiction's traditional relationship to tension, action, and pursuit-of-goals. It is also the nature of the characters, specifically their ability to enter each other's minds. In the novel, it is never quite clear how far these powers of possession go, how exactly they work, or even who has them versus who lacks them (although the I, as their name implies, are especially adept at thought travel as well as all sorts of identity bending). Still, such fluid character borders make it hard to get a fix on what is happening in terms of psychological motivation. Which sensibility is thinking or speaking is always mildly indeterminate in the book, muddling the question of what is at stake and for whom; moreover, almost every character appears as a deep twin of a least one other character. In this way, reading *Ultravioleta* illuminates, by its absence, the degree to which most fiction—including ostensibly "experimental" fiction—tells the story of the development and growth of clearly delineated personalities with distinct personal histories.

Ultravioleta's subversions go beyond plot and characters, as well, extending down into the structure of the narrative itself. A long chapter in the center of the book, "The Astrologer: Prisoner of Mars," provides a microcosm of the alternative narrative model conditioning the book as a whole. The chapter liberally borrows the structure, as well as doppelgängers of the characters, from Bernard le Bovier de Fontenelle's *Conversations on the Plurality of Worlds* (1686), a French popular science book considered one of the first works of the Age of Enlightenment. Fontenelle's work was progressive for its day, featuring some advanced ideas about alien life as well as an intelligent female main character who—almost radical for the times—grasps her male teacher's ideas. Its form is a modified Socratic dialogue, an extremely common framework at the time for philosophical speculation. Crucially,

Moriarty thus takes one of her most overt sources from an era just before the novel develops into approximately the form we still see today; just prior, that is, to its ascent into mass, middle class appeal. Daniel Defoe's *Robinson Crusoe* (1719) and Samuel Richardson's *Pamela, or Virtue Rewarded* (1740)—two books that scholars frequently use to mark the rise of the contemporary novel as such—are still decades off from Fontenelle's great work. As it happens, both *Crusoe* and *Pamela* are particularly short on dialogue as well (*Crusoe* because the main character lacks an interlocutor, *Pamela* because it is in epistolary form). Perhaps this lack of dialogue was partly, if perhaps unconsciously, an attempt by those writers to mark their new literary form off from philosophy and its Socratic influences. In the end, dialogue swiftly became a central component of the novel proper, although what came to matter for fictional dialogue was not its ability to convey conceptual ideas but its realism—a "realism" very much constructed by Defoe and Richardson. Regardless, in place of the didactic, abstract, artificially oratorical form descended from Socrates, the bourgeoisie novel was soon striving to approximate, or at least appear to approximate, how people actually exchange in speech.

Moriarty's book very nearly performs the opposite operation, using the architecture of the philosophical dialogue—a form out of fashion for four hundred years—to mark her novel off from contemporary fiction. Not only does "The Astrologer: Prisoner of Mars" rely heavily on speculative exchanges between characters, but the rest of *Ultravioleta* contains a diversity of dialogues that are spoken or thought by characters, usually without the least pretense of realism. Some are so long they border on monologues, while others actually are monologues—all of it, perhaps, little more than material fuel for the paper ship that is, in both metaphor and reality, the novel itself.

Of course, anti-realism has had many canonized advocates in the history of fiction proper, so it would be hard to defend the position that unrealistic dialogue is a characteristic of the poet's novel per say. There is even a small tradition among innovative modernist novelist of the early 20th century to extend dialogues to unlikely lengths. In Robert Walser's novels, for instance, or in the endless speculative exchanges of Matthew O'Connor and Nora in Djuna Barnes' *Nightwood*, the implausible ornateness of the dialogue ruptures the formal framework of "realistic" fiction, replacing it with a foregrounded awareness of language as such. At the very least the monologic tends to raise questions about the narrator's reliability or the nature of identity and reportage. In *Ultravioleta*, however, this borrowing from the philosophical tradition goes even further, since the monologic / dialogic exchanges in Walser or Barnes are still embedded in vaguely substantial, vaguely "lived" situations. In other words, there remains some semblance of the actual in those books, often breaking through most clearly in the voice of an omniscient narrator. Commonly, it is possible to locate at least the suggestion that the nature of the narrator's own experiences account for the warps in the dialogue's realism. In the world of *Ultravioleta*, by contrast, even the voice of the omniscient narrator is syntactically and logically structured as if the speaker were one of the book's indeterminate characters. Supposedly neutral, Moriarty's narrator is firm, declarative, and analytic in tone, yet expresses paradoxes, doubts and metaphorical ambiguity at every juncture, as in the following passage:

> As a hybrid, Dayv has a unique perspective, but he doesn't care. As I he wants to eat. And as I he realizes he is always eating. It is the beautiful thing about being one of the boys. They are not really all boys. But they are always eating. As human Dayv wants to be in the library. He believes there is someone he should meet. Some bit of organizational culture he should share but the war rises back up in his mind as soon as he seems to get there. Dayv looks into the middle distance seeing the endless battle beyond his eyes. Ada writes. She watches. She finds two women struggling to survive. She sees Stella. She sees herself as someone else. She writes against gravity, knowing herself to be running and falling and flying. (105)

The problem of whether Dayv wants to eat or is always eating or both, and what the actual differences are between those various states, does not seem to be the concern of whoever is narrating the passage. Same with whether the I are boys or not. In more standard novels, narrators step in with explanation—no doubt Percy would insist on the importance of doing so—but here the narrative voice only raises more questions, more problems (even if those often masquerade as statements). How is wanting to be in the library a characteristic of humans? Is Dayv literally seeing a battle or only figuratively? Is the "she" in "she sees herself as someone else" modifying Stella or Ada? Or is it a disembodied pronoun? Or is a "she" a new kind of alien? In *Ultraviolata*, with all those I's running around, the last possibility is entirely conceivable.

This extreme antipathy towards expository explanation—even towards simple discursive sequitur, at times—is why the text reads so much like poetry, and why many readers would be comfortable with a classification like "poet's novel" for the book. Each sentence feels subtly cut off from the previous sentence, in turn barely getting a rope over to the next. But, while Ultravioleta's parataxis is perhaps easiest link to poetry, and certainly echoes some stylistic elements in Moriarty's poetic output, it is also useful to keep Fontenelle in mind. By writing in the tradition of didactic forms, a form wherein Percy's anxiety about "urgency" and "tension" is far less important than languorous, speculative exploration, the Frenchman creates a work as disinterested in determinate plotting, characters, or narrative as any poem. Moriarty's text draws on Fontenelle's *Conversations* because she is interested in any formal structure—not just poetry—that can offer an alternative to the shape of fiction. In this respect, the book is less an anti-realistic novel than a realistic anti-novel.

To be clear, the anti-novel has a history that is nearly as long, rich and canonically accepted as the history of the novel itself. Truth be told, the line between the poet's novel and the standard issue anti-novel is hazy to the point of irreality. Critics like the Russian formalist Viktor Shklovsky went so far as to take the act of undermining preceding forms of literature via formal revivification—a technique Shklovsky called *ostranenie*, or "enstrangement" in some translations—as the very definition of literature. Hence, Moriarty's attempt to contradict literary conventions is, in this sense, entirely within the lineage of someone like Lawrence Sterne (a favorite of Shklovsky's), a writer whose books no one confuses with poetry. We are back to square one in our attempt to mark off some specific characteristics of the poet's novel. In fact, as long as we keep strictly to the level of aesthetic principles and techniques my feeling is that there is no simple way to separate the contemporary "poet's novel" even from fiction written fifty years ago by, say, Jean Genet, Nathalie Sarraute, or for that matter Virginia Woolf.

Still, I believe there is probably something unique—if difficult to pin down—about spending many years working within one genre, then suddenly attempting a work in a different framework. Quite a few novels written by poets—and I would include *Ultravioleta* among them—attempt an estrangement of not just, say, certain conventional fictional objects and forms, but rather take on the genre as a whole, treating it as a single object, as *the* object, in a way very few experimental novels think to do. Frequently the poet's novel doesn't just jettison Percy's ticking clock, but imagines a formal universe where the clock never mattered in the first place. Still, in the end it proves necessary to turn to the sociological meaning of "poet's novel" to make the term meaningfully distinct from the many anti-novels, new novels, and just plain novels out there.

I realize I have left open the question as to precisely why *Ultravioleta*—or, really, any formally subversive novel—might set out to thwart the dominant paradigm. Many critics posit a connection between aesthetic subversion and political resistance, with an equal number finding that connection specious, and to my mind those are useful and important debates. Yet they don't quite line up, in my mind, with *Ultravioleta's* ambiance. The drive to resist schemas and fixed premises, to foreground contradiction and the freedom of thought as an absolutely primary route to feeling, is inscribed into every page of *Ultravioleta*, making it hard to generalize its aesthetic argument without violating its intense anti-hierarchical spirit. In *Ultravioleta*, everyone speaks (at length), everyone's thoughts are both real and unreal, everyone loves and betrays across regulations, everyone is forever in the midst of deciding their politics and the relation of those politics to thought and art. The novel strongly suggests a utopian space in continual danger of dissolution—specifically, dissolution by functionalism, by discursive certainty, by the reverse of contradiction.

Here, we begin to slide precipitously into the contradictions of literary subversion as an approach, as well as the elusive borders of genre classification itself. Is the "resistance" the novel displays truly resisting the normative, or does it merely reinscribe a new norm? This essay has used Percy's tenets as a foil for *Ultravioleta* since they make the novel's basic concerns starkly clear; however, it is much more challenging to figure out how a book like Moriarty's fits into a classification system that itself aims to be subversive. Consider, for example, Fredric Jameson's paradigm for the "postmodern" novel. It is hard to deny that Ultravioleta fits fairly well into the "constitutive features" for postmodern cultural objects laid out in *Postmodernism, or, The Cultural Logic of Late Capitalism*. These are: depthlessness, a weakening of historicity as a result of such depthlessness, an emotional "ground tone" that Jameson describes as a return to the sublime, and a "constitutive relationship" to new technology. Moriarty's book undeniably manifests all four features. At the same time, the book's characters are given such extreme agency to think and rethink their own (aesthetic) conditions that it is hard to imagine placing the work comfortably into *any* classificatory system. In a sense, *Ultravioleta* is stuck—marooned, to keep with its nautical themes—in a paradox. It is "postmodern" even as it would clearly detest the category; strangely, it is postmodern *because* it would detest the category. In the end Jameson severely critiques the political efficacy of such paradoxical aesthetic understandings, but even then *Ultravioleta*, with all those "boys" moving in with their mind control, their slick takeovers of thoughts and experiences intimate to the largely female and hybrid characters, essentially thematizes a dispute it has with anyone trying to theorize political and personal space, be they radical, complex, or even accurate. Who gets to say? Which framework gets to contain the other? In this respect a deep contrarian spirit lies at the heart of *Ultravioleta*, a spirit which—in its basic prickliness, its aesthetic indeterminacy, and its subcultural sociological position—might also constitute the only reliable marker of the "poet's novel" as a distinct creature.

WORKS CITED

Jameson, Frederic. *Postmodernism, or, the Cultural Logic of Late Capitalism.* Durham: Duke University Press, 1991.

Moriarty, Laura. *Ultravioleta.* Berkeley: Atelos, 2006.

A Ghostlike Interference
Jack Spicer's Detective Novel

DANIEL KATZ

"Bohemia is a dreadful, wonderful place" Jack Spicer wrote to a more conventional boyfriend who had jilted him, sometime in the early fifties, "It
is full of hideous people and beautiful poetry. It would be wrong of me to
drag a person I love into such a place against his will. Unless you walk into
it freely, and with open despairing eyes, you can't even see the windows"
(*Collected Poems*, 442). However, it is precisely into such a Bohemia that
Spicer drags his protagonist, Jim Ralston, in his unfinished detective novel, dubbed by his editors *The Tower of Babel*. The background to Spicer's
project has been brilliantly detailed by Lewis Ellingham and Kevin Killian
in both their afterword to the novel and their biography of Spicer, *Poet Be
Like God*, where readers can find a full account of its gestation.[1] The book,
probably started in 1957 but principally composed in 1958, was meant to be
a money-making project—or so, at least, Spicer tried to convince himself
at the outset. Spicer enjoyed crime fiction and thought he could produce
a successful contribution to the genre, but the prime selling point of the
book would be its setting: with the sensational reception of Kerouac's *On
The Road* and the *Howl* obscenity trial, San Francisco was now in the national news as center of the fascinating, scandalous, and perplexing "Beat"
phenomenon.[2] "Every social system, every Bohemia, has an aristocracy, a
middle class, and a poor-white class" (13), Ralston muses as he tries to assess
the (counter)cultural capital possessed by a young woman he has met in a
bar his first day back in San Francisco after a seven-year absence. And it is a
version of the Beat "social system"—the demi-monde or underworld with
its foreign rules, slang, rites, rituals and arcana, so vital to the crime fiction genre—that Spicer set out to chart for the titillation of what he hoped
would be a sizable reading public, ready to pay for the vicarious pleasure of
the journey. And Spicer would follow another common generic convention
in making his guide a rather reluctant Virgil—not a police officer or a private detective, but an "ordinary man" who becomes accidentally embroiled
in someone else's criminal affairs. In this, Spicer followed a motif dear to
one of his favorite film directors, and one who certainly knew how to foreground the city of San Francisco in a murder mystery: Alfred Hitchcock.[3]

But the book had a largely autobiographical aspect too, which came increasingly to drive its concerns. J. J. Ralston, as he is known to his readers, is a poet who left the San Francisco Bay Area around a decade before the story begins for a career as a college professor on the East Coast, where he has published a first book of poems to mainstream critical acclaim, and a favorable review from Randall Jarrell. But his success notwithstanding, Ralston harbors serious doubts about the ultimate value of his well received but unadventurous recent work, and feels impelled to visit his former haunts, either to be inspired by or ultimately reject the new poetry of San Francisco, which has everyone talking: "And you've come to dig the San Francisco Renaissance?" (4), the woman in the bar asks him, revealing his distressing legibility. Jack Spicer, too, had recently returned to San Francisco after an absence spent on the East Coast. His had only lasted from June, 1955 to November, 1956, but like Ralston he returned to a scene that had greatly changed, and from which he felt displaced. There was never the slightest danger of Spicer falling into the fate which worries Ralston, who betakes himself to San Francisco "at least to make an attempt not to be what he had undoubtedly already become—an, face it, academic poet [sic]" (10). On the contrary, what worried Spicer was that his own Bohemia, in which he, Robin Blaser, and Robert Duncan had been the "aristocracy," had now been entirely superseded by a new one of *arrivistes* under the kingship of Allen Ginsberg with his full court of notable and notorious figures, whom Spicer viewed as newcomers, interlopers, inauthentic Californians, and poets of questionable importance. Spicer's rivalry with Ginsberg extended all the way to his very last poem, addressed to Ginsberg in July 1965, just weeks before Spicer's death. Moreover, John Vincent has stressed that as Spicer was writing the novel he was watching his lover, Russell FitzGerald, progressively break from him as he fell in thrall to the high-profile Jewish and African-American Beat poet, Bob Kaufman. If the second, late-breaking crime in the novel is the death of black beatnik artist Washington Jones (a possible murder which Spicer's unfinished manuscript leaves unsolved), Vincent suggests that the true "murderer" must be read as the jealous and vindictive Spicer himself: "he could find one world in which Bob Kaufman could be neatly removed from the scene: his novel" (79). However, whatever bitchiness, meanness, or downright murderous rage Spicer might have channeled into the novel, returning to Hitchcock it is fair to say that the murder mystery and crime story are nothing if not a "MacGuffin."[4] For the real mystery is whether Ralston will ever manage to write the poem he came to San Francisco in order to create, and rather than what might be called a "police procedural," this novel is nothing if not a "poetics procedural"—both a study and an allegory of where poetry comes from, how it comes about, and how it can be given and received. Here, for all their enormous differences, Ralston's difficulties, evasions, inhibitions, and parapraxes regarding the poetic task ask to be read as echoes of Spicer's own. Detective stories, like Dante's *Divine Comedy*, which Spicer had studied with Ernst Kantorowicz, are not only tales of the underworld but also very frequently of redemption, and if Spicer's "dark wood" was different from Ralston's, no less than his protagonist was Spicer at this time searching for the new poems he wanted to write. *The Tower of Babel* is an integral part of this exploration, not least of the then still embryonic sense of poetry as "dictation," whose first stirrings are found in the motif of translation as haunting in *After Lorca*, written shortly before Spicer began his novel. Indeed, the work couldn't be more entwined in the idea of the "serial poem" or composition by book, which Spicer theorized in his famous letter to Robin Blaser from *Admonitions*: in the notebooks which contain Spicer's pencil holograph manuscript of the novel, the narrative is occasionally interrupted by pages containing poems and drafts of lyrics from *Admonitions*, as well as *A Book of Music* and *Billy The Kid*.[5] We know that Spicer eventually decided to put the novel aside until he could get a contract or advance from a publisher, at which mythical point he promised to set about writing out the rest—an eventuality which never came to pass. It's worth remembering, however, that he put it aside to make room for the kind of poetic blossoming it's not clear Ralston was destined by his author to know.

And that question or mystery, of course, is the one which dominates the book, even more so as Spicer never completed the manuscript (though even a finished novel might have left the question open, of course; there are mystery novels in which the crime remains unsolved). But against the grain of some interpretations of the novel, I would like to argue that the seemingly triumphant note on which the extant story ends is ambiguous, to say the least. The manuscript breaks off shortly after what appears to be a conclusive accomplishment for Ralston: he has written the poem he felt he had to write, has resolved his ambivalence concerning the seductive and charismatic young San Francisco poet Rue Talcott, and has therefore decided to leave San Francisco and resume his middle-class, professorial, New England life. This resolution is interrupted, however, by the unexpected news of the death of Washington Jones (an event which for various reasons makes it harder for Ralston to cut his ties with Rue than he had hoped) and the abrupt ending of the manuscript. Ellingham and Killian rightly suggest in their Afterword that if the novel stops where it does, it is because in many ways Spicer had at that point closed major aspects of his narrative arc. I would only like to add that they also point to the elements which hint at how that dénouement might have been reknotted, had Spicer decided to finish the book. For example, Ralston succeeds in writing his poem, but only at the price of losing the sheaf of poems handed to him by Rue, which he has spent the entire novel managing not to read. Moreover, his unease at seeing Rue naked in the final scene brings more fully to the fore the erotic attraction of the married and putatively heterosexual Ralston than any of the various hints that had been given previously. If Spicer leaves us, as it were, a finished strophe in the portion of text that he completed, I think it's also possible at least to outline the antistrophe and catastrophe—when the actions, certitudes, and decisions reverse themselves across the narrative stage—that Spicer left unwritten.[6]

To start with, Ralston's jubilation at having written his poem is expressed through the focalized narration in terms which couldn't be further from the poetics Spicer was elaborating at just this time:

> He opened the notebook and glanced at it again with satisfaction. It was one of *his* poems. . . . I am myself, Ralston thought with surprise, and my poems are my poems. (152-3)

Ralston will go on to conclude that "the energy behind this poem" derived not from coming to San Francisco but was rather "the product of his leaving it," and the narration continues the jubilatory narcissistic tautology: "He was himself and his poems were his poems" (153). Obviously, this is a very far cry from Spicer's poetics of dictation, as evidenced, for example, in his late declaration in the Vancouver lectures, "I really honestly don't feel that I own my poems" (*House*, 15). And as for Ralston's happy assertion, "I am myself," one need only think back to Spicer's Lorca project, finished very shortly before the novel was begun, in which it is precisely the loss of identity brought about by translating and the concomitant "haunting" of an alien poetic voice that makes poetry possible. If the poet must be a "dead man" (*Collected Poems*, 150) to write, that means he writes when and where he is not himself. Going even further, it's hard not to hear Charles Olson's "Projective Verse" behind Ralston's evocation of "energy" above. In the Vancouver lectures, Spicer specifies, "Olson's idea of energy and projective verse is something that comes from the Outside" (*House*, 5). Yet for Ralston, the "outside" represented by San Francisco is exactly what he has rejected in order to find "energy" for his new poem. For all these reasons, it seems clear that what Spicer presents as Ralston's sense of breakthrough and renewal is precisely what would have been the target of an ironic come-uppance in the remainder of the novel.

However, if Ralston is on a false track at this juncture, early on he expresses concerns which the novel treats more sympathetically. What first drives Ralston back to San Francisco is a lingering anxiety that his poems are too safe—that ul-timately, in them nothing is really at stake. This is brought home to him watch-ing a college football game, in which a third-string quarterback comes off the bench late in the contest to erase a large deficit and lead his team to an improb-able victory, by virtue of embracing risk in the face of hopeless odds: "What I'm trying to say is that I suddenly realized in that fourth quarter that I had never written a poem using the energy that they used, taking the chances that they took" (6). When the woman in the bar disingenuously asks if this means he's never written a poem about football, Ralston responds, "Football doesn't have anything to do with it. I mean pitting the energy, the chance-taking, or even a fraction of it against the eight-man line of language. . . . I realized that I had never done it, but that I wanted to do it more than anything else in the world—and not with a football" (6). Ralston goes on to share this story with an old friend from Berkeley, who subsequently writes him an extended letter on the subject. Upon reflection, Henry concludes that the football analogy contains a "fallacy," which he relates to the distance of art from the realm of "satisfaction"—the realm, that is, proper to the appreciation of food and sport: "and art, whatever it has to do with, has precious little to do with satisfaction" (80). Again, Henry here sounds a lot like the Spicer of the Vancouver lectures, who declares: "I don't think po-etry should be a pleasure for the audience any more than it should be a pleasure for the poet. I don't think it's meant as a pleasure" (84). Interestingly, however, in this instance the distance from pleasure likens poetry to sports, rather than separating them, "I think it's very nice to get kicks out of poetry, but I don't think it's for pleasure any more than I think baseball is for pleasure or chess is for pleasure" (85). This could represent an evolution in Spicer's views about sports, but it might also reflect his differing senses of football and baseball. As has been much discussed, baseball is central to Spicer's poetry and poetics, as well as his biography: many of his contemporaries recount his predilection for listening to San Francisco Giants' games on a portable radio in Aquatic Park.[7] Even more to the point, his "Four Poems for *The St. Louis Sporting News*" are entirely devoted to baseball, with only the slightest mention of football, which comes in the last poem of the sequence:

> God is a big white baseball that has nothing to do but go in a
>   curve or a straight line. I studied geometry in highschool
>   and know that this is true.

Given these facts the pitcher, the batter, and the catcher all look
   pretty silly. No Hail Marys
Are going to get you out of a position with the bases loaded and
   no outs, or when you're 0 and 2, or when the ball bounces
   out to the screen wildly. (416)

To the best of my knowledge, the term "Hail Mary" has no application
in baseball. In American football, however, it refers to a low-percentage,
long, forward pass made when a team has no choice but to try to score extremely quickly: basically, the quarterback just throws the ball as far as possible, and hopes a team-mate manages to come down with it. As its name
indicates, a "hail Mary pass" is the equivalent of a desperate prayer, with
very small chances of being realized. Spicer's lines above might be read as
referring to the unforgiving nature of baseball, which has extremely little
room for the high-risk, high-return tactics which can always be initiated
in football. Here, baseball is the Calvinist sport in which God exists only
as the immutable laws of physics, rather than, say, a more "Catholic" football, where tactical appeals for divine intervention are given more room by
the sport's very structure.[8] Is one of Ralston's failings, then, his fetishisa-
tion of risk and chance-taking? Such an argument is difficult to make for
many reasons, of which one would be that Spicer's resistance to the notion
of "pleasure" is precisely that it reduces and contains the stakes of poetry,
rather than heightening them. But I do think the football analogy can be
read as suggesting that Ralston's understanding of the risks and chances of
poetry and poets is mistaken. For in his football analogy, Ralston's figure of
identification is the quarterback. This seems logical, as in football the quarterback is the ultimate decision-maker on the field—the one who has the
ball, and determines where it will go, forcing defenders to react as well as
team-mates, too, if he or she is the kind of improviser that Ralston models
himself on. However, when Spicer turns to baseball in the Vancouver lectures, his figure of the poet couldn't be more different from that on which
Ralston seizes: "Actually a poet is a catcher more than a pitcher, but the
poet likes to think of himself as a pitcher more than a catcher" (117).[9] The
point to be made is that unlike the quarterback, the pitcher, or the batter,
the catcher is in a fundamentally receptive position; as the name indicates,
he or she is there mostly to "catch" whatever might come their way, rather
than initiate a pitch or a swing. In this way, the catcher—like the poet as
radio—is essentially receptive, and not "projective" in an Olsonian sense.
Of course, one speaks of a radio *receiver*, and in football, "receiver" or "wide
receiver" is one of the standard player positions: the receiver is, precisely,

the player whose task is to catch the pass—hail Mary or not—thrown by the quarterback. The implication, then, is that Ralston has read football wrong as a lesson for the poet, has in fact fetishized the wrong task. What Ralston needs to do is learn how to catch—catch the poems that will not be "his" but will instead come from the Outside, catch the passes that Rue seems to be making throughout.

The first of these passes constitutes the culmination of the opening chapter, which recounts Ralston's first afternoon back in San Francisco, spent in the new Birdcage bar, privileged meeting-place of the new Bohemia. There, Rue asks to look at Ralston's copy of the *Partisan Review* and then suddenly rips it to pieces, provoking Ralston's unsurprising ire as the latter explodes at him in rage. Seeming shaken and chastened, which is more surprising, Rue leaves, only to return again in high spirits, with a gift for Ralston: "a fairly large black fish" (20), "not quite dead" (21), with a "tightly folded" (21) piece of paper in its mouth. Ralston removes and unfolds the paper to discover it's in fact "two pages of poetry written in large childish handwriting" (21), which he rips to pieces without reading a word, causing Rue to exit almost weeping, repeating softly "You Bastard. Oh, you bastard" to Ralston as he does so. This inaugurates Rue's dogged insistence that Ralston read his work, and Ralston's equally dogged evasion, which culminates in the ultimate parapraxis of losing Rue's poems at the very moment he writes his own. Indeed, the entire action of the novel is framed by this encounter more than by any crime, real or imagined. But this encounter itself contains not a little mystery, which is not that of Ralston's desire, but of Rue's. Given Rue's ostentatious provocation of Ralston, why he is surprised and upset that the latter reacts so violently? And even more, why would Rue, of all people, care what a stuffy, academic poet thinks of his work, and want so much for him to read it? If *The Tower of Babel* is not a roman à clef,[10] it very much is a fantasy or dream-stage based on people and events from Spicer's life. As Ellingham and Killian note, Rue Talcott is in some ways a composite of Russell FitzGerald and James Alexander, who arrived in San Francisco in 1958 and whose work is evoked in the description Rue's poetry as "a sort of combination of wild French stuff and the Wild West" (72).[11] But if Ralston is in some ways a distorted mirror-image of Spicer, as we have seen—a jaded Spicer imagining James Alexander's talent and beauty can lead to a rejuvenation, perhaps—it's worth noting that he also projects some of his characteristics onto Rue. The latter's "large childish handwriting" is a precise description of the script in which so many of the only drafts of Spicer's work survives. If it's true that in fantasy the subject in some way occupies all the positions, we can see how Rue is a projection not only of Spicer's real and ideal love objects, but of Spicer himself, in his desperate and ambivalent desire to be read, and heard (even by academics!), along with his violent address which defeated its own purpose. Throughout the novel, Rue is shouting at Ralston Spicer's own ambivalent dyad: "No one listens to poetry" and "No / One listens to poetry."

But will Ralston—would Ralston—get the message? The message being nothing other than the poet as receiver of messages, the poet as receiver or catcher rather than quarterback? There are indications that perhaps he might have. In a letter to his wife, Anne, Ralston writes:

> Certainly San Francisco is neither as good or as bad as I had pictured it. I have met some fools and no angels. The announcer of common sense discloses the cast. But if I could force myself not to listen to him, there is a station underneath trying to get through (like those Mexican stations that make a ghostlike interference to the programs I listen to on my portable radio here)—a mysterious bit of almost unheard music or five words uttered in a strange tongue—and I will not believe that, good or bad, the sounds are merely static. I could not afford to believe it. (103)

This is one of the very earliest instances of Spicer's trope of the poet as radio receiver picking up alien signals in strange languages like Martian, the view which dominates his late sense of poetry as dictation. Or as an exhausted and discouraged Spicer put it in *Language*, "The trouble with comparing a poet with a radio is that radios don't develop scar tissue" (373). But six years earlier, when Spicer has Ralston stop to reflect in the middle of his letter just where that fragile signal could be heard, his protagonist cannot fool himself: "And where in the last few days had he heard even a hint of the ghostly voice of the Mexican radio station? With the fish perhaps—and he turned the whole radio off" (104).

No trace has been discovered of Spicer's plan regarding the murder mystery itself, its resolution or lack thereof. But in a draft of a letter to his agent, Spicer offers a very brief synopsis of the novel regarding what are in fact its central questions. Near its end, Rue will set Ralston up for a marijuana bust and then regret it, calling to warn him just as the police knock on his door. Spicer explains, "Ralston, in the few seconds real time while the police are knocking at the door of his room spends half an hour subjective time deciding whether to get rid of the cigarette (which he still has time to do) or to open the door and deliberately make his former life impossible. He opens the door."[12] Ralston will choose the hideous people and beautiful poetry.

A slightly different version of this essay first appeared in Raritan 39:4 (Spring 2020)."

NOTES

1. See the "Afterword" to *The Tower of Babel*, pp. 165-169, and *Poet Be Like God*, especially pp. 128-132.

2. Both these events date from September, 1957.

3. Spicer's friend Joe Dunn claims he and Spicer stumbled across the filming of *Vertigo* during one of their rambles through the city. The film was released in May, 1958, at which point Spicer had probably written more than half of the manuscript. See *Poet Be Like God*, p. 155.

4. "MacGuffin" was the term Hitchcock favored to describe plot devices which keep the narrative moving, but are ultimately incidental to a film's deeper concerns. For example, the MacGuffin can be the pretext that brings two characters together.

5. For a few speculations on how work on the novel fed the marvelous poetic work Spicer was drafting concurrently, see *The Poetry of Jack Spicer*, pp. 174-183, which scratches the surface. Clearly, this is a promising topic for more extended study.

6. As I've argued elsewhere, I think the novel ends just at the point where a series of Ralston's decisions, conclusions and stances will begin to be systematically reversed. In this, I suspect that Spicer is following Henry James, whom he mentions in the novel (93), particularly the structure of *The Ambassadors*. For the full account, see my *American Modernism's Expatriate Scene: The Labour of Translation*, pp. 140-148.

7. For a brilliant account of baseball in Spicer, see Peter Gizzi's Afterword to *The House that Jack Built*, pp. 192-199.

8. For an extremely useful discussion of the vexed question of Spicer's "Calvinism," to use the term Duncan often employed to characterize Spicer's poetics, see Norman Finkelstein's "Spicer's Reason to 'Be- / leave.'"

9. This analogy mostly holds in the "Sporting News" poems too, but it's worth noting that in the Vancouver lectures Spicer does modify it, complicate it, and consider abandoning it. At one point he concedes "You're both catcher and pitcher, I guess, as a poet" (118) but his displacement of the poetic figure away from the two most obvious roles—pitcher and batter—remains noteworthy.

10. With the exception of Arthur Slingbot, who is clearly a parody of Kenneth Rexroth, though Rexroth is also referred to independently in several places in the novel. This points to the hole gaping at the center of the novel: what is most obviously "missing" from the San Francisco it charts are

nothing other than the leading figures of the scene it is concerned with—Spicer, Duncan, Ginsberg, Snyder, and Kyger themselves, to name just a few.

11. See *Poet, Be Like God*, pp. 156-159 for Alexander's impact on Spicer at this time.

12. This document is found in the "Jack Spicer Papers," BANC MSS 2004/209, Bancroft Library, University of California, Berkeley, Box 12, Folder 1.

WORKS CITED

Ellingham, Lewis, and Killian, Kevin. *Poet Be Like God: Jack Spicer and the San Francisco Renaissance*. Hanover: Wesleyan UP, 1998.

Finkelstein, Norman. "Spicer's Reason to 'Be- / leave,'" in *After Spicer: Critical Essays*. Edited by John Emil Vincent. Middletown: Wesleyan UP, 2011.

Katz, Daniel. *American Modernism's Expatriate Scene: The Labour of Translation*. Edinburgh: Edinburgh UP, 2007.

— —. *The Poetry of Jack Spicer*. Edinburgh: Edinburgh UP, 2013.

Spicer, Jack. *The House that Jack Built: The Collected Lectures of Jack Spicer*. Edited and with an Afterword by Peter Gizzi. Hanover: Wesleyan UP, 1998.

Spicer, Jack. *Jack Spicer's Detective Novel: The Tower of Babel*. Hoboken, NJ: Talisman House, 1994.

— —. *My Vocabulary Did This To Me: The Collected Poetry of Jack Spicer*. Edited by Peter Gizzi and Kevin Killian. Middletown: Wesleyan UP, 2008.

Vincent, John Emil. "Pinnacle of No Explanation: Jack Spicer's Exercise of the Novel," in *After Spicer: Critical Essays*. Edited by John Emil Vincent. Middletown: Wesleyan UP, 2011.

III

Interior Lyric /
Displacement/
Cartographic Time

She wanted to climb through walls of no visible dimension
—H.D., *HERmione*

Hilda Hilst's *The Obscene Madame D*
A Derelict Reader's Guide

TRACI BRIMHALL

Who is Hilda Hilst?

Born in Brazil in 1930, in the state of Jaú, Hilda Hilst would become a well-known author in three genres in her lifetime. Her literary career started young. She published her first collection of poems, *Presságio*, at age 20. In her late 30's she began to write plays, and in her 40's moved on to prose. In each genre she collected numerous national literary awards. Though her texts often contain supernatural or magical realist elements, the hallmark of Hilst's work is transgressive intimacy, sometimes viewed as pornographic. For example, her writing blends eroticism with theology, and incorporates incest or libidinous abandon. Some have compared her to Artaud and de Sade. Hilst moved to a country house, Casa do Sol, outside of Campinas in the 1960s and lived there until her death in 2004.

The Obscene Madame D showcases many of Hilst's obsessions—madness, theology, and the aforementioned interest in the transgressive. The book opens with a poem, is formatted as prose, and contains heavy use of dialogue like one of her plays, thus unites her divergent interests in genre. Sometimes it's difficult to know which genre one is reading in the book. Her blending of genres is seamless or completely fractured or both. *The Obscene Madame D* creates a reading experience like that of reading poetry—a mind in tumult, a heart in grief. The book is crude, sarcastic and sincere. There's a speaker, but she's not an easy protagonist to zip into. This is not a book about a protagonist, or plot, but a quest for memory. Most questions contained within are unanswerable.

Speaking of challenging novels, if its questions are unanswerable, why read this book?

Because I don't want reading to be a passive pleasure; sometimes I want to think alongside someone, try on their mind for fifty pages. Books have so often helped me feel and find the language for that feeling, but I want books to stretch my brain and not just my heart. I want to be shown ways of questioning, the rhetoric of the internal, the circular, the inscrutable, the places of recognition where my thoughts mirror someone else's, and the wonder and terror at the places they diverge. Experience is not external, and sometimes books fail to offer one of the principle pleasures of art—voyeurism, to think I know something private about someone, even if that someone is fictional. What do they desire? What haunts them? How close is the mind, always, to madness? I need some books to be difficult because life is difficult. I don't want it reduced to platitudes and parables.

Terror has long been the most interesting part of art to me. Anytime I walk into an art museum, I scan the room and wait for something to hit my nervous system. I stand in front of whatever piece terrifies me for twenty minutes until the fear subsides and a kind of understanding takes its place. For me, fear seems to be the incomprehensible expressing itself as instinct. Sometimes what is beyond me feels like a failure of intellect, but horror always feels like a failure of complete feeling.

Hilda Hilst's *The Obscene Madame D* has the same sense of the incomprehensible, of a terror that can only quelled by abandoning order. Though it is an incredibly short novel, it has a largeness, a "brain is wider than the sky" canvas. The scale is so big you can't look at it; you have to look in it. But there's no tranquility; there's a self-interrogation through discussions with a dead lover, father, the self, and God that slips in and out of a present time in which the speaker is in a cupboard under the stairs holding two paper fish. That is the most literal, grounded image in the novel, and it's what the reader imagines the rest of the time, less like a lantern in a darkness and more like a lantern that's extinguished, that little thorn of fire is gone—the sureness of that amidst the fear of the unknown and unseen, that reassuring weight in your hand.

Do you have to always go in search of terror? What is this book's terror?
That's the beauty of a book. It can land in your mailbox or jump off a bookstore shelf into you hands. A book's terror can be experienced in the most intimate places. You are not limited by museum hours to your experience. You can seek it at night, at home, in daylight, in public, whatever complements or contrasts the emotional experience of the book.

Ah, the terror of not-knowing. Of accepting that. It's not a book for answers, but a book for feeling, intuiting, digressing, exploring, pleasuring, fearing. The terror is never getting to the bottom of things. The terror is that there may be things in this life (and all these deaths) that we may never overcome.

Why so many names? Hillé, Madame D, I, Nothingness, Name of No One— What do I call her?
Call her Hillé. Or at least I like to. The beloved's name, Ehud, means love.

The father is known only as the father. God has the most monikers of all, and she chooses "Lord," a call back to that old feudal power, and her surrender so necessary and inevitable. Hillé is called so many things, but Madame D. seems a pet name. Affectionate in its dismissal, or perhaps reduction of her, but it only says one thing about her. Pet names say something about what you mean to a person but not about what you are, and Ehud says the D stands for Derelict, her baseness, her love of that profane set of pleasures offered by the body. Given names have set definitions studied by parents with baby naming books across the world, but they also contain multitudes. A name is a meaning and a person. And yet the book is named for Hillé's inexhaustible, erotic, feral, Derelict side.

Why the dialogue with the dead? And why focus so much on the body if everyone she's talking to is dead?
Why not? Isn't that what we're all hoping for? Aren't we all looking for ways to touch the invisible? To commune, to talk, to find answers? Isn't that why you're here? Hasn't this love of terror and books always been about making the invisible visible?

Let's talk about how the living and the dead talk to one another. Let's start some place easy, where a beginning is clear:

> Every month I ingested the body of God, not in the way one swallows green peas or agrostis, or swallows swords, I ingested the body of God the way people do when they know they are swallowing the More, the All, the Incommensurable, for not believing in finitude I would lose myself in absolute infinity.
>
> lie down, open yourself pretend not to want to but you do, give me your hand, touch yourself, you're all wet, so open up, Hillé, hold me, please me
>
> I ingested the body of God and I must continue . . . (5)

Hillé begins, as she so rarely does, with a capital letter. She begins, and then she runs on and on in her sentence, her monologue, he explanation and defense for her experience of God. There is, equally rarely, a finality. A period. A closure. And then we hear Ehud's voice, coming in the middle of things. It's as though he has been giving her instructions for erotic pleasure this whole time, as though her speech and his erotic instructions were happening simultaneously but we could hear her voice above his. His entreaties are also left without conclusion and Hillé's voice resumes with force. Her exchanges with the dead look like this so often—layered, interrupted, a confusion of too much desire to communicate breaking down into fragments. Every figure seems to be existing in a different moment. Like watching all the gears in the clock, every moment—whether imagined or remembered—turns at once.

She's always going on about the body because the body is where heaven and earth meet but do not mingle. No wonder Hillé is so eager to escape it by going through it. The paths to God seem to be asceticism or the bacchanal. Either deny yourself everything and find that purest, whitest light. Make the body a veil, a wisp, and let the soul reconnect with its image. Or make the body animal like Hillé. But fucking one's way to God needs a partner. A physical surrender to reach the spiritual one. Ehud is the tool for self-abnegation. Or he was when he was alive. But Ehud is also the one continually making logical arguments. He's also always asking for coffee. Love is the raw, alive everything. It is also logic and distraction.

The inconceivable seems to require that logic, punctuation and order be abandoned willingly or through madness. I've always been more interested in John of Patmos the man than in the book of Revelation. Although bowls of plagues spilling out on the earth and a dragon chasing a pregnant woman has the thrill of drama, they were born of the imagination of an exiled man. He has his vision alone, witnessed the end of the world because God required it of him. What shell of a self is left after that? Was it a relief to be broken and broken down? To surrender to the awe of power holding itself back for the future? Or is every interaction with the God and the dead a depletion of a well-constructed and ordered psyche?

I don't know. That's why I'm asking you. Is grief breaking down the self for her in a way pleasure never did?
Did you notice "the eye of the beast is a dead question" (13)?

You seem to think it's all a conversation with the dead. Could they also be memories? Isn't it the movement between the internal and external what's important?
But if they are already dead, there is no external; there is only the memory of the external. Even all that feralness, that delicious and bacchanalian embodiment is a memory, a construct of the mind. And she tried to use the body to unhook herself from this fearful circularity, this entrapment of memory, but she couldn't get away from "the body, a nacreous, pearled outgrowth" (14). It is disgusting and pleasurable and too much and not enough. No wonder she wants to get out of it.

To make the body a primal thing, to unlearn all the manners and social niceties and morals might be an escape. Hillé becomes an animal to escape language, but language is her tool:

> I don't come to terms with people, with the world, the sun out there
> is not a sun of gold, I want to go without end and I search for you, I
> vomit, Pig Child, I gallop buffalo zebra giraffe from the beginnings,
> I crumple brutally on my four hoofs, and I slump breathless in the
> grass, I am a very fat animal, humid, lucid, who continues to search
> for you, now I don't articulate, but I am also not mute, some roars,
> some strident violent, come out of my throat—buffalo at present I
> dive—some darkness (9-10)

There she is again with run-on sentences trying to mirror her consciousness, its leaps and repetitions, the way an "I" can want to become every word it skips over. Why do we want a meaning with equal signs? Why can't something sing rather than say?

Perhaps part of the problem is that we are used to moving from the believable into the unbelievable—our hero goes on a journey, crosses the threshold, experiences something new and so narrates for us the encounters with the unbelievable. But here, we skip the introductions to the journey and already are in the belly of the beast—which in this case is a closet playing with paper fish. We always want more context, more story. There is no clean resolution.

Before we get to endings, can we talk more about God?
Isn't God an ending?

Isn't God a beginning?
Let's talk about God. Or better yet, let me talk about beginnings and then we will go back to God. Hillé made the body a tool to escape the body. Then she made language the tool through which to escape the body. But first she used language to give us our beginning. We tend to think prose is a form for clarity and poetry as a form for multiplicity, contradiction, obfuscation. But I think she is clearest of all when she opens the book with a poem. It feels like a prayer, a benediction:

> To be able to die
> I keep the insults and sarcasms
> Between the silks of mourning. (3)

As if death is something to make progress towards, something to achieve rather than to flee. And look, she repeats:

To be able to die
I disarm the traps
I stretch out between the walls
In ruin. (3)

Ah grief, sometimes it is a luxury. It accepts the body it confines. Sometimes I, too, get greedy for it.

To be able to die
I wear batiste
And direct my eyes
Toward new lives. (3)

Little christening dress, darling chemise, promise me there is a world elsewhere.

To be able to die with appetite
I cover myself with promises
Of memory. (3)

And yet memory is not a vow. Those traces of time left in you may or may not summon the absent beloved's on the other side of life. But yes, hunger while you can. Hunger if you must.

Because this is necessary
For you to live. (3)

Is it? Is suffering someone's resurrection through memory the only way for them to survive in the world? Can grief not accommodate a little forgetting?

Are you saying now that covering herself in memory as a way to make someone live again is actually a way to forget?
I'm saying forgetting can be a mercy. But I don't think this book is about mercy. I think it's about labyrinths without exit signs. So many books want you to get in, learn something, watch a character change, and get out, but this book is not about easy catharsis. There's no quick rise and fall to give you a take away to discuss in a book club or cocktail party. I think it's actually about resisting those things, about trying to find language for something as abstract as the self. I think it's about accepting discomfort. Ease can be

so seductive. There's a place for the spellbound, but there is also a place for questions. Questions that come out slightly malformed. Questions that have desire, but no desire for resolution or knowledge. Questions that drive towards dereliction, abandonment. It is a place for the parts of the self that are confused, the fragmented parts of the self that aren't trying to save themselves from confusion.

You promised me God.

I did. I did promise that. What is it to both want to be and fear to be chosen? The best annihilator is not death—see how alive Ehud and the father are? How memory insists on pulling them back? Nothing can destroy Hillé quite like God, and I believe that no matter how much she uses her body to seek nothingness, and no matter how well she uses language to that effect, it is still a fearful fucking thing.

Her body has wanted "cords, a mesh of steel wire around me, for years I have wanted to belong, do you hear?" (29), as if pain and confinement were part of the belonging but her brain keeps on untethering and drifting elsewhere. And words, she's tried those, too: "sometimes we want so much to crystalize the instant in the word, translate the spark and disgust in lucid parameters" (28). God, she wants both. Both! That crystallizing, that confinement, and also an escape. Could they be simultaneous? Can a limitation inspire freedom? Ah, but that implies annihilation is the same as freedom . . . Although Hillé does talk about the story of Job as a love story. All those glorious lamentations an exercise in argument about suffering and God. Job wins the argument because his metaphors are better. What do you think Hilst's meatphor is?

Isn't Hilst's metaphor Hillé?

Oh God, real critics will hate us. The author is not a character, and yet isn't it nice to conflate the two? But back to God, maybe this time in Hilst's own words:

"Is there room for flesh in your heart, Lord" (35)?

" . . . it's more than enough to keep living, Hillé, to question does not tame the heart" (41).

It would be hard to find a moment in the text where Hilst does not contradict herself, though perhaps it is better to say that every assertion always finds itself a paradox. She seems to want to assert that both are true rather than privileging one interpretation over another. The body is degrading, or the body is the way to the spiritual. The anus is disgusting, or the anus is God. Ehud is the One, the Only, or he is like every man. She is saved. She is damned. Why have one truth when you can have two or twenty or two hundred?

What about the ending?

You don't want to end on "the obscene gaze of my God" (52)? Very well, you want some clarity. I don't know if I can get clear, but I can get personal. I can be fearful. I can be jealous. Though I've stood in front of paintings to get more acquainted with fear, in Hilst I'm learning about my envy. Jealousy blistered each chamber of my heart when I read her. The dead are so painfully real to Hillé. I thought of my mother whose heart failed, my grandmother's cancer that crept out of her lungs and up to her brain, my beloved murdered by the roadside. They are all now more apart from me than they've ever been, but Hillé has wonderful luck with the dead. She can recount or recreate or create wholly new conversations with those she's loved. What a wonder to be able to use memory and imagination to such fruitful ends—if the annihilation of the self is an end that can be seen as fruitful.

And that ending, dear God, language has fallen apart into these nice, neat little columns. But by falling apart, it makes all these alternate endings possible. The more that becomes possible, the less clear she becomes. Or I should say she becomes clarified by diffusing into the possible rather than confined to what is. And that's not terrible but isn't it terrifying? God has too many faces. I think reading Hillé's mind is "an obscene adventure from so much lucidity" (43). One can barely stand to be everything that one must. All that possibility seems impossible, but you must try it.

But tell me how to make sense of it all.

Be "A being that peels. Godless. Weary sinister . . . shine dark in your bones again" (52). And if you can't be that, keep asking questions. It seems to me that questions can be a tool for annihilation. All that dialogue with the dead was really just a conversation with the self, a Q&A where the self is an actor playing both parts. The form is really just a way to peel away layer after layer and find a self that could either be released or a self that is so fundamental it could be touched. Not only to see the face of God, but to lick the white of his eye.

WORK CITED

Hilst, Hilda. *The Obscene Madame D.* Trans. Nathanaël and Rachel Gontijo Araujo. New York, NY: Nightboat Books, 2012. Print.

Narrating the Financialized Landscape
The Novels of Taylor Brady[1]

ROB HALPERN

Taylor Brady's two novels, *Microclimates* (Krupskaya 2001) and *Occupational Treatment* (Atelos 2006), are hybrid works of hypertrophic narration crossed-hatched with passages of lyric verse, at once full-throated and broken. Situated in relation to the built environment of South Florida whose cycles of financialization could be felt long before the subprime collapse of 2007, the novels perform self-consciously in the manner of a *Bildungsroman* as they recount the constitution of its narrator's subjectivity, "an inevitable history poised to birth a subject," like an inverted ouroboros delivering its own head (*Microclimates* 89). Emerging as a bastard child of Language Writing's critique of narrative (Lyn Hejinian's *My Life*) and New Narrative's embrace of storytelling (Robert Glück's *Jack the Modernist*), Brady's novels pursue a rigorous critique of subjective plenitude without disowning the excesses of narrative in a critical effort to grasp, in the words of the narrator, "my full relation to my time" (*Microclimates* 15). Drawing on poet's theatre and critical theory, economic analysis and procedural constraint, cartographic plotting and musicological echolocation, the work's conceptual, thematic and formal horizons are dynamic, and they traverse resources as varied as the socio-aesthetics of Sun-Ra's Afrofuturism and Rosa Luxemburg's analyses of crisis and accumulation, among a thick reservoir of cultural allusion. Most significant here is the way both *Microclimates* and *Occupational Treatment* find a model in the maximalist prose of Marcel Proust to whose sentences, in the Kilmartin and Moncrieff translation of the first two volumes of *In Search of Lost Time,* Brady apprentices himself often with remarkable fidelity. Indeed, one question that will orient my reading of the novels concerns the enriched semantic resonance of "lost time" in an era of financialization beginning in the mid-1970s whose mystifications can be characterized by "the deferred temporality of financial speculation," when buying power in the present becomes increasingly drawn "from the profits of future labor," to borrow Annie McClanahan's phrasing in "Investing in the Future: Late Capitalism's End of History" (90). This is a period when the stretches of suburban development that occupy the ambient surround of Brady's novels seem to fulfill Robert Smithson prescient predication of "ruins in reverse" in his "Tour of the Monuments of Passaic, New Jersey." Alluding to "all the new construction that would eventually be built" throughout the suburban expanse of Passaic, New Jersey in 1967, and with an acute sensitivity to temporal contradiction, Smithson writes, "This is the opposite of the 'romantic ruin' because the buildings don't *fall* into ruin *after* they are built but rather *rise* into ruin before they are built" (72). For Smithson, this "ruin" has an aura of something eternal about it—"a clumsy eternity," he calls it—as if he were already able to sense how the present had been, or would become, subsumed by a deferred crisis lurking in the wings, "a present already abandoned" (Smithson) to a state of emergency as tomorrow becomes nothing more than an extension of today (73).

But before pursuing the novels further, it's important to draw attention to the fact that Brady is an accomplished lyric poet, and that his novels often become poems in their own right. From the verses that interleave the pages of the novels themselves, to the volume of poems called *Yesterday's News* (Factory School) and the forthcoming *In the Red* (Compline), Brady's poems offer—to this ear at least—one of the most rigorous and sonorous lyric accomplishments of recent memory. This is a poetry characterized by the critical examination of self-expression at a historical moment when the objective world of financial calculation and globalized circulation are no longer separable from the subjective fiction we call a self.[2] And while lyric poetry may be well suited to interrogate the construction of our contemporary subjectivities under financialized conditions of life, Brady's turn to the novel complements the lyrics' concerns by submitting them to the demands that narrative makes on our effort to grasp our personal histories in relation to collective situations and events.[3] In doing so, the novels locate the narrating subject within the often illegible processes of neoliberal capital's accumulated dead labor, its concentration and trickle-down through South Florida's exurban development tracts, its flows, blockages, and waste-producing apparatuses.[4]

Poised on the edge of an era defined by consumer credit defaults and collateralized debt obligations, when future earnings are already underwriting the present, Brady's novels anatomize the "structures of feeling" and affective epiphenomena—the histories of particular bodies and selves—that accompany or resist the damage of crisis. In doing so, the prose of both *Microclimates* and *Occupational Treatment* makes the logic of intractable economic force legible, as Brady himself notes in "Narrative Occupation and Uneven Enclosure": "part of the desire for narrative is the desire to produce precisely such an intelligible account" (190). Most significant, however, are the effects on a novel's form when that desire exceeds what can in fact be rendered intelligible as narrative, or when the very material of narrative—as well as the temporal medium through which it moves—resists its own intelligibility. As Brady formulates it: "narrative fundamentally has to miss something of historical experience in order to render it narratable at all" (190). Indeed, as the novels aim to feel "the full relation to my time," a relation inseparable from the local processes and global crises whose displacements make the narrating subject what it is, they can only strain the logic of narrativity, a logic that always involves a tension between the two axes of composition—the spatial axis of equivalence with its vertical pull toward dilation and the temporal axis of combination with its horizontal pull toward termination—while maintaining as its limit the wholesale displacement of the one onto the other, which in Roman Jakobson's formulation constitutes the "poetic function," and whereby narrativity would be minimized.[5]

In so far as these processes and crises test the limits of narrative possibility itself, Brady's novelistic form approaches that of non-narrative as the writing locates itself within a concatenated set of unnarratable dynamics. The novels consistently confound the generic distributions of poetry, prose, and theory—as well as narrative and non-narrative—as each writerly modality participates in all the others. With respect to non-narrative, Carla Harryman offers this useful précis in her introduction to a special feature of the *Journal of Narrative Theory* devoted to "Non/Narrative":

> The theoretical work of the socially engaged non/narrative text stems from its production of a crisis of understanding. Works that shift between genres disturb categorical frames, foregrounding language such that narrative seems to disappear. They radically break rules of story-telling to stage a necessary disruption of asymmetrical power relations, the limits of knowledge, psychological and social operations of recognition and misrecognition, the complex connections between private experience and larger social forces, and the cooperative construction of meaning. The radical formalism identified with nonnarrative is thus not a 'mere formalism' within the sphere of the politically and aesthetically radical work. It is a strategy of intervention. (2)

What Harryman refers to as a crisis of understanding might also be thought of as a crisis of representation wherein the relation between subjective perception and objective force becomes radically disjoined when the historical specificity of any socio-economic event belies its overdetermination by a plurality of forces. And while narrative can never capture the fullness of such an event, it can make the expansive feeling of that fullness perceptible, if only in its negative outline, by performing a relation to its own receding horizon, enacting a dialectic of narrative and non-narrative characteristic of Brady's novels as they leaven with that feeling.

With the sort of experimental precision one might otherwise attribute to the very forces the novels witness, Brady's narrative desires to feel the shape of its own time by throwing the narrator's past into relief against the ground of the present, which itself can't be felt except insofar as it emerges against the ground of that past. First, there is the time of the narrator's childhood and adolescence during a transitional period of capital accumulation argu-ably inaugurated in 1973 with the abandonment of the gold standard. This is told, however, from the historical horizon of the early 2000s as the effects of the earlier period are coming to fruition in what will result in our contem-porary financial crisis. Brady himself draws attention to this historical peri-odization in "Narrative Occupation and Uneven Enclosure" when he writes,

> My own recent narrative writing has attempted to articulate the var-ious scales of experience in a working class Florida suburban ado-lescence in the late seventies and early eighties. As it happens, this experience coincides with a period in which the rolling wave of accu-mulation crises dating, for the sake of convenience, to 1974 begin to exert an exaggerated pressure on real estate, and the intensification of relations between social landscape and speculative capital becomes, for a certain class and region, a matter of direct experience. In my nov-el *Occupational Treatment*, this process culminates logically, and orig-inates experientially, with a series of police raids on escheat zoning plats on the exurban fringe, which have until now been squatted by homeless families and used for various illicit pleasures and conflicts by young people housed in the surrounding low-rent neighborhoods. (192)[6]

"A matter of direct experience," but of what? Perhaps of nothing more than the structures that mediate our experience. Just as "contact with the land" once connoted a more immediate experience of nature, one whose direct-ness has seemingly eroded with modernization, the idea of making direct contact with the financialized landscape of monetized plots—like "a hand trailing absently along a blond cinderblock wall"—can still connote imme-diate contact with "universal experience" under contemporary conditions, only this is an experience—and a nature—entirely mediated by capital (*OT* 276). Often, however, Brady's narrative will perform this sense of direct experience by way of more extravagant juxtapositions, "as if it were my existence in someone else's mind, were it laid out as fine tissue from power plant to port to culvert to kumquat tree, and threaded through the chain-link in every kind of knot, would have been the membrane around the balloon payment, the final installment on the property" (276-7). Thus does the South Floridian "vista full of property" manifest in both novels as "an excess of vacancy:" the plenitude of a void heavy with the body as it gets contracted by the logic and structure of state violence, identity and ownership (206,74).

"Plot structure" means everything here, and it contains a residue of a so-called "universal experience" once associated with traditional storytelling. While de-emphasizing a generic fidelity to narrative plot, Brady's writing deftly makes use of character and story; but whatever we might call "plot structure" in Brady's novels appears as an effect of the irreconcilable temporalities that the writing formally negotiates: the phenomenological time of the body, for example, and the economic time of the market. With respect to the idea of "plot" as it might be heard as a homonymic pun, however, *Microclimates* and *Occupational Treatment* remain remarkably faithful as they map the subject's relation to the social economy of unevenly developed plots—grids of cartographic measure, real estate, and ground rent, whose "plots" the novels regularly thematize in the form of strip malls, tract homes, vanished woods, as well as stories—all of which shape our experience of time, while harboring time's socio-material substrate in exploitative structures like wage labor and credit debt. Thus, the novels arouse the tension between seemingly disparate structures of economic force and experiential time as if this tension were its specific material.

This tension between what Brady refers to as "combative temporalities" has implications for an understanding of narrative form, and it realizes itself in the structure of Brady's novelistic prose where the verbal sequencing that constitutes one's narration of a personal history—memory, interlocution, analysis, recollection—is pressured by the more elusive temporality of "landscapes and built environments," the terra firma of capital investment against which those verbal sequences become audible as sound figures (*Occupational Treatment* 252). "What I'm reaching for," he goes on to write, "is a disposition of narrative that addresses this experience riven between two or more time-space scales, in the sense of knowing that to elaborate a track across a landscape is ultimately to impoverish or underdevelop some constituent of the vectoral multiplicity of possible developments it initially poses" (252). Whereas realist fiction takes its "landscapes and environment as accomplished facts (i.e., with a view of history that irons out contradiction)," Brady's approach to narrative aims to arouse the material of all those flattened contradictions, "to mark the tempo of the administered relation to place," while self-reflexively acknowledging in itself a residue of "those strategies for make-believing away the divergence between the narrative of place and its historical occupation" (252).

Brady refers to this temporal dissonance as a kind of perennial "stutter"—not at all a gratuitous metaphor—whereby one's utterance, at the level of its very embodiment, registers a "fault" that makes a dissonant relation palpable at the level of physical sensation itself, as the spatial axis of verbal selection fails to coincide with the temporal axis of its own sequencing. "Stuttering in this case would be the constant catching-up this stance necessitates, as the administrative consciousness is always having to adjust, like a bad dancer, to a reality that has shifted subtly away from it, even as its gesture is in part an attempt to efface its own recognition of that shift" (252).[7] This becoming-perceptible of otherwise unseen structures works like a phenomenology of natural history set against a backdrop of capital's laundering machines, where the signs of force are impressed into the lived environment, then washed away or bleached. Brady's narrative presences the invisibility of capital's structural violence—"the displaced violence of foundation"—a violence that shapes our field of vision, so that "to see" the developed landscape in South Florida is to feel the effects of incoherent sites and the strain of seeing that incoherence coherently (216). In this way, the novels themselves become akin to what Robert Smithson calls *nonsites* whereby submerged processes and dynamics become visible as if for the first time. In short, the novels' narrative preoccupations make the terms of a foundational violence perceptible, even as that violence recedes, not into the historical horizon of visibility, but into an unspeakable zone of embodied life whose kernel contains "the sumptuous stuffs of our ability to recognize a common history in this place," an ability to recognize and speak a common history that has become disabled, not by way of either prohibition or taboo, but as an effect of positive convention, the most banal and everyday ("Narrative Occupation" 185).

In the blurb that I wrote for the back cover of *Microclimates*, I referred to the novel as "an awesome construction committed to producing the vanishing moments of its own historical truth." I wrote this while thinking about how the book materializes a negative imprint of a withdrawn catastrophe that challenges the very possibility of narrative and around whose damaging effects the book organizes a vast architectural form. The first page of *Microclimates*, for example, presents a facsimile of a handwritten poem captioned by a footnote attributed to the work's fictitious editors: "[Eds.] In the manuscript this space was occupied by a Polaroid photograph set between corners [...] Unfortunately, severe water damage—perhaps inflicted by the events narrated in pp. 63-73—has rendered the photograph unrecognizable" (7). But the catastrophic cause of the work's damage remains at the limit of what the work itself can represent, so that when the reader turns to the noted pages—which of course one wants to do immediately in search of some narrative explanation for the effect that has already captured one's attention—they discover that these pages don't exist. Instead, one finds an inexplicable insertion of pages 235-245 where pages 63-73 ought to be, a mysteriously displaced supplement to this novel of 164 pages, and no mention of a flood. *Microclimates* goes on to assume a shape around this hole, which situates the work on the edge of its own narration, a threshold where the book becomes *ek-static* and fails to coincide with itself, turning on the axis of its dislocation. Thus the novel bears the impress of an occulted violence that shapes its local specificity, producing a material record of its own history together with an absence of any real evidence.

Occupational Treatment only deepens *Microclimates'* constructions as it finds its form around a series of blanks and voids, silences and vacancies, dead spots and holes, placeholders and apostrophes all of which mark a perennial crisis, leaving the figural stains of trauma everywhere unavailable for straight representation. For example, the novel opens with the line: "Here is the catalogue of the construction disasters I promised," a catalogue that later arrives at the boundary of the self's own narratability with a series of blank film stills in the novel's central section, "Production Notes for Occupation," where the writing works, in its own words, to recover from oblivion some "invisible event obscene relation," an event whose indeterminacy hangs on its being both psycho-sexual or socio-economic, "an event whose exclusion from our experience first set in motion the series of forced equivalents by which we have staked out this miniature horizon" (15, 119, 228). Insofar as it attempts to narrate the narrator's own formation as a subject, *Occupational Treatment* occupies the space of unrecoverable loss and foreclosed possibility, while locating itself in relation to capitalism's endless depredations and military occupations.

Within the shared framework of both novels, socio-aesthetic problems can be thought of in terms of time and vision as the writing shows our situation to be one in which the light that we depend on in order to see the world turns out to be the residual glare emitted by all our apparatuses of social production: military, industrial, sexual, urban, environmental, like the "night gases rising brightly from the bay," with which *Occupational Treatment* comes to a close (277). This underscores the aporia of vision wherein the writing situates itself. Here, "the sun has risen. And is false. Layer after

unbearably bright layer. This is the opacity of light in the barrens of architecture" (239). Melissa Dyne's cover image for *Occupational Treatment* illustrates this idea exquisitely: the scene is one of a dark room in which the only
light is the light emitted by a *camera obscura* projecting an inverted image
of a desert motel and a pool on a blank wall. Karl Marx draws on the image
produced by the *camera obscura* in his effort to describe the inversions in
perception and cognition that structure ideological consciousness, and the
rigor of Brady's writing amounts to a counter-force commensurate to that
structure. But this is a counter-force that refuses the consoling illusion that
the ideological image can be simply overturned or corrected. By contrast,
Brady's work is painfully aware that it is the image-apparatus itself that generates the light enabling our vision in the first place.

> As I pondered what this revelation might mean for the course of our
> migration across the plains of redevelopment, residual brightness
> continued to dazzle, in decorative shards that ate into the structure
> they purported to reveal, the picture I was beginning to reassemble
> of my location in the world, and for the second time in my life I was
> graced with a vision of dancers just behind the level blank of visibility
> [...] (242)

Like the underdeveloped tract of suburban landscape, this blank is never
neutral. Rather, it's saturated with uneven relations of power so refined and
thinned as to admit the illusion of its own transparency, except at those
places of bodily contact where power thickens: for example, "I had so much
skin, collapsing on me like an abandoned lean-to" (276-7). This one extravagant simile offers a point of departure whereby Brady is able to create,
through a series of substitutions or "forced equivalents," an image of direct
bodily contact with the stuff of suburban development: money and matter.
Thus the passage moves from "so much skin" to "an abandoned lean-to" to
"translucent drapery" to "fine tissue" only to resolve itself in "a membrane
around the balloon payment" and "a tarp on that scale, stretched over the
building materials" (276-7).

Just what kind of sentence enables one to feel those uneven power relations or the blank in the landscape that harbors them? What kind of sentence can apprehend its own inadequacy when sensing something ungrasp-
able within its own experience? Any answer to this question must consider
the role of syntax, or the conventions governing the sequencing of linguistic
units as they organize themselves in relation to a terminal period, constantly
being deferred and anticipated. Brady's sentential syntax is always in the
process of trying to stabilize its meaning from a horizon that can never quite

be seen but can be tensely felt through a disorienting thicket of conjunction and subordination, a whole labyrinth of clauses, and "this predictability and constant predication were founded on an essential dislocation, both his own and others', that allowed him nonetheless to 'hold the line'" (*Microclimates* 116). As the sentence approaches its limit, the volatility of its syntax becomes amplified, as if the sentence itself could feel the imminence of a terminal moment when the fiction of its own fixed relations can only belie its appearance of stability. Syntax thus becomes a kind of social material, at once resistant and pliable, by which the writing recursively enacts a relation to relation itself, even as the very terms of relation, terms that the sentence longs indefatigably to feel, have been withdrawn into a structure of effects without a narratable cause.[8] As Brady himself notes,

> The total effect is one of forward motion that continually falls back upon itself, maximal fullness of syntactical elaboration becoming an odd kind of lack, as if the world were to eject us in order to form itself in the image of our voices. (*Occupational Treatmet* 262)

Recalling the stutter, this auditory "image" intimates a formal allegory as it registers the breakdown of relation under a mode of production constantly reaching its own saturation. Thus, the paradigmatic (spatial) axis of selection—along which the vast array of commodities and financial instruments expands by suppressing any perception of time—fails to correspond with the syntagmatic (temporal) axis of combination, along which that same vast array is produced. In other words, spatial equivalence and temporal sequence become consequentially detached in such a way that cannot adequately account for its own "disjunction," itself a formal figuration of crisis; and this crisis is constitutive of the so-called "narrative tension" that the novel itself can only fail to fully narrate. This particular use of spatial and temporal disjunction is just another characteristic feature of Brady's method and it registers something critical about the subjective experience of value—what the ongoing crises of capital might actually *feel* like, not only in its effects (although that, too) but in its very structure—an experience at the displaced center of both *Microclimates* and *Occupational Treatment*, "the experience of a vanished plot of woods, for example" (*OT* 252).

> But even this precision fails to account for the production notes secreted by the scenario, not as its interior, as in the familiar trope of the film within a film, but as its necessary and missing anterior, a place prior to the tempo of non-occurrence where the problem of missing time resolves into a paradox of space through the essential technique

of an absent social mass for being in more than one 'once' per place, so that packets of life in excess of this body spread through our script and the scene of circular relation into which it calls us, making the question not the easy one of a founding absence, but the irrational numerical expression of our own reflections distributed among all the objects and territories we survey in the form of their non-reflective obverse, in which even the pain of a prior disappearance cannot stabilize around those whose dead labor or labor of dying our situation here assumed for *there is now the possibility of meeting them again later on; they have ceased merely to be silhouetted against a horizon where we had been ready to suppose that we should never see them reappear.* [Brady's italics] (228-9)

This sentence is exemplary not only for its form but for its thematization of its own formal problem. Here, the displacement associated with the temporality of finance capital becomes legible as "the problem of missing time," a problem whose tensions and contradictions can't be contained by the familiar phrase according to which one might be in two places at once. Instead, the sentence transfigures the spatial paradox through semantic stress and syntactic torque to one of "being in more than one 'once' per place." Brady's turn of phrase estranges the cliché while enabling us to think about the phenomenon whereby a seeming absence—let's say, of laboring bodies—becomes an uncontainable excess of effects "distributed among all the objects and territories we survey," like an immense accumulation of commodities that spatializes the time of production, just as it temporalizes the space of relation. More than just the same fragment of labor time appearing simultaneously in multiple iterations at any one place, Brady's figure complicates the idea even further as it imagines an "absent social mass," like abstract labor power itself, whose socialization is only accessible in its numerical effects, turning "a founding absence" into an "irrational numerical expression of our own reflections," while placing "ourselves" in relation with "the dead labor or labor dying our situation here assumed." Even "the pain of prior disappearance"—the "missing time" of living labor—manifests in the present as the most unstable relation with "our situation."

Brady's sentences expand as they seek the structure of present time itself. In its effort to register the specific structure of time under intensifying processes of financialization, a structure immanent to its vast array of effects and which we are still in the process of apprehending, Brady's sentences dilate toward the horizon of a future from which the temporal resource of its own medium has been borrowed, a future which acts as a lender of an abstract surplus that becomes concrete in its effects, endowing the present by displacing its center of gravity. Both the structure of time and the structure of feeling that informs Brady's first-person singular subject—grammatically and thematically—are thus intimately related, and it is the nature of this relation that the writing aims to grasp as the sentence itself participates in a search, not of lost time, but rather "my full relation to my time," or the present's temporal form. It's worth quoting one more emblematic sentence as a final illustration:

> I understood that, while my entrance had made quite an effect, the effect was all there was, drifting free of the entering body that was its cause and masking even the fact of the entrance itself behind the bibliographical occasion to which it gave rise, or rather fall, converting the potential energy of the encounter to a cold lump of ballast, the battle having been fought, decided against me, and entered into the chronicle by the time I folded myself into a too-small child's rocking chair in a dark corner and prepared for the inevitable moment when one of the family would back into me and, thinking they had discovered some rare and valuable coincidence, offer to pay an inflated admission to the privileged affective states I carried in the air around my head as the sublimate of all the knowledge of the wide world I had managed to assemble for my own index, reading the travel section of the *Tampa Tribune,* its lavish far-right raise for the bucolic splendor and radical quiet of the pacified Honduran back country, while waiting for my no-frills student haircut. (*OT* 66-7)

At stake, in the end, is the question of what a "poet's novel" can do that other forms of writing cannot in an effort to perceive a whole phenomenology of crisis, the spatio-temporal compressions of globalization and debt, the experience of no experience and the "empty horizons of futurity" that enclose it. What are the limits of narrative's capacity to sense, perceive, and cognize the dynamics, contradictions, and occulted relations that structure our contemporary crises? This is not necessarily a question of representation, but rather one of feeling, sensing, and perceiving the processes that shape our world—production, circulation, consumption— *as if for the first time* through a method of embodied subjectivization enabled by a radical approach to first person narration. As an extension of the very situation it attempts to narrate, Brady's novels perform what Joshua Clover refers to as "narrative's mediated dissolution into structure," a structure whose relation to the novels' grammatical "I" becomes impossible to articulate fully insofar as that structure has already penetrated body, landscape, and utterance alike (39). Nevertheless, the sentence acts as that relation's most precise instrument of registration—an exteriorization of the system's sensorium—and the placement of the subject within its grammatical and syntactic terms enables a reader to feel the structures that exceed it.

In short, Brady's narratives bring the banalities of everyday life—"dinner had grown cold"—into relation with global processes whereby "some unheralded disaster" might at any moment have "swept away another bit of infrastructure"(*Microclimates* 36). The novels achieve this by cutting a paradigmatic figure against which any banal particular might come into focus as a part of the inarticulate whole in which the seemingly trivial detail is embedded:

> Once understood thus, the whole pattern cast my episodes in the shower, previously understood to be caught in the contradictory grip of private impulse and administrative reason, in the far more quotidian and public light of what I remained naïve enough to call civil society, making it clear that what I sought was the trace of recent history in the varying smells of urine atomizing and diffusing through the superheated steam that fogged the windows, mirroring exhalations of the streets themselves that evening as the rain let up, just in time for us to drag the TV out into the yard and gather round to watch a bit of wrestling. (37-8)

No doubt, *Microclimates* and *Occupational Treatment* are inexhaustible, and without even touching on the novels' incorporation of lyric verses whose persistent interruptions offer another formal horizon against which to measure the work's non-narrative limits, I have at least managed to skim the surface of the novels' depths with the hope of drawing attention to the promise they offer those of us committed not only to the formal possibilities of experimental literary form, but to what those possibilities are capable of showing us about our current situation.

NOTES

1. A longer version of this essay first appeared in *Mediations: Journal of the Marxist Literary Group*, 28:2 (Spring 2015). Online at http://www.mediationsjournal.org/articles/financialized-landscape. Many thanks to the editors.
2. For my reading of *Yesterday's News,* see "Sensing the Common Place: Taylor Brady's Dialectical Lyric."

3. For a full engagement with the concept of "financialization" in relation to Brady's novels, see the longer version of this essay in *Mediations,* 84-86.

4. It is worth noting here that Florida has been referred to as the epicenter of the collapse of speculative financial instruments based on property mortgages. See Robin Blackburn, 92-93.

5. According to Jakobson: "The poetic function projects the principle of equivalence from the axis of selection into the axis of combination" (358).

6. A variant appears in *Occupational Treatment* (263). I've chosen to quote "Narrative Occupation" for its direct and reflexive reference to composing the novel.

7. For excellent explorations of the poetics of stuttering that extend and deepen Brady's allusion, see Jordan Scott, *Blert*; Craig Dworkin, "The Stutter of Form"; and Gilles Deleuze, "He Stuttered."

8. The allusion to Althusser's theory of structural causality, whereby the structure of the social whole—the so-called "totality"—can only be apprehended in its particular effects, ought not to go unmentioned. Brady acknowledges his debt to Althusser on the first page of *Microclimates* by way of an epigraph—"The characters of the time seem strangers to the characters of the lightening"—a sentence that appears in one of Althusser's few essays on aesthetics, "Notes on a Materialist Theatre" (*For Marx*).

WORKS CITED

Blackburn, Robin. "The Subprime Crisis." *New Left Review* 50 (March-April, 2008) 63-106.

Brady, Taylor. *Microclimates.* San Francisco: Krupskaya, 2001.

—. "Narrative Occupation and Uneven Enclosure." *Biting the Error: Writers Explore Narrative.* Eds. Burger, Glück, Roy, and Scott (Coach House Books 2004).

—. *Occupational Treatment.* Berkeley: Atelos, 2006.

Clover, Joshua. "Autumn of the System: Poetry and Finance Capital." *Journal of Narrative Theory* 41:1 (Spring 2011) 34-52.

Deleuze, Gilles. "He Stuttered." *Essays Critical and Clinical.* Trans. Daniel W. Smith and Michael A. Greco. Minneapolis: University of Minnesota Press, 1997.

Dworkin, Craig "The Stutter of Form," in *The Sound of Poetry/The Poetry of Sound.* Ed. Marjorie Perloff and Craig Dworkin. Chicago: University of Chicago Press, 2007.

Halpern, Rob. "Sensing the Common Place: Taylor Brady's Dialectical Lyric." *ON: Contemporary Practice* (Brooklyn: Cuneiform Press, 2008).

Harryman, Carla. "Introduction: Non/Narrative." *Journal of Narrative Theory*, 41:1 (Spring 2011) 1-11

Jakobson, Roman. "Linguistics and Poetics." *Style in Language*. Ed. Thomas A. Sebeok. Cambridge, Mass: MIT Press, 1960.

La Berge, Leigh Claire "The Rules of Abstraction: Methods and Discourses of Finance." *Radical History Review* 118 (Winter 2014) 95

McClanahan, Annie. "Investing in the Future." *Journal of Cultural Economy* 6:1 (2013): 78-93.

Scott, Jordan, *Blert.* Toronto: Coach House Books, 2008.

Smithson, Robert. "A Provisional Theory of Non-Sites." *The Collected Writing of Robert Smithson*. Ed. Jack Flam. Berkeley: University of California Press, 1996.

—. "Tour of the Monuments of Passaic, New Jersey." *The Collected Writing of Robert Smithson*.

Structure as Philosophy in Inger Christensen's *Azorno*

DENISE NEWMAN

Perhaps the poem cannot speak any truths at all; but it can *be* true, because the reality that comes along with words is true.

INGER CHRISTENSEN

The term "poetic novel" is often associated with fiction that emphasizes description over plot, but my favorite works earn the name because they have a total enactment of meaning through form and language. For example, in Italo Calvino's *If on a Winter's Night a Traveler* and Virginia Woolf's *To The Lighthouse* form is an indirect but essential part of the expression and in the end something new is revealed about our language-constructed reality. Inger Christensen, the esteemed Danish author who died in 2009, was one of these masters of form.

Inger Christensen is known in the US mainly for her poetry (New Directions has published four collections, all translated by Susanna Nied) but she also wrote essays, short stories, plays, children books, and three novels, two of these I've translated, *The Painted Room*, and *Azorno*, (the latter, also published by New Directions). I don't believe that either Christensen or her readers considered her novels as departures, but rather, they are viewed as integral parts of her oeuvre. Each book grew out of the preceding book, and the forms they took were intrinsic (and original) to the particular inquiry. In other words, from time to time, Christensen had something to investigate that could only be done in the expanse of a novel and the artifice of fiction.

Christensen was deeply engaged with form. Each of her works is highly structured, and the way it's written has an active relationship with the contents. Often her forms are so integral that they are easily overlooked, the way one might not notice the proportions of a room perfectly suited for its use. Christensen goes beyond the Olson/Creeley claim, "Form is never more than an extension of content," in that her forms are also content, though they never dominate; ultimately, she controls the form. Once, when we were working together on a particularly long slippery sentence in *Azorno*, she commented, "With sentences like that you don't need many of them."

In an interview in the Danish press she stated: "Probably not many people consider that we're thinking about how the world is arranged when we write poems and novels. People don't see the structure of a work of art as a kind of philosophy. But that's how I think of it, and I believe I've been doing so since my first poetry collections" (7).

Perhaps the most stunning example of the structure as philosophy is her single-poem collection *alphabet*. Here form enacts growth and cosmic patterning by calling attention to how objects accumulate and are organized. We feel the relationship between the general laws of nature and grammar. Christensen uses the alphabet to loosely determine and organize the sections. In addition, the Fibonacci sequence (a mathematical system where the sum of the two previous numbers equals the following number) is used to determine the line length of the sections, which increase gradually at first, but then multiply exponentially. Characteristically, Christensen did not feel obligated to play the poem out to the letter z, but rather ends it at n. The number and letter systems create a tight grid that allows for accumulation, repetition, and variation, an enactment in language of life following its constructive and destructive course.

In addition to her deep understanding of human consciousness and language, she was interested in the sciences. (She had planned to become a doctor and was enrolled in medical school but had to withdraw for financial reasons.) Nature in her writing is not simply used as a metaphor, but rather she views human beings, our forms and actions, within the context of natural systems. Eva Ström, the Swedish writer and critic, mentions Christensen's foundational experience of reading Noam Chomsky's theory of universal grammar, and quotes her as saying, " I have the same right to write as a tree has to produce leaves." (2) It's interesting to compare this to Goethe's description of a tree when he used it to defend his free verse style. According to Rosmarie Waldrop, he believed, "[a] tree does not need to be symmetrical to have form. Its branches do not have to be regular to combine as a whole . . . " (199). Christensen, who was influenced by the German Romantics, meets Goethe somewhere in the middle, with the cool neoclassical style on one side, and the 20th century "organic form" on the other, both poets placing equal value on process, structure, and lyricism.

The biological freedom to produce words comes through in her proliferating forms and love of lists, but, as in the plant kingdom, restraints and patterns keep growth organized and in check, the structural methods she uses are as much a part of the story as the dazzling surfaces, so that the reader is constantly made aware of the ways language shapes and defines existence. This is the territory of *Azorno*, her prescient novel published in 1967, and the book I'd like to focus on in this essay.

Azorno is a short novel, set in modern Europe, and told in the first person. Beyond these facts, it's as difficult to summarize as it is to draw a map of a labyrinth from the inside. It concerns five women and two men—a novelist named Sampel, and his main character, named Azorno. They each have personality traits—some mutually inclusive, some mutually exclusive—and four dwelling places. The challenge is to figure out which character has which traits and lives where.

At first we're given to believe that the novel is about love and betrayal. A woman meets her lover. The lover has other mistresses. Some of these women know each other and write letters back and forth. Several characters are involved with the novelist and he may include one or more of them in his book. As Christensen's novel progresses, the reader begins to notice odd discrepancies. Images and passages recur, often with variations. The exact steps to making a salad are repeated, for example, with the addition of a new ingredient, hemlock. Disquieting questions arise. The narrator is one of the women, but which one? The narrator shifts, but from whom to whom? Has someone been killed? Is someone insane? Is someone being held captive? Are some of the characters fabricating others? Is the whole story part of Sampel's book?

Like a nest of Russian dolls, there are fictions being written and discussed within Christensen's *Azorno* and you're never quite sure which fiction you're in at a given time. Despite the apparent artificiality of the situation, it's easy to find yourself grasping after the "real" story and the "real" identity of the narrator.

From the first sentence on the first page, we're swept up into two narratives: "I've learned that I'm the woman he meets on page eight" (1). At the end of this two-page description of a meeting with Azorno in Tivoli, we find out that the entire passage is a letter and the reason the new narrator has been summoned down through Germany to the lake house in Switzerland to help the author of the letter, "understand that she's caught in a daydream," because, so we're told, the woman in possession of the letter is actually the one he meets on page eight. At the end of this account, which takes us to Rome, we find out we've been reading yet another letter: "And my dear Katarina, I know you won't be sad or angry when I send you this letter about how I ended up with Xenia's letter, which I am also sending you" (11). In no time at all, we find ourselves in the middle of a thick knot of contrasting perspectives and overlapping details, unable to discern who's telling the truth, let alone who's doing the telling.

This proliferation of narratives follows the biological "right" mentioned earlier of language-oriented humans, and is presented here almost as a sort of madness—"It was a habit I had from when I wrote letters as often and painstakingly as you wash your hands" (27)—though it's not far from the truth, especially today with compulsive texting and tweeting. Christensen puts this out front with the novel's epigraph by the Polish writer Witold Gombrowicz:

> Human Beings, as I see them, are:
> 1. created by form
> 2. creators of form
>   its tireless executors.

Form works two ways: it makes us who we are (visible), and we're constantly creating them, but who we are influences the forms we create, whether it's a letter or a salad, and in turn, these forms influence the course of things, sometimes gaining the upper hand (think of the smartphone). It's difficult to discern who's influencing what or what's influencing whom. This reciprocal quality of form is embedded in the construction of *Azorno*, on a large scale, with fictions generating and influencing new fictions, and on a small scale, with recurring images, thoughts, and situations in new contexts. There's a fractal-like quality of the repetitions. We meet Goethe, Sampel's dog, in several scenes in different roles, and towards the end, a little black porcelain dog is placed on top of a wardrobe in a hotel room in Paris, which the couple names Goethe (96). Literally, the dog is shown at a smaller scale, and it's discrepancies like these that keep the repeated elements active. The malleability of details relates to Wittgenstein's proposal, "1.1 The world is the totality of facts, not of things" (5). Things are simple and suggest discreteness, whereas facts include multiple parts, relations, and context, and when Christensen continually reshuffles the "facts" she calls attention to the constructedness of our world. In a sense, the world of the novel is a small-scale model of the world as Wittgenstein conceives it.

One scene that functions as a sort of fractal for the whole work occurs early in the novel when one woman supplants another in her home, puts on her too-small clothes and garish makeup, and sits admiring herself at the supplanted woman's dressing table mirror:

"When the image was complete I blew life into it with the cigarette holder, and when I was looking around for cigarettes in order to get the entire machinery of the artwork to work, I happened to find Xenia's letter to Bet Sampel. Nothing could've gotten it to work more perfectly" (24).

She makes herself up, clown-like, using her rival's garb, calling attention to the mutability and dependence of one form on another. She creates a new image of herself that is comprised of parts, and, as with the machinery of the entire novel, one key element sets everything in motion. In this case it's the incriminating letter, and she says, "It could've been Bet Sampel herself indignantly lighting one cigarette after another while reading this letter" (24).

If this scene represents a part of the whole, then what sets the entire machinery of the novel in motion? Perhaps the answer is in the quote from the Danish philosopher Søren Kierkegaard with which Christensen ends the novel:

> When the sea heaves and is rough, the seething waves in their turbulence form pictures resembling creatures; it seems as if it were these creatures that set the waves in motion, and yet it is, conversely, the swelling waves that form them. Thus, Don Juan is a picture that is continually coming into view but does not attain form and consistency, an individual who is continually being formed but is never finished, about whose history one cannot learn except by listening to the noise of the waves.

This description, concerning the character of Don Giovanni in Mozart's opera, illuminates how Christensen engages the forms of fiction. From waves, which are literally the disturbance of water, and the opposite of still water, (an image often used in Zen literature to describe a calm mind), we get "pictures resembling creatures." As Kierkegaard points out, you might think that the "creatures," or characters, have agency but actually, it's the waves, or you could say thought/language, that are in control. Repeatedly, Christensen's characters comment on the hold language has on them, how it is "encroaching on the freedom to experience" (99).

Kierkegaard's use of the word "picture," I believe, relates to Wittgenstein's subsequent proposal, "3. The logical picture of the facts is the thought" (11). Picture is both a noun and a verb, and as Ray Monk points out, "It is because facts have parts that they can be pictured, the elements of the picture corresponding to the objects that constitute the fact" (41-42). The "pictures resembling creatures" are comprised of a great many details that exist in thought/language, which, like the waves, give them appearance, whereas, syntax keeps things moving.

Mid-way in *Azorno*, Sampel's wife, Bet, after speculating about who the woman on page eight in her husband's novel might be modeled after, decides to write a novel including all the possible women in order to illicit a reaction from Sampel, thus revealing the actual mistress. "My only chance of tracking down the right one depended on my ability to read Sampel's reactions" (64). Her novel sets in motion two unexpected turns of events. First, she begins to think more about Azorno (his character) than Sampel, and second, she begins to identify with her writing to such an extent that she feels she needs to meet the other women before she can proceed with her novel. This leads to the most suspenseful part of *Azorno* where all five women, who are pregnant by Sampel, meet in his lake house in Switzerland. We see how a story may start with one intention, but at some point it begins to take on a life of its own.

In "When Fiction Lives In Fiction," Borges comments on De Quincey's observation about the play within the play of *Hamlet*. De Quincey believes that the heavy-handedness of the minor play makes the play that includes it seem all the more convincing, and Borges adds, "its essential aim is the opposite: to make reality appear unreal to us" (156). This is exactly the effect of the fictions within the fiction of *Azorno*. Christensen attains through overtly artificial means a real picture of the unreality of our society. The proliferating letters with their discrepancies are similar to how actual events get spun, in the media and between individuals. After translating *Azorno*, I would become self conscious in exchanges involving a third party: was I speaking about X or about X's character? (to use the complaint that runs through *Azorno*). It was as if I were in Christensen's novel, continuing its story. As the poet and Zen priest Norman Fischer has written, "We are what we tell ourselves we are in language" (4). And this extends to our descriptions of others, sometimes at the expense of reality.

Where are all these proliferating, re-circulating fictions headed? Again, Christensen presents an image of biological processes that might be understood as a kind of philosophy in this regard. She describes two different ways a tree can die: either from *within*, "by giving the tree poison and quickly paralyzing the tissues in their multiple functions," thus pulling everything down, leading to disintegration, or from *without*, "by giving the tree freedom, an excess of space, light, air, water, nourishment." By this method, the plant first blooms profusely, and is then "abruptly followed by exhaustion, withering." In both cases, the plant ends up as "a mute block that is slowly consumed by itself. By everything" (49). At a macro level, this describes the situation of the women who are either locked up or wandering about, as Douglas Messerli points out in his review (2), and, at a micro level, it describes the course of all the bits of circulating propositions that at some point lose their hold and terminate. The sunroom that's noted throughout the novel for its light, for example, is revealed one day as actually a dark room, shaded by large trees on one side, mountains and a large rock outcrop on the other two. The reputation of brightness, Bet speculates, "may have come from a memory of the architect's vision, which he must have had one cold winter's day . . . " (59). In other words, it began as an abstraction, you could say a "picture," which usurped the "real" picture of the room, until one day it's refused and replaced by another.

Towards the end we realize that all the characters are from the imagination of the writer Azorno, (who admits to using the pseudonym Sampel) and finally it is he who narrates the story. A great quantity of the circulating images and descriptions appear in rapid succession, creating the sensation of time speeding up because few new elements are being added. But, like a coda, we also learn the background of certain descriptions, like the one of the car trip south over the mountain passes that first appears on pp. 10-11. Azorno admits that "regardless of the actual circumstances, I always return to exactly that description, as though gripped by language, as though it set a limit on my freedom to experience, as though when a personal expression has taken shape it reveals that that expression has its own life and actually takes shape without my help, or intervention. Almost as if it were impersonal. Something I ultimately don't have power over, maybe not even a say in the matter" (96). We see that Kierkegaard's wave, or language, has been the main subject all along, and finally there are only two characters, a man and a woman, struggling through the mental constructions that keep them from each other and the world.

Bathsheba, who no longer goes by Bet at this point in the story, explains to Azorno that his pet names create a role, "and without knowing how it actually happened you're suddenly stripped of your freedom to experience or be experienced" (102). Like his rose garden, she is an image, no more than an abstraction to him. But Christensen does not end here. Bathsheba tells Azorno she's pregnant, they kiss, then walk silently around the Luxembourg Gardens. Repeated images continue to circulate around them, but then, suddenly Azorno has a new thought: "I was thinking that this was my only life," (103) and at the same time, he realizes that someone somewhere was having the same thought simultaneously. Finally, as the gardens are about to close, and the water jets stop so that the surface of the water is calm, and in a moment of soundlessness, they get up and kiss each other, "for the first time." Language is left "three steps behind" so they can experience each other, and become, in fiction at least, autonomous creatures, rather than "pictures resembling creatures."

WORKS CITED

Borges, Jorge Luis. *On Writing*. Trans. Suzanne Jill Levine. New York: Penguin Books, 2010. Print.

Christensen, Inger. *Azorno*. Trans. Denise Newman. New York: New Directions, 2009. Print.

Christensen, Inger. *Hemmelighedstilstanden (Essays)*. Copenhagen: Gyldendal, 2000. Print.

Fischer, Norman. *Experience: Essays on Thinking, Language, Writing, and Religion*. Tuscaloosa: University of Alabama Press, 2016. Print.

Messerli, Douglas."Pictures Resembling Creatures," *Rain Taxi* Vol.14 Feb. 2009/2010: Print.

Monk, Ray. *How to Read Wittgenstein*. New York: W.W. Norton & Company, 2005. Print.

Skyum-Nielsen, Erik. "Man får lyst til at holder det hele I bevaegelse." Copenhagen: *Information*, 4 Feb. 1982: 4-9. Print.

Sørensen, Rasmus Bo. "Så kom Inger Christensen til Sverige," Copenhagen: *Information*, 13 Jan. 2012. Online.

Waldrop, Rosmarie. *Dissonance (if you are interested)*. Tuscaloosa: The University of Alabama Press, 2005. Print.

Wittgenstein, Ludwig. *Major Works*. Trans. C. K. Ogden. New York: HarperCollins Publisher, 2009. Print.

The Point of Robert Creeley's *The Island*

MARCELLA DURAND

Even as it provides the title for what is simultaneously autobiography/nov-el/long poem, *The Island* doesn't address so much an actual island, as the claustrophobia of being within a limited geography. It seems at first rather un-Creeley-like, this invitation to think of an island as a metaphor—the is-land being marriage, or not even marriage, but the state of being an individ-ual dealing with other individuals. Creeley's own introductory note inclines us to take it so:

> They want an island in which the world will be at last a place circum-scribed by visible horizons. They want to love free of a continuity of roads, and other places … I have found that time, even if it will not offer much more than a place to die in, nonetheless carries one on, away from this or any other island.

But, as in Creeley's poetry, a seemingly simple metaphor is never always that. "There is the sign of / the flower—/ to borrow the theme. // But what or where to recover / what is not love / too simply" ("The Rhyme," *For Love*). The island in the novel is also a geographical actuality that intensifies the characters' isolation, and that geographical isolation (heightened by a cultural isolation from the island's inhabitants) in turn intensifies the issues that drive the narrative forward. The main character, John, trapped by the island of his own existence, turns inward, losing the ability to escape his own boundaries. Similarly (or simile-like), almost every encounter with the waters that surround the island turns close to mortal for those characters who swim in them. Thus the island exists both as parallel metaphor and literal element.

The Island is intensely mono-perspectival, which furthers the relation of island to individual, but also makes the novel difficult to read, suffocat-ing even. Almost every action of the main character, John, is set in context with all his other actions, his emotions, and his past, and this often appears to become justification. So time, too, is a device that drives the novel, and how incidents occur to affect what comes after. "By some means or other, this demanded, a man must make of his narrative a cohesion of things there occurring, must give them demonstrable relation. Which is order of a kind; and we've gone wrong, only, in believing it to be of one kind, no other to be admitted," Creeley writes in "How to Write a Novel." The other kind, he posits, is a division: "[T]here are two ways of evoking a reality: that it has a place in time, or that it is existent in space. There is some choice between them, at least for the novelist." But in *The Island*, he makes both choices—the novel occurs in the specific space of *the island*, and the novel's action occurs as incidents accumulate in a sense to increasingly contextualize consequent action. For instance, the actions of John's wife, Joan, are more responses to his actions—his actions are the contexts for her actions even her one last thrilling attempt to disappear off the island (into the water!) and away from the consuming interiority of her husband:

> ... he began to make her up, to invest her with his own mind, no matter the twists, the shifts, the distortions of her, talking in his voice, from hers, impatient when she did in fact speak to him, now, came from whatever place she did live, out, to look for a moment at what he was, what they were, together.

Trained Pavlovian-like by popular culture, I kept waiting for Joan to die, as women are so often physically erased in so many narratives. I thought a cyst would be cancer; I thought somehow the book would punish her for abortions described in honest brutal detail or her attraction to another character; and at the end, I certainly expected a near-death scene to become actual—and was almost giddy with relief when she was allowed to live (spoiler alert!). How rare! How compassionate, particularly of a male writer in the early 1960s! But rather than death, or even erasure, she is pushed further and further out as a character by the expanding bubble of John's self-absorption, joined in external orbit by their children, their friends and the island's inhabitants, the "locals." The latter seem to speak, or exist, primarily as a group. Further on, when gypsies arrive, the complications of where he stands in relation to "others" becomes more so, highlighted again by place, by geography.

> In that sense, the whole town was a conspiracy, even his family. It wasn't that he didn't want his own children to have even the grotesqueries of the place, if they really were that. How can you be somewhere without being all there, and if they took on the superstitions of the town, he was almost proud. They were doing clearly what he couldn't.

What John "couldn't" do is fully inhabit *the island*, his marriage and his relationships as he isolates inward. There's been a fair bit written on how in *The Island* Creeley depicts this process: his skill as a narrator, the devastating details he includes so that we readers are not quite fully absorbed into John, but retain our distance. We can still stand apart—and judge. Perhaps, in some odd oblique way, this novel distantly opened a path for a poet like Bernadette Mayer to work toward getting fully away from readerly judgment and instead inhabit the mind's interior and document its every small movement in similar close detail.

At the same time, there's something else going on in this novel that speaks not so much to fiction innovation, but to what was really a detour from poetry in the life career of a great poet. What I find mattering to me is the poet behind the construction of the novel—that is, the poet who wrote the poems of *For Love* that span the decade before *The Island*'s publication in 1963 and who, after this novel, returned to poetry and poems like "Numbers," published in *Pieces* in 1969. What then, poetically, I want to know, is important in this break?

"Form is the extension of content," Creeley says. So, as Marjorie Perloff has identified in her essay "Four Times Five: Robert Creeley's *The Island*," *The Island* has a form: each chapter is approximately five pages within five chapters to four parts. 5:5:4. *For Love* includes the poem:

"The Names"

When they came near,
the one, two, three, four,
all five of us sat
in the broken seat.

Oh glad to see,
oh glad to be,
where company
is so derived
from sticks and stones,
bottles and bones.

Creeley's famous quatrains, and fine control over, are in ample evidence throughout *For Love*, but in this poem, the focus is on the syllables and the numbers within the syllables: 4, 5, 5, 5/ 4, 4, 4, 4, 4, 4. It's not one of the better known poems in the collection, but it's evidence of Creeley's sense of numbers within both content and form—as aural skeleton, as link to tradition that extends enough to accommodate his breaks with it, as the percussion most organically echoing the body and breath's own length and sound. Form here is the natural number of the human body, and it accommodates the "others" within—the structures within language that are human beings interacting with each other (even if with sticks, stones, bottles and bones). In "Numbers," a longer piece written for Robert Indiana, Creeley provides some insight into why the syllabic beats or stanza lengths of four or five in poetry may accommodate relation:

> and two by two
> is not an army
> but friends who love
>
> one another. Four
> is a square,
> or peaceful circle,
>
> celebrating return,
> reunion,
> love's triumph
>
> "FOUR," Numbers
>
> ...Somehow the extra
> one--what is more than four--
>
> reassured me there would be
> enough. Twos and threes or
> one and four is plenty.

> *

> A way to draw stars

The structures of four and five can create a geometry that accommodates interaction and conversation within human scale. Problem is that this perfect poetic structure—the human quatrain—this beautiful form that extends the content of relationship doesn't actually work as well for *The Island*. Instead, the four/five/five structure overlays somewhat uneasily content that is essentially the structure of one—John. The epigraph for *The Island*: "It is all one to me where I begin;/ for I shall come back again there" is echoed years later in "ONE" from Numbers: "What/ singular upright flourishing/ condition . . . / it enters here,/ it returns here."

John's relationships with others are too ghostly or plural or faceless to create a dialog. Moreover, *The Island*'s sentences and paragraphs of prose extend past the natural four or five beat of a human breath, and often become overpunctuated, choppy—so very unlike Creeley's precise sense of line breaks in poetry.

> The long car one had, had taken them all in, but he was left, later, somehow, still unclear, he was running down the street after the fading image of it, trying to catch it, calling to her.

To return to *For Love*, as this book seems closest in time and intention to *The Island*, I see that Creeley knows how to use—and how to escape, beautifully—the quatrain, and to compress and stretch the line into and past the breath enough to become exhilarating.

from "The Rain"

Love, if you love me,
lie next to me.
Be for me, like rain,
the getting out

of the tiredness, the fatuousness, the semi-
lust of intentional indifference.
Be wet
with a decent happiness.

Four and five transform gorgeously to 13, 9, 2, 7 . . .

But in *The Island* there is no such escape, not really much transformation—it is what it is, and so I look for the form more suited to this content, and find the island not only metaphor, but structure itself in how it holds the situation of the novel—it is solitary, it is irregular, it is mute and not mutable—it, too, is ONE. Rather than allowing for dialectic, or dialog, it restricts and inhabits, and all that enters, returns. Joan returns to John and John never leaves. Perhaps not such a satisfying form after all for a poet to continue in, so I speculate that this experiment—for that's how I see it—led to certain doors being necessarily closed and others opened. *The Island* acts somewhat as magnifying glass and prism—not so interesting an entity on its own, but fascinating in the light it casts on the poetry prior to and after its writing.

WORKS CITED

Robert Creeley. *A Quick Graph: Collected Notes & Essays*. Four Seasons Foundation. San Francisco: 1970.

Robert Creeley. *For Love: Poems 1950-1960*. Charles Scribner's Sons. New York: 1962.

Robert Creeley. *The Collected Poems of Robert Creeley 1945-1975*. University of California Press. Berkeley: 1982, 2006.

Robert Creeley. *The Island*. Charles Scribner's Sons. New York: 1963.

Marjorie Welish. "Four Times Five: Robert Creeley's *The Island*," *boundary 2* : Robert Creeley Special Issue, 6, no. 3 (Spring/fall 1978): 491-507.

Attention and Attunement in Forrest Gander's *As A Friend*

SUSAN SCARLATA

People know this story. Poets and writers and people from Arkansas, especially from Fayetteville, especially in the late 70s, know this story. People who follow Forrest Gander's work probably know this story; those who follow his late wife C.D. Wright's work definitely do. People who know about Frank Stanford know this story about his untimely death. Forrest Gander, the author of *As A Friend*, has lived within and alongside and behind and beyond this story for many years. Thus it is both entirely natural and wholly uncanny that Gander wrote and published his first novel based on the true story of the death of Frank Stanford, his wife's former lover.

As someone who knows both Gander and Wright, who runs Lost Roads, the press Wright inherited from Stanford and captained for over twenty years, the mere idea of this book has had me not wanting to read it. The premise of the maladaptive onlooker, "the friend," obsessed with Les, and that obsession being the plotline that puts all of the elements in place for Les' eventual suicide have all had me not wanting to get close to it. The doubling, mirroring and ghosting of the author being the husband of one of the women whom experienced this story in real-time, has made me want to look away. But in my most recent move I found I had saved my copy of *As A Friend* despite thinking I had given it away. Upon re-reading it I find that Gander convinces me. He does this in spite of the surrounding context and despite all of my preconceived notions; he does this because he is a poet. People know this story, and every story has been told, but Forrest Gander's poetic prowess and sensibility make this a novel worth reading and returning to.

The text has the ultimate narrative arc of a writer's life. It starts with a birth and ends with outtakes from an interview. These sections act as bookends around Clay's ("the friend" in the book's title) narrative perspective and the grief-stricken point-of-view of the lover, Sarah. With its short sections and shifting perspectives, *As A Friend* takes some cues from other verse novels. More than being a novel with sections that break into verse, however, this is a novel that could not have been written by anyone other than a poet, and certainly not as well by anyone other than a poet intimately entangled with the aftermath of the lives of the two poets and one painter at the center of this true story.

Researching and considering what it means to be a poet writing a novel, it is quickly clear that it is the opposite of simply inserting a poem into a work of fiction. This method can be a crutch for a fiction writer when words fail a given character, as if extremity transforms people into speaking and thinking in verse. Gander, in contrast, is first a poet and then he is telling a story; the ultimate grief he catalogs in this text is absolutely poetry, but the narrative sections are as well. This story is one that has arced, arched, and likely reared around he and his life. It takes sparseness, nimbleness and often the lightest of touches to not succumb to re-hashing this simply as literary myth. Gander holds the story up and clears the poetry of the clutter of years of legend in each of the four sections of the book with grace and acuity; he makes all of it real.

Two of the four characters developed with depth in *As A Friend* are po-ets, which is another way to define what a poet's novel is. As central as that is though, ultimately, it is because Gander is a poet that this is a fully realized novel. We are led in with a question as the very first sentence.

And where is he, the biological father of the unborn child? States away. On a New Orleans tugboat in violent Gulf water. Nor will he make it so far up the river gain, with five weeks' pay and anaconda boots, looking for a lovely girl's ear to nibble, and with half a notion, steadily declining, to betroth his charismatic loathsomeness to what-ever sad someone might part her lips for him, take in his torrent of lies, and mistake him for whatever he surely is not. (3)

This description of the main character, Les', biological father—never anywhere to be found—is the only mention of the one word most semi-nal to this story and text, charisma. Tellingly, it is "charismatic loathsome-ness," and in that personality descriptor is the rise and fall of the story we are about to read. Throughout Gander puts to good use the skill with and attention to language he has earned and utilized as a poet. Inverting the syn-tax of certain stock phrases, he calls the reader to attention as he has done in books of poems at least from his *Eye Against Eye* forward. This is a poet's novel because it was written with a poet's attention to language. Gander's sharpened visions of detail show us what we need to follow this story and its aftermath; the spotlight on Les' physical presence grounds him as a fully drawn character in the novel and beyond. The recognition of play with and warping we experience through the sonic then all carry us through Sarah's grief. This disparateness is written with grace and focus making it integral to the narrative even as it conveys fragments that will only ever be fragments.

As A Friend becomes increasingly less narrative as you move through its sections. Things break apart as Stanford did. With a myth as looming as this, this structure is the only way the narrative, or lack thereof once the main character's heart has been split open, could have been captured. This outsized event gains nuance in Gander's hands; the focus is on the event as told by the friend who churns the players into action. This is a story told by a living poet, and when Sarah's section arrives as a collage of poetic musings it is not solely because the event to end her relationship with Les was baffling to the most severe degree. Gander is never using poetry as a gateway to altered mental states.

This is a poet's novel in every sense; a novel written by a poet about two other poets who thought and loved through poems. And though elements less-than-clandestine may lead readers to wince, they also present the reality that only Gander, with access to the details, real and imagined, and only after twenty years time, could have written this story down.

Gander focuses on existence as grounded in the body and the animal self as a way of capturing the character of Les through other's eyes. Each description is so specific, whole and aptly conjured that we not only see and understand whom Les was, but can feel into this character and person as well. These are all impressions from the friend, Clay's, perspective:

> Les let himself in without knocking and two at a time shot up the stairs like he was escaping a bear. (17)

Les is someone who could have escaped a bear.

> . . . I knew his shape and the way he moved, rolling on the balls of his feet, all swing and curve like a big cat. (19)

Les has the animal capacity, the smoothness and speed, of a big cat.

> When people saw Les, they touched him. Coming into the bar or into the surveyor's office before work, he would pass through a gauntlet of hands extended in greeting. He was like a votive stone. . . . Men and women alike . . . hugged him hello and goodbye or touched him on the shoulder, people who saw him every day, people who weren't physical with anyone else. (31)

People were so drawn to Les they wanted to touch him without knowing why. Gander deftly portrays the physical realities of the character; Les is not a thinly sketched character there for the sake of poetry. From birth to death and in-between Les' character in *As A Friend* is fully fleshed. Through these metaphors and descriptions we are drawn the clear picture that Les was at ease inside his physical self. And this ease, assurance and confidence, what abstractly we would call charisma, Gander describes through Clay's eyes again with perfection as the reality that, "You looked at him, at the loose way he walked, and you thought about sex. His torso rode on his hips like a snake on its coil" (31). All these dexterous accounts express how Les had an air of otherness, the intrigue of being almost more than human while still existing among mere mortals.

These observations come from the third person point-of-view of Clay, Les' workmate; and eventually these feelings mutate in Clay so much that he wants to be Les. The obsession never turns fully sexual, but Gander handles this with the skill of a practiced novelist, giving us every element to think that it might while walking the thinnest of lines.

Gander plants this objectifying of identity early on with Clay describing, "Les liked staging dramatic interactions from which he could exit quickly, leaving a charged space behind him. His resonance" (17). As readers we are shown that when seen from great enough distance, anything can appear planned or pre-meditated. Clay spends so much of his time thinking about Les he comes to think everything about him is not just deliberate but also calculated. Gander's attention to minute details pays off in the narrative making the shift in Clay's perceptions entirely believable; his extremely calculated actions are natural outgrowths of his seething emotions.

Gander's skill in conveying inner dialog carries us through this section and the entire novel. As here Clay notes, "Maybe he wasn't even fully conscious of the effect he had on me. But part of what he awakened in me was a horrible awareness that I would never be the only person I now wanted to be" (31). The hatred Clay harbors for Les fully burgeons into being with the two of them drunk at Mr. Burger. Watching Les place his order at the counter Clay compares it to how he approached the situation and let the servers behind the counter in on the joke of their drunkenness. Les, in contrast, plays it straight, fully "in control of the material." These perfectly placed; novelistic details shine the brightest industrial light on the rest of the text. The situation is entirely innocuous and we see Clay taking it wholly personally. Gander provides readers the dual perspective to guess that Les is likely not thinking much about how Clay orders while Clay replays the difference between them ad infinitum. His observation that for Les it all hinged on "controlling the material," and that Les could inherently do that continues to highlight his own lackings. With acuity, Gander plants this entire progressive seed, demonstrating in perfect narrative the birth of envy. Then he writes, "It all reversed." Clay takes a series of actions that lead to what he figured would be confrontation and the end of Les' current ruse, but instead lead to Les' death.

Sarah's words enter the novel as piles of memories, and we get an entirely different perspective. Sarah's point of view includes the desire when over-taken with grief to make any sort of sense and the repetition in the inability to do so. More than anything spoken aloud, this section is thinking-to-one-self and thinking to someone who is gone. It is stream-of-conscious, but a step beyond or deeper than that since that connotes consciousness, which is not all that much a part of the overwhelm of grief. Gander intersperses Les' notions about poetry and sound through Sarah's section, which tether her collaged perspective together.

Early in this section Sarah remembers Les saying, "I don't think poets tell things at all, you said. Poetry listens" (68). From there we are given touchstones about the aural and sound throughout Sarah's pages. These sonic references are often scientific and in that they provide readers with a semblance of grounding. They are remembrances of facts beyond grief when the grief is so close to being everything. "The greater the cilia vibra-tion, the louder the sound." Sentences and phrases such as these are woven within and between memories and sensual, bodily things such as Les clean-ing Sarah's ears about which she thinks, "What a strange, complex intimacy, your at once maternal and sexual tenderness" (72).

Smartly, the sonic elements that Gander calls attention to are not all tender or factual. Sarah describes the ultimate picture and sound patterns of grief as eels, "They say the South American ghost eel makes a high-pitched piercing hum. Sometimes, it seems like the air around me must be full of them. Invisible. Screaming" (81). This is the body in grief, unable to screech and scream any longer yet still experiencing the resonance of oth-er beings doing the same. Gander's larger tableau presents this ultimate comparison of Sarah's body in grief against the earlier descriptions of Les' body in motion.

This story is about being torn apart, and concentration on the body's inti-mately small receptors is, if nothing else, a place to exist within that tearing. "And the brain determines pitch by the stimulated hair cells" (82). Gander's poetic sensibility engages here with the scientific in the tiniest of observa-tions. All is reduced to its most elemental degree in times of such solid grief. Things come down to vibration and pitch. Content is no matter; the va-lences of surrounding structures become all. These are things a poet, quite practiced at his craft, is able to capture.

Gander also interlaces Sarah's section with perspective on Les' physicality, and, as one would expect from a lover, these observations are much less externalized than those we get from Clay. Sarah is aware of Les' "economy of . . . gestures" (72). She sees and understands "The subtlety of [Les'] visual attention. . . . Alert me or change the subject with a contraction of your iris" (71). And then a combination of the physical and aural as Sarah depicts Les, "You laughed like a roller coaster" (94). Also, a fine point put on Clay's envy from Sarah's broadening position "The rest of us made you the point where our astonishments and our projections converged." Then this is echoed with Sarah's need to move on and wanting "For my conviction and my action to be of a piece" (82, 100).

After Sarah's section, a collage of interwoven observations, memories, and requisite attentions, Gander moves us to the last section, a curation of Stanford's own observations. More maxim than poetry these thoughts encapsulate the mental underpinnings going on in the body and soul we have come to know well from the other points-of-view in this novel. Here, as throughout, Gander's choices move us into and through this poet's novel.

We get:

To be unreflective about language, you limit the frequencies of meaning and even, I'd say, of experience . . . (101)

This reflects evenly back onto Sarah's notions of pitch, registers and vibrations. Frequencies fit well on that list. Facts about sound are interwoven into Sarah's section, Les and Clay are collecting factual data sets about land as surveyors, and as readers we wonder what in this novel is "factual." As this passage goes on we know that Les' perspective on life and what leads where is much more true to the lives we all lead than facts ever are.

Frank Stanford as Les in *As A Friend* spoke to a documentary filmmaker,

But the sequence of random inconsequential incidents that led you here . . . those forgotten, stupid, inconsequential moments form beds of substrate underlying all the logic on the surface. (103)

So it is here, and Gander, the amateur geologist, could not have held himself back from including this excerpt. The visual of "substrate" fits so perfectly into these notions of tuning in and tuning out, piling layers upon layers, and the underbellies that are inherent to this story and the humanness in us all.

Gander allows these quotes to speak for themselves and lets this section demonstrate, as does Stanford's work, that although young and impulsive, he possessed eerie amounts of wisdom. On these pages Les talks of all of the things that "insulate" us from the "real encounter," and captures what has become even more the case since his untimely death in 1979. Frank/Les refers to people's first reaction to seeing photos of themselves when they have had no exposure to pictures before. He says they are unable to recognize themselves because nothing about a black and white flat, scentless photo has the "kick of being" in it. Having spent much time with Stanford's work and with the archive of his press I have more than once looked at pictures of him and considered this very thing. Not until Gander's *As A Friend*, a poet's novel in every sense: written by a poet, about a poet and utilizing poetic gestures and attention throughout, did I have any semblance of the true "kick" of Stanford's being.

Les/Frank's final tangent in the novel is reminder that Gander likely worked backwards as much as forward, constructing the narrative out of what we have Stanford saying on film. In contrast to what Clay thinks about him, and perhaps to Les/Frank's actions, he realizes he is never in "control of the material."

> We don't know what will happen, we aren't alone at the wheel, despite our best efforts, we're at risk, but that vulnerability is all we'll ever know of the sacred, it's what we don't comprehend and what calls us to be responsible for others, for everything, the source spring of what we call our conscience. (104)

Here is the sense too of why the gun, in the bedroom, in the heart. As his best self, Stanford believed in this deep-rooted responsibility to and for other people. Then there were two. Two women he loved in the one house, and Stanford took a way out.

He said,

> ... [A]ll that feeling of interrelation and vulnerability is enough to scare anyone, so we fight it off, we cultivate boredom, we try to assert control by talking shit, talking shop, doing the same old same old, sopping up the impersonal drone of facts, newspapers, sales pitches, the disembodied language of real indifference that eclipses poetry every time. (104)

He talked shit, talked shop, did a rote job day in and day out, and then concerned himself with poetry, the type of language that is not disembodied or indifferent.

With superb insight, Gander lets all the last words be Stanford's own. Stanford said:

But what it means and how it means and who is saying it and who is dying it —I'd like to think there is some hope anyway to be found in paying attention to the words. (101)

Hope found in paying attention to the words —as poets and writers, of poems and of novels, we like to, we do, and we must think that. And Stanford said:

Poetry with its subterranean insights and amphetamine rushes lighting us up, lighting up whatever it is we call our inner selves, that holy now that gives us a hold on what we actually feel. (104)

WORKS CITED

Gander, Forest. *As A Friend*. New York: New Directions, 2008.

Out of Marsh and Bog
"H.D., Imagiste" and the Poeisis of *HERmione* Precisely

JENNIFER SCAPPETTONE

In *End to Torment: A Memoir of Ezra Pound*, written the year Pound was released from St. Elizabeth's Hospital (1958), H.D. recollects her own coming into being as a poet—with her inscription as author taking place via Pound's pencil in the British Museum tea room:

> "But Dryad," (in the Museum tea room), "this is poetry." He slashed with a pencil. "Cut this out, shorten this line. 'Hermes of the Ways' is a good title. I'll send this to Harriet Monroe of *Poetry*. Have you a copy? Yes? Then we can send this, or I'll type it when I get back. Will this do?" And he scrawled "H.D. Imagiste" at the bottom of the page. (*End to Torment*, 18)

The author of the Pound memoir reconstructs how through a few phallic slashes and scrawls, this former lover liberated Hilda Doolittle of her inauspicious surname, emptying the appellation as a whole in favor of depersonalized initials, and definitively launched her poetic career. The poems "Hermes of the Ways," "Priapus" (later "Orchard"), and "Epigram" were soon published in *Poetry*'s fourth issue, in January 1913, under the deflecting heading "Verses, Translations, and Reflections from 'The Anthology,'" and signed "H. D., 'Imagiste.'" These poems would launch H.D.'s reputation for a radical impersonality realized via finely cut images: she is often heralded as having inaugurated the Imagist style whose principles Pound would lay out explicitly in the next issue of *Poetry* (with "A Few Don'ts by an Imagiste"). Pound would later summarize in "A Retrospect,"

> In the spring or early summer of 1912, "H. D.," Richard Aldington and myself decided that we were agreed upon the three principles following:
> 1. Direct treatment of the "thing" whether subjective or objective.
> 2. To use absolutely no word that does not contribute to the presentation.
> 3. As regarding rhythm: to compose in the sequence of the musical

phrase, not in sequence of a metronome. (*Pavannes and Divisions, 95*)

As Richard Aldington acknowledged in a letter to H.D., "Ezra may have 'invented' Imagism but, after all, you wrote the poems" (Letter dated 20 March 1929, *Richard Aldington and H.D.* 17).

H.D.'s early "Imagiste" lyrics strike the page through their austerity and oblique formulations of agency; they antedate the stances adopted by the male authors routinely credited with the modernist precept of impersonality, Pound and T.S. Eliot. Presenting the poems to Monroe, Pound wrote, "Objective—no slither; direct—no excessive use of adjectives; no metaphors that won't permit examination. It's straight talk, straight as the Greek!" (*Selected Letters,* 11). "Epigram *(After the Greek),*" an adaptation of an anonymous epigram from the Greek Anthology, reconstructs the inscription of a woman as an absence in the life of her lover Atimetus, stripped of pathos:

The golden one is gone from the banquets;
She, beloved of Atimetus,
The swallow, the bright Homonoea:
Gone the dear chatterer;
Death succeeds Atimetus. (*Poetry* 1:4 122)

When translated by J.W. Mackail for a 1907 anthology much treasured by the Imagist circle, where H.D. is likely to have encountered it, the epigram was voiced in the first person of the deceased ("I Homonoea, who was far clearer-voiced than the sirens . . . "); H.D.'s version achieves a starker, more haunting, chilling effect by removing the voice of the chatterer gone as well as that of her lover, so that a vantage point as removed as the funerary stone itself is all that is left to reconstitute this birdlike presence.[1] Though the first lyric of the group published in *Poetry,* "Hermes of the Ways," does contain a first person, its subject is something of a hollow, defined by the encroachment of an aggressive environment, via dialogue with the messenger god:

Hermes, Hermes,
The great sea foamed,
Gnashed its teeth about me;
But you have waited,
Where sea-grass tangles with
Shore-grass. (*Poetry* 1:4, 120)

The god of transit and translation, represented on boundary stones (*hermai*) and poised here at the threshold of land and fluidity, provides a somewhat inscrutable bulwark against the sea that threatens to swallow this stanza's implicit I.[2]

The label (and associated name) for which H.D. had Pound to thank was and remains something of a prisonhouse for the poet; the Imagist designation has restricted H.D.'s reception for decades, despite the range of her works composed beyond the temporal, conceptual, and stylistic boundaries of that storied moment in the history of modernism (which was soon enough eclipsed by Vorticism, and definitively losing traction by 1917). Any number of male interlocutors advised her not to abandon the precision of her poetry for prose. Yet a desire to work through an unremitting series of traumas at once intimate and collective—the early battle for a fluid sexual identity that would not subject her to the authority of another; the trauma of her husband Aldington's fighting in the trenches of WWI and erratic sexual adventures, and their marriage's disintegration; the death of a brother to the same war; then almost dying in a boardinghouse in childbirth to her daughter Perdita in 1919—led this author to prose's ampler discursive space. In *End to Torment*, Hilda notes polemically of her Imagist verse, "I was in hiding ... *H.D.—Hermes—Hermeticism* and all the rest of it" (*End to Torment* 40).

HERmione, completed in 1927 but not published until 1981, twenty years after her death, is one of several texts by H.D. that come out of hiding—to a degree: works that are routinely classified through the contradictory term "autobiographical fiction." She wrote this roman à clef at age forty about events that took place roughly between 1906 and 1911, when she was college age—and suffering a crisis of identity following her withdrawal from Bryn Mawr. Having performed poorly in math ("'I failed in conic sections'") and, of all subjects, English, this "odd mind" is now subject to "fresh barriers, fresh chains, a mesh" (*HER,* 12). *HERmione* is a memoir of self-hermeneutics in thin disguise—suspended behind the unsatisfactory masks of "Hermes—Hermeticism" and Hermione, the Queen of Sicily in Shakespeare's *A Winter's Tale*, a figure who is unjustly accused of adultery ("How will this grieve you, / When you shall come to clearer knowledge, that / You thus have publish'd me!") and reconstructed as a statue until her climactic reanimation by music (*A Winter's Tale,* Act 2, Scene 1). Why the need for disguise? *HERmione* is the record of an inchoate woman artist's tormented search for a name, an agency, distinct from both the Hilda Doolittle of inheritance—freighted with her father ("Carl")'s reputation as a professor and scientist, and the expectations of femininity of her mother ("Eugenia") and society at large—

and the "H.D., Imagiste" of literary destiny. Yet Her Gart recalls that it was a grandfather's idea to name her something out of Shakespeare; no name is purely Her's own. Throughout, the name of the father and its arrangements will threaten the membrane protecting her but also impeding her ability effectively to defy a hostile symbolic order:

> Words beat and sizzled and a word bent backward like a saw in a saw-mill reversed, turned inward, to work horrible destruction. The word 'father' as [her sister-in-law] Minnie spoke it, reversed itself inward, tore at the inner lining of the thing called Her Gart. (*HER,* 15)

As a consequence, Hilda Doolittle was constantly adopting new names, new personae: as Susan Stanford Friedman notes, the title page of *HERmione* bears the signature Helga Doorn, a personality the author created for her three films (*Penelope's Web,* 42).[3]

That Her is an object rather than a subject pronoun suggests some impasse in the solution, some stoppage along the way to formation of a *Bildungsroman.* Her will be suspended in a circular, vertiginous, lyrically afflicted present tense: "Her Gart went round in circles. 'I am Her,' she said to herself; she repeated, 'Her, Her Her'" (3). A competing refrain asserting the self's integrity and even divinity affirms, "I am AUM": "Clear throat, Em, Um, Hem. Aum. It was AUM. I am the word AUM. God was in a word" (38). Throughout narration of her struggle for self-definition, Her Gart remains yoked to what Rachel Blau DuPlessis identifies as "psychocultural scripts" (*Signets* 406-08). These include those of a claustrophobia-inducing family, on the one hand, and on the other, a love triangle between herself, George Lowndes (the fictionalized Pound, her first love), and Fayne (the fictionalized Frances Gregg, an art student and writer) that only partially relieves the gender binaries of what DuPlessis calls "romantic thralldom" ("She dragged things down to the banality, 'People don't want to marry me. People want to marry me. I don't want to marry people'") (5). Following psychic and cognitive breakdown and recovery, Her's tempestuous lesbian relationship with the rebellious and "dangerous" Fayne is weakly triumphant at the roman à clef's abrupt close: Hermione will in the end go to Europe accompanied by Fayne, thus escaping the bonds of family and the fate of Philadelphia "faculty ladies" (7), and breaking free of the overbearing male lover as exclusive bridge to the Continent and its culture.

In a letter to John Cournos written around 1919, H.D. divulged that she was beginning a novel. When pressed to explain why, she noted that

I want to clear up an old tangle. Well, I do not put my personal self into my poems. But my personal self has got between me and my real self, my real artist personality. And in order to clear the ground, I have tried to write things down—in order to think straight, I have endeavoured to write straight . . . .

You must remember that writing poetry require[s] a clarity, a clairvoyance almost . . . .

But in the novel I am working through a wood, a tangle of bushes and bracken out to a clearing, where I can see ~~clear~~ again. (Qtd. in *Penelope's Web,* 34)

Like the "four-conveyer system" of John Dos Passos's *U.S.A.* trilogy, wherein the "Camera Eye" sections provide the author "a way of draining off the subjective by directly getting in little bits of [Dos Passos's] own experience," this author's discursive ecology spawns prose arenas in which to grapple with the tangles of personhood, that they might not snarl her poetic lines and reduce visionary poetry to less capacious testimonials of confession ("An Interview with John Dos Passos," *First Person,* 289). This does not mean that *HERmione* is a confessional work; on the contrary, Her's trouble is that she resists being "suffocate[d] with sentiment" (9). The tulip tree, oak, and dogwood literally (and perhaps figuratively) deflowered at which the incipient woman gazes recall the tree imagery equated with young Hilda in the poems of Pound's handbound love poem sequence, *Hilda's Book* (composed from 1905 to 1907), but as infinitely more complex networks resisting identification: "She was nebulous, gazing into branches of liriodendron, into network of oak and deflowered dogwood" (3).

Her's struggle to define herself is played out in the metaphorical economy of *HERmione,* which draws heavily on overdetermining tropes of fluidity and solidity, muddiness and clarity then ascendant in characterizations of the sexes, that were particularly abundant in the contemporary work of Pound, from his writing on Remy de Gourmont to *The Cantos.*[4] A 1919 letter from Pound to Marianne Moore (H.D.'s classmate at Bryn Mawr) confides, "Thank God, I think you can be trusted not to pour out flood," and follows with a poem that celebrates the admixture of gender binaries: "The female is a chaos, / the male / is a fixed point of stupidity" (qtd. in *Gender of Modernism* 361). Pound's "Hell" Cantos, published shortly before H.D. began *HERmione,* mobilize tropes of swamp and ooze to decry "the state of English mind" in an inferno of profiteers, usurers, and "the perverters of language," represented as engulfed in dung, mud, and "bog-suck" (*Selected Letters* 239;

Cantos 14/61, 15/66). H.D.'s self-characterization through tropes of lucidity and muddiness resonates strongly with her ex-lover's damning metaphorical economy, the same that defines the modernist aesthetic by privileging clarity: *HERmione* begins, "She could not see the way out of marsh and bog. She said, 'I am Hermione precisely'" (3). The "bog" recurs, but without a satisfactory corrective, as *HERmione* is equally suspicious of scientistic classifications for things: "She had not then dipped dust-draggled, intellectual plumes into the more modern science that posts signs over emotional bog and intellectual lagoon ('failure complex,' 'compensation reflex') to show us where we may or may not stand" (4). Between the poles of quagmire and science's feeble taxonomies, the young artist searches for a vision, an image to still: "she tried to concentrate on one frayed disc of green, pool or mirror that would refract image. She was nothing. She must have an image no matter how fluid, how inchoate" (5). H.D.'s transcription of multifaceted, multidimensional and multiscalar visual compositions in Her's mind parallels the painterly consciousness of Lily in Virginia Woolf's masterpiece *To the Lighthouse,* published the same year and itself characterized in 1927 as "a psychological poem" (*Diary of Virginia Woolf* 123). However, even compositions in the visual realm cannot satiate this heroine, for "Pictures were conclusive things and Her Gart was not conclusive" (7). The paradoxical task of *HERmione,* its chief experiment, is to represent, in writing, the frustrations of consciousness in one who has not yet alighted on her vocation as a writer:

> There was a sort of 'composition' of elements that her mind, fused to the breaking point, now apprehended. The catch was that her perception was ahead of her definition. She could put no name to the things she apprehended . . . .
>
> The boom of the bee in her ear, his presence like an eclipse across the sun brought visual image of the sort of thing she sought for . . . it had not occurred to Her to try and put the thing in writing. (13)

Little by little Her realizes that "there was hope in blocks of substantiated marble, words could carve and set up solid altars" (76)—and yet both George and Fayne, comrades in writing, threaten Hermione with petrifaction. Her feels "smudged out" by George's kisses (83-84, 120-21), as a blackboard "smudged at edges with cloudy chalk stuff" (83); he turns her head and hand to marble weight, "dehumanized" (77). He renders Her a decorative muse, not a poet worthy of laurel: "There was something stripped of decoration, something of somewhat painful angles that he would not recognize. George saying 'choriamics of a forgotten Melic' was flattering her, tribute such as some courtier might pay to a queen who played at classicism; he did not proffer her the bare branch that was the strip of wild naked olive or the tenuous oleander" (230). At the same time, Fayne taunts Her with compliance, saying "Like Lot's wife you are a frozen pillar" (162), though she vows, "I'll make you breathe, my breathless statue" (163).

In "Romantic Thralldom in H.D.," Rachel Blau DuPlessis points out that

> Whenever H.D. writes 'Her realizes' or 'Her says,' she is using the wrong form of the pronoun in subject place; and every time this un-grammatical usage occurs, one is jarred into a recognition of the sit-uation of generic woman. Though "Her" is the object form, the very ungainly quality of the name used as the subject of a verb . . . suggests that we are in the presence of some resistant, stubborn matter which will not be captured. (*Signets,* 408)

Intriguingly enough, in the end, Her will escape America, for "there was nothing in America . . . but rows of desks and stabilization and exact for-malization (Uncle Sam pressing things down in test tubes)" (233). In per-spective, "Things piled up became a sort of hecatomb for some god . . . . Hermes more exactly" (234). The trip to Europe will be her marriage: her dowry spent on being "Practical and at one with herself" (234). Intriguing-ly enough, the narrative of inner torment of this privileged young woman, her intellectual strife, comes to a close on a moment of awareness of her mistreatment of others, and on her "barg[ing] straight into" the racialized speech of the family's cook Mandy, who reports that Fayne is waiting in Her's "little" studio: "Oh, Miss. I thought you was back long since. I done left Miss Fayne all alone upstairs in your little workroom" (234). Critics have emphasized the implications of *HERmione's* last sentence for its protago-nist—both its affirmation of Her's bisexuality, and its implied suffocation of Her within a destructive relationship. Yet the novel's final word, delivered in the approximated speech of a minoritized character, also embeds lessons about the suffocations of race and genre. It holds out the promise of hetero-glossia—a concept to be theorized by Mikhail Bakhtin shortly thereafter, in 1934—in the evolving poet's novel. These final sentences given to Mandy reinforce that the discursive vehicle of lyric finely hewn (as in the still over-determining heyday of H.D.'s "high" modernism) could never have strayed so far to expose the limits of its recognition of psychocultural difference, or of a barbed subject's integrity.

NOTES

1. See John William Mackail, ed. and trans., *Select Epigrams from the Greek Anthology* (Longmans, Green, and Co.: London, New York, and Bombay, 1911), XLVI, 165. The technical possibilities for modernist poetry presented by the Hellenistic epigram are presented by Eileen Gregory in "H.D. and the Classical Lyric," in *H.D. and Hellenism: Classic Lines* (Cambridge and New York: Cambridge University Press, 1997), 129-78. David Ayers points out that H.D. is "not simply rendering the Greek epigram, but transforming it into an idiom which is, if possible, even more epigrammatic"—therefore treating it as an encapsulation of Imagist ideals. See "H.D., Ezra Pound and Imagism," in David Ayers, ed., *Modernism: A Short Introduction* (Malden, MA, Oxford, and Carlton: John Wiley and Sons, 2004), 4.

2. Represented as looking in three directions, this Hermes must be read in relation to the Hermes Trismegistus whose writings form the basis of Hermeticism. In her reading of H.D., which relates *HERmione* to the Victorian Decadent tradition, Diana Collecott notes that Mitsuru Kamachi has unearthed the relation of Hermione-as-statue in *The Winter's Tale* to Hermeticism. See her *H.D. and Sapphic Modernism, 1910-1950* (Cambridge: Cambridge University Press, 1999), 61-63.

3. Susan Stanford Friedman's book is an invaluable resource for the student of the poet's novel, providing a full account of the impulses of H.D.'s fiction.

4. The 1920 essay "Remy de Gourmont," preface to *The Natural History of Love,* was reprinted in Ezra Pound, *Literary Essays* (New York: New Directions, 1968), 339-60. For an analysis of tropes of flooding and swamps and their application to the politics of the day, particularly in the swells of Fascism, see, especially, Klaus Theweleit, *Male Fantasies, Volume 1: Women, Floods, Bodies, History,* trans. Stephen Conway, with a foreword by Barbara Ehrenreich (Minneapolis: University of Minnesota Press, 1987).

WORKS CITED

Bakhtin, M. M. *The Dialogic Imagination: Four Essays*. Ed. Michael Holquist. Trans. Caryl Emerson and Michael Holquist. Austin: University of Texas Press, 1981.

Friedman, Susan Stanford. *Penelope's Web: Gender, Modernity, H.D.'s Fiction*. Cambridge: Cambridge University Press, 2008.

————, and Rachel Blau DuPlessis, ed. *Signets: Reading H.D.* Madison: University of Wisconsin Press, 1990.

Gado, Frank, ed. *First Person: Conversations on Writers and Writing*. Schenectady, NY: Union College Press, 1973.

H.D. *End to Torment: A Memoir of Ezra Pound*. Ed. Norman Holmes Pearson and Michael King. New York: New Directions, 1979.

———. "Epigram: After the Greek." *Poetry* 1:4 (January 1913): 122.

———. "Hermes of the Ways." Poetry 1:4 (January 1913): 120.

———. *HERmione*. New York: New Directions, 1981.

Pound, Ezra. Pavannes and Divisions. New York: A.A. Knopf, 1918.

———. *The Selected Letters of Ezra Pound: 1907-1941*. Ed. D.D. Paige. New York: New Directions, 1971.

Scott, Bonnie Kime, and Mary Lynn Broe, ed. *The Gender of Modernism: A Critical Anthology*. Bloomington: Indiana University Press, 1990.

Woolf, Virginia. *The Diary of Virginia Woolf, Volume 3: 1925-1930*. Ed. Anne Olivier Bell. San Diego: Harcourt Brace Jovanovitch, 1980.

Zilboorg, Caroline, ed. *Richard Aldington and H.D.: The Later Years in Letters*. Manchester: Manchester University Press, 1995.

Message in a Bottle
A Brief Introduction to *Radical Love: 5 Novels* by Fanny Howe

KAZIM ALI

"Little word, who said me? Am I owned or free?" The questions that occupy Fanny Howe's characters are always ridiculously serious. I say "ridiculous," because they almost always know the joke's on them. If there was a Rapture in which knowing people were taken into Heaven, these are definitely the "left behind," confused, unknowing—"social losers," as Howe calls them. The drama of these five novels is the drama of the individual body and soul trying to find herself in the confusing matrix of social reality.

The body of the child is abused, a body passes for white, a woman's body cannot get pregnant, bodies are broken into and dispersed into parts.

Unlike many writers of innovative or experimental fiction, in her novels Fanny Howe trusts the ability of the novel to not only depict American life using social realism but also what is often seen as an opposing extreme, its ability to depict the interior and thinking life. In this she may trust the novel's capacity but not its received structure. Howe's interest in marginalized figures (women and children primarily but not exclusively) and in borderlands (the actual US-Mexico border, but also the liminal space between races, closets, the wasteland of Utah desert used for nuclear testing, etc.) places her closer to 19th century pre-modern novelists than with the more typical postmodern and post-post-modern of the contemporary lyric novel. Thomas Hardy would be a closer ally in terms of craft, structure and character than would Gertrude Stein.

The concept of "radical love"—complete focused and devotional attention to the creatures and beings of the existing world—is key to understanding Howe's intention in writing. She also chose when collecting five earlier novels into one volume to title the omnibus edition *Radical Love: 5 Novels.* And indeed they are stories of how people try to love each other. Most of the families depicted are "non-traditional" ones. In *Nod* both parents decamp, leaving the two sisters in the charge of an Irish nanny and layabout Norweigan translator who may or may not be the former lover of the mother. In other stories a strong strand of fraternal incest haunts the relationships, confusing intimacy of family and sexuality.

Childhood is an important state in these books and some characters, like Cloda, never escape it. Not only does she "have the same appearance at thirty-nine as she had at nine," she also rejects the forward momentum of a life that requires her to "settle down," or get established in a profession. All of Howe's characters seem to be artists and free-thinkers, defined by their rejection of society's material demands. Their innocence allows them to create—poetry, films, music—and when others intrude on that process (Cloda's sister Irene steals her poem; Echo trashes Kosta's film studio) the results on the personal psyche are devastating.

Storytelling is also important. In *Nod*, Irene tortures her younger sister Cloda with stories that end badly while in *The Deep North* Tonio expresses his not-quite platonic love for his younger sister Gemma with wild fabrications of which he soon tires. The stories (and lies) we tell ourselves are at the heart of *Saving History,* to the point where the characters themselves no longer agree on what happens at the story's conclusion, and *Indivisible* is one long story that Henny tells to God, leaving out—as the young child Julio notices—the most crucial component.

That missing piece of the story, the part we can't—or are unable to—share with others haunts many characters. Cloda, in her child-like innocence makes the wildest and best attempt at communication: she writes a note—"Help! I'm being held hostage! SOS!"—and seals it in a bottle she throws into the ocean. Other characters do not have the required naiveté to make such a leap of faith and stumble about in their efforts to understand one another and be understood.

The novels seem to encourage this by their sometimes lack of clear chronology, geography, consistency of narrative point of view, of theme, of direction. Howe further encourages this de-centering by her ordering of the books not by date of publication but rather by the progression of the protagonist's age—in the first novel she is a 12-year old girl, then a young woman, after that a young mother, then a mother of adult children and then finally as a mature woman. As the reader progresses through *Radical Love*, she has to decide—if it's closure and formula she wants she will slowly perhaps work hard to uncover the secret significance of the episode being described; but if she is rather on carried along by the experience and the music of the language and the flow of the characters' internal sensibility, ranging from the child Cloda wondering about fairies to Henny musing philosophically about the Indian saint Ramakrishna, who held that all religions were one and equally valid. The individual novels are similarly non-linear or cavalier with their treatment of time; and the final novel *Indivisible* takes place before, during and after the events of all the previous novels and revisits most, if not all, of the characters from the previous books.

One way to experience the books then is as a "geography," traveling through them across the landscape the way the novels themselves travel across the country, from *Nod,* set in rural Ireland, to *The Deep North,* set in New England and across the country to California. The final novel takes place during a cross-country journey in which Henny, the protagonist, drives from New York City to California, accompanied by Tom, a character who previously took the same journey with the character Felicity from the previous novel *Saving History.*

The term "saving history" has a double meaning. Firstly, it is a term that can be used alternately with "salvation history"—a concept in Christian historiography that views all events in human history as part of God's plan for the ultimate salvation of the human race. But it also has a particular political intention the way Howe uses it—the idea of "saving" history "from the doom of duality," as Howe puts it. After all, both the title of *Indivisible* and Henny's obsession with Ramakrishna point to an interest in the Vedantic concept of nonduality—that all people are manifestations of God's energy and are one. "The word 'two' is a joke," Howe wrote in *Glasstown,* "that's why I'm always laughing."

And it's true that there is a certain kind of dark humor that haunts the characters of these books. Gemma, a dark-complected white woman in 1960s Boston, suddenly finds herself passing as Black after rescuing an African immigrant from a gang of hooligans on a train platform. Felicity, a hapless housewife without health insurance and unable to afford transplant surgery for her sick daughter, is drawn into a cross-border organ trafficking ring accompanied by an itinerant monk and a transgendered prostitute named Money. Henny, in love with God and fleeing the wreckage of an old relationship and the death of two close friends, locks her abusive husband McCool in a closet with a box of saltines and a jar of peanut butter in order to better care for her new foster child, Julio. His mother is Gemma.

It makes sense that time sends you backward and forward in these books. Their closest forebear in fiction would seem to be Anaïs Nin's *Cities of the Interior,* another collection of five novels that treated their characters and plot in an extremely lyrical fashion. Of that collection the critic Sharon Spencer wrote the novel was "a mobile hanging in space," that it should be experienced spatially and visually, that all the details of plot were less important than the unfolding of the characters' awareness and perceptions.

Gemma chose a sublimation of her own body (by passing as Black) in order to escape her upbringing and be embraced by a community, but that same deception took away any potential she had for personal growth. In the end she gives herself a "new name and disappears." It is not until her reappearance in *Indivisible* that we discover the depth of her personal unmooring that occurred in that act of self-occlusion. Perhaps the desperation could be traced back—like the theft of Cloda's poem by Irene—to the betrayal of Gemma by her brother Tonio in their childhood games. He would play imaginary games with her, sometimes even pretending to run away from home, and then at the height of the story he would abandon her, once even literally leaving her sleeping outside in the middle of the night.

The Deep North manifests the first of the shifts between first and third person that will continue throughout the novels, most specifically in *Saving History* where Felicity and Tom alternate in first person narration and then later in *Indivisble* where chapters of Henny narrating the story are interspersed essay-like chapters of her lyrical and philosophical musings.

In her introduction to *Radical Love* Howe wrote that in addition to their time in history, the five novels were linked "by the presence of children and the effort to hold childhood high." And though each novel does have a plot and a narrative structure Howe claims that "each page can be in most cases glanced over as if it were a prose poem, a complete unit." It is tempting—it's the wish of the lyric poet, or perhaps of all poets—to leave language at the moment of the pitch into empty space, at the moment of the dare but not the dare's fulfillment. The novelist must continue past the moment of language's leap into the unknown. Howe's novels have traditionally drawn characters, strong narratives that progress in ostensibly Aristotelian ways and function as books more or less in the traditional mode of the novel. Howe's novels, and Scalapino's for that matter, are all the more radical because they asked to be read as "novels" while departing radically from the commercial commodity that form has come to settle in.

The novel in the center of the collection also serves as its center conceptually. *Famous Questions,* which I first read in Central Park waiting for the Dalai Lama to speak, juxtaposes the supposedly radical but actually nearly quotidian life of New England transplants Kosta and Roisin cohabitating in suburban California with the new-age spiritualism of a wandering drifter named Echo whom they invite to stay with them; this shaky arrangement is complicated by the radical anti-nuclear politics of Kosta's mother, dying of cancer; Kosta's own aspirations as a filmmaker and Roisin's troubling past and first marriage.

The narrative, in its originally published form, is punctuated by Roisin's recounting the story of her first marriage to her young son, Liam. At the end of the novel Liam goes missing. Roisin falls asleep, unaware of his fate. She asks, as she drifts into sleep, the "famous question" of the novel's title: "are my children safe?" In the revised version of the novel, she never asks the question. Instead *Famous Questions* concludes with a conversation between Roisin and a safe Liam about her past in Ireland. She feels a kinship with her old lover: "His laugh I knew as well as the bark of a dog or the slam of a car door or the cough of a child . . . the meeting of two people who share one story and agree on its meaning. That's what I had always been looking for."

This dream of Roisin's takes on additional poignancy when one remembers Cloda's desperate desire to be understood manifested by her message in a bottle, or Gemma's pathetic secret life passing as a mixed race woman. Throughout the novel *Famous Questions,* Kosta, Roisin and Echo misunderstand each other. The confused household is presided over by Kosta's eccentric mother, called simply Ma, the first of a series of older women who have managed, through their age and experience, to see through confusion and misapprehension to be able to see things as they truly are. Ma wants no bullshit domestically—she wants Echo out of the house immediately—or politically—at the climax of the novel she has decided to go and expose herself to death in the Utah wilderness of nuclear testing grounds.

At the confusing conclusion of *Saving History,* Felicity's aunt suddenly appears and utters a single nonsensical line that reads like pure prophecy—it successfully bears the weight of meaning of the entire novel which came before it. And Henny in *Indivisible* is finally able to integrate her perceptions with the reality around her. She is called Ma by most of the other characters, including McCool, her deadbeat husband. She also integrates the other five books in her body. She cares for Julio, who is Gemma's son. Roisin knew her husband McCool back in Ireland and she herself knew Kosta before he left for California. Her companion Tom once accompanied Felicity to Mexico.

When Howe says "linked by their time in history," she means the full range of the second half of the twentieth century. *Nod* is set in World War II Ireland. In it two sisters are left alone while their mother travels to France and their father fights in the war. By *The Deep North*, as mentioned above, the action has shifted across the Atlantic to a segregated and racially tense Boston. *Famous Questions* is a quintessential Reagan-era 1980s novel set in the city sprawl of Southern California and *Saving History* shifts weirdly from first and third person narration as it crosses and recrosses the US-Mexico border. In *Indivisible* the fates of various of Howe's characters—including characters named above but also characters from her other novels *First Marriage* and *Bronte Wilde*—are resolved as the millennium quietly turns.

Howe isn't interested in her characters transcending and the novels themselves do not bring them to fair conclusions. As her spiritual interest is in the concept of 'doubt,' Howe is interested in difficulty. She describes her characters as "social losers" who are "attuned to the forces of history" and who "think about survival as a sign of meaning." Like characters from Lispector or Duras, they are caught in a social web of class, race and industrialism. How they struggle is what interests the novelist. She says, "each of them could be called a pilgrim trying to make progress as they struggle under the signs of sexuality, war, poverty, work, body parts, film, friendship, race, parenting and church."

"Unable to rest because unable to know," begins *Saving History,* appropriately having neither subject nor clarifying indirect object. Felicity, the heroine of this book, has the strongest moral center of any of the characters that came before but she is the least able to act upon it. Her allegorical allies, the shady businessman Temple and his associate Money, each drive Felicity to a defining act: will she smuggle organs across the border in order to procure one for her sick daughter? Her companion Tom, on his own quest to meet his stepbrother's imprisoned father Pedro, tries unsuccessfully to convince her to pursue legal avenues. This mistrust of authority and social institutions, the unfixity of identity, the changing of stories and name-changing (both by Pedro, by Gemma, by Money, by Felicity herself) point to distress in the relationship between a human body, its space and place in society and the soul or spirit's existence as an "individual."

In her case, Felicity becomes concerned with the nature of evil, mostly because she is worried that she is evil or will become evil by going through with the smuggling scheme. The internal thinking it provokes are some of the novel's most beautiful and odd sections. "When you are living on the edge of your society," she wonders, "are you closer to the center of the next era?" Now that we ourselves live in an age where biotechnology, cybernetics and genetic modification of food sources have transcended the corporeal limits of bodies, human and otherwise, Felicity's question seems disturbingly prescient.

It is figures on the "edge" of society—the traveling Gypsy family in *Nod,* the group of students and organizers that Gemma tries to join in *The Deep North,* the wandering drifter Echo from *Famous Questions*—that the main characters of the novels always want to connect with. Those figures on the edge seemed to have been able to release themselves from material concern in a way that liberates the spirit. Felicity, deep in her dilemma, confesses, "I never met a kinder man than the homeless alcoholic who introduced me to the father of my kids." A former street person herself (she claims—by this point in the story one does not know the truth of anything Felicity says because her story has changed so many times), she says, "Extreme affliction frees you, finally, from desire, and so we sought the longest and most difficult route to the nirvana of a woodland setting, hand in hand, mind you, and imagining a prospect both physical and internal."

Saving History presents the dilemma of the individual caught in larger forces—god, "history," morality. Even Tom, who finally believes he is productively imitating Felicity by reinventing himself and going incognito in an anonymous place—is caught up in Temple's devious machinations. "Who owns the individual?" Felicity wonders. In the end, she makes the only choice she can. Having abandoned Tom, her family, her society, Felicity again wanders and it is on her wanderings she meets two older women. The first is Cloda, who had ridden a bike around the world, "a Peace placard taped to her back." The second is her aunt, sitting in the center of a frozen lake, fishing, a bottle of Southern Comfort between her feet. Though she is "terrified of expanse," Felicity makes her way over and her aunt offers her the bottle. "That's how we do it down here," the old woman comments and though Felicity is desperate to understand and empathize—she answers "I know what you mean"—she hasn't yet. Howe says, "the bewilderment in her eyes lasted far longer than the sound of her words."

The lingering and ongoing questions of identity, moral responsibility, eschatology and phenomenology are all taken up in the final novel of the cycle, *Indivisible*. In certain ways it is the most radically innovative, formally speaking. The shifts in time are pronounced and the main character, Henny, shifts between recounting her past with Lewis and Libby, her present with Tom and Gemma's child Julio. These narrative chapters are interspersed with Henny's religious and spiritual musings. At one point in the novel, Tom is driving east from California and while he drives he writes what could be an ars poetica for the novel on a legal pad which sits beside him on the passenger seat: "To paraphrase an experience is heresy, unless you can turn the paraphrase into an organic part of that experience . . . I must reproduce the feeling of the original moments."

In this Howe suggests that *thinking* has a place, a relevant and physical place, in contemporary American life. Of all of *Radical Love's* radical proposition, this one may be the most essential and extreme. "There is a kind of story, God," says Henny to herself later, "that glides along under everything else that is happening, and this kind of story only jumps out into the light like a silver fish when it wants to see where it lives in relation to everything else." *Everything* about this final novel is about "relations." It's the care of Gemma's child—care that is necessitated by Gemma's continued inability to adapt the needs of her spiritual search to the material condition she finds herself in, a conflict later resolved by Felicity but at great cost—that forces

Henny to break out of the pattern of her past, to finally take action against the abusive McCool.

Abuse has formed another pattern throughout the novel, but none of the victims of abuse—Cloda, Roisin, Felicity—are able to more than escape from their circumstance. Only Henny is able to take action against her tormentor and actually inflict punishment. Though she helps him to avoid the police she also steals his passport and buys him a plane ticket, not to Ireland where he wanted to disappear to, but instead to Southern California, a place he has no affection for. She recognizes, on some deep level, that she still believes in the doctrine that suffering might make her more beloved to God: "I would do any amount of slave-work in order to be free."

The care of another, in most cases, a child, forces Howe's characters out of their own dilemmas and into a larger engagement with the spiritual and material matters of the world. Gemma and Felicity failed because they were unable to achieve a higher level of empathy or "radical love" for the people around them. Roisin and Henny each were able to choose the other—the vulnerable Liam and the blind boy Julio. Each of their stories conclude with the mother telling the child a story. As Henny recounts the story of the Sun who became human proving himself worthy of a princess' love, it becomes clear to the reader—who has heard Henny muse on topics from Ramakrishna to Catholic liberation theology—that the story is about God and a spiritual search. The brief fairy tale manages to sum up all the sound and fury that has come before it. And then the child, wild in his naivete and wise, says, "But you forgot something, Ma." And he asks a question that will stop you cold in your tracks.

It's Cloda, after all of it, who has the last laugh. Howe may be influenced by Beckett in her sensibility and her use of language and form but in terms of her construction of plot it's still Chekhov who rules her roost: that bottle that Cloda cast into the ocean with her despairing cry for help? You better believe it shows back up again and in the most extreme of circumstances: sighted by a boy soldier, thrown from his boat by a blast, floating there in the middle of the ocean, holding the red bottle "though anyone, including himself, would know that a bottle could not hold up an 18-year-old boy in Army gear."

What happens next—to the boy, to the bottle, to the message inside—is perhaps one answer to Julio's haunting final question.

The School of Fears
Rilke's *Notebooks of Malte Laurids Brigge*

BRIAN TEARE

Rainer Maria Rilke published *Die Aufzeichnungen des Malte Laurids Brigge* in 1910, after the rise of the great modern metropolis but before the First World War. Equal parts little poems in prose, journal of a nervous condition, anthology of ghost stories, theory of love, spiritual autobiography, and archive of obscure episodes from European history, Rilke's *Malte* stands grandly at the origins of modernism. Its publication was followed in 1913 by Proust's *Du côté de chez Swann*, in 1915 by Dorothy Richardson's *Pointed Roofs*, and in 1916 by Joyce's *A Portrait of the Artist as a Young Man*. These unprecedented novels preceded the great flood of the twenties, when Proust, Richardson, and Joyce published further installments in their ambitious life projects, and Woolf, Stein, Mann, Toomer, H.D., Kafka, and many others both continued and complicated the legacy of the early modernist novel. Rather incredibly, *Malte* was the earliest of all of these, and the fact that it was written by one of twentieth century Europe's greatest poets raises the interesting question of the relationship between modernism and the poet's novel.

Did the poet's novel exist before modernism? Certainly it did in German literature, though when compared with the much shorter tradition in English, which spans the twentieth and twenty-first centuries, the novels of Goethe and Hölderlin seem rather more bound to novelistic conventions. For when I write "poet's novel," I *might* think of Goethe's semi-autobiographical *Die Leiden des jungen Werthers*, but would I think of *Wilhelm Meisters Lehrjahre*? And though both *Werther* and Hölderlin's paean to Greek ideals, *Hyperion*, employ heightened diction and emphasize their protagonists' subjectivity in ways more typical of the poet's novel than the conventionally plotted *Wilhelm Meisters*, I have to admit: the quality I most associate with reading a poet's novel is the thrill of watching a text find a nonce form fitting its own occasion, an experience that neither Goethe's nor Hölderlin's epistolary novels quite provide.

It just might be that the poet's novel in English is largely a legacy of modernist aesthetic thought and creative practice, and that the textual thrill of which I speak above is essentially a modernist one, borne out of the very qualities Virginia Woolf praises when she describes Joyce's *Portrait of the Artist as a Young Man*:

> It attempts to come closer to life, and to preserve more sincerely and exactly what interests and moves [him] by discarding most of the conventions which are commonly observed by the novelists. Let us record atoms as they call upon the mind in the order in which they fall, let us trace the pattern, however disconnected and incoherent in appearance, which each sight or incident scores upon the consciousness. Let us not take it for granted that life exists more in what is commonly thought big than in what is commonly thought small . . . the problem before the novelist at present, as we suppose it to have been in the past, is to contrive a means of being free to set down what he chooses. (33-35)

Indeed, it strikes me that much of what Woolf singles out for praise in this 1919 essay on "Modern Novels" could also be qualities attributed to many poet's novels from the past one hundred years, from Rilke's 1910 *Malte* to Eileen Myles's 2010 *Inferno*: a) the attempt to come closer to everyday life; b) the discarding of most novelistic conventions; c) the emphasis on sensory and aesthetic patterns within human consciousness; d) the re-evaluation of what is deemed valuable and important; e) the emphasis on creative freedom. "Any method is right, every method is right," Woolf claims, "that expresses what we wish to express" (34). If these are the kinds of freedoms offered by the novel after modernism, it makes sense that poets interested in innovation would sense an analogy between their relationship to poetic tradition and the novelists' relationship to the genre conventions of the novel. By which I mean that for modernist novelists as for poet-novelists, the *idea* of the novel and not necessarily the genre itself makes the search for new forms and methods possible.

• • •

Insofar as *Die Aufzeichnungen* is interested in conventions of plot, it is very simple: Malte Laurids Brigge, a young poet and descendant of Danish nobility whose fortunes seem to have dissipated, has drifted to Paris, where he lives in a shabby furnished room, walks the streets and observes the urban poor, visits the *Bibliothéque Nationale* to do research on his chosen poet, and returns to his room to write much of this down in his notebook. These facts create the present tense of the notebooks, whose opening pages focus quite viscerally on Malte's heightened response to Paris, but as Malte adds to the notebook, he begins to counterpoint the present with increasingly elaborate meditations on his childhood in Denmark as well as pocket chronicles of obscure European history, among other subjects. Malte's notebook allows for a formal logic that is not bound to genre—rather than genre, *Die Aufzeichnungen* relies largely on thematic repetition and analogical linkages between scenes or subjects to carry it forward. So if the notebook's opening pages are saturated with the sights of Paris, and its closing pages are crowded by figures from Malte's past and Europe's forgotten histories, it's not plot but rather a chain of largely figurative associations Malte has followed.

Given its loose affiliations with genre, why call *Die Aufzeichnungen des Malte Laurids Brigge* a novel?[1] In no German or English edition have I seen the subtitle "ein Roman" or "a novel" following the title. *Die Aufzeichnungen* translates as *the sketchbooks* or, more commonly, *the notebooks*, and Rilke in letters written during its composition and after its publication usually calls his text *Die Aufzeichnungen* or, more affectionately, *Malte*. His preference for calling it after its title or title character speaks to how he thought of the book less as generic than as experiential and metonymic. In letters to his wife Clara he either explains what the experience of composing it has taught him, or emphasizes how Malte has become a figure for the lessons he's drawn from writing the text: "The book of Malte, once it is written, will be nothing but the book of this knowledge, exemplified in one for whom it was too tremendous" (157). But my favorite description comes from a letter written to his confidante Lou Andreas-Salomé in May of 1904, a few years after the first Paris experiences from which *Malte* sprang. "The work I am undertaking, to engage my attention by turns," he writes from Rome, "is as follows:"

1. The *Prayers*, which I want to go on with.
2. My new book (whose firm, close-grained prose is like a school and an advance that had to come so as to enable me, sometime later, to write all the others ...)
3. An experiment in drama.
4. Two monographs on:
   The writer: Jens Peter Jacobsen.
   The painter: Ignacio Zuloaga. (*Selected Letters,* 49)

Of these five projects, only two would see completion: his book of prayers, *Das Stunden-Buch*, known in English as *The Book of Hours*, was published the following year; his "new book" of prose would become *Die*

Aufzeichnungen, but it would take another six years to finish. In fact, Rilke's comments are uncannily prescient: the experience of writing it indeed became "a school" whose curriculum would enable him to write the late, great work of the *Duiniser Elegien* and *Die Sonnete an Orpheus*. To the degree that Rilke gets schooled by the writing of *Malte*, Malte himself is schooled by the writing of his notebooks, which borrow extensively from Rilke's own letters detailing his somewhat rootless life in *fin de siècle* Paris. Despite Rilke's words being always ouroboros-like in Malte's mouth, it's best not to think of Malte as Rilke's fictional alter; he's better considered metonymy for Rilke's experience of getting schooled by life.

• • •

The origins of *Die Aufzeichnungen* lie in Rilke's first sojourn in Paris, where he lived from 1902 to 1903. Rilke moved to Paris in August of '02 in order to research and write a monograph on the sculptor Auguste Rodin; he finished the manuscript by December and the book was published in the spring. Rilke found Rodin to be both a model and an ideal, providing him with the most potent example of a successful working artist he had yet encountered. "He is a learner and beginner and spectator and imitator of the Beautiful," Rilke enthused to Andreas-Salomé, "And this way of looking and living is rooted so firmly in him because he acquired it as a craftsman" (*Selected Letters,* 31). Personal interviews with the master and time spent browsing his sculpture garden inspired in Rilke the desire

> to get down to the making of things, not plastic, written things, but *realities* springing from some handcraft. Somehow I too must discover the smallest element, the core of my art, the tangible yet insubstantial technique for expressing all things . . . I do not want to sunder art from life; I want them, somehow and somewhere, to be of one meaning. (36-7)

Rodin's art allowed Rilke to understand that technique could create reality, and that such skill was in fact necessary if art and life were to be made one. And though his work with Rodin went well, Rilke seemed to see Paris as one big hospital full of the ill, the disfigured, and the dying, uncannily like the modern metropolis Walter Benjamin describes in his essay "The Paris of the Second Empire in Baudelaire": "The resistance that modernity offers to the natural productive élan of an individual is out of all proportion to his strength. It is understandable if a person becomes exhausted and takes refuge in death" (104). So while in Rodin's studio Rilke drew strength and inspiration from the example of his craft and dedication to his work, upon returning to the streets Rilke found that the people struck him as "a new kind of animal, for whom misery had fashioned special organs, organs of hunger and dying" (*Selected Letters,* 25). And at night in his rented room with its shabby furniture, he read Baudelaire's *Le Spleen de Paris,* and admired in particular "A une heure du matin": "Horrible life! Horrible city! . . . Annoyed by everyone and annoyed by myself, I'd like to be redeemed and gain a little self-respect in the silence and solitude of the night" (18). So it is from a consciousness split between high idealism and rank abjection that *Die Aufzeichnungen* springs, and much of it reads as though Rilke took Rodin's work ethic and applied it not only to the making of realities but also to the making of terrors.

• • •

Most critics and biographers agree: in 1902 and 1903 in Paris, Rilke experienced a profound psychic crisis whose after-effects would haunt him for the duration of the composition of *Die Aufzeichnungen.* Rilke's letters and Malte himself would agree that this crisis took one form: fear. "I am afraid," Malte writes, "One must take action against fear, once one has come down with it" (7). And though Malte indeed takes action by sitting up all night and writing, the remarkable fact is that this fear does not localize itself as a singular phobia, but rather sinks the city entire in its shadow, endlessly proliferating. Fittingly, *Die Aufzeichnungen* contains, among other things, brilliant catalogues of terrors, and its most virtuosic passages are inspired by neurotic fright, paranoid fantasies, hypochondriacal conjecture, paranormal encounters, and nightmarish hallucinations. In a letter written in July of 1903 after his departure from Paris, Rilke describes to Andreas-Salomé his experience in language that will serve as a model for Malte's notebooks:

> I want to tell you, dear Lou, that Paris was the same sort of experience for me as military school; just as then a great fearful astonishment seized me, so that once again I was attached by the terror of what, in some unspeakable confusion, is called life. Then, as a boy among boys, I was alone among them, and how alone I was now among all these people, how continually denied by all that I encountered! (24)

Whether at the Militär-Unterrealschule at St. Pölten, an experience he considered the low point of his life, or in Paris as an impecunious young adult in his late twenties, or in the six years spent composing the prose that would change his writing forever, the school at which Rilke persists as a perpetual student has one curriculum. But why study fear for so long? Rilke's perennial problem lies not in being alone, but in the constant denial of recognition by others, and in the denial of oneself *inside* others' alleged recognition, denials that result in terror so consuming that it threatens reality's stability. For instance: after experiencing such denials as an adult in the anomie of the Parisian crowds, Malte discovers that "here and there on my blanket, lost feelings out of my childhood lie and are like new" (*Die Aufzeichnungen,* 63). Indeed, as Freudian critic Andreas Huyssen writes in his essay "Paris/Childhood," Rilke's and Malte's Parisian experiences strikingly "suggest . . . connections between early childhood experiences and the disrupting, fragmenting experience of the modern city" (116-17). "All the lost fears are here again," Malte laments in his notebook before beginning an exquisite list of fantastic anxieties in which appearances deceive and the most innocent domestic details conceal imminent disaster:

> The fear that a small woolen thread sticking out of the hem of my blanket may be hard, hard and sharp as a steel needle; the fear that this little button on my night-shirt may be bigger than my head, bigger and heavier; the fear that the breadcrumb which just dropped off my bed may turn into glass, and shatter when it hits the floor, and the sickening worry that when it does, everything will be broken forever . . . (63-64)

At the School of Fears, nothing seems to be what it seems, neither substance, scale, or causal logic: in the same way that a woolen thread may disguise a steel needle, so a shirt button might be bigger than one's head, and a falling breadcrumb cause an apocalypse. Rilke's skillful narration lets us know Malte knows his fears could be unfounded, but it also informs us that he is *physically* convinced of them, as incapable of shaking the sensations of terror as a child waking from a nightmare. "Malte does not see holistically," Huyssen argues, "Rather he perceives fragments, and this bodily fragmentation causes his anxieties . . . of excess, of flowing over, of unstable bodily boundaries" (118). But if School is in session, in what manner are these anxieties pedagogical? Does Malte learn from his fears in the manner that Rilke learned from Rodin to see? Though *Die Aufzeichnungen* is in fact famous for Malte's hopeful declaration, "I am learning to see," it is less famous for the more unsettling sentences that follow:

I don't know why it is, but everything enters me more deeply and doesn't stop where once it used to. I have an interior that I never knew was there. Everything passes into it now. I don't know what happens there. (5)

Not unlike the shirt button that could be bigger and heavier than a child's head, or the breadcrumb that, when dropped, might destroy everything, the "interior" Malte discovers through the effort of learning to see disconcertingly escapes the usual measures of scale and causality. This interior is of unknown dimensions, and what happens there is likewise unknowable. As if that weren't alarming enough, Malte also can't help but take everything personally; his boundaries simultaneously expanded (*everything* enters him) and contracted (everything enters *him*), he experiences continual vertigo and synesthesia. "I can't give up the habit of sleeping with the window open," he writes, "Electric trolleys speed clattering through my room. Cars drive over me" (4). They drive straight into his interior, into the School of Fears where *something* happens. What?

· · ·

In *Eros the Bittersweet*, Anne Carson suggests that not only do reading and writing encourage "a heightened awareness of personal physical boundaries and a sense of those boundaries as the vessel of one's self," but that "To control the boundaries is to possess oneself" (44). If the curriculum is fear, and the problem is one of boundaries, then perhaps one can only learn one's lesson by writing, by possessing oneself in language. Huyssen invites us to read Malte's inaccessible interior as "the intense modernist longing for another kind of language that would . . . correspond to a phase preceding the development of language," and though I am persuaded by the claim that aspects of Malte's psychic organization are inherently historical, I remain as skeptical of this alleged longing for a pre-verbal phase as I do of most traditional Freudian readings of *Die Aufzeichnungen* (126). Biographer Donald Prater points out in *A Ringing Glass* that Rilke may have avoided entering analysis, but his own writing tended to function as a form of self-analysis: "his instinctive feeling . . . was that he must be his own healer" (200). Similarly, language seems in the end to save Malte from what remains too much outside of his conscious awareness. Malte after all begins his notebooks in the hope that writing will fend off his fear: "I have taken action against fear. I sat up all night and wrote" (16). Perhaps the totality of *Die Aufzeichnungen*, the writing of the notebooks, *is* what happens in Malte's interior, *is* The

School of Fear. "And I am still defending myself," Malte writes later, "For the time being I can still write all this down, can still say it" (52). But does writing actually save Malte?

> In spite of my fear, I am still like someone standing in the presence of something great, and I remember when I often used to feel this hap-pening inside me when I was about to write. But this time, I will be written. I am the impression that will transform himself. It would take so little for me to understand all this and assent to it. Just one step, and my misery would turn to bliss. But I can't take that step (53)

Some critics think Malte never takes that step, and describe Malte the character and *Malte* the text as failures, citing the book's second half as par-ticularly disappointing. Huyssen, for example, claims it is "the culmination of a series of evasions of the splits and tensions that tear the protagonist apart," and asserts that while the ending is not "a tragic failure," it nonethe-less "just comes to a dead end" (137). But you can only claim a text a failure if a) you believe it should accomplish something, and b) it fails to accomplish it. Huyssen believes he is reading a novel, as do many other disappointed critics, and I wonder—how deeply are their expectations shaped by *a priori* notions of genre?

If *Die Aufzeichnungen* isn't a novel, and if Rilke wasn't interested in psy-choanalysis proper, then it seems foolhardy to demand that Malte's note-books deliver novelistic and analytic resolution. And yet Malte *does* change, though to describe the internal mechanisms at work over the course of *Die Aufzeichnungen* isn't easy. Upon its publication, Rilke himself wrote, "the present content of the book is by no means complete. It is only as if some-one has come upon a heap of disordered papers in a drawer and had found no more for the moment and had to make do with those" (*Selected Letters* 178). But others might argue that such a description undercuts the persua-sive design of *Die Aufzeichnungen*, seen most clearly in Malte's transforma-tion from midnight fearmonger to rapturous chronicler of the European past and theorist of spiritual experience. Though he begins his notebooks sensing "that his relation to the things around him is blurred and indistinct," critic Eleanor Honig Skoller writes, by the end of *Die Aufzeichnungen*, Malte "suspects some sort of delineating process [has taken] place in his psyche" (15). Indeed, the notebooks *do* seem organized by internal logics and the emotional tenor of the entries alters as we move from Paris into annals of the past, the entirety moving temporally backward, rather than forward, a historical retrogression that paradoxically counterpoints Malte's psycho-

logical progression from a childhood of terrors to an adult state of mind less
dominated by outsized fears.

• • •

Malte graduates from the School of Fears, but how does he do it? In the
same way that Rilke begins *Die Aufzeichnungen* with his own Paris address
of 1902—*rue Toullier*—the end of the notebooks reflects his own life at the
time of their completion. So if the book's last third is relatively calm and reflective, it's not only because "Malte reads and muses on the books and the
episodes from French and Russian history that Rilke absorbed," but also because Rilke finished the book during almost two years fully funded by a patron, and he completed work on the manuscript in January 1910 during two
weeks in residence at his publisher's own house (Prater, 173). His worldly
situation had changed a great deal during those eight years: he had not only
published many of the books that provided him a modest income and so-
lidified his reputation, but also established the relationships that essentially
created an elaborate patronage system that left him free to write without
other employment. And in the same way that "the longest period of *Malte*
did not strike [Rilke] as a decline so much as a strange, darksome ascent
into a remote and deserted part of heaven," so Malte moves from a state of
agitated fear to one of inquisitive and reflective ambition (*Selected Letters*,
185). "But now that so much is changing, isn't it time for us to change?" he
asks midway through his notebooks, "What if we went ahead and became
beginners, now that much is changing?" (135).

At the center of *Die Aufzeichunungen* hang the six sixteenth-century tapestries that make up *La Dame á la licorne*—tableaus Malte describes with
luxurious detail, a care mirroring the five senses upon which the first five
tapestries are named. The entries in Malte's notebook are also a series of
tableaus, variations on themes that gradually transform through repetition:
terror, life, death, art, love, God, and distance. The notebook's major themes
culminate, as the tapestries do, in a single tableau: The Prodigal Son, which
could be read as Malte's version of the sixth tapestry, *À mon seul désir*. Malte
reads *La Dame's* final tapestry as an allegory, "another festival" to which "no
one is invited," and yet "Everything is here. Everything forever" (130). The
tapestries propose an erotic aesthetic in that they're paradoxical, on the one
hand a "chain of signifiers whose movement is fed by desire," and on the other hand a series of images eternally fixed on chase and capture (Skoller, 21).
But Malte proposes a less conventional reading of desire when, for his final
tableau, he rewrites The Prodigal Son as "the legend of the man who did not

want to be loved," who leaves home in search of a "profound indifference of heart" and achieves it in a life of poverty and dedication to God before returning to his family (251). If, as we recall, Rilke "as a boy among boys . . . was alone among them," and was also alone "among all these people" in Paris, and in each case was "continually denied by all that I encountered," then it would in fact be a kind of progress to reverse the power dynamic, to become the one who refuses the chase, who eschews relations that promise love but instead deliver a denial of oneself (*Selected Letters*, 24).

Perhaps critics have had a hard time with Malte's final tableau because it's a valediction that seems to forbid loving, a passionate valentine to the man who refuses the love of those who give it without seeing who he really is. Or perhaps because it begins with Baudelaire's Paris and ends with the Bible, and what kind of teleology is that? But both Malte and Rilke are clear: to be misrecognized at all is terrifying, but to be misrecognized by the ones you love is potentially annihilating. To grow up and graduate from the School of Fears, you have to give up both being badly loved and always wanting to be loved. Of course in doing so, The Prodigal "was now terribly difficult to love," Malte reports, and "felt only One would be capable of it" (260). But it doesn't mean he gave up love entirely. It doesn't mean he gave up on God, though, as Malte writes, "He was not yet willing" to love the Prodigal (ibid). The chase over and all fear subsided, the final tableau depicts the soul's only desire: the patience to endure being a soul.

NOTE

1. One of the few novelistic conventions Rilke draws upon is that of the text having been "found" and "edited," a convention shared with *Werther* and other epistolary fictions. But this aspect of *Die Aufzeichnungen* rests almost entirely on rare signs of an editorial presence, the pretense of an editor only occasionally suggested by the employment of bracketed passages marked by an asterisk that leads to the footnote "Written on the margin of the MS." So though we might then briefly imagine the interpreter who delivered the manuscript to a publisher, any other paratextual evidence of the editor is otherwise absent, leading us back to the text instead of into a rich layer of metafiction.

WORKS CITED

Baudelaire, Charles. *Paris Spleen: Little Poems in Prose*. Trans. Keith Waldrop. Middletown: Wesleyan University Press, 2009.

Benjamin, Walter. *The Writer of Modern Life: Essays on Baudelaire*. Cambridge: Harvard University Press, 2006.

Carson, Anne. *Eros the Bittersweet.* Normal: Dalkey Archive Press, 1998.

Fuerst, Norbert. "Three German Novels of Education III: R. M. Rilke's Malte Laurids Brigge."*Monatshefte*, 38.3 (December 1946): 463-478.

Hillard, Derek. "Rilke and Historical Discourse, or the 'Histories' of Malte Laurids Brigge." *German Studies Review*, 29.2 (May 2006): 299-313.

Huyssen, Andreas. "Paris/Childhood: The Fragmented Body in Rilke's *Notebooks of Malte Laurids Brigge.*" *Modernity and the Text: Revisions of German Modernism.* Eds. Andreas Huyssen and David Bathrick. New York: Columbia University Press, 1989.

Junyk, Ihor. "'A Fragment from Another Context': Modernist Classicism and the Urban Uncanny in Rainer Maria Rilke." *Comparative Literature*, 62.3 (Summer 2010): 262-282.

Kleinbard, David. *The Beginning of Terror: A Psychological Study of Rainer Maria Rilke's Life and Work.* New York: New York University Press, 1993.

Prater, Donald. *A Ringing Glass: The Life of Rainer Maria Rilke.* Oxford: Clarendon Press, 1986.

Rilke, Rainer Maria. *The Notebooks of Malte Laurids Brigge.* Trans. Stephen Mitchell. New York: Random House, 1982.

——. *The Notebooks of Malte Laurids Brigge.* Trans. Burton Pike. Normal: Dalkey Archive Press, 2008.

——. *Selected Letters 1902-1926.* Trans. R.F.C. Hull. London: Quartet Books, 1988.

Skoller, Eleanor Honig. "Threads in Three Sections: A Reading of *The Notebooks of Malte Laurids Brigge.*" *SubStance* 10.3 (Isssue 32, 1981): 15-25.

Woolf, Virginia. "Modern Novels." *The Essays of Virginia Woolf, Volume Three.* Ed. McNeillie, Andrew. New York: Harcourt, Brace and Jovanovich, 1988. 30-37.

IV

Prose Poem /
Concatenation /
Novel Borders

An ambulatory fig tree strolled down a street crowded with seminarians, streetwalkers, and geometry professors—a thousand aging gentlemen, dirty collars, sticky fingers."
—MARTÍN ADÁN, *The Cardboard House*

Impressions of Martín Adán's *The Cardboard House*

MÓNICA DE LA TORRE

The Latin American 20th-avant-garde canon has its share of oddballs and fringe characters, and the Peruvian poet Martín Adán (1908-1985) figures prominently on the list. A consummate bohemian and renegade, he changed his name from the stodgy Rafael de la Fuente Benavides to Martín Adán—the result of pairing a monkey's name (the San Martín titi) with that of the first man—since he aspired to be accepted by all, or so he argued. Not only was his nom de plume more memorable, it had the added benefit of making the aristocratic background he renounced less conspicuous amongst his mentors and peers, who embraced him from the outset upon the publication of his uncategorizable first book, *La casa de cartón* (*The Cardboard House*), in 1928. In the late 1930s and '40s, an orphaned Adán would live alternately in hotels and psychiatric hospitals in Lima into which he would check himself when in need of sanity, since he believed "that the sane [were] in the madhouse and the crazy on the street" (*Entrevistas*, 87-99). After 1960, he essentially lived in a mental institution until his death.

Unconcerned with leaving behind a cohesive body of work, he wrote the majority of his poems on scraps of paper, hotel stationary, napkins, and other disposable printed matter—they would then be devotedly transcribed and compiled by his friend Juan Mejía Baca. Despite these and probably many other eccentricities, Adán became one of Perú's most revered 20th-century poets along with César Vallejo. It was none other than José Carlos Mariátegui, one of Latin America's leading socialist thinkers, who first published excerpts of *The Cardboard House* in the journal *Amauta* in 1926.

No one has seemed particularly perturbed by the fact that the book fails to fit tidily within any particular genre, judging from the favorable critical reception it garnered from the start. However, one cannot help but notice the various ways in which the book has been framed in English- and Spanish-language editions. The back-cover blurb for the 1986 Casa de las Américas edition, for instance, echoes other editions when summarizing *La casa de cartón* as a young man's "reminiscences of a summer break in the Peruvian resort town of Barranco" composed of "his own memories and those harvested by reading the diary of Ramón, his friend, rival, and alter-ego at the time." The book's protagonists are evocatively described as remaining "suspended in the creative discourse of the narrator who is playing demiurge," and, except for the mention of characters, other nomenclature around genre is avoided. In contrast, the flap copy for Katherine Silver's superlative revised translation, published by New Directions in 2012 (while an earlier rendering was put out by Graywolf in 1990), assures readers that they are holding Martín Adán's "only work of fiction."

As one would expect, barring the realm of trade fiction, in Latin America a work's genre is less likely than in the U.S. to determine the type and scale of the economy in which it circulates. Whether *The Cardboard* House is fiction or prose poetry is not a decisive issue; the book's place in the pantheon is secure. Yet regardless of the various exigencies of the continent's different literary cultures, at its core is a resolute probing of conventions. Adán's compact and plotless prose displays indifference toward the consistency of the reminiscences it purportedly delivers. Readers are in the hands of a narrator who cunningly shifts points of view as he rehearses multiple registers, including first and third-person accounts, poetry, extended similes and their deconstructions, and inventories of old loves, as well as of the people and things inhabiting the surroundings. What is more, a heightened awareness of language unexpectedly articulated and occasionally taking neological turns does not complicate *The Cardboard House*'s narrative as much as erect it as the very problematization of genre.

It goes without saying that authors are rarely authorities on their own work, but it is telling that Adán himself, in an interview published in 1981, stoutly denied that *The Cardboard House* was a novel. What follows is an excerpt of the interview, the first he gave in 25 years (those who knew him claim that dialogue was not Adán's forte) and one to which he might have agreed only because of the clout of the team of interlocutors querying him, Mario Vargas Llosa among them:

> Max Hernández: What is the relationship between poetry and your dreams?
> Martín Adán: None, I write awake, fully lucid and attentive to grammatical rules.
> MH: What about the relationship between your poetry and your life?
> MA: None. Life imposes itself on me; poetry, I choose.
> MH: And between your poetry and Peru?
> MA: None.

[...]

Javier Sologuren: Last year *The Cardboard House* turned 50. Rereading it made me wonder about its genre: Is it a novel? If the answer is no, how would you define it?

Martín Adán: It is not a novel. It is a series of impressions of the Barranco I knew as a child. (*Entrevistas*, 60-63)

One need not dig too deep to notice how Adán's laconic exchanges might contradict each other. If *The Cardboard House* is not a novel, then it must be poetry or nonfiction. If Adán's poetry bears no relationship to Peru or the poet's biography, and *The Cardboard House* is made out of his impressions of Barranco, then the book must be a nonfiction one. Yet it isn't one either; there is nothing diaristic about it. The point is not to obfuscate, but to identify the gray area on which *The Cardboard House* stands. The book is indeed divided in thirty-nine distinct vignettes about Barranco, the seaside resort town only a cable-car ride away from Lima where Adán summered with his family during his childhood. Although the novel's narrator convincingly portrays place with the conviction of having experienced it first hand, the luxurious resort town he depicts had been long gone even when Adán visited it in the 1910s. By 1928 Barranco was already becoming a suburb, but it had started to become engulfed by the capital decades before, and nowadays it is one of Lima's historic neighborhoods. So effective is Adán's prose—inspired by an earlier, grander era's vestiges scattered "amongst mansions and hovels," as scholar Mirko Lauer puts it—that it creates the anachronistic illusion of the narrator's actual experience of the Barranco of the Peruvian Belle Époque.

This comes not as a surprise given that Adán signals a healthy dose of disregard for sincerity in *The Cardboard House*: "The truth!—the enthusiasm of a missionary priest, the theme of a frantic cuckold, the worst part of a good book" (29). The work—no less radical because of its elegant and indeed-perfect grammar, given that its experimentation refrains from disrupting normative syntax—trumps linearity and proposes an alternative to the sequence of events as they occur in history. Its temporal unfolding parallels how its focus moves from fragment to fragment associatively, testing the limits of verisimilitude, its connective tissue being memory, which inevitably construes what it can only partially retrieve.

Adán's prose tells no other story than that of its narrator's kaleidoscopic, synesthetic, and superimposed perceptions and desires:

I have gone to the countryside to see the clouds and the alfalfa fields. But I have gone almost at night, and I will no longer be able to smell the scents of the afternoon, tactile scents, that are smelled through the skin. The sky—affiliated with the avant-garde—creates out of its dusty whiteness round, multicolored clouds that at times look like German balls and at others, really, like the clouds of Norah Borges. Now I must smell colors. And the road I take turns into a crossroads. (45)

This narrator is a cultured young man jarringly refined and skeptical of the haute bourgeoisie, cosmopolitan and disdainful of foreigners, vivacious and world-weary, derisive of the adult world and nostalgic for a lost past:

And the sea is one of Salgari's rivers or Loti's shores, or Verne's fantastic ships, and the sea is never glaucous but rather has pale, colorless zones, lined with the tracks of ducks, full of minute coasts and feeble backgrounds. The sea is a soul we once had, that we cannot find, that we barely remember as our own, a soul that is always different along every esplanade. And the sea is never the cold and vigorous one that squeezed us, with estival lust, throughout our childhood and our vacations. The esplanade is full of German shepherds and English nursemaids, a domestic sea, family stories, the great-grandfather was captain of a frigate, or a free-booter in the sea of Antilles, a bearded millionaire. (39)

The prose's only loyalty is to the textual dynamic that it sets in motion, which is characteristically self-reflexive. Taken apart, many of *The Cardboard House*'s components reveal the work's stance on process and genre. Early on, for instance, the speaker says of his friend, which one surmises is the poet Ramón who appears in the next passage and later, out of the blue, will die:

I feared hearing your secrets—always sincere—so, to prevent you from speaking, I recalled out loud a distant afternoon that, like in a joke, was a huge fried egg, an embossed sun of brilliant gold almost on the periphery of the rugged and aqueous porcelain sky, a nutritive afternoon that stained gluttonous poets from their foreheads to their noses with sunset hues. (9)

This is exactly what Adán supplies in *The Cardboard House*: feverish, partially fabricated recollections substituting traditional narration and dialogue in a refusal to put words in the mouths of anyone but the speaker and Ramón. If the latter has a voice, it is heard only in the rapid-fire succession of mostly colloquial yet elliptical first-person statements in his "Underwood Poems"—a single long poem appearing in one of the book's sections which the narrator claims to have found scribbled on the margins of the contents page of one of Ramón's books: "You have a shirt and no great thoughts of any kind. [. . .] I like the colors of the sky because they are definitely not German dyes. [. . .] I have no past and an excess of future."

Denying the reader access to anyone else's consciousness but those of the narrator and Ramón (if rather obliquely) seems consistent with Adán's almost ethical stance on the traditional novel, described later in *The Cardboard House* as a "conflict of hysterias" (25) perhaps since its conventions dictate that it display the construed interiority of fictive characters who in order for there to be a plot must find themselves at odds at times. In contrast, the main protagonist of Adán's book is the narrator's own perception, zooming in and out and tuned so finely to the slightest of multisensory stimuli that its findings often verge on drunken hallucinations. That is, in *The Cardboard House* outside stimuli *appear* to be perceived and not imagined, filtered and processed through the speaker's consciousness, to be returned treated to the realm of shared reality. Hence Adán's prose might be understood as performing the opposite operation to that expected of the traditional novel, which deploys a maximum degree of illusionism in order to create a seamless effect of realism. Adán's prose, on the other hand, distorts reality to the point of rendering it almost implausible, and wears its illusionism on its sleeve: "At six in the morning, at six at evening, the streetlamps are the most vegetable thing in the world, in an analytic, synthetic, scientific, passive, decisive, botanical, simple way—the upper edges of the trunks support crystal jars that hold yellow flowers" (61).

The brief passage in which the remarks on traditional fiction appear features a man who, aboard a ship to Europe, is at work on a novel: "one thousand pages blackened by letters that threatened Manuel's sanity, mad things, shouting, all without motive" (25). This character knows not how he arrives in Paris and then returns to Lima, but the narrator establishes a contrast between both places that seems in keeping too with the *The Cardboard House*'s stance on genre as well: "Manuel awoke, and now it was Paris with its smell of asphalt and its factory sounds and its public pleasures. [. . .] Now it was Lima with its smell of guano and its private pleasures" (26). In this equation, it is as if the economic and cultural machinery supporting the public Parisian spectacle found a literary counterpart in the novel, and in Lima's less-industrialized economy, the matching genre were the less loquacious, more introverted, and perhaps for that reason more unregimented one of poetry.

The dichotomy between the native and the alien is another prominent aspect of the book. The narrator trains a particularly satirical lens on foreigners; depicted with telling broad brushstrokes, they are devoted individual vignettes. In the "Underwood Poems" the following line appears: "The flesh of Yankees is too fresh, almost cold, almost dead" (71). And the cast in the prose includes Herr Oswald Teller, a traveler from Hanover "wearing thick-soled shoes and smelling of leather and disinfectant" who "rented a room full of spiderwebs in Ramón's house" (33) and an Englishman with "a high, thick nose on his long terra-cotta face; below, the mouth of a priest, drawn and still, the lips sunken" who works as a travel agent and idiotically spends hours fishing with a rod, to not even catch "a piece of seaweed with a drop of water on its tail" (13). There is also a somewhat crazy Englishwoman named Annie Doll—one of Ramón's love interests—characterized as a "photophobic gringa photographer," a "sinewy, mobile thing that carries a Kodak over its shoulder and asks questions that are wise, useless, and nonsensical" (19). More than the alliterative charm of her epithet is at stake. There is nothing unconventional about Miss Annie Doll's desire to capture quaint local culture with her portable camera; she is a tourist, after all. As for her photophobia, it might be symptomatic of (particularly American and European) travelers', if not resistance, then obliviousness, to the fact that they too might receive the exoticizing or othering treatment they inflict on those they gaze upon. *The Cardboard House* not only turns the realist novel upside down, it also performs one of the first Peruvian critiques of the Baedeker, and this might be one of the clues to its place in the canon.

Contemporary readers should know that Martín Adán's scorn of foreigners seeking to turn Peru into the backdrop for their experience of authenticity spared no one. In the 1960s Allen Ginsberg made a trip to Peru to try ayahuasca, and poet and translator Jorge Capriata arranged for him to meet with Adán at a local café (11). One would think that between psychoactive infusions and Adán's hallucinatory writing, they might have found a conversation topic, yet Capriata reported that during their brief encounter both poets chose to hurl hostile gibes at each other, occasionally interspersing them with silence.

WORKS CITED

Adán, Martín. *Casa de cartón*. Havana, Cuba: Casa de las Américas, 1986.
The Cardboard House. Katherine Silver, tr. New York: New Directions, 2012.
Entrevistas. Lima, Peru: Fondo Editorial, 2011.

"What Am I to Do with All of This Life"
Gwendolyn Brooks's *Maud Martha*

JULIA BLOCH

When Gwendolyn Brooks's novel *Maud Martha* was published in 1953, it was described in the *New Yorker* as "really not a novel but a series of sketches." Rather than a narrative in the cumulative or progressive sense of the genre, the review suggested, *Maud Martha* was marked by Brooks's signature "impressionistic style—a hopeful piling up of small details to achieve a single effect." That style, the reviewer noted, "is not quite sharp or firm enough to do justice" to Brooks's narrative "gifts"—even if that style, the reviewer conceded, "seldom gets in the way" ("From Poet to Novelist" 15).

To set "style" against "narrative," or to suggest the ways in which style interferes with whatever other strengths a text has, as if "style" were decorative or empty of content, is a popular way to dismiss the poet's novel—or to dismiss poetry in general. The *New Yorker*'s fixation on Brooks's "small details" as a sort of "style" in her novel similarly betrays an assumption about the "smallness" that characterizes *Maud Martha*'s uses of poetic language, particularly its allusive detail. Characterizing detail, especially domestic detail, as "small" is a typical way to dismiss the cultural work of women's literature; as Naomi Schor argues, the detail is "gendered and doubly gendered as feminine" (4).

In Brooks's case the word "style" also functions as a sort of code in the discourse of race and literature at midcentury. "Style" was the term readers used to describe Brooks's early uses of received poetic forms, particularly the sonnet and the ballad; "style" was also the word used to dismiss the shortcomings of her 1949 long poem *Annie Allen*, the work that made Brooks the first African American to win a Pulitzer in any category. With *Annie Allen*, Brooks came to be identified among a number of other U.S. poets writing in the middle of the century who used the long poem to experiment with inductive assemblage, seriality, and cultural critique; even though *Annie Allen* incorporates the sonnets and ballads other modernists rejected ("To break the pentameter, that was the first heave," notes Pound parenthetically in Canto 81), Brooks's poem also draws on the densely allusive practices of H.D.'s *Trilogy* or William Carlos Williams's *Paterson*. And in "The Anniad," the middle section of *Annie Allen* in which Brooks wryly alludes to the formal encodings of heroic genre, punning on Homer or Virgil to elevate her central character to heroic subject, Brooks appears to share the approach H.D. takes in *Helen in Egypt* to set her central figure at the intersection of kinship drama, classical analogy, and psychic quest. Finally, in polyphonic representations of a Chicago increasingly beset by racial and economic tension, *Annie Allen* belongs within a sphere of U.S. long poems that take treatise, argument, or history as their major ambition, turning outward from first-person lyric expression and toward collective critique.

And yet the cultural ambitions of Brooks's midcentury work—including *Annie Allen* and *Maud Martha*, written within four years of each other—have been frequently described as hindered by an overindulgence in "style": the European sonnets and English ballads of *Annie Allen* and the close domestic sphere of *Maud Martha* were seen to assimilate Brooks for a white audience. *Annie Allen* and *Maud Martha* are frequently read as belonging to the first of two major periods in Brooks's literary practice: the first, beginning with her 1945 collection *A Street in Bronzeville*, encompasses a body of work that Haki R. Madhubuti (writing in 1972 as Don L. Lee) described as "strained" within European and English poetic forms, too wedded to "style" at the expense of historical urgency (82). Brooks's second period, inaugurated by her 1967 radicalization at the Black Writers' Conference at Fisk University, characterizes the range of work Brooks herself described as motivated "to write poems that will somehow successfully 'call' [. . .] all black people: black people in taverns, black people in alleys, black people in gutters, schools, offices, factories, prisons, the consulate; I wish to reach black people in pulpits, black people in mines, on farms, on thrones" (*Report* 183). Brooks borrows a crucial term from Amiri Baraka's articulation of the disaporic aims of the Black Arts movement in his poem "SOS": "Calling black people / Calling all black people, man woman child / Wherever you are, calling you, urgent, come in" (218). This second body of Brooks's work, seen as freed from the metrical confinement that conditions or strains otherwise urgent historical content and favoring free verse and more overt political declaration, includes works such as *In the Mecca, Riot,* and *Family Pictures.*

Some readers have compared the formal traditions of Brooks's early work to an internal conflict between strands of identity, a Du Boisian double consciousness: in 1972, Houston Baker describes her work as "composed of 'white' style and 'black' content—two warring ideals in one dark body" (qtd. in Gery 45), and more recently A. Yemisi Jimoh writes that Brooks's early work consists of "two conflicting definitions of African American identity: a prevailing and debilitating European American definition as well as a more self-determined African American definition" (167). The way identity gets intertwined with literary form in writings about Brooks anticipates similar reception of Melvin B. Tolson, whose 1965 work *Harlem Gallery* extends a long deliberation of how "the Great White World / and the Black Bourgeoisie / have shoved the Negro artist into / the white and not-white dichotomy, / the Afroamerican dilemma in the Arts— / the dialectic of / to be or not to be / a Negro" (335). Tolson recalibrates Hamlet's well-worn soliloquy as a question about identity, but this question is always, for Tolson, also about literary form: Tolson metaphorizes "the split identity / of the People's Poet" as a contrast between "the racial ballad in the public domain" and "the private poem in the modern vein" (335).

Contrasting the two periods of Brooks's work has served to contextualize her place within the formal revolutions of the Black Arts movement as well as within a broader discourse around the cultural encodings of poetic form; however, as a number of scholars have argued, readings of Black aesthetics have not always been able to account for the formal heterogeneity within works like *Annie Allen* and *Maud Martha*. In fact, as Evie Shockley points out, Brooks's works in particular have been among those marginalized both from the African American poetic tradition and from histories of the avant garde, and yet both *Annie Allen* and *Maud Martha* illuminate crucial turns in post–World War II Black aesthetics (1, 37).

If the "split identity" of the African American poet is metaphorized by Tolson as a choice between ballad or modernist (free) verse, that identity might also be metaphorized as a choice between the poem and the novel. Although I have been heavily mentioning *Annie Allen* because of its pivotal significance for Brooks's work and because it helps unpack the significance of using "style" to describe *Maud Martha* as a poet's novel, the two works invite comparison. Both are intricately numbered in sequence and follow their heroines from early childhood to later adulthood; both are structured by titles and segments that range from the descriptive to the elliptical; both are built out of "small details" that among other things paint a portrait of postwar Chicago; and both construct a central figure who foregrounds her own competing impulses toward singular self-expression and outward-directed cultural critique.

Maud Martha appears at times as herself as a kind of detail. In the sixth vignette of the novel, Maud Martha, at sixteen, attends a concert at Chicago's Regal Theatre and reflects on fame. "She had never understood how people could parade themselves on a stage like that," Maud Martha thinks; "The applause was quick. But the silence was final, so what was the singer's profit?" (21). The performance having left her feeling cold, Maud Martha articulates an alternative vision for what her own creative efforts might entail:

> To create—a role, a poem, picture, music, a rapture in stone: great. But not for her.
> What she wanted was to donate to the world a good Maud Martha. That was the offering, the bit of art, that could not come from any other.
> She would polish and hone that. (22)

Maud Martha contrasts the experience of assuming a role on stage, creating a painting or a piece of music, or carving a sculpture with the notion of self-cultivation. The way she imagines herself as a "bit of art," "good" rather than "great," renders her literally into an object, a diegetic detail.

The passage might suggest that Maud Martha simply wishes to be "good": a good wife, a good mother, a good keeper of the small kitchenette apartment in the "great gray stone building" she occupies with her husband, Paul (60), a normative female moving dutifully through the various female economies that serve as backdrop for the novel's vignettes: millinery, beauty shop, the home of the white woman who employs her as housekeeper. Arguing with her young husband over his suggestion they take a "stove-heated flat" over one heated by steam, Maud Martha reflects on the demands of femininity, imagining the kind of women who would defer to these conditions:

> Was her attitude unco-operative? Should she be wanting to sacrifice more, for the sake of her man? A procession of pioneer women strode down her imagination; strong women, bold; praiseworthy, faithful, stout-minded; with a stout light beating in the eyes. Women who could stand low temperatures. Women who would toil eminently, to improve the lot of their men. Women who cooked. She thought of herself, dying for her man. It was a beautiful thought. (58-59)

Maud Martha invests a lot of its time in its main character's heteronormative domesticity; here and elsewhere, she worries over what it is to be a good wife, a good mother. But the structures start to break down with the details: when she sees a cockroach in her kitchenette, Maud Martha becomes ever aware of "The sobbings, the frustrations, the small hates, the large and ugly hates, the little pushing-through love, the boredom" (63) of married life.

Maud Martha falls a little out of love when she realizes Paul doesn't seem to like libraries; she resents him when he won't stand up to the racist white box office girl at the theater; she reflects that giving birth feels "as though her whole body were having a bowel movement" (96). As these details accumulate, the novel starts to forge implicit parallels between the racist norms Maud Martha encounters outside the home and the misogynist norms inside it. In "tradition and Maud Martha," the disconnect grows between her desire for intimacy and permanence and the drudgery of her routine of service to her husband:

> What she had wanted was a solid. She had wanted shimmering form; warm, but hard as stone and as difficult to break. She had wanted to found—tradition. She had wanted to shape, for their use, for hers, for his, for little Paulette's, a set of falterless customs. She had wanted stone: here she was, being wife to *him*, salving him, in every way considering and replenishing him[.] (102)

"Solid," "form," "stone": Maud Martha's desired object has moved from the realm of self as art into procreation. But the tradition breaks down and loses its contours—not just its shape, but its very form.

Maud Martha's words on losing the form she had wanted to "found"—to melt and mold—echo "the children of the poor," a poem in *Annie Allen* in which a mother confronts the impossibility of caring for her children by using the vocabulary of abstract form:

> My hand is stuffed with mode, design, device.
> But I lack access to my proper stone.
> And plenitude of plan shall not suffice
> Nor grief nor love shall be enough alone
> To ratify my little halves who bear
> Across an autumn freezing everywhere. (*Blacks* 116)

The mother in *Annie Allen* imagines her hand holding "mode, design, device": the image is tactile without thingness, gesture rather than object. The phrase "proper stone" suggests the mythical philosopher's stone that can turn base metal to gold or can heal illness—or lift from poverty. The mother in "the children of the poor" is unable to "ratify" her diminutive "little halves": the legal rhetoric here suggests validation, but also consent. Brooks's lines suggest a speaker with certain formal tools at her disposal who lacks the one tool that would be of most use: a form that could meet the structural demands of her social bonds.

In *Annie Allen*, the problem of adequate or proper form is held in the speaker's hands; in *Maud Martha*, this problem is first the figure of Maud Martha herself. Metaphorizing herself as a piece of "good" rather than "great" art suggests that Maud Martha goes further than imagining herself to be good at being female, however. Imagining she might "polish and hone" herself, her own "good Maud Martha," and "donate" herself to the world, Maud Martha both makes a claim to the singularity of her subjecthood—"that could not come from any other"—and suggests the way her subjecthood becomes estranged and objectified. A counterpoint to the *New Yorker* review in *Crisis* lauds Brooks's "subtle, close-lipped control over her style" and describes Maud Martha as "a finespun, fractional specimen" (Winslow 16). When Maud Martha tells us she wants not to be "great" but "good," that she will "hone that" quality in herself, she recognizes her own vulnerability to being allegorized, made more than character, made type. And when she later laments that she has lost the solid family "form" she had wanted, she is lamenting that instead of stone, she got this: domestic diminishment.

Detail enables *Maud Martha* to go larger than its story, to become a critique of the forces that would otherwise shape and hone its central figure. Note, for example, Brooks's penetrating invocation of intersectionality when Maud Martha observes that while World War II combat may have ceased, racialized gender norms live on. Her brother Harry has come home from the war, the spring light is coming into the kitchenette, and the spring air coming through the window figure as possibility: "What, *what*, am I to do with all of this life?" (178). Maud Martha's "sharp exhilaration" is interrupted by thoughts of the war's dead and wounded and of the racial climate in the U.S.:

And the Negro press (on whose front pages beamed the usual representations of womanly Beauty, pale and pompadoured) carried the stories of the latest of the Georgia and Mississippi lynchings. (179)

Maud Martha turns away from these thoughts, choosing to focus on the living. "And in the meantime," she thinks, "while people did live they would be grand, would be glorious and brave." This is where Brooks's novel ends, with survival hinging on the style of the details that make up all of a life.

WORKS CITED

Baraka, Amiri. *The LeRoi Jones/Amiri Baraka Reader.* Ed. William J. Harris. New York: Thunder's Mouth Press, 1991. Print.

Brooks, Gwendolyn. *Blacks.* Chicago: Third World Press, 1987. Print.

———. *Maud Martha: A Novel.* Chicago: Third World Press, 1953. Print.

———. *Report from Part One.* Detroit: Broadside Press, 1972. Print.

"From Poet to Novelist." In Wright, *On Gwendolyn Brooks: Reliant Contemplation.* 15. Print.

Gery, John. "Subversive Parody in the Early Poems of Gwendolyn Brooks," *South Central Review,* 16.1 (Spring 1999): 44-56. Print.

Jimoh, A. Yemisi. "Double Consciousness, Modernism, and Womanist Themes in Gwendolyn Brooks's 'The Anniad.'" *MELUS* 23.3 (Autumn 1998): 167-186. Print.

Madhubuti, Haki R. "Gwendolyn Brooks: Beyond the Wordmaker—The Making of an African Poet." In Wright, *On Gwendolyn Brooks: Reliant Contemplation.* 81-96. Print.

Pound, Ezra. *The Cantos of Ezra Pound.* New York: New Directions, 1996. Print.

Schor, Naomi. *Reading in Detail: Aesthetics and the Feminine.* New York: Routledge, 2007. Print.

Shockley, Evie. *Renegade Poetics: Black Aesthetics and Formal Innovation in African American Poetry.* Iowa City: University of Iowa Press, 2011. Print.

Tolson, Melvin B. *"Harlem Gallery" and Other Poems of Melvin B. Tolson.* Ed. Raymond Nelson. Charlottesville and London: University Press of Virginia, 1999. Print.

Winslow, Henry F. "Soft Meditations." in Wright, *On Gwendolyn Brooks: Reliant Contemplation.* 16. Print.

Wright, Stephen Caldwell, ed. *On Gwendolyn Brooks: Reliant Contemplation.* Ann Arbor: University of Michigan Press, 1996. Print.

A Book and Other Fractured Pages
Nicole Brossard's Early Novels

ANGELA CARR

1970 was the year of the October Crisis in Montreal: an escalation of revolutionary activity that reached a crisis following the kidnapping and murder of members of the Quebec government by the FLQ (Front de libération du Québec). In response to the crisis, the Canadian government, under the direction of Pierre Trudeau, famously invoked the War Measures Act, effectively subjecting Quebec to martial law, flooding Montreal's streets with soldiers and creating a state of exception whereby anyone could be arrested without any clear charges being brought against them. Such a drastic punitive response angered political moderates and outraged those who were more radical. For Quebec was, at the time, emerging from the Quiet Revolution (la Revolution Tranquille) with a vision for its liberation through self-government. The imposition of Canadian martial law, the brute police force of the federal state, was not welcome.

In the same year, Nicole Brossard published her first "novel," *Un livre* (soon after, it was translated as *A Book* by Larry Shouldice). Reading this book again today, in the summer of 2013, just one year after protests shook Montreal every night again for months and forced an election, I find myself looking with fresh eyes on the scene that Brossard gives us with *"la foule"*— the crowd—comparing the scenes of *Un livre* to recent marches, grafting similar affects created by current political tension onto my reading of her book. Montreal: characterized by its passion for political liberty and its passion for pleasure. Protest and pleasure combining in whimsical and wildly absurd protests when all the city's citizens gathered after supper on the streets to bang on metal pots together, marching through the streets in spontaneously forming crowds with makeshift percussion instruments from their kitchens, from the very old to the very young: small children clanging away with happy abandon, all calling for the resignation of Quebec's leader, Jean Charest. Bicycles with metal pot lids affixed to the frame, men pushing barbeques through the streets and banging on them ... all of which was captured by Concordia University students and live-streamed every night on what came to be known popularly as the "Casseroles Channel." How strange—how old-fashioned, really—that the word "casseroles" had been adopted to designate pots and pans. People stood on rooftops and banged their pots in unison with all who walked past. If they went out to the theater or for dinner one evening, all were sure to bring a small metal pot lid and a wooden spoon in their purse, in case the banging began, to show solidarity. And yet—this playful surface concealed an alarming situation, a potentially dangerous state of affairs; wasn't it disturbing to observe the velocity at which the affects of outrage and anger spread among even the most politically apathetic Montrealers? Affects spreading like an epidemic, the contagion of the crowd threatening to dissolve in its wake individual opinion. For everyone participated; the protest would start outside everyone's kitchen every night and everyone would be drawn out with domestic implements in hand. It is this embedded, pervasive political context through which I read Brossard's early novels: a later development of the context that shaped her early novels.

There are five letters in "foule" (just as in the English word "crowd")— and thus five characters in *Un livre*: O.R., Dominique, Mathieu, Dominique C., Henri. However, self-reflexively the text explains that rather than denoting people, these character names refer to "variants;" they are open signifiers. Later, the reader is informed that the characters' experience is marginal to that of the experience of the text—that is, to the experience of writing and reading. "Ainsi cette page. Parce que le texte cherche à se concentrer sur lui-même . . . " (Thus this page. Because the text seeks to focus on itself) (47). When Brossard published *Un livre*, she was the author of five books of poetry. Not at first glance conforming to our expectations for a novel, *A Book* is formed of elliptical prose poems, with only the upper part of every page filled with text. The prose narrative is dominated by a questioning of its own scaffolding, an interrogation of conventional novelistic devices and narrative techniques. Rather than set out to write a conventional novel, with *Un livre*, Brossard created a poetic investigation of the novel as such, in what is her earliest experimental novel. Even though the narrative situation of *Un livre* is "discontinuous" from page to page, fragmented and broken, there are consistent narrative elements at play in the book, dominated by the themes of romantic love, writing and political action. The characters come together variously, write manifestos, make love (with gender ambiguity; e.g. Dominique can be a man or woman's name as could O.R.), all against a background of political turmoil. A book that functions as a hybrid-genre work, *Un livre* is at once an open letter, a narrative, an essay, a reflection on the book, a poem, and ultimately: a text that focuses on itself.

Following *Un livre*, Nicole Brossard went on to publish several poem-novels in the 70s, including *Sold Out. Étreinte-Illustration* (translated
as *Turn of a Pang* by Patricia Claxton), *French Kiss. Étreinte/Exploration*
(translated as *French Kiss, Or: A Pang's Progress* by Patricia Claxton). (In
English, these novels were part of a series known as the Blue Books, published by Coach House, with plain blue card stock covers). *Turn of a Pang*,
the second "novel" in this series, develops the political tensions that were
impressionistically conveyed in *Un livre*. In this case, the crisis of the 1970
War Measures Act is juxtaposed with Quebec's Conscription Crisis of 1943
(another moment in history when Quebec's majority was trammeled by
the federal government: in this case, Quebec was the only jurisdiction in
Canada to vote against conscription, and the Canadian government imple-
mented the law against their vote). The parallelism of these two historical
moments of tension, both indicative of a Quebec with a will differing from
that of Canada, a will in discord with that of Canada, bears another level of
reading as well. For Brossard is of the generation whose lived experiences
span these two very different eras in Quebec history, with the long difficult
reign of DuPlessis dividing them. Therefore, although I am not given to biographical readings, Brossard's generation is clearly evoked in the following: "Absolutely describable; the thirsty paper drinks black soaks up fluid
and germinates letters (splash) word for word I we back to the start of the
text recounting with absolute authority the years lived from 1941 to '71."
(*Turn of a Pang*, 61)

However, on the level of content, the narrative in this novel is delivered
impressionistically (if we can say a narrative is delivered at all); temporal
and spatial constraints, even the constraints of character development, are
all secondary to the experience of language and the pleasure contingent on
that experience: "Because wanting one thing means unconditionally sensing the reality of its opposite, and by that very fact formulating an impossible concordance of language to fit what has to emerge as some instance of
pleasure" (63).

Again, as in *A Book*, this novel does not conform to our expectations of a
novel; in fact, in many ways, *Turn of a Pang* is even less like a novel than *A
Book*. Although numbered "chapters" are delineated in *Turn of a Pang*, the
framed page of text that follows each such chapter break draws attention to
its own framing, as though to parody the convention of its framing, display-
ing form itself as "fictional form" crystallizing a sequencing of "real" events
(47). Throughout *Turn of a Pang*, Brossard's language is experimental, impressionistic, fleeting and challenging, as should be the case for poetry, and
as it was in *A Book*. Unlike a standard work of fiction, the text breaks into

stanzas, most often stops near the top of the page, and does not flow from margin to margin or page to page (again, we find a lot of white space on the bottom half of most pages). However, unlike *A Book* where Brossard gestures toward character narratives, there are very few mentions of any character's proper name. Cherry does not take on a name until the middle of the book in *Turn of a Pang*. Here additional graphic features stand out, for example, the faint reproduction of an old photograph depicting an anonymous woman walking along a city street, handwritten graffiti, and other interventions on the level of typography (creative use of underline, of capitals, of punctuation): an attention to the visual experience of reading that is usually associated with poetry, rarely prose.

The third book in this series, *French Kiss*, continues to develop the theme of narrative resistance, which becomes inextricably associated with desire and more specifically with lesbian love; as a result, the political conflicts of *A Book* and associated tensions are replaced with overtly feminist struggles, e.g. against the "symbolic pollution" of patriarchal authority (as represented by the written word). During this period, Brossard was part of a radical feminist movement to re-appropriate women's bodies and language from patriarchal discourse, a movement that implicated the symbolic order of language on every level to the very fundaments of syntax and grammar. Although Brossard was not interested in representing women's struggles in patriarchal terms or with patriarchal authority and syntax, with *French Kiss*, for the first time in Brossard's novels, we encounter characters who express internal dialogue, conflicted feelings and complex desire for each other. Here are characters whose stories are not so marginal to the experience of the text, as Brossard had stipulated in *Un livre*, characters who ask that the reader feel if not *for* them then *with* them (their pleasure), characters who emerge as individuals rather than variants in a crowd, even though the author has not described them in any linear fashion. This book resembles a novel more than the others also on the level of paragraph and page flow (continuous text between the margins and from page to page). However, on the level of syntax and the sentence, Brossard's language in *French Kiss* is resolutely ludic.

The self-reflexivity on the level of form that is displayed in Brossard's early novels place them in a category that defies genre. (As an aside, an interesting note: the word "genre" in French can be used to refer to either "gender" or "genre," and Brossard was certainly resistant to the imperatives associated with both these categories). In all three early novels, devices and elements of fictional narrative are present but only as subjects of inquiry and doubt. Form itself becomes an element of the story, and the medium of inscription—the written word—loses its transparency, its gloss of authority. By calling the frames of narrative conventions and oppressive systems into question, Brossard's novels convey the atmosphere of the 70s in Quebec, a period of tension, elation, rupture and hope. Furthermore, Brossard's early novels evoke the blossoming feminist movement of the period. These three poem-novels—the mythical blue books—convey the spirit of radical revision and expansion that characterized both of these political movements, two movements that profoundly informed Brossard's thought and writing.

WORKS CITED

Brossard, Nicole. *Un livre*. Montreal: Éditions du Jour, 1970.

Brossard, Nicole. *Sold-Out: Étreinte/Illustration*. Montreal: Éditions du Jour, 1973.

Brossard, Nicole. *Turn of a Pang*. Translated by Patricia Claxton. Toronto: Coach House Books, 1976.

Brossard, Nicole. *French-Kiss: Étreinte/Exploration*. Montreal: Éditions du Jour, 1973.

Brossard, Nicole. *The Blue Books*. Translated by Larry Shouldice and Patricia Claxton. Toronto: Coach House Books, 2003.

To Seek Air
Barbara Guest's Inter-layered Fiction

KARLA KELSEY

One of the to-be-loved, loveliest things about Barbara Guest's work is its mystery. A master of lucid prose on art and artists, as witnessed in her writing for *Art News* and her biography of HD, *Herself Defined*, Guest is best known for lyric poetry that outstrips recognizable categories. Her poems interact with us as uncharted experience, rather than as exercise operating within ready classifications of meaning. We might frame this mystery's story in terms of clarity vs. opacity: the content-oriented prose, bell-clear. The poetry a layered experience as visceral as fog-on-skin, as elusive as the source of a bell heard from far out at sea.

It is tempting to want the prolific poet's only novel, *Seeking Air,* to be a book that operates *between* the poles of the clear and the obscure, a normalizing text that will allow us to unlock the secrets of her oeuvre. In a 1992 interview with Mark Hillringhouse published in *APR* Guest said of the book, which she called "my novel and my prose poem:" "I wanted to write a novel. And I think that what was wrong about the novel was that I was trying to write a conventional novel. I was trying to write nonconventional and conventional" (29). The concept of "betweenness" however, is not quite right. "Between" implies a middle ground, a blend, or muted combination. But this isn't the novel's case at all. Rather, at its essence, the novel occupies both ends of the spectrum at the same time, rarely blending in the middle. And so more apt, perhaps, is the thought that *Seeking Air* inter-layers convention with non-convention into a single narrative frame creating less a text that blends modes, than a form for them to exist simultaneously in service of expressing the mysteries of creative consciousness.

• • •

"(I wonder if he had taken my poems away with him.
I could find no smell of it, the poem. I understood"

—FROM *THE TÜRLER LOSSES*

The content of *Seeking Air* is conventional, I suppose, particularly for the 1970s in which it was written. The story is of a couple, the primary narrator a man—Morgan Flew—moody, controlling, and unsolicitous of Miriam, his long-term lover, who is a sophisticated, educated woman, but who also, old-fashioned, defines herself through him. Along with this fairly conventional domestic situation, the book bears multiple hallmarks of novelistic convention. For example, a consistency of setting and objects: the 103 short chapters of the book take place mainly in Manhattan and bear the facticity of place. Morgan's apartment, Guest tells us in her preface to Sun & Moon's 1997 reprint of Black Sparrow's 1978 edition, is modeled on her own apartment in the East 90s where she lived while writing *Seeking Air* as well as *Moscow Mansions* and *The Türler Losses.* The novel also includes moments set in California, the Caribbean, and Long Island.

Physical location, however, is secondary: Guest composes the narrative primarily in the first person as an internal stream of consciousness monologue, voiced by Morgan. As such, the space of the novel is essentially internal. Morgan's central conflict unfolds into a desire for control over not only the people around him, but also over his own psychological states and moods. We witness Morgan from the inside, as he monologues memories, a nervous breakdown, an affair, friendships, work. Miriam and a mysterious internal/external force called "Dark" are the objects he most often obsesses over, and the book ends with a novelistic resolution of sorts: in the final chapter Morgan realizes that Miriam offers a necessary "White" to his "Dark" and the book's last line reads "I think I've found the way."

Of course, convention in novel-writing, as with anything else, relies upon not only *what* a novel does, but *how* the novelist executes the book's work. Many of the stretches of prose detail the anxieties and movements of the story in a direct narrative fashion, matching the conventional domestic content of the novel with conventions in style. In Chapter 2 Morgan monologues towards an absent Miriam. Here is the first of the chapter's three paragraphs:

> The next morning after you had left I was neatening your traces. You do leave behind you an extraordinary disorder. That was what I thought when first I knew you. Now I recognize your assortments. There is a lucidity in your placing of personal objects. On one table the hair pins. On another the powder. Here is a half-eaten pear. In the bathroom the soap has slipped to the floor. A lipstick lies on an ash tray in the middle of the bed. And yet there is "order, clarity, lucidity." And there is a purity in your design, like a Matisse painting of "Studio." It took me a long time to learn this (14).

Through this portrait of interior setting we learn that Miriam is not tidy and does not appear to worry herself over Morgan's space. The hair pins, lipstick, and powder show a stereotypical feminine care towards presentation and beauty. The half-eaten pear and the middle-of-the-bed ash tray suggest light distraction. Of Morgan we learn a desire for order, clarity, lucidity and purity. We learn his affection for—and vocabulary of—fine art, a lens for viewing the world that is essential to Morgan's rather literary and artistic nature.

This description also reaches after the underlying epistemological anxiety of the novel: to what extent can we know another—even an intimate other—given that we have no direct access to their interior mind? What can we deduce from the concrete details that they leave behind? How do we know the extent to which our understanding of another is merely a projection of our own desires? It is no surprise that Miriam, treated by Morgan as an object, makes sense to Morgan as an object of art and we note that Guest follows the novelist's convention of establishing this dynamic early on in the plot through concrete physical details. These epistemological questions, relevant to the particular scenario of *Seeking Air,* are of course also fundamental to the genre's investment in representing interior consciousness, interior states.

At the very same time as the novel operates through literary and domestic convention, Guest's estimation of the unconventional nature of the book rings equally as true. First, there is the mysterious figure of Dark, not so much a central character in the book as a somewhat burdensome, hungry, and destructive force that Morgan must care for, but often also seeks out. While Dark seems to be a tangible experience for Morgan, it remains vague and abstract to us. In one of the rare chapters of the book *not* voiced in first person we see Morgan externally as he interacts with Dark: "He kept picking up his pen, like a painter's brush, laying it down, as a dentist places his tools on the tray. Selects another and begins his digging. He was digging a trench around Dark. Dark was in the center . . ."(119). Here Morgan's interactions with Dark morph from page to canvas to body to land. Such descriptions give us a general sense of Dark's overwhelming, central importance to the text—in fact, we might read the entire book through the lens of Morgan's quest into the mysteries of Dark—but, even as the quest ensues, Dark remains too indeterminate to fit within the clean categories of characterization. Is Dark internal? external? abstract? animal? Is Dark a mood, a state of art-making? All of the above?

A further mark of non-convention is what Guest locates as a second subject in the novel, which operates simultaneously with Morgan's struggles for knowledge and control. This subject constitutes not so much a secondary plot, for it has no rising and falling action, no resolution, no essential cast of characters. Rather, as she describes it in an interview, it is an "account of what happens every day in New York City and about Paris, and what somebody is thinking while looking out the window, and about memory, about the collision of ideas, about coincidence, the brevity of ideas, about time, disorder, flux, etc" ("Interview," 29). Guest presents the collisions, brevities, and disorders of *Seeking Air* in the fashion of a poet, that is to say, they are presented in such a way that enacts and creates collision, rather than simply describes it.

For example, Chapter 47, which begins with an italicized parenthetical *"(The next chapter drew its source from Miriam's fingernails.)"* and proceeds:

Toward dawn waking and finding her hand outstretched upon the coverlet.

Regarding the fingernails. Including the cuticle. Their slenderness and length. Like the Ptolemies. One, the brother of Cleopatra, cut off in his youth. Then the elegance of their curve, the clumsiness of a blunted arch, a buried difficulty somewhere a . . .

Farmers scratching in the ravine there where the finger's lake currents washed across the pavilions as in a village where walk the country girls lake casting everywhere the pine scented air of Sochi. (79)

Such moments illustrate the description Kathleen Fraser gives of the novel in her essay "One Hundred and Three Chapters of Little Times: Collapsed and Transfigured Moments in the Fiction of Barbara Guest." Fraser characterizes the book as a "disrupted narrative text . . . a strikingly innovative fictional model based on discrete units and intervals, strengthened by peculiar juxtapositions that resemble certain Cubist paintings or experimental films in their overlapping planes and abrupt shifts" (241). As Fraser further points out, such passages of disruption and shift accentuate the fragility of the characters' personas in the world. In addition, juxtaposing this Cubist, shifting description of Miriam with the more conventional passage I've quoted from Chapter 2, the epistemological questions of the novel deepen, asking not only what it is we can know of another, but also: to what extent is our knowledge dependent on the way we articulate what it is we understand? Morgan's direct, simple description of the absent Miriam expresses a different texture of knowledge than his Cubist portrait. Finally, Guest privileges neither mode of understanding; rather, she offers the novel as a form for both conventional and unconventional modes of understanding, creating space for the interplay of tensions between them.

• • •

"At home she recorded this event in her DIARY, JOURNAL,LETTERS, and the Sundry Shopping Lists later discovered nestling in the shrubbery outside her workroom."

— FROM *THE TÜRLER LOSSES*

Guest's preface to the book locates sources for Morgan and Miriam in Jonathan Swift's *Diaries* and Dorothy Richardson's early 20th-century stream of consciousness novel *Pilgrimage,* whose 13 volumes follow the life of a woman named Miriam. Guest tells us she uses Richardson's heroine as a model for Miriam. And, to create Morgan, who she describes as "Selfish Morgan, in a Swiftian way, obsessed with himself," Guest funnels Richardson's third-person stream of consciousness technique through his often-diaristic first-person point of view.

Many essays could be written about the aspects of convention and non-convention embodied by such figures as Swift and Richardson, but let us just note that stream of consciousness, itself, is a layering of the conventional and the non-conventional, of the transparent and of the opaque. Virginia Woolf's famous passages championing the technique accentuate the resistance to convention motivating the form, stating that in stream of consciousness writing "the accent falls differently from of old; the moment of importance came not here but there" and that "if a writer were a free man and not a slave . . . if he could base his work upon his own feeling and not upon convention, there would be no plot, no comedy, no tragedy, no love interest or catastrophe in the accepted style . . . "(160).

However, although the impulse towards stream of consciousness arises from a resistance to convention, the narrative technique has, naturally, accrued its own array of conventions. In *Transparent Minds, Narrative Modes for Presenting Consciousness in Fiction,* Dorrit Cohn cites Édouard Dujardin's 1888 *Les lauriers sont coupés* as the first novel based entirely upon interior monologue. She provides a comment by Joyce about the novel to outline the two fundamental conventions of first-person stream of consciousness texts. Joyce muses: "In that book the reader finds himself established, from the first lines, in the thought of the principal personage, and the uninterrupted unrolling of that thought . . . conveys to us what that personage is doing and what is happening to him" (173).

The form's two primary conventions—"the uninterrupted unrolling of thought" and the establishment of the reader "from the first lines" in the thought of the principal narrator—create constraints that exceed, in strictness, those placed upon stream of consciousness texts voiced from other perspectives. Third-person narratives or narratives that employ multiple first-person narrators—for example—employ an "outside" layer that allows the author to take us in and out of the character's minds. First-person interior monologue can make use of no such devices to show us the character from various vantage points. From the *first line* we are in the narrator's head and we must—uninterrupted—stay there. This implies that even the author must stand, invisible, behind the crafted consciousness of her narrator. This is the contract of the form's narrative frame.

Given these conventions, an author such as Guest, building a novel on first-person interior monologue, is quite limited in the ways she can provide a context that creates a believable occasion for the narrator's telling of the story, and also allows a depth for viewing the narrator from multiple perspectives. Narratives of memory do this beautifully because the remembering narrator essentially doubles herself, cuing the occasion for the telling with a simple "I remember," and allowing us to watch the narrator from both inside and outside without breaking the narrative frame. But, in the hands of a writer other than Proust, an entire novel built on first-person interior monologue has need of a wider array. The genres of writing that Cohn cites as precursors to the first-person interior monologue suggest the additional ways a writer of this mode can match this task: confessional literature; diary and epistolary novels; digressive narration; the essay; the prose poem; the dramatic monologue; and the stage monologue (175). In the case of confessional literature, diary, and epistolary novels it is interesting to note that the context is, at essence, writerly, providing not only an occasion for narration, but an occasion for narration that self-consciously deploys the conventions of crafted, written language.

Guest gives many of her chapters the tone and trappings of a diary—Morgan mentions typing on a new typewriter, the size of his handwriting, and, in Chapter 18, he comments on the writing of the previous chapters saying "I really am ashamed of the previous passages. Because in relating them I have used the mannerisms of a foreign correspondent or a third embassy secretary, or at least what I think are their *gestes*" (37). Further, in Chapter 88 our writerly Morgan breaks into a poem, writing "Miriam into Miriam/ Morgan into Miriam/ Water into bottle/ Seed into bread" (159). And, even more to the point, Chapter 48 takes on the letter form, beginning with the address "Miriam," and continuing, on the next line, with "Today, Sunday, I find I can no longer sing 'Ancient of Days.' In fact I can no longer sing more than a few notes of anything. It was the strep throat that did it . . . " (80). In considering these sentences it is remarkable to note how much work the letter form does to contextualize and provide the passage with clarity. The sentence, "Today, Sunday, I find I can no longer sing 'Ancient of Days'" is— by itself—quite mysterious. It might be a line from a poem and suggest a spiritual and metaphorical weight. But, provided with the conventions of letter-writing—set under a salutation and followed by the mundane details of an illness—the sentence becomes simple, clear, literal.

Letter-writing, diary-writing, and trips down memory lane provide useful conventions for expanding the territory inside the narrator's head, but the greater challenges of the first-person interior monologue come to the fore when the narrator gives to us present-tense moments, or ranges of experience that are not based in language—what, in the words of Joyce, the narrator "*is* doing and what *is* happening to him"(173). Because we are alone inside the narrator's head without an authorial presence or third-person narrator to step in and frame these moments, the reader gets plunged into the image, syntax, and style of immediacy and feeling without mediation. In many ways, such present-tense sensation is quintessentially a poet's territory. For example, in Chapter 31, which takes place while the couple vacations in the Caribbean, Guest enters the plunge beautifully, lyrically, creating impressionistic vibrations of consciousness. I quote the chapter in its entirety:

> Dark, indeed, must always have been mixed with that planter's crop of dream and isolation. Surrounded by sea and palm. With the shaded house. The women in the house sequestered, the migraines with their raging heat and darkness. What was it like there on the land, the black astuteness hiding there numbly? Screens and birds. Rain. Looking at that planter's chaise in the department store, the chaise with its dark leather cushions and oiled wood. The evenings . . . (56).

Because in other, narrative chapters Morgan shows himself to be so very literary and sensitive to the aesthetic nature of the world it is easy for us to believe that these images and sensations take place inside of Morgan's head, and that we are there, witnessing the turnings of consciousness that occur between the fixities of narration. In moments such as these, through the poetic techniques of fragmentation, association, and sharp cuts between interior and exterior imagery, Guest creates a powerful atmosphere that—even absent the conventions of narrative—continues the "uninterrupted rolling" of the narrator's thought, maintaining the boundaries of the narrative frame.

• • •

"Words
   after all
are syllables *just*
and you put them
  in their place"

—"PASSAGE," *MOSCOW MANSIONS*

It is essential to note that while shifts from narrative mode into the lyric genre of the prose poem draw us more deeply into the interior of the narrator's mind, the novel contains several highly unconventional shifts in genre that send us in the opposite direction. In such chapters we are sent away from the inner regions of Morgan's consciousness, out into the world of artifice and text. The most dramatic generic shift occurs in Chapter 99, when the couple is in Long Island with friends. The chapter spans a single page and is formatted as a play written in faux-Shakespearian diction. The chapter is typeset in italics and bears the parenthetical *(Act the first)* and opens with the following:

> *Miriam: Noble one whence go we hence?*
> *Morgan: Yon ship repaireth to our harbour and methinks there if fortune*
>   *kindly nod, its Captain shall heed our request and bed us board.*
> *M: Certain art thou 'tis a friendly bark?*
> *M: As certain as Sirius, the Dog Star, rises that brings the heat at noon.*
>   (174)

The dialogue proceeds down the page and ends with the "M" that is Miriam proclaiming, "*And thou to whom I now appear like Imogen, newly drest and garbed with faithful rubies, to thee I pledge whatever place to which we hie, my soul shall constant be.*"

On one hand, although the highly stylized language is a far cry from Morgan's quotidian language, we might read this chapter as quintessentially Morgan: Morgan performing for himself (for us?) on the page of his journal or inside of his mind. Of course, we might think, rolling our eyes, Morgan ("Selfish Morgan, in a Swiftian way, obsessed with himself") apes the diction of Shakespeare and has his lady Miriam pledge to him her faith and rubies. In this way the text could be read as an extension of Morgan's interior consciousness, pushing the narrative frame into the genre of Shakespearian drama to include this little one-act play. While the break into this dramatic genre is unconventional, such an interpretation leaves the conventions of the first-person interior monologue intact.

On the other hand, by typesetting the passage in italics as a dramatic text, Guest draws our attention to the materiality of the words in front of us. Even if we are happy to imagine the scene taking place in Morgan's mind, the fact that we are reading an intentionally typeset text commands our attention. In the artificiality of this moment, should we read Guest's "hand" in the frame? If so, we must admit that here Guest breaks the rules of the game that, by convention, require the author to remain hidden behind her narrator. Remarkably, Guest refuses to privilege one interpretation over another, creating a moment that simultaneously offers both absorption into Morgan's inner states *and* insight into the constructed nature of written personae.

Such frame-shifting also happens on the level of textual material itself. As a visual collagist will place an advertisement next to a shopping list, Guest inserts written material that exists, in "real life," independently of her novel, into the text. Most often the material is inserted without comment and includes a range of text—from quotations taken from Goethe, Poe, and Alexander Blok to a 1920s cookbook—*A Thousand Ways to Please a Husband*—and an annual report from the Occidental Petroleum Corporation. Much of this material feels like text Morgan would be drawn to—perhaps as research into Dark—and we can imagine that the novel is working much like a commonplace book, with quotations and cuttings copied or pasted in. But we might also read the additions as traces of the author, extending the text beyond the natural break of a narrative frame into the documents of the nonfictional world. If we think of the novel as a model of interior consciousness, does this imply that the texts around us constitute, in significant measure, our consciousness? Is Guest slyly proposing that Morgan, who tries so very hard to affect impermeability, is part-Poe, part-Petroleum Report?

Less obvious than these shifts in genre and material, but perhaps the more significant, are shifts in point of view that take place in 11 of the book's chapters. Chapter 46 is voiced entirely by Miriam, and the third person is used in 10 other chapters of the novel. These third-person narratives are most often focalized through Morgan, but, at times, focalize through Miriam or through both of the characters. Chapters 76 and 103 include both first and third-person perspectives. Due to such shifts all 11 chapters break the conventions of establishing the reader "from the first lines" in the thoughts of the principle narrator and interrupt the "unrolling of" his thought.

However, there is a way of interpreting these shifts that leaves the conventions of first-person interior monologue intact. Given that Morgan is a writerly narrator, we might propose that when the book moves into third person, Morgan is simply referring to himself as a character. When the novel shifts to Miriam's "I" we might suspect that it is not Miriam who speaks to us, but Morgan, imagining that he is her—co-opting her voice. This interpretation not only keeps the conventions in their places and the narrative frame intact, but it deepens our sense of Morgan's solipsism (my writing of Miriam is just as much Miriam as Miriam's), our feeling that everything the novel touches has been controlled and mediated by Morgan.

In another interpretation, however, we might just as easily propose that by shifting point of view Guest has, for a moment, freed us from Morgan's mind. This interpretation acknowledges the violation of the two primary conventions, breaking the narrative frame. Morgan's agency in this reading is not primary, despite his desperate attempts at control. Such an interpretation might propose that while what we think and know of ourselves and the world is fundamentally an interior game, we have roughly 11 chapters to the book-of-ourselves that open out into a different, mysterious epistemology created by unmediated connections with others.

•   •   •

"There is the mysterious
traveling that one does outside
the cube and this takes place
in air."

—FROM "ROSES," *MOSCOW MANSIONS*

In an essay titled "Shifting Persona," Guest says of Jane Austen's characters that "They are persons who are capable in their minds, even in an obtuse mind, of looking outside themselves into another place, of shifting their persons. They are relieved of ordained claustrophobia, as is the reader, who might be stuck in the drawing room, who is lifted by the author's inked quill, her euphemism for time, to project beyond singularity"(*Forces of Imagination,* 38). Such projecting beyond singularity, such interior/exterior capability, is what *Seeking Air* achieves in virtue of its inclusion of extremes. As absorbing as it is to linger in Morgan's mind, the novel's layering of opposing modes draws our attention to the materiality of the novel—to the fact that it is a work of fiction, of artifice, of written language, and *not* simply a window into someone named Morgan's mind, as the conventions of the narrative frame would have us believe. This inter-layering constitutes a gesture of opening, affording readers access to ambiguities, opacities, and unresolvable questions—access to the very mysteries that catalyze art into being.

WORKS CITED

Cohn, Dorrit. *Transparent Minds: Narrative Modes for Presenting Consciousness in Fiction.* Princeton: Princeton University Press, 1978.

Fraser, Kathleen. "One Hundred and Three Chapters of Little Times: Collapsed and Transfigured Moments in the Fiction of Barbara Guest." from *Breaking the Sequence: Women's Experimental Fiction.* Ed. Ellen G. Friedman and Miriam Fuchs. Princeton: Princeton University Press, 1989. pp. 240-249.

Guest, Barbara. *Collected Poems.* Ed. Hadley Haden Guest. Middletown: Wesleyan University Press, 2008.

——. *Forces of Imagination: Writing on Writing.* Berkeley: Kelsey St. Press, 2003.

——. *Seeking Air.* Los Angeles: Sun & Moon Press, 1997.

Guest, Barbara and Hillringhouse, Mark. "Barbara Guest: An Interview by Mark Hillringhouse." *The American Poetry Review,* Vol. 21, No. 4 (July/August 1992), pp. 23-30.

Woolf, Virginia. "Modern Fiction" from *The Essays of Virginia Woolf.* Volume 4: 1925 to 1928. Ed. Andrew McNeille. London: The Hogarth Press, 1984, pp. 157-169.

Carnal Knowledge
Carla Harryman's *Gardener of Stars*: A Novel

LEE ANN BROWN

A leonine brow
pads summerly up to
Carla Knowledge

Early in my encounters with Carla Harryman's work, I wrote this strange haiku-like fragment around my desire to approach and understand her multi-generic writing practice, at once deeply cerebral and viscerally moving.

I wondered why a poet would want to write a novel. What tools would become available in this way that would not normally be accessible? Could there be writing which accesses the strengths and permissions of poetry, at the same time making worlds unfold in forward momentum?

The "leonine brow" is of course, a pun on my name, as a feeling and thinking human animal / reader who craves fulfillment of both body (Carnal) and mind (Knowledge). That is the kind of work I wanted to approach. When people would criticize "language centered" poetry as being disconnected from the body, or sexuality, I would pull out the example of Harryman's multi-genre book *Animal Instincts* to prove this generalization simply wasn't true. The very titles of her fractal-like books prove that critique wrong. Many of Harryman's titles contain two words which are opposites. This deliberate doubling aims high and low. *Animal Instincts* is both sharp and sweet. Her title *There Never Was a Rose Without a Thorn* is both earthy and celestial. *Gardener of Stars* manifests that walk along the edges of narrative and poesis falling and roiling into the abysses of excess and pleasures of that dialectic throughout. The work is once viscerally accessible:

> "Prometha pulled down her ripped-in-the-crotch pants, opened his pants with her sweet hand, and sat on him with an indulgent calm until each suffered the greatest ecstasies of pleasure"

and syntactically visionary:

"Girl she screamed as if she were screaming for the person she could no longer be."

I first encountered Harryman's work in the late 80's during the latter part of college. I was a member of a pack of young women writers hungry for new forms. We were curious about reading beyond what was assigned in our classes. We were hunting for linguistically innovative and radical poetry. We were studying semiotics, feminist theory and poetry, and in hot pursuit of examples of the poetry that would manifest some of the linguistic exploration suggested by French feminist theory. We sought writing and syntax that resembled our ways of thinking. We were fascinated by Luce Irigaray's theoretical writing which spoke of the multiplicitous and non-linear, and the fact that the theory embodied the very principles it sought to illustrate. What we didn't understand was why theorists such as Kristeva only provided male-authored exemplars such as Joyce's *Ulysses,* and we were especially searching for women writers who practiced these experimental trajectories.

As extracurricular research we started reading the so-called 'language poets.' We discovered Stein through their lenses. We had not encountered any of this literature in coursework in English, American literature classes, creative writing or women's studies courses. It was a Utopian moment for me—one of the first times I united with others in search of knowledge that had not been provided to us in school. We found utopias and dystopias and heterotopias such as Monique Wittig's *Les Guérillères.* This was the era of Donna Haraway's Cyborg manifesto, Kathy Acker's massively multi-referential mash-ups, Monique Wittig and her island of radical text: *Les Guérillères* which used a split non-monumental "J/e" instead of "I." We read Angela Carter's "rewired" fairy tales, Nicole Brossard's *Mauve Desert.* We read Djuna Barnes's *Nightwood* with its lush tribadism. Is *Gardener of Stars* a Cyber-Nightwood after the end of the world as we know it? Is this how thinking in language could be if the novel is reinvented by a poet? Octavia Butler's *Parable of the Sower* actually has poems at its heart alternating with "clear style" narrative. But here in *Gardner of Stars* even the prose is intensely poetic:

Are the curses licking you on the breast plate.
Or the mind, since you are gone.
Left with sweet salt.
Without company. Wandering. Is it me or you?

Harryman's practice traverses an ambitious landscape. She engages with and transforms a wide range of genres melding poetry, prose, theory, essay and experience-based writing. She does this as Stein does without sounding like Stein. Not only does her writing explode the limitations of genre, her work serves as a HINGE between the almost opposite vectors of "language-centered" writing and strategies of new narrative where frank language and explicit description combine to compel personal narrative forward. Harryman takes these permissions and runs with them. There are markers in her book that parallel her own experience (having a male child for example) but totally transformed and wild.

I recall (and paraphrase from my notes) a talk Dodie Bellamy gave on Kathy Acker in which she said that reading and thinking about Kathy Acker is always profound, the way she fucks rationality and always returns to the body, and that having to translate all this into a conventional essay is torturous. Harryman's work is in dialogue with Acker in its interest in radical, transgressive collage, as well as the exploration and explosion of the novel form.

Gardener of Stars functions in multiple genres. The novel is imagination in action. This impulse can be called utopian, even if not ideal; in reality things change by disappearing and dissolving. In a novel things change (happen) over the course of the book and you can always re-inhabit the world at any point in the story—but you are a different person then.

Gardner of Stars defines the embodiment of the poet's novel. The book makes a world that the reader can drop into—be fully immersed in—that makes "sense" within itself. The book immediately plunges the reader into a shifting medley of connected landscapes and atmospheres that are highly unsettling in their mise en scène. If this book were a film I imagine an alternately lush and barren Mad Max post-apocalyptic atmosphere conjured non-linearly with intercuts of poetic fragments interrupting the more linear "recognizable "scenes." Poetic fragments function as reordered genetic code, pantoum-like permutations splice through narrative space, as utopian architectures of dream.

This flow, flowering and reinvention of genre spans Harryman's career. The text is full of openings, a falling of clear exegesis and story that resolves / revolves to a chapter or section ending ("I haven't seen a car since they were outlawed"). Associational, hallucinatory, dreamlike yet somehow very clear images and descriptions are of a reality never encountered or seen before. Here's an imaginal utopia, palpable in its sensory detail—then we turn the page and fall into the canyon of a poem which interrupts the landscape of the book as no normative novel ever did before.

Gardener of Stars was published as the tenth book in a projected fifty volume project by Lyn Hejinian and Travis Ortiz's ATELOS whose mission is described as being "devoted to publishing, under the sign of poetry, writing that challenges the conventional definitions of poetry, since such definitions have tended to isolate poetry from intellectual life, arrest its development, and curtail its impact." *Gardener of Stars* is presented "under the sign of poetry" yet labeled "a novel." This calls to mind other contemporaneous works such as *Pamela: A Novel* by Pamela Lu, (published as Atelos #4) and Sianne Ngai's work, *My Novel*. The fact that these books are *labeled* "novels" implies that the writer wants them to be read through that lens even though the works may not be immediately recognizable as fiction.

One of the first clues I received about how to approach the book is in the dedication. In *Gardener of Stars* the dedication reads: "in memorium: Warren Sonbert." Having seen this master experimental filmmaker's streaming associational images or rather images that stretch the bounds of free association, I knew to let the reading experience wash over and through me without having to understand each logical piece as it unfolded.

Ron Silliman's essay *The New Sentence* is illuminating as to why much of this postmodern 'language' poetry was in prose and used the sentence as a basic unit of composition. Stein's book *How to Write* (with Stein's posit "A sentence is not emotional a paragraph is") as well as her essays at once make clear in-depth observations on the intimate relationship of "Poetry & Grammar." An understanding of these innovations are essential to numerous manifestations of a "poet's novel."

Gardener of Stars engages in both the "clear-style" sentence-based narrative mode and the disjunctive poetic mode, creating a dialogue between them. This alternating mode of poetry and prose is also present in Harryman's collaborative book with Lyn Hejinian *The Wide Road* which takes its name from (and as converse of) Bashō's *The Narrow Road to the Deep Interior* and alternates prose diary entries with haikus and tankas that grow out of the specific contexts described.

In thinking towards a definition of the poets' novel, I take Harryman's *Gardener of Stars* to be a landmark exemplar of the possibilities of that form. This kind of sensory, mental, bodily integrated, utopian and dystopian mode is at the heart of Carla's practice. It did take me a while to inhabit the world of *Gardener of Stars*—but rereading it now is like opening a portal into a strange yet familiar, always surprising world. One of the most remarkable things about the work is that it's one of those books that after you live with it a little while, things from the book uncannily begin to appear. As the book unfolded it powerfully illustrated the complex and sometimes abject situations that struggles for "love" and power can illicit.

Are you going to hold me to my words? asked Gardener.

I haven't decided yet, said M.

Because I was talking about my thoughts said Gardener, not what you can see.

If I could see your thoughts said M.

We would be having the same ones.

M and Gardener are both female: M is characterized as younger, Gardener as older and more experienced, but sometimes they seem to be two halves of one self or manifestations of Self and Other navigating "the paradise and wasteland of utopian desire." There is a power play of fantastic proportion that erupts in glyphs such as Gardner "saying" of M, "I want to enslave myself to M the way she wraps herself around him."

This results in a radical reformation of character and subjectivity itself in a landscape where things definitely "happen" but are also strangely permutational.

Later in the book, after "Gardener" has a baby named Caesar the sentence "Everybody was his mother" recurs in various permutations. The name "Caesar" for the male baby references "sees her" and "seize her" as well as an imperious male presence.

Being immersed in the strange new word world Harryman creates in *Gardener of Stars* I began to hear it everywhere. A New York Times article entitled "The Art at the End of the World: A pilgrimage (with children) to see ''Spiral Jetty,'' Robert Smithson's profound testament to catastrophe" read to me as if it could have been a part of Harryman's book with its inclusion of stark poetic language and poetic child-song:

The littler crow stared out the window and sang a soothing song to itself, the lyrics of which consisted of one repeated sentence:

No people.
No people.
No people.
No people.

I am especially excited by the fact that Carla Harryman is now collaborating with performers and musicians to perform *Gardener of Stars* as Opera, furthering the performative mode of the work and engaging her expanded practice of poets theater to the poet's novel form.

WORKS CITED

Barnes, Djuna. *Nightwood*. London: Faber & Faber, 1936.

Harryman, Carla. *Gardener of Stars*. Berkeley, California: Atelos Books, 2001.

Silliman, Ron. "The New Sentence" *The New Sentence*. New York City: Roof Books, 1987.

Stein, Gertrude, "Poetry & Grammar," in *Lectures in America*, (Boston: Beacon Press, 1935)

Wittig, Monique. *Les Guérillères*, 1969 in France and in 1971 in English.

Rereading Emmanuel Hocquard's
AEREA dans les fôrets de Manhattan[1]

AEREA IN THE FORESTS OF MANHATTAN, TR. LYDIA DAVIS[2]

NORMA COLE

une . nue

—EMMANUEL HOCQUARD, *ALBUM D'IMAGES DE LA VILLA HARRIS*[3]

a formal type of work[4]

—EMMANUEL HOCQUARD, *FROM AN INTERVIEW WITH SERGE GAVRONSKY*

Dear Stacy,

In the airport, at the gate, very early for the flight leaving Philadelphia to come home to San Francisco. Leaving Philly, where I saw Jena and Laynie. We spoke about you, missing you.

I'm reading, in Hélène Cixous's *Ex-Cities*[5], the introduction by Eric Prenowitz, where he gives a brief yet thorough account of her bio. I'm reflecting just now about the relationship(s) between biography and fiction because of the anthology Laynie is editing, about poets who write novels, poets who also have written a novel. Laynie has just written a novel herself—she's in New York this weekend for her book party.

I am writing, or will be writing about Emmanuel Hocquard's *AEREA*, imagining I need to think more about this palindrome, how it must parallel the text in terms of... characters? narrative? setting, which proliferates and becomes characters? Ah, grammar. AER, air.[6] What, if anything, does this "AER" have to do with *AEREA*? Is it true that more literal means more abstract?

Dear Stacy,

I'm rereading the book as if in a dream, as though haunted by past readings, or rather feelings; at the same time, as though never having read these words before even though recognizing every sentence in its order. Surprised and not, I pluck from the pages of the book a photo I took of Emmanuel Hocquard in my sunroom or living room when he came to visit in 1986 or '87, not much in the room, a wicker armchair, a small table beyond it—I'd just moved into the house. Sitting in the wicker chair, he looks directly at the camera or at me, his right hand on his forehead, unsmiling, "time frozen in space." [7]

"Imagine, reader, Ulysses far away from his own people . . . ."[8] Ulysses. Not Odysseus, the Greek name, but Latin for the character from ancient Greek literature.

Dear Stacy,

Remember how he's reading Lucretius? I mean, all the time? Emmanuel once asked me how that book, *De Rerum Natura*, was translated into English. I said, *"On the Nature of Things."* He snorted and said something in French like "you can't be serious!" When I got home to SF, I xeroxed the cover and sent it. That was of course before you could go online and just send the link.

Emmanuel Hocquard, who writes in poetry, in prose or in between, thinks about the fiction of grammar, works on it. Doesn't need or use "genre" as his port of call. Reads Wittgenstein, Reznikoff and Chandler, as in Raymond[9]. Always trying to get closer to literality, word = thing, tautology. "The world is a collection of letters."[10]

There's a paragraph, a close-up, near the end of *AEREA*, where Hocquard communicates in detail the movement of the fishing line, the fish, the water, the air, the lava rock, "a business concluded by death," where the literal transforms abruptly into metaphor, as Francis Ponge's *Savon* (*Soap*),[11] begun in 1942 but not completed until 1965. This pivotal work, in its literality veers with its/his address to the French, to the Germans—during WW2, when Germany had marched into France and taken over—becomes at once metaphor and metonymy. And yet, "The sound of the leaves is just the sound of the leaves."[12]

As the photo of the Lucas Cranach painting of "Eve tempted by the serpent," on the covers of both French and American versions, means all the words in the book. "Night has fallen on the trees and on the great plains of the middle of the world. As I listened to the ice cubes clink in my glass, I admire the delicate nudity of my smooth-bodied companion, Eve by Cranach the Younger."[13] On the back cover of the P.O.L 1985 edition, C 1350 is given as the date for that painting, whereas on the back cover of the Lydia Davis translation, published in 1992 by The Marlboro Press, the dates for Lucas Cranach the Elder are 1472-1553. Younger, older, the thirteen hundreds or fifteen hundreds, disparities abound. What is literal?

Dear Stacy,

I am writing about Emmanuel Hocquard, whom we both adore and love to think about, about whom we say to one another the next time we're both in Paris we'll make a plan, rent a car, drive south and west to the Pyrénées, find that farmhouse where he's living with Juliette Valéry. I'm writing about Emmanuel Hocquard and "the novel." And other things.

Along with these musings I'm also thinking about how early in my writing life I knew writing a novel wouldn't work for me because I believed it would have to skate too close to reality, too familiar and familial. And now, suddenly, coming up to map's edge, finding purpose in remembrance of things that happened, sliding horizontally into the mental landscape like rocks on a platter,[14] "To be at the same time somewhere and nowhere."[15]

In his interview with Henri Deluy,[16] Emmanuel Hocquard speaks about how, from the time of his editing (and making with his own hands, i.e. type-setting etc.), with Raquel, the Orange Export series, from 1969 to 1986, he did not see himself as "part of a generation" or his writing and the writing of others as one genre or another, "poetry" for instance, but as writing: writing as an instrument, a tool for experimentation, to push against the rules of the game. No interest in boundaries. Erasing the circumscription between prose and verse; liminal.

AEREA reads rhythmically but lines up as normative prose in narrative or quasi-narrative little sections, with tiny line drawings or icons between the sections (like these asterisks, but small trees, apples). No lines of verse. A "broken series."

Dear Stacy,

I'm sitting at a table in Café Fiore, where Samantha and Yedda just came in to have a belated birthday lunch for Yedda; all the May birthdays, hers, Michael's, yours, mine. When they came in, I was reading a piece by Youssef Ishaghpour in his *Archéologie du cinema et mémoire du siècle*,[17] mostly an interview with Jean-Luc Godard, but at the end, his fine text called "J-L G cinéaste de la vie moderne: Le poétique dans l'historique," a significant reference to Baudelaire's famous "The Painter of Modern Life."

I have come to think of *AEREA* as a suite of scenes, vignettes instead of *récits*. Actually, Emmanuel Hocquard makes a shift over time from thinking of *récit*, that elusive French genre, as narrative prose (I'm thinking here of his "Il rien,"[18] where he writes about Treasure Island as a *récit*, and there is nothing more narrative than that novel) to a paratactic form, with no chronology, no causality[19]—montage, in fact. Emmanuel Hocquard doesn't care or want to think about genre(s). Unless of course he's writing a grammar. He and his sometime collaborators, for example Juliette Valéry, and Alexandre Delay, work in video, photo/text, sculpture/text, architexture, installations et cetera.

Take *Allo Freddy?*[20] for instance, in which the first half of the book is pages of blank frames or windows with bits of narrative or dialogue in them; the second half, photographs, kind of helter-skelter on the page. You don't have to but the movement of the narrative tells you to find the photo that "goes with" a particular frame with the bit of text in it. It's a fictional piece, a "noir" mystery with characters, but with real people in the photographs, including or two I could swear are Emmanuel seen from behind, his hair, the trench coat, the set of his shoulders, etc.

I always relate *Allo Freddy?* to Godard's *Lettre à Freddy Buache: à propos d'un film court-métrage sur la ville de Lausanne.*[21] There is no quick association between the two, besides having the same name in the title, but there are many deep and pertinent affinities between Hocquard and Godard, as in the foregrounding of the address. Godard's *"Lettre"* begins with an address (in remembrance of) to Robert Flaherty and Ernst Lubitsch. I knew Lubitsch but had to look up the other guy. Robert Flaherty (1884-1951) was an American filmmaker who directed and produced the first commercially successful feature length documentary film, "Nanook of the North" (1922). I knew that title, may have even seen it way in the past, in Canada. Flaherty is the one who pioneered ethnofiction and ethnographic film. In other words, his work was the wellspring from which the ethnographic film work of Jean Rouche *et al* began. And then Godard, who, addressing Freddy and everyone else ("Dear Reader," as Emmanuel Hocquard is wont to say; he addresses texts to Claude, Olivier, Juliette, Oscarine, Norma, Paul, Alexandre and others; his *Grammaire de Tanger* to Juliette de Laroque, his daughter), by detours, points out the signs, the signatures that figure into his vast undertaking, Bonnard, Picasso, Wittgenstein, Baudelaire to name just a few in the first pages of the unpaginated *Lettre*.

Godard is looking at, bringing into focus, things "scientifiquement," trying to find rhythms in movements of the crowd; finding the origins of "fiction" because the city is a fiction. The sky (blue) and the forest (green) become the *"roman,"* the novel, which becomes abstraction. Godard states, "C'est juste une note d'intention. Ça ne fait pas une mélodie. Mais Rome n'est pas faite en un jour." ("It's just a note of intention. That doesn't make a melody. But Rome wasn't built in a day.") The first showing of the film that was to celebrate the 500 years of Lausanne's founding was at the Swiss cinématèque, 19 October 1981, but the book about its making came out in 2001. No one liked the film.

Unlike *récit*, something called *la dérive* comes into focus, detournement, poetry as drift, as presentation, not representation. Assembling fragments, phrases. Arrange together equals syntax. Not exactly fiction, not exactly non-fiction.

Forest, mountain, lake (or sea perhaps). In the fiction of *AEREA*, memory is everywhere, "empty recollections, which can't be tied to anything."
Think of Médé and the pears, Médé and the Great Sokko, Médé and the
grasshoppers, the coal fire and his smile; of Montalban and his table, the
pottery shards. The book could be a hymn to Médé, who is or was a real person in EH's young life in Tangiers, as well as an elegy for Aerea (a fiction?)
who says at the book's close:

"these words in which honey was tenderly mingled with venom:
'Don't forget me! Don't forget me!'"

Dear Stacy,
Looking through another book by Emmanuel Hocquard and Juliette Valéry,
Le Commanditaire: Poème (a private eye, Thomas Möbius, is the "I" in the
story, if it is a "story": "Here, Thomas Möbius, you will not have anything
to do with pronouns, just people.") A noir b/w photo/text work. Flipping
pages, there you are, or there is you:

Dear Stacy,
Osip Mandelstam, in his major essay, "Talking about Dante,"[22] "mean(s) to
say that a composition is formed not from heaping up of particulars but in
consequence of the fact that one detail after another is torn away from the
object, leaves it, flutters out, is hacked away from the system . . . " whereas
in his "Addenda to Journey to Armenia"[23] he says, and this is substantively
how Hocquard writes about writing, "Prose which corresponds to reality, no

matter how expressly and minutely, no matter how efficiently and faithfully, is always a broken series . . . . a broken sign of the unbroken continuum."

Giorgio Agamben writes in his elegant "Preface" to *Infancy & History*,[24] "Every written work can be regarded as the prologue (or rather, the broken cast) of a work never penned and destined to remain so, because later works, which in turn will be the prologues or the moulds for other absent works, represent only sketches or death masks. The absent work, although it is unplaceable in any precise chronology, thereby constitutes the written works as *prolegomena* or *paralipomena* of an non-existent text; or, in a more general sense, as *parerga* which find their true meaning only in the context of an illegible *ergon* . . . . the counterfeit of a book which cannot be written."

In various of his texts (novel, poems, chronicle) Hocquard writes about this particular absence in terms of his old friend the archeologist Montalban who is forever trying to piece together shards of a pot that once existed and now exists in his mind or in mind's eye. The continuum is not about origins but about rhyming space/time, as in timelessness, the ever present.

Dear Stacy,

The more I reread *AEREA*, the more of a dream I find myself in. In each section, more of a sense of smell, touch. As though touching each letter, as in Emmanuel Hocquard's "Comment j'ai écrit une (chronique)" ["How I Wrote One (chronicle)"].[25] "I learned how to write with the help of an alphabet whose letters, cut out of heavy cardboard, were painted with red varnish. From one letter to the next, the red was not exactly the same. I learned to trace each letter by walking my index finger over the smooth surface."

From the same book, "Assis à ma longue table . . . " ("Sitting at my long table . . . "), first published in 1981 as a limited Orange Export chapbook, with an original watercolor by Raquel. And in the beginning of *AEREA*, we see him "Sitting today at my long table . . . ".

As Wittgenstein has written, "We are asleep. Our life is a dream. But we wake up sometimes, just enough to know that we are dreaming."

I just saw on Youtube a poem I don't think we've seen from Emmanuel Hocquard, "Je ne sais pas si Fernando Pessoa a vraiment existé," read by him on May 10, 2010, in Merilheu. With a photo. "I don't know whether Fernando Pessoa has ever existed."

Who has?

NOTES

1. P.O.L, 1985
2. The Marlboro Press, 1992
3. Page 59 [Hachette, 1977]
4. EH interview, p.229. *Toward a New Poetics: Contemporary Writing in France. Interviews, with an Introduction and Translated Texts*, by Serge Gavronsky. [University of California, 1994]
5. Edited by Aaron Levy and Jean-Michel Rabaté, foreword by Eric Prenowitz. [Slought Foundation, 2006]
6. *Latin* aer: air, atmosphere, ether, weather. "AER," *Album*, p.61 ff.
7. *AEREA*, p.30
8. *AEREA*, p.7
9. cf. epigraphe to EH, *Un privé à Tanger*
10. *Privé*, p.45
11. *Le Savon* [Gallimard, 1992]; *Soap*. Tr. Lane Dunlop. [Jonathan Cape, 1969]
12. *Privé*, p.19
13. *AEREA*, p.7
14. Barbara Guest, *Rocks on a Platter*. [Wesleyan, 1999]
15. *AEREA*, p.37
16. *Action poétique* 131. "Les maîtres chanteurs," p.31-34
17. Jean-Luc Godard, Youssef Ishaghpour, *Archéologie du cinema et mémoire du siècle*. Dialogue. [farrago, 2000]
18. *Privé*, p.51-58
19. "Le récit," *Une grammaire de Tanger*. Unpaginated. [cipM/Spectres Familiers, 2007]
20. Emmanuel Hocquard and Juliette Vaéry, *ALLO, FREDDY?: Elégie 9*. [cipM/Spectres Familiers 1996]
21. [editions demoures, 2001]
22. Tr. Clarence Brown & Robert Hughes. Reprint from DELOS 6, 1971
23. p.394, *The Collected Critical Prose and Letters*. Tr. Jane Gary Harris & Constance Link. [Ardis, 1979]
24. Tr. Liz Heron. [Verso, 1993]
25. *Privé*, p.41

WORKS CITED

Hocquard, Emmanuel. *AEREA dans les forêts de Manhattan.*
Hocquard, Emmanuel. *Aerea in the Forests of Manhattan*. Lydia Davis, translator. Evanston, IL. Marlboro Press, 1992.

"The Greek Fragment"
Irreal Salvation in Mina Loy's Gnostic Text *Insel*

KIMBERLY LYONS

Something Unknowable Had Entered into My Intuition.

—MINA LOY

At an early, anticipatory moment in Mina Loy's novel *Insel*, narrator Jones remarks to the character Insel:"You've inherited the keys your father made . . . you whose life will turn on a key." There is a further key reference: " . . . his salvation depended upon keys." The word "key" is a clue to the hidden secrets of *Insel* and offers readers a sly suggestion that there are "keys"(and secrets) to the text. The words "father" and "made" and "salvation" also allude to the frameworks her novel works within. The poet and artist Mina Loy wrote *Insel* between 1933 and 1936 as far as is known from the Loy archives at the Beinecke Library at Yale University. According to editor Elizabeth Arnold, Loy may have worked on the book in later years as well. The novel was not published and waited for discovery and notice like the Berlin Codex, until Elizabeth Arnold unwrapped its pages in the Yale Beinecke Library archives and heroically pushed through the novel's first publication in 1991 by Black Sparrow Press.

The narrative is of a first-person account of a Mrs. Jones, an artist living in Paris, who is introduced to the German painter Insel (based on Mina Loy's friend, the German painter Richard Oeize and possibly, also Stephan Haweis, her first husband) on the eve of World War II. Jones becomes intrigued by the contradictions within this itinerant artist's personality and his compelling, surrealistic styled paintings. They hang out in her apartment and look at art. Jones and Insel walk around Paris together for a night. She lends him a sum of money. She allows him to stay at her place for a few days while she is away. They go to cafés and have a few, sudden meetings. Jones worries that Insel must be starving to death, or is vulnerable in some way and rescues him in an imbroglio with his two girlfriends. There's lending of cigarettes, interludes of the cleaning of his suits, her own dresses being fitted and made, more looking at paintings, more poetic dialogue until she divests herself of her weird obsessive bond with him, and they both go away. Such is the surface knot of described occurrences that configures this modernist, enigmatic novel.

The chimerical, multivalent poetic imagery of the novel, Loy's commentary and the novels position within Mina Loy's oeuvre compels various readings. Scholarly readings that inform our understanding of the novel include Hilda Bronstein's feminist analysis of the novel's rebuttal to the Surrealists (from a doctoral dissertation available online in 2013); David Ayer's reading of Christian Science, mystical, surrealist contexts and Tyrus Miller's understanding of the modernist artist's conflicts around issues of representation, reproduction and originality,

I agree that it is certainly true that *Insel* makes fun of the surrealists, whom Loy skewers as falsely pretending to the mystical and magical. Is there no more hilariously deadpan insertion than "Man Ray came up and sat with us and went away." (61). Loy beats out Hemingway. Yet, Man Ray will not go away. The German "strahlen" which denotes a psychic "ray" is used as a cipher running throughout *Insel*. Furthermore, in relation to the character Insel "ray" is employed as in: "light, to arrive in rays focusing on the brain at a minimum akin to images on retinas." A statement which may also allude to Man Ray's invented Rayographic process. Sandeep Parmar alerts us also to a drawing by Loy found in her "Metaphysical Notes" archive, on which is written: " rays of awareness, descend from above and are absorbed . . . " The *Thrice Greatest Hermes*, translated by GRS Meade in a 1905 edition, may have been known by Loy and also referenced : "Depart, O holy ray; depart, O fair and holy light of highest God!" (97). Mystic rays are a significant entity within Loy's spiritual vocabulary and serve as one of the persistent puns of *Insel*.

The unequal relations between men and women are critically important generators of Loy' writing (as has been explored by Rachel Blau DuPlessis) and Loy's acerbic points and despair about the relations of women and men are consistently woven into all of her works. She states starkly in the novel, "the effort to concentrate on something in which one takes no interest, which is the major degradation of women, gives pain so acute that the mind disintegrates." (40).

For all of the validity and applicability of these readings, Loy's intention with *Insel* goes beyond feminist irony and parody. I suggest that gnostic and magical themes surmount any other reading. *Insel's* hermetic, magical, possibly mystical Jewish sources and Chrisitan Gnosticism, in particular, are the meta narratives of the project that Loy refers to as "In conception vast enough to absorb the centuries it survived, now in defiance of time to surpass it . . . the eternal Thing was looking at us with the fullness of the future" (85). The surface wit and skeptical, ironic tone of *Insel* serves to quixotically disguise the mystical urgency of its project.

Readers know from her body of poetry that Loy is highly receptive to that which Jones in *Insel* reports as "my parasitic clairvoyance" and as manifestations of the "irreal." I suggest that Loy was a serious reader of hermetic texts and wove in and transformed hermetic concepts, images and imbedded keys incredibly subtly into her work to compel the attentive reader and most essentially, work out wisdom mythology in a modernist, poetic context. Which practice aligns her work with alchemical and hermetic texts throughout the centuries with their imbedded messages and metaphors to be recognized by advanced readers. I believe Loy would have aligned herself with such practices for the joy of it and yet with an underlying seriousness and belief.

This reading is bound to be as hypothetical in some aspects as are all the other theoretical frameworks by which we may read Loy. A reader who searches for certainty of absolutely certifiable textual origins for Loy's gnostic tale is compelled to wander the realms in search of home. And so, the reading that follows is theosophical in its dependence on correspondences, correlations and ultimately on speculation.

Yet, Loy inserts clues. Jones and Insel walking in Paris see," a book lying open on the sidewalk . . . an early Greek fragment. I do not remember which." (86). If us dunderheaded readers cannot recognize this surrealist chance encounter with a key to the "profane mysteries" found in the various Greek papyri fragments whose content serve as templates to the novel, then we are offered another opportunity with the diagrams Loy placed in the text of the novel. In two instances, geometric diagrams are described. Insel leaves a square set of papers on Jones's table: "its squareness was instinctively exact replicates the hexagons of wasps." If the table is imagined as a round, then the square of the paper upon it creates what appears to be a magical circle. This diagram may correspond to the glyphic diagrams contained in the so-called *Book of Jeu* within the Bruce Codex and possibly also to diagrams in the grimoire of magic, *Solomon's Key*, translated into English in 1889 by Golden Dawn practitioner, MacGregor Mathers. A related possibility for the source of the diagram is of the famous magical diagram described at length by Celsius later refuted by Origen (and which is evaluated by contemporary scholar April DeConick). Another possibility is the GRS Meade-Blavatsky diagram of the Monad or any number of other alchemical or even Rosicrucian related diagrams.

Jone's vision of Insel as "a man of light—of aerial substance . . . as the Greek fragment" (97) is a third clue to Loy's intentions. "Man of Light" is referred to in the Coptic language Bruce Codex, housed in the Oxford Bodleian Library since 1848. Loy may have known of the text from the

F. Lamplugh 1918 translation into English or the Baynes translation of 1933 from Cambridge University Press, or most likely, the GRS Meade 1896 translation, published in the Theosophical Lucifer Magazine with notes by H.P. Blavatsky herself. The GRS Meade 1906 *Fragments of a Faith Forgotten*, a study of Gnosticism and related threads, would have offered a scholarly, readable, speculative survey that would have appealed to Loy. There is no underestimating the influence on the British modernist writers who kept up with hermetic and occult developments of Meade's *Thrice Greatest Hermes* and his 1906 series of pamphlets, *Echoes of the Gnosis*, published by the Theosophical Society. Another compendium Loy may have looked at is the Montague James *Apocryphal New Testament* published by the British Clarendon Press in 1924, for many years a primary source for these materials. It is also possible that Loy would have read *Against Heresies* by Irenaeus if she were especially engaged by Gnosticism. That text is particularly demanding as the interpretive obscuring by the early church fathers distorted the information that they relayed.

The Gnostic core narrative of the suffering, creative, redemptive figure of Sophia offered Loy a workshop of materials. Historian Hans Jonas' summary and synthesis of the gnostic concepts in his classic primary study, *The Gnostic Religion: The Message of the Alien God* defines "the goal of Gnostic striving" as "the release of the inner man from the bonds of the world and his return to his native realm of light" (44); the essential drama that I believe would have compelled Loy.

It appears that there is no single Gnostic narrative to which *Insel* adheres. Just as far is as known there is no unified Gnostic corpus, school or religion. And yet, it is not known for certain that there is not. The branching, diverse and diffuse origins of the Valentinian, Sethian and Mandean philosophies (to name the most well- known communities) are complex. Scholars and readers have discerned Jewish, Egyptian, Persian and Hellenistic underlays to the extant texts. There are tangents within *Insel* that suggest a familiarity with, and possible use of, related sources including: early Christian Apocrypha, hermetic and magical traditions and Kabbalah. Loy's Jewish heritage and interests, her considerations of her mother's mainstream Christianity and Loy's Christian Scientist beliefs all figure into her complex, theological-magical-hermetic ideas and interests.

The marvelous innovations of her poetic language and the sculptures, collages, lampshades and installations created by Loy, such as "Christ on a Clothesline" reproduced in the tantalizing photographs in the Carolyn Burke biography *Becoming Modern*, demonstrate Loy's iconoclastic practice across all media. Loy's Gnosticism conjoined with Christian Science and her own creative Christology. There are also issues of textual accessibility, translation, and edition that require sorting (with which I am presently engaged) to establish with more certainty Loy's sources. Her Gnosticism appears to be a mix of concepts and experience: the creative, suffering, redeemed and redeeming Sophia; the concept of a cosmological spectrum of aeons realized in circled spheres of experience and the arrogant demiurge in contrast and relation to the thought creating Sophia. Gnostic signatures in the novel include the realm of the Pleroma (a totality of the 30 created aeons and emanations; the completion of perfect knowledge) as a home only attained by suffering, acts of purification and contrition; and, finally, the singular intercession of a loving Christ figure.

The Gnostic core of *Insel* is this: Jones for a phase in the novel mirrors the Sophia (Wisdom) function and Insel also for a phase is a demiurgic/archon figure (similar to a demon); who is the creation of Sophia/Loy. If this correlation seems outlandish, consider that Burke noted in a 1912 or 1914 story or journal entry that Mina Loy depicts a "Sophia" who represents Loy. Jonas summarizes the Sophia/Archon dyad as:

> We have met before in gnostic thought two different symbolic figures to represent in their fate the divine fall, the male Primal Man and the female thought of God . . . who personifies the fallible aspect of God, usually under the name of "Sophia." (176)

Jonas goes on to elaborate how "the causation of her fall (is) more in the nature of a mishap brought upon by her offspring" (177). The 13th Aeon (which I suggest is the basis for the realm of interaction in the novel) is described by Jonas, based on his reading of Gnostic texts, as a realm where: "a series of progressive subtractions which leaves the "naked" true self . . . free to enter the divine realm and become one with God" (166). In the *Pistis Sophia* translation by Meade, this passage clarifies Sophia's search:

> The emanations of Self-willed again oppressed Pistis Sophia in the chaos and desired to take from her whole light; and not yet was her commandment accomplished, to lead her out of the chaos, and not yet had the command reached me through the First Mystery, to save her out of the chaos. It came to pass then, when all the material emanations of Self-willed oppressed her, that she cried out. (Chapter 41)

Becoming embroiled in the phantasmagoria that was life with Insel, Jones instructs herself.. ". . . keep out of this . . . you'll get me into an unnecessary jam" (37). Here is the gnostic concept of the Sophia's proliferation of thought that engenders further productions of material entangling reality. Loy may also have conceived of the necessity of poetic creation as drawing herself, the Sophia, further in to the material chaos.

Amid *Insel's* signals and coded occurrences, Loy creatively reworks the Gnostic drama. The two characters only obliquely refer to this level of their function and struggle as though they were carrying the incrustations of gnosis without knowing fully their burden. Neither of them believes the other recognizes who they are: "Let us not be too precise as to what I am," (50) Insel says to Jones. She acknowledges his "having no idea of whom he alternately bewailed upon and beamed upon. Whom that is would be his creatrix" (92).

Loy describes Jones' descent into the embroilment with Insel as "the visionary lethargy of the primeval chaos" (137). From her hotel, "The St. Cloud," she muses, "I felt if I were to go back, begin a universe all over again, forget all I am familiar with . . . evoking a chaos from which I could draw forth incipient form, that at last the female brain might achieve an act of creation" (37). This statement alone is a singular clue to the gnostic frame-work of the novel. Jones recalls, "at the back of that memory stands another memory of having had the power to create whatever I please" (107). This is not only an ironical revelation but also refers to the Gnostic mythos of So-phia, who mistakenly (the nature of her creation is treated differently with-in differing gnostic texts) made a demiurge son out of her own thought as she was drawn down out of the aeons, thus bringing matter and nature into existence (which crudely summarize the intricacies-and variances- among gnostic texts).

Insel becomes the demiurgic/archon/artist created by Sophia/Loy and all of his conflicts in the novel derive from his status as a creature cut off from gnosis of his origins and holy source; yet who is drawn to the wisdom and path to salvation that Sophia/Jones offers. (Whether or not the demiurge may be reunited in the Pleroma/home is a complex, contrary point within Gnostic texts). "The demiurge is a creature from the mother of psychical substance," Jonas explains (193). Insel, as an artist that has parallels to the demiurge without gnosis, magnetizes Jones with "fixed enchantment turned to a staggering stare." The account of that enchantment and her consequent escape is the core tale.

Insel is diaphanous and shifts from solid to transparent, from powerful to weak from ugly to beatific, from good to evil. He tells Jones that he has been released from a "haunted house" (Sophia's body) by the pounding on the "last door" (of the circles of creation, the aeons) and is "jailed" for "9 months" (in the utero of Jones/Loy's creation) as a "forger" (gnostic mistaken falsifier of creation). Insel's peculiar skeletal state is reiterated throughout the text. He appears as an immaterial being "Abandoned of all quality except the opaque" (101). His repulsion at being touched and insubstantiality when he is—a fragment of his arm comes off in Jones's hand—alerts the reader to his status as a stunted being driven by creative powers who knows neither himself or his true relation to creation. "I can create anything," he states hubristically. His powers of projection are coupled with Loy's descriptions of the "elemental mist," "invisible herbage," "carpeted chaos of his paintings." The gnostic demiurge is known to have created primeval earthly conditions in some versions of the Gnostic cosmology. Jonas clarifies: ". . . anguish became dense like a fog . . ." (183). This fog will be described throughout *Insel* as inhabiting rooms, Insel's paintings and the atmosphere of their relation: "the mists of chaos curdling into shape"(49).

What does Insel as emanation want from his creator Jones/Sophia? He seems to need to bind to her "hunching into materialization" (128) so as to keep her in the material zone to mirror and feed him. Insel craves meat (meat stands for materiality) and yet never seems to gain weight or to overcome his hunger (for Gnosis). He "had need of a food we knew not of" (30). "Everyone imagines I'm the devil" (42). "He preferred any discomfort to going home" (34). Insel tells Jones that he is called "alien" (alien being a well- known gnostic concept).

The compact theatre of *Insel* is crowded with incident and poetically extended metaphor and simile. The language conveys a charged singularity within the gnostic framework and it is in this synthesis that Loy's tremendous poetic realization and creation is apparent. Paragraphs float like autonomous prose poems and "Words, like roomy cupboards, dipped into the reservoir of excited honey . . . " (77) electrify the novel. Loy creates an effect of ruptures in space, states of being and matter. Within the web of the novel's metaphors, surface dimensions compact, fold, collapse, encompass and expand as "a possible trans-occupation of cubic space" (38) as ". . . in the smoothed out air there was a suspicion of a collapse in time" (44) in which ". . . eternity spins round and round" (70). Loy's concept of time is both poetically permeable and philosophically complex and the reader's experience of time is consequently permutated and collapsed. The purpose for bending time in *Insel*, adheres to a schema and combination of contexts not yet fully determined although it is reasonable to surmise that the variability of time emanates from the purposes of the gnostic soul's journey.

Insel offers a "hallucinatory dimension" which I contend is poetry; that is, a universe of forms that constantly transform. Through metaphoric recostuming (and more later on clothing in *Insel*) the narration follows how soul essence changes within its skin, or container, and function to become something—many things. As the tissue of the novel rumples and creases, locations and even species are altered. A reader may wonder: is this a hash or opium induced experience? The super-delineated electrical traces of the realities Jones and Insel imagine as they move about Paris read like the account of a trip that anyone who has read the classic literary descriptions—or experienced one personally—would recognize. Ayers states, reasonably: "*Insel* may be a lost classic of drug literature." However, Loy foresees such assumptions and warns us off: "Drugs meant nothing to me. I supposed they were a substitute for imagination" (126).

The shape-shifting flow within *Insel* further emphasizes the hallucinatory flux of being that may be traced in the following quotations of Loy's descriptions of Insel as: "an embryonic mind locked in a dilapidated structure."(19); "an invisible will-o-the wisp"(21). "He is permanently a skull"(21); "a stork on one leg" (22); "As a honeyless bee"(25); "a rigid crow with folded wings" (42); "Dissolved into a strange mirage" (45); "He looked like a lamppost alight" (pg.49); "As if he were growing a set of soft invisible fur" (50); "like a quicksand"(54); "a porcupine"(150); "like seeds fallen upon an iron girder, a wounded feline" (65); "a witch's cat . . . turned into a sugar dove" (137); "immaterial algae" (69); "moldy wood"(69); "A double starfish" (79); "a termite . . ." (79); "a dazed gnome with a spider's silk"; "a lithe tree struck by its own lightning" (93). All of these transformations are reminiscent of the shape-shifting within the Welsh epic poem, "Taliesin" translated into English by Lady Charlotte Guest in 1877 which surely was known to Mina Loy. The statement, "Their art takes on such shapes as would seethe from a cauldron" (22) specifically alludes to that mythology.

Loy creates and discards each appearance and momentary reincarnation in search of the divinely fitting true apparel. Tim Armstrong alerts us in his discussion of Loy, to Christian Science founder, Mary Baker Eddy's phrase very likely known to Loy: "The eternal is sustained by serial metamorphosis" (208). Further, GRS Meade's writes in *Thrice Greatest Hermes*:

The Mother in higher natures contemplates the Eternal Cosmos . . . copies its beauties by means of the permutations and combinations of her elements and the generations and transformations of her lives or souls. (31)

Loy identifies with the creative, permuting, combining powers of the Gnostic female creatrix with "A supersensibility so acute it shattered itself to splinters." Each manifestation of materiality as it spins before the poet's eye is discovered to contain an elemental essence such as "Elementals formed of a submarine snow" ... " ... like drowned diamonds." ... "Dynamically compressed as the carbon of a diamond" ... "dissolved in its wire caging with the craft focus of sight to set the content free"(85). Jones imagines rescuing the "immaterial essence" of Insel by "some ruthless extraction of a Supreme Good from a fallible pulp" (102) and "his exquisite nucleus" (68). Here, Loy may allude also to the Kabbalistic idea of an essential God particle within a Kelipot or husk. The dynamically compressed elemental carbons are the vital essence of imaginative particles of poetry. It is in the relentless flux of Loy's language that her ecstatic creatrix powers are demonstrated.

True to the figure of the demiurge in the Pistis Sophia story, Insel demonstrates a longing for Jones/Sophia. "I could never find you ... for where you trod there were little fragments of stuff"(46). "I prayed that you would come back." ... "You must come over" (56). He looks at her over the rim of an empty plate which corresponds to the Gnostic conception of Sophia being sought in the divine concentric circle "at intervals of the aeon"(174). He cries, "There you are ... pointing to the center" and asks "Promise to be my guide and companion?" (169). These utterances mirror the complex relation of the demiurge to the Sophia figure which inadvertently created him.

Jonas describes their Gnostic drama, "The darkness is seized with greed for the lightness" (162). "Towards a terrible magnet" characterizes the intensifying binding of Jones to Insel (55). Jones "obtained a corpse like sack, and stuffing it full of scribbles I tied it up, and threw it into a superfluous room." Superfluous room equals aeon, corpse like sack, equals Sophia's repentances and magical banishment. Jones muses that she feels herself "grow to the ruby proportions of a beef steak" as her gnosis becomes the food Insel seeks.

To redress and purify the demiurge and release the Sophia/poet from the mal effects of creation. Sophia must seek the pleroma (fullness) of home as escape from her creation, and return and attain union with the Christ. Jones " ... finally gives Insel the key" (143). This key is the magic that will advance their mutual spiritual journey. What follows is a peculiar instance in which Jones remembers a mixture of flammable clear "dissolvent" lying about in "antique bottles" that she must warn Insel away from drinking. In Against All Heresies, Irenaeus, transcriber of the so-called heresies cites: "He (the Demiurge) also created ... from an invisible substance consisting of fusible and fluid matter" (25).

After bringing Jones to his apartment, Insel "shuts the door ... like all automatism we take for granted, stupendous in its implications" (50). Jonas informs us that in Gnosticism doors represent the separations between the aeons which souls must traverse back to the Pleroma/home. Essential to the Sophia release are her cries for help/repentance (eventually responded to by Christ after she has attained a sufficient state of initiation). Jones states "any such patroness would have cried for help" (58). As she and Insel sit together "a sound of anguish was hovering above us" and "... a prayer repeated over and over" (66). Jones has a sense of the "outlines of a giant" which may be read as an immaterial savior nearby (66). At this point Insel cries: "To seek after a woman, a vanishing woman and find nothing, to find in her stead nothing but pins" (46). He then, strangely, steals a packet of her dressmaking pins. Jonas describes the Gnostic crisis thus:

> Whenever we hear of the doffing of garments, the slipping of knots, the loosing of bonds in the course of the upward journey, we have analogies to the Poimandries passage. The sum of these knots is called "psyche..." we find a successive putting on and off and on of seven garments. (GR 186)

This clarification is significant in view of the interludes that follow between Insel and Jones. While visiting him, she puts him to sleep and then assiduously tries to stain his black suit white with a potent substance while "cleaning" it. Meanwhile, Jones throws "a white blanket over my dress" (109). And then as abruptly she is wearing a "huge white sail." She finds herself "encumbered with an enormous shell white as plaster... trailed in a sail of mist" (66). These 'garments of light" and rituals of purification have gnostic and Christian apocryphal reference to baptism and the garment of the bride (the soul). For example, as in a passage quoted by the Church Father Clement in *The Apocryphal New Testament*:

> When Salome inquired when the things concerning which she asked should be known, the Lord said: When ye have trampled on the garment of shame, and when the two become one and the male with the female is neither male nor female. (11)

A quotation from Irenaeus in his account provides another instance of soul/clothing language:

> the whole creation which we know to have been formed, having been made by the Demiurge, or by the angels is contained ... as a spot is in a garment. (363)

At this juncture the critical intervention occurs. Jones imagines "the dove that, when had been still for awhile would seem to have taken his place" (63). The dove may be the presence of the Holy Spirit as a Christ emanation. And: "The afternoon wears on "as if a dove had flown through a window and settled upon a chair"(20) like "a vapor . . . thin infiltration of half-light softly brushing the dark" (109). "I could discern among the uni-fied flood of customary light an infiltration of rays . . . a white incandescence that made the air look shinier" (139). These visions would realize the Sophia Pistis narrative of ascent with the aid of the Christ (in the Sophia Pistis, a divine brother/partner/savior. (Other Gnostic texts have other forms of di-vine intervention). "Black as was the stain on my name" Insel sings to Jones, "ever so white I would wash it in glory" (57). It is a mysterious litany with echoes of Revelation 7:14 as found in the King James Bible: "These are they which came out of great tribulation, and have washed their robes, and made them white in the blood of the Lamb."

Jones is then subjected to various sensations of lightness and disintegra-tion. "I felt so airy" "being carried away to infinity" in "a sudden dynamism other than my own rushed in to fill the interstices" (150). Jones relates "a maddening desire for a thing I did not know . . . something unattainable" (151). This interlude is Loy's working of the salvic Sophia ascent in which by her desperate cries, a Savior figure/Christ/the Holy Spirit envelops her and releases her from torment. As the narrative progresses, Insel gives Jones back her key which he no longer needs. They have become healed. Or he is impervious to healing through all the interactions of the novel culminating in her ritual actions of cleansing the dark, protecting the white garments and other divine interventions.

Insel is no longer magnetically drawn to her, nor is Jones attracted or bound to his aura, rays or projections any longer. She finds Insel completely material and a bit of a creepy bore. They each have become homesick and strangers to each other. Their very state of mind is described as preparation, search for, and reception to gnosis. In further preparation for the Sophia ascent the longing for "something unattainable" now heralds a new stage. "I received a lateral invitation to wholly exist in a region imposing a supine inhabitance. Being parallel to paradise" (110). For Jones/Loy, a journey to Manhattan would serve as the promise of liberation from the Insel complex as well as safety from the threat of the oncoming war. New York is where her daughters and many artist friends were to welcome her. Loy may have fig-ured spiritually that her endurance of the torment of Insel's obsession and her subsequent healing had earned her this miraculous journey to home. Out of the 13th Aeon and on to the Pleroma of Manhattan!

In the concluding phase of the novel, Jones holds out to Insel an object: "the box he desired was . . . a small object by the American Surrealist, Joseph Cornell . . . under the glass lid, a slim silver slipper and a silver ball and one of witch's blue" (168). On receiving this object, "he was completely cured of his obsession" (169). Cornell's charged object effects the healing of Insel Jones had enacted; an elfin conveyance for spiritual departure from negativity to the etheric arena of healing thought. The object also served as a talisman of Christian Science understanding between Jones/Loy and Cornell.

Loy explains the multiple functions of these characters as "a sort of doubling of space where different selves lived different ways in different dimensions at once" (117). Insel's last words to Jones are "Thanks for everything" (178). This recalls the wording in Irenaeus that "The holy spirit taught them to give thanks on being all rendered equal among themselves, and led them to a state of true repose" (10). Jones, now fully herself, coolly takes stock: "how far my mind had travelled . . . Whatever I had found out was for future generations." She concludes: "I had for dabbling in the profane mysteries got more than was coming to me" (153). The same may be said for any reader of the novel *Insel*.

NOTE

1. A new edition of *Insel* was published by Melville House after this essay was written.

WORKS CITED

Armstrong, Tim. Loy and Cornell: Christian Science and the Destruction of the World. *The Salt Companion to Mina Loy*. London: Salt Publishing, 2010.

Ayers, David. "Insel and its Contexts". *The Salt Companion to Mina Loy*. London: Salt Publishing. 2010.

Burke, Caroline. *Becoming Modern*. New York: MacMillian, 1996

Bronstein, Hilda. *Mina Loy and the Problematic of Gender for Women Poets of the Avant-garde*. London: University of London. 2002

Clement, *The Apocryphal New Testament*. Clarendon Press Oxford, 1924.

DeConick, April. "The Road of the Soul is Through the Planets: The Mysteries of the Ophians Mapped." *Practicing Gnosis: Ritual, Magic, Theurgy and Liturgy in Nag Hammadi*. The Netherlands: Brill, 2013.

Irenaeus, *The Ante-Nicene Fathers: Translations of the Writings of the Fathers Down to 323*. Ed. James Donaldson. Charles Scribner's Sons, 1913.

Jonas, Hans. *The Gnostic Religion*. Boston: Beacon Press, 2001.

Loy, Mina. *Insel.* Ed: Elizabeth Arnold. Santa Barbara: Black Sparrow Press, 1991.

Mead, G.R.S. Trans. *Pistis Sophia.* Reprint. 2005. Mineola, NY: Dover Publications, 2005.

Mead, G.R.S. Trans. *Thrice Greatest Hermes.* Gnosis.org. London. J/M. Watkins, 1921.

Miller, Tyrus. "Everyman His Own Fluoroscope": Mina Loy's *Insel* Between Aura and Image Machine." Ed. Maeera Shreiber and Keith Tuma. *Mina Loy: Woman and Poet.* Orono, Maine: National Poetry Foundation, 1996.

Parma, Shandeep. "Mina Loy's 'Unfinishing Self': 'The Child and the Parent' and 'Islands in the Air'. *The Salt Companion to Mina Loy.* London: Salt Publishing, 2010.

Gertrude Stein and the Poet's Novel, Thank You

RACHEL BLAU DUPLESSIS

Gertrude Stein is like an outsider artist inside modernism. She makes obsessive, relentless, repeated (and repetitive) works. Even the vagaries of her reception did not stop her eager and determined production. With a "both/ and" affable intransigence, Stein uses language semi-semantically—some definable meaning sometimes emerges, and semi-semiotically—playing intensely with *pulsions* and bodily-mental sing-songs, rhyming-rhythms, and repetitions (see Julia Kristeva). She writes a text of bliss, in Roland Barthes' terms and is the best illustration that such a text is "frustrating" (precisely as Barthes says) in its suspension of finish and its constant multi-directional arousals.

Stein has a slightly comic, slightly naive sound—a knowing-innocent sound—which she carries through with a shameless panache and a magisterial largesse. At the same time her propositions can be startling and paradigm shifting, particularly when they implicate literature, genre and the nature of language. For Stein addresses the building blocks of literary production—down to the letter, the phoneme, the word, the sentence as syntactic unit, up to the text, and she also scrutinizes and undermines the conventions of form and genre—a poem, a prose poem, a novel, a work of critical prose, a poet's novel.

Saying "poet's novel" evokes two gripping words: a genre (novel) and a practitioner (poet), both precipitating a cornucopia of cultural associations and historical uses. These associations veer in different directions. Novel = narrative, perhaps even realist narrative, and poet = person who specializes in the sublime, transcendent and lyrical. Those are some first-thought ideological associations. A "poet's novel" is, then, an oxymoron, a contradiction in terms. This makes it terminologically similar to "prose poem"—another contradictory phrase.

A prose poem amalgamates modes and genres to resist contemporaneous norms of the literary and social worlds. In France with Baudelaire and Rimbaud, that genre involved a critique of the rigid rules of French prosody and of the insistent idealist claims of poetry. In England with Wilde, the prose poem occurred as a fable counter-hegemonic in religious and sexual terms. In the US, the prose poem drew on journalism and newspaper feuilleton and a Whitmanic list impulse (in Fenton Johnson), but also was a zone of language experiment (in Stein's own *Tender Buttons*). Because it combined the terms *prose* and *poem* in one phrase, such work seemed to offer a third path, a place for "third" impulses to settle; in its hybridity, it is anti-binarist. Hence the prose poem is a subversive genre historically undermining verse literally by its sentences of prose and undermining prose formally by allowing something "poetic" to enter the fiction (Margueritte Murphy). Words to "define" the prose poem are *critique, counter-hegemonic, anti-binarist, contradictory*. Yet these words might well be used to describe / define the aspirations of many varied works in the contemporary period.

A prose poem is a poem-sized work in free prose without line breaks or fixed meter, but using image, rhythm, association, disjunction and juxtaposition. A key trait is that the visual text is cued with justified margins as a prose extract and is written in sentences or phrases, not in lines (poetry deploys sentences, phrases <u>and</u> lines). Line break does not matter, but sentence break emphatically does. So a prose poem often depends on a torque or disjunction between its statements, as Ron Silliman suggested in "The New Sentence." The practice called prose poem may draw on fable, essay, sermon, parable, sketch, or other genre traces from short prose. The prose poem is sometimes <u>called</u> a prose poem, but sometimes not; it can be an "improvisation," an "impressionist novel," "portraits" of things not people. The work is situated purposefully / deliberately on some border between prose and poetry, and is thus dependent on the cultural-ideological meanings ascribed to each and is propelled by specific stagings of their interchange. The mode is hybrid and claims the oddity and perverseness of that zone.

Is there a parallel category—poet's novel—with a plausible definition, or is this designation simply an amalgam of practices, a series of one-off's unified only by the suggestive, oxymoronic name? Subversion seems equally to be the outcome ascribed to the poet's novel—for a boundary crossing act occurs when a "poet" (an unrewarded writer? a non-novelist? a writer of poems?) writes a "novel," though the designation "poet" seems, in some cases, only an honorific. "The poet's novel" could be a novel-sized work in prose where there are disjunctions among the larger building blocks of narrative, an inter-generic work, inflected with the culturally changeable meanings of poetry. For this mode, like "prose poem," depends on what "poetic," "poetry" and "poet" mean. A long and inconclusive discussion of this might follow, with snarls of cliché about "poetry" trailing everywhere. For example, writing or literary criticism about a poet's novel could be "poetic" / "evocative," creating genre-identification by stylistic mirror; however, this is true of writing about prose too, as in Virginia Woolf. A poet's novel may be said to care about word choice, repetition, sentence rhythms, as does poetry. But of course, so do writers of most prose. Few writers treat language as transparent. Or people say a poem is "musical"—but so is prose (including in structure); a poem uses "cadence" and "rhythm"—but so does prose. These strictures and qualifications reveal why definitions are not as easy as they may look.

Is a poet's novel a slide away from plot—taking the apotheosis of the novel to be the police procedural (clues decoded in realistic time) and making plot be all? A novel does rest on the claim that something needs to happen. Even "thinking as an event of consciousness," or "talking about nothing" occur or happen. Sometimes these "things that happen" do get causally related to other things. And however attenuated or tenuous, those "somethings" are indeed related by "something" overarching. That's a novel.

A poet's novel, for Stein, is a step away from even these linkages. Does "poetic" means the suspension of sequential causality? A poet's novel may be "realistic" but it trumps pure logic. In Stein, this is true first for the micro-scale of syntax. Stein often suspends or disturbs the normal sequences within a syntactically complete sentence and in the sequential relation of one sentence to the next. Further, in a related move on the macro-scale, Stein calls narrative itself into question as retrograde and uninteresting. Or, as she puts it "novels . . . which tell a story are really then more of the same much more of the same" (*Lectures*, 184). Perhaps plot and normal networks of causality are deemphasized in a poet's novel. Sequencing of the elements occurs differently and for different ends.

Both terms, poet and novel, seem to depend on implicit norms from the 19th or 18th centuries, not the 20th or 21st. Virginia Woolf's poetics of the novel—desiring a "luminous halo" not well-spaced lampposts to illuminate the terrain—already incorporates the poetic turn. Yet in Woolf's great essay "Modern Fiction" (1925), this angelic haze versus the "gig lamps" is very binarist (Woolf, 631). Woolf seems to think that the poetic part of the novel, or (to extend her observation) that the "poet's novel," offers sense of an atmosphere away from the prose of fact, away from materialist realism.

Yet there is no marker of the twentieth-century novel that is not also "poetic." Sentence rhythm, word choice, image can be as important in a novelist like Joseph Conrad as in the work of "a poet." Is it interiority or "stream of consciousness" alone that are decisive for a poet's novel? What about Miriam in Dorothy Richardson's *Pilgrimage*, Stephen in James Joyce's *Portrait*? It's clear that a poet's novel certainly does not and cannot simply mean a beautiful evocative writing style, since many novels are poetic in this way, novels by Marcel Proust, for example. An evocative emotion of wonder, oddity, the baroque, "the poetic" managed by the writer—is this all that "the poet's novel" could mean? Then Djuna Barnes has written a poet's novel. Indeed, if you start pointing to modernist masters of fiction, you have to observe that most significant novels of the 20th century are "poet's novels"—which is either very satisfying (we've captured them at last!) or a situation in which the category has become overly inclusive (and therefore useless).

Furthermore, what some people want and appreciate is a materialist-inflected poetry—the poetry out of William Carlos Williams' sense of writing, or out of the documentary impulses in late modernism, or out of the essay-poems and projective poems of our era. Being anti-materialist and calling that stance "poetry" is not helpful. Hence our definition of poetry has really shifted, and the term "poetic" or "poet's ANYthing" cannot be counted on to do the cultural work it had been doing. It has been the work of many avant-gardes and many experimenters to "de-poeticize" poetry. (Not everyone agrees with this move, and there are little tucks and compromises in it, but willy nilly, it has occurred repeatedly over the 20th and into the 21st century.) Therefore it is hard to stop qualifying the terms "poet's novel" or "prose poetry," since both seem to depend on keeping a monologic definition of poetry as a practice, while poetry itself has, in the mean time, become unfixed, destabilized, dialogic and polyphonic (Mikhail Bakhtin).

This has been a discussion without a firm conclusion.

Gertrude Stein's work *A Novel of Thank You* is not exactly a poet's novel in a simple definition of poetry (transcendent, sublime, lyrical, "poetic"). Nor, incidentally, did Stein call it a poet's novel. But generalizing from this one example, the poet's novel is a meta-novel—giving self-conscious attention to the mechanisms of the novel: an approach to the novel from the far outside, from an epistemological overview. It is a novel's meta-language, the abstraction of a novel, questioning knowing and the languages for knowing. Written in 1925-26, not published until 1958, it connects to Stein's 1926 decisive essay in poetics called "Composition as Explanation" (Meyer, Introduction). That essay's thesis statement proposes "a constant recurring and beginning" (Stein 1962, 517); then "beginning again"; finally "there is using everything" (Stein 1962, 518).

"Who can think about a novel. I can" (113) may seem like an empty bluff in one light, but in another it says—you all want to write a novel; I want to analyze it, literally to break it down into components in order to "think about" it. Stein writes an experimental novel as an experiment in thinking about a novel (not a specific novel but a novel or a novel-item in general).

This book has 240 pages and more than 315 short chapters, short ones (like prose poems . . .), and it pursues a *Tristram Shandy*-like playfulness with chapter numbering, as does her later work, *The Geographical History of America*. Chapters might be in the wrong numerical order, for example, or called only "Chapter" (there are lots of these). To top this off, in the work's last four pages, a Part Two and then a Part Three are rapidly introduced, a perfectly dada move, especially since there is no Part One named as such, and even if there were, it would be 236 pages long. Symmetry and balance are discarded in this allusion to the "three volume" novel. The chapters might be taken as abstractions, as if made to "abstract" a novel or short stories, an abstraction devoid of continuous plot, action, causality or outcome, but alluding to the mechanisms of the novel. What are some of these mechanisms?

Plot. Classic plots of the novel come up in a shadowy and attenuated form—family novels, romance plots, novels of manners, even the "regional novel" (41) are mentioned. At one point, the question is raised—can a novel be changed (in mid-stream?) to a story of adventure or to a historical novel (112-113). The answer seems to be—yes, why not? There are arch and mannered plot summaries for novels unwritten (56-57, 65-68). Such novel-oriented plot thoughts recur sporadically—on marriage and adoption (80), on an illegitimate daughter (105)—the list could go on, but nothing is made of those hints. There are conceptual postulates of plots: "Supposing Henry Harper had a mother . . . " (9), but one doesn't have to write that work, or any other, just project or postulate it diagrammatically.

In reading Stein, there are always perfectly idiomatic sentences that one could imagine someone stating in some specific context, some set of actions, some plot. But no context is built, given or maintained. Examples would be "she said not to say" (21). Or even the far more complicated and promising (insert punctuation if you need to): "And what it was it was a wedding and she married him having been more or less in love with someone else" (26). Or "We are very sorry that we are not seeing Katherine again" (140). Or "He never wishes to see either Dora or Minnie Meiningen. [after a few similar statements, different names] And no one knows why" (79). These moments of coherence are unsetting.

Character. "Letting out names in novels" (93). There are lists of names of characters and potential characters, often the oddest ones, such as you might find in Henry James' notebooks. These names are comic, suggestive, yet rarely repeated. So there are no filled-out characters. And the names are never used in sequences, confrontations, conversations, events—in plot. Meyer calls these names "subject positions"; they are barely even this, as they have no "position" to defend. The names are pronominal even if color-ful ("Emmet Addis," 212), filling a place otherwise called <u>he</u> or <u>she</u>. Some-times there are patterns—as a spate of names all beginning with the letter "C" or "H" (95, 96). At one point, there is a flurry of names that later re-peat ("George is one name Paul is one name James is one name John is one name . . . " [183, 188 and 211]), but nothing establishes them as "characters." They are empty signifiers the way numbers are, holding a place as an entity and waiting for a function.

So rather than characters, the work has pronouns. The pronouns that predominate are third person singular and plural: *it, she, he, one, they, who, also some, somebody, everybody.* "This is a long history of them" (140). The second most used pronouns are first person (*I* and *we*); the pronoun that emerges toward the end of this work is *you* but in much sparer quantity. For the bulk of this work, the effect is to hold things at arm's length with no intimate address. A good deal of this pronoun use is general, unspecific, and abstract—a constructivist set of entities. This work in general is always abstracting and attuned to the pictorial (but not illustrative) use of language elements.

However, Stein does begin using *you* in the latter part of the novel. Be-ginning at Chapter CCIV (173 ff.), chapters tend to end with versions of the title phrase. "Once more I thank you" (173), "And now and then thank you" (195), "A novel of thank you is historic" (198), "Thanks" (214), "Very nice and please and thanks" (215), "Thank you very much" (220) are just a few examples, clustered in the latter third of this book, and making a pattern in a work in which predictable patterning is rare.

So this is "a novel of it" (20). It is a novel of pronouns, which are often words functioning as deictics—that is, words whose reference is thoroughly situational. (Explanation: "She" might mean the student in your class in one conversation and your mother in another.) But what would happen if con-text and dialogue and interactive understandings were erased and reference was not functioning? You could not then tell who "she" was and in what "story" to put her, or even what her name is or what she does or says. And the same with "he" and with "they" and "everyone." Everything becomes vague, general and indeterminate, yet collective and populated, too.

Stein's pronouns are consistently deictic without referent—that is they seem to refer to characters or situations not otherwise described, analyzed, given air-time, developed. Similarly, time-marker deictics like *once* or *then* or *yesterday* are also situational. They are meaningful only in relation to the establishment of a clear—if temporary and site-specific—framework of ref-erence. There are many adverbs of time and manner, for in this work the adverb is as vital to Stein as are pronouns. But time markers are similarly un-referential. So about sequence (perhaps) or time (perhaps), one might say "It is if it is at all needful to have it come after or before it came when they were after all in plenty of time every once in a while" (124). Thus *A Novel of Thank You* is (on no matter what page) a maze of deictics—both as pronouns and as adverbial time markers. That is the work's purpose and one of its central points.

Stein's goal is to abstract these words from semantic meaning and frameworks; so in this work, as in others, pronouns point, but here they do not point to an understood referent. Instead, the opposite happens, they are deturned from their normal function and become perverse: there is so much "they" without any reference that the indistinct plethora becomes the point (or the frustration). Similarly adverbs modify everything ("then") or nothing. That is, instead of pointing to one thing in one specific situation (as they are designed to) these deictics pluralize many things in many situations (all of which have only the vaguest content). It is in this sense that Stein can say about this work "Everything happens" (187) when, looked at from another perspective, it really doesn't; in fact, almost nothing "happens."

"Back to back. Who knows. Plenty of time. Who knows. Had the same name. Who knows. When as in the meantime. Where is where is where is where where it went when when and when is always always in a while by that by that returns to and in conclusion" (97). That about sums it up. Stein offers words about time relationships as novelistic markers only, not as informational content. These adverbs and adverbial prepositional phrases are given for their own sakes, not to declare useable sequences, causality or events connected to a chain of events. The same thing happens with space or setting ("there" and "here"). These too become pure deictics without specific reference: "And as it was when she was near when she was here when they were there . . . " (99). Adverbs (modifying verbs, showing the manner in which something is done) are orphaned with blanked-out semantic content, because the manner in which something was done is normally connected to semantic meanings of events, actions, sequences. Here, no.

"This follows that and after that this follows and after that this follows that after that" (115). This is another example of Stein's abstracting the features of the novel in a general way, like a graph or diagram of any novel's mechanisms. Reiteration, not causality is a well-known feature of Stein, mainly because pure repetition never happens (in her view)—every repeat is slightly shifted; there is difference not sameness, even when words are repeated. A climactic passage contains seven lines of looping variations of this basic statement: "You understand very well what I mean every once in a while and yesterday and to-day and to-morrow Every once in a while and to-morrow and yesterday and yesterday ... " (163). What happens in this passage is that time markers are loosened from their possibility of referring and become a rhythmic weave of words. One might well call this poetic.

Instead of any plot sequence, many times in this novel Stein uses number sequences—sometimes pure lists of numbers (approximately up to ten), or numbers used to list items or language events. This numbering is a motif. Numbers are like a subset at once of characters and actions. They are primary, by which I mean fundamental elements of signage.

The Theme of this Novel. "The central theme of the novel is that they were glad to see each other" (72). While some of Stein's statements in this work have a meta-textual, explanatory quality, this one is probably the most accurate and succinct, not to say the funniest. This *is* a novel of thank you, and of other virtually meaningless, bland but pleasant moments of almost phatic communication around social interchange. The work features set-ups of meetings, visiting, calls (paying a call on), all the mechanisms of the social in the novel in general, bringing "characters" (i.e. names and pronouns) together one way or another. Stein postulates abstract social connections: forms of politeness, or sheer sociality without "content" or conflict, simply having them (the pronouns) begin to talk to each other by greetings and other bits of chit-chat. So this novel is constructed of patterns of inane, charming, filler conversation and social set-ups—the glue of sociality without the content of social interactions. And everyone, as in Lake Woebegone, is extremely nice: "they had explained that they were very very admirable very very responsible very very careful very very pleasing and very very welcome, welcome as well" (164).

There is some paternal [!] advice late in the work: "if you must do it do it graciously" (212). This is the pleasant ethos by which the names and pronouns abide. "How do you do how do you do said easily" (74). So being "Kindly and kindness" (100), being agreeable, being polite, being socially pleasant, circulating, inviting people, arranging invitations, visiting (the beginning and ends of visits only—the "how do you do" and "thank you" parts), and being nice and sympathetic ("She might say oh Josephine. He might say oh Katherine," 98) are vital and repeated moments. "Coming again" (98) is pleasant, and includes a slightly sexual implication, but seems to be mainly about getting together with others by visiting them, coming and going, leaving and being "called back" (136). There is an implicit "list of addresses and who went to see them" (169). Stein's Prufrockian motto might be: "Oh, do not ask, 'What is it?' / Let us go and make our visit."

"They are back again again from there" (173). This work might be indexical to a novel. But many novelistic markers are missing. There is no description (setting, clothing, mood changes, feelings). Well, there are a few windows mentioned (165) and a taller person (164), but that's about it. There are
no social cues of class, status, bearing. However, there is a one word chapter
("Chapter CXCVII Religion"), and the provocative observation toward the
end of the novel in the context (?) of a "christening": "Jews do not like the
country, yes thank you, christians [sic] do not all like the city. Yes and thank
you" (237). There are no interests or motivations (spite, envy, lust, despair,
greed and so on), though there are extremely rare flashes of negative feeling
("Stupidly agreeing if you like it that that was that that that was for" 143) or
even a one and only statement regarding morality, on liars (165). There is no
nature, just a few bouquets and gardens, including "pansies." There is a little
food mentioned here and there, but no sit-down dinners, no menus, no interactions over eating. There are definitely visits, but no rationale for them
nor any outcome but more visits and leaving and arriving. There are no time
markers in a sequence and hardly any words like Wednesday, or February,
although there are a few.

Poet's Novel?

What does a poet do that Stein does? That's one question. And what is "poetic" about this work by Stein is another.

Poets rhyme. (Yes, they do. They have and they still can. Or may.) Rhyme
is a clear marker of poetic practice rhetorically and historically. And Stein
rhymes—something generally avoided in prose. Rhyme is considered jarringly inappropriate—a fascinating convention to consider—possibly because it spoils the looser rhythms of prose with a sing-song beat of recurrent
sound. Or because it calls attention to words' materiality. A-normatively,
Stein offers various definitions and statements in the theory of the novel
and some potential plots in rhyme words. That is, when talking about "the
novel," Stein often speaks in "poetry."

Here are examples. "What can a novel do a novel can tell everything that
is true it and tell everything truly it can tell that it comes it comes it comes
out not fancifully but really" (134). Or plot in rhyming doggerel: "Telling
that she went away and to stay. Telling that she went away so that they might
say that she had not gone away right away. Telling that she had to-day to go
away as she had to say anyway . . . " (139). Or "Daily daily every day what did
they say" 165), which is the whole of Chapter CXCII.

There are too many examples for this trait to be totally random.

"A novel makes more than a third, it makes less than is heard it makes more than is inferred" (35, repeated backwards on 36).

or

"Will they lend us money. Will they lend us will they lend us will they send us will they send us honey" (36).

or even

"George had a bother he said he had a brother but that was not as important as one another" (148).

Or—in poem-like line breaks

"It is easy to change novels to two.
    One and two.
    Through and through.
    You and you.
    One and two.
    Too many bow to two.
    Too many." (45)

In a 1927 essay entitled "Poetry, Fiction, and the Future," Virginia Woolf again proposes that the new novel, the modern novel will have a poetic feel to it.

It will give, as poetry does, the outline rather than the detail. It will make little use of the marvelous fact-recording power, which is one of the attributes of fiction. It will tell us very little about the houses, incomes, and occupations of its characters; it will have little kinship with the sociological novel or the novel of environment. ... It will give the relation of the mind to general ideas and its soliloquy in solitude. (435)

Woolf's is a brave, anti-materialist, anti-sociological definition of the poetic potential of the novel, but for me, it is not the blur, the hazy outline, but rather the detail that is "poetic" and helps to define a poet's novel. What details? Stein is quite interested in small phonemic differences (*think* and *thank*; *this* and *that*; *in* and *is*) that drastically shift meaning. Emphasis on this kind of detail is central to poetic language in its sound, its calculation, its demand for specificity: "heard and had and headed" (10); "said and sat and saw" (10). Stein is also interested in a "wrong-word," letter-shifting method that calls attention to the surface of things, shifting the expected: "They went to go" [want] (47) or "wishing windows" [washing] (42); "he has heated war" [hated] (31); or using "white" instead of "while" (27). One aspect of "the poet's novel" is a focus on the material detail.

A poet's novel is also conceptual, abstracting, meta-textual as well as materialist.

In Stein in general, writing is perverse. It is writing evacuating writing of most of its markers—clear time frame, semantic meaning, distinctive place, and a logic of setting, conventional genres, continuous characters, memory in the reader (the ability to remember what went before), and any sense of causality (the goal to extrapolate sense and sequence from what already happened).

Perverse writing means writing pluri-filled, exorbitant, so stuffed with conflicting plethoras of time, place, characters, genres, everything on over-load so that prioritizing, establishing a sense of hierarchy of materials is impossible. There's no before or after, just the sensation of word pleasure or frustration in a loosely bounded field. There is no before, no after; there is only the sequence of words in an often torqued or split sentence. There is little remembering. This is a curiosity of the reverie that gets created. That is—by jiggling the detail in a wash of endless repetition, and despite the sense of abstract "diagram," Stein creates that hypnogogic state that has, historically, been one property of poetry; while she also rests on two other, material properties of poetry—precision of the detail, and the now-unfashionable joys of rhyme. Her fictional "narrative" is not an event in the world reproduced or replicated. "Narrative" is an event of language on the page.

The novel's last sentence is "This is the difference between this and that" (240).

WORKS CITED

Bakhtin, M.M. *The Dialogic Imagination: Four Essays.* Ed. Michael Holquist. Austin: University of Texas Press, 1981.

Barthes, Roland. *The Pleasure of the Text.* Richard Miller, trans. New York: Hill and Wang, 1975.

Kristeva, Julia. "From One Identity to An Other." *Desire in Language: A Semiotic Approach to Literature and Art.* Trans. Leon S. Roudiez, Alice

A. Jardine, and Thomas Gora. New York: Columbia UP, 1980. 124-147.

Murphy, Margueritte C. *A Tradition of Subversion: The Prose Poem in English from Wilde to Ashbery.* Amherst: University of Massachusetts Press, 1992.

Silliman, Ron. *The New Sentence.* New York: Roof Books, 1985.

Stein. Gertrude. "Composition as Explanation" (1926). *Selected Writings of Gertrude Stein* (1946). Carl Van Vechten, ed. New York: Modern Library, 1962: 513-523.

———. *The Geographical History of America or The Relation of Human Nature to the Human Mind* [1936]. Intro. William H. Gass. Baltimore: Johns Hopkins University Press, 1973.

———. *Lectures in America.* New York: Random House, 1935.

———. *A Novel of Thank You* (w. 1925-26). Steven Meyer, Introduction. Normal, IL: Dalkey Archive Press, 1994. All references to this work are in the text.

Woolf, Virginia. "Modern Fiction" (1925). *The Gender of Modernism: A Critical Anthology.* Bonnie Kime Scott, ed. Bloomington: Indiana University Press, 1990: 628-633.

———. "Poetry, Fiction, and the Future" (1927). *The Essays of Virginia Woolf: 1925-1928,* Vol. 4. Andrew McNeillie, ed. London: Hogarth Press, 1994: 428-441.

Fidelity and Form
Rosmarie Waldrop and the Poet's Novel

ELIZABETH ROBINSON

In "Form as a Response to Doubt," Lydia Davis writes that the doubt or dissatisfaction an author experiences with writing in existing forms can result in new forms. Davis goes on to affirm the value of an "interrupted" or fragmented work because

> [a]ny interruption, either of our expectations or of the smooth surface of the work itself—by breaking it off, confusing it or leaving it actually unfinished—foregrounds the work as artifact, as object, rather than as invisible purveyor of meaning, emotion, atmosphere. (35)

Rosmarie Waldrop's novel *The Hanky of Pippin's Daughter* exemplifies writing that refuses the transparency of narrative expectation. In enacting its complex investigation of history and memory, the novel works shrewdly with form and formal expectation in ways that deliberately bring the reader up short in surprise. Waldrop works with the reader's knowledge of form in order to undermine expectation. Form becomes, in a sense, its own betrayal.

Summarized reductively the content of *The Hanky of Pippin's Daughter* turns around a series of infidelities. The narrator describes her mother's extra-marital affair with the best friend of her father; she discusses her husband's and her own infidelities. Each betrayal burgeons into greater complexity, no one instance easily resolvable into "right" or "wrong." The cuckolded father, for example, seeks redress that entangles him in a larger imbroglio and treachery. Set in Germany in the years just prior to World War II, the novel gestures toward the crushing load of reparations Germans were required to shoulder after World War I and the growing anti-Semitism and Nazi Socialism that lead inexorably to the Second World War. Within this historical and familial context, the author points to the great tangle of affiliations and fickleness that knot around the attempt to justify any given approach to rectitude.

The Hanky of Pippin's Daughter is thus a novel that can in some ways be read in a straightforward narrative manner. There are distinct characters, discrete events, and these motivate narrative movement. Waldrop creates a narrative environment of oscillating intimacy and antagonism by setting up the novel as an address from one sister to another. Lucy, the protagonist, writes to her sister Andrea, alluding to letters from the latter which the reader never sees. In this, one experiences the partiality of an interaction that purports to be somehow dialogic or reciprocal. Here, then, is yet another infidelity, for as Lucy argues against Andrea's ostensible memories and opinions, Andrea is never given the opportunity to make any rejoinder, and thereby to portray herself.

Of course this reductive summary fails to capture the complicated currents of memory and attestation that sweep through the book. The author forces the reader to repeatedly interrogate what a narrative *is*, how trustworthy any statement may be, and whether memory can serve as a reliable vehicle for truth. Arguably, a conventional novel could achieve the same ends. It could not do so, however, with the same level of nuanced critique, humor, and ambiguity that Waldrop effects. It is the formal shaping, deeply informed by Waldrop's work as a poet and translator of poetry, that makes this writing so resonant. Waldrop's assessments, though sharp and sometimes even scathing, retain a formal and emotional sympathy that leaves the reader implicated, in jeopardy, uneasy. Waldrop is incapable of writing anything without engaging intensively with ethical questions, and her formal mastery is a central tool by which she wrestles with the ethical.

In her introduction to the novel, "Between, Always," Waldrop notes that she felt that she had exhausted the utility of the increasingly short lines of her poetry of that time, and so she developed an interest in the formal elasticity of the sentence: "I began to hanker for subordinate clauses, for digressions, meanders, space to amble" (viii). Her conception of the novel was of a spacious site, where there was "room for anything" (ibid.). At the same time, her experience as a poet militated against any facile sense of the novel as a tidy container, no matter how spacious, how able to hold the "anything" of digressive thought. Rather, looking toward Merleau-Ponty, Waldrop adopts a concept not of spaciousness, but of space itself: form therefore renewed not as "'the space *in which*' but 'means *through which*'" (ibid.).

Process, then, and not product, is where emphasis of the novel resides. Given the charged and often overdetermined historical narrative that characterizes Germany in relation to World War II (and here let me clarify that what I mean by this is the foregone ethical conclusions that fail to consider the difficulties and ambiguities of everyday survival for Germans during this period), it's useful to break up conventional narrative patterning in favor of multiple narratives that overlap, echo, and alternately repeat and contradict each other. Waldrop deliberately causes characters to blur: Lucy's husband

Bob struck in the same chord with Lucy's father Josef, for example. The contemporary merges with the historical and the individually recollected. Given Waldrop's personal experience of growing up in post-war Germany, there is the added haziness of that accrues in trying to sort through personal experience while shaping a fiction. Waldrop acknowledges as much, saying that when she prepared to write the novel:

> I realized if I wrote about my childhood I would in some way have to address the Nazi Germany into which I was born. A subject so over-whelming, a knot of connections so complex I knew it would be impossible to treat head on. I would need room to approach it indirectly, via detours, from various angles, from the margins. (ix)

Thus, the emphasis on approach, detour, digression—in short, on process as it evolves rather than the container we know as completion.

Before I continue on to offer a more specific reading of the book, let me pause to apply a little pressure on the word "connection" in the quote above. The modernist sensibilities that inform, I would argue, much of Waldrop's writing are engrossed in the question of connection and fragment. Ezra Pound famously noted that "Points define a periphery." This statement can be understood in a paradoxical way. On the one hand, it's possible to read it as an affirmation of ultimate continuity: eventually, our outline will coalesce into something complete. Simultaneously, it can affirm the obdurately disconnected: there are patterns, yes, and we are able to recognize them, but they never entirely solidify; they merely project possible patterns onto the random and the transient. The fragments clatter, but they do not come together in a monument to the whole.

Waldrop is a writer who has long expressed a preference and a motivating involvement with the latter perspective. (Her collection of critical essays is, after all, called *Dissonance (if you are interested)*. The adjunct of process in a poem, or in this case, in *The Hanky of Pippin's Daughter*, is the displacement and digression that Waldrop invites in with her *"through which."* "My novel," Waldrop notes, "would have to stake its progress on not knowing where it was going. It would have to be an imagining and testing of models . . . It would have to do and undo" (xi). The author insists that discontinuity is the natural state of the human, and to be true(r) to this discontinuity, it's necessary to permit gaps to remain unfilled.

Lest the reader of this essay fear that *The Hanky of Pippin's Daughter* became the "loose and baggy monster" that Waldrop initially imagined it would become, I suggest returning to our Poundian dictum, "Points define a periphery." *The Hanky of Pippin's Daughter* doesn't abjure form in a way that would render content irrelevant. Instead, in this novel, the author recognizes a multiplicity of patterning points and her formal design layers one atop another, much in the way a chord layered with too many notes still makes a discernible sound, but it is a sound that fuzzes over with discordance, aural contradiction:

> I am rehearsing *Pierrot Lunaire*. I am struck how "Nacht" is drawn entirely from a 3-note motif, the way we both are trying to construct this story from the two or three meager facts we know. Only the patter is clearer in Schoenberg, his transpositions, inversions, retrogrades, the E, G, E-flat as melody, or built up into a chord. But there, as in our story, all grows into contrapuntal ramifications which it is hard to believe came out of such simple material and which, by the end, have pushed alarming pockets into the tonal and moral systems. (108)

My discussion will proceed by studying two of the distinctive formal elements of *The Hanky of Pippin's Daughter*. My claim is that these elements borrow from poetic pattern and, in so doing, they permit Waldrop to leap over conventional narrative expectations to create a novel that is unusually ethically searching and provocative.

When the reader opens this book, she is immediately struck by Waldrop's use of visually bold, capitalized "headlines" or "captions" between sections of prose. For instance, the book starts as follows:

LAST SEASON'S BESTSELLER WAS *GREED*.

These captions are eye-grabbing and they break up the page. Initially, the reader expects them to serve as section headings, organizing the content of the section that follows. In that way, they cue the reader to anticipate a conventional narrative linearity and order. In fact, these captions work in the opposite way. The novel shifts abruptly between present and past, between first person epistolary passages and third person narrative, between moments of dialogue and meditations on the nature of story, time, memory, and truth. The writing cultivates a certain degree of chaos. In one two page spread (26-27), "THE VOCAL TISSUE OF FREDERIKA SEIFERT, THE SINGER" introduces an abstract portrait of the mother's voice (e.g., "Timbre: trees falling.") that moves on to "FREDERIKA WAS PROUD," a heading that enjambs into the following section with "to have a lover." This section proceeds with a fairly straightforward account of Frederika and

Franz (the friend of her new husband) becoming lovers, only to transition again with "ANDREA, ANDREA, ANDREA," thereby effecting a remove into the contemporary and a rather admonishing first person address to the sister, who, it is implied, objects to a comparison between her own romantic practices and that of her mother.

Earlier, I noted that the orientation of this novel is not toward narrative resolution but functions as an exploration of process. It asks, "How might history, memory, identity be explored?" The answer, it appears, is not through smooth evolution. Waldrop's sectional shifts can be jarring. Sometimes they effect transitions, but sometimes they pause narrative entirely—"PORTRAIT OF FREDERIKA AS A CONTROL TOWER"—or tersely combine musical, mythical, and historical allusion as with "WOTAN'S OAK." In the latter reference, Waldrop conjoins Wagnerian music and Nazi history, though later in the section, Waldrop employs that reference as a springboard that permits her to depict the absurd mystical preoccupations of the father, Josef, along with the story of Kitzingen and Pippin's daughter-of-hanky-dropping-fame.

Though nothing in this formal device *looks* like poetry, it functions much as poetry does. It implicitly refutes narrative linearity as the only pattern by which understanding can develop, favoring instead metaphor, association, and analogy. These elements liberally seed the essentials of narrative that do come to play in the book. One might recall that the "stanza" of the poem comes from the Italian word for "room," and this is apt here, where the captions set up walls that alternately guide and stop movement through the rooms and maze-like passageways of the novel. The reader, compelled by these interruptions and their visual blare, must remain alert in the way that a mirrored funhouse requires alertness, for our perceptions in the funhouse are unsteady. The reader, as do the characters, must continually ask: what is real and what is illusion?

To describe each section as its own room is not quite adequate, however, because that would be to focus on each section as neatly contained. This deemphasizes the ways the sections find indirect ways of creating mobility and linkage. The captions do segment the book into sometimes counter-intuitive "rooms" but in so doing, they not only disrupt our sense of "meaning" within the novel, they force the reader to question the nature of temporal movement—what is forward, backward, sideways? What is this narrative and/or historical geography? I will make a perhaps-surprising formal equation and say that *The Hanky of Pippin's Daughter* has something of the quality of a haibun. The haibun originated in Japan in the 17th century. It's a malleable form, able to compass both narrative and essay. Haibun is characterized by shifts between prose and very short imagistic poems, most often haiku. Typically, haibun has been a way to juxtapose the sequential ordering of narrative with the extra-narrative sharpness of the image. Many haibun, for example, have recorded the movement of a journey punctuated by the meditative stops of haiku imagery. Waldrop certainly intends to provoke thought, albeit not in the tranquilly thoughtful mode of most haiku. Moreover, the journey of this novel is not from discrete point of origin to endpoint. The narrator is herself engaged in a search for a variety of origins. The prose of the novel might better be compared to a scavenger hunt, replete with objects of discovery and salvage that are improvised, imperfect, lost along the way, retrieved haphazardly. Or, again, the funhouse: what is a door and what is a mirror?

In this unusual haibun-like prose journey, the captions serve as a startling alternative to the haiku. Rarely do they constellate on an image and promote focus per se. If you will excuse my mixed and proliferating metaphors, they are more like hard rests in a piece of music. The sudden stops remind the reader that she has after all been moving. By disrupting the trajectory of attention, they recreate attention and attention's sometimes piecemeal continuities. In an interview with Johnette Rodriguez in *The NewPaper*, Waldrop appreciatively cites Valery's assertion that a poet enters the forest of language with the intention of losing his way, "Because only this way will you see something unexpected—if you stay on the path, nothing happens" (3). The journey so characteristic of the haibun is distorted here. Waldrop works with formal ingenuity in a distorted haibun whose haiku are abolished in favor of caption-roadsigns that may create a sense of progress through the funhouse, or may lead fruitfully astray.

Another of the notable formal motifs of the book is Waldrop's distinctive use of names. One section of the novel even leads with the caption/headline "DO YOU KNOW HOW YOU GOT YOUR NAME?" There, the narrator observes her father's fascination with names because of their "echoes from the past," yet he also laments the frivolous, miscast nickname his wife has given him, for a name can also place an individual "in the wrong context." As though to remove him from his home in Germany and displace him far away, his wife gives Josef an Italian nickname. But the name that can put one in the wrong context is more ominously figured in Frederika's grimace to her niece, "It's a shame you're called Esther. Not a nice name. It's Jewish. We'll call you Anna" (63). When the family later moves, they take the former domicile of one Eduard Grossman. And here, the very name equates with exile, with the catastrophically wrong context of disappearance.

Names are not only context. The further value and perplexity of names is that they "are rhythm" and the narrator observes that the church has coordinated "this rhythm of names with that of the stars: a calendar of names"

(62). Hence, naming is profoundly linked to history, as though history has its own recurring seasons. Many reviewers have noted that the twin sisters are named Andrea and Doria, clearly a reference to the Andrea Doria, a luxury liner that sank in 1957 when it was rammed by another boat as the result of fog, darkness, and the captains' miscalculations. At a later juncture in the novel, the reader learns that the name of the narrator is Lucy. Wryly, she asks her sister, "By the way, do you think it is possible that I was not named after St. Lucy, but after the Lusitania?" (112) Another famous shipwreck, the British Lusitania was once the biggest ship in the world, but was torpedoed by a German U-boat in 1915. Over a thousand people died as a result. While some readings of the book have aptly noted the names as suggesting "submerged histories," the other dimension of these names is in the idiomatic reference of the term "shipwreck" which is to be stuck somewhere without a way to get home, escape, or get out of the situation. The recurrence of history as the contemporary overlaps and merges with the past demonstrates throughout the novel just how "at sea" the characters are.

In a similar splitting of names, the narrator's father is named Josef, and his friend and the man who cuckolds him is Franz, conjuring of course, the Austrian Emperor Frank Josef who ruled from 1848 until 1916, but whose reign was troubled by struggles to retain territory and keep unity amid uneasy alliances. (He fought constitutionalism and was considered a reactionary besides.) The two men orbit around Frederika, the absolute ruler, for "one does not bargain with Fredericus rex, with the king of Prussia." (20) Frederika exercises such power over these men, it's as though, like Andrea and Doria, they fail to be quite complete in themselves. The initial friendship of the men, as war comrades, was complementary, but this balance shifts into shards as they betray each other in Frederika's wake. Amid all the naming, Waldrop has raised questions of identity that work against the sharpness of her wittiness. Franz and Josef can be described in the same perplexing terms that Andrea and Doria are, toddlers who are harnessed together with a yardlong leash between them. Lucy, recalling the twins, speaks in terms that apply equally to Josef and Franz, (but also to Lucy and her mother): "Anchored. To what? . . . A shape which should be you, but is not? A double trying to get away? A refrain? An echo?" (59) A bystander looks on the twins and asks tellingly, "Can you tell them apart?" (ibid.)

The names are significant indeed in this novel, and yet names, which tend to tie themselves to an individual as a stable marker revolve in this narrative around persistent gaps. On the one hand, the story is largely set in a town that gets its name from the action of an unnamed woman: Kitzingen is named for the handkerchief dropped by Pippin the Short's daughter; it was later retrieved by a shepherd named Kitz on the site where the town was to be. If Pippin is historically legitimated in this action, his daughter is not, "who had no choice at all, with her one gesture, stuck at her window, forever dropping her one hanky . . . Without so much as her name entering the legend" (102). What is the reader to make of this absence? Why is the novel titled for the gesture of an unnamed woman when names are so important here? And what other absences crop up in this exercise of otherwise profuse naming? Toward the end of the book, Josef uses a pendulum to magically read the fates of those missing in the war. In Josef's acts of divination, what names does he fail to divine, to spell out? "Names which he'd rather not know, which might mark the death of Franz whom he'd rather forget?" (148)

At the conclusion of the novel, Lucy returns to the import of the name, for it is she who has told her sister Andrea the name of the man who might be her biological father, Franz Huber, with whom their mother had an affair. The name has consequence. It is not resolution, but a pivot, and Lucy agrees with her sister that "You are right to insist that I help you find out what happened to him. After all, I have given him to you, Andrea, given you his name" (152). In the converse of the unnamed daughter of Pippin, what we now have is a name without its bearer.

In her use of the captions and the charged use of names, Rosmarie Waldrop has brought distinctive formal design to this novel. The effect—as with the aim—of this original writing is not merely dazzling technique. Embedded in this sophisticated and often very funny novel is an urgent ethical struggle. Joan Retallack, addressing Waldrop's fiction, cites "the nerve to resist packaging unruly materials in the nineteenth-century conventions" (85). Retallack sees in the turbulence, even violence of this resistance, that the "contemporary paradox of storytelling is that the disturbance that comes from the 'drive to know your own story' must enter the *form itself* thereby making the desired knowledge impossible" (ibid.). It is not easy to live amid the impossible and forgo a bank of seemingly stable knowledge. What results is an epistemological crisis that Retallack helpfully labels a "navigational project" (86).

And this is where the theme of infidelity in *The Hanky of Pippin's Daughter* returns to us in different guise. Fidelity: loyalty, faithfulness, reliability, trustworthiness, conformity. In depicting a lengthy series of infidelities, sometimes with sympathy and sometimes with antipathy, Waldrop forces the reader to navigate the fluid modulations of fidelity. Indeed, her novel is admonishment against one monolithic fidelity. Witness Josef's growing and disturbing sense of fidelity as he acquiesces to Nazism:

If one could trust Hitler. Believe in him. What an immense relief, giving yourself up to someone larger, stronger. Being a muscle, a mere fibre of a muscle in a larger body, an atom of a larger force. (124)

What then is fidelity? Waldrop suggests that it is an illusion, a capitulation. The reader discovers why fidelity must always, more properly, be plural: fidelities. As Lydia Davis notes, "Roland Barthes justifies his own early choice of the fragment as form by saying that 'incoherence is preferable to a distorting order'" (36). The genius of *The Hanky of Pippin's Daughter* is that Waldrop's formal eccentricities and inconsistencies uphold an ethics in which there are many necessary and viable fidelities. Human action does have consequence, but our efficacy as ethical agents lives within quick-changing patterns of value and experience. In one oft-quoted passage, the narrator reflects wistfully:

You wanted a story. Something with form, like a sonata: beginning, development and resolution. Where one thing would lead to another. Of course, it's my own fault that I tried to comply. I was carried—and deceived—by your version. It seemed easy, or at least possible, to give a different interpretation, to fill gaps, to look at it from another angle. Now, as the paragraphs wear on, I wonder if it is too late to give up the desire to control, to shape a story, and just let things surface as they may. (110)

Despite the pain of relinquishing control, Waldrop does prove that it is possible to shape a story wherein coexist any number of stories, and where versions and forms multiply their urgent, if fleeting, verities. The betrayal of form, finally, gives way to gaps which open to necessary, unanswerable questions.

WORKS CITED

Lydia Davis, "Form as Response to Doubt," pp. 35-37, in *Biting the Error*, edited by Mary Burger, Robert Gluck, Camille Roy, and Gail Scott. Toronto: Coach House Books, 2004.

Joan Retallack, *The Poethical Wager*. Berkeley: University of California Press, 2003. Johnette Rodriguez, "Rosmarie Waldrop: Poetry and Prose," p. 3, in *The NewPaper*, April, 1987.

Rosmarie Waldrop, *The Hanky of Pippin's Daughter* in *Two Novels by Rosmarie Waldrop*. Evanston: Northwestern University Press: 2001.

V

Portrait /
Documentary /
Representation /
Palimpsest

I've read many stories of revenants and apparitions, but my ghosts merely disappear. I never see them.
—KEITH WALDROP, *Light While There Is Light: An American History*

Etel Adnan's *Paris, When It's Naked*

BRANDON SHIMODA

THE CITY—a bounded infinity. A laby-rinth where you are never lost. Your private map where every block bears exactly the same number.

  Even if you lose your way, you cannot go wrong.

—KOBO ABE, *THE RUINED MAP*

(TRANSLATED BY E. DALE SAUNDERS)

Paris is a working proposition

—ETEL ADNAN, *PARIS, WHEN IT'S NAKED*

A poem lives in Paris. Whether it has taken temporary or permanent residency there does not change that's where the poem lives. By living, I mean, the poem is not complete. Though being a poem, not even death will complete it. What then is a poem? And how does it live? A poem is the form poetic consciousness takes. It is a relationship between the mind and what is outside the mind. It is, therefore, a dynamic, which the mind can choose to engage or ignore. It does not seek completion. The activation is ongoing. Only the human dies.

The poem lives by being open. It is not that the form is inappreciable, but, like Paris, holds either a temporary or permanent relationship to the poem, so that what begins to grow in what is called "the world," is a series of increasingly complex forms compensating for the substance of the world being ultimately incorporeal. Paris, being a city, is the pageant (par excellence) of a city. It is an incarnation of the history of Paris, therefore the history of each of its citizens, living and dead, each who occupy some part of the scene. *You can say that you're a container of cities.* That is also a form the city's consciousness takes. But what is the difference between the mind and what is outside it? Is consciousness fixed, with the relationship between consciousness and what is perceived strengthening the attributes of consciousness without fundamentally changing it? Being an incarnation of the history of Paris, as a pageant, and a city, Paris is a monster. It has innumerable faces, two of which are primary, oppositional: the city as an idea and the city as a concrete reality. The idea proliferates along, and radiates out from, the margins. Concrete reality unfolds upon entrance. Both dissipate upon contact. One face is always looking out, the other always looking in. Which is which? With which is the consciousness of the city in relation?

What matters most to a poem being a poem is that it is the form poetic consciousness takes, and not the predestination of poetic consciousness. It has no form without it. It is the city as an idea. *Yes, Paris is inseparable from the idea of poetry.* Though even concrete reality is a series of increasingly complex ideas *applied.* The city is always the pageant of a city. Furthermore, a city is a *rehearsal* for the pageant of a city; not a re-creation, but the preparations made for the interpretation of the city that will be entered and eternalized into the historical record. The city itself will be gone. There will only remain, as for everything else, the wake of consciousness in the form of writing.

• • •

Etel Adnan's *Paris, When It's Naked* is a book about a city. What about a city? It *is* a city. It is a complex system of relations and interactions among citizens. It reveals the relationship between a person—Etel Adnan—and a city—Paris—revealing both as compositional processes. But when *is* the last time Paris was naked? It is, or appears to be, steadfast, overprotective; it resists alteration, which would require it to become at least temporarily naked. It takes Etel Adnan to *see* Paris naked. No, her energy and insight *actually denude* it.

Etel is the consummate solitary walker. Her task is *collecting perceptions.* It's not a task; her looking carries her through the window and into the streets where she becomes elemental. She encounters friends, strangers, paintings, monuments, buildings, gardens, cathedrals, instantiations and reminders of herself and the city. *Doesn't the act of looking at an object become also one of its definitions?* (See also: Jacques Réda's *The Ruins of Paris* and the documentary films of *Agnès Varda).* When one is reminded, their mind is brought back into itself *as a mind.* Etel is acutely sensitive to the weather, the news, history writ, rewritten and erased, in infinite cycles; the reflection of Europe, colonial, the imperium. *And then, look at Paris, do it in your imagination if your eyes can't find it, and see what a solid mass of a city it is, what a fugue in its composition, what an epic story in its stones, what an evanescent spirit in its rain.* It feels, in part, retrospective; there is a tireless capacity to know, to want to know, and to experience the world in multiple tenses, not out of restlessness, but in a way that understands the world as a continuum with a shape not yet settled into itself. I keep hoping for the discovery of new fragments, uselessly.

Paris is the center of a certain kind of economy. By "about" I mean also movement. The kind that comes from a continuously renewed curiosity, though even more so agitation. Kinesthetic agitation. *Paris* moves by chance and intuition, the way one proceeds after forgoing a scheme, every turn as rich with possibility as it is unthinkable. Every threshold lines an abyss. Though *Paris* is written, formally speaking, in prose, its economy is poetry. Prose makes the city visible. Without poetry, however, the city would die. It would never have been born. Etel lives in Paris. She was born and raised in Beirut. Her mother was Greek. Her father was Syrian. She was educated and started writing in French, though formalized her commitment to poetry during the Vietnam War, against which she wrote poems in English, while living in the United States. She's a poet. She also paints, writes fiction, was for many years a journalist, but what coheres the work is Etel's poetic consciousness. Poetry arises from crisis, even as crisis protracts into order. If she possesses it, then is Etel herself the poem? *A birth certificate tells me that I was born. I repudiate this certificate: I am not a poet, but a poem. A poem that is being written, even if it looks like a subject.*

Paris is a book about how to *read* a city. It is composed of thirty-four passages, each titled *Paris, When It's Naked*. Each time the title is repeated the mantra is further infused. Within the rehearsal for the pageant is the reminder of the city's existence. It is inseparable from its name. I don't mean that *Paris* is its own explication, as a poem into which an exegesis has been stitched, but the opposite: all understanding is contingent upon one's faith in standing inside, or under, what is being read. One of the patron saints of *Paris*—at least, the first to emerge—is Baudelaire. He appears in the first passage, in a mention of *Le Spleen de Paris*—in reference to young women in the Metro who, Etel surmises, have *never* read it; one's relationship to a book, or a work of art, can be as profusely life-changing as it can be ghostly, isolating—and in the last: *Baudelaire is in a state of perpetual reincarnation.* He appears on the cover of *Paris*, in a photograph of a statue beneath a leafless tree, his body rising out of a stone plinth bearing the austerity, though in abridgment, of the twentieth century. Is it a monument or a tumor? At first, the leafless tree behind Baudelaire dwarfs him—Baudelaire seems listless, lost, out of place—but then the tree seems literally Baudelaire's protégé, as Paris begins to seem, by the occasion of the book, Etel's:

> Should I get to know myself in order to know why Paris is so central to my life, or should I know this city even more than I do to find out at least a few essential things about myself? (75)

Baudelaire, as quoted at the end of *Paris*:

> Ivresse religieuse des grandes villes.—Panthéisme. / Moi, c'est tous; tous, c'est moi. (113)

And again, and hereafter, Etel:

> Paris is a working proposition. (69)

> When I walk in this city I plunge into an abyss, I lose myself in contemplation, I experience ecstasy, an ecstasy which I know to be also a defeat. (7)

> Walking in the streets, you could literally be in a series of innocent villages. And still, much hatred is living here, always in the name of reason. (34)

> You never experience the feeling of having gone far, in Paris. It's always familiar. The unity of its architecture makes it shrink, because you constantly move between the sumptuous and the intimate. You never fall into wilderness. (17)

> It's quite an odyssey to turn in circles in a section of the same arrondissement: you either encounter centuries fixed in stones, or people from all the lost civilizations of the earth. (25)

> The repetition is incarceration, for some. It's also, for others, a relentless initiation to the self. (93)

> Paris becomes a place, a location with which I can't measure myself, not an alien, no, never, but some beast that consumes me, as well as others, and remains equal to itself. (92)

> You don't resolve problems, in Paris, you chat, you measure the extent of your powerlessness. That's what it means to be marginal. (36)

> This city has the power to propel you out of it, vigorously, and I can't fight that ultimate power which makes me feel not only not here, but not existing at all. (67)

It's only through this ultimate solitude reached by the very fact of living, that one can find the kind of peace that makes tangible the accumulated absurdities that constitute every one's personal truth. Yes. Paris has to be reduced to energy points, has to be obliterated, and then rebuilt by one's mind, to be livable. (105)

Paris is a book on how to read Paris. It is a book on how to read. Many, if not all, of Etel's books are: a city, a mountain, a voyage, the sea, a painting, the sun, civil war, a killing, one's exile, love, the view from a window. *I do not want to become involved in the strictly historical sequence, I wish to recall the impressions, or rather I wish the impressions to recall me. Let the impressions come in their own way, make their own sequence.* They elaborate consciousness as a process and an act, and instill within the parameters—as within a city or a book—the possibilities of consciousness as strengthening not only the poetic attributes, but the spiritual and social. They are not separable; they are indispensable. We have within the problem that is the human condition, ecstasy, defeat, hatred, reason, repetition, incarceration, power, marginality, solitude; confrontations with the self, filiations, the strictures of an essentialist, imperialist system; the relationship between citizens, struggling to be more than ornaments acted upon by the force of their vision, while always wedded to it.

Who *are* the citizens of *Paris*? Not only the people who populate the city, but the people who are populated *by* it, the communities and movements rejected and dispossessed by, in this case, Paris, France, western Europe: North Africans, Algerians, the Arab world. Two faces: *one turned East, as under Charlemagne, and one turned South, where its underbelly lies.* The conflict is personal; Etel's life in Paris is that of an exile: from the country of her youth, from the Arabic language, from the landscapes that possess her, the mountains, the sea, in the ever-flattening plane of the city spiraling like a rose slipped loose of its carpel. The consequences manifest a commitment to interrogating the places that compel and repel, simultaneously.

The State is a cold concern, which cannot inspire love, but itself kills, suppresses everything that might be loved; so one is forced to love it, because there is nothing else. Etel's work exists within the tension between the Arab and western worlds, and her reading of politics, culture, in fact, the book that is the landscape before her, is informed by her relationship to these entwined yet disparate worlds. Is she writing or rewriting history? Her disrobing of Paris—successful or not; the defenses are always perfectly maintained, even when the rain makes them run—is hopeful. And yet, the future is apocalypse. When Etel does not find herself enshrined in her vision of mountain or sea, she envisions a fate as catastrophic as the machinations by which the future is being delivered. Her book is a mirror taking plasma from the sea. She is writing and rewriting history insofar as history does not arrive complete in its moment but across emanations and fragments and revelations of itself. *Do I feel exiled? Yes, I do. But it goes back so far, it lasted so long, that it became my own nature, and I can't say I suffer too often from it. There are moments when I am even happy about it. A poet is, above all, human nature at its purest.*

• • •

To read, to write; to read or write a city, a novel, a poem; to collect perceptions—is to engage a process of fiction: invention, discovery (uncovering, apocalypse). *Paris* calls attention to itself as a work of fiction. It is as an ongoing, raveling invention—a "working proposition." *In order to write a single line, one must have seen many cities.* It is pure narrative; there is no plot, so to speak, outside the narration. It moves with the swiftness of reportorial intuition. The narration, when it is really moving, lifts the entire mass of discourse off the page and into the solemn yet ecstatic presence of the reader, as if the writing, the consciousness through which the writing emerges as narration, is a plate of the earth, pressed with each word, and into the reality of the presence: earth meeting earth with a skin of sun-forged language between. The reader becomes sanctified idea. *Paris* is like a painted scroll of Heian Period, Japan, illustrating a narrative, unbroken, that can be viewed—perceived—across many directions at once. The effect can be vertiginous. It's the perspective of oracles and gods. The commonplace becomes mythological. The viewer has to make an incision in the scroll for light to cast a shadow as a principle on the hands and legs of the reader by which to delineate time and space. The scroll, *Paris*, encompass the epic and the infinitesimal, refusing to reduce what is encompassed into a scheme.

Does imagining mean to invent what is immanent? The novel—at once the towering monument and the intimate transcription of the ways we live—has existed for me—since the days when I, a young reader, first approached it—as the period, the space, of it's being approached. The space was of fear, trepidation, and wonder. The novel was epic and empyrean. It was never not fully formed and in motion. I was the novel's late-blooming interloper; I would have to be transfigured to get there. All novels, especially great novels, were to me the memory of them having been anticipated and then finally, somewhat idiotically, and breathlessly, entered. The anticipation of, for example, a city: the idea, prior to the concrete reality, becoming more desperate and rarefied, paradoxically, in the realm of the common-place. This is perhaps overstating the feeling, while understating that of the experience of reading, of being *inside* of the novel. But the fear, trepidation, and wonder—the feeling of being transfigured—enlarges, paradoxically, as the novel moves from being the towering monument to the intimate tran-scription of the ways we live.

The novel is, I think, the perfect form for the poet—the perfect form in which the poet might write. It allows the poet to participate in the positive space of life without forsaking the negative, positive and negative not be-ing judgments but qualifications of space. *The novel is the one bright book of life.* Is calling attention to one's self as fiction an act of resistance? The engagement of both positive and negative space, the circulations of both as speculative, stem, in a sense, the totalizing onrush of death. A poem is, or can be, the manifestation of the unspeakable. See, for example, another of Etel Adnan's books, the profoundly beautiful and urgent *The Arab Apoca-lypse*, which begins in communication with the sun and leads to an incalcu-lably powerful articulation and imagining of the Arab world in apocalypse. *If you're a novelist, you know that paradise is in the palm of your hand, and on the end of your nose, because both are alive; and alive, and man alive, which is more than you can say, for certain, of paradise.* Can a novel be the manifes-tation of the unspeakable? Transmutation into poem; it is already poetry. I see it in corporeal form contingent upon the non-corporeal, as an object overlaid on the sky versus the sky itself.

Yet "the novel" seems an insufficient term. I prefer "the book." In "Sur-gery for the Novel—Or a Bomb," D.H. Lawrence bemoans the split between philosophy and fiction, citing the time of Plato's Dialogues, after which "the novel went sloppy, and philosophy went abstract-dry." The book as a form is capacious. There are innumerable splits to bemoan. Is it true there were fewer distinctions made between kinds of content; in which philosophical works that endured were those that endured for their poetry; the great epic works and dialogues and compilations of fragments, allegories, narratives, tales, notes, all inventions of consciousness in relation to a world that per-mits each sense a shape upon discovery, being those immanent expressions of life? The poet is compelled to write. To see, interpret what is seen; rein-carnate experience by compulsion or as a relic of what has already been lost or erased. A poetic consciousness undergoes transmigration into a book. *Then, just as the tremor of the unreal turned into language gleams only to go out, simultaneously the unfamiliar presence is affirmed of real things turned into pure absence, pure fiction: a glorious realm where "willed and solitary celebrations" shine forth their splendor.*

• • •

It is nearing midnight in Paris. There is a bowl of oranges on a dining table. We are sitting in an apartment one block west of the Luxembourg Gardens; we have just finished dinner, and are eating oranges. At one end of the table, before a wall of tall windows, is Etel Adnan. I ask Etel if she feels at home in Paris, which is maybe not the same as asking if Paris is her home. What is the difference? One can feel at home anywhere, and I suppose that makes a home of that place. One can, for example, feel foreign to one's home, where they live, but then that is not their home, but where they live. Etel lives full-time in Paris. In her apartment she is surrounded by windows and books and art on the walls, a lifetime of articles of travel and what she's working on, the people she loves. Throughout *Paris,* Etel's heart hangs over the sea, purifies in fog. *There is no use living in Paris when all one cares for is the sea.* She is tempted, always, to leave, her mind running *furiously* to distant places. She says she does not feel exactly at home in Paris, and when I ask where she does, she says, Beirut and Marin County, California, which are, in some phases, certainly works, represented by the Mediterranean and Mt. Tamalpais. In what ways have these been distilled in this present location that is not merely a present location but the fulcrum of a life against which two very different worlds continue to evolve? *I spend little time with the individuals I love, and never live in the cities that matter the most to me. That's the way it goes.*

We talk about her work, accumulating and evolving over many decades; her relationship to her earlier work; and of the archive, or the archivist's impulse to collect the fragments of life and work for purposes external to it. The archive suggests a relationship to death Etel does not possess. It is an illusory approach to mastering death by proliferating the materials by which the self might be ordained, or preordained; the archive is a function of religious fervor. Is it faith? *Ivresse religieuse des grandes villes.* Paris is an archival city; it views itself as complete, or believes in the possibility of establishing of itself a total view. Perhaps it is not external. Isn't writing, or any act of creation, therefore a similar approach to mastering death? The poet is already the archive.

One begins at the point of death. The series of increasingly complex forms that is the world creates a counter-archive. The counter-archive institutes a tremendous distance between the point of death and the invention of the soul. Poetry dispels, in part, that distance. It becomes instantaneously, through the form poetic consciousness takes—a poem,

a novel, a book—a living paradox. What is created is a voluminous error, being an imaginative, therefore fictive, fragment of consciousness,
including consciousness measured broadly across people and places, as
well as the ultimate successor of it, by which all people and places either
choose or choose not to abide. In the infectious bemoaning of the demise of the book, and the ongoing debate on what constitutes one, the
technology that seems to be suffering the most amazing decline is not
the book but the human being. The suffering is a matter of distance. The
demise, or extinction, of the relationship between the human and their
ability to maintain and evolve alongside the technology that has proven,
by the fact of history, to be infinitely more durable and lasting, is precisely the demise, or extinction, of the human. What does the poet impress
upon memory? The poet is the transcendence of the technology. That is
a possibility. What comes out is the evidence of consciousness, or maybe
the other way around. Only books will remain. *Paris, When It's Naked*
is, in part, a testament to "bounded infinity." What we have are working propositions. Etel's open out into life until they becomes ours. I have
walked many dozens of circuitous miles in cities on all sides of all waters
and have felt the movement to be a poem; I have exiled myself from those
cities and miles and have felt I am revising the poem that once was. It
returns where consciousness meets itself within the ensemble of forms,
withdrawing and asserting itself as a book being continuously written in
correspondence with life, that is, *living in one's mind like the turning center of everything that is.*

• • •

NOTE

All italicized quotations are from *Paris, When It's Naked,* except for the following: *You can say that you're a container of cities.* Etel Adnan, *Fog. Doesn't
the act of looking at an object become also one of its definitions?* Etel Adnan,
Of Cities & Women. A birth certificate tells me that I was born. Jacques Lacan, The Four Fundamental Concepts of Psychoanalysis. *Ivresse religieuse
des grandes villes.* Charles Baudelaire, *Intimate Journals. I do not want to become involved in the strictly historical sequence.* H.D., *Tribute to Freud. The
State is a cold concern.* Simone Weil, *The Need for Roots. Do I feel exiled?*
Etel Adnan, To Write in a Foreign Language. *In order to write a single line,
one must have seen many cities.* Rainer Maria Rilke, *The Notebooks of Malte*

Laurids Brigge. The novel is the one bright book of life. D. H. Lawrence, *Why the Novel Matters. If you're a novelist, you know that paradise is in the palm of your hand.* D.H. Lawrence, *Why the Novel Matters. Then, just as the tremor of the unreal turned into language gleams.* Maurice Blanchot, *The Space of Literature. I spend little time with the individuals I love.* Etel Adnan, *Of Cities & Women.*

"Mme Wiener," the French Novelist and her Masks
Reading Stacy Doris's Two French Novels

VINCENT BROQUA

I want this book to be a way to love Chester in or with another language to which we are both finally so attached yet fundamentally so foreign.[1]

—STACY DORIS, *LA VIE DE CHESTER STEVEN WIENER ÉCRITE PAR SA FEMME* (23)

How far can a novel be a poetic act? Why does a poet choose another language to write a novel? Why did Stacy Doris translate herself into "sa femme" ("his wife") and "Mme Wiener" ("Mrs Wiener") when writing her two French novels directly in French? What was she doing to the French language and to French literature?

Doris's two novels, *La Vie de Chester Steven Wiener écrite par sa femme* (1998) and *Une année à New York avec Chester* (2000)[2], were published by P.O.L, a French press, now part of the Gallimard group, which also publishes Emmanuel Hocquard, Claude Royet-Journoud, Christophe Tarkos, Anne Portugal and Suzanne Doppelt, to name a few. They are, respectively, an incomplete biography of Chester Steven Wiener and an auto-fictional chronicle of her life with Chester in New York in 1998. Therefore much of her life is reflected, mirrored and, thus, distorted in these two books. As Stacy spent many years in France, she kept up an ongoing conversation with the French literary scene, to the point where many thought of her as something a French author.

Borrowing from 16th and 17th century fictitious prefaces (from Defoe to Diderot and Choderlos de Laclos), from 17th Century French memoir authors, from Stein's masks in *The Autobiography of Alice B. Toklas*, and from Proust, Balzac, Montaigne, De Sade, and medieval romance, her two books are a set of mirrors, functioning as a diptych. Thus, *Une année* is not a sequel of *La Vie*. Although set in a defined time, the first novel is about the creation of a legend and often resorts to the language of tales, while the second one is a series of chronicles anchored in 1998, also the year of the writing of the novel and the year when the first novel was published (1998). While the first novel is less political than the second one and feels Parisian, the second novel is overtly political and reads like quasi-diaries that document life in New York. In addition, one of the stark differences between the two novels is

Chester's hyper-presence in *La Vie* and his quasi-absence in *Une année*. But the main striking difference is the satirical tone of the second book. While the narrator claims that the first book is "deprived of political opinion" (*Vie*, 9), *Une année* is a critique of authority and politics, specifically the politics of gender. It takes former New York Mayor Guiliani as one of the recurring clownish figures. Towards the end of the book, the narrator opposed Guiliani to Hillary Clinton, who appears as a legendary heroine, and yet is also subtly criticized by Mme Wiener's powerful irony. The sense that the first novel is History while the second one is history is made blatant by the extraordinary tale of exile of Chester's Jewish family fleeing the Shoah in the first novel as opposed to the "exile" of the inhabitants of a damaged building in Manhattan told in the second novel.

I want to read Doris's novels against this backdrop of opposition to suggest how they relate to and yet differ from French novels of love, and I want to examine how she wears "[her] less than rudimentary knowledge of French" (*Vie*, 15) as a mask, performing "His wife" or "Mme Wiener" or even Chester himself, disguising into the multiple identities of the novelist.

I. Hypertrophy of a lover's discourse

"ADORABLE. Not managing to name the specialty of his desire for the loved being, the amorous subject falls back on this rather stupid word: *adorable!*"

—ROLAND BARTHES, *LOVER'S DISCOURSE* (18)

Stacy Doris's *oeuvre* constructs fragmented and protean figures of a lover's discourse, of which *Paramour* was the paragon. Her two French novels are no exception; they deploy such figures in a lover's discourse that she terms, after Chester, "the theory of hypertrophy" (*Vie*,183).

Ending on a dedication to "HUMAN PERFECTION AND ITS FRIENDS" (*Vie*, 254), *La Vie de Chester...* uses all the *topoï* of the unsurpassable excellence of "our hero," to the point of being outrageously funny: "Chester was an extremely curious baby as a consequence of being so bored" (*Vie*, 61), so that when he was supposed to be napping, he instead went on "reconnaissance missions" (*Vie*, 61), like an extremely precocious baby-adventurer overcoming the inimical world around him. In keeping with her theory of hypertrophy, even Chester's bad sides are praised as "signs of his superior intelligence" (63), and his technique of making faces becomes "a very refined art" (*Vie*, 64). Gradually Chester becomes a hero and a legend, and like mythological heroes, Chester's birth is actually not a birth at all (69). The character therefore becomes both too human and non-human, he is a "genius." Much of the language used is that of legends and courtly love. Almost posited as Chester's origin, the romance of his grandfather, a Jewish prince from Prussia, and his grandmother, the daughter of a haberdasher, is a tale mixing wonder, commonsense and elevated discourse (*Vie*, 83-94).

Chester and his family become the principle of a language-machine, generating text and new words, such as "mignonneté" (*Vie*, 68, 136)[3]. Indeed, naming Chester, or thinking about his habits, unleashes a lexical and syntactic swirl. Pages are replete with "—able" adjectives such as "adorable" (*Vie*, 58), "100% loveable" (*Vie*, 31), remarkable (*Vie*, 183), his PhD is "unbelievable" (*Vie*, 71). Such adjectives *grow* into adverbs "adorably"[4] (*Vie*, 16, 158), or develop into sentences that are so hyperbolic that they become pleonastic "il était mignon à un point vraiment hors du commun" (*Vie*, 68), or again morph into a baroque poetics of parentheses (*Vie*, 181-184):

> At the age of sixteen [. . .], Chester, who was beginning to express the remarkable theory (mainly concerning literature) that he eventually named Hypertrophy (he will explain it to you with gestures evoking a sort of sublime and almost tangible tactility) according to which the genius of some works resides in that they exaggerate out of proportion one or several (depending on each specific case) qualities characteristic of their form of expression. (183-184)

These parenthetic lines belong to a two-page web of sometimes excessively long sentences that are stretched by digressions, appositions, and accumulations. The narrator's exposition of the hero's own exposition of his theory is done under the influence of the theory itself and seems to espouse it totally, so that she is imperceptibly but visibly drawn to creating these syntactic circumlocutions with a language that performs his as well as her theory in writing. But is it *his* theory? Who is Chester in the book? And what does this language say?

One of the figures of Barthes' *Lover's Discourse* is titled "Adorable." In this figure, as in others such as "Écrire," the French critic argues that the totality of beloved also creates an aesthetic vision of totality which, counterintuitively, is epitomized by an empty and almost silly word, "adorable:"

> By a singular logic, the amorous subject perceives the other as a Whole (in the fashion of Paris on an autumn afternoon), and, at the same time, the Whole seems to him to involve a remainder, which he cannot express. It is the other *as a whole* who produces in him an aesthetic vision: he praises the other for being perfect, he glorifies himself for having chosen this perfect other; he imagines that the other

wants to be loved, as he himself would want to be loved, not for one or another of his qualities, but for *everything*, and this *everything* he bestows upon the other in the form of a blank word, for the Whole cannot be inventoried without being diminished: in *Adorable!* there is no residual quality, but only the *everything* of affect. (Barthes, 19)

Mme Wiener's playful recourse to such emphatic and hyperbolic language, and her overt use of this empty lexicon conditioned by the appearance of the generating machine that Chester's name is, reflects what Barthes calls "that region of hysteria[5] where language is both *too much* and *too little*, excessive (by the limitless expansion of the *ego*, by emotive submersion) and impoverished (by the codes on which love diminishes and levels it)" (99). The two novels hesitate between the two interrelated polarities of the language of love: the language overflows with words and is sometimes redundant or tautological, and yet such tautologies as "Chester is Chester" also reveal that language lacks something, that it leaves something out, or, that is, in true baroque fashion, it creates hypertrophy to underline mortality: *La Vie* begins with the narrator thinking of "the angst of mortality" and ends with the hero's "deepening despair," "he was afraid of his existence and of his wish to die. He decided to wait for the unlikely event of a new life" (254).

Although Mme Wiener's joyously proliferating discourse of love could be read just as the ingenuous celebration of her beloved, it is in fact aware of its own critical limits. Such limits are particularly marked in French by the repetition of "adorable" and such adjectives, but also by the somewhat un-grammatical use of adverbs, which are often placed in the wrong position. The quirky French syntax, which we will analyze further in the conclusion of this essay, destabilizes language and says something about her lover's discourse: speaking love *is* to forge a foreign tongue (*Vie*, 23).

II. Stacy Doris's mask-making

The first time that Aurélien saw Bérénice, she struck him as definitely plain.

—ARAGON, *AURELIEN* (3)

À cause de sa perfection globale, son côté miracle (. . .), je suis obligée de me demander non pas rarement si Chester est vraiment un être vivant, au lieu d'être juste un rêve parfait.

—MME WIENER, *LA VIE DE CHESTER STEVEN WIENER ÉCRITE PAR SA FEMME* (17)

In *Aurélien* (1944), his long epic novel of failed love, Louis Aragon makes his hero—the young Aurélien—gradually fall in love with Bérénice both through literature—Bérénice is loveable because her name alludes to a play by Racine; and through the macabre mystery of the death mask of a woman who had drowned in the Seine. When Bérénice sees the death mask hanging on one of the walls in Aurélien's Parisian apartment, Bérénice understands that it is her rival. She asks that her own face-mask replace the death-mask, thus playing with her own becoming-ghost. *Aurélien*'s discourse on love is in keeping with a long line of French novels from *Madame Bovary* to *Le rouge et le noir*. Just as in *Tristram and Isolde*, whose Wagnerian version Aurélien listens to, Aragon's novel tells a story of tragic love and responds to a *topos* of romantic love, which Aragon himself used explicitly in one of his poems in *la Diane française*: "il n'y a pas d'amour heureux" ("there is no happy love") (25).

In many ways, Doris's two novels are the exact opposite: the ingenuous gaiety of her narrator is more closely related to Gertrude Stein's brisk prose and ode to her "Ir Re Sis Ti Belle" than to Aragon's fated love-story, and yet, the reference to *Aurélien* is not just counterintuitive. Not only is Mme Wiener's innocence not so obvious in the end, but her two novels are strikingly haunted by her mask-making.

I cannot think about *La Vie* and *Une année* without seeing masks and ghosts, not just because Mme Wiener forecasts her untimely death in the novel and Stacy Doris died too soon, but also because a lover's discourse produces ghosts and "imaginary beings" (*Vie*, 17). As a direct effect of the narrator's lover's discourse, Chester's existence is cast into doubt: "because of his total perfection, his being a miracle, to tell the truth (it is very difficult for me to give you a relevant idea of what this miracle is), it is not infrequent that I have to wonder if Chester truly is a human being, or whether he is merely a perfect dream I have been having for almost eight years now"[6] (*Vie*, 17). In French, the idiom is "faire un rêve," "to *make* a dream," so that if one reads closely one has the clear sense of the narrator's creation of Chester into a co-author. Indeed, early on in *La Vie*, in a gesture that seemed witty when the book was published, the narrator says that she will not complete the biography of Chester, that she will only write his story up to the moment when they met. Referring evidently to Dante's *Vita Nuova*, the narrator adds that the second volume of Chester's life will be titled *La vie nouvelle de Chester* (*Chester's New Life*) and that, since she, like Beatrice will die before him, "he will eventually have to write the second volume, using the notes [she] will have accumulated" (*Vie*, 22-23). The death of the narrator-author, her proleptic transformation into the ghost of Beatrice, is also the rebirth of the character-become-author. It is striking that with such prescribed authorship, Doris should question the comedy vs. tragedy pattern that most love stories espouse. In an endless series of reversals, the narrator and the character become masks of each other. Although she casts herself into a future ghost, reinventing him as her alter ego, the figure of Chester haunts both books and is written into a principle of authority, if not of authorship. Chester—not just Chester whose story is told, but the husband he has become—is frequently summoned not only as a validating source of her information (*Vie*, 96, 106) but as co-authoring the book by editing it (105). Despite Chester-the-character's conspicuous absence from most of the second book, he functions as an underground presence helping the narrator, or trying to twist her narrative: "when he read the manuscript, Chester tried to change it twice" (*Une année*, 148, see also *Vie*, 92).

Going further than Stein's conundrum in *The Autobiography of Alice B. Toklas*, Doris constantly reverses positions of authority, creating interchangeable masks. But although the narrator relies so much on her character for information, and although so many of Chester's theories are put into practice in her narrative, *she* is the one writing the present novels and granting him his present quality of "general hallucination" (17) as well as his future authority as a novelist: he is her mask. As often in her performances and books, Doris plays with this "idea of the interchangeable mask of personality" (*Vie*, 223)[7]. These reversible positions of authority set the context for the reflection on masking, role-playing[8], and artifice, which unfolds in the two novels and is displayed with much force as a short manifesto in the very last pages of *La Vie*: the problem is that of creating screens and veils between knowing and being (*Vie*, 253), "the main object of knowing thus becomes the awareness of its failure" (*Vie*, 254).

The performance of identity as artifice, which these masks prepare, is mostly dealt with in *Une année*, which lays bare the phantasmagoria[9] of the society of the spectacle. In fact, her two novels could be said to mirror each other in terms of Debord's book: the first is not to be tainted by the spectacle, whereas the second one is made up of amused and satirical stories told by "Mme Wiener." Here she documents the heart of the society of the spectacle: Times Square and its surroundings not riddled with just images, masks, and simulacra but with "social relationship[s] between people that [are] mediated by images" (Debord, 12), in which "truth is a moment of falsehood" (Debord, 19). Buildings are like "false castles" (*Une année*, 107), a restaurant becomes "Ali Baba's cave" (101), this area of Manhattan is "like the Champs Elysées transposed to Pigalle" (105), and even the Wieners' apartment is scripted by France (99). Essentially, the surface of the city is like a "joyful palimpsest," (107) but people are constantly wearing masks or transforming their realities to resemble a desired image; for instance, poets borrow dogs from others in order to be photographed and appear in a magazine doing an issue on poets owning dogs (51). But this goes even further, and sets the lover's discourse of *La Vie* against the alienation of sexual bodies. Ovaries become "a commodity" (*Une année*, 94)[10]; similarly, using irony, Mme Wiener criticizes an anthropologist of contemporary sexuality who argues that "women are always seduced by money" and that men look for "remuneration" of their "male efforts" because they are "alienated from their means of reproduction" (98), which puns on the Marxist phrase *means of production*, to be also found in Debord. In the society that the narrator observes, the hypertrophy of love presented in the first novel has been turned into legislated sex and into the power vs. impotence dichotomy in the opening chapter on the wonders of Viagra. In these hilarious pages about the sex industry and "prudish education," Mme Wiener mischievously reports that sex toys are "almost made banal by the ceremonial and solemn atmosphere" of a big "convention of venereal industry" (95); she reports that campaigns are launched to legislate touch such as in "dance shows, in which risks and physical contact are entirely reduced" (93), and that youngsters are asked to play basketball instead of making love, because "you cannot make love when you play basketball" (93): "love can wait" (92). The texts thus drift from the context of masks and ghosts to a poetics of distortion applied to the law and order of the spectacle.

III. "THINK/CLASSIFY," the twisted rules of law and order

Very tempting to want to distribute the entire world in terms of a single code. A universal law would then regulate phenomena as a whole: two hemispheres, five continents, masculine and feminine, animal and vegetable, singular plural, right left, four seasons, five senses, six vowels, seven days, twelve months, twenty-six letters. Unfortunately, this doesn't work, has never even begun to work, will never work.

—GEORGE PEREC, "THINK/CLASSIFY" (186)

I aim for my poetry to measure and codify observations; not necessarily "my" observations; observations that come to me and that I gather. I love the impossibility of achieving that.

—STACY DORIS, "POETICS STATEMENT" (275)

In the beginning of *La Vie*, the narrator places much importance on Chester's meticulous way of arranging his T-shirts and his underwear, which she finds utterly irresistible and imaginative (*Vie*, 16). This anecdote is the first of a series of motifs in the book showing how Chester orders the world, and is linked to his becoming an amazing poet (213). As discussed above, being human too human, that is real-unreal, Chester functions as a theoretical and poetic guide to the novels. Following his perpetually reinvented methods, Mme Wiener goes on to say that her novel will consist in "archiving these series of exceedingly pleasing habits" (*Vie*, 20). It is as if her repeated emphasis on his habits of ordering the world in lists and categories acts as the formal engine of the novels: she will create lists in *La vie*, she devotes the entire chapter of May 17th 1998 of *Une année* to an "assortment" of seven ludicrous trials held during the month, and she is systematic about not revealing the end of the trials, as if the chapter was "an organic plate" (15)[11], and again in her Christmas chapter, she describes the "frozen kitsch" (113) of Christmas decorations in a street in Brooklyn, giving the exact addresses by their number in the street (113-118). These means of ordering life and the city in her novel have much to do with Perec's "ineffable joys of enumeration" (Perec, 194), but they are also whimsical ways of ordering the world, both creating rules and constraints and yet twisting them so that her novels have a formal elasticity which relates to her elastic mode of thinking. And indeed, law and order, turned into a spectacle of endless trials and soap opera[12], have become mad: Mayor Guiliani files lawsuit after lawsuit just for the sheer enjoyment of it. The second book looks into the poetics of what Perec called "think/classify," and links it with narratives in which law, justice, and the police have gone out of control. "There is something at once uplifting and terrifying about the idea that nothing in the world is so unique that it can't be entered on a list" (Perec, 194). Lists, enumerations, and such poetics of classification are two sides of Doris's thinking about law and order: on the one hand the freeing and forever moving constraints that Chester applies to his world and that respond, as Perec says, to "that need to name and to bring together without which the world ('life') would lack any points of reference for us" (Perec, 194), and on the other hand, the constricting and coercive rules related to the absurd world of surveillance and punishment, trying to make everyone conform to terrifying laws. This is expressed in the embedded tale of Chester's European family in an anti-Semitic Poland—either fleeing it or not being able to escape extermination camps, and being dispossessed of their lives and homes (*Vie*, 102). In *Une année,* law and order doesn't have such dreadful consequences. It consists mainly in a recurring string of trials, rendered humorous notably by a play on names: for instance, the first two people who oppose each other in a trial are called "Mme Fass" and "Mme Binder" (*Une année*, 15), thus alluding to the name of the German filmmaker Fassbinder and his staunch criticism of society, such as in *I Only Want You to Love Me* (1978). The tortures are now those of tortoises (*Une année*, 43), but order, power, flawed justice, and the police are recurrent. The dehumanizing effects of "zero tolerance" leads to the murder by the police of a completely innocent African young man. "Zero tolerance" is also connected to the police statistics on the number of bullets fired in 1998, and the rate of resulting deaths (*Une année*, 140).

Conclusion: Trans-, the negative capability of the migrant

I have also published two books in French, which I wrote by translating the style of seven-teenth-century French noble memoir authors into the antistyle of an American Girl Scout troop leader residing in Paris.

STACY DORIS, "POETICS STATEMENT" (276)

In her "Poetics Statement," Doris says: "I am a poet because I don't agree with form as assigned" (274). That probably answers many of the questions that her two French novels raise. Her wish to translate herself into another form—that of the novel, albeit in a deformed and interrupted reinterpreta-tion—and into another language, as well as into evolving masks of herself, is contained within what remains when all is said and done: her French lan-guage. Doris's syntactical boldness and idiosyncratic spelling will no doubt seem heresy or at least dubious to the guardians of the law, be they "MM. de la Police" whom Mme Wiener begs to be indulgent for her "lamenta-ble americanisms" (10), or Académiciens, the supposed legislators of the French language and its stringent grammatical rules. In fact, although it is undoubtedly faulty, the French idiom that she creates offers her a way to gain new ground from relative unmastery, a way to transform her identity, make it foreign, and escape the strictures of standardization, or, as Mme Wiener says: "it is deeply depressing to try to display one's similitude, one's conformity" (*Une année*, 49). Sabine Macher, a German poet writing in French whom Doris knew, first deliberately wrote in French although she knew only a limited amount of French. She needed this constraint to be able to write, in a movement probably akin to Kathy Acker's saying "I was unspeakable; therefore, I ran into the language of others" (161). Indeed, es-caping is one of Mme Wiener's motivations for using French: "this is a good exercise to escape from my American seriousness" (*Vie*, 24). Other writers such as Rosmarie Waldrop, who has written her work in American English, Cole Swensen, who has done experiments in self-translation, and Caroline Bergvall, who uses multilingualism to explore the porosity and obstructions of language, have *foreigned* their language or listened to the foreignness contained in their language. Doris has also created an idiom, i.e. a language within the French language whose effects can be identified beyond the typi-cally French anxiety of making mistakes, which she plays with in the preface of *La Vie* and throughout her two novels, referring to "her badly mastered French" (*Une année*, 248). With a malleability not unlike that which she claims for her forms and genres ("Poetics Statement," 274), her French is a series of manipulations in translation. She sometimes translates literally such phrases as "gay pride" ("l'orgueil gay," although in France, gay pride is "la gay pride") (*Une année*, 45), "underdog," as "chien d'en dessous" (*Une année*, 210), or "couch potatoes" as "pommes de terre en robe de chambre" (*Une année*, 120), which is particularly funny because it puns on "pomme de terre en robe des champs" ("baked potatoes") and "robe de chambre" ("nightgown"). Sometimes she translates someone's odd pronunciation: "vraiment une mauvaise fille" becomes "*w*raiment une mau*w*aise fille" (*Vie*, 36). Here she translates the mother into French and transfers her immigrant pronunciation into an invented vernacular. Sometimes she transliterates the cultural context; although the scene is set in the USA, people shop at the once typical French supermarket chain "Mammouth" (*Une année*, 188), or Hillary Clinton's tour across the US is described as "a personal Tour de France" (*Une année*, 225). Writing two novels in French is therefore a poetic project in itself: a project in the trans- and de-formation of one's self, a project in one's exploration of language, and a project in the translation of the history and culture of the novel, to which Doris constantly alludes (Balzac and Proust as well as 17th Century memoir authors, among others), but it is also an experiment with the history of language; her language uses outdated words, such as "remonstrer" (*Vie*, 38), "mortdieu" (*Vie*, 120) from 16th and 17th Century French, or the *subjonctif imparfait* (subjunctive perfect) next to hyper-contemporary words, so that such survivals of the stratification of the French language participate in her contemporary idiom. In *La Vie*, the narrator says that when she was 15 years old, "[she] refuse[d] to ever own the slightest identity" (*Vie*, 64). And speaking on the matter of form and formlessness in her "Poetics Statement," Doris alludes to genre and gender trouble: "because I have always had many certain problems with form, I consider myself a poet. I have never agreed with form in the sense that it was assigned to me at birth with my body. Why this form and why stay in it for more than an instant? There is no stability of form" (274). And tellingly, she performs the forms of her identity, be it as masks, as a series of genres, parodies, and what Gérard Genette calls burlesque travesties (67), or as styles and theories she espouses for a moment. Just like the artist she evokes in *Une année*, her manifestations are "one and multiple," or, that is, she forges the negative capability of the migrant/translator.

NOTES

1. The two novels are not translated into English, all translations are mine.
2. The titles translate respectively as *The life of Chester Steven Wiener Told by his Wife* and *A Year in New York with Chester*, I'll refer to them as either *La Vie* or *Vie*, and *Une année*.

3. Based on "mignon" ("cute"), "mignonneté" sounds like an invented form of cuteness. It is perhaps as strange as "cuteliness."

4. In French, "adorablement" is considerably longer.

5. It should be noted that "hysteria" is probably an overinterpretation of Barthes' text. His term is actually "affolement" (115) and not "hystérie," a term which, to my knowledge, has almost the same extension in French as "hysteria" in English. *Affolement* means something between panic and agitation. Barthes' sentence could actually also refer to a region of perturbation in the language itself, and not just a psychological form nervousness.

6. In French the syntax of "me demander non pas rarement" is as strange as "it is not infrequent that I have"

7. For instance, speaking of *Paramour* Caroline Crumpacker notes that "all that is written reverses itself" adding that This and Thus, the two characters are "erotically entangled" in "this *Through the Looking Glass* structure" (282).

8. Role playing and thinking about the thin limit between fiction and non-fiction is furthered in Emmanuel Hocquard and Juliette Valéry's *Commanditaire*, when a film with Stacy and Chet as characters is mentioned and photographs of Chet are included in the book.

9. I am using "phantasmagoria" in the sense that Adorno gives to the term in *In Search of Wagner* (74-85).

10. The French word she uses is "marchandise," i.e. exactly Debord's word for the second chapter of *La société du spectacle*.

11. The French term is "plateau organique", and although she borrows the metaphor of French wine and cheese, Doris seems to be also playing with Deleuze's notion of *plateau*, but his thousand *plateaus*, have transformed into plateau de fromage, a plate of cheese (*Une année*, 15) and the assumption of the metaphor is that in the USA trials are consumed as frequently and which the same delight as cheeses in France.

12. The narrator recounts the shooting of an episode of *Law and Order* (*Une année*, 246), which she typically juxtaposes to a remark about Chester's skill at packing their suitcases (247), therefore mastering a certain kind of practical order.

WORKS CITED

Acker, Kathy. *Body of Work*. London: The Serpent's Tale, 1997.

Adorno, Theodor. *In Search of Wagner*. Rodney Livingstone (tr.). London: Verso, 2005.

Aragon, Louis. *Aurélien*. Eithne Wilkins (tr.). New York: Duell, Sloan and Pearce, 1947.

——.*La Diane française*. Paris: Seghers, 1946.

Barthes, Roland. *Fragments d'un discours amoureux*. Paris: Seuil, 1977.

——.*A Lover's Discourse. Fragments*. Richard Howard (tr.). New York: Hill and Wang, 1987 (1978).

Crumpacker, Caroline. "The Poetics of Radical Constraint and Unhooked Bedazzlement in the Writing of Stacy Doris," in Claudia Rankine and Lisa Sewell (eds.), *American Poets in the 21rst Century: The New Poetics*. Middletown: Wesleyan University Press, 2007. 278-289.

Debord, Guy. *La Société du spectacle*. Paris: Gallimard, 1992.

——.*The Society of the Spectacle*. Donald Nicholson-Smith (tr.). New York: Zone Books, 1994.

Doris, Stacy. *La Vie de Chester Steven Wiener écrite par sa femme*. Paris: P.O.L, 1998.

——.*Une année à New York avec Chester*. Paris: P.O.L, 2000.

——.*Paramour*. San Francisco: Krupskaya, 2000.

——."Poetics Statement", in Claudia Rankine and Lisa Sewell (eds.), *American Poets in the 21rst Century, The New Poetics*. Middletown: Wesleyan University Press, 2007. 274-278.

Genette, Gérard. *Palimpsestes*. Paris: Seuil, 1982.

Hocquard, Emmanuel, and Juliette Valéry. *Le commanditaire*. Paris: P.O.L, 1993.

Perec, Georges. *Species of Spaces and Other Pieces*. John Sturrock (ed. and tr.). London: Penguin Books, 1997.

Thalia Field's *Ululu (Clown Shrapnel)*
A series of detonations

JENA OSMAN

Thalia Field's writing presents a challenge—especially to those who need to categorize literary works into neat fields of genre. Her three books with New Directions Press (*Point and Line, Incarnate: Story Material,* and *Bird Lovers, Backyard*) are labeled poetry, although Field considers them to be fiction. Her collaboration with Abigail Lang, *A Prank of Georges,* was published by Essay Press—a press that "extends or challenges the formal protocols of the nonfiction essay." Field's "performance novel" *Ululu (Clown Shrapnel),* published in 2007 by Coffeehouse Press, is labeled for the bookstores as fiction but is also a documentary essay and a textual opera. Mac Wellman has called it "a lunatic screenplay and a highly articulated literary polyhedron." No matter what the label, Field's work occupies an interdisciplinary space that opens up the possibilities of what literary work can do.

Ululu (Clown Shrapnel) provides, as the parenthetical suggests, a zany yet aggressive fragmenting of wholes. Its pages are Joycean in their layers of reference and their multi-level punning. Like *Ulysses,* or *Finnegans Wake,* sentences and phrases spool outward in a complicated weave of historical and literary citation. The book is bursting with allusions, but rather than taking a generally known classic like the *Odyssey* for its schematic, *Ululu* uses Alban Berg's 1934 opera *Lulu* as an organizing principle.

Field's book offers a variety of reading experiences. There is the associative dream-world where the reader senses the lexical echoes and thematics that follow certain characters. There is the research-oriented essay where readers can lose themselves in the wormhole of the internet following the trails of the historical figures and events encountered. There is the linear world of the plotline and the nonlinear world of the scattered detail; the poetry of puns and coincidence, and the prose of fact. In any case, it's a book that shows cultural history to be a slow detonation; its multi-generic expansiveness shows the present to be just a fractured iteration of multiple pasts.

Detonation One: Lulu
Technically, shrapnel is a hollow shell filled with bullets and a fuse or charge at its center. When the fuse bursts the shell, the bullets splinter and scat-

ter. Over time, shrapnel has come to be understood as the splinters themselves. In *Ululu*, shrapnel is a trope for the way stories cascade and fragment
through time. The fuse of this book is the character Lulu, who has appeared
in a variety of works of art; although she is clearly an archetype, nobody
can seem to agree on what she represents. Is she a monster? An innocent?
A sexual predator? A reflection of others' desires? In all interpretations, she
is a woman with power but seemingly no agency, and her indeterminacy
continues to be a point of fascination.

The Lulu character made her first appearance on the cultural scene in
1870 when a young acrobat appeared in European theaters as "The Beautiful
Lulu, the girl Aerialist and Circassian Catapultist." The Beautiful Lulu astonished crowds as she was catapulted from under the stage to a trapeze above
by a complicated contraption—until 1878, when a stage accident revealed
that Lulu was actually a young man named El Niño Farini (a.k.a. Samuel
Wasgate of Maine).

Inspired by Lulu the "girl" aerialist, as well as the Commedia dell'arte
stock character Columbine, novelist Félicien Champsaur created a pantomime in 1888 called *Lulu*. In this performance, Lulu is a dancer whose lost
heart is discovered by Arnold Schopenhauer. Schopenhauer is determined
to understand how the heart works, but Lulu tricks him in giving it back to
her. She then hands it off to Harlequin.

The German playwright Frank Wedekind saw Champsaur's pantomime
and it inspired him to write his Lulu plays, *Earth Spirit* and *Pandora's Box*.
The plays tell the story of a woman and her many relationships. Each man
(and one woman) turns Lulu into a personification of his/her own desires.
She is Pygmalion's creature—shaped by each person that touches her. As
the torrid events of the play escalate, and as each lover meets a gruesome
fate, Lulu seems to have no emotional response; she lacks a moral center,
and in that way reflects the corrupt culture of Wedekind's era. The story
does not end well; Lulu is ultimately murdered by Jack the Ripper (who
was killing prostitutes in London in the same year as Wedekind first saw
Champsaur's *Lulu*).

After Wedekind's plays premiered (in 1895 and 1904 respectively) and
were subsequently censored, Lulus proliferated—first in the silent films of
Leopold Jessner (*Erdgeist*, 1923) and G.W. Pabst (*Pandora's Box*, 1928, star-
ring Louise Brooks as Lulu), and then in the 1937 opera *Lulu*, by Alban Berg.

Thalia Field's *Ululu* continues the chain of adaptations, but her version
puts all of the prior renderings in conversation with one another. Thus,
Field's novel functions as a cultural biography of a character, taking all of
Lulu's interpreters into a multi-form account.

Detonation Two: The Plot

The structure of Alban Berg's *Lulu* is a close adaptation of Wedekind's plays; Field, in turn, has used the shape of the opera as the structure for *Ululu*. Each chapter of the novel correlates with acts and scenes of the musical composition; capitalized subtitles are mostly translated quotes from the libretto. In fact, these subtitles can be read in sequence as a "play within the play," a linear story within a decidedly non-linear novel.

The plot of Berg's *Lulu* is comic in its excesses; this is a work of social commentary rather than dramatic realism. Lulu is saved from the streets by a newspaper editor named Schön, who becomes her lover and calls her Mignon. But the editor has no interest in marrying her; he wants a better match for himself, so he marries Lulu off to Dr. Goll, who calls her Nelli. Goll brings her to get her portrait painted by Schwarz, who paints her as a Pierrot (this painting is a major prop throughout the opera). Things get amorous between Lulu and Schwarz, until her husband unexpectedly shows up and upon seeing them together, has a stroke on the spot. Lulu then marries the painter, who calls her Eve, but she continues to be Schön's mistress. Trying to get rid of her before his marriage to another, Schön tells Schwarz about her lurid past; in response, Schwarz slits his own throat. Lulu then becomes a dancer, sponsored by Schön's son Alwa, who is also in love with her. Lulu convinces Schön to break off his engagement and they marry. One day Schön returns to find a host of lovers (his son Alwa, an Acrobat, a Schoolboy, the Countess Geschwitz and the Manservant) trying to woo Lulu. Schön tells her to shoot herself, but she shoots him instead and is arrested for murder.

These events take us only to the mid-point of the opera. A silent film (rarely presented in performance) which portrays Lulu's imprisonment, illness from cholera, and jail-break, serves as a bridge between the plots of Wedekind's *Earth Spirit* and *Pandora's Box*. Field represents the cinematic transition with text accompanied by film stills by Bill Morrison (best known for his film *Decasia*, which is made from found footage from decaying silent films).

By the final act, Lulu has become a prostitute in London. A palindromic structure (which was present all along in Berg's score) becomes clear in the narrative as well; Lulu's lovers in the first act reappear as johns in the last. The newspaper editor, Schön, comes back as Jack the Ripper. By adding a "U," Field has turned Lulu's name into a palindrome; she also plays with the fact that the letter "U" is a palindromic shape in and of itself.

In Field's hands, the subtitles follow the "U" structure of the opera, but the texts below them are shattered fragments of historical and literary data.

Facts from various centuries are placed side by side with details from the opera's plot and with the biographies of Wedekind and Berg. The relationship between fact and fiction is not causal—one does not illustrate or explain the other; rather the elements co-exist, revealing radical connections that our usual modes of story-telling resist. Documentary materials collide with fictional archetypes. Pierrot from the commedia dell'arte, Arnold Schoenberg's "Pierrot Lunaire," the history of clowning, and Lulu painted as Pierrot, are fragments shot from the shell of history onto the field of Field's page. They intertwine and interconnect, but reject simple "this leads to that" logic in favor of a kaleidoscopic complexity.

I THINK YOU'RE A NOVICE
Coming from Jack the Ripper that might be a compliment—since he too was never caught—just a figment of historical imagination—coming together: JACK AND ULULU canceling each other out. His letters to the police just as crucial as the sightings of the little girl selling flowers—This is it, the evidence fractures, but the attraction between them can be as real as moonlight in the river. (241)

What is compelling about Field's method is that Jack and Ululu do not actually cancel each other out; rather their stories become more present as part of an epic accumulation that includes characters such as Casanova, Columbine, Tilly Newes (Wedekind's wife), Adorno (a student of Berg's), Berg's sister Smaragda, Louise Brooks, and a host of others. The fictional and essayistic exist in a system of mutual significance. Coincidences and trans-historical points of contact reverberate madly. Field shows the hidden connections between the biographies of Wedekind and Berg and their respective artworks, as well as how their narratives are part of a much more extensive cultural resonance.

Detonation Three: Secrets
In an interview, Field stated that she "started *Clown Shrapnel* in 1994 as an inquiry into the porousness of an unfinished opera derived from a play derived from a whole culture's worth of secrets . . . ." Frank Wedekind (whose *Spring Awakening*, is perhaps his best known play in the United States thanks to a Broadway musical version) rejected the bourgeois naturalist theater of his time, and used the stage to showcase all that was politely hidden behind the theatrical curtains. Because his work treated sexual issues openly, it was frequently censored throughout his career. As Field's book notes, Wedekind was imprisoned in 1898 for disrespecting

the Kaiser in his satires; he was condemned as "an arch-pornographer, destroying culture, unpatriotic, immoral, undermining values of the Reich" (111). In 1904, performances of *Pandora's Box* were banned until 1918, the same year that Wedekind died. Field quotes the judgment of the Royal District Court: "The second act, taken independently, lacks all tragic stature or apparent purpose, and submits the reader to a quite inexhaustible flow of sexual filth" (112). While Wedekind's work was intent on staging a "return of the repressed" where sexuality was concerned, his characters also revealed the corrupt inner core of capital. His plays anticipated expressionism, but also influenced the theater of the absurd and Brecht's epic theater, presenting the characters as representative of a system rather than as an enactment of "universal" human emotions.

Field's inquiry is also intent on making visible hidden systems of connection, but of a different order. For example, *Ululu* continually refers to Frank Wedekind as Benjamin Franklin Wedekind. This was in fact his full name, and the humor inherent in a German expressionist playwright, whose works fight against the "rational" controls required by societal standards, being named after one of the most pragmatic of America's founding fathers is evident. In the first chapter of *Ululu*, called "Clown Particles," Field continues to play with this whimsical linkage:

> Open for lies (theater) and closed for animals (George Washington was there) the first American Circus introducing its first **clown** in Philadelphia, 1793 (Benjamin Franklin was there) A nation founded on pantomime later to explode with sentiment . . . (19)

Wedekind was at one time a publicist for a circus, and his Lulu plays open with a circus scene: the ringmaster of the play introduces all of the animals, with the final animal—the snake—being Lulu. Facts about Wedekind's life, American circus history, Pierrot and clowning, and the fictional Lulu all collide in just a few concentrated lines. Similar to her playful correlation of Wedekind and Benjamin Franklin, Field also connects the character Alva with Thomas Alva Edison: "Alva Edison generated enough juice to kill animals by shocks . . . " (147). Names are puns that expose the long-hidden connections between historical moments, between fact and fiction. These connections are kept secret because they don't follow linear logic; Field's *Ululu* questions that limit.

Unlike Wedekind, Berg wasn't interested in revealing society's secrets; rather he used his work to keep his own. Although Berg ultimately finished the libretto for *Lulu*, he died in 1934 (from an insect bite) before he completed the orchestration. In the introductory note to *Ululu*, Field writes that Alban Berg's widow Helene "prevented the unfinished third act of *Lulu* from being orchestrated until her death in 1976, when it was revealed that a 'secret score' was written into the notes." Helene had actually tried to get Berg's former teacher, Arnold Schoenberg (spelled "Schönberg" throughout *Ululu* in order to pun with the character Schön) to complete the orchestration. However, he declined the request after discovering anti-semitic stage directions in the libretto: "He is stopped by the SAUJUD/ 'Jew-pig.' . . . How could Alban write that?! he wonders" (213). Field does not apologize for Berg's word choice, but contextualizes it when she includes the fact that "In the early late days at the premier of the *Lulu Suite*—days before his death—Berg had to prove his Aryan ancestry to be certified for the concert . . . Secrets are not kept by the Secret Police—they hunt them out and kill them" (213).

And what about the "secret score" that Field mentions in her note? In 1907, Berg set a Theodor Storm poem ("Schliesse mir die Augen beide") to music for his future wife, Helene. In 1925, he set the poem again in his first twelve tone composition; the letters A, B, H, and F figure prominently in this composition, and it is now understood that this piece was an anagrammatic love letter to Hanna Fuchs-Robettin, the sister-in-law of Alma Mahler, who was one of Berg's close friends. Berg, who believed in numerology, determined that his number was 23 and Hanna's was 10; these numbers were used to determined tempo or bars in a section of music. A similar anagrammatic and numeric coding was found in Berg's *Lulu* when Friedrich Cerha finally completed the orchestration after Berg's widow died.

Field's *Ululu* revels in Wedekind's code-breaking and Berg's hidden codes. At a certain point she quotes from the sixteenth book of *Natural Magick* ("If Invisible Writing: Wherein are handled secret and undiscovered Notes"), written in the 16th century by John Baptista Porta: "How characters may be made, that at set days shall vanish from the paper." Such references are combined with the invisible connections that the reader can infinitely decode (à la *Finnegans Wake*) throughout *Ululu*.

Detonation Four: Epic Engaged
In a pedagogical essay titled "Writing as Experimental Practice," Field writes

> Though the history of the novel began with an approach to the book flexible enough to contain letters, found texts, dialogues, treatises, etc.—this openness receded with the rise of the naturalistic psychological novel and the convention of the "invisible" author and seamless narrative. Instead, try playing with a collage of three or four

distinct languages or texts. Don't smooth them over into one whole but let the braided edges and untranslated parts create fortuitous connections. (309)

Such an instruction provides insight into Field's own practice and the motives behind it. She is not only trying to open up what's possible in contemporary fiction (which is currently dominated by the demands of psychological realism), but she sees that opening as a necessary return to the freedom that existed when the novel was a new form.

Field's rebellion against naturalism echoes Wedekind's—as well as the resistance of composers such as Schoenberg and his students Alban Berg and John Cage to the seeming unities of romantic harmonics. Field joins these artists in their search for a creative mode that more honestly maps the complexity of the world as it is actually experienced. For Field, the hyperbolic form of opera is ideal for this purpose. As she said in an interview with the playwright Suzan-Lori Parks,

> In opera you have the entire spectrum of speech, from silence to song to shrieking. And music automatically denaturalizes the situation and does this kind of intense social thing to it . . . it absorbs and eats up whatever's around, from film to satellite technology.

Bertolt Brecht was also a fan of "opera with innovations." In his famous essay "The Modern Theater is the Epic Theater," he explains how his opera *Mahagonny* improves the classic bourgeois form. His epic approach "turns the spectator into an observer" (rather than absorbs the spectator so she forgets herself), "the spectator stands outside, studies" (rather than shares the experience), "the human being is the object of the inquiry" (rather than something taken for granted), and the form is "in curves" (rather than linear). Whereas Wedekind's Lulu plays presaged the tenets of Brecht's epic theater, *Ululu* finishes the job, creating a textual equivalent for that performative mode. Brecht used a system of constant disruption so that the spectator could maintain a critical attitude and see the actions of the play in relation to a more expansive context. Field's *Ululu*, with its capitalized subtitles, its lively push of historical facts with the pull of a fictional plot, its jumps and curves, strives for a similar relationship with the reader. *Ululu* asks for the same kind of heightened awareness and sense of epic scale. In that regard *Ululu* could be considered a modernist text written with the tools of the postmodern era. But it is more than that.

Cole Swensen, at a conference on conceptual writing, described Field as one of a group of writers that are "consciously or inadvertently echoing models of distributed cognition, an area of the cognitive sciences which recognizes that individual minds are not self-sufficient, independent entities, but part of complex networks incorporating communities and objects." Such a claim, made in the context of a conference on appropriative and conceptual works, is complicated. The networked referentiality and fragmentation that dominate a work like a *Ululu*, could feel almost old-fashioned in comparison to the internet-based "information management" strategies used by someone like Kenneth Goldsmith. For Goldsmith, citation is no longer about working a weave of found fragments, but of resituating massive blocks of text culled from the everyday atmosphere of any present moment. The conceptual method, as represented by practitioners such as Goldsmith, requires an indifferent mirroring of culture, the kind of recontextualization we associate with Marcel Duchamp's readymades. But there is another side to the Duchampian project; for every readymade, there is a note in the Green Box, Duchamp's "guide" to his Large Glass (otherwise knows as "The Bride Stripped Bare by Her Bachelors, Even"). While the readymades seem complete in and of themselves, the Large Glass presents a web of semi-comic mysteries. While the readymades are ultimately about the viewer and his/her response to relabeling an everyday object as art, the Green Box and the Large Glass ask the reader to forge a narrative out of symbols and mechanical parts. While the readymade is easy to access and gives you all the information you need in a quick glance, the Large Glass asks the viewer to parse the shards into a larger story. Similar to *Ululu*, the Large Glass is about analogy, difficulty, and a conversation of fragments.

Perhaps the most crucial aspect of a book like *Ululu* is not how it rethinks genre, but how it makes no apologies for its systems. *Ululu* is a book that values the modernist command to "make it new," but is well aware that the reader's active curiosity is the fuse that will *make it explode*.

WORKS CITED

Field, Thalia. *Ululu (Clown Shrapnel)*. Minneapolis: Coffeehouse Press, 2007.
—. "Writing as Experimental Practice." *The Handbook of Creative Writing*, ed. Steven Earnshaw. Endginburgh: Edinburgh University Press, 2007.
—. "Playing with Indeterminacy: Thalia Field interviewed by Suzan-Lori Parks," *Theater*, Winter 1996, 26(3).
Miranda Mellis. "Interview with Thalia Field." https://www.dalkeyarchive.com/interview-with-thalia-field/
Swenson, Cole. "What to Do Besides Describe it: Ekphrasis that Ignore the Subject" (presented at Conceptual Poetry and Its Others conference, University of Arizona Poetry Center, 2008)

Turning Poetry into Prose
Not Without Laughter and Langston Hughes

W. JASON MILLER

The blues are non-denominational. Langston Hughes invokes the non-denominational aspect of the blues in *Not Without Laughter* (1930), the semi-autobiographical novel about his childhood. No small feat, *Not Without Laughter* outsold all Hughes's collections of poetry and prose by 1938 (Kutzinski 182). In fact the novel was so successful that it has been translated into eight languages (Miller 362). Before all this success, the famous Cuban poet Nicolás Guillén remarked to Hughes in a private letter that he was looking forward to receiving a personal copy of the novel once it was published so that he could use it to improve his English (Kutzinski 161). As we might expect from Hughes, the novel highlights the fact that the blues are America's signature form of artistic expression. Even more significantly, *Not Without Laughter* gave Langston Hughes an opportunity to turn poetry into prose.

Before directly exploring this tact in Hughes's work, it is important to provide a general overview of the novel. *Not Without Laughter* mirrors Hughes own experiences living in Lawrence and Topeka, Kansas, during his youth. It also documents the migration towards the cities of the north which Hughes himself eventually followed as he became so intimately associated with Harlem. To capture the tensions associated with the Midwest and the Great Migration, Hughes's novel centers on the Williams family. Hagar Williams is the great matriarch of the family. Her three daughters each play a significantly different role in the upbringing of the youngest boy Sandy. Annjee (Sandy's mother) leaves Stanton, Kansas, to re-join her husband Jimboy (first in Detroit and later in Chicago). Jimboy is a traveling bluesman who encourages Hagar's second daughter Harriet to sing the blues for a living. As the most undependable sister in the family for most of the story, she nonetheless ends up earning the title "The Princess of the Blues" and playing to packed audiences throughout the country. Tempy is the disassociated sister who takes Sandy in for a short time after Hagar dies. Her character allows Hughes the opportunity to take a "jab at the black bourgeoisie (who figure prominently in the novels of Jesse Fauset and Nella Larson, among the leading novelists of the Harlem Renaissance)" (Hubbard

4). Sandy is all too glad to leave her well-meaning but exacting instruction when he is reunited for good with his mother and Jimboy in Chicago at the end of the novel.

Mirroring his own life, Hughes's novel is attune to both art and politics. Hughes's poetic descriptions give us characters with "alive nostrils" and mouths that "split into a lighthouse smile" (*CW* 4: 70). Because the young Sandy is all too often privy to information he knows he should not share, he sees things "with his eyes, but not with his mouth" (*CW* 4: 85). Through Sandy, the epitome of the young Hughes, the novel provides insights on the relationship between poverty and the emergence of what might be labeled blues culture. As adept at social commentary as he was at compressed expression, Hughes identifies poverty as the source rather than the result of this blues lifestyle: "But was that why Negroes were poor, because they were dancers, jazzers, clowns? . . . The other way around would be better: dancers because of their poverty; singers because they suffered; laughing all the time because they must forget. . . . . It's more like that" (*CW* 4: 202). In the published version of his novel, such commentary is present, but muted. Hughes's latent views are more explicit in his manuscript drafts. This is due in part to the fact that during this time, Hughes was living on a $150 a week stipend from a white patron named Charlotte Mason. In comparing the early draft manuscripts written by Hughes with the editorial letters and published revision it becomes possible to see how "Mrs. Mason's involvement with Hughes's composition of *Not Without Laughter* . . . seems more like censorship" (Shields 603). Ms. Mason's influence lead Hughes to tone down (or omit) some of the social commentary found in his drafts.

Writing the Blues: Poetry Masquerading as Prose

Above all else, (in poetry or prose), Hughes is often at his best when he is describing those who were singing, dancing, and playing the blues. While capturing the dynamic aspects of music in language can overwhelm many writers, this is a space where Hughes always flourished. Some readers have gone so far as to suggest that "Like a character itself, the blues becomes a constant and central presence in Hughes's novel" (Burkhardt 116). In the chapter titled "Dance," we are privy to some stirring performances of the blues as Hughes represents dance itself as a communal event. Against the brasses loud repeating, Hughes tells us that the banjo at first joined in "like timid drops of rain" (*CW* 4: 74). However, its role begins to change as the song continues. Later, as a coronet tilted in pain, the banjo "cried in stop-time" (*CW* 4: 74). And by the time the trumpet "panted as though it were out of breath," the banjo "scolded" (*CW* 4: 75). Caught up in the dream-like sensuality of the song, the song goes as "cruel, desolate, and unadorned" as the "body of a ravished woman on the sun-baked earth" (*CW* 4: 75). Every listener (reader) enjoys this interplay as the "High yallers," "Brown skins," and "chocolates-to-the-bone" start "eagle-rocking" with their faces gleaming like circus balloons" (*CW* 4: 75-60).

Hughes then extends his metaphor of seduction suggesting that each boy is a balloon being pulled by strings held by girls. The dancer's feet stomp so hard they go down "through the floor into the earth" as "the 'St. Louis Blues' spread itself like a bitter syrup over the hall" (*CW* 4: 76-7). As Sandy falls to half-dreaming in the music hall, his conscious experience ends as he seems to hear "the sparkling bubbles that rise on deep water over a man who has just drowned himself" (*CW* 4: 77). The blues have intensified Sandy's attentiveness as he enters a state of sleep that mirrors death. Symbolically rising from this transformative sleep, he sees "stars faded to points of dying fire" (*CW* 4: 80). To find his dreams he looks up, and the night stars hold the reminder of the light he has seen. Rarely has the summative experience of hearing the blues seemed so simultaneously vibrant, visceral, sensual, and forlorn. The persona of Sandy allows Hughes's readers to simultaneously celebrate this erotic experience as if life itself were something new.

But when dealing with the blues, things are not always as they seem. In fact, readers are often encountering words that blur traditional boundaries between prose and poetry. Poetry and prose intermingle throughout the novel, and Hughes's descriptions of the blues also took the shape of verse. Hughes's personal copy of his manuscript included the unpublished poem titled "Poem for a Dance" on a separate page at the very front of the chapter described above:

> The earth rolls relentlessly,
> And the sun blazes forever on the earth,
> Breeding, breeding, breeding.
>   But why do you insist like the earth,
>   Music?
> Rolling and breeding,
> Earth and sun relentlessly.
> But why do you insist like the sun?
> ~~Insist~~ like the lips of women?
> Like the bodies of men, relentlessly?
> "Aw, play it, Mister Benbow!"
> But why do you insist, Music?

Who understands the earth?
Do you Mingo?
Who understands the sun?
Do you, Harriett?
Does anybody know—
Among you high-yallers, you jelly-
  beans,
You pinks and pretty-daddies,
Among you seal-skin browns, smooth
  blacks,
~~Sweet papas~~, Easy risers,
  chocolates-to-the-bone—

Does anybody know the answer?
"Aw, play it, Benbow!"
It's midnight.
De clock is strikin' twelve, an' . . . . .
"Aw, play it, Mister Benbow!" (Shields 609)

What is so striking about this separate and unpublished manuscript poem is that it aligns word for word with descriptions Hughes portrays in prose on pages 75-76 of his novel. It reminds us that even when Hughes was communicating in prose, his internal rhythms and ideas were often poems. This is but one of many instances in this novel where we are unconscious of the fact that Hughes's poetry is masquerading as prose.

In fact, Hughes eases us into this proem by deftly preceding these lines with a gradual buildup of rhyme. Immediately before the above proem, he rhymes "sun" with "done," "flesh" with "emptiness," and "hoarsely" with "board":

Cruel, desolate, unadorned was their music now, like the body of a ravished woman on the sun-baked earth; violent and hard, like a giant standing over his bleeding mate in the blazing sun. The odors of bodies, the stings of flesh, and the utter emptiness of soul when it's done— these things the piano and the drums, the coronet and the twanging banjo insisted on hoarsely to a beat that made the dancers move, in that little hall, like pawns on a frenetic checker-board. (*CW* 4: 75)

Hughes activates the ambiguities of metaphor leaving us to ponder what is being implied by these poetic descriptions of giants and pawns. Who are the dignitaries that stand silently behind the pawns as they spend themselves? Is this merely a way to describe dancers who freely give themselves away, or is this a veiled observation about white ownership? Is it coincidental that Hughes offers such implications after providing imagery that clearly suggests rape? Why does Hughes choose the elusive distance between vehicles and tenors in these metaphors to raise such issues? Like religion, the blues are more than just an opiate. In this chapter, Hughes is demonstrating exactly how the blues collectively and covertly transcode and sublimate life's troubles.

Turning Poetry into Prose: "Mother to Son" and "Brass Spittoons"

Hagar shapes the imagination of Sandy just as Hughes's own grandmother Mary Langston shaped the author's own ambitions. Like the biblical character her name itself activates, Hagar's life has been shaped by displacement. Her name also draws our attention to the 1921 blues song "Aunt Hagar's Children's Blues" which was recorded over two dozen times by 1942 (Tracy 27). In addition to these two connections, she also holds fast to her dreams for young Sandy's future: "'I wants you to be a great man, son,' she often told him, sitting on the porch in the darkness, singing, dreaming, calling up the deep past, creating dreams within the child. 'I wants you to be a great man'" (*CW* 4: 202). Hagar's worldly wisdom results in poetic conclusions where she suggests "Ever'thing there is but lovin' leaves a rust on yo' soul" (*CW* 4: 132). The connection is no coincidence. Translating rather than redacting his poems, Hughes intentionally braided together ideas from his poetry into his first novel. More specifically, Hughes extended ideas from one of American literature's greatest dramatic monologues as he invoked the hardships expressed in his poem "Mother to Son" (1922) throughout *Not Without Laughter*. In his poem from 1922, life's obstacles are symbolically expressed as a set of ragged stairs filled with tacks and splinters. The mother tells her son she has continued climbing these stairs "even in the dark" (line 12). She firmly implores her son he should not "turn back" just "Cause you find it's kinder hard" (15-16).

Hughes not only includes the motif of struggle in his presentation of the key mother figure here with Hagar, he actually reactivates the very imagery and diction included in the poem itself throughout the novel. Aunt Hagar tells her daughter: "don't trip on none o' them boards nor branches an' fall" just before she herself "climbed slowly over the door-sill" (*CW* 4: 27). Later, Hager uses the exact same phrase from the poem when she says there is no reason to stop loving others "cause things is kinder hard" (*CW* 4: 129). The language continues. When Hagar is exhausted from washing white folks clothes, she exclaims: "I feels kinder tired-like, that's all" (*CW* 4: 156). Because the novel is so unpretentiously semi-autobiographical, Aunt Hagar certainly resembles the inspiration provided to Hughes himself by his own mother Carrie as well as Mary Langston who instilled in him a sense of his potential to make a significant contribution on behalf of the race.

Hughes also recasts another poem in the form of prose in chapter twenty when he details Sandy's job of cleaning out brass spittoons at the Drummer's Hotel. Published just a year before Hughes began writing *Not Without Laughter*, "Brass Spittoons" (1926) finds some small compensation in the act of a job the poet himself once held. Despite the ever-present sense of financial need and an assault of racist directives, the poem also claims that "A bright bowl of brass is beautiful to the Lord" (32). Where "Mother to Son" serves as a type of theme Hughes has reactivated, "Brass Spittoons" appears to simultaneously extend the idea of the influence that Aunt Hagar has had on young Sandy. Hughes begins this chapter with a description that amplifies her influence:

> He liked to clean things, to make them beautiful, to make them shine. Aunt Hagar did, too. When she wasn't washing clothes, she was always cleaning something about the house, dusting, polishing the range, or scrubbing the kitchen floor until it was white enough to eat from. To Hagar a clean thing was beautiful—also to Sandy, proud every evening of his six unblemished brass spittoons. Yet each day when he came to work, they were covered anew with tobacco juice, cigarette-butts, wads of chewing-gum, and phlegm. But to make them clean was Sandy's job— and they were beautiful when they were clean. (*CW* 4: 148)

Early uses of the words "slimy" and "gold" that precede this description lead to even greater connections to the actual poem as the section above includes the word "shine" as well as three repetitions of the very word "beautiful" that Hughes includes in "Brass Spittoons." Just as Hughes would continue to upcycle his poems in dramatic works performed across numerous stages over the rest of his career, here he was already learning how to reinvigorate his poetic ideas in the genre of prose. In fact, even his poem "Red Silk Stockings" (1927) can be connected to the reactions Harriet gets when she auditions for a job at the carnival (Stone 275).

Hughes clearly reveals himself to be a poet writing prose. The vast majority of instances in which his works blur boundaries reveals that the poems were the source works that were written first. That is, Hughes most often took his poems into another genre rather than getting new ideas for poems as a result of working in another field. This very process reveals why Hughes always defined himself as a poet first, and he ventured out into other fields armed with the short lyrics he both gravitated toward and trusted as a result of responses he had already received from audiences.

Praying the Blues

As time progresses, Sandy blurs blues and religion just as Hughes himself is set on blurring poetry and prose. Sandy's prayers take on the unmistakable rhyme that characterizes the traditional turnaround of the twelve-bar blues. Hughes gives us four lines of an oft repeated prayer only to show us how easily these lines can be reframed as blues. Mirroring the dozens of blues lyrics included throughout the novel, these lines are also set off as their own separate text. We read:

> Now I lay me down to sleep.
> Pray the Lord my soul to keep.
> If I should die before I wake,
> Pray the Lord my soul to take. . . . (*CW* 4: 110)

Immediately after, we are given an additional two lines to complete this stanza. Sandy can almost hear the laughter of a slide guitar that might easily accompany the end of his own riff:

> And let Santa bring me a Golden Flyer sled,
> Please, Lord. Amen. (*CW* 4: 110)

The slant rhyme between "sled" and "Amen" turns this simple child's prayer into a blues man's plea.

Here, Hughes blurs prayers and blues while succinctly reshaping poetry and prose. To covey this idea to full effect, Hughes sets the first four lines off as verse rhymes, while the final two lines above are originally portrayed in prose. Like the blues itself, Hughes's novel is slowly becoming non-denominational. Sandy is praying the blues in a form that grafts song with prose.

The blues, of course, is more than the sum of its songs. Hughes himself reveals the blues's ability to transcode social pain into metaphors that are as cathartic as they are elusive. Hughes notes that the blues have "not only double, but triple meanings" (*CW* 4: 50). The blues lifestyle can also be expressed in the narrative of traveling. Furthermore, insight learned from a story based on "out-bragging and out-lying" is where the novel unveils its title. Just before allowing readers to listen in on the depths of blues culture, we are introduced to Uncle Dan Givens. We learn that no matter "how hard life might be, it was not without laughter" (*CW* 4: 175). It should be noted that, like poetry, "laughter is . . . associated with sound" (Tracy 22). In a section of the manuscript draft, Hughes wrote: "don't think they're all happy people—like the white man does, just because a nigger grins" (Shields 612). Those we see smiling are often hurt the most. In this pool hall, Uncle Dan can be heard giving ample evidence of this as his performances have earned him the title "worlds' champion liar" (*CW* 4: 175). Because this is cast within the context of blues culture, this is a title of distinction, not ignorance. Uncle Dan's self-described prowess in love fulfills the transcoding prerogative of the blues as he tells of how many children he has fathered. The story is humorous on the surface because of its outrageous claims and seasoned delivery. However, it masks the pain of truth as it subtly (but unmistakably) weaves together the narrative of how Uncle Dan was once his owner's prime "stud-nigger" (*CW* 4: 176). The blues man's narrative turns the horrible reality that slaves were sometimes bred by their masters like livestock into a tale where humor can conquer. In this way, Hughes presents people who laugh to keep from crying.

While Uncle Dan's blues are rewarded here with free food and liquor, the blues songs sung by Harriet earn her the money that eventually keeps Sandy in school. As such, she "represents how the religious and the secular may be brought together in peaceful and natural coexistence" (Tracy 24). She saves Sandy from being a worker as he is about to quit so that he could take up a full-time job to help his mother pay the rent. He was destined to work as an elevator operator who literally travels up and down all day without moving forward. This is how Sandy is saved by the blues. In place of work, Hughes elevates the thing he himself now has as a recent graduate of Lincoln University: education.

Dramatizing a Spiritual

Extending his earlier example where Sandy prays the blues, Hughes ends his novel by dramatizing an old spiritual. Hughes physically sets off the first two lines from the refrain of the famous hymn "We'll Understand it Better By and By." He begins by writing: "By an' by when de mawnin' comes, / Saints an' sinners all are gathered home" (*CW* 4: 209). Then, Hughes deliberately turns to prose. While talking with his mother on the streets of Chicago, where the hymn itself can be heard coming from the opened church door, Sandy recalls his early childhood in Kansas. The final line of the novel, again set off as verse, is the fourth and final line of the refrain from the hymn: "An' we'll understand it better by and by!" (*CW* 4: 209). The paragraphs of prose in-between these off-set lines of verse are highly representational. However, even the most attentive readers can hardly identify this unless they actually know the third line from the hymn's refrain that Hughes omits: "We'll tell the story how we've overcome." Hughes's imaginative substitution literally leaves the prose of the novel standing in the place of this line. Infused with poetry, the prose of *Not Without Laughter* amplifies this hymn's lyric truth. In terms of genre, this is dramatic: this substitution epitomizes what Hughes's entire novel comes to represent. The best prose is often lyrical.

The hymn's heroism and struggle coalesce for the young Sandy as Aunt Harriet's blues performances pave the way for him to have the opportunity to be the great man his grandmother helped inspire (and prayed for). It is hard to miss the parallels to Hughes own life, as his own discovery that the blues medium could be translated into poetry literally became the first cornerstone of his distinguished career in letters. That he would by the early 1960s stand as the unquestioned ambassador of African American Poetry makes this connection all the more resonate. Having already discovered that the blues could be transmitted in poetry, in *Not Without Laughter*, Hughes explores transmission of the blues through prose.

Sandy "overcame" as a result of many influences, including his grandmother's industry and inspiration, time spent with his Aunt Tandy experiencing the limitations and advantages of refinement, his mother's love, and the fruits that came from his father playing and living the blues. For conservative readers, Hughes's novel keenly dramatizes a Christian hymn; for those who study culture, Sandy is saved by the blues; in terms of class, the protagonist represents some of the hopes of the proletariat by recognizing that he is more than a mere worker; and, all the while, poets find Hughes's poetry masquerading as prose. Hughes brought all these readings under the same tent cover by giving us a novel that models what it means to be inclusive. *Not Without Laughter* reveals that Langston Hughes was not only a poet exploring the realm of prose, he was also testing the bounds of genre now through the music that became his muse. Like all who were segregated, art's categories, titles, and divisions were things waiting to be united. For this reason, Langston Hughes's artistry became non-denominational.

WORKS CITED

Burkhardt, Barbara. "The Blues in Langston Hughes's *Not Without Laughter*. *Midamerica: The Yearbook of the Society for the Subject of Midwestern Literature* 23:1 (1996): 114-123.

Kutzinski, Verna M. *The Worlds of Langston Hughes: Modernism and Translation in the Americas*. Ithaca: Cornell University Press, 2012.

Hubbard, Dolan. Introduction to the Novels. In *The Collected Works of Langston Hughes*, edited by Dolan Hubbard. Vol. 4. Columbia: University of Missouri Press, 2001.

Hughes, Langston. "Brass Spittoons." In *The Collected Works of Langston Hughes*. Edited by Arnold Rampersad. Vol. 1. Columbia: University of Missouri Press, 2001. 82.

Miller, R. Baxter. " 'Done Made us Leave Our Home': Langston Hughes's *Not Without Laughter*—Unifying Image and Three Dimensions." *Phylon* 37.4 (1976): 362-369.

———. "Mother to Son." In *The Collected Works of Langston Hughes*. Edited by Arnold Rampersad. Vol. 1. Columbia: University of Missouri Press, 2001. 60.

———. *Not Without Laughter*. In *The Collected Works of Langston Hughes*. Edited by Dolan Hubbard. Vol. 4. Columbia: University of Missouri Press, 2001. 11-209.

Schultz, Elizabeth. "Natural and Unnatural Circumstances in Langston Hughes's *Not Without Laughter*." *Callaloo* 25.4 (2002): 1177-1187.

Shields, John P. " 'Never Cross the Divide': Reconstructing Langston Hughes's *Not Without Laughter*." *African American Review* 28.4 (1994): 601-613.

Stone, Joan. "Circles of Liberation and Constriction: Dance in Not Without Laughter." In *Montage of a Dream Deferred: The Art and Life of Langston Hughes*, edited by John Edgar Tidwell and Cheryl R. Ragar. Columbia: University of Missouri Press, 2007. 259-283.

Tracey, Steven C. "Langston Hughes and Aunt Hagar's Children's Blues Performance: 'Six-Bits Blues.' " In *Montage of a Dream Deferred: The Art and Life of Langston Hughes*, edited by John Edgar Tidwell and Cheryl R. Ragar. Columbia: University of Missouri Press, 2007. 19-31.

The Explorer Narrative as Silence
M. NourbeSe Philip's *Looking For Livingstone*

SONNET L'ABBÉ

It may seem somewhat of a false project to approach Marlene Nourbese Philip's *Looking For Livingstone* ([1]) as a novel, when the poet herself writes that the book was "conceveived as a poem in prose and poetry. It does have certain narrative features," she writes, "but it is a poem to my mind" ([2]). Kate Eichhorn and Heather Milne, naming a genre in which they include *Looking for Livingstone*, define "innovative poetry and poetics as writing that, at the very least, approaches language as an inherent problematic and subject of inquiry rather than mere vehicle for representation" ([3]). This definition easily fits *Looking for Livingstone*, which takes as one of its key epistemological concerns a mistrust of the word, particularly of the English words in which Philip must write. The simultaneous impossibility and necessity of articulating the experience of African diasporic identity in a colonizer's language, a problem which pushes the author toward syntactical rupture and open self-reflexiveness, is foregrounded in all Philip's writing except, perhaps, her more conventional young adult novel *Harriet's Daughter* ([4]). *Looking For Livingstone* is indeed closer in formal strategies to the ground-breaking poetry collection, *She Tries Her Tongue, Her Silence Softly Breaks* ([5]), which preceded it, and to her equally phenomenal book-length poem *Zong!* ([6]), which followed, than to her novel, a tender story about two pre-teen girls who long to return from Canada to the Caribbean.

Nonetheless, the back cover of *Looking for Livingstone* describes the book as "an elegant and compelling novel" and presents Philip first as a novelist, then as a poet, a framing that invites the reader to experience *Looking for Livingstone* as a story told poetically, rather than as a poem with narrative features. I'm not convinced that a genre label makes much difference to the philosophical and historiographical work the book enacts. If we describe the poet's novel as Laynie Brown does, insisting that "in a poet's novel action is not more important than quiet, arc is not the same as plot, character is not necessarily person or portrait, and time is often a character or operative device," ([7]) then *Looking For Livingstone* fits the bill.

Importantly, however, the problematization of language and disruption of lyric in *Looking for Livingstone*, and indeed in Philip's oeuvre more broadly, arise out less out of shared interests in Euro-American postmodernism's interrogation of the subject, or in the language play that has its roots in modernist avant-gardes, and more out of the project of Afro-Caribbean writing to effectively represent Caribbean consciousnesses of the forces of creolization, subjugation to colonial people and practices, and sense of forced exile and displacement from their own language and history. Despite Philip's frequent association with Language school poets, because of her insistence on the materiality of language and her willingness to "look at language ... as an artist looks at paint," ([8]) her drive in *Looking for Livingstone* is toward an affirmation of interiority, not a negation of it or of lyric subjectivity. *Looking For Livingstone* uses the strategies of innovative poetry to narrate her Black subject's successful quest to "open a way to the interior or perish" ([9]) and articulates, through involutions of the traditional European colonial quest narrative, her discovery of what Kevin Everod Quashie calls "the sovereignty of quiet." ([10])

Looking For Livingstone begins with a narrator setting out on a journey to discover something as yet unidentified. She begins her search before she knows exactly what she is searching for, but suspects that her compulsion to discover is related to the fervor that propelled the nineteenth-century Scottish physician and missionary, Dr. David Livingstone, into the interior of Africa. "Where was I going? I had forgotten where I had come from—knew I had to go on. 'I will open a way to the interior or perish.' Livingstone's own words—I took them now as my own—my motto. . . . [He] was shown the falls of Mosioatunya—the smoke that thunders—by the indigeonous African and 'discovered' it . . . Livingstone now lies buried at Westminster Abbey because he 'discovered' and explored Africa . . . Perhaps he discovered something else—the same thing I search for—." ([11])

The narrator, whose name we never learn and who asks only to be referred to as The Traveller, identifies Livingstone (and Henry Morton Stanley, who was later sent to find Livingstone) as "white fathers of the continent. Of silence" ([12]). The scare quotes around the word "discovered" indicate the Traveller's skeptical perspective on the narrative of Livingstone as the "discoverer" of Africa. Writing in 2006, Edward P. Antonio describes the the missionary and "civilizing" activities of David Livingstone as "nothing short of ground preparation for efficient colonization," and his legacy in Africa as "one of racial segregation and discrimination, imperial domination, apartheid and violence" ([13]). To Philip's Traveller, Livingstone is the father not only of this tangible legacy of violence but of vast, intangible absences: the erasures, obliterations and silencings of African peoples, their cultures and their languages. This silencing is inscribed and reinscribed by narratives that painted Livingstone as the bearer of enlightenment to a dark continent, and that shaped representations of Africa and its peoples for the next century and a half (Joseph Conrad, for example, had the stories of explorers "whispered to [him] in the cradle" and read Livingstone as a boy ([14])).

The Traveller's consciousness exists outside the chronologies of European history. Her journey begins on: "THE FIRST AND LAST DAY OF THE MONTH OF NEW MOONS (OTHERWISE KNOWN AS THE LAST AND FIRST MONTH) IN THE FIRST YEAR OF OUR WORD 0300 HOURS)" ([15]) and ends, in a hundred-thousand-year-long encounter some 18 billion years later, on a date that is "THE SAME AS THE END OF TIME, WHICH IS THE SAME AS THE FIFTEENTH DAY OF JUNE, NINETEEN HUNDRED AND EIGHTY SEVEN IN THE YEAR OF OUR LORD" ([16]). Her geography is also ephemeral: she travels "in circles," referring to maps that are blank, arriving periodically in "the lands" of various peoples—though these "lands" are sketched only enough to give huts, dirt and fires to the various people; they are lands without geography; it is not even given that the Traveller begins in Africa.

Each people has a name that is an anagram of SILENCE. The ECNELIS, the first people the Traveller meets, tell her she will recognize what she is looking for when she sees it, that it is something to be recovered, not discovered. Each group the Traveller meets teaches her, either through example or lesson, about the nature of conscious silence. The ECLENIS share their creation myths; the uncommunicative LENSECI are examples of brute labour without culture—while with them the Traveller realizes she needs to follow in Livingstone's footsteps. The SCENILE, a gentle and learned society, who understand what the Traveller is looking for, but will not tell her straightforwardly what it is, offer her anagrams. The CESLIENS are silent by choice and teach the Traveller a language of Silence; their ceremony upon the Traveller's departure involves enclosing her in a circle, and culminates when the Traveller finds safety within a space she delineates for herself, within the contours of her confinement. The sensual CLEENIS invite the Traveller to sweat out all the words from her body in their sweat lodge; and finally, amongst the NE-ECLIS, who are weavers and needlewomen, the Traveller meets a lover who tricks her into confinement, commanding her to stay in a room until she can "piece together the words of [her] silence" ([17]).

It is in this solitary confinement, which lasts seven hundred years, most of which is taken up by rage against the betrayal that put her there, the Traveller finally begins to understand:

[T]here were two separate strands or threads—word and silence—
each as important as the other. To weave anything I first had to make
the separation, and before I could do that, I needed to find my own
Silence. . . . Silence does not always mean the absence of sound, because in all that sound, of my own voice, I was able to find and hear my
own Silence. . . . when SHE finally arrived, I had woven a tapestry,
and had pieced together a multicolored quilt—of Silence—my many
silences—held together by the most invisible of stitches—the invisible
but necessary word." ([18])

With this new awareness, the Traveller is able to move on and find Livingstone, but not before coming across the Museum of Silence, "erected
to house the many and varied silences of different peoples . . . I recognized
the displays—these silences were mine as much as they had belonged to the
people they had been taken from" ([19]). She demands that these labelled and
collected silences be returned to their owners, but the curators only laugh.

When the Traveller finally catches up with Livingstone, she finds she has
little to say to him except to correct his version of the story of his exploits.
She explains the nature of her journey, her discovery of Silence. He recoils
from her request for a kiss. Philip draws out their encounter; the Traveller
tries to use words to impart her sense of Silence to him whose journey is
the antithesis of her own. The two remain together for an indeterminate
period, and rather than culminating in a triumph of Silence over Word, or
of the rewriting of history, the Traveller's journey closes with the touch of
her hand and Livingstone's.

The traveller's journey is appended by a frame, a fictitious note from a
fictitious archivist who explains that this work is based on two volumes that
rest in the Bodleian Library, and that in the second volume are Polaroid
photographs: one of Livingstone, one of a white person and Black person,
blurred, identified as Livingstone and the traveller, and a third photo "entirely black, rendering nothing visible" ([20]). Though the librarian believes
their holdings to be the only copy of "Diary of a Traveller," the archivist
informs the reader that a note, in a hand assumed to be the Traveller's, states
that the library volumes are a facsimile, and that the real physical document
of her travels has been left with the CESLIENS, who are the only ones who
know how to keep their Silence. The library displays the books in a glass
case, accompanied by a note that contradicts the statement.

Interspersed between these many chapter-like episodes of cultural encounter are poems, poems of very short line, in a separate font from the
diaristic entries, in an almost fragmented breath. The poems speak of birth-

ing silence, of female embodiedness, of the seductive and phallic nature of the Word, the womb- and mouth-like spaciousness of silence: these poems reach for metaphor and line break that evoke the embodied longing for a voiced representation of extra-vocal knowledge. Though the first poem speaks with an "I," the rest of the poems speak of the Traveller and of silence in the third person, and express in lyric mode, as a chorus might, a kind of deindividualized observation of human desire.

Looking For Livingstone is subtitled "An Odyssey of Silence," and though the Homeric epic had no chorus, Philip's subtitle locates her work within a logic of the oral traditions, narrative poetics, cultural mythologies, and practices of written transmission of cultures that predate the Judeo-Christian literary culture of Western Europe. In this light, it makes sense that Philip should refer to Looking For Livingstone as a poem because its historical engagements so clearly predate the beginnings of the novel in English, and take up more than once the question of a tongue's poesis, the first makings of language itself. Still, a work that engages and criticizes the epic poetry tradition nonetheless engages the mechanics of cultural hero-making that inform such landmarks of the novel form as Miguel de Cervantes' Don Quixote (1605), Moby Dick (1851), Heart of Darkness (1901), The Wonderful Wizard of Oz (1900) and James Joyce's Ulysses (1922). So I will return to Laynie Browne's description of the poet's novel for the terms by which we can take inventory of Looking For Livingstone's intervention into the Western narrative tradition.

1. Action is not more important than quiet: This is practically Looking For Livingstone's manifesto. In fact, the book is an affirmation of the equal importance of quiet and the action of putting-into-words, if not of quiet's superiority as a space of knowing in the context of the enforced silence of the African in the writing and laws of the colonial consciousness. Where the traditional Western novel focuses on putting action into words and stitching these together with "invisible seams," that is, with simple line breaks that enact shifts in scene or chapter and broach broad expanses of time and relative inaction, the Traveller uses stitches of "the invisible but necessary Word" to make unvoiced consciousness itself visible, tangible and productive.

2. Arc is not the same as plot: novelistic convention, particularly of the adventure genre, plots a story such that the protagonist reveals his character through his navigation of conflicts encountered in pursuit of a goal. Without conflict, without antagonists that jeopardize the hero's possibility of success, there is little in the way of conventional Western narrative. Philip's Traveller is already seeking when we first meet her; there is no initial stasis out of which she is triggered and launched into action. Once her search

materializes into an idea of its object (Livingstone), the Traveller encounters no real antagonism — she moves freely over uncharted geographies and through time. Her free movement is in powerful contrast to the imagery of the white man's struggle against dense impenetrable jungle and native savagery in the lexicon of European explorer narratives. Where the sound of drums, heard by Conrad's Marlow in his excruciatingly slow progress into the "heart of darkness," signal threat and a schizophrenic confrontation with aspects of humanity that the Western psyche would disavow, Philip's Traveller meets ancient peoples as her fellows. She is slowed in her movement not by ambush or inhospitable landscapes, but rather by decisions to meet, spend time with and learn from the people, the women, she meets as she moves. Their communities offer her the opportunity to pour her energy into periods of stasis that reveal new dimensions of silence. Hence she opens "a path to the interior" not by the action of cutting of jungle paths or "civilizing" adversaries but by entering into the non-doing of introspection. The learning the Traveller undergoes is non-linear, random, rather than occuring as one event forces her to choose one direction or another, and her arc is a product of the "going in circles" that is propelled not by individualistic desire but by the forces that connect individuals to ancestors and that move bodies across lands. Which leads us to:

3. Character is not necessarily person / portrait: If the conventional Western novel leaves us with the effect of having spent time with individuals, individuals whose successful characterization involves setting them in a particular time and place, *Looking For Livingstone* confounds us by leaving us with no image of our narrator other than a blurred, faded photo of a smiling Black person, and no physical setting in which to ground her, other than her body, which we understand is female and black and whose sympathies lie with indigenous Africans; and no temporal one other than her conscience, which spans the duration of the known universe. Philip resists simply adding an individualized, realist black female character as a contribution to Western literature's hero-protagonists. *Looking For Livingstone* challenges the dependence of Western quest narratives, and hence of one key figuration of individual self-actualization and valour, on the objectification and exoticisation of others, and on racism and violence. The book particularly indicts the mutual reinforcement of such hero-making stories and the colonial violence perpetuated by similarly structured "exploration and discovery" expeditions such as Livingstone's. *Looking For Livingstone*'s silence-discovering heroine is a figure of historical awareness, the silenced feminine, and speaks both as the voice of a singular embodiment but also of the continuous, unspoken awareness of an intergenerational consciousness.

The fragmented choral lyricism of the poetry reinforces the disjuncture of the narration from personage and reframes it as engaging an ongoing, polychronous process of languaging.

4. Time is a character or operative device—time travel in *Looking For Livingstone* gives the book the flavor of science fiction, of Madeleine L'Engle's *A Wrinkle In Time* or Octavia E. Butler's *Kindred*. But where science fiction often uses time travel playfully to give characters access to the past, or to other worlds, Philip's Traveller is tired, her movement feels chronologically directionless, and the time / distances she travels only suggest the constructedness of time itself, and of the vastnesses of silent presence that can be stitched together, and elided, with little bits of narrative. At the end of the book, the Traveller and Livingstone encounter each other in a moment that is simultaneously the end of time, a date in the 1980s, chronologically both before and after Livingstone's death. Philip eschews a novelistic telling that consciously flashes back or forward in a narrator's memory for a deliberate foregrounding of historical consciousness as always occuring now.

Marlene NourbeSe Philip's project has been, over the course of her career, to create forms that might "speak silence" and "tell the story that cannot be told" ([21]). In so doing, Kate Eichhorn argues, Philip has demonstrated to a generation of writers that "sometimes the most politically urgent writing necessitates innovation at the level of language and form" ([22]). In *She Tries Her Tongue, Her Silence Softly Breaks*, for example, Philip works visually and typographically to set a voice that narrates a matrilineal, bodily transmission of wisdom from mother to daughter literally at right angles to, at cross-purposes with, legal language prohibiting slaves to speak their own languages, and the thin, reedy plaint of the lyric voice that speaks the anguish of having to use English ([23]). In *Zong!*, Philip fragments the text of a legal document (Gregson v. Gilbert) that records the death of 150 Africans on a slave ship as a disputed insurance claim, again using visual and procedural techniques to disperse the original text into never-fully reconstituted words and utterings. Yet to use the word "innovation" to describe what Philip does with genre feels a bit incomplete, because the implication is that a spirit of progression is at play; that a language's technologies, having been pushed to the upper limit of their functionality, find through the poet's innovation their serviceability expanded, updated, to meet contemporary demands. For Philip, the English language is functionally and normatively incapable of enacting the consciousness she is compelled to articulate. This lack of capacity will not be built upon; there is no "innovating" on an impossibility.

For the consciousness seeking to decolonize itself, English itself is violence, is flaw, is constraint. Responding to a question about how her work fits into practices that choose constraint in order to find new ways of generating and ordering language, Philip comments: "The very idea of the freedom to choose a constraint signals the existence of . . . pre-existing constraints and serves to mask them by the very idea of freedom to choose the constraint. Further, the apparent absence of constraints in certain groups, which requires one to go out and find one . . . actually depends on the overabundance of constraints in the lives of others. . . . I think the constraint begins a lot earlier than the act of artificially seeking a constraint" ([24]). Philip's project can be understood as always-already working within this constraint, while still trying to break open what she has called "the hard kernels of silence." The phrase first appears in *Looking for Livingstone* (the cruel between of teeth / crush / grind / the hard kernels / of silence) ([25]) and later Philip describes these kernels as "places where longing and desire come up against history, the lacunae in history, where, for instance, you can't ever know what tribe or group they came from, what your mother tongue was . . . The ever and ineffable unknowable. In the face of a culture that purports to know everything it knows and promises that what it doesn't it will" ([26]). For Philip, the legal document which *Zong!* opens up is a hard kernel of silence, "because locked in that text is the story of unnamed Africans who like many, many others have been erased from history or memory" ([27]).

We might then understand *Looking For Livingstone*, as one step in the evolution of Philip's strategies of germinating these kernels into consciousness. If in her early work Philip expresses hopefulness about "recreat[ing] our histories and our myths," ([28]) and then in *Zong!* evinces a wearier, almost defeated stance, telling "the story of be-ing which cannot, must, be told," ([29]) we might read *Looking For Livingstone* as a bridge between those energies of hope and cynicism. In the space-time of *Looking For Livingstone*, an idealism and expressivity that at first believes it possible, or enough, to tell her side of the story, finds, through a fantastic exploration of freedom of movement and desire, the harsher apprehension that "a fact is whatever anyone, having the power to enforce it, says is a fact." ([30]) And if we see in her early poetry Philip taking a wide-angle perspective on the colonial violence of the entire English language, addressing in lyric-formal play the broad shapes and textures of its silencings, and if on the other hand, later, in *Zong!* we read Philip as focusing on the smaller, denser and more violently euphemistic kernel of one legal document, which she fragments, then *Looking For Livingstone* is framed as engagement with a kernel of silence somewhere between the extreme poles of entire language and single document: the kernel of a entire genre, one that spans fiction and non-fiction—the European explorer narrative, the exoticizing travelogue, the adventurer's tale.

When the traveller tells Livingstone that through her journey, she has discovered silence, her silence, he hardly registers the meaning or nature of the accomplishment she is claiming. She says to him:

> You want to know whether I have written any books about my disco-eries, or my exploits . . . you ask for proof that I discovered my Silence . . . you want facts, dates and years . . . and titles of books like TRAVELS WITH MY SILENCE, or MY LIFE WITH THE CLEENIS . . . ([31])

Upon reading these lines, a reader is reminded that she holds in her hands exactly what some would take for proof: a book about the Traveller's discoveries. The evidentiary pose of the travel narrative, and the contingency of its authority on the context of its reception, will be emphasized again by the "author's note" that indicates that this book is not an original account but is based on records bound and held in the Bodleian Library, a source text that has already been indexed and interpreted by "someone other than The Traveller" ([32]). Philip suggests that like the objects in the Museum of Silence, the text of *Looking For Livingstone* is a silence severed from its source, and therefore risks being a cold structure ([33]) cut off from its meaning. In this metatextual move, which resonates with the convolutions of story and book object and archive we might see in the work of Dionne Brand, Jorge Luis Borges, and Italo Calvino, Philip demonstrates the impossibility of holding the intergenerational knowledges of indigenous African peoples in Western genres and systems of literary production.

Through breaches of narrative convention, employing strategies on travel narrative that may be common to other poets' interventions into the novel genre, Philip seems to release her protagonist from the constraints of the explorer's tale—allowing her Traveller to move freely through time, to require no conflict in order to experience her own heroism, to experience silence as the most compelling action to tell. But despite freeing her narrator from the realist and historicist pretensions of the genre, we find that the Traveller's tale is still produced within a system of power that will can decide what is or isn't fact. In its more recognizably poetic modes, *Looking For Livingstone* performs what, within a paradigm of genre-as-technology, may be read as genre innovation and expansion. But in Philip's context of English language as lacuna, and its forms as potential "hard kernels of silence," her poetics expose something absolutely not-new, the unvoiced constraint and unknow-abilities that are continually enacted by genres in their most basic forms.

NOTES

1. Philip, Marlene NourbeSe. *Looking For Livingstone.* (Stratford, ON: Mercury, 1991).

2. Letter to author, March 14, 2015.

3. Eichorn, Kate and Heather Milne, eds. *Prismatic Publics : Innovative Canadian Women's Poetry and Poetics.* (Toronto: Coach House, 2009), 9.

4. Philip, Marlene NourbeSe. *Harriet's Daughter.* (Toronto: Women's Press, 1988).

5. Philip, Marlene NourbeSe. *She Tries Her Tongue, Her Silence Softly Breaks.* (Charlottetown, P.E.I.: Ragweed, 1989).

6. Philip, Marlene NourbeSe. *Zong!* (Middletown, CT: Wesleyan University Press, 2008).

7. Browne, Laynie. "A Conversation with Bhanu Kapil: The Poet's Novel." *Jacket2.org.*

8. Mahlis, Kristen. "A Poet of Place: An Interview with M. Nourbese Philip." (*Callaloo* 27:4 Summer 2004), 693.

9. Philip, *Looking For Livingstone,* 7.

10. Quashie, Kevin. *The Sovereignty of Quiet: Beyond Resistance in Black Culture* (New Brunswick, NJ: Rutgers University Press, 2012), 134.

11. Philip, *Looking For Livingstone,* 7.

12. Ibid.

13. Antonio, Edward P. *Inculturation and Postcolonial Discourse in African Theology.* (Peter Lang, New York, 2006), 210.

14. Rubery, Matthew. "Joseph Conrad's 'Wild Story of a Journalist'" (*ELH* 71:3 Fall 2004), 751.

15. Philip, *Looking For Livingstone,* 7.

16. Ibid., 60.

17. Ibid., 51.

18. Ibid., 54-55.

19. Ibid., 57.

20. Ibid., 78.

21. Betts, Gregory. "Not Against Expression." *Jacket2.org.* 29 March

22. Eichorn and Milne, 139.

23. Philip, *She Tries Her Tongue,* 56

24. Eichorn and Milne, 144.

25. Philip, *Looking For Livingstone,* 8.

26. Eichorn and Milne, 139.

27. Ibid., 143.

28. Philip, *She Tries Her Tongue,* 25.

29. Philip, *Zong!,* 200.

30. Philip, *Looking For Livingstone,* 67.
31. Ibid.
32. Ibid., 77.
33. Ibid., 57.

WORKS CITED

Antonio, Edward P. *Inculturation and Postcolonial Discourse in African Theology.* Peter Lang, New York, 2006.

Betts, Gregory. "Not Against Expression." Jacket2.org. 29 March 2013.

Browne, Laynie. "A Conversation with Bhanu Kapil: The Poet's Novel." Jacket2.org.

Eichorn, Kate and Heather Milne, eds. *Prismatic Publics : Innovative Canadian Women's Poetry and Poetics.* Toronto: Coach House, 2009.

Mahlis, Kristen. "A Poet of Place: An Interview with M. Nourbese Philip." Callaloo 27:4 (Summer 2004) 682-97.

Philip, Marlene NourbeSe. *Harriet's Daughter.* Toronto: Women's Press, 1988.

—. *Looking For Livingstone.* Stratford, ON: Mercury, 1991.

—. *Letter to author,* March 14, 2015.

—. *She Tries Her Tongue, Her Silence Softly Breaks.* Charlottetown, P.E.I.: Ragweed, 1989.

—. *Zong!* Middletown, CT: Wesleyan University Press, 2008.

Quashie, Kevin. *The Sovereignty of Quiet: Beyond Resistance in Black Culture.* New Brunswick, NJ: Rutgers University Press, 2012.

Rubery, Matthew. "Joseph Conrad's 'Wild Story of a Journalist." ELH 71:3 (Fall 2004), 751- 774.

Coming through Slaughter
Michael Ondaatje's Buddy Book

C.D. WRIGHT

A book that follows its nose, trusts its nose, a book that has its own rhythm, its own melody; a book that opens with a damaged photograph and a quote from a long-dead musician from the band of another long-dead musician along with three sonographs of a dolphin. That's how it starts. Under the tent-flap of poetry.

Then comes a slow low ride, through the old neighborhood. Then Buddy Bolden, the great jazz cornetist, a progenitor, springs to life, shaving a man in his barbershop, circa 1905. His drinking habit, his sleepless habit, his loving habit, his personal broadside, *The Cricket,* circulated to satisfy his gossip habit. "He was the best and the loudest and most loved jazzman of his time, but never professional in the brain." The sentences start to nab you, snatch you by the arm, lure you into the alleyways; prowl between sets.

Bolden's wife Nora Bass "for instance, believed in the sandman when putting the children to bed whereas even the children didn't." The characters come clear in a one-sentence stroke.

Bolden's sound, "Nora's Song": "Dragging his bone over town. Dragging his bone . . . " a little song, the same line over and over, broken on a jag. Already the prose has to stand on the sidelines while the horn makes its rounds.

Already our main man has disappeared and his oldest friend, Webb, a laconic detective, is out looking for him.

A page is given over just to naming the tunes: Funky Butt, Take your big leg off me, If you don't like my potatoes why do you dig so deep? Poetry of the vernacular: alive, undisciplined, metaphoric, erotic, and recorded by a very distinctive, very selective Sri Lankan ear. On a certain level it is a ready-made match. A kinship with the ways of a place. Not just the place, but its ways. Not just the ways but the warp of its time.

A shiver of the magical is hard to resist. The wife's mother arrives with her Audobon prints and her retired python. A week later she is discovered strangled in her Envictor. That's right, her Envictor. Shades of Isadora Duncan. When Nora and Bolden come across the mother's body, they drive her stiff in the automobile to the police station where corpse and car are stolen while they are making their report. An unlikely scenario, but who cares. You're up to your gumbo now.

A line is laid in and repeated: "There were his dreams of his children dying."

A riff of a scatological order for texture: In his search for Bolden, Webb questions a fellow player who talks only about taking an epic crap.

Cut to Bolden, watching another friend's wife cutting carrots. Bolden lost to his friend, lost to his wife, lost to his friend's wife, lost first and last to himself.

Coming through Slaughter does not walk through its paces as a full-fledged story, but frames up like a score and segues like a film and phrases like a poem. A short paragraph is a page; a paragraph is an entire scene. Every paragraph is a polished work. He is building his poem. It is wrapped in a novel. Suggestions, coincidences, scattered pieces of hard information, interviews, archival material, and a man with a scantly documented past, leaving his last gig with nothing but a mouthpiece in his pocket. Gone. "He woke to see the train disappearing away from his body like a vein." Bolden walked away from his life and stumbled into someone else's.

It is not until the second section that he speaks. It is not a chapter but a section. He speaks. Sort of. or, at least in his head he is heard talking to Webb.

The actual chronology allows the real Buddy Bolden to fictionally befriend the real (reputedly) hunchbacked Storyville photographer, E.J. Bellocq. The lone archived photograph of Buddy Bolden's Band is fictionally linked to Bellocq. A description of another actual photograph is fictionally linked to Nora, Bolden's wife. When Nora Bass was a whore. Bellocq photographed whores. Bolden bedded them. We get a slide show of Bellocq's pictures. Click. Click.

There is always a dog somewhere in the frame of an Ondaatje work.

There is always a line that comes back around, "passing wet chicory that lies in the field like the sky."

There is always a love scene, attained with incomparable lust and loveliness.

Usually a tragic quality gets caught up in it, most often a betrayal. An enactment of which most prose writers rarely seem to nail. He does.

A fictional account of Bellocq's death by suicide. Ceremonial. A little over the top, a little operatic, but who cares. You bought the ticket, got a front and center seat.

There is often a reflexive hint dropped in, [Webb]: "entering the character of Bolden through every voice he spoke to." The interior of Bolden's mind is explored as it gradually dissolves. "Swimming towards the sound of madness."

Another character is introduced, Tom Pickett, a pimp, through whom Buddy's madness is made manifest, as he takes a razor to Pickett's nipple and face. Nora intervenes. The formerly beautiful Tom Pickett staggers off. The rain comes into Bolden's head. Another character is introduced, likewise contributing an element of Bolden's state at the time. "Impossible . . . In any argument he'd try to overpower you with yelling . . . . Buddy didn't leave at the peak of his glory you know. No one does. Whatever they say no one does . . . But he was still playing fine . . . ."

Webb tracks his old friend down. Taking his own Louisiana lag time. Pacing is all.

Train Song. "Passing wet chicory that lies in the fields like the sky." One line repeated on a jagged score.

One more night of love. "Already travelling on the morning bus tragic." And it's over. "There is no need to turn. . . . There is no need to turn my head for Robin is gone." And "the morning bus tragic" brings on a random sexual interlude . . . . "cruel, pure relationship." He rides out this rainy head spell in his friend Webb's cabin. There is always room for another hound dog story. There has to be solitude in the story of a musician going mad. The poet knows how to charge the silence with space. The dog follows.

The poet jimmies in some music history. Inventory-style. Music making history. Radio. Live music. Mutt Carey, Bud Scott, Happy Galloway. Music experiments. Carey dying in Bolden's house, "in the middle of a shake." Fuckit.

Buddy Bolden woodsheds in Webb's cabin. With the dog. Shaving. Practicing. Talking to Webb in his head, in a letter? The talk is always along the oblique. Half interior, half sounded out. He's "got more theoretical with no one to talk to."

His friend Crawley pays an uninvited visit. Tells him, "You learn to play like that and no band will play with you." Tells him, Nora is living with Cornish, another player.

A six-line interview. That's a page. Comes the information you have been dreading, "He died in the bug house."

"All my life I seemed to be a parcel on a bus. I am the famous fucker. I am the famous barber. I am the famous cornet player. Read the labels. The labels are coming home."

The names of the bands. Another inventory. That's a page.

Buddy comes home to live in his house with his wife Nora and his friend Cornish. All his labels. Ready to play in Henry Allen Sr's Brass Band . . . in the parade . . . "crazy, at the Liberty-Iberville connect."

"And Buddy watched her large hip as she lay on the floor of the room, the hill of cloth, and he came into her dress like a burglar without words . . . ."

"The home of his wife's mouth coming down on him."

"The diamond had to love the earth it passed along the way, every speck and angle of the other's history, for the diamond had been earth too."

Nora: "You look like a favorite shirt I lost."

"He lies back with his head in her lap. Looking up at her. The home of his wife's mouth coming down on him."

Bolden "had wanted to be the reservoir where engines and people drank, blood sperm music pouring out and getting hooked in someone's ear. The way flowers were still and fed bees" until his friend Webb came for him and Bolden had turned "glinting and sharp and cold . . . turned into metal at [his] mouth."

The four days before the parade are told in outline. Broken down into the days and the evenings. In and out of Bolden's head. The kids, the musicians, the whores, the photographer now among the dead, "Dear small dead Bellocq." Bolden who never shut up, fallen silent. Sober . . . "Just his face laughing at the jokes."

"The home of his wife's mouth coming down on him."

Flashback to Buddy shilling for Bellocq, so the women will let the hunchback photograph them.

Dreams roll out. Including the dreams of children.

The parade takes place on the fifth morning. Bolden is playing to a woman.

Horn seduction. Blowing his vessels, blowing out his mind.

His stats: Insane at 29 in 1907. Taken to the House of Detention. Taken to East Louisiana State Hospital. Where he lived until his death in 1931. It is not until the penultimate page that we learn that the trip from Baton Rouge to the State Hospital, by horse and wagon, passed through Slaughter.

The inmates cut their tendons. Conditions were that bad. Same as at Louisiana's Angola State Prison, in 1951, where they were called heel stringers. Not Bolden. He did not cut himself. He was already gone.

Talking to a wife of Willy Cornish (not Nora), Webb picks up a piece of long lost vital information. Talking to her about Buddy, about Buddy's death. Except it's 1924. Buddy dies in 1931. Buddy was still in the state hospital. Since 1907. The first Webb heard.

Bolden never speaks. He just touches things.

Then reels of interviews are transcribed from the Tulane Library, edited by the writer, retold in abbreviated syntax. Reel by reel.

So sparely and sympathetically does Ondaatje fill out the legendary musician's life, making him one of us, but going down hard.

Most of the story is pure invention. Of course there was a Buddy Bolden. He could really really play. He had training. He could read music. He could improvise.

He was Louis Armstrong's idol, but had none of his own. He was the first of his kind. According to Willy Cornish, an actual sideman, there was an Edison cylinder recording but it has never been found. Bolden was never steady on. His father died when he was six. He was almost a redhead. He alienated his first wife who left with their son; his second wife was hard-pressed to put up with him, as were his players. He was said to hit wife Nora Bass's mother in the head with a pitcher. He did for a stone cold fact totally lose it in a parade, Labor Day, 1907. He was never a barber. According to city records he was a plasterer. He did not put out a broadside called *The Cricket*. He did not know Bellocq though both were habitués of Storyville. He was buried in Holt Cemetery. There is a monument now, but no one knows where his bones actually lie. It took a poet, telling it slant, to bring him back.

"Light" in Keith Waldrop's *Light While There Is Light: An American History*

LAURA MORIARTY

Keith Waldrop's *Light While There Is Light: An American History* is a fully realized autobiographical novel composed in a subtle, expressive language redolent of the author's poetry—and yet not. Though the story is simply and elegantly told, Waldrop tends not to rely in the narrative on the multiple connotations of words or the collaged presentation of lines that are a familiar to readers of his poetry. That said, he does place things in the text (incidents, lines, characters) adjacent to things (nextily, as Gertrude Stein says) without excessive explication in a way that allows the reader to draw her own conclusions. He also uses Dickinsonian dashes and a metaphorical richness in language not unlike the exquisite phrasing of Emily Dickinson and suggestive of their mutual sources in hymns, the Bible and Shakespeare. The section names are allusive and poetic ("A Pilgrimage," "Tibet," "Discerning Spirits, "The Call Asserts Nothing"), rather than explanatory. Still, the narrative remains a clear, linear history easily accessible to the reader who is not an enthusiast of poetry. One of its powers is in making us wonder how this narrator with the challenges of his particular life could ever have managed to survive and grow up to tell this story with such stunning brilliance.

Light While There Is Light is called "*An American History*" and Waldrop puts some pressure on its genre by his use of his own name and the names of his family, as well as the inclusion of family photographs. The book can be, and often is, read as a memoir but the invention of some characters, place names and events and the fact that the narrator is not the main character, or not the only main character, tends to support the author's assertion that the book is a work of fiction which simply, in the great tradition of novels, utilizes material from life.* This question of genre might seem relatively straightforward but continues to be of interest as one reads *Light While There Is Light*. The reader experiences a strong sense of a life remembered, a portrait, from her son's point of view, of Opal Mohler who is rarely named in the book but almost always referred to as "my mother." The history in the title is of a certain kind of religious fervor present in the middle of the last century and still an important part of American life. The book is a coming of age story and a hilarious, almost slapstick, comedy of family life. It is also the tragic tale of the anguished unfulfilled life of Waldrop's mother, a woman born into the last century with much more intelligence and sensitivity than the available resources could support. There is much pathos, history, memoir, story-telling and reflection in this book—but most of all there is "light."

For the purposes of this essay I plan to present the instances of the word "light" in the text as a way doing the kind of close reading you might expect in considering a poem. On the way, for this will be a kind of pilgrimage to the "light," I will provide commentary. This way of reading the novel will allow me to present an almost random collection of passages from throughout the novel that contain the work "light" in all of its connotations.

I present this poem-like collage of the "lighted" passages out of admiration for this book, which is surely one of the masterpieces of fiction, but also as an offering of delight to its readers and potential readers for whom I propose to pose and answer the question of how much "light" there is in *Light While There is Light: An American History*.

• • •

> Walk while ye have the light, lest darkness come upon you: for he that walketh in darkness knoweth not whither he goeth. While ye have light, believe in the light, that ye may be the children of light. John, 12:35-36

Though the book has two epigraphs (see below) the passage above from the Gospel of John is not one of them. It is included in Jaimy Gordon's excellent introduction to the reprinted edition just out from Dalkey Archives. By not including the quotation, Waldrop seems to suggest that the Bible is a reference text to the book, a key that forms a backdrop and frame for the work that he expects you to know and go to in all its historical enormity and yet which he does not place in his own text as an authority, saving Emily Dickinson for that role. But, to back up slightly, let us start with "light," as a word. The first definition of "light" in Merrium-Webster is "something that makes vision possible," an intriguing definition that can be read as doubling the double meaning of both light and vision to what is the fifth definition, "spiritual illumination." "Light" comes from Old English (lēoht) and from an Aryan root similar to the High German (lioht), presumably along with other "ight" words like "might" and "right." In both cases the word seems to mean the light that shines. The association of light with knowledge and divinity is probably as old as the word. "God" comes up in the first citation in the Oxford English Dictionary from Ælfric of Eynsham in the year 1000 in a line that appears to be Genesis 1:3, and can be rendered in current English, "And God said, Let there be light: and there was light." None of this information is in the novel but, of course, the Bible is there in the title.

Waldrop's mother's love and knowledge of the Bible and inclination to argue its doctrines and his father's love and similarly exact knowledge of Shakespeare form two of the main literary heritages of the *Light While There Is Light*, along with, perhaps strangely, Djuana Barnes' *Nightwood*. In an extensive, multi-year interview with Peter Gizzi published in two issues of *The Germ*, Waldrop references this book as of great importance to him when he first began the novel that was later merged into this fictionalized story of Waldrop's family.[1] As a tale of obsession and madness, *Nightwood* can be seen as another sort of coming of age story and a book that, like *Light While There Is Light*, stands alone in the writer's ouvre. The form is not exactly similar and Barnes' language is a bit more stentorious than Waldrop's but when I read, in the interview of Waldrop's interest in *Nightwood* I began to see it and *Light While There Is Light* as the same kind short, intense masterpieces of great tragedy and incredible humor. Both are books you read again and again like a poem. Another influence that comes up in the same interview and elsewhere (it is mentioned in the introduction) is Henry James, who Waldrop confesses to liking more than any poet. James' use of the narrator whose point of view reveals a complex stake in the narrative, and who is deeply implicated but also somehow distant from the inevitable outcome, is another way to look at this master work. Still another is to focus on the carefully crafted and precise prose managed by both writers. There is a stately progress to Waldrop's approach which suggests the nineteenth as much as the twentieth century's prose rhythms.

Here, however, I would like to view *Light While There Is Light* (and even deconstruct the text into) the poem it clearly is not. To this end I have transcribed the sections in which "light" appears and will present them with comments divided by asterisks. I have not commented on every use of "light" in the book though it seemed right to include them all. While the book tells a great story—reminding one as much of Mark Twain as the writers mentioned above—it is the words that fix my attention as a reader who is also a poet familiar with Waldrop's immense poetic legacy. The deft execution of a series of tropes using the word "light" forms a sort of superstructure within the text that I hope to uncover by presenting these excerpts. Aspects of the work should also be legible in these collected texts—as, for example, the themes of perception and death that are present throughout the book. The actual deaths are those of Waldrop's mother, his father, his brother and others in the story. Waldrop remembers his dead and the story is about them and yet he also can't remember them. Memory becomes another important theme. Very often these concepts are introduced with a mention of "light" (and also with words that rhyme with "light") and it is these I propose to follow—beginning, however, with the two "lightless" epigraphs that suggest both the situation (the deaths of loved ones) and the solution (work) with which the author identifies his task.

The overtakelessness of those
Who have accomplished death . . .

—EMILY DICKINSON

Work, for the night is coming . . .

—OLD HYMN

These quotations set the stage with the suggestion of death, as night or absence of light, and the fierce, examined Protestantism that form the backdrops of the events in the novel. Waldrop open the first section, "A Pilgrimage," with a passage that does not use the word light, though it is present in the scene. Though the light of the sun is described as being "without a shadow," it is the ghostly lack of shadow, this dark brightness that one is left with in this first line. This dark light appears often in the text.

> I've read many stories of revenants and apparitions, but my ghosts merely disappear. I never see them. They haunt me by not being there, by the table where no one eats, the empty window that lets the sun in without a shadow. [p. 11]

• • •

> "Probably, I am ignorant of her most exquisite pains. I know enough not to make light of lamentations. . . . Sometimes I could get her to play the piano." [p. 11]

Intimated by its rhyme with "night" in the second epigraph, "light" first appears in the book in this line about Waldrop's mother with the meaning of lessening or making less important. This use seems to fly in the face of my earlier suggestion that Waldrop does not use the connotations of words to move forward in the narrative, although in my defense I note that the use of the word "light," in this line is unambiguous. It is simply other than its use in the title. The indirection here is subtle in a way that becomes evident in the novel as you move through it word by word, instead of merely succumbing to the fascinating story and memoir. The effect is of being hypnotized by sound and connotation without noticing it is occurring, as if the argument is being sung to you rather than explained. The use in this case, with the biblical feel of "lamentations" sets the stage for the tragic figure of Waldrop's mother, Opal Mohler, who is the other main character, with the narrator, of *Light While There Is Light*.

• • •

The stasis described and, I think, produced by the following section is not the only or even the first light-related critique of memory in the book (because, as above, light appears in the text without the use of its signifier) but it is one of the most intense, told, as it is, like a ghost story, yet with all the familiarity of an often-related family tale. This event literally appears and disappears in and out of the light in a way that comes to mind later when Waldrop describes the use of lighting in a performance of Shakespeare that was and is quite common but which was revelatory to the young narrator.

And then he ran across the room and turned the lights off.

And it was dark then, of course, but it was not a darkness that she recognized. It was as though there lacked not light, but the flow of time. It was not, across the black room, a distance in steps, that even the blind might feel their way, but a space of centuries, a loss total and immeasurable. And she could not get out of the cradle, which she felt rocking. She could not even struggle. With the utmost effort, she managed to form her friend's name, but cried it so feebly that she knew it would never carry across the emptiness.

He meanwhile, as it turned out, was feeling much the same thing as she and was searching, terrified, for the light switch, which he could not find again. Finally his hand, groping blindly, hit the right spot and the room burst into light—the same room, with its paneling, its four-poster, its cradle in the fireplace, and her, clambering out of the cradle. They were both terror-stricken and refused to stay the night in that room. [pgs. 21-22]

• • •

The relating of the following incident, one of those that ended Waldrop's mother's second marriage (to his father; his brothers and sister were the children of her first marriage), uses "light" in a way that is often repeated as one follows the word through the text. In this novel "light" often produces shadows and darkness or is harsh and glaring. It appears not to illuminate but only to obscure, plunging things into confusion and darkness and yet, also, rest from its garish intrusion.

> Now she raced back to her own room as he switched the lights on. "This is what happens," he was yelling, "as soon as I turn my back." The giant doors cracked shut again, leaving me dazzled with the light that was now shut out. His shouts continued on the other side, Elaine's voice sometimes chiming in from a distance. (Neither Charles nor Julian were there—Charles was in the war in the South Pacific.) I lay tense while the shouts got louder. I heard Sister Eliot's name. Finally there were other sounds: movements, doors. Then a blow and my mother's scream and Elaine howling. [p. 25]

• • •

> The lamp gave a brilliant white light from its ash mantle, but I dropped off before we made it into Newton and was only half awake to clamber across the immense freight yard where, strangely, there were blinding lights all through the air, and yet the crisscrossed rails seemed endless and unlit. [p.26]

Waldrop narrates his father's somewhat nightmarish world of work where there is a lot of light and yet little that is illuminated by it.

• • •

> She took this dipper from the hook, without lighting the lamp. And in the shadows she scooped a drink from the water bucket and swallowed, along with the water, a black widow spider.

> "No one knew this was going to happen," my mother always said at the end of this tale. "Not even the angels knew. But the Holy Ghost knew. [p. 35]

This unnerving event suggests the sense of predestined but unknowable tragedy embraced by Waldrop's mother from the very beginning of the story. It is also one of the many occasions when "light" appears in a passage about death.

• • •

The black cloud that belched out now blotted the daylight and we could hear nothing but the engine puffing and grinding. [p. 48]

In order, however, to make things a little lighter for himself, he left his waycar to a younger man and became (by a process trainmen called "bumping") flagman on a passenger streamliner called El Capitan. [pgs. 50-51]

"Light" appears in the first section above only to be obscured. In the next part we find out the second use of "light" in the sense of lessoning, as it was first used in the text. These lines make us feel the heaviness of Waldrop's father's job as a railroad man and the lifelong demands he was able only to "lighten" as an aging worker.

• • •

I'm not sure, to this day, whether my aim was to find out something I didn't know—some fact unnoticeable in the light of day—or rather to celebrate that no one knew I was there. [p. 57]

"[L]ight of day" appears here in contrast to the religious light that suffuses the novel, though it never leads to any sort of enlightenment.

• • •

What puzzled me, as I watched him gaze at the moonlit bulk, was that there was really nothing to look at. I don't mean that none of the girls was worth a glance—I mean there was, across the whole expanse, not one light burning. [p. 58]

The bright darkness of adolescent desire appears to light our way to the character of Evangeline (below) whose name meaning "the good news"

belies the doomed love that occurs between her and the young Waldrop.
She is, like her namesake in Longfellow's poem about the heroine of Aca-
dian history, a tragic spiritual wanderer who seeks the light, but not of this
world.

> And then, while the car rattled through the harsh daylight and unusu-
> al snow (with an old man at the wheel who looked at things through
> thick blue lenses), while I tried to see Evangeline in some other light
> that would show me who she was and why—*Why?* [p. 60]

• • •

> One bulb directly above J.W. gave a harsh downward light, leaving the
> end of the vault in shadow. The windows were less bright than they
> had been and I noticed something like snow falling far on the other
> side of the bars. [p. 64]

> Stella rose and stood under the discolored light, unsubstantial without
> her instrument, both her hands clutching at a handkerchief. [p. 64]

> ''Amen!'' shouted old LeFebvre and his ancient white head moved
> shining into the light. [p. 65]

> "Lord," said J.W., "we thank thee for this opportunity to bring the
> message to these in need of thy great power and light." [p. 68]

These lines are from the story of the preacher J.W.'s visit with students
Evangeline, Stella (whose name, which means "star," suggests light) and
Waldrop, fellow students at Sharon College, to a local prison to minister to
the prisoners. Waldrop goes in pursuit of Evangeline, who is sick with an
enlarged heart from rheumatic fever and even more with a kind of spiritual
sickness that causes her to want to die and go to heaven rather than stay in
the world, be in love or do anything else. The word "fire" appears in relation
to the strictly religious passion of the scene and produces a lightless heat
that drives Waldrop away. It is here in the face of this young beauty's choice
of eternal death rather than the common "light of day" that the narrator first
seems to lose his faith or at least something like spiritual innocence as an
inner voice declares:

Nobody, nobody could want to die. But the voice was artificial and almost extinguished, a voice rapidly dissolving away, a voice of my naïveté. [p. 70]

• • •

I noted the way, common enough I now know, in which each scene, instead of being marked off by raising and lowering the curtain, was brought up out of the dark and at the end returned to dark, so that the entire play became a series of moments articulated by light on a background of darkness. [p. 70]

The reader is struck by the connection of the stagecraft in this presentation of the "G.I. Hamlet" in which scenes are lit and then fade away with the framing of events that has already occurred and continues throughout the novel.

• • •

It was even odder, however, that sprinkled among the collection now were works by Darwin and even by Ingersoll. (Also a long eulogistic poem called *The Light-Bearer of Liberty*.) [p. 73]

The "liberty" here in the first poem to appear in the text after Dickinson's might be the freedom that allows for Waldrop's eventual escape from this life into the world of Darwin and Ingersoll. (Robert G. Ingersoll was known for his defense of agnosticism.)

• • •

Then the wall disappeared altogether, but the neutral light remained, as if I were in a dense fog; there was sound, too, but indistinct. When the congregation stood up to sing I stood up too, gazing at Shebbajean's knot, and can recall no transition. [p.78]

This story of being entranced by Shebbajean's auburn hair "twisted and braided into a knot" ("her name was written Shelby Jean but pronounced Shebbajean") is another instance of a scene disappearing and then reappearing before the young narrator's eyes, as was mentioned in the passage above about the lighting of Hamlet, and, again, much as the incidents in the text artfully appear and disappear for the reader.

• • •

The pianist switched tunes and we were singing J.W.'s favorite:

> To be lost in the night, in Eternity's night,
> To sink in despair and in woe—
> But such is they doom if thou turn from the light,
> Refusing his Mercies to know. [p. 78]

In this second case of a quoted hymn, the dark light of the fundamentalist religion that infuses the first two sections of the novel appears. The "light" here is full of "doom," "despair" and "night."

• • •

He pointed across the campus toward the boy's dormitory and I saw a light go on in a second story window. It went out and in a moment the window next to it was lit. Then the next, and so on, with quick regularity, until there was a longer pause of darkness and then a light on the third floor commenced its round. I started up the steps to our apartment, but on the porch there was a dead cat. Even in the moonlight I could see that it was brother's favorite brindle. [p. 79]

Light is used for the first time in this passage in its role as signal, comprising a kind of writing with light and creating a pattern, a sort of prosody, meant to be legible to its "readers." The deadly import of the message takes the form of the death of one of Waldrop's brother's endless stray animals.

• • •

And if she dreamt at night—one of those nights when I was restless and, without thinking, paced the kitchen floor—of a dazzling young man, hero or poet, approaching her bed as an angel of light with cloven hoof. [p. 89]

This line, about a teacher called Miss Yodle, is notable as the only occasion in which the word "poet" occurs in the book. The word is associated with the heroic but devilish individual that, perhaps, the narrator is on his way to becoming.

• • •

By one of memory's common tricks I remember him as witty but cannot produce an example of his wit—which has, all the same, a definite quality for me, a light understatement that was effective partly because set in a matter-of-fact, open personality. [p. 90]

The phrase "matter-of-fact" can possibly be equated with the positive "light of day" which appeared earlier. "[L]ight understatement" is a good short description of Waldrop's own style which includes a value for focusing on the nuances of ordinary perception and the slight differences that distinguish one particular from the other. The words "slight" or "slightly" are used almost as often as "light" in the novel, forming a rhyme within the ongoing song of the story, as well as suggesting the fineness of the observations used to discern and relate what is happening in it.

• • •

(He also was the school's chief carpenter and it was noticed that in the newer buildings all the light switches were on a bias.) [p. 91]

Sharon College, one of the invented places in the novel, is shown to be troubled in its very structure by a misaligned light.

• • •

Charles, from his wide reading, revealed that chickens can be made to grow faster by leaving a light on at night, roosting time indefinitely postponed by a crude and stationary imitation of the sun. [p. 94]

Julian got tired of it. I complained. Charles had asthma-like attacks at night. The eternal light bothered everyone. [p. 94]

Charles is Waldrop's other brother. These lines constitute another case where light is intrusive and unhealthy.

• • •

At closing time (Liberty is not big enough for the bus station to stay open past business hours—my brothers, indeed, had often closed early) Mr. Himble would hoist his wife, help her into the car, turn the lights off, and lock up. Then they roared down the street with, strangely enough, Mrs. Himble at the wheel. [p. 97]

This domestic scene is notable for being the second use of "Liberty," though clearly there was little in the situation of the freedom suggested by the word. The aspirations of Waldrop's siblings and the people around them often seem to reach toward a kind of light and liberty only to find darkness, limitation, frustration and failure.

• • •

"The devil is possessing more souls than ever. And he's doing it in the name of religion. There are devil cults in California. And even right here . . . "

"Around here?" I said.

"He's subtle," she went on. "He's in cahoots with churches that call themselves Christian. He confuses them. He takes over and makes them babble. They gargle—and they call it speaking in tongues. And they're deceiving millions." I conceived then and there a desire to hear the tongues she attributed to Satan, but in the meantime—it was several years before I got to a Pentecostal service, and then under unexpected auspices—I went through the New Testament looking for light on this strange phenomenon. My mother was delighted that I took such an interest. She wanted to compile—the two of us together, that is—a scriptural refutation of all false doctrines. [p. 99]

I include an extended version of this passage because of its important use of "light" to refer to textual knowledge and understanding, while also suggesting a familial basis for the life of the mind eventually pursued by the narrator. The narrator's deep connection to his mother and to her sacred text and his turning to a kind of figuring out that was text-based are aspects of his character that allow us to see how the writer of this account can possibly be the same person who experienced the difficulties he describes.

• • •

Bare bulbs were strung between tent poles, and the light was harsh. A wiry song evangelist started things off by getting the whole crowd to sing "My God is Real." [p. 103]

My God is real
For I can feel
Him in my soul [p. 103]

Bright moonlight picked out the curves of the tent from among the dark fields. [p. 107]

This hymn and scene are another case where the dark light of religion is starkly portrayed.

• • •

I was the exception (so I told myself), moving against the pull, farther away at each turn. It is only now, searching thorough memories, circling among the figures who fail to appear—a tenuous history shows through them like sunlight—that I find my getaway less than complete. [p. 156]

This section echoes the opening lines of *Light While There Is Light* characterizing this engrossing account as a "tenuous history" and reminding the reader of what connects the narrator to the milieu he has left behind, but which has also left its mark, a kind of shadow, on him.

• • •

I remember, for some reason, a film I once saw, in which sequences resembling old, contrasty photographs faded, not into darkness like the usual fade, but into a bright white empty screen, so that the story seemed sketched in elaborate shadows against a field of perpetual light—shining now through pictures, illuminating them, and now supplanting them, shining on its own. [p. 159]

This sentence opens the section "The Call Asserts Nothing" which, with its line from Heidegger seeming finally to negate the religious fervor that has existed among the characters in the story, tells the tale of Waldrop's departure from the religious life. It is yet another use of light as a thing which obliterates rather than illuminates what it touches.

• • •

"'These Ouija boards,' someone once told me, 'it's all wish fulfillment. It's the same mechanism as dreaming.'" No doubt there's something to that. The planchette moves where the fingers, lightly pressing, desire it to go." [p. 161]

This final use of "light" in "lightly pressing" meaning to make less leads to a situation in which a séance is desired but then refused by Waldrop's sister Elaine as being devilish—so again "light" ends by being associated with its opposite.

• • •

My imagination is poor. In my dreams, for instance—where one would suppose wishes can be fulfilled without hindrance—if I dream the events this account describes, they are not usually changed, but in what should be a world nearer to the heart's desire, they play again, just as I tell them here, exactly as already experienced. It is as if despairing, even of imaginary improvement, I contrive instead to set my affections on the damned world, this very world, as it was and as it is. (Thus I record subjunctively my own conversation.) And waking, my ghosts are as before: neither soul nor body, but the lack of obstacle to sunbeams coming in the window or light from a light-bulb or any everyday reflection. [p. 171-172]

This paragraph, citing particulars and "everyday reflection" on "this very world, as it was and as it is" as the thing missing in the ghosts of the story is key to the central impulse of *Light While There Is Light*. The autobiographical material is not remembered with complete exactness but carefully, lovingly observed to make the novel. The most imaginative thing about the story is the words used to tell it. The most engaging thing about the novel is the humor, intelligence and humility of the narrator.

• • •

Well, you know how it says we'll not all die, but we shall all be changed—well, Kate thinks if we're children of the light not children of the dark, we don't have to die. [p. 181]

This section is yet another instance of the dark light of the false prophet who tells us what we want to hear in a manner that is quite opposite of Waldrop's mother, who never claimed to have found the light and ultimately seemed not to find any solace in a life spent seeking it:

I asked her then (it's unlike me, such a question—perhaps I was more upset than I knew, or had not yet taken in the dreadful possibility of faith outliving the loss of hope) if her religion gave her no comfort. And she replied immediately, without any emotion in her voice, "No." [p. 187]

The image that appears on the page opposite this passage is surely the darkest of the many family photos in the book.

My mother,
after her operation

•   •   •

I went roaring over to Beulah Chapel and was ready to bite nails, and he was all sweetness and light and smiled and said God told him to buy the house. [p. 194]

Waldrop's brother Charles, who relates this incident, becomes himself something of a cult leader, living among others who are lead by their god, and presumably the dark light often observed in this history, to make cut-throat business decisions.

•   •   •

My own sense of 'reality,' never perhaps all that strong, has changed over the years. I used to think that, the sum of things being obviously unreal, I should cling to what is at hand, the minute particulars of my immediate experience. I still try, but less and less seems particular. What I find now is more often like a play of light—that is, of shadow— in which the objects of my attention are ripples, or notches, or bumps, or bubbles, on a surface otherwise inarticulate, a field which, but for these defects, would be empty. [p. 195]

This passage from near the end of the novel seems to summarize Waldrop's approach to memory, reality and light. Death is suggested by the emptiness pictured as the ultimate object of the narrator's attention. Waldrop's mother's death is appears in the text soon after this section.

•   •   •

Julian carried his cigar, which he would never light in a church, looked around when we were seated—he liked a sumptuous ceremony, as he liked suits and Cadillacs. The church looked right to him, the ushers, the minister, the minister's wife at the keyboard, a bank of flowers around Mother in her hijacked coffin. It all met his approval and he tapped the cigar as if it had an ash, crossed his legs—a difficult gesture for him—and said to me quietly, with satisfaction, 'Giving Mama a good send-off. [p.195]

Julian's cigar, and his performance of one last con on behalf of his mother, constitute points of light in this dark time of her death.

• • •

Just yesterday morning, I woke slowly and found that opening my eyes gave me a view of blanket and bedroom in the usual half-light (it was broad day, actually, the curtains were closed) and then—what would have startled me perhaps if I had been more awake—found that if I closed my eyes again, which I did several times, I continued to see precisely the same scene, but slightly brighter, and all over the blanket (only if I kept my eyes closed) there were innumerable flies. [p. 199]

Light, finally, is related very directly to this deathly image of the narrator's body covered with flies. We follow the instances of the sound—"eyes," "half-light," "eyes," "precisely," "slightly brighter," "eyes," and finally "flies" into an observation of mortality that utilizes the narrator's finely tuned perception to intimate but not actually say, perhaps, that he and we are all always dying.

There is much to celebrate and admire in *Light While There Is Light: An American History*. I have chosen to follow the use of one word and puzzle out some of the connections of this word, "light," to darkness, shadow, death, the sun, heat, emptiness, memory, perception, a quality of touch and, potentially, with all of the words in the novel with which it rhymes. The richness of this text is quite infinite and I could have approached it in any number of other ways. I concur with its publishers (the first edition came out from Sun & Moon in 1993) and reviewers, almost all of whom proclaim that *Light While There Is Light* should take its place among the best books of the last century or of this one. In the interview mentioned above, Waldrop surprised Peter Gizzi, his wife, poet, Rosmarie Waldrop and this reader by citing it as his master work.

I want to close with three passages from Keith Waldrop's *Haunt,* a book of poetry that comes up in the same interview as being from the time as the novel. The loveliness of these lines belies Waldrop's conclusion above, written, as they are, in a language similar to but distinct from that in which the novel is written. However, these passages allude to a relationship with darkness and with a questioning sense of the divine and of writing itself. They also seem to comment on the novel and the intensely lived life reflected in its pages.

He walks in darkness, sits in darkness, dwells. Darkness falls, clouds, covers. [p. 81]

He is no more present to himself than objects in his view—the journey, long for so short a life, promising agate, chalcedony. He attends to changing expression, flickers of shadow, to keep his thought from running inward to inward light. [p. 83]

He cannot decide if the experiment is local, all life composed on this periphery, or if along the wall of stars there's by chance another creature—farther than faintest signals—signifying. [p.83]

With *Light While There Is Light,* the writer is this creature and this novel is his song.

NOTES

1. Page numbers refer to *Light While There Is Light: An American History,* Keith Waldrop, Dalkey Archives, 2013 and to *Haunt,* Keith Waldrop, Instance, 2000.
2. An introduction to *Light While There Is Light: An American Histroy* by Keith Waldrop was published, along with a chapter of the novel, in *Conjunctions* 20 (1993).
3. "Real Shadows," Keith Waldrop interviewed by Peter Gizzi, 1993-1997, appeared in two parts in *The Germ* #4, Spring 2000, and *The Germ* #5, Summer 2001.

"I'm All In The Dirt And On Fire Or Something. Get Me Out Of Here"
The novels of Philip Whalen: *You Didn't Even Try* and *Imaginary Speeches for a Brazen Head*

NORMAN FISCHER

I first read these novels not long after they came out—*You Didn't Even Try* was published in 1967 by Coyote Press; *Imaginary Speeches of a Brazen Head* by Black Sparrow in 1972 (both books were reissued in a single volume in 1985 by Zephyr Press, with an introduction by Paul Christensen, under the title *Philip Whalen: Two Novels*). At that time I was a young writer obsessed with how to write, how anyone made poems and novels. I was looking for writing per se, its forms, so that the content of the novels, what they may have said about their author, his life and times, was of almost no interest to me, or, at any rate, I was blind to it.

What amazed me about these novels was their language, their line by line brilliance and strangeness (as with Whalen's poems, simple and straightforward in disarming ways, and, at the same time—from time to time— surpassingly wild and crazy). Also I was impressed by the fact that as novels, the texts didn't seem to go anywhere. You couldn't tell what was at stake for the characters, what they were after, what their problems, if any, were. I remember putting down *You Didn't Even Try*, marveling at how it went all over the place yet nowhere at all. There seemed to be no plot, no conflict, no problem, no resolution—just a bunch of very interesting, if unusual and aimless, people crashing into one another. And then it ended. Since I was then (and remain) fascinated by things that seem to move around with great energy but not to particularly go anywhere identifiable, or to say anything you can grab hold of, I loved the novel. Later I read *Brazen Head* and had a similar experience, though I was more challenged by this text that seemed to contain some kind of subterranean point, although I didn't get the point.

Also—and this is very important—at the time I read the novels I didn't know Philip Whalen personally, as I later came to, practicing Zen and writing with him for nearly thirty years, when we were fellow students at the San Francisco Zen Center, and after. In San Francisco we lived down the hall from one another at 308 Page Street, and later practiced together as monks at Tassajara Zen Monastery in Carmel Valley, California. When Phil returned to San Francisco after a few years in Santa Fe in the late 1980's, we saw each other regularly, and I was one of his helpers and protectors during the last years of his illness, when he lived first at Zen Hospice and then (having flunked hospice, as he liked to say) at Laguna Honda, the public hospital in San Francisco, where I visited him regularly.

When Phil died on June 26, 2002, I was teaching at Naropa. I was able to say good-bye to him on the phone in his last hours, and spent my teaching weekend celebrating his work and life, which was a great comfort. He meant a lot to me because he was a great writer with immense ambition, knowledge, and reach, but also a tender-hearted and kind person, always, to me and everyone else ... except when he wasn't, after which he was always deeply regretful and mad at himself. He was often mad at himself, usually for good reasons. Certainly knowing Phil formed my life as a writer and a Zen priest. In both these spheres, he gave me permission to be who I was.

I came to the novels after having already been hooked on the poetry—introduced to it when I was struggling with writing at the Iowa Writers' Workshop. One of my teachers there (the novelist Bob Boles) probably saw better than I did what my problem was, and, as medicine, gave me a copy of *On Bear's Head*. I was thunderstruck. I had never seen anything remotely like it. You really could do this? Just write down whatever was going on, inside or out, without trying to make any profound literary points, or even organized sense? And shape it into terrific, lively, poetry? I was instantly liberated from my struggles.

A few years later I was astonished when I knocked on the door of the Zen Center and Philip Whalen opened it for me, his big fuzzy orange beard (featured on the backs of the several books of his I owned) making him instantly identifiable.

All of which is to say that now, rereading these novels, which are, more or less, conventional novels, that is, with characters, scenes, chronologies, and all usual the machinery of ordinary novels (Phil always said that he never intended to be a poet: he thought he'd write novels and become rich and famous, like Hemingway) I see what I entirely missed the first time around—Phil's heart and soul, his dreams and wishes and frustrations and struggles. Even more than the poetry (if possible—and more on this later) these books express the life that Phil was living from the late 1950's to mid the 1960's and beyond: the life that nearly drove him crazy and caused him to leave first the United States, and, finally, the world itself, when he ordained as a Zen Buddhist monastic, in 1972.

Both novels are group portraits. Though both feature central characters who seem to be stand-ins for Whalen, both also include a full cast of others who figure equally at the heart of the action. I'm sure the novels are romans à clef, and some detective work could suss out who is who, but the ensemble of characters is, in any case, interesting enough in its own right. That the novels are built on such assemblages of characters seems to be the point I missed thirty years ago: that there are no persons apart from other persons, that we exist as communities of association, each of us helping every other of us to come alive to similar experiences at similar times in similar places— that together we make a human problem and grope about for a solution we probably never find. The books are about human relationship—its necessity and its ultimate impossibility—about the group of friends (the Beat writers, their friends, lovers, and associates) Phil depended on, loved, and was driven crazy by in that formative period of his life

Try opens with an epigraph from the notebooks of S.T. Coleridge:

The sick and sleepless man, after the dawn of the fresh day, is fain to watch the smoke now from this and then from the other chimney of the town from his bedchamber, as if willing to borrow from others that sense of a new day, of a discontinuity between the yesterday and the to-day, which his own sensations had not afforded. (Notebooks 1811-1812,page 3 in *Philip Whalen, Two Novels*)

Not incidentally, this epigram also suggests another implicit theme of the novels—the strange and arbitrary nature of time. *Try* is written in three parts, with large gaps of time—in which important things have happened— separating the parts; *Brazen Head's* time sequence is fractured and discontinuous—events that precede other events in time are reported long after those events appear, so that the reader is often confused about who is married to and divorced from whom and when.

The characters in *You Didn't Even Try* are restless young creative people, born in the 1930's, living now in late 1950's San Francisco, when the city felt homey and affordable. The War they've all just lived through is seldom mentioned, but it seems to loom over or under them as a kind of dread. These are not happy people. Nor are they troubled by anything in particular. And this goes for the female as well as the male characters—in fact it is quite striking, considering the time in which these novels were written, how liberated and lively Whalen's women characters are in their creativity, their strength, and their full sense of agency. Reading these novels you'd never guess that the period was one in which women were struggling for even basic recognition. Whalen's women are every bit as restless, troubled, and brilliant as his men are.

Kenneth and Helen are married but not happily, mainly because Kenneth (who, we are told in an offhanded way, was slightly wounded in the war when a mortar shell blew up nearby) is profoundly out of step with the world. He can't seem to find any motivation to do anything much. Ordinary daily tasks drive him to distraction. He has a constant need to get away, go for long walks, look at things, dream. He's interested in philosophy, reads a lot, and jots things down, but none of it goes anywhere. But it's clear that our author's sympathies lie with Kenneth—that it's the world, not Kenneth, that's out of whack. Life really doesn't make any sense; it's just simply a mess; there's no truth and beauty to be found anywhere except in escape from the world as it's conceived of. "It occurred to him at last that what he wanted was a quality of life something like looking through a grove of trees at a creek tumbling down over the rocks. The ferns and moss are green, five p.m., early spring. Nothing will sustain me, my entire weight and being, except the unexpected." (page 25 in *Two Novels*). Or, later, "I never saw a world system yet that was so funny as this one. My laughing at it won't hurt it any. Just don't expect me to take it for what its label claims for it—officially, scientifically, legally real. The whole thing is a big hype." (page 50, *Two Novels*).

So life is a trial for Kenneth, and he refuses to, can't, submit. Nor can he, in his funk, pay attention to others. When Helen—an intelligent woman, a trained art historian (all Whalen's characters are brilliant and accomplished)— gets pregnant, she doesn't tell Kenneth. Instead, she goes home to Seattle to get an abortion. But after the time gap between Parts I and II we learn that after she left Kenneth, abruptly, she moved back to Seattle, actually had the child, re-married, is pregnant again, and Ron, her current husband (a much better catch then Ken) is running around on her. (Sexual fidelity in Whalen's novels doesn't exist, and sexual infidelity seems to be no problem for anyone).

Joan and Bruce Chatwin are also married and divorced. Bruce is an artist who makes all kinds of funny assemblages that hang in galleries, and Joan is an importer who travels round the world buying and selling exotic things. Both are so independent that they can't stay married for long, but they remain friends, and one of the novels striking passages describes a dinner Joan cooks for Bruce featuring steamed fish "served in the Chinese way" with a fruit sauce, artichokes with melted butter, pommes a la batard, eggplants Bottacinni, green salad "with little homey touches . . . and the soup is real turtle." All this is preceded by Joan's spectacular martinis: "simply holding

358 • PORTRAIT / DOCUMENTARY / REPRESENTATION / PALIMPSEST

a glass which contained this fluid had an immediate effect upon the person holding it: he would smile quite unconsciously, as if in anticipation of his coming translation." (p 103 in *Two Novels*).

The novelist Marilynn Marjoribanks is married to Travis, who is a genius scientist in great demand with governments and great universities. Meantime Marilynn tapes phone conversations of her friends' rants and intimate revelations, edits the tapes daily, and then goes out to record appearances and conversations of people on the street and in restaurants and shops, amassing huge amounts of material from both sources that she eventually collages into three immense novels for which she receives much acclaim—and then gives up novel writing. (This likely describes, more or less, Whalen's own novel-writing procedure).

In short, these are brilliant resourceful people whose immense lives and accomplishments are depicted in the novel as quite ordinary—and futile. Though there is plenty of sex, the novel seems not to include any "love" scenes. People just have sex, sometimes it isn't even much fun, sometimes it is. Something is wrong, something is missing. It's as if all the characters—not only Kenneth—are constricted in this ordinary world, like a too-small shoe pinching a foot. There's got to be something larger. But what?

The novel ends with an epiphany of sorts. Bruce, Kenneth and Travis go on a trip to the High Sierras where Kenneth learns that Helen wants him back, Marilynn is in love with him, and so is Kate (Marilynn's cousin, a professor of French). Pitching some stones over an alpine lake Kenneth reflects on the situation. "The actual immediate presence of a woman could occupy his consciousness, evoke his love in the same way, but no single woman he could think of could bear the whole weight of his love; he must build a work of his own which would bear the rest of the weight, that pressure, distribute it to the rest of the world. He sighed. He was thinking., 'For a short towhead Swede I must be the biggest megalomaniac now at large. Nevertheless I believe I've got it; The problem is—logistics, the transport of material? Communications—drama? But always the main question: how to tell my love, how to act it out." (p 120 in *Two Novels*).

In actual life, it appears that Whalen wasn't nearly as irresistible to women as the novels main male characters seem to be. Yet the characters (both male and female) seem consistently—as Kenneth here—to reject love relationships as any sort of solution, or even comfort. As Kenneth—like Whalen himself I think—their love is too big, too all-encompassing to be contained. Here's how Roy Aherne, the poet who's the main character in Brazen Head, puts it, "All I really like is fucking and food and poetry and landscape and music. But I get tired of people too easily—and they get tired of me: I talk too much and too loud. I want too much from them. I want to consume them, get so close that we both disappear. They don't like that, they get scared, bored ... I belong in a monastery ... an asylum ... jail."(p 135 in *Two Novels*).

• • •

Imaginary Speeches for a Brazen Head employs the device of a"brazen head" (called "The Grand Mahatma") who appears now and then to comment metaphysically on the action. A brazen (brass) head was a legendary machine, in the shape of a man's head, usually owned by a medieval sage, that could answer any question, a kind of magic oracle. Friar Roger Bacon, who lived in the early 13th century England, was said to possess one. The first speech of the Grand Mahatma appears on the novel's second page:

> The Grand Mahatma says: "SHE comes along and lights up each of our senses, then SHE selects a different partner and moves away. The numbers on our watch dial glow for a while after they've been exposed to the sunshine, then their light finally dies away. They remember for a while, then they rest. The circulation of the blood, the flow of the breath, what did I have for breakfast—each of these trips a different brain electric relay network chain, brain clouds of light, thy great Andromeda nebula, other universes outside this one which we usually think of as true and real, which we in fact keep insisting is the only one ... bright billowing clouds that mix together into "I" "I want" "I see" "I remember;" ... and more of the same sparkling fog produces the earth we're sitting on, produced Queen Victoria, Ashurbanipal, the cobalt bomb, all kind of gods, buddhas, unicorns, the fried egg sandwich we shall eat for lunch." (p 126 in *Two Novels)*

Once again, as with *Try*, we have a large ensemble of brilliant and accomplished characters all of whom are married to and/or sleeping with one another in the webbing of, in this case, a fractured time-frame that's designed to confuse the reader's sense of narrative flow. Roy Aherne, the celebrated poet who reads on college tours, drinks too much, takes too many drugs, sleeps with anyone who will have him, and eventually burns out and moves to Japan (as Whalen did) is a central character. As is Dorothy, a linguist, (maybe modeled on Joanne Kyger?) who is married to Tom, a photographer (who sometimes takes porn pictures of young boys), but used to be married to Clifford, an organist and scholar who mostly lives in Nepal (and might be modeled on Gary Snyder) and sleeps with Roy, who wanted to marry her but ceded to Clifford's priority (as Whalen was in love with Kyger before and after Snyder married her). Roy shoots up methadrine with the artist and actress Margaret Gridley, from Radcliffe (via a small town in Oregon), they stay up for four straight days, after which they drive to Reno and marry, a condition in which they remain until one day Margaret runs into Herbert Wackernagle, her childhood sweetheart, and determines she must now live with him. When her husband protests she says, "Oh Roy, come on." Earlier—or later?—Margaret marries Beefy Johnson, the African American jazz musician. Other important characters include Max and Alice Lamergeier (he's a leading psychiatrist) and Beth and Mark Sanderson (he's a composer who is in possession of Flora McGreevey's all-important piano— more on this later), Sarah, Clifford's English painter girlfriend, who was married to Max Gardner, an even more famous painter, who left her in Europe to run off with his ex-wife. At any rate, the point seems clear enough—these are colorful, unconventional people who are busily rushing around living their lives like so many beams of light bouncing off one another, while the Grand Mahatma (like Nero fiddling in Rome) comments:

> The Grand Mahatma says: "We must practice doing everything right. We must practice being perfect. The Saints, the Bodhisattvas, the Confucian Sages—all of them practiced at it until they could do everything perfectly, and they were perfect themselves, of course. Any one of us can do the same thing. What else is there to be done after all?" (p 132 in *Two Novels*)

Brazen Head includes spectacular passages about food, psychedelic highs, and mystical transports. There's an hilarious three page description of breakfasts— in cafeterias, the Army, his grandmother's hotel room, at Clifford's ancestral home in Idaho, on railway cars, hiking trips, elegant breakfasts served by Dorothy—eaten by Roy (p 173 in *Two Novels*), as well as one of the most detailed and baroque descriptions of a hashish high, Tom's, that I've ever read (p 230 ff in *Two Novels*).

> Dwarf slaves with huge golden trays of roast suckling pig passed among the throng; others bore trays of swans and peacocks and pheasant all served up in their own gorgeous feathers. . . . wine slopped over jeweled hands, naked bellies, gold, fruit, veils, brocade and velvets, asses, tits, bellies, hands, shoulders, eyes, fantastic headdresses, mouths, big eyes above transparent jeweled veils, arms and legs glistening with

sweat oil, mouth eyes—Tom . . . swam joyfully out among them, his penis visiting here a pretty momentary cunt, there a pretty mouth, a pretty ass . . . a silent lake where he floated among lilies and lotuses, alone in silence of summer night, then Dorothy was floating with him, quiet and understanding, everything resolved, all peace . . . TELE-PHONE ??? PARANOIA DOORBELL? where's Dorothy? Flying horse ladies above a ring of fire where she lies golden asleep . . .

· *Brazen Head* ends much less conclusively than *Try*—possibly in the years between the publication of the two books Whalen had given up on the idea of becoming a successful novelist (failure as a writer was and remained throughout his life a major theme) so, feeling no need to come up with an acceptably novelistic epiphanic conclusion, was content to leave things up in the air. The novel closes with a few short vignettes—Roy (in a flashback, if the novel could be said to have flashbacks or flash forwards), happy, hav-ing just received a letter from Dorothy in Asia with Tom, nearly gets hit by a bus in Golden gate Park, near the aquarium; Dorothy and Tom drinking hot chocolate in Vienna, Dorothy reading a letter from her mother, the re-doubtable Flora McGreevey, who wants her piano back. (The disposition of Flora's piano, that passes from Dorothy to Clifford to Mark Sanderson is a constant refrain in the novel). And the Grand Mahatma:

> They ask me all the time: why is the world this way? Why is it all messed up? And I shock them with my answer: Somebody's making a pile of money out of it, that's why . . . Say, I need help. I hurt. Isn't anybody going to come and help me? Isn't there any human being around here going to give me a hand? I hurt! Why don't you get me a doctor? Why don'tthey take me to the hospital? Why don't they give me a shot of something? Say, what kind of outfit is this, anyway? I'M ALL IN THE DIRT AND ON FIRE OR SOMETHING. GET ME OUT OF HERE. (p 250, *Two Novels*)

• • •

All this raises the question—what do the novels add, if they add anything, to what readers have come to appreciate in Whalen's poetry?

What's radical and important about Whalen's poetry is its directness, its nakedness. It's as if, in many of the poems, Whalen isn't even writing poetry at all, he's doodling, ranting, improvising, letting off stream. In fact, it is almost surely the case that Whalen wasn't writing poetry—at least at first. That he really was (or felt he should be) interested in writing novels, but that this was hard work (though Whalen wrote all the time, he was also famously lazy and distractible: complaints about these personal failings run through the poems) so that often he goofed off, doodling in his notebooks, and that this goofing eventually became more important that the novel-writing—in any case it was easier and quicker to do, and eventually Whalen was getting much more cred-it for it than he was getting for his novels. (His notebooks indicate that he had started some thirteen novels, abandoning all but these two).

The novels do, as one would expect, reflect the same concerns as the poems, but as novels, dramatize these concerns. Because they are built on characters who exist in some version of a temporal frame, they make two points the poems can't make—first, that character exists only in ensemble; that a coherent separate psychological entity around which other, minor, characters revolve (as others are separate from and incidental to one's self in life) is a false notion: there is no such thing. I am sure this was Whalen's own experience, and is, not incidentally, a key tenet of the Buddhism he was interested in and later to devoted his life to: there is no independent self, only the mixing of beings in a network of being.

And second, time—that there is no linear time in narrative, no sense or rationality to what happens in literature or in life. Things just go on. They are not going anywhere. There is no movement, no coherence. And therefore no redemption.

There are very few novels with poets as characters, and in the novels that do feature poets the characters are seldom seriously realized (probably be-cause the novelist's world and the poet's world are so radically different). But Whalen's novels are about poets. They dramatize pretty clearly a poet's despair and deeply ambivalent feelings about life: like Roy Aherne, Whalen was a grand sybarite, he loved food, landscapes, colors, art, poetry, beauty, intelligence; but also, like Roy, and like Kenneth, Whalen found the world absolutely pointless and impossible, even at its best. In the end, he had no choice but to leave it, and, little by little, let go of everything (including poetry) but his pious religious practice and quiet life. In his own way he did, I think, achieve the peaceful wisdom that was beyond even the Grand Mahatma: contentment and kindness.

In the poetry all this is enacted rather than dramatized. In the poetry we see the word by word line by line inner life as it enfolds on the page. The poems aren't about anything. They are so personal, so idiosyncratic, that they transcend the personal. They are the mind that experiences a per-plexing and marvelous world, the heart that feels more than it can bear or understand, the hand that writes words on paper. They are about the words themselves, the struggle to express something: the rants and ravings of an essentially inarticulate person (that is, insofar as any of us is inarticulate when we try to get down to what, really and exactly, we are about) struggling with the need to express.

FAILING

The practice of piety. The practice of music. The practice of calligraphy. These are exemplary pastimes. The practice of re-reading the novels of Jane Austen. The practice of cookery. The practice of drinking coffee. The habit of worrying and of having other strong feelings about money. All these are vices. We must try not to write nonsense, our eyes will fall out.

> *In answer to all this my head falls off and rolls all messy and smeary across the floor. KEEP TALKING squelch slop ooze. (Whalen, 1.i.67 in Collected Poems p 538*

As in the novels, whose characters can't find a place to land, and are never satisfied, the poems, at their best and most characteristic, do not afford any comfort. Insofar as life really is, when you pay attention, basically impossible and unsatisfactory (the First Noble Truth of Buddhism), poems, when they are nakedly honest, will have to express this—as Whalen's do. His genius was that he could say this in desperate seriousness while maintaining not only his sense of humor and play—but also a clear and sane knowledge that the whole thing is actually as ridiculous as it is tragic.

> *To Henrik Ibsen*
>
> *This world is not*
> *The world I want*
> *Is Heaven*
> *& I see*
> *There's more of them*
>
> *
>
> *I've seen most of this world is ocean*
> *I know if I had all I wanted from it*
> *There'd still not be enough*
> *Someone would be lonely hungry toothache*
> *All this world with a red ribbon on it*

Not enough
Nor several hells heavens planets
Universal non-skid perfection systems

Where's my eternity papers?
Get me the great Boyg on the phone.
Connect me with the Button Moulder right away.
(Whalen 3:i:67 in Collected Poems, p 539)

WORKS CITED

Philip Whalen, *Two Novels: You Didn't Even Try, Imaginary Speeches for a Brazen Head,* introduction by Paul Christensen, Zephyr Press, 1985.
Philip Whalen, *The Collected Poems of Philip Whalen,* edited by Michael Rothenberg, Wesleyan University Press, 2007.

VI

Metamorphic /
Distance /
Aural Address /
Wandering

Everything in the poem was in transition
—PETER WATERHOUSE, *Language Death Night Outside*

Fernando Pessoa's *The Book of Disquiet*

JOHN KEENE

Livro do desassossego por Bernardo Soares, usually truncated and translated into English as *The Book of Disquiet*—or *Disquietude,* as translator Richard Zenith rendered it[1],[2]—did not exist in completed form during the lifetime of its author, Fernando Pessoa (1888-1935). His longest prose work and his only novel, *The Book of Disquiet* instead was an extended dream project Pessoa initiated around 1912 and continued until his death. Toward that goal, he drafted hundreds of fragments ranging from phrase- and sentence-long prose entries to extended, multi-page reveries, mostly but not all numbered, a few dated chronologically as well, according to a system that later editors have had to puzzle out, though Pessoa left numerous clues and placed three hundred and fifty of the fragments in an envelope marked *The Book of Disquiet.*[3]

Although Pessoa did publish a dozen of the fragments in his lifetime, the published novel did not appear in Portuguese until 1982, in two volumes, nearly five decades after Pessoa's death; Jacinto Prado Coelho, in collaboration with Teresa Sobral Cunha and Maria Aliete Galhoz, served as its editors.[4] Subsequent editions in other languages have led to differing versions, most slimming it to a single volume, removing material thought to be extraneous or redundant, and reordering the texts to create a different narrative line than the original Portuguese version. *The Book of Disquiet* was not translated into English until 1991, when a handful of publishers began issuing editions by four different translators: Zenith, who also edited his editions; Iain Watson; Alfred MacAdam; and Margaret Jull Costa.[5]

As the full Portuguese title indicates, Pessoa, who gained fame not only for his poetic prowess and output but also for his extensive use of heteronyms (and semi-, para- and proto-heteronyms, along with pseudonyms), or distinct, differently named personae, also assigned the authorship of the text to one of these. In total he created eighty-one identities under which he penned and published his poetry, prose and translations. Some of these he also designated as characters populating his published and unpublished writings. One edition of the book, Margaret Jull's Costa's 1991 translation for Serpent's Tail, edited by Maria José de Lancastre for the Italian publisher Feltrinelli, in 1986, has Bernardo Soares, a heteronym and semi-heteronym for Pessoa, signing its introduction, though this is not the case for her 2017 New Directions translation, in which the introduction remains unsigned, nor for Zenith's 1996 edition for The Sheep Meadow Press, which attributes the introduction directly to Pessoa himself.

Bernardo Soares was not one of the three primary heteronyms—Alberto Caeiro, Álvaro de Campos, and Ricardo Reis—under which Pessoa wrote and published most of his poems. Soares, however, provided Pessoa with a (light) mask behind which he could share his musings in prose, toward the novel that became *The Book of Disquiet*. As the author himself stated:

> My semi-heteronym Bernardo Soares, who in many ways resembles Álvaro de Campos, always appears when I'm sleepy or drowsy, so that my qualities of inhibition and rational thought are suspended; his prose is an endless reverie. He's a semi-heteronym because his personality, although not my own, doesn't differ from my own but is a mere mutilation of it. He's me without my rationalism and emotions. His prose is the same as mine, except for certain formal restraint that reason imposes on my own writing, and his Portuguese is exactly the same—whereas Caeiro writes bad Portuguese, Campos writes it reasonably well but with mistakes such as "me myself" instead of "I myself," etc.., and Reis writes better than I, but with a purism I find excessive... (Pessoa, Zenith, 1991, 474)

Yet alongside Bernardo Soares, the novel's original editors detected a second (semi-) heteronym, chief among them the symbolist Vicente Guedes, an "office clerk" like Pessoa, according to the novel's "Commercial Register" (Pessoa, Jull Costa, 2017, 183). Vicente Guedes also occupied the professions of translator, poet, director of the Ibis Press, and essay author, and shared his last name with several similarly last-named heteronyms— Gervasio Guedes and Inspector Guedes—who appear at various points in Pessoa's literary corpus. Editors and critics have discerned that Guedes' entries constitute the earliest fragments, from the 1910s, while Soares takes control of the narrative, and the novel, as the 1920s and 1930s roll in. Jerónimo Pizarro's 2017 edited version, translated by Jull Costa and published by New Directions, appears to follow this timeline, dividing the book into two sections, the first centering on Guedes's voice, the second one that of Soares. Amid these two key voices, a scattering of others, including the aristocratic Baron of Teive, virtually indistinguishable from Soares, and the author's direct voice, are detectable throughout fragments. Pessoa's heteronymic play in this text suggests a multiplicity, if not exactly Whitmanian, within a unified stylistic and tonal spectrum, a hallmark of Pessoa's overall impressive literary production.

Since its initial Portuguese publication, *The Book of Disquiet* has been classified as a novel, though Pessoa himself suggested in one of the fragments that it could also be read as an "autobiografia sem fatos," or "factless autobiography." Yet there is little in the text overtly resembling autobiography or memoir, at least in the terms we understand these genres in contemporary American, European and global literature. It nevertheless and in multiple ways tracks closely the mundane quarter-century of life that Pessoa led in Lisbon from the second decade of the 20th century through the early years of the Estado Novo, or Second Republic, the authoritarian, national-corporatist regime that seized control of Portugal's government in 1933. In *The Book of Disquiet* there is no direct mention of the First World War, which Portugal initially sat out until 1916, nor representation of the coup and dictatorship with its increasing restrictions, or of the creeping financial depression that gripped Europe, in the narrator's meditations and statements. The book also contains no discussion of Portugal's colonial history or its then-extant colonies in Africa or East Asia.

In fact, though Pessoa does depict numerous aspects of petit-bourgeois experience and labor, little of the larger social, political or even cultural field, at least in realist terms, appears in this novel. As Pessoa's "factless" designation suggests, verisimilitude is not the point. Nevertheless, a reader does encounter the often banal vicissitudes of a lower middle-class bachelor's life, including scenes in the office as he copies and checks accounting figures, his thoughts at restaurants and eating-houses, and his observations of people he works with or those he encounters in the street. Even those quotidian events are, as Soares announces early on in the 1991 Jull Costa edition, reflections of or at the very least mediated by "the journey in my head." (Pessoa, Jull Costa, 1991, 1).

In the brief sections that follow, I will aim to offer a few thoughts about how to read *The Book of Disquiet* in different ways that underscore a small portion of its literary significance. Its repetition of affect produces tedium—and it is, to put it mildly, a book of almost unrelieved narrative tedium intercut with cyclical accounts of psychic distress. The narrator highlights this when he speaks of "a tedium that contains only the prospect of more tedium" (Pessoa, Jull Costa, 2017, 239). Yet Pessoa produced—or was in the process of producing—a novel that can stand as an exemplary work of Portuguese, European and global Modernism. *The Book of Disquiet* is also harbinger and forerunner of post-Modernism, a profoundly poetic anti-novel, eschewing most, if not all, of the components scholars and critics of the novel tend to associate with that genre, even as it represents a model for the lyric novel and later developments in autobiographical and memoiristic nonfiction, and a paradigmatic account of psychological depression. Pessoa's novel, whether this was his explicit aim or not, unsettles the very categories of genre, of fiction, nonfiction and poetry, and perhaps, like Arnold Schoenberg's great, unfinished contemporaneous opera *Moses und Aron* (1932), could never be fragments fully shored against the gathering ruins of industrial capitalism, which is to say, never completed because its intrinsic conceptualization and nature made completion, at least by the author, impossible.

"How modern all this sounds": A Modernist Novel

The Book of Disquiet is, at first and repeated glance, a collection of fragments. This formal quality, coupled with the era in which Pessoa drafted the novel, immediately marks it as a Modernist text. The carefully structured realism of the preceding generations, exemplified by Pessoa's Portuguese predecessor José Maria de Eça de Queiroz (1845-1900), as well as the symbolism of European counterparts like Maurice Maeterlinck (1862-1949), yields to an approach to the novel melding experimentation in both form and content. Pessoa's lack of instructions, or even implicit guide for assembling the novel died, might suggest sloppiness or a haphazard plan, but as the novel's narrator states, the aim was to collect impressions rather than produce a representative novel, even a Modernist one. Richard Zenith argues that, "*The Book of Disquietude* should be published in a loose-leaf edition, permitting the reader to order and re-order the fragments according to the dictates of his or her own intuition" (Pessoa, Zenith, 1996, xiv), much as B.S. Johnson would do thirty-five years later with his 1969 novel *The Unfortunates*.[6] This is not to say that Pessoa offered or imposed no order whatsoever; in addition to the distinctly Guedes and Soares texts, fragments he wrote in and around the last decade of his life were sometimes chronologically marked, while these and others were numbered, aiding editors in constructing possible narrative sequences. Pessoa's clues can be found in the continuities and shifts in narrator's voices, moods, implying thematic and narrative centers and movements.

To put it another way, Pessoa imagined and wrote about a completed work, even if he did not know what that completed work would or should look like. One can infer, as well, in the constancy of the vision inherent in and across the fragments a sense of wholeness that simultaneously eludes any definitive editorial approach, including Pessoa's. The novel *form* itself, though it changes with every edition of the book, and certainly with any reading of a given edition, invokes a formal completion that Pessoa's narrator at times expresses a desire to achieve, that already haunts him. He is, however, like the book he cannot bring to a close: "I am composed of the ruins of things unfinished, and the landscape that would define my being is one of resignations." (Pessoa, Jull Costa, 2017, 336) At another point, he lays out his modus operandi, guiding the reader through his process and sharing his literary aim: "During one of those periods of sleepless somnolence in which we entertain ourselves intelligently enough without recourse to our intelligence, I re-read some of the pages which, when put together, will make up my book of random impressions." (ibid, 347-8)

In addition to the fragmentation of Pessoa's novel, its insistent psychological and spiritual angst and its defamiliarization of the everyday, not through radical syntactic or imagistic juxtaposition, but rather through a repetition that begins to blunt the disruptive breaks between texts—"One must make the everyday so anodyne that the slightest incident proves entertaining" (ibid., 418)—are in keeping with the literature of Modernism, both in the English-speaking world, a literature that Pessoa, who spent nine years in South Africa, knew well, as well as with Europe's, Iberia's, and Portugal's own canons. Pessoa captures the profound *disquiet*, which is neither unhappiness nor fear, nor sorrow or anger, but a mental and spiritual tumult, endlessly roiling and deeply tinged with irony and alienation, that accompanies modernity's transformation of the physical and psychic world for a white, European working-class clerk whose salary—"Money is beautiful, because it is a liberation..." (ibid, 24)—has liberated him from the demands of the prior, older familial and social order.

A "Romantic" (ibid, 276) in soul who instead only reads the classics, the narrator spends most of the book showing that his horizons on the one hand stretch far beyond observable reality into Orientalist fantasy, reveries, and the waking nightmares produced by grief, sadness and insomnia, while on the other they remain tightly tethered to Rua dos Douradores, his boss Mr. Vasques and his fellow employees, the city of Lisbon, anchored to the office desk at which he inks figures into ledgers, the home desk where he records his thoughts. He is, he emphasizes, pining to get away, to travel and experience a world that may or may not exist, to exceed his daily circuits and the drudgery they represent. Yet like James Joyce's eponymous short story character Eveline, Soares is unable to leave, a captive not just of his limited earnings and class, but of the modern world, whose salvation, art, he strives to create even though he mourns that he cannot do so. Yet though Soares views art as his liberation from the affective and psychic labor he performs in the accounting firm and in his journal, he will never live to see it realized, even as, ironically the reader has his efforts at hand through this novel.

Showing the influence of literary symbolism, which marked Vicente Guedes' voice in the early fragments and which took root in Portuguese literature as it did across Europe and Latin America, people he encounters transform into symbols for him that "come together to form occult or prophetic writings," reflecting "shadowy descriptions of [his] life" (Pessoa, Zenith, 1996, 42). Everything—people, life, and the world around him— dissolves into the aestheticized, often abstracted but still painful viewpoint he has of life and himself. As a result, the narrator Guedes-Soares becomes an emblematic Modernist stand-in, as tragic as he is pathetic, as constricted in his life and his attempts to record and understand it as his text, once out of his hands, is free.

"Anonymous, prolix, unfathomable present": A Post-Modernist Novel

In as much as *The Book of Disquiet's* formal fragmentation brands it as a key text of Modernism, its incomplete—despite the "complete" stamp that appears in various translated editions—form and structure also can be read as emphasizing process and openness. Simply put, the text demands the editor's, translator's, critic's, and reader's active participation. Indeterminacy is one of its guiding principles, linking it to the post-Modernist turn that would occur only a few decades after Pessoa's death. As already noted, there is no final or authentic version because Pessoa, despite the marked envelope, left none, and any assembly of these fragments, let alone reading, could constitute a correct one as well as a possible mis-assembly and mis-reading. Soares-Pessoa ironically underlines this when he notes, "The only true art is that of *construction*," (Pessoa, Jull Costa, 2017, 183-4), going on to add that "the only thing in which construction plays a part today is the machine; the only logical argument is a mathematical proof," echoing both the early, Modernist Ludwig Wittgenstein of the *Tractatus* and the later, proto-post-Modern Wittgenstein of the *Philosophical Investigations*. The narrator models and thematizes the concept of "construction" throughout the text, yet leaves the onus on those who follow to see it through.

Though Pessoa was primarily a poet, and though metaphors appear throughout the book, one of the *The Book of Disquiet's* crucial figure is the metonym. Guedes-Soares, the putative everyman and exceptional figure, as well as the firm where he works, the street where he lives, his boss, his co-workers, his experiences, all stand in for the larger social, economic, and spiritual condition in which he and others like him find themselves. The novel's reliance on and use of metonymy presses the text outwards, beyond the suffocating confines of the narrator's mind and immediate world, giving it a broader, deeper resonance. Melding grandiosity and humility, the narrator is aware of his imagined communities, evoking the counterpublics that his words, these fragments, speak to, for and of.

> It consoles me to think that I have as brothers the creators of the consciousness of the world—the unruly playwright William Shakespeare, the schoolmaster John Milton, the vagabond Dante Alighieri [...] and even, if I'm allowed to mention him, Jesus Christ himself who was so little in this world that some even doubt his historical existence. The others are a different breed altogether—Councillor of State Johann Wolfgang von Goethe, Senator Victor Hugo, heads of state Lenin and Mussolini.
>
> It is we in the shadows, among the errand boys and barbers, who constitute humanity. (ibid, 210)

A reader might also view the novel's chapters as rhizomatic in their origin, function and progression. Each proceeds via an associative, non-hierarchical logic from what has come before, yet each also appears to spring from deep interior spaces within the narrator's head and soul. No single chapter or a dozen will reveal the whole text's correct schema, since none exists, but rereading them slowly and in clusters often rewards insight beyond their surface meaning and content. The novel's title telegraphs its focus, the neurotic author's anxiety, in essence giving away the game, but the text's cumulative effects and meaning can only be grasped by delving into its entirety. The impressions, analyses, and lyrical passages connect paratactically via Guedes-Soares' plaintive, pessimistic tone, suffused periodically with an anti-humanism verging on misanthropy. In the Zenith translation Soares ends the novel's first paragraph by decrying humanism outright, stating "The cult of Humanity, with its rites of Freedom and Equality, always struck me as a revival of those ancient cults in which gods were like animals or had animal heads." (Pessoa, Zenith, 1996, 7)

But these same chapters, in their individuality of statement and effect, mirror the isolation, loneliness and marginal position their author recounts and bemoans in them: "I...am the sort of person who's always on the fringe of what he belongs to, seeing not only the multitude he's a part of but also the wide open spaces around it." (ibid, 7) One also can view the fragments through another term associated with the post-modern, anarchy, over which the novel form, and the participating reader (editor, critic, translator) appear to impose control, through the act of organizing the texts and reading them. The narrator, in one of many moments of visionary lucidity, understands this truth about this text, which reflects the spiritual dispossession and liberation the new world has unleashed, stating, "What I would like to create is the apotheosis of a new incoherence that could become the negative constitution of the new anarchy of souls." (ibid, 106)

"The ineffable poetry of those sentences": A Poetic Anti-Novel

If it is true that a good deal of European and American Modernist fiction dispenses with some of the conventions of fiction from preceding eras, it is nevertheless also the case that it often retains fundamentals such as characterization, plot, pacing, tone, voice, theme, and structure, even as it transforms them. Pessoa, steeped in the experiments of then-contemporary literature, as his essays that became *The New Portuguese Poetry* indicate, nevertheless eschews all of these fundamentals in what became his entry in the genre. Beyond his narrator, he dispenses with character altogether. His boss Mr. Vasques, the object of the narrator's fascination and desire; the office "boy" who heads back to his village; coworkers like Moreira, are all nothing more than cardboard stand-ins for the figures Soares interacts with daily. We get no sense of them *as people*, as living beings with personalities or inner lives. Instead, as Pessoa himself noted of the work, its solipsism is autobiographical, with but a few details and passing incidents to flesh out scenes, to anchor the narrative in what we think of as "reality." Telling is the near total absence of dialogue, except of an idealized or apostrophized kind. He is not the man without qualities, as in Robert Musil's eponymous, unfinished 1943 novel, but he is the man for whom little occurs, beyond the pedestrian, outside the offices of his mind.

Besides its lack of round or curved characters other than the narrator, *The Book of Disquiet* is plotless. The narrator ends up where he begins, writing and thinking, the journey almost completely in his head. "Action," he argues at one point, "is a disease of thought, a cancer of the imagination. To act is to exile oneself." (ibid, 105), thereby not only defending his own inertia, but also negating a key element of most extended fictional narrative. There is no narrative telos here, no point toward which incidents flow. Soares possesses wisdom, keen perception, a razor-sharp capacity for irony or wit, as well as a lugubriousness that hovers like a fog around so much of his thought. But he also has seldom boarded a train or dared risk the stability of his tedium or torment by voyaging beyond nearby cities, let alone Spain or France, or the "Orient" or "islands" that so fascinate him, canceling out another source of plot. Soares recounts banal events at his job, but they add up to nothing more than impressions for him to philosophize about or decry. An orphan who lost both parents during childhood, his mother to an early death and his estranged father to suicide, Soares also has no apparent extend family and is friendless, so these traditional sources of plot also cannot germinate. Moreover, given Soares' "horror of real women, sexual women" (ibid, 18), and the lack of "sexual attraction in dreaming about" his imaginary, idealized "Our Lady of Silence," there are no romantic or physical encounters, nor a relationship, involving the opposite sex, while those involving other men, if they occur, are also never mentioned. Thus no domesticity, with the rich plot possibilities it might offer.

Instead, having announced, presumably at one of his desks, that between his work and home life, with their coruscating monotony, he has become a shadow of himself, Soares concludes morosely: "In the chair in which I sit, I forget the life that so oppresses me. The only pain I feel is that of having once felt pain." (ibid, 514). All of the dreaming, thinking, writing, and brooding lead nowhere, except back to the same spot, the rooms in which his mind races and his life clock ticks down. In Jull Costa's 1996 translation, the novel ends with Soares telling the reader:

> I feel nothing because I feel nothing. I think this is because this is all nothing. Nothing, nothing, just part of the night and the silence and of whatever emptiness, negativity and inconstancy I share with them, the space that exists between me and me, a thing mislaid by some good. (Pessoa, Jull Costa, 1996, 262)

Here a negative space has opened within Soares, but this is a journey we could have predicted from the book's opening lines. In Zenith's 1996 version, the novel ends on no less of a bleak note: "And all that I do, all that I feel and all that I live will amount merely to one less passer-by in the daily scenery on the streets of one more city." (Pessoa, Zenith, 1996, 303)

What unites these disparate, non-advancing entries are the insistent theme, tone and voice, rather than the fiction novel's usual conventions and components. While metonymy is one of *The Book of Disquiet*'s key figures, anchoring the narrator's mundane experiences in the realm of fiction and grounding him as an everyman, Pessoa's metaphorical gifts and his lyrical, imagistic approach to narration also situate the text within a larger poetic field. The lyric passages often serve as hinges, binding the text together by hasping image to theme, and vice versa, while also enabling a forward flow of thought. In essence, numerous chapters are also prose poems of varying length, and a reader might even view the entire text as a collection—a series—of prose poems that together constitute a novel. One example of the author's metaphorical prowess lies in Chapter 75 in the 2017 Jull Costa translation, "Imperial Legend," in which the narrator expatiates in an Orientalist reverie:

> My Imagination is a city in the Orient. Its composition in real space has the voluptuous feel of a soft, lavish rug. The crowds that multicolour its streets stand out against some kind of backdrop which is not somehow theirs, as if they were embroidered in yellow or red on the palest of blue satins. (Pessoa, Jull Costa, 2017, 109)

He continues:

> The sands of my non-existence were carpeted in intimate softnesses, and clouds of algae floated in my rivers like shadowy exhalations. Thus was I porticos in lost civilisations, febrile arabesques on dead friezes, ancient black stains on the curves of broken columns, solitary masts on remote shipwrecks, the steps up to vanished thrones, veils veiling nothing, only shadows... (ibid, 210)

Pessoa's novelistic logic, like his narrative toolkit, is the poet's, not the traditional fiction writer's. His anti-novel is a poet's novel.

Another possibility for reading Pessoa's poetic anti-novel is as a work of proto-*autofiction*, a term French writer and critic Serge Doubrovsky coined in 1977 to describe his novel *Fils,* which merged the autobiographical and fictional in productive tension. Doubrovsky defined autofiction like this: "Fiction of strictly real events or facts, if we want, autofiction, of having entrusted the adventure of language with the language of an adventure, outside the wisdom of the traditional or new novel."[7] As noted at the beginning of this essay, given that Bernardo Soares—like Vicente Guedes and the Baron of Teive—was a semi-heteronym of Pessoa's, and that their experiences closely track each others' (with the psychological and social complexities of Pessoa's life distilled into the written, highly emotional thoughts of Soares'), one might recall that the author himself states that their "personalities" are nearly exact, the difference being Soares' unfolds as a "mere mutilation" of Pessoa's, and that their prose is "the same" as Pessoa's save the "formal restraint" of the real-life author. If *The Book of Disquiet* evacuates most of the characteristics one would expect of a novel of its era or preceding or successive ones, it also prefigures, in its fidelity to the emotional truths, spiritual torments and tedious patterns of Pessoa's life, a form of the novel and of literature that would reappear forty years later.

"I only suffer more" : A Novel of Depression

Though psychology as an academic and professional discipline existed during Pessoa's lifetime, our contemporary understanding of psychological depression did not. I thus hesitate to initiate such a reading in relation to *The Book of Disquiet*, which despite its exploration of psychology is not a psychological novel, for fear of imposing a potentially reductive, present-day medical diagnosis on a past work of art, or diagnosing a character whose social and cultural contexts differ from today's in a variety of ways. A focused exploration of Soares' entries might nevertheless lead a reader to conclude that alongside a spiritual and metaphysical explanation of the narrator's anxieties, he is also negotiating and recording a sustained emotional crisis. Additionally, rather than obscuring the psychological challenges, the traumas he lives with, his lyrical descriptions manage to amplify recognition of them.

The spiritual sickness and the unrelenting disquiet, which Pessoa avoids psychologizing by recourse to Sigmund Freud or similar figures, and which Soares professes almost like a refrain, map onto the DSM-IV's criteria for major depressive disorder (MDD), even if imperfectly. The narrator expresses "decreased interests or pleasure in most activities," "change[s]" in sleep resulting in insomnia, "fatigue," feelings of "worthlessness," and even thoughts of self-annihilation.[8] Soares' diurnal accounts of his existence often present a poetic version of what the DSM-VI outlines, employing day and night as tropes for his depression. For example, he writes:

> The life I drag around with me until night falls is not dissimilar to that of the streets themselves. By day they are full of meaningless bustle and by night full of an equally meaningless lack of bustle. By day I am nothing, by night I am myself . . . Men and objects share a common abstract destiny: to be of equally insignificant value in algebra of life's mystery. (Pessoa, Jull Costa, 1996, 35)

A few pages later, he calls forth the specter of self-annihilation, apostrophizing to the night, "make me, body and soul, part of your body, and let me lose myself in mere darkness, make me night too, with no dreams to be as stars to me, nor longed-for sun to light the future. (ibid, 37). In the next chapter, speaking of his insomnia, he shares with the reader his idea that "anyone wanting to make a catalogue of monsters would need only to photograph in words the things that night brings to somnolent souls who cannot sleep.... They hover like bats over the passivity of the soul, or like vampires that suck the blood of our submissiveness." (ibid.) A few paragraphs later, still following the same vein of negative imagery, Soares says, "They are doubts from the deep that settle in cold, sleep folds upon the soul." And a few paragraphs later still, he punctuates this lament by saying of himself, "The moment I find myself, I am lost; if I believe, I doubt; I grasp hold of something but hold nothing in my hand. I go to sleep as if I am going for a walk, but I'm awake. I wake as if I slept, and I am not myself." (ibid) The liminal state of un-sleep produced by the insomnia exacerbates his abjection, confusion, and desire for self-negation. The insomnia is not the cause, but a symptom of Soares' depression.

To give a few more examples, just pages later, Soares waxes lyrically about his suffering, but he does not shut down, at least not at first: "I am a widowed house, cloistered in upon itself, darkened by timid, furtive specters. I am always in the room next door, or they are, and all around me great trees rustle." (ibid, 39). This self-reading leads him not to despair, initially, but to "wander around," both outside and in his mind, like a sleepwalker yet unable to sleep, summoning childhood, which appears to him "dressed like a pinafore." (ibid.) The "widowed" house metaphor and childhood apparition correlate with the multiple losses and resultant trauma Soares has already shared: his mother's death when he was very small, his father's suicide as well as the more recent one by a fellow worker at Vasques & Co., and his own psychic displacement from the modern world around him. Nature and night, however, offer only temporary respites. Concluding the chapter, he announces that "all [he] feel[s] is tired, tired, utterly tired!" not just from the lack of sleep, but from the turmoil in his mind and soul.

Finally, just a few chapters later, Soares begins by telling the reader that

There are some deepseated griefs so subtle and pervasive that it is difficult to grasp whether they belong to our soul or to our body, whether they come from a malaise brought on by pondering on the futility of life, or whether they are caused by an indisposition in some chasm within ourselves—the stomach, liver or brain. How often my ordinary consciousness of myself is obscured by the dark sediment stirred up in some stagnant part of me. How often existence wounds me to the point that I feel a nausea so indefinable that I can't tell if it's just tedium or an indication that I'm actually about to be sick! How often....

My soul today is sad to the very marrow of its bones. Everything hurts me—memory, eyes, arms. It's like having rheumatism in every part of my being. (ibid, 45-6)

Here, the *self*-diagnosis, and the physical effects of the depression lie right before our eyes. Pain, sorrow, the deep well of disquiet—depression—burrow through him—mentally, and throughout his body.

One might ask what use is it to read clinical, psychological depression into, or out of, this text. It is important to consider how Pessoa, via Soares, represents the reality and totality of depression within *The Book of Disquiet*, showing its totality and effects on the person experiencing it. The narrator may be so self-focused that he misses global wars and economic crises, and secure enough in his petit-bourgeois position to ignore the dictatorship headquartered several neighborhoods away, but his overwhelming depression, which these larger forces, including capitalism itself and the constraints it places on him, is one of this novel's true subjects, and constitutes its imaginative core. While *The Book of Disquiet* is not the first text to anatomize psychological pain and trauma, often in prose so beautiful it achieves the condition of poetry, it may be the first to present it as constitutive of a novel's protagonist, showing how it immobilizes him and how he navigates its effects in order to produce, to the extent possible, a work that might offer others a reflection of their suffering, as well as an example of how art can portray one of modern and now post-modern life's most persistent challenges. Though this is but one if its achievements, it is amid the others a significant one.

NOTES

1. Fernando Pessoa, *The Book of Disquietude: by Bernardo Soares, assistant bookkeeper in the city of Lisbon*, translated, with an Introduction by Richard Zenith, Riverdale-on-Hudson, New York, The Sheep Meadow Press, 1996.
2. One could also translate "desassossego" as "restlessness" or "anxiety," but neither of these two English words captures the particular contextualized sociocultural and psychological connotations of the original Portuguese *desassossego*.
3. Pessoa, tr. Zenith, 1996, xiv.
4. *Livro do Desassossego por Bernardo Soares*, 2 volumes, edited and with a preface by Jacinto do Prado Coelho, collection and transcription of the texts by Maria Aliete Galhoz and Teresa Sobral Cunha, Lisbon: Ática, 1982.
5. *The Book of Disquiet*, translated by Iain Watson, New York: Quartet Books, 1991; *The Book of Disquiet*, translated by Alfred Mac Adam, New York: Pantheon Books, 1991; *The Book of Disquiet*, translated by Margaret Jull Costa, London, New York: Serpent's Tail, 1991; *The Book of Disquiet*, translated by Richard Zenith, New York: Penguin Classics, 2002; *The Book*

of Disquiet, translated by Margaret Jull Costa, New York: New Directions Publishing Company, 2017.

6. *The Unfortunates* was initially published (and later republished) by Panther Books in the UK and Secker & Warburg in the US as a box filled with a sheaf of loose pages, empowering the reader to order them as desired, save for specifically designated "First" and "Last" chapters. New Directions later republished the novel in this format in 2009.

7. Quoted in Catherine Cusset, "The Limits of Autofiction," online draft of a paper written for an NYU Conference on Autofiction, New York, April 2012.

8. *Diagnostic and Statistical Manual of Mental Disorders,* 4th Edition, Text Revision (DSM-IV-TR) New York: *APA, 2000.*

WORKS CITED

Cusset, Catherine, "The Limits of Autofiction," online draft of a paper written for an NYU Conference on Autofiction, New York, April 2012,

Diagnostic and Statistical Manual of Mental Disorders, 4th Edition, Text Revision (DSM-IV-TR) New York: APA, 2000.

Pessoa, Fernando, *Livro do Desassossego por Bernardo Soares,* 2 volumes, edited and with a preface by Jacinto do Prado Coelho, collection and transcription of the texts by Maria Aliete Galhoz and Teresa Sobral Cunha, Lisbon: Ática, 1982.

The Book of Disquiet, translated by Iain Watson, New York: Quartet Books, 1991.

The Book of Disquiet, translated by Alfred Mac Adam, New York: Pantheon Books, 1991.

The Book of Disquiet, translated by Margaret Jull Costa, London, New York: Serpent's Tail, 1991.

The Book of Disquiet, translated by Margaret Jull Costa, New York: New Directions Publishing Company, 2017.

The Book of Disquiet, translated by Richard Zenith, New York: Penguin Classics, 2002.

The Book of Disquietude: by Bernardo Soares, assistant bookkeeper in the city of Lisbon, translated, with an Introduction by Richard Zenith, Riverdale-on-Hudson, New York, The Sheep Meadow Press, 1996.

Malina, Murder
Death In Ingeborg Bachmann's Writing

METTE MOESTRUP

TRANSLATED FROM DANISH BY MARK KLINE

1.

Malina. Animal. L'anima.

I keep coming back to the ending of the novel.

I keep coming back to the last sentence.

The haunting last sentence of *Malina*:

"Es war Mord."

"It was murder."

2.

Is it already midnight? I sit at my desk in the dark; the only light comes from my computer monitor. Books written by and about Ingeborg Bachmann lie on my desk. Born in Klagenfurt, Austria, 1926; died in Rome, Italy, 1973. She's been called a diva. She's been called everything from feminist icon to fallen poet. Some of the books lie open and are filled with notes written in pencil; other books are closed with colored post-its sticking out from between the pages. Many of the pages are adorned with black-and-white photographs of Ingeborg Bachmann at various ages. With the wind in her hair. Smiling. Wearing a vinyl raincoat. With somber eyes. And in my mind I see her face (short hair, heavy lipstick) at a tender young age on the cover of *Der Spiegel*—the 1954 cover that signaled her breakthrough as postwar German poetry's great new hope.

3.

"Es war Mord."

The black of the final period.

The white following it.

The last sentence.

The white preceding, surrounding it.

The fact that it stands alone.

Its immense power.
Its brevity, simplicity, clarity.
Subject, verb, object.
The crystal-clear grammar's haziness.
The transparent, the opaque.
Its openness, its occludedness.
Its surface, its depth, luster, pull.
Its enigma: a 3-D structure in my brain.
The sentence enters me, or I enter the sentence.

4.

I leaf through *Darkness Spoken: The Collected Poems*, and I think about how the language of Bachmann's poems are permeated with, or perhaps more precisely, *haunted by* the horrors of the Second World War. In a way it's paradoxical that she of all persons, she with her ambivalent relationship to the German language—"I who cannot live among humans//I with the German language" (313)—completely renewed German poetry. I recall Adorno's famous words: "To write a poem after Auschwitz is barbaric." And I think, where would German poetry be today without her—and Paul Celan?

And why, unlike him, did she stop writing poetry?

Whereas Celan moved further and further into an increasingly isolated "speech-grille" (one of his books of poetry was called that, or, in German: *Sprachgitter*), Ingeborg Bachmann abandoned poetry for the novel. Trauma and the guilt of survival, on the other hand, are found in both their writings, not only thematically but in the ways they wrote—maybe even in what initiated their writing.

The eyewitness bears witness to horrors not with the body, as do the dead, but only with the word. The word is the witness's only means to bear witness for the dead, but it also carries along with it the guilt of survival. That someone is even able to bear witness with words means that they couldn't save the dead. That they didn't sacrifice themselves for the victim. That they are alive while others paid with their lives.

But who bears witness for the witness?

"Niemand/ zeugt für den/ Zeugen"
("No one/bears witness for the/witness")—Paul Celan (198)

I browse through *Herzzeit (Heart's Time)*, Bachmann and Celan's nearly life-long, heartrending correspondence, and I reflect on whether their relationship with each other ruined their relationships with others, or if their relationship with others ruined their relationship with each other.

I close my eyes and sigh.

Paul Celan twice tried to kill his wife, Giselle, before jumping into the Seine.

Ingeborg Bachmann had a nervous breakdown after her split with fellow writer Max Frisch.

All those pills, all that alcohol. The self-destruction. I believe it's the trauma, the war trauma. Possibly something exists that could be called "verbal guilt," the unsolvable ethical dilemma for the writer: is it more unethical to remain silent about the horrors than to create from the horrors? I think this is why they both radicalized their writing.

5.

Es war Mord.
But what *is* Es?
Es *war* Mord.
But *what* was Mord?
Es war *Mord.*

It was murder.
The sentence is unambiguous and free of metaphor.
But can it be read literally?

If there is no body.
If no murderer.
No proof of a crime.

"Es war nicht Malina."
Written on the penultimate page of the novel:
"I have walked over to the wall. I walk into the wall, holding my breath. I should have written a note: It wasn't Malina. But the wall opens, I am inside the wall, and Malina can only see the fissure we've been looking at for such a long time. He'll think I've left the room." (223)

6.

When a poet becomes a novelist, sometimes it's a sign of conventionalizing or commercializing. But in Ingeborg Bachmann's case, turning to the novel was a radicalization; her writings became wilder, fiercer, more experimental. It's as if she needed to shatter all boundaries after the success of her first two books, the poetry collections *Die Gestundete (Borrowed Time)* (1953), and *Anrufung des großen Bären (Invocation of the Great Bear)* (1956). Her short story collection, *The Thirtieth Year* (1961), which includes mystical, political, and lesbian stories, was criticized by (male) reviewers who earlier had praised her to the heavens. Now they lamented her status as a "fallen poetess." It didn't stop her from continuing her boundary-breaking (and even more criticized) journey further into prose. In writing the *Todesarten* cycle, which she began after the short story collection, she seemed to want to create an enormous space, to maximize everything—scale, tempo, temperament, volume, breadth. To give room to everything from the philosophical to the trivial, from the progressive narration of the novel to dense, complex passages. Pathos, violence, adventure, dark laughter.

Whereas Celan's radicalization consisted of minimizing and condensing his poetry to the point where he almost wrote without language. As if the language of muteness could grow out of a stone.

I sense a grace, tiny as a comma, in Celan's and Bachmann's mutual attempt to at least keep in contact, even though they often hurt each other. Bachmann, the daughter of an Austrian Nazi, and Celan, son of a Romanian victim of the Holocaust. Maybe they tried (in vain?) to bear witness to each other?

At any rate, writing about death as if they were possessed is something they had in common. In literature's arguably most famous poem about the Holocaust, "Todesfuge" (Death Fugue), Celan wrote, "Der Tot ist ein Meister aus Deutschland" ("Death is a master from Germany") (40-41). In one of her poems, Ingeborg Bachmann wrote, "Tot ist Alles. Alles tot." (Dead is everything. Everything dead.) (*Darkness Spoken*, 488-489)

7.

Es war Mord.

But: Es war nicht Malina.

So the murderer wasn't Malina?

But: before the passage that includes "I should have written a note: It wasn't Malina." she writes:

"I stare at Malina resolutely, but he doesn't look up. I stand up, thinking that if he doesn't say something immediately, if he doesn't stop me, it will be murder, and since I can no longer say this I walk away." (223)

So "If he doesn't stop me, it will be murder."

But the murderer isn't Malina? (He thinks that she's left the room.)

Es war Mord.

But the narrator is alive inside the wall, or what?

Like an immured woman.
Immured alive.

Es war Mord.
But did she kill herself?
Or is Es/It the wall?
Is the wall murder/a murderer?

8.

The window is open a crack, winter cold seeps in. I light a cigarette and enjoy looking at the red glow in the darkness, the smoke billowing, and then it hits me: her nylon nightgown caught fire from a cigarette. As I snuff mine out, I think about the words of Flaubert: "With my burned hand, I write of the nature of fire." In the film portrait, "Portrait von Ingeborg — Ähnlichkeiten mit Ingeborg Bachmann," Ingeborg Bachmann says that she would have liked to have written that sentence herself, and she adds, "For if the hand isn't burned, you can't write about it."

Her writing is ruthless.

As with the cult poet, Sylvia Plath, and the Iranian writer, Forugh Farrokhzad (who died in a car accident in 1964 at the age of thirty-two), Ingeborg Bachmann's abrupt and tragic death, which to a frightening degree echoes her poetics, influences the perception of her works. In other words, Bachmann's own death has enhanced the myth surrounding her.

But the reason her name is interwoven with the word "death" in my head is, first and foremost, that death is a complex leitmotif in her writing that crosses her shift from poetry to prose and culminates in her magnificent—though unfinished—*Todesarten* project.

9.

Es war Mord.
But is Es in the last sentence the same Es as in the next-to-last sentence?
Es war/Es ist

The wall: so spatial that the temporal aspect is overlooked?

"Es ist eine sehr alte, eine sehr starke Wand, aus der niemand fallen kann, die niemand aufbrechen kann, aus der nie mehr etwas laut werden kann."

"It is a very old wall, a very strong wall, from which no one can fall, which no one can break open, from which nothing can ever be heard again."

I think it's important:
That the wall isn't just a wall no one can break out of, but also a wall from which no sound can ever emanate.

10.

In *Malina* (1971), the female protagonist and narrator, who is an author, is torn between two men, Ivan and Malina. Seen from an autobiographical perspective, the love triangle drama sometimes is interpreted as referring to Ingeborg Bachmann, Paul Celan, and Max Frisch. The complexity and level of abstraction in the novel alone should problematize this view. Both Ivan and Malina are difficult to nail down as characters; Malina in particular is ambiguous and at times abstract. As "animal" and "l'Anima" (anagrams of "Malina") imply, Malina is both the corporeal and the spiritual. The name Malina has been interpreted in relation to Jung's anima and animus as the female side of men's unconscious and the male side of women's unconscious. Sometimes Malina is a male figure distinct from the first-person narrator, a lover in the love triangle drama; other times Malina is a side of the narrator, with whom she struggles inside herself. Sometimes, such as in the fight with the violent father, Malina is a helper; other times he's a threat.

Towards the end of the novel, Bachmann writes: "I have lived in Ivan and die in Malina."

Ivan is strongly opposed to the protagonist writing about death; he thinks she should write about happiness. "You're always mad with joy yourself, so why don't you write like that." In the three-part novel's first chapter, "Happy with Ivan," it can be said that happiness completely takes over:

"At night Ivan asks: Why is there only a Wailing Wall, why hasn't anyone ever built a Wall of Joy?

Happy. I'm happy.

If Ivan wants it I'll build a Wall of Joy all around Vienna, where the old bastions were and where the Ringstrasse is and as far as I'm concerned, a Happy Wall as well around the ugly Vienna Belt. Then we could visit these new walls every day and be so happy we would leap for joy, for this is happiness, we are happy.

Ivan asks: Should I turn off the lights?

No, leave one on, please leave one light on!

Some day I'll turn all the lights out, but now, go to sleep, be happy.

I am happy.

If you're not happy—

Then what?

You won't ever be able to accomplish anything good.
And I tell myself that if I'm happy I'll be able to.
Ivan walks out of the room quietly, turning off each light as he goes, I listen to him leave, silently I lie there, happy." (35)

Stylistically the dialogue between the first-person narrator and Ivan is absolutely unforgettable because of the unfinished sentences:

"I don't stutter, you're imagining things But I told you the day before yesterday. There must be some mistake, I wanted to say . . . ." (96)

Even though *Malina* is so violent, painful, and filled with horror that, as the protagonist yells in the chapter with the abusive father, it may well be said to be "A book about Hell! A book about Hell!" (115), it also contains laughter that sometimes is nearly burlesque, other times sardonic.

In one of the dialogues with Malina, the protagonist and Malina talk about sex and relations between men and women. The derision of the protagonist is bitingly sarcastic and tragicomic:

If he likes kissing feet, he'll kiss the feet of fifty more women, why should he risk occupying his thoughts with a creature who is right now enjoying letting him kiss her feet, at least that's what he thinks. A woman, however, must come to terms with the fact that now her feet happen to have their turn . . .

In this passage, Bachmann also has her protagonist say, " . . . every man really is sick," which echoes her own statement in an interview in the aforementioned documentary film:

Ingeborg Bachmann: "Männer sind unheilbar krank."
Interviewer: "Wieso sind sie krank?"
Ingeborg Bachmann: Wieso sind sie nich?"

Ingeborg Bachmann: "Men are incurably sick."
Interviewer: "How are they sick?"
Ingeborg Bachmann: "How are they not?"

I can't keep from lighting another cigarette.
Outside, the moon shines through clouds, a train passes by.

11.

Es war Mord.

I emailed the passage about the wall to my German translator, Alexander Sitzmann:

"Es ist eine sehr alte, eine sehr starke Wand, aus der niemand fallen kann, die niemand aufbrechen kann, aus der nie mehr etwas laut werden kann."

I wanted him to tell me more about "laut werden."

He answered:

"It's a very old, very strong wall that no one can break up, a wall from which no sound can escape, but this is a bit difficult because 'laut werden' can mean several different things, not only the literal meaning, but, for example, also 'to become known' or 'to say something out loud' or 'to be outraged and say something out loud.' In any case, I would interpret it as: That which is inside the wall can never again come out and never be heard, it can never be known."

TO SAY SOMETHING OUT LOUD

12.

In *Ways of Death*, Bachmann unfolds and investigates a radical idea: "People don't die, they get killed." In the introduction to one of the unfinished novels, *The Book of Franza*, she writes:

"I've often wondered, and perhaps it has passed through your minds as well, just where the virus of crime escaped to—it cannot have simply disappeared from our world twenty years ago, just because murder is no longer praised, desired, decorated with medals, and promoted." (3-4)

And then she continues:

"For today it is infinitely more difficult to commit crimes, and thus these crimes are so subtle that we can hardly perceive or comprehend them, though all around us, in our neighborhoods, they are committed daily. Indeed, I maintain and will only attempt to produce the first evidence that still today many people do not die but are murdered." (4)

The view that war didn't cease at the end of World War II, that only war exists, not peace, is found already in her debut poetry collection. It is expressed in "Alle Tage" ("Every Day") (38-39), a poem that unfortunately feels intensely contemporary:

> War is no longer declared
> but rather continued. The outrageous
> has become the every day. The hero
> is absent from the battle. The weak
> are moved into the firing zone.
> The uniform of the day is patience,
> the order of merit is the wretched star
> of hope over the heart.

In our time, when xenophobia is again baring its teeth in Europe, I salute Ingeborg Bachmann's legacy. I find it more important than ever. Her work, her words make me aware of my problematic European heritage. She was concerned about the lost European soul, and she knew it could get lost over and over again. Did the notion of cultural superiority ever leave Europeans for good? She somehow predicted that the threat wouldn't end even after the Holocaust. Now, in 2016, the anger and fear is targeted at Muslims, not Jews. And she whispers in my ear: You have to be alert. She makes it impossible for me to indulge in flowers, stars, love.

13.

TO SAY SOMETHING OUT LOUD
"Write yourself. Your body must be heard,"
Hèléne Cixous wrote in "The Laugh of the Medusa" in 1976.

"It's all about persisting in writing,"
Ingeborg Bachmann wrote in a lecture in 1960 ("Literatur als Utopie):
"Es gilt weiterzuschreiben."

14.

Ingeborg Bachmann's face appears on my computer screen. She blinks her eyes. Her lips move, she says: Exil (Exile). It looks painful for her to pronounce the word. She blinks her eyes over and over again, rapidly. Now she begins to read a poem, "Exile."

How can I describe her voice? Not dark, not light. Not hoarse, not crystal-clear. Grave alto. Her diction is direct, but there is a hesitant, nervous vein in the tone. She reads the poem slowly and solemnly, she concentrates, as if each and every syllable could ruin the reading. The black-and-white recording is from 1961, the year in which the construction of the Berlin Wall was begun. And it almost makes me cry. Sometimes intensity and intimacy is incompatible, but not in this reading, no.

It is a poem about the German language, therefore I have to quote it in German:

> Ein Toter bin ich der wandelt
> gemeldet nirgens mehr
> unbekannt in Reich des Präfekten
> übersählig in den goldnen Städten
> und im grünen Land
>
> abgetan lange schon
> und mit nichts bedacht
>
> Nur mit Wind mit Zeit und mit Klang
>
> der ich unter Menschen nicht leben kann
>
> Ich mit der deutschen Sprache
> (…)

Exile

> I am a dead man [person]* who wanders
> registered nowhere
> unknown in the prefect's realm
> unaccounted of in the golden cities
> and the greening land
>
> long since given up
> and provided with nothing
>
> Only with wind with time with sound
>
> I who cannot live among humans

I with the German language

. . . .

(*Darkness Spoken,* 312-313 (* the gendered translation to "man" is probably due to the German grammatics, but in other translations it is just "person", and I think "person" is closer to the original).

Shockingly, the narrator of the poem is declared dead in the first line. Therefore the language of the "I" is also infiltrated with death from the first breath of the poem. Then the "I" is described as a refugee, a person with no rights, home, or future. A homo sacer to Giorgio Agamben, a person in society without the rights of a citizen, a naked body, not human yet among humans. This clearly echoes the status of the Jews during the Holocaust (and refugees now), and by identifying with the victim, these lines may be taken as pointing to a lack of empathy. Then the poem makes an inversion: The "I" who cannot live among humans is none other than the "I" with the *German* language. It is ambiguous, of course, but I tend to read it as a way of connecting the writing of poetry in German (after the Holocaust) with an inescapable guilt. The crimes committed in the name of this language bleed through the doomed "I" of the poem.

The "I" of the German poem is always already dead.

15.

Es war Mord.

The wall is a wall that eliminates the possibility of saying something out loud.

The wall is soundproof.

The acoustic aspect (in "laut warden") is important, because it—in the novel—points to a voice.

And by voice I mean not only the narrator's voice,

which is part of the fiction (the fictive body's voice);

I also mean the voice of the writing (the voice of the body who is writing).

I also mean the tension between the implicit and explicit narrator.

The temporal ultimate—nie mehr, never more—in the novel's penultimate present tense sentence is contradicted by the last sentence, which is in past tense.

It is paradoxical:

The last sentence means that something is making a sound, even though no sound can ever again be made.

16.

> There was one specific moment that shattered my childhood: the march of Hitler's troops into Klagenfurt. It was something so horrible that my memory begins on that day, with a premature pain, perhaps stronger than any I would ever feel again. I didn't understand everything the way an adult would, of course. But this monstrous brutality that you could feel, this shouting, singing and marching—my fear of death was born.

In this terrible childhood memory, Ingeborg Bachmann expresses her initial fear of death, which in light of her work seems not only to be the fear of her own death, but also of the death of others. Death in the shape of Nazism and Fascism. One could argue that although her father was a Nazi, she was—psychologically—a victim of Nazism. The way in which she was broken is in no way comparable to the horrors experienced by the Jews. This difference, by the way, is always present between the lines in her correspondence with Celan. However, with her radical idea that "people don't die, they are murdered," she seems to expand the understanding of the victim. And of where and how Fascism takes place. In the aforementioned documentary portrait, she talks about Fascism as something that takes place every time a person wants to dominate another person. As mentioned, she also states that "men are incurably sick." In one of the unfinished novels from *Todesarten*, *The Book of Franza*, she writes, "Why does one only refer to Fascism when it has to do with opinions or blatant acts? Yes, he is evil, even though you can't use the word 'evil' today, but rather only 'sick.'"

Later, Franza is raped in Egypt by a white man, a rape that ultimately kills her. Here, Fascism and "the whites" are unmistakably connected, and it is fair to say that Ingeborg Bachmann's critique of Fascism includes a quite early incorporation of colonialism and whiteness.

Her focus on the bond between patriarchy, violence, and Fascism (and Nazism) is a common thread throughout her work; it's extremely visible in her masterpiece, *Malina*, the only completed novel from the *Todesarten* project. Its main character is brutally attacked by her father, and this silences her. But somehow, via the diversity of languages, she also says no:

> I can't say nothing, since I have to escape my father and get over the marble wall, but in another language I say: Ne! Ne! And in many languages: No! No! Non! Non! Nyet! Nyet! No! Ném! Ném! Nein! For in

our language, too, I can only say no, I can't find any other word in any
language. (115)

17.
Es war Mord.

When a sound can never again escape from the wall:
When nothing can ever again be spoken out loud,
how then is the last sentence possible?

WHO IS SAYING SOMETHING OUT LOUD?

after the soundproof wall
through the soundproof wall
through after (space, time)

There is this enormous chasm between *Malina's* penultimate and last
sentence, in the shift from present tense to past tense. The relation between
the narrating and the narrated time is toppled.

It is not impossible to read the statement as the explicit narrator's posthumous statement, or as the voice of the immured woman, a type of ghost
statement.

But that is a simplification. It's more precise to say that the implicit narrator emerges from the explicit narrator. Yes. The implicit narrator (and its
attachment to the living, writing body (not, parenthetically in parentheses
noted, the concrete biological body, the Ingeborg Bachmann-body, which
unlike the implicit narrator's more abstract body no longer exists)) emerges
from the explicit narrator, which is inside the wall from which nothing can
be spoken out loud, and says, in and with the writing:

Es war Mord.

The implicit narrator emerges from the wall into space, concurrently
with the shift from present tense to past tense.

The force of the sentence results from the fact that it transcends the
wall's—and the novel's, the narration's, the fiction's—space in *time*.

This is what makes the closed sentence so open that it forces me to think
about violence against women *now* and gendercide, globally. As Nicholas
D. Kristof and Sheryll Wudunn writes in *Half the Sky* (xvii): "More girls are
killed in this routine gendercide in any one decade than people were slaugh-
tered in all the genocides of the twentieth century."

Death and gender.

The last sentence gives the dead woman a posthumous voice AND speaks the living, writing female body's language.

The last sentence.

Inside me, with me

everywhere, constantly.

Es war Mord.

WORKS CITED

Adorno, Theodor W.: *Kulturkritik und Gesellschaft I. Gesammelte Schriften. Band 10.1.* Suhrkamp, 1977.

Agamben, Giorgio: *Homo Sacer. Sovereign Power and Bare Life.* Translated by Daniel Heller-Roazen. Meridian, 1998.

Bachmann, Ingeborg: *Darkness Spoken: The Collected Poems.* Translated by Peter Filkins. Zephyr Press, 2006.

Bachmann, Ingeborg & Paul Celan: *Herzzeit Briefwechsel.* Suhrkamp, 2009.

Bachmann, Ingeborg: *Letters to Felician.* Translated by Damion Searls. Green Integer, 2004.

Bachmann, Ingeborg. *Malina.* Suhrkamp, 1971.

Bachmann, Ingeborg: *Malina.* Translated by Philip Boehm. Homes and Meier, 1990.

Bachmann, Ingeborg: *Sämtliche Gedichte.* Piper, 2015.

Bachmann, Ingeborg: *The Book of Franza & Requiem for Fanny Goldman.* Translated by Peter Filkins. Hydra Books. Northwestern University Press, 1999.

Celan, Paul: *Die Gedichte.* Suhrkamp, 2005.

Cixous, Hélène: "The Laugh of the Medusa." Translated by Keith and Paila Cohen. In *Signs,* vol. 1, No.4, 1976).

Kristoff, Nicholas D. and Sheryll Wudunn: *Half the Sky: Turning Oppression into Opportunity for Women Worldwide* (2009).

Lennox, Sara: *Cemetery of the Murdered Daughters: Feminism, History, and Ingeborg Bachmann.* University of Massachusetts Press, 2006.

Silkeberg, Marie & Ingrid Z. Aanestad, ed.: *Att fortsätta med att skriva — om Ingeborg Bachmanns Malina.* Litterär Gestaltnings Skriftserie N:11, 2011.

Sources of Poetry in Carroll's Novels

AARON KUNIN

1.

Here one of the guinea-pigs cheered, and was immediately suppressed by the officers of the court. (As this is rather a hard word, I will just explain to you how it was done. They had a large canvas bag, which tied up at the mouth with strings: into this they slipped the guinea-pig, head first, and sat upon it.)

"I'm glad I've seen that done," thought Alice. "I've so often read in the newspapers, at the end of trials, 'There was some attempt at applause, which was immediately suppressed by the officers of the court,' and I never understood what it meant till now."

(*WONDERLAND*, 99-100)

How does Alice know the exact word for what happened to the guinea pig?

I know that the word is "suppressed," because I have read Carroll's explanation. Alice, who is not reading the novel, should not have access to this information. Something other than narration intervenes between what she reads in English newspapers and what she sees in the courtroom at Wonderland, so that she knows herself to be seeing what she has previously read.

Alice's relationship to language is special in a few different ways that Carroll specifies. When he observes that her use of "curiouser" to compare intensities of curiosity is not "good English," he implies that she and the creatures she encounters both in Wonderland and in the Looking-Glass World actually speak correct English most of the time (16). When Alice repeats the word "jurors" to herself, Carroll affirms that she is right to be proud, since "very few little girls of her age knew the meaning of it" (95). Alice is naturally clever, intellectually curious, and well educated: she can speak well, provided that she "remembers" to pay attention to her speech (16), and her vocabulary distinguishes her from other children "of her age" (95). These are special kinds of knowledge that Alice acquires from her teachers, and by reading novels and newspapers.

(In a letter to one of his sisters, Carroll proposes that reading old novels is the best way to learn correct English; he seems to mean early 19th-century novels, and singles out books by Scott, Austen, and Edgeworth for praise. Newspapers, on the other hand, "are largely responsible for the bad English now used in books" ["Alice on the Stage," 302].)

Alice's knowledge of "suppressed" is not like her knowledge of "jurors." "I'm glad I've seen that done." How does she know that "that" is what was "done"? In this essay, I am going to argue that her knowledge comes from the same place that poetry comes from.

2.

The distinctive texture of both *Alice's Adventures in Wonderland* and *Through the Looking-Glass and What Alice Found There* is prose studded with poetry. Nearly every chapter has a poem in it. Unlike Bely's novel *Petersburg*, or genres such as haibun, where prose can turn into verse without warning, and the shift can occur within a sentence, the Alice novels strictly separate the prose narrative from the poetic performances. The poems are never spoken in Carroll's voice. (The only exceptions are the dedicatory poems.) Instead, they are recited or sung by the characters. Most of the poems in *Wonderland* are spoken by Alice; most of the poems in *Looking-Glass* are spoken to Alice.

Note the frame around each recital. The most elaborate frame is around the Knight's Song in *Looking-Glass*. Before the White Knight performs the song, he names it; before giving it a name, he has another job to do, giving a name to the name. In the Penguin edition, this series of frames goes on for more than a page: what the name of the song is called ("Haddocks' Eyes"), the name itself ("The Aged Aged Man"), what the song is called ("Ways and Means"), what the song really is ("A-sitting on a Gate")—which is different from the actual words of the song. Alice contributes one more layer when she disputes the originality of the tune; the knight claims that "the tune's my own invention," but Alice identifies it as "I Give Thee All, I Can No More" (*Looking-Glass*, 213-14). I have just added a new layer to the frame by referring to the poem as the "Knight's Song."

The frame separates prose from poetry. That is really all that it does. It does not name formal features that distinguish prose from verse, or narrative from lyric. Between the knight's conversation and his song, five names stand as obstacles. One of the names is supposedly identical to the song, but merely refers to it. This name has a nickname ("only what [the song] is *called*, you know" [214]), as though the utterance of the original name were too crude, and could only enter polite conversation in the form of euphemism. Neither of these is the song's name, which also can't be named, and requires another nickname for circulation in polite society. So far, the only point of this proliferation of names is to emphasize a distinction between the song and talking about the song. The name of the tune, which Alice contributes, makes a different distinction between two of the song's formal features, the tune and the words, or between the words of the original song and the new words.

This proliferation of names is hardly unique to poetry in Carroll's novels. There is a similar cluster of names around the character Alice. Carroll always refers to her as "Alice"—it's the first word in *Wonderland*—and when Alice introduces herself to the Queen of Hearts (*Wonderland*, 71), or when she is called to testify in court (101), she readily produces and responds to this name. She responds to other names as well: when called "Mary Ann" (31) or "Serpent" (47) or "Monster" (201), she simply does what she is told, without insisting on being called by her given name. Flummoxed by sudden changes in the size and shape of her body, Alice tries applying other names to herself, concluding that "Mabel" is most likely (19).

The rule might be that any name applies to any object. Or names might be distributed unequally, so that Alice can appropriate any name, while Tweedledum and Tweedledee have barely one name to share between two distinct characters. In any case, Carroll is interested in what happens when names detach from objects. (In *Looking-Glass*, Alice passes through a forest where nothing, including herself, has a name — which is a problem for the characters, but not for the narrator. The things still have names, and Carroll continues to use them, but Alice and the fawn she meets are troubled by a tip-of-the-tongue feeling, and can't manage to bring the names into conversation.) What happens to Alice is that her names, instead of referring to her, become external objects that stand between her and her speech.

The poems don't require all of these extra names, because they are always called poems or songs, and thus clearly distinguished both from Carroll's narration and from the polite, grammatically correct speech of the characters. The accommodation of poetry in the voices of the characters has two implications. The first is to keep poetic activity separate from the task of writing the novel. Carroll does not deal in poetry directly. He protects himself by farming the poems out to characters. The second is that poetry is an activity, something the characters do as part of the story of the novel. (By contrast, verse in Shakespeare's plays is not an activity, and not part of the story; it's a medium that Shakespeare uses, as though without telling the characters.)

3.

Why are there so many poems in Wonderland?

The diegetic explanation is that Alice wants to confirm that she has not changed into a completely different person. Her identity is in question because the size and shape of her body change significantly when she eats or drinks. Instead of a "little girl," she has become a "great girl" (*Wonderland*, 17) or a much smaller, caterpillar-sized girl (46), or a "serpent" rather than a girl (47). She can't take her body for granted any longer; she relates to her limbs not by proprioception, but as distant acquaintances to whom she is obliged to send cards and gifts on special occasions (16). In response to these challenges, Alice repeats her lessons. The theory is that maybe she retains the same knowledge as before, although her body has become unrecognizable.

Alice has previously encountered poetry as part of her education. She has memorized Isaac Watts's "How Doth the Little Busy Bee" and "Tis the Voice of the Sluggard," Robert Southey's "The Old Man's Comforts and How He Gained Them," and other homilies and rhymes. These poems are didactic, and their didacticism is directed toward the world rather than toward literary history. These are not the kinds of poems that Alice would study in order to become a critic, or even a practicing poet like Watts or Southey. These poems do not imagine becoming a poet as possible or desirable. Their wisdom encourages correct speech, polite behavior, decent living, cleanliness, forthrightness, and industry. These, as opposed to wonder or curiosity, are values that Alice has learned to associate with poetry.

Thus, in moments of crisis, she turns to poetry, expecting it to perform the function it has in her schooling: recognition, the establishment of continuity between herself and a shared social world. "Who in the world am I?" Alice asks (*Wonderland*, 17-18). To determine whether her true name is Alice, Ada, or Mabel, she recites, "How Doth the Little." "Who are *you*?" "I—I hardly know, Sir" (40-41), and she recites, "You Are Old, Father William." Poetry is supposed to answer the question, "Who are you?", and attach her name to her body. She recites a poem as one might glance in a mirror to make sure that everything is in its place.

However, mirrors in Carroll's novels do not reflect the world. They are more like windows, offering a view into another world, the "Looking-Glass World." Similarly, when Alice recites a poem, two things happen: her voice changes, and the words change.

> . . . her voice sounded hoarse and strange, and the words did not come as they used to do. (19)

> Some of the words have got altered. (45)

> . . . the words came very queer indeed. (91)

... she went on in a trembling voice. (92)

Alice's voice becomes "hoarse and strange," and it "trembles," and the words are "altered" and "queer." To put it another way, this isn't her voice, and this isn't the poem. Different sound, therefore different voice; different words, therefore different poem.

What's interesting is that Alice knows something is wrong. She is not suffering from the delusion that she has recited the poem perfectly. In fact, she hasn't forgotten the words, and she hasn't forgotten how to use her voice. Her knowledge and her voice remain under her control. Another voice, over which she has no control, speaks the words of a different poem.

4.

There are poems in Wonderland, and in the Looking-Glass World, but there are no poets. The characters recite poems from memory, or find poems in books, but never compose them. The White Knight claims to have invented the tune of his song, but Alice denies him even that much originality.

Where does poetry come from?

You might argue that poetry is imported from England. All of Carroll's great poems are parodies of other poems. For example, the source text for Carroll's poem "You Are Old, Father William" is Southey's poem, with which it shares the same first line. The parody of *Beowulf* in "Jabberwocky" is less explicit, but becomes apparent in the context of the poem's early private publication in *Misch-Masch* (1855) a magazine produced by Carroll and his sisters for circulation within the Dodgson family, where the poem is presented as a "curious fragment" of "Anglo-Saxon poetry" with a glossary and textual apparatus (*Looking-Glass*, 328n).

But the source texts are never the real sources. Carroll imports style and form from the earlier poems, but does something to make them immeasurably better. I do not think it is controversial to say that Carroll's parodies are, without exception, better than the poems they parody. This is undeniably the case for the poems by Watts and Southey that readers know only because Carroll worked with them. I would go further: Carroll's parodies are better even when he is working with acknowledged masterpieces such as *Beowulf* or Wordsworth's "Resolution and Independence," the source text for the White Knight's song.

The origins of poetry in Carroll's novels fall into two distinct categories. On one hand, there are sources with traceable names: Carroll, the author; his characters, who recite the poems; previous generations of English and Saxon poets, who composed the originals. This information has almost nothing to do with the poems as they appear in the novels. (The only remnant in *Looking-Glass* of Carroll's interest in the revival of Old English is the March Hare's habit of "wriggling like an eel" in "Anglo-Saxon attitudes" [195-96].)

On the other hand, there are hidden, unnamed sources. An elaborate series of frames separates them from the author, the characters, and the earlier poets. Alice becomes a radio or ventriloquist's dummy, transmitting a voice that she knows is not her own and that does not belong to Carroll or Watts either. The use of poetry in her education has been to form polite speech and behavior, but the voice with which she recites poetry is impolite, "harsh and strange."

The same goes for the newspaper. Carroll despised journalism nearly as much as he despised the writing of Watts and Southey, but constantly uses the newspaper in his art. In *Looking-Glass*, a man "dressed in white paper," and also reading a newspaper, gives Alice useless advice for traveling to the third square by railway. (Tenniel portrays this man as Disraeli, and Empson glosses this identification in the following words: "Disraeli, the new man who gets by on self-advertisement, the newspaper-fed man who believes in progress, possibly even the rational dress of the future" [*Some Versions of Pastoral*, 256].) I have already noted that Carroll blamed newspapers for "bad English." Further, he wrote in "Alice on the Stage," unlike himself, journalists do not work by inspiration.

> If you sit down, unimpassioned and uninspired, and *tell* yourself to write for so many hours, you will merely produce . . . some of that article which fills, so far as I am able to judge, two-thirds of most magazines. (294)

According to Carroll, newspapers and magazines produce no "original writing." They add nothing new to the world. However, he has no objection to adding something new to the world using the style of the newspaper as a gateway. The source of "suppressed" is journalese, and Carroll turns it into nonsense by introducing a new meaning into the newspaper. The source of the Knight's Song is "Resolution and Independence," and Carroll turns it into nonsense by introducing a new vocabulary into the poem.

The identifiable sources of Carroll's poetry are merely contextual, a line from a newspaper or a textbook from a schoolroom. A common mistake is to treat context as origin. And it's true that Carroll did not make up all the sources of his creativity from scratch. But it's also true that he added something new to the world when he put them together.

WORKS CITED

Carroll, Lewis. *Alice's Adventures in Wonderland and Through the Looking-Glass and What Alice Found There: The Centenary Edition.* Ed. Hugh Haughton. London: Penguin Books, 1998.

Empson, William. *Some Versions of Pastoral.* New York: New Directions, 1974.

A Space for Bhanu Kapil

LAURA MULLEN

Experimental prose, as a category, has allowed me to work out the texture notes of a sentence in a way that fiction, or even the essay, has not. Is this true? Perhaps the more useful
question is: What is a sentence for? Could a sentence, as it's written in English, function as
a possible record of boundary "awards," and of the carnage that follows such decisions?
I think of semi-colons, for example, as a kind of scar tissue. Their reversed curvature as
formal: the way they are moving in the opposite direction to the content or subject matter of
the sentence. Towards what? What comes before, as registered, as marked, in the present,
but delayed, so that memory, too, is held in another place. . . . In a shamanic or trauma
theory model, the body streams towards the place where a scrap of it is held. In the butch-
er's shop. On a hook. And so on. A recursion.

BHANU KAPIL (*HTMLGIANT* INTERVIEW)

An American citizen of Punjabi origin who grew up in a working class,
South-Asian community in London, Bhanu Kapil is one of the most inventive, exciting, and important voices in contemporary literature, and someone whose writing explores and expands received ideas about genre. Kapil
received her MA in English (with a minor in Creative Writing) from SUNY
Brockport, and a BA with honors in English Literature from Loughborough
University. Working, since the mid-1990s, in "experimental prose," Kapil has
been producing urgently necessary investigations of identity: gender identity, colonial (and post-colonial) identities, human (and nonhuman) identities. Focused on subjects who are, as she says, "segmented and seeking"
(immigrants, cyborgs, wolf-girls, "monsters" or those whose bodies become
the marked site of political conflicts and cultural issues), her work is remarkable for an astonishing degree of courage, as well as its honesty, intimacy
and immediacy. Refusing the pretense of disembodied "objectivity," each
work emerges from autobiography and every perspective on the material is
located *in the material*, always returning to the body as the measure of truth,
so that the beginning and end point of each flight of imagination is located.
The vividness of Kapil's imagery and the width of her range of reference call
to mind writers like Clarice Lispector and Anne Carson but Kapil's voice is
her own, and her work is recognizable for intensely sensual language that
gives readers immediate access to the author's rigorous thinking. Shaped

by a deeply intuitive and spiritual intelligence, as well as a practical under-standing of the body—the writer and teacher is also a licensed massage ther-apist—Kapil's writing is grounded by research in physiology, psychology, and cognitive science, along with an impressive understanding of theory.

Kapil's first full-length book (*the Vertical Interrogation of Strangers*) was published by Kelsey Street in 2001 and her sixth (*How to Wash a Heart*) was published by Pavilion Poetry in 2020. She blogged for years (generously and gorgeously) at "Is Jack Kerouac a Punjabi" and has participated, by invi-tation, in conversations at *Poetry* magazine's "Harriet"; Kapil has also writ-ten plays and established a reputation as a performance and visual artist. In the context of such genre fluidity labels become extremely vexed (when her books are labeled at all it's likely to be as "Literature"), but there are significant overlaps with ideas about the form of novel in her works that make it appropriate to discuss her writing in the present collection, as each of Kapil's books engages ideas about genre while posing a challenge to pre-conceptions about what a story is and how it gets told. It might be useful to think about Colonialism itself as a story (or one of Jean Lyotard's "Grand Narratives") and to contextualize Kapil's resistance to the more usual modes of fiction with Audre Lorde's oft-cited query about how effective it is to try using the Master's tools to bring down the Master's house. Kapil (influenced by Gayatri Spivak, Theresa Cha, Rosi Braidotti, and Donna Haraway, among others) is fiercely aware of the way in which an unquestioning obedience to given forms forecloses the possibility of vision. Genre and gender are equal-ly interrogated in this author's work, as are a host of other assumptions and prejudices: writing is always, for Kapil, a means of improving our ability to recognize and honor a life force which transcends social identities. There are, in other words, powerful and inescapable reasons that these books are not presented as easily recognizable "novels" and that, in fact, writing—as fragile and hesitant action—must pass through the possibility of nonexis-tence in order to find a new way forward. And so Kapil's writing repeatedly, on the level of form, but also on the level of content, faces the possibility of failure, loss, and the veer toward incoherence and silence:

> "I understand that it will not always be possible to write this book" (*The Vertical Interrogation of Strangers* p, 82)

> "I said, 'What is a monster?' You said: 'Anybody different.' I thought that was so amazing and I wrote it down in my notebook, in which I have been writing to you. Tearing out the pages as I go." (*Incubation: A Space for Monsters* p 16)

"In the aeroplane from London to Kolkata and in the jeep to Midnapure, I put my nib on the page and let motion wreck the line. My notes were a page of arrhythmias, a record of travel." (*Humanimal* p. 43)

"On the night I knew my book had failed, I threw it—in the form of a notebook, a hand-written final draft—into the garden . . . " (*Schizophrene*, introduction)

"I wrote a companion series or sequence of childhood stories to lie next to Ban, but when it was time to publish them here . . . I pressed the delete button . . . " (*Ban en Banlieu* p. 9)

"The project fails at every instant and you can make a book out of that and I do . . . " (*Ban . . .* p. 22)

Surviving loss is, arguably, a foundational experience for the immigrant, whose "next life" (*Ban* p. 82), is also an *after*life—and Kapil demonstrates a sharp awareness that any *re*membering takes place at the scene of a prior *dis*memberment (or what she calls, in the quote which functions as an epigraph, "carnage"). Assembling disparate fragments of memory while resisting the pressure to *assimilate* or falsify / erase particularity in order to totalize is a project as important as it is difficult, and it is more often a poet's project (Kapil's commitment to this effort aligns her work with that of poets like Susan Howe, Myung Mi Kim, Juliana Spahr, and Claudia Rankine). Though the work of memory and imagination may allow, near each book's end, for a new, freighted understanding resembling—as experience—a kind of climax, progress is anything but linear in Kapil's oeuvre, and "story" is a distrusted structure under an extremely sophisticated critique. Precisely because expectations are being tested and transformed rather than met, her books may seem, to the inexperienced or inattentive, unfinished: clear plot lines are unlikely, where narrators pause to consider the quality of a feeling or (re)adjust a description, or to examine the way the question of addressee shapes an utterance, or to count the cost of so called progress for those whose lives are confined by discursive structures, or in order to dwell on associatively related subject matter a more standard sense of the form might exclude. But Kapil reveals her extensive knowledge of the genre in the way her work responds to and resists traditions and histories (always plural). Analogous to that post-colonial ("corrupt, humanimal") landscape Kapil calls "a severed fold," her work bears the traces of an original eco-system and the consequences of Colonialism: "the British erased sections of the forest, then re-planted it like a Norfolk copse, brutally. Linearity is brutal. Yet, now, the jungle is more luminous and spacious than it would have been naturally." (*Humanimal* p 34)

Arranged *not* by the invisible constrictions of the realist novel (whose craft consists in hiding craft), but by the modes of organization and categorization endured and mobilized by those trying to gain access to citizenship or to better their social position, Kapil's works display and play with an anxiety about literature's *usefulness*. Her books often seem to wish to raise the possibility, in other words, that they be used as guides or read for information rather than entertainment. This should be familiar as a gesture stretching from Gertrude Stein (*Useful Knowledge, How to Write*) to Lyn Hejinian (*Writing As An Aid To Memory*): literary experimentalism often engages the desire for instruction, and, with it, tends to prefer the exposure of structure and ordering devices to an internalized and well-hidden discipline. "Chapters" involve the pretense that life unfolds with a seamless logic whose order is natural, but *lists* make vivid the arbitrary, unstable order of a particular representation.

Kapil's engagement with both didactic promises (familiar from "self-help" books) and exposed structuring devices is a continuation and revision of the experimental tradition, and can be seen throughout her body of work. *The Vertical Interrogation of Strangers* is shaped by a list of questions and "interviews" (as if for a kind of ethnographic project) are the form which (loosely) organizes a peripatetic account of past and present loves. But it is unclear who answers the survey which appears to elicit the text, and, from the start, identity is under "interrogation." In Kapil's work the boundary between self and other is blurred: "Who are you and whom do you love?" (9) are presented in/as the same question. *Incubation: A Space for Monsters* (about which there will be more to say below) is organized by various list strategies (numbers and an incomplete alphabet) and includes a chapter of definitions as well as a "guide to hitchhiking." *Humanimal* (the text which takes as its subject the story of the Bengali Wolf Girls: their "rescue" and subsequent death) is subtitled "A Project for Future Children," and features a doubled ordering structure involving both numbers and another incomplete alphabet (*Incubation* goes up to "L" and *Humanimal* gets as far as "O"). *Schizophrene*, a meditation on the attempt to "make a map of healing" (48) charting the effects of trauma on immigrants from Britain's former colonies, puts the category of "book" into question throughout, but includes a chapter titled "A Healing Narrative." *Ban En Banlieu* uses a numbering system (which keeps starting over rather than adding up) to structure its turns and returns to subjects rendered incoherent or actually destroyed by racism and sexism (among other forms of despair). And in this text the author's familiar gesture of advice-giving is more broken up, tentative, and arguably more obviously self-directed than in her earlier works: "Focus hard on life to write a novel. / Try not to be afraid." (60) While the realist novel internalizes and naturalizes its information-giving gestures and ordering structures in order to hide, in part, the fear that make information and order so urgently necessary, Kapil reveals those disciplining gestures and arbitrary systems of organization in order to expose the terror behind the desire for guides and instructions and the efforts at control and mastery.

At the start of her first book Kapil asks herself and others (including the reader) to describe an original space of fearlessness: "Describe a morning you woke without fear." (9) In the text that will form the focus of the remainder of this essay, *Incubation: A Space for Monsters*, fear is evoked, investigated, complicated, and arguably—to some degree—ameliorated. Fear is, of course, an aspect of vulnerability, and in Kapil's work as a whole vulnerability is a crucial part of the content as well as the form—but *Incubation*'s protagonist, a solitary female hitchhiker, is extraordinarily exposed. Dependent on the kindness of strangers and open to the chance encounter, her heroine's mode of travel—"Mate with surfaces. Okay. Hitchhike." —makes vulnerability a crucial aspect of the journey. Anticipating writer and director Ana Lily Amirpour's film *A Girl Walks Home Alone at Night*, Kapil's book focuses on a situation that either serves as a prime example of foolishness (insofar as the victim is blamed) or danger (insofar as sexism's violence is acknowledged). Both Kapil and Amirpour are interested in flipping expectations: both make a "space for monsters" in which a lonely girl can *be* frightening, as well as confront fear. "Perhaps it is useful to point out that one in every three hitchhikers is a murderer . . . " Kapil notes (in the "Guide to Hitchhiking"), adding, "However, as a hitchhiker you are certainly vulnerable to . . . I don't want to scare you." (73) Those ellipses are filled in by the book's end: Kapil's book includes explicit images of the female hitchhiker's all too usual perils (involving rape and dismemberment). But the fear of violation and murder facing women who walk home alone at night or hitchhike alone is a fear faced as well by women who fall in love—and Kapil, like Amirpour, means us to be aware of that. In *Incubation* the connection between "hitchhiking" and finding love is made vivid in a number of ways, not least by the narrator's advice to "Divorce and remarry the road" (72). But Kapil's book is unusual in its direct treatment of the physical and psychic vulnerability of her heroine, even as the book's significant formal deviations enact the "risky" or daring choices made by the "girl." However, *Incubation* is also remarkable for the writer's embodied imagination of the hitchhiker's possible survival, and readers of Kapil find that the author manages to transform fear into hope and encouragement for the woman who wants to follow her desire.

In *Incubation* "Laloo"—cyborg, monster, "Punjabi-British hitchhiker on a j-1 visa" (3), "inevitably female" (4) and also "What a girl or boy becomes by accident in the deep of the body" (23)—sets off on a picaresque adventure which is both a voyage in space (mostly America) and time (a sentimental journey). Aspects of the work which make it appropriate to consider *Incubation* as a "poet's novel" would include the protagonist's protean quality, the book's concentrated, vivid language and fragmented form, and the easy movement between the exterior and interior voyages (mileage and memory), as well as swift the changes of tack from realism to fantasy. Here questions about the "hazardous travels that brought you to a different place" can go like this: "Were you a girl then a woman, a boy then a man? Did you grow wings when you were a cat, and fly away to a different but no less lucrative scene, complete with mice and milk and massage therapy . . . " (89). There is an explicit quest motif, as Laloo "sets out to see things as they are" (4) and a romantic fantasy (wonderfully, the American actor George Clooney is invoked as impossible object of desire). *Incubation* could be usefully included in a course on travel / quest narratives: Kapil's book can be compared to *On the Road* and read with *Don Quixote* (both Cervantes' original and Kathy Acker's take) or combined with movies like *The Vagabond* and *Thelma & Louise*. But race, as well as gender is part of the story here, and because of the way in which Donna Haraway's theory of the Cyborg is mobilized in *Incubation*, but also because the term "alien" is used for both visitors from other countries and—imagined—visitors from other *planets*, adding movies like *The Man Who Fell to Earth* or *The Brother from Another Planet* might round out this suggested syllabus. Presenting Kapil's book in the context of works with a similar theme is a good way to demonstrate how such themes are transformed over time, leading to a productive discussion of the means the author finds to expand the tradition to include her experience and make "space" for a different kind of protagonist.

Indeed, some of what is most interesting about Kapil's work emerges via comparison with the tradition(s): where readers are led to ask first *How is this different from what I have been led to expect?* and then *Why is it different?* Or *Why was I trained to expect something else?* In other words, some of Kapil's accomplishment involves making a space for readers to confront and question the certainties they bring to the encounter with the work of art. Used to following the protagonist through a novel by way of his / her unchanging name (and pronoun), stable gender, physical description, and possessions, for instance, readers of Kapil's work are encouraged to track in new ways, shifting their ideas about "character" and narrative. Sometimes seen and reported on in the third person, sometimes appearing to have taken over the first person narration, "Laloo" undergoes a variety of trans-formative (and never complete) (re)definitions. However, there is always a particular color (red) linked to or inked on the protagonist: "Laloo means red because Lal means red, so Laloo means 'the red one'." (39) Though if Laloo is a "red girl" (67), she is also a "read" one. "Are you red?"—a question apparently posed to the book's reader—is followed by "Did you read books on a windowsill all morning like a Bronte heroine . . ." (89). This recursive image of a reader who is read (and, in Bronte's *Jane Eyre*, was shut up for punishment in a *red* room) is not chosen at random. "Red" as a color is first introduced in *Incubation* as the direct consequence of writing (and shame):

> "I'm embarrassed by this book. It makes my blood roar to think of you reading it. So intimate. A text. Then it is a document related to shame flooding the body to make it red." (4)

It is only later that the color appears to be a consequence of travel:

> "This is the story of how I become a red girl, which sounds bad, but I don't know how else to say it. I turned red over the course of my journeys" (39)

"In a conventional novel," as Laynie Browne points out (in her essay on the book for *Jacket2*), "readers expect to be told—what happens to Laloo? Is she a reliable source of her story? Who is she in any one moment and how can we trace who she has become by the end of the novel? A progression is demanded." But at the end of *Incubation* Laloo is seen "in her red dress . . . like a girl in a fairytale" (possibly a reference to Little Red Riding Hood) "in a forest," just before both girl and forest are transformed again (as dress becomes body and forest turns into a word): "Yes. A red girl goes into this yes and is never seen again . . ." (92)

Indeed, on the book's final page the narrator literally loses sight of Laloo ("I can't see her") and the first initial of the heroine's name is loosened from that reference: "L is for love which is blood: the gathering speed of a pulse . . ." (93) "Red" in other words, emerges from "blood" and returns to it, and Laloo's movement through the text should be seen in the context of other kinds of circulatory systems, including the work of imagination and memory involved in reading / writing as well as the flow of gossip, rumor, and myth: "I'm sure you must have heard the myth of the hitchhiker whose heart was found next to her body, wrapped in a T-shirt." (74) Rather than putting her immense skill to the task of presenting Laloo as a recognizably (oxymoronically) "*realistic* character," made up of stilled and disparate parts, Kapil uses a color to evoke a figure who flows, who is both the same and different, who both disappears and survives, whose living heart is embodied and—felt as "pulse"—*beating*. Kapil engages her readers in the work of recognition, presenting a protagonist who is, as it were, both particle and wave: responsive to the "conditions of surveillance" (27) that conjure and transform this figure. While charting the movement of a particle is work more familiar to physicists, and tracing a color through a movie or painting might be the kind of activity more often expected of critics of film or visual art, Kapil offers readers the chance to think about literature in radically interdisciplinary ways. "I want a literature that is not made from literature," the author states (*Ban* p. 32), and readers who confine inquiry to the framework of a restricted literary hermeneutics are likely to miss a large part of the experience of reading Kapil's work.

In her essay on *Incubation*, Laynie Browne explains:

> Readers of poet's novels want our relation to the text to be released from the expected conventions of telling. We want instead, to be shown one of any manner of ways in which a text can behave. We desire our own definitions of multiple intelligences, which may require multiple readings . . .

And Oliver Bendorf, writing about Kapil's *Schizophrene,* noted that "writing is capable of healing to the extent that it pays attention to the visual—to what we see and have seen, but also, importantly, to what we cannot or will not see . . . " Kapil's work invites us to pay attention to what we see, and when, and where, and how we feel about what it is we are seeing (or not being allowed to see), and her writing is capable of healing those who are willing and able to read.

WORKS CITED

Amirpour, Ana Lily. *A Girl Walks Home Alone at Night*. 2014. Film.

Bendorf, Oliver. "Bhanu Kapil, Schizophrene." *Devil's Lake*. 1 Mar. 2012. Web. 1 July 2015.

Browne, Laynie. "Incubation: 'A Space for Monsters' by Bhanu Kapil The Poet's Novel." *Jacket 2*. 18 Apr. 2013. Web. 20 July 2015.

Haraway, Donna Jeanne. *Simians, Cyborgs, and Women: The Reinvention of*

Nature. New York: Routledge, 1991. Print.

Higgs, Christopher. "What Is Experimental Literature? {Five Questions: Bhanu Kapil}." *HTML Giant*. 1 Mar. 2011. Web. 20 July 2015.

Kapil, Bhanu. *Ban En Banlieue*. Callicoon, NY: Nightboat, 2015. Print.

Kapil, Bhanu. *Humanimal: A Project for Future Children*. Berkeley, CA: Kelsey Street, 2009. Print.

Kapil, Bhanu. *Incubation: A Space for Monsters*. New York: Leon Works, 2006. Print.

Kapil, Bhanu. *Schizophrene*. Callicoon, NY: Nightboat, 2011. Print.

Lyotard, Jean, and Geoffrey Bennington. *The Postmodern Condition: A Report on Knowledge*. Minneapolis: U of Minnesota, 1984. Print.

Rider, Bhanu Kapil. *The Vertical Interrogation of Strangers*. Berkeley, CA: Kelsey Street:, 2001. Print.

Circumambulation
Cowrie Shells, Bottle Caps and Balloons in Nathaniel Mackey's
From a Broken Bottle Traces of Perfume Still Emanate

TYRONE WILLIAMS

Quotidian and surreal, Nathaniel Mackey's narrative of musicology, musical performances, lectures and dreams, resists its narrativity by deploying rhetorical contradiction, paradox and qualification while valorizing musical/vocal stutter, nasality, and hoarseness. Even the mode of this writing—fiction, criticism, philosophy, mythology, etc.—resists generic identity and genetic history (a poet writing a novel, a novelist writing a prose poem, for example) since the earliest epistles (and Mackey's serial novel is primarily epistolary in form) first appeared as "Song of the Andoumboulou: 6" and part three of "Song of the Andoumboulou: 7" in *Eroding Witness*, Mackey's first book of poetry. However experimental they may be, the writings that dominate this first book are recognizable as poetry. Thus one could justifiably read these two epistles as prose poetry or literary criticism. Still, given the fact that Mackey had not conceived the idea of the serial novel at this point in his career,[1] that the book is largely comprised of poems, one would be on safe ground asserting that *From A Broken Bottle Traces of Perfume Still Emanate* represents the work of a poet writing a serial novel. Because its matrix is wedged between poems in that first collection of poetry, the serial novel not yet conceived as such, only manifesting itself after several collections of poetry, represented a turning back to, a repurposing or partial cannibalization of, those early epistles in *Eroding Witness*. This arc or spiral describes the general trajectory of Mackey's novel in progress.

Of course, the middle section of *Eroding Witness* also contained the first poems entitled "Song of the Andoumboulou," although the themes that would emerge in subsequent Andoumboulou poems and sections in subsequent books permeate the entirety of *Eroding Witness*. One of those dominant motifs is incessant, restless, travel and movement. Thus, insofar as the Andoumboulou poems may be understood as a self-generating machine or algorithm, the serial poem meshes form and content. Because one could apply the same description to the serial novel, it is clear that Mackey's writing projects have, from the very beginning, contested the very concept of genre even as the writings manifest themselves in recognizable generic forms. Individually, the discrete poems and novels push against the constraints that invariably pull them back. Another, and perhaps more pertinent, way to visualize the dialectics of these writing projects is to imagine them in an elliptical orbit around their respective genres. As it happens, this bent circularity or elliptical circumnavigation appears in a number of illustrations throughout the serial novel.

In what follows I want to briefly focus on what I believe are just a few of the metonyms that imply a "whole" underpinning this work of fiction. As a "whole" this object or idea is utopia, literally nowhere, but the question this novel (and I daresay, the poems too) relentlessly pursue is whether or not nowhere has always been the case. That is, the serial novel worries over, sifts through, what it imagines (or hopes, or believes) are the remains of a somewhere, a *topia* once extant or accessible.[2] These remains—bits of glass, bottle caps and cowrie shells—are thus analogous to or part of the balloons that appear in the novel, themselves analogous to or part of sphericity in general. Thus, I want to examine how the part/whole dialectics that constitute these metonyms manifest themselves thematically and formally throughout the serial novel. Specifically, I want to argue that *From a Broken Bottle Traces of Perfume Still Emanate* works against, even as it works "for," the suturing of the spiritual and cultural, the personal and the social, the musical and the literary, facets of these metonymic relations. In short, I argue that the serial novel calls into question the concepts of both the "part" and the 'whole," undermining the very conditions for the possibility of genre per se. At the same time, the novel is a delineation of its calling, its being hailed, by that which, however deconstructed, remains a potent center of gravity.[3] However elliptical its orbit, the novel revolves around genre, a movement which, deliberate or not, "mirrors" circumambulation and thus sanctifies genre.[4]

To thematize and pigeon-hole this writing, one could say that this ongoing serial novel concerns the cultural, musical and philosophical "travels" and tribulations of an improvisational jazz band, variously named Deconstructive Woodwind Chorus, East Bay Dread Ensemble, The Mystic Horn Society, and Molimo d'Atet. This open-ended self-naming reflects the band's incessant critical reassessments and reinventions of its musical philosophy. At the same time its free-form jazz replicates the ancient ritual of circumambulation, the deliberate movement around a sacred space or object. In this novel, circumambulation is anchored by what is not, not yet, no longer, or never was, present. This negative center is nonetheless active, transitive and migratory, as suggested by the manipulated Venn diagram on page 134 of the first book, *Bedouin Hornbook*. This space is less an absent center, however, than the "drawn blank" that Penguin, one of the band members, evokes in the third installation of the novel, *Atet A.D.* (152) Penguin's reference to the "comic-strip" balloons which "first"[5] appear in this novel's third volume, the "drawn blank" is, by all appearances, a bounded emptiness whose boundary shifts, is shifting, shape. However, like all inflated balloons, it is, in fact, inflated by what cannot be seen—air—just as the Venn diagram is filled in by graphic marks and the very paper on which it appears.[6]

The "comic-strip" balloons emerge, at least initially, from wind instruments played by Penguin and N., the narrator in all four books of the novel. However, these comic-strip balloons (often lettered with serious aphorisms) are presaged by "soap bubbles" that emerge from Penguin's and N.'s horns near the end of *Bedouin Hornbook*. (204) These soap bubbles appear in the wake of a "real balloon" that shows up at the end of a concert N. attends. The "real" balloon, inscribed with the phrase "Only One," anchors, perhaps gives rise to, its more "comical" manifestations; the relationship between the "real" balloon and its spectral "copies" may be understood as analogous to the relationship between the black dots and the Venn diagram.[7] The diagram itself may be "read" as a phallic and/or clitoral abstraction alluding to the heterosexual, heterosocial, and homosocial dynamics that underpin and infiltrate the band and its music.[8] By *Atet A.D.*, the original quintet—two men, two women, and N.[9]—has become a nebulous sextet, having added, on a trial or semi-permanent basis, Drennette, a drummer and percussionist. Because Angel of Dust, N.'s correspondent, and N. are never gendered, their joint neutrality, their solely epistolary relationship, "balances" the explicit sexual tensions and rivalries that arise among Lambert,[10] Penguin, Aunt Nancy and Djamilla. Moreover, the relationships and differences between the glass bits/cowrie shells/bottle caps-induced "headaches" N. experiences mirror the "headaches" the band experiences when comic-strip/talismanic balloons begin appearing during live performances throughout *Atet A.D.*[11] In short, the apparent oppositions—glass bits/cowrie shells/bottle caps on the one hand, "real"/soap bubbles(comic-strip)/talismanic balloons on the other, constitutes a sextet as a "reflection" of the band's six members.[12] If we understand the black dots as an absent real, a negative space, they might be encapsulated by the glass bits on the one hand and the "real" balloon on the other. But if the diagram is indeed in motion, always in transition, then the bits of glass and "real" balloon are manifestations of one another.[13] In terms of narrative time, the glass bits precede the "real" balloon by several pages in *Bedouin Hornbook*, but the glass bits may be as phantasmal as the spectral balloons that show up in book two, *Djbot Baghostus's Run*. Though N. associates the bits of glass embedded in his forehead with his childhood when he hit his head on the windshield of a car his mother was driving, he also believes the Crossroads Choir "planted" the glass bits in his brow. However, at the beginning of the chapter that follows this assertion, N. notes that, "This time around they feel more like shattered cowrie shells than bits of broken glass." (125) Given N.'s penchant for metonymic substitution—he will refer to the objects almost exclusively as cowrie shells until they are supplanted (or supplemented) by bottle caps in *Djbot Baghostus's Run*—he is an "unreliable" narrator only within the epoch of modernity, the era of "realism" and "objectivity." Within this tradition, the "real" balloon he sees at the end of the previous chapter may well be a hallucination, to say nothing of the soap bubbles, (204 BH), bottle caps (172 DBR) and comic-strip balloons (54 A A.D.). Within *and* outside this tradition, the dots in the diagram may well be black holes that nonetheless cannot consume everything within their gravitational fields. What remain, what escape, are bits and pieces, remainders, remnants, circling at different levels, on different planes, of the serial novel.

Given the multidimensional, transitive facets of this work, it isn't surprising that at least one critic has aligned Mackey's project with the "thousand plateaus" of Deluze's and Guattari's multiple, simultaneous, universes even if this critic does so to demonstrate the superior complexities of nomadic fiction vis-a-vis nomadic schizophrenia.[14] Here are three of the plateaus this serial novel operates on: at the narrative level, the band travels up and down the West Coast and back and forth across the country, playing gigs; at the musical level, avant- or post-garde improvisation (one musician after another gets to "lead" or play a variety of wind, string and percussion instruments) enacts the ritual of circumambulation;[15] at the level of gender politics, the male band members "take turns" desiring and pursuing "actual" and "dreamt" female band members. In general, circumambulation functions throughout the novel as it does in religious rites: to discover what no longer exists, to recover or forge access to what is still extant. Here, the traces of what has been almost lost, and so must be almost invented, include cultural histories, non-Western modes of knowledge, alternate universes, and altered states of mind. "Almost lost" manifests itself as traces of the sacrosanct, if not sacred, spheres, around which the narrator, N., circles. These traces are "ordinary" materials—cowrie shells, bottle caps. "Almost invented" appears primarily as the soap bubbles and balloons, lettered with cryptic statements that call into question the gestures toward romantic idealism to which Penguin and N. are particularly susceptible. Like Benjamin's chips of messianic time, these "manifestations" serve as correctives to both worldly realism and otherworldly idealism (e.g., Wordsworth's numinous spots of time).[16] Bobbing between earth and heaven, the balloons disrupt the metaphysics of linear time associated with Western modernity for a more "Eastern," that is, pre- and post-modern Western, concept of temporality.[17] That is, because the balloons are neither residues of a settled "past" nor auspices of a determinate "future," they, like the soap bubbles, cowrie shells and bottle caps, may be recovered, discovered, and/or invented again and again via circumambulation. For all that, circumambulation is never a return to the same "ground"; the balloons are unpredictable in terms of appearance: they sometimes have statements written on them, they are sometimes simply blank. Nor can N. predict when he will experience bits of glass, cowrie shell or bottle cap attacks. Circumambulation presupposes the arrival of what the sacred powers deem necessary, not what the penitent desires. The essential gap between the divine and the human, between the past and present, means that one can never be sure where to step, where to look for what he wants/needs. In taking a step forward and a step backward[18] in alluding to musical, mythic and folklore sources, this serial novel announces its metaphysical gestures, gestures beyond the boundaries of a fixed tradition, genre or culture. Yet, if change is one facet of the human condition, so too the desire for stability, for the resistance to changes (except those that, like sacrifice and death, are construed as necessary transformations *toward* a final stability—immortality or nirvana), is also human. As it happens, the "real" balloon" and the "mystical" balloons appear in the context of the desire for fixity, for oneness, for stability. And the most stereotypical and iconic figure for that kind of fixity is, at the personal level, romantic love and, at the cultural level, ethnic, racial or national unity, both of which are "analogous" to traditional literary genres.

The *Bedouin Hornbook* chapter in which the "real" balloon appears begins with Mackey's rendition of the crossroads motif, the place where three roads meet: think Oedipus Rex or Robert Johnson. N. has been trying to make contact with a mysterious band called, not surprisingly, Crossroads Choir. One night he receives a mysterious phone call telling him to go to the intersection of three roads and blindfold himself. He does so, and shortly after is stuffed into the back of a van that takes him to some "place" where he is allowed to remove his blindfold. He cannot make sense of his surroundings:

> One moment it seemed I was in an intimate nightclub, the next a domed arena with a seating capacity of thousands....a cramped garage...a huge, drafty warehouse...a cathedral...a storefront church. (111-112)

In the midst of applause Crossroads Choir strolls onstage where its band leader announces that the first piece will be "an Indo-Haitian-Sufi nocturne" called "Head Like A Horse's, Heart Like A Mule's." (113) The title summarizes the division between hard-knocks reason—we always know better—and stubborn desire: As N. concedes, "'Better fool's gold than no gold at all,' they seemed to insist—a conviction after my own quixotic heart." (113-114) The gold in this context is the band's insistence on oneness;[19] they "wasted no time going for the audience's jugular, laying claim to blood and to kinship ties as though they mined us for gold." (113) Later, after the flutist intones into the mike, "'As for me,' he muttered, 'who am neither I nor not-I, I have strayed from myself and I find no remedy from despair,'" the audience leaps wildly to its feet. A man near N. breaks off two glasses, places them upright on his table, rams his palms into their jagged edges, and holds them up to the band—sacrifice as appreciation. N. then feels bits of glass embed themselves into his forehead, and though his heart wants to believe they were "heavensent" his head reminds him of his childhood involvement in a car accident, "that it was the windshield of my mother's car when I was eleven,,," (115-116) When the band begins playing "one of the most dangerous standards around, 'Body and Soul,'" (117), N. joins the band and "narrates" via his horn a seven-day love affair he had with a woman. As the crowd joins in, singing the lyrics to the song, the balloon appears and is batted about by the audience. However, swept up in his nostalgia and sentiment, N. mistakes the balloon for a "ball of cabalistic light our week-long courtship had sparked, a promise of one day overcoming division." So says his heart. After his head reminds him that the "cabalistic ball" was also "a blank, bouncing check," N, like the balloon, comes back to earth.[20] (124)

This chapter seems paradigmatic of the entire novel. One of the central dramas throughout the four books is Penguin's tortuous, and torturous, pursuit of Djamilla. His longing mirrors the band's pursuit of a female drummer over the objections of Aunt Nancy who plays both bongos and violin. Penguin, whom N. refers to as a "grounded bird," struggles for completion; so too the band. Their individual and collective desires are played out amid the rubble that was the Black Arts Movement and Sixties and Seventies black militancy, both, to varying degrees, yearning for "collectivity," "the people," and "Africa." At a more molecular level, the problem of performing their own compositions (they often stutter, falter, limp, etc.) is also the source of ruminations and problems for the band. Within and beyond the band, N. shuttles back and forth between both the appeal and danger of "every flat, formulaic 'outcome'." (116) The balloons, while almost always appearing in the context of unity frustrated (romantic or cultural), also serve to dampen the exorbitant attention (academic and popular) given to African-American music as *the* cultural "gift" to the world as a consequence of the Diaspora.

Because the balloons emerge from Western musical instruments emitting African-European music (i.e., jazz), they suspend the stereotypical schema that would define African Diaspora cultures as primarily "oral/aural" and Western cultures as primarily "visual/optical." Their very visibility—reinforced by the occasional "message" written on their skins—serve notice that the oral and visible, the aural and visual, are as much a part of African and African American history as that of any other people. For all that, the balloons embody an expansiveness that risks the inflation of excessive differentiation (N. worries about the potential 'elitism" and coterie affectations) and, conversely, the deflation into identity politics. Excessive differentiation nurtures nostalgia—N. awash in the memories of a week-long affair during the Crossroads Choir concert, the valorization of indigenous "African" values, etc.—while identity politics fortify reductionism. This circulation of sentiment that unites inflation and deflation is dramatized at the beginning of the second missive of *Bedouin Hornbook*. N. has "the pleasure" of "walking past the aftermath of a motorcycle/automobile crash on the way home, one that, predictably, draws the attention of "the great beast.'" (10) N.'s "pleasure" in the conflation of separate vehicles is one with his reduction of human beings, as different from one another as a motorcycle and sedan, to "the great beast." For N. "the great beast," a reduction, likewise reduces music to messages ("Only One"). To the extent N. is a part of, apart from, the "beast," reductionism is part and parcel of his own self-inflation, he is a latter-day descendant of Ellison's narrator in *Invisible Man*.[21]

N., however, is the only band member—thus far—who suffers cowrie shell and bottle cap attacks. If Penguin's "problem" is Djamilla (and Djeannine, avatar of Drennette), N.'s may well be his epistolary relationship with Angel of Dust. More bluntly—if Penguin concedes too much to his heart, N.'s tendencies to intellectualize give too much to the head. In both cases, distance is key. Both Penguin and Djimalla circle one another like boxers in a ring, sexual desire and professional relationships (they are musicians in the same band) at the center of their dance. N.'s letters to Angel of Dust, his, hers or its to him, however attenuated (N. cites titles and even quotes from the letters Angel sends to him), also enact circumambulation, however elongated, an elliptical orbit of letters punctuated by N.'s dreams and lectures. Not once does either N. or Angel express a desire to see one another. There is simply N.'s logorrhea and Angel's near "silence." Angel of Dust is not only the proper name shorn of its history (it exists but has been forgotten) but also the nickname of the objects that give rise to N.'s headaches: bits of glass, cowrie shells and bottle caps.[22] All three are remnants of histories, parts of wholes, from which they have been dislodged:

a windshield, bottles, Polynesia.[23] These histories have not been lost; they form the sacred/secular spaces announced by the proper name Angel of Dust. And these histories, lost, forgotten or mythologized, trigger searches: N. returns to the scene of the car accident, "creates" both Djbot—shard of glass—and Jarred Bottle (seeking no doubt his bottle cap), whose figure may also be "read" in the Venn diagram; and of course N. suffers devastating headaches that force him to be frequently hospitalized. The bits of glass, cowrie shells and bottle caps embedded in N.'s forehead allegorize the risks one takes in circumambulation, as though ambulation is always pursued by the possibility of the ambulance.

NOTES

1. As Mackey writes in an interview with Peter O'Leary, "I didn't have a plan when I first started writing them [the letters]...I just saw them...as a way to speak without the constraints of verse. There are constraints in verse that disallow certain kinds of statement and certain declarations." Later, in the same interview, Mackey explains that "one of the impulses [for including the letters] was to unpack the poetry in some ways but not do it in verse."

2. Needless to add, this elsewhere may be extant without being accessible; this is, in general, the formulation of hope as conceived within the novel.

3. I am resisting the temptation to read the more spectacular events and manifestations in the novel as metaphor since this concept depends on a disjunction between tenor and vehicle. While the sense of loss and absence that suffuses the novel might justify deploying metaphor, Mackey's insistence on the paradoxical presence of what is absent, what has been lost, suggests that the threads, however tenuous, between past and present, absence and presence, remain intact.

4. Paul Hoover also notes the modes of circularity in the novel, movement that he relates to the Stations of the Cross. See his "Fair of Figures for Eshu: Doubling of Consciousness in the Work of Kerry James Marshall and Nathaniel Mackey."

5. In fact, the first balloon appears in the first book, *Bedouin Hornbook*. Unlike the apparently "metaphysical" and "cartoonish" balloons that emerge later, the balloon that appears at the end of a rousing concert is "real," though N. mistakes it for both "a ball of cabalistic light and the blank, bouncing check" he'd had "inklings of earlier." (124) I discuss this chapter in detail below.

6. The diagram is marked by two black dots and several words. I discuss the significance of two of the words and the two black dots below.

7. The words that partially frame the first dot—"Bleeding" and "Voice"—can

be understood separately as references to the exaltation of slavery and racism on the one hand and the oral/aural dyad on the other as the definitive attributes of African American culture. Needless, to add, this reductionism, especially during the Black Arts/Black Power Movements, both attracts and repulses N. Read together, as "Bleeding Voice," the hoarse, raspy and/or nasal voice would serve as the fulcrum of a Western culture that valorizes clarity, control and timbre—in short, opera singing—as the highest achievement in vocal music.

8. These dynamics depend, of course, in part on N.'s gender. See footnote 3. Absent, thus far, is any hint of homosexual dynamics.

9. N.'s gender is under- and over-determined. On the one hand, it is never made explicit. On the other hand, as a male reader, I project and infer stereotypical masculine characteristics onto, from, N. Because N. must be understood then as a kind of neutral, perhaps neutered, blank, he/she is the equivalent of the black hole at the center of the novel's circumambulating narratives. He/she is, however, not alone "there"; the same gender neutrality marks Angel of Dust, N.'s correspondent in every sense of the word. However, for the sake of convenience, I use the masculine pronoun when referring to N.

10. N. does have sexual fantasies about the female band members and mystical women that show up in his dreams and writings. However, unlike Penguin, he does not overtly pursue any one.

11. . In book four, *Bass Cathedral,* balloons emerge from the vinyl (the serial novel takes place during the 1980s) when N. plays the band's first album, *Orphic Bend.*

12. N.'s ungendered status is mirrored by Drennette's ambiguous status in the band; she sits in with them but it isn't clear that she's a permanent member of the band. Absence and uncertainty are thus at the center of the band.

13. If, on the other hand, the circle and ellipse are two overlapping planes, then we may understand N.'s various personas or avatars—Djbot, Jarred Bottle, Flaunted Fifth, et al—as "N." on different, incongruous, levels of existence. For the purposes of this brief essay I read the ellipse as a later stage of the circle because I read, in the English (as opposed to, say, Arabic) tradition, left to right.

14. See J. Edward Mallot's "Sacrificial Limbs, Lambs, Iambs and I Ams: Nathaniel Mackey's Mythology of Loss" in *Contemporary Literature.*

15. Fritz Gysin notes that the trajectory of jazz drumming has also been described as elliptical. See his "Double-Jointed Time in Nathaniel Mackey's Jazz Fiction" in *Amerikastudien/ American Studies.*

16. That is, two orientations toward temporality are invoked by the bal-

loons, the past and the future. But what they have in common is the attempt to ward off, place into abeyance, modes of temporality other than the,-selves. In that respect, each—the past, the future—collapses into "time," an ever-present "now."

17. On the complex notions of time, temporality and history, complexities irreducible to the binary opposition "African time" and "Western time," see Ulfried Reichardt, "Time and the African-American Experience: The Problem of Chronocentrism," in a special issue of *Amerikastudies/American Studies*.

18. Or two—in an early section of *Bedouin Hornbook,* a college roommate of N. notes that we "may be worse off than ever."

19. The reference to "blood and kinship ties" notwithstanding, N. provides no explicit evidence of the substance that undergirds this union when he describes the audience as comprised of "hairless, mannikinlike men and women, each of whose faces wore itself like a tight tautological mask." (112) The oblique reference to Dunbar's poem, "We Wear The Mask," itself a poetic version of Du Bois' "double consciousness" as delineated in *The Souls of Black Folk*, presumably corroborates the "blood and kinship ties" reference as racial and/or ethnic.

20. "Finally a woman tapped it with a sharp flick of her finger, sending it towards the ceiling. It rose with ever-increasing speed, taking my breath away, only to come down even faster." (124)

21. In the opening paragraph of *Bedouin Hornbook*, N. relates a dream he has had of a trombone emerging from a manhole. All three—manhole, dream, jazz—recall the beginning of *Invisible Man* which finds the narrator, Ellison's unnamed N., living beneath the streets of Harlem and recounting a drug-induced dream that involves, among other things, references to slavery, blues and the responsibility of the individual. Indeed, there are so many direct and indirect allusions to Ellison's novel that the subject warrants an essay—at the least—on its own.

22. Given the hallucinatory intensity of some of N.'s headaches, one can be sure that the remedy offered by Angel of Dust is also, simultaneously, the poison of its anagrammatic "twin," angel dust.

23. Though they are often linked to indigenous markers of African female sexuality, itself an avatar of a water goddess, and were used as currency by some Indian and African cultures, cowrie shells are believed to have been brought to Africa by traders and explorers from the South Seas.

WORKS CITED

Du Bois, W.E. B. *The Souls of Black Folk.* New York: W.W. Norton, 1999.

Dunbar, Paul Laurence. "We Wear The Mask." *The Complete Poems of Paul Laurence Dunbar.* Philadelphia: Hakim's Publications, 2004.

Ellison, Ralph. *Invisible Man.* New York: Random House/Vintage International, 1952.

Gystin, Fritz. "Double-Jointed Time in Nathaniel Mackey's Jazz Fiction." *Amerikastudien/American Studies*, 45: 4. Time and the African-American Experience (2000), 513-518.

Hoover, Paul. "Fair of Figures for Eshu: Doubling of Consciousness in the Work of Kerry James Marshall and Nathaniel Mackey." *Lenox Avenue: A Journal of Interarts Inquiry*, Vol. 5 (1999), 3-20.

Mackey, Nathaniel. *Eroding Witness.* Urbana and Chicago: University of Illinois Press, 1984.

———. *Atet A.D.* San Francisco: City Light Books, 2001.

———. *Bass Cathedral.* New York: New Directions Books, 2008.

———. *Bedouin Hornbook.* Los Angeles: Sun & Moon Press, 1997.

———. *Djbot Baghostus's Run.* Los Angeles: Sun & Moon Press, 1993.

Mallot, Edward J. "Sacrificial Limbs, Lambs, Iambs and I Ams: Nathaniel Mackey's Mythology of Loss." Contemporary Literature, 45:1 (2004), 135-164.

O'Leary, Peter. "An Interview with Nathaniel Mackey." *Chicago Review*, 43:1 (1997), 30-48.

Reichardt, Ulfried. "Time and the African-American Experience: The Problem of Chronocentrism." *Amerikastudien/ American Studies*, 45: 4. Time and the African-American Experience (2000), 465-484.

"the equal instant space of action"
On Leslie Scalapino's *Dihedrons Gazelle-Dihedrals Zoom* (2010)

JUDITH GOLDMAN

In one of his *Epistolae familiares*, Petrarch gives a famous account of his ascent of Mount Ventoux: having gained the mountain's peak, the poet finds himself tortured by thoughts of a decade wasted in love for Laura. As he resolves to cultivate virtue, he turns to bibliomancy for guidance and, in a variation on *sortes virgiliae* (Virgilian lots), opens his pocket copy of Augustine's *Confessions* at random. Of course, as Petrarch himself remarks, his gesture repeats the very action through which Augustine precipitated his own conversion, through divination with the New Testament. Like Augustine, Petrarch not only converts to a new life, but also converts his brush with chance to a form of fateful, personalized address. For after all, as with Augustine, so fortuitously fitting is the hazarded passage, that Petrarch must take it as peculiarly meant for him.

Yet another version of bibliomancy opens the volume of Leslie Scalapino's poet's novel *The Dihedrons Gazelle-Dihedrals Zoom*, but as with every other imaginable element of this posthuman tour de force, its terms are completely transformed.[1] She writes in her "Author's Note":

> *The Dihedrons Gazelle-Dihedrals Zoom* was written by leafing through *Random House Webster's Unabridged Dictionary* choosing words by process of alexia, not as mental disorder but word-blindness: trance-like stream overriding meaning, choice and inhibition. The intention to bring about an unknown future was changed by this action of alexia making as it happens sensual exquisite corpses—leading to the discovery that there isn't any future, *isn't* even any present. Such an exquisite corpse, read, is in an instant yet not even in 'a present.' Outside's events unite gluing to each other in a single object. That which had already existed is by chance . . . the writing is not the *idea* of the whole framework of occurrences *after* without its existence ever being. (DGDZ vii)[2]

As with her earlier, related novel *Floats Horse-Floats or Horse Flows*, Scalapino asserts here that the book has been composed through a cultivated "alexia," as applied to the dictionary. "Alexia," or "word-blindness," is, technically, an acquired inability to read resulting from brain damage; Scalapino's torqued, figural alexia, by contrast, is a strategy for non-intentional composition that treats the dictionary as a repository of radical lexical and narrative potential rather than a reference work. And, indeed, rather than as a pronouncer of fate: for here chaotic encounters with the dictionary are not retroactively framed as purposive and motivated but stand instead as a nonlinear process of emergence, a process that yields productive, autonomous assemblages of reciprocally affecting words that stretch and morph language to the point of total conversion. Likewise, instead of revealing "an unknown future," the alexic composition of *Dihedrons* demonstrates a deconstruction of linear temporality altogether, giving onto a temporal scheme in which future, present, and past happen at once and mutually influence one another, producing a stream of occurrence as existence and "event" rather than plot.[3]

Most deeply informed by Mahayana (Zen) Buddhism and Western phenomenology, Scalapino's *oeuvre* in general, but perhaps most outstandingly *Dihedrons*, reflects tenets of all beings' openly processual interdependence: "Being cannot be anything but being-with-one-another," as Jean-Luc Nancy writes, "circulating in the with and as the with of this singularly plural coexistence," in which condition the world is continuously actively worlded by a "reticulated multiplicity, which produces no result." (Nancy 3; 9). In a 1993-5 interview, discussing Gertrude Stein and Indian Buddhist philosopher Nagarjuna (in which she notes that Stein represents "character or mind as action not entity"), Scalapino states: "As nothing has inherent existence, in that it is dependent on other factors, it can't begin or have an ending as an inherent object; nor can a view of its *nonexistence* be accurate either. Poetically, this implies change/transformation being the principle or 'structure' itself (as from all points or perspectives) of the writing." (Scalapino & Frost 22).

I thus apply the term "posthuman" to Scalapino's novel advisedly and with the profound implications suggested by R. L. Rutsky: "the posthuman is ... an autonomous, ongoing process of mutation ... that takes place not as a narrative, but as an event." (Rutsky 110). Most significantly, as Rutsky formulates, posthuman mutation is a decentered mode of unfolding that denies Western culture's anthropocentric dichotomy between linear causality and chance or accident even as mutation is itself contingency: "Mutation ... cannot be seen as an *external* randomness that imposes itself upon the biological or material world—nor, for that matter, on the realm of culture. Rather mutation names that *randomness which is always already immanent in the processes* by which both material bodies and cultural patterns replicate themselves" (111; my emphasis). Modeling the noncausal webs of becoming of organic and nonorganic life, *Dihedrons* enacts a formal aesthetic of mutation; so, too, is its main content precisely a resplendent, ebullient, and timely presentation of the expressive and affective transmutation of lifeforms. Given its ethological bent, *Dihedrons* also operates an aesthetic of the aesthetic, becoming a rigorous inquiry into capacities for affect, devoted both to a fully dimensioned monism (equal, shared, experiential being or reality among all things) and to differential plurality.

• • •

There is a sense, then, in which writing must resist meaning . . . Why? Because meaning exists before writing. (Consider, not just the rationale, but the power of the dictionary.) Writing is always belated, comes to a world already determined, already written.

—BRUCE CAMPBELL, "NEITHER IN NOR OUT:
THE POETRY OF LESLIE SCALAPINO" (1992)

a be ce dar i um. Not an abacist.

—SCALAPINO, *DIHEDRONS*

Incorporating technical jargon, strings of verbatim definitional language, and even the numbers that separate (and hierarchize) words' meanings — as formally striking, miniature indexical paroxysms in an otherwise verbal stream, *Dihedrons* is recognizably the rhizomatic efflorescence of the dictionary. It thus participates in 21st-century writing's obsession with the database, though situated cannily adjacent to what Craig Dworkin has called "database literature." Troping on engagement with the new media environment, which requires everyone to use tools to manipulate information in quantity, database works, Dworkin writes, "are composed by establishing rules with which to organize large amounts of 'ready-made,' found material" (32), austere "arbitrary procedures" that compile deracinated data into unpredictable texts characterized by "chance moments of local coherence" and "preposterous molar incoherence" (38), as by pattern and anomaly. By contrast, Scalapino's appropriative novel neither elaborates procedures, nor accumulates lists of inert data that may or may not be enlivened by the reader, even as the reader must nonetheless co-create the text. "There is space yet is only in one's experience at night's delative reverse-out. 'Then' delaminates" (18). Lifted language proliferates events that generate or involve hyper-vivid affective assemblages; these scenarios flash out fragmentarily only to repeat or continue later, with added elements or recombined with yet other scenes.

In this, *Dihedrons* also differs from other literary experiments specifically with the dictionary, such as Stefan Themerson's *Bayamus and the Theatre of Semantic Poetry* (1949) "a novella [replacing] certain words with their dictionary definitions" (a poeticizing tactic Raymond Queneau proceduralized in the 1973 *Oulipo* compendium) (Rubenstein 33). Better known is Clark Coolidge's *The Maintains* (1974), entirely made of words and phrases borrowed from the dictionary. In part, the work improvises with what Coolidge saw as the dictionary's peculiar syntax: "in its definitions it has phrases like 'that which is blank,' that sort of syntax . . . helped hook the work together" (cited in Golston 303-4). If *The Maintains* indexes this syntax to point to its role in the dictionary as a metalinguistic apparatus for "maintaining" language, as Michael Golston observes, Coolidge's work also short-circuits the extra-linguistic referential function of the dictionary (302-306), Ron Silliman argues, for instance, by dragging various kinds of functional and deictic words and phrases out of their context in full definitions. Because such strategies block the production of an "image track," Siliman notes, "they create a blind language" ("Ubeity" 21).

Likewise flouting the reference work's disciplinarity, its status as compendium of authoritative information, Scalapino nonetheless inverts the "blind language" to which Coolidge reduces the dictionary by using alexia ("word blindness") to make *Dihedrons*: allowing words their autonomous life propagates images galore. The liveliness *Dihedrons* liberates goes beyond Lyn Hejinian's suggestion in "The Rejection of Closure" that, "Even words in storage, in the dictionary, seem frenetic with activity, as each individual entry attracts to itself other words as definition, example, amplification," for the very laws of their attraction have changed. Indeed, I will suggest that one biopolitical dimension of *Dihedrons* is its status as a *reflexive genetic text*, not just through its self-conscious foregrounding of its compositional process but of its source, the dictionary, as the very "genetic code" of language. In this, *Dihedrons* refuses the myth of DNA as "master molecule," becoming instead an exemplary post-genomic text that acknowledges a wide array of actants and non-linear processes in the generation of lifeforms.[4]

· · ·

Alexia, not disordered mine unknown streams as word-blindness make an open (non-)future
wood B closed a person by unknown words 'our' illusory sequencing there is sequencing
also of flesh

SCALAPINO, DIHEDRONS

Over against the geo- and biopolitical thematics central to her writing through decades, her outspokenness regarding the politics and ethics of aesthetics, and her practice of incorporating often violent, urgent current events into her texts—in *Dihedrons*, her allusions to conflict between Han and Uighur factory workers in China in 2009, to vice presidential candidate Sarah Palin's support of aerial wolf killing, to protests surrounding the Iranian presidential election of 2009—Scalapino's works have also been playful in content and especially form (one thinks, for instance, of her engagement with the comic book through a number of works).

Most playful by far, I would venture to say, is her last novel, *Dihedrons*—so entirely in-formed by word-play that not only do the bulk of its characters enter the text as incorporated dictionary entries, *but they also retain their mode of being appropriated words while participating in the narrative.*[5] One of the main characters/word-protagonists of the book is the "base runner." On one hand, the "base runner," a functional position in baseball (and cricket), is initially imbricated as the exponent of one of the novel's narrative strands through intermittent references to a 2009 attack on the Sri Lankan cricket team visiting Lahore, Pakistan; further, various aspects of the game of baseball, such as being at bat, the diamond, or the very dynamic of contest, are continually depicted as "actually" occurring in the narrative even as they become analogs of elements of narrative structure. On the other hand, while the "base runner" comes to have non-baseball-related experiences and to interact with other characters, the very phrase "base runner," so often accompanied by (perhaps ersatz) explanatory phrases from its lexicographical entry, cannot but register very literally as a term continually being defined with language from a reference book.[6]

Dihedrons might thus be viewed as a virtuosic exemplar of the poet's novel, for it explores every possible nuance of textual materiality while continually returning the reader to a *scene* of representation. Part of the novel's art, too, is its means of transporting the reader between these levels or modes of attention, as well as its canny ability to keep its reader in equipoise among them. Here, for instance (to continue with the base runner's strand), the image of a bat hitting the ball derives straight from the visual presence of the word "pop" in the obviously dictionary-tendered term "apophyge" (pronunciation of which does not contain the sound "pop"), even as the text comments on the incalculability of the linkage: "empty links planted set to a cycle or future roaming to meet and roam not at the links originating it apophyge pop the ball struck by the bat arises simulates (how can the ball be action) the ball striking the bat in dawn links no sequentially though dawn is" (37). Earlier, to reverse this schema, it is the baseball narrative that provides a means of linking an appropriated term: "The contester reaches the red chela into the streaming crowd cheliform extracting the dark blue poppies . . . The hand thrust in. The red claw, the mitt reaching the poppies" (1). Here the unlikely "cheliform"—"having the shape of a pincer or claw"— is visually elided with a baseball glove.

Such lucid, 'pataphoric dream logic is at work everywhere in the text and runs the figural gamut, relying as much on the sonic as the visual.[7] Scalapino describes *Dihedrons'* chapters as "sensuous exquisite corpses" (as quoted above), yet I would argue that at its most literal material level, the text mobilizes "hidden nonlinear relations" to stage "the recombinant infinity that is the Western alphabet in operation" (to use Steve McCaffery's terms) as a transgenic poetics (vi; xxiii). One way that *Dihedrons* performs a reflexively genetic recombination and reinflection is through complex forms of punning. ("Homophony," as McCaffery writes, "registers a certain autonomy of language outside of referential constraint and systematic relations but also unleashes a dynamis of vertiginous, uncontrollable transformations" (29).) "The ctenophors first giving birth when the parents are still larvae that give birth again in the middle of their life the same as lives/thought as being/ all the surroundings their structure existing at once differently from its organ, organization, the *new borne* on the ocean waves" (80; my emphasis). The text continually adverts to its paranomastic proclivities, often proffering its doubles directly, as with "or/oar," "maw/ma," "would/wood," "halving/having," pairs that appear throughout ("Or/Oar is not existing (time). The old by *not* having ability *have* even as *halve* things . . . Or/oar just not knowing?" (22; emphasis original)), and always dexterously folding in such happenstance twins, who share genetic material by chance. Here the character "deb" (debutante) thinks of her mother, a chrysanthemum (another pun here!): "having been lifted out of herself halving by raging emotion then carrying with her always red Mongolian death-fan Chrysanthemum, reacting to her maw (ma who's) elsewhere sieve-fucking red petals eating speaking" (49). Filiation by sound is made more literally filiative, while paranomasia also stretches synesthetically, since the red bloom is figured as an open mouth.[7]

Dihedrons also draws the reader to textual materiality (and genetic origin) by subsuming the dictionary's disciplinary signatures in citations from its entries: "Because the first ga•ril´•as attack elsewhere the cricketers on the bus the policeman and a cricketer killed augend *then* others explode the hotel guerrillas first head-quartering (in Mumbai) in an discovered afterwards Augean kitchen kill its works that event including the ga•ril´•a boy asleep on the car motor" (116). As noted above, the novel, too, materially incorporates the dictionary's hierarchical ordination of word meanings in each entry by taking in the numbers (2; 4) and letters (B) that order that system, yet turns them into puns: "the men leading this civil war havoc on the 2 sides forced to the peace table by the women" (137); "as grizzly can't burn immune 2." (41); "the trees fractionaters future only, a forest 2 states a tree" (1); "4 as a child one hasn't emotion or it is as crystals clinging crumbling at touch remembered as flesh object 4 there is no death" (138); or even, "in a fo4est and indigo sand sky at night trees wave on wave of skies forest" (52).

In an insightful discussion of her "negative poetics" and "disontological writing," Jason Lagapa argues that, consistent with Buddhist tradition, Scalapino employs an insistent rhetoric and paralogic of negation, paradox, and contradiction to push beyond duality and to point to the fallibility of language ("Opposite climes are not opposing" (79)), exposing the groundlessness of both being and writing and proposing entity as ongoing action or process.[8] *Dihedrons* notably also uses puns to arrive at this sense of the coincidence and abolition of opposites, of a reality beyond normative perceptions, concepts, and categories. The character "the Distaffer," a pilot who transports orphans and is shot down over the ocean, is associated with "dor," a homonym that conjoins two words with entirely separate etymologies, one meaning "beetle" (as in dung beetle) and one "mockery." Scalapino uses "dor" to symbolize the Distaffer's female difference (and political/ethical resistance) to the other pilots: "the Distaffer however a young-tough halo equals demoted works assigned to the planes . . . the other pilots men regarding her subsumed as dor, beetle and mockery, between two entirely different poles unwanted haloed interloper" (52). If here the word's undecidability marks the Distaffer's exclusion, elsewhere "dor" is glossed, precisely due to its paralogical homonymy, as a kind of porthole for transcending language towards processual being: "Word on the door 'dor' is 'beetles' and 'mockery,' both. Meet midway where there is no language" (43).

Marked as a poet's novel through its materialist artistry and its adept shuttling between materiality and representation, its equipoise between surface and depth, opacity and transparency, *Dihedrons* might also be counted one given the following paradox: *if narrative is re-presentational, a mimesis of events that is dependent on those events as prior to narrative,* Dihedrons *is a radically genetic text, reflexively announcing its events as produced by the act of narration.* Here we see the gorgeous genetic drift of the text as it foregrounds the nonlinear dynamics of recombination and mutation that compose both *words* and *worlds* by weaving narrative out of the aleatory, alphabetic juxtapositions one finds in the dictionary:

> Nightshift released do walk at the end of their shift. That's how she got there. No nidation occurring in the workers and that connected she sees suddenly to nidana, boschvark peering later their people standing outside at night . . . watching the night jar/the farmer rather the nightshift released floods of people out into the factory yard. Nicker of the horse in the dark. (39)

Dihedrons is, impossibly, at once ostentatiously performative and hyper-vividly descriptive, as found words—obtruding upon the reader as "mere" words—create and propel the narrative, yet simultaneously—as they give rise to images and storylines—describe seemingly independent occurrences.[9]

While never losing sight of writing as process, others (including Scalapino herself) have focused on such narratological issues in her texts as the layering of world, perception, and the act of writing, with accompanying disjunctions and sudden conflations of interior and exterior, mediation and immediacy, as well as her works' disruption of linear sequence and causal schemas especially through the repetition and re-representation of events. In *Dihedrons*, perhaps what foments the near-magical coetaneity of creation and mimesis is how the novel's generative exploration of the transgenic vivacity of the material text recapitulates the very dynamics of the postgenomic affective assemblages it also depicts. Indeed, it is often Scalapino's anarchic genetic dérives through the dictionary that instigate those assemblages, as she allows a panoply of unusual lifeforms and qualities—so often left to rest as unused "jargon" between the lexicon's covers—to non-teleologically co-evolve.

• • •

One persists in order to see something that has come up in the writing, it seems to be attached to other things, those things may on the surface have nothing to do with each other . . . it's not that you wish to explain the connections, or to break the connections. It's that you want to find out what they are . . . I was thinking how someone could, with a kind of humane rationalism, simply put one thing next to another thing and let it be there and see something about it. As opposed to my own tendency which is to have things really hit the fan . . .

—LESLIE SCALAPINO, INTERVIEW WITH SARAH ROSENTHAL (2001)

If Scalapino enacts a transgenic poetics in composing with sensitivity to words' shared genetic material, she also attends to words as "vibrant matter" in treating them, along with their definitions, not as information with predictable narrative vectors but as expressive and affective actants prone to "unnatural participations and nuptials" (Deleuze & Guattari 241).[10] Thus, her text may be considered postgenomic both in the sense that its events are not preprogrammed or controlled by a master code and in the sense that its morphology is exuberantly expressively and affectively driven, in ways indifferent to function (such as normative logic, narrative probability, linear causality) and in ways devoted to exploring function non-deterministically.[11] Radically divested of presumption, *Dihedrons'* ethological literary form is predicated on finding out, to use Deleuze and Guattari's famous phrase, "what a body can do": it is a textual environment for lively, autonomous assemblages of words, ensembles motored by continual affective inter-modification. In turn, the matrix of character-space in *Dihedrons* is also anarchic: the narrative structure produced by its complexes of word-protagonists radically equalizes characters' interior and exterior representations and their potential to catalyze events and affect one another; indeed, the novel distributes narrative agency and attention to the extent that figure-ground distinctions are mooted: the settings themselves become characters (see Woloch, Chap.1). Thus, the text not only *takes shape* through these groundless, nonlinear processes but it *depicts* such processes, which is to say that the text not only *behaves as* affective assemblage but also *represents* such ensembles with an extraordinary degree of insight and imagination.

Filled with "transversal communications" and events of becoming, the aesthetic mode through which *Dihedrons* portrays its "animal reality" performatively transcends the sequentiality of prose in stretching it to represent complex events and networks of relations all at once. In a passage that recalls the discussion of the skateboarding film *Gleaming the Cube* in her novel *Dahlia's Iris* and her use in *Floats Horse-Floats* of the tennis star Venus Williams as character, Scalapino asserts a likeness of motion between a child's and a dog's body at play, describes trees as vomiting their leaves, torques the meaning and grammar of the word "deterge" ("to wipe clean"), and graphs the intersecting trajectories of leaves, car, and skateboarder:

> The little white wolf-dog Distaffer's avatar is that of many children who play the shape of it in the air as their (each child's) shape is left there many are above the rose horizon Venus is resting red and brown crisp curled huge flowing leaves millions deterge by Venus resting that fallen from trees hurl vomiting the blue sky of the car flowing toward the leaves (flying that vomit the car's blue sky coming hurtling to them) through the coursing flow of red-brown leaves a man skateboards crossing toward/and the skateboarder is *before* the windshield of the car's flow overflow elation at brim or rim without horizon color or sides. (9)

Each oscillating actant in this aggregate is presented as passive and active as once, in the midst of sympathetic movement. The ensemble is shown as a *whole*, the analytic bent of detail harnessed by gestalt, just as the phrase "red and brown" is turned into a compound adjective "red-brown" closer to the act of apprehension.

In an event that recurs through the novel, the base runner runs through a forest fire set by the nefarious "ocker" character (Australian slang for "uncouth male"):

> Even temporarily apyretic, the base runner [. . .] there cling to him collecting on him swellings-torulosis of other boojums hangers-on apyrous fur non-human they are apulmonic have empty chests with no lungs and having thus come through the fire storm of the flaming forest aren't clinging deer dreamlike are large hanging on him as if while not breathing with lungs in being apulmonic assemble dissemble inflated their breathing breathe through their whole skin. The base runner's action is always vivacious conatus forms intermittent. The forest's conatus effort of the young pre-fiery green shapes of trees passes into the running base runner as feelings. (20)

Reconfiguring the "boojum," a species of desert tree, as a parasitic animal, Scalapino here plays on the negating prefix "a" to imagine the creatures: they are "apyretic" and "apulmonic," the text in turn fascinated with these "non-human" capacities for fire-resistance and lungless breathing, as with the organs that sponsor these capabilities. Yet the text focuses not just on the affective assemblage of base runner and boojums, but also the larger haecceity involving deer and trees. Here Scalapino directly alludes to Spinozan ethology: "conatus" is the tendency of bodies to persist, which paradoxically requires each body to change, so "to creatively compensate for the alterations or affections it suffers" vis-à-vis other bodies, a process whereby it inevitably modifies them in turn (Bennett 22). The defendedness of the trees "passes into the running base runner as feelings."

Of the many questions Scalapino pursues in *Dihedrons,* perhaps the most formative is: What is sensation, and how is the sensory mediated and felt? Here the novel goes well beyond finding out "what a body can do," its capacities unknowable outside the events and relations that draw out these powers, but seeks more profoundly *how it is* that a lifeform affects or is affected. With what organs does one feel, and what is the experience of sensory perception and response such organs afford? *Dihedrons'* approach to this inquiry is posthuman and anti-determinist. As the novel so often envisions, inside and outside, the particular sensory apparatus each lifeform contrives to experience its experience, it is clear that the functional parts allotted a body do not straightforwardly delimit its affects. Participants in "symbioses that bring into play beings of totally different scales and kingdoms, with no possible filiation," lifeforms both incalculably remake themselves and find their limits (Deleuze & Guattari 238).

Dihedrons pays particular attention to plant experience, privileging flowers for the immediacy of their mode of being; they impose no false temporal constructs on reality: "flowers *haven't* future or present-*that-now not* having present is their having sensation of living never separate from their blooming or after/before/*then* haven't concatenation even blue (not ever or [not and] *"when"*) blooming/*that's* empty" (30). Yet the text also goes further to posit floral sensation and to imagine how sensation might be "translated" between "chordates" and non-chordates, among flowers, animals, and humans:

> Not chordate then. in their radiant colors. The flowers hadn't spines
> [. . .] Flowers have sensations as being their only living not doing
> actions outside—can be sensations of others' living in these other's
> actions since there others have become outside our own sensations,
> flowers being mute substitute 4 animals people's sensations not being
> known by the flowers. The flowers plombs of night as being day [. . .
>] are *have 'seen'* involute to 'return' to the animal shape size state un-
> aware. Neither hearing or seeing. As vertebrates' sensations translated
> to be only visual to others amidst them flowers oar radiant color. (21-
> 2)

Flowers here become an inter-species interface through which "vertebrates" feel other vertebrates' feelings—they are conduits of the specifically desubjectified, transpersonal affect of non-alienated being, which they express through color. But flowers only function this way because of their difference, their limits.

As it reimagines relations among organs and functions, *Dihedrons* also envisions expressive morphologies that go beyond function. Here the hatable ocker acquires a cetaceous "blood-spout":

> the ocker FoxP2 no language faculty for dorsal fins in the air; in it his integumentary expansion [. . .] yet there his dorsalis the blood vessel serving the back part of him that parts the air moves spouts blood breathing it in jets in the air from his dorsalis children covered with the blood-spout are wiped off with dossils. Used to wipe him. (19)

Here zooform "dorsal fin" and blowhole are elided with the human "dorsalis" blood vessel to create a new organ that may "serv[e] the back part of him" but less functionally simply sprays blood over everyone—everyone being the children he abducts and sells as slaves (19). On one hand inverting his biopolitical traffic in bare life, the grotesque blood-spattering expresses on the other the ocker's megalomania. This passage also introduces "FoxP2," a gene required for the formation of brain regions associated with speech and language. It was discovered in the late 1990s through studies of three generations of a family with a rare language disorder; those with the disorder were found to have the same mutation (Marcus & Fisher). By making the FoxP2 mutation one of the ocker's traits, Scalapino also incorporates it into descriptions of *Dihedrons*' dystopian political setting: an "ochlocracy" (rule by mob) has chosen the ocker as "exarch": "the mobs oar chosen the exarch who's to speak for the family family ocker Fox P2 gene has no language *faculty*! the Distaffer thinks . . . Fox P2 he's made oral deputy! thinks Distaffer incredulous" (27).

As with the apulmonic, apyretic boojums, with the ocker's language deficit Scalapino deploys yet another mode of "negative poetics" germane to the poet's novel, involving experiments with specified lacking affects and capacities. Scalapino announces this privative poetics in the statement in her author's note about "dysaphia," a disorder of the sense of touch: "Dysaphia: as if the people can have no sensations, the writing becomes the sensations that are then felt by everything" (vii). The description recalls an assertion from her essay "Fiction's Present Without Basis": "Sensation itself is in part socially derived, constructed. A characteristic of being now in the imperial present: one is conceptually divided from one's own sensation (from tactile even), isolated from one's physical motion in real-time (as also *from real-time*, as it's occurring)" (42). In *Dihedrons*, allusions to dysaphic experience, too, stem from immersion in a culture of radical alienation from the affective flux of reality: "As the senses mistrusted are born by doctrine, they emerge dysaphic" (151). Such privative disorders are remedied by prostheses, the author's note suggests, as bodies under construction seek out immediate affective experience.

So what of the dihedrons? The very first words of the volume are: "Dihedrons and Gazelle-Dihedrons are human-like creatures. Profoundly injured, they roam jetting space in the form of vertical severed halves" (vii). The creatures carry fetuses, yet cannot reproduce: "they don't give birth? [. . .] fetuses whole are seen nestled curled in the sides (of the sides-dihedrons) but are never born" (29). Yet the novel in fact seems undecided whether these half-bodied creatures *are* human and foregrounds the ambiguity: "Humans become dihedrals their sides spatial open or were not ever people, only halving human frames organs open appear" (29); "on which apparent but no longer people or weren't ever their sides open seen gazelle-dihedrals" (30). At what point does morphological and affective deficit cross the species limit? The novel formally stages this query with dihedrals that are split cranes:

> hepatoportal system even is seen in the sides (the dihedrons) whooping. Also. Whooping that is from both the whole-cranes sound of birds and apparently from invisible middles of the sides-dihedrons-halves of them. Crowd though not acting together (as do the cranes)? But are they (sides) existing in or as cranes or as cranes on elephants ride for instance elephants and bears are *they* ever dihedron-planes are there such versions of them? Or permanent one-life forms in that one life? (61)

The dihedral birds can whoop just as the whole birds can: affectively equivalent, are they *really* cranes? Do all species accommodate this degree of self-difference? How do species mutate?

• • •

I'd like to create a place that is a free state as a terrain in the writing. I haven't done it yet so
I have to go on finding a way to make that.

LESLIE SCALAPINO, INTERVIEW WITH ANNE BREWSTER (1997)

Dihedrons is a novel obsessed with the figure of the network and, thus,
not surprisingly, with (new) media technologies. But Scalapino is strongly
skeptical of these technologies: she is elegiac about the newspaper ("(all are
closing, newspaper as anachronism, any people who read)" (40)) and critical of the assumption that books are linear, while digital media are not (48).
A recurring landscape in *Dihedrons* is an urban space filled with inescapable
billboard monitors: onscreen is "an avatar starfish . . . speaking for everyone" (4), "substituted for anyone to be able to speak" (7), an acephalic em-
blem that only seemingly represents "the Collective the People, that doesn't
exist anyway" (31), since "in the oscillating universe infinitely governed by
the mob no one *real*-ly the corporations always" (28). Here the implications
of ubiquitous computing are simply propaganda and surveillance; there is
even a scene, in the budding romance between the Distaffer and the base
runner as political dissidents, that recalls Orwell's *1984*: "Still in its blank
they are in its blind place out of the range of the monitor the base runner is
speaking sitting across from the Distaffer in the café" (91).

If the rhizome has here been arrogated to a sinister governmentality, the
trope is transvalued in the pleasure of the political efficacy of the more authentically populist technology of Twitter, used to protest the 2009 Iranian
presidential election:

> Certain joy gemma in the outside in one [allowed] at hearing the
> people coasting surfing after the Iranian election was rigged usurped
> they're posting on Twitter coordinate times of protest marches serv-
> ers closed down find Twitter-feeds servers outside their country (7)

Even as Scalapino acknowledges violent crackdowns against the pro-
testers (27), preeminent in her allusions are the strategic relations at play,
through which Twitterers, through forms of decentered, anarchistic coor-
dination, creatively resist dominance, releasing worldwide joy. Yet Twitter,
too, comes to grief in *Dihedrons*, as it is turned against the novel's political
resistance: "showing the three on Wanted notices posted on Tweeter-feed
and projected on the roaming monitors the screens 'on' continually outside" (99)

But all is not lost: communication is nonetheless the ultimate expression
of biopower from below. Throughout the novel, Scalapino portrays a

network of girl orphans, to be sold as prostitute-slaves, using a hand-language of their own device: "Their flashing of messages reading in the air with their hands was a dactylology invented by them, the girls, and passed on wild-fire" (6); "the dactylology of the thousands of silent girl orphans speaking in trees" (47). A sign-system of the body, a swarm-language, an idiolect of bare life, dactylology functions in a mode of affective immediacy in an "outside" beyond language: "the abandoned orphan girls in lines concurrent outside create dactylology as are bumblebees' signals nests holes entirely outside" (90); "people texting flesh cells aren't speaking even as, say, the deb, base runner, and Distaffer are" (88). What Scalapino offers here is not a romanticized subaltern, cannot be, because it is so thoroughly and recognizably a component of a total vision she has imparted in every aspect of the novel: an imagination of a possible and necessarily always changing affective field free from all dominating constructs. A language beyond language. Like *Dihedrons*.

NOTES
1. My thanks to Lauren Shufran for her insight that Scalapino's procedure is bibliomancy.
2. The first italics are the author's; italics in the last sentence are my own, to emphasize Scalapino's point that the action of writing is not an abstraction from or representation of occurrences after they have already taken place— the writing is coeval with existence.
3. However, to clarify, this is not to say there are no plotlines in the book. This essay will neither summarize the plotted events of *Dihedrons*, nor will it address the many (autobiographical) anecdotes embedded in the work, whether these simply erupt in the narrative or are contained in the diegesis by somehow being attached to a character. Working at a certain level of abstraction, my discussion is thus not an assay at "figuring out" what is "actually happening" in the book. Rather, I am interested in the genetic context of the book—by which I mean its (portrayed) scene of composition and the traces of that process within it, how it unfolds (the way its elements interact), and the way the content recapitulates these dynamics. Thus, I focus on *Dihedrons'* exhilarating radical, formal tendencies, which I argue mirror aspects of complexity theory and theories of nonlinear systems as these bear on organic and nonorganic "life," as well as postgenomic understandings of lifeforms. Hopefully, such discussion lays ground for future analyses of *Dihedrons'* specific events (and its representation of temporality and memory).

4. For arguments against viewing DNA as "master molecule," see Evelyn Fox Keller, "Master Molecules" and James C. Wilson, "(Re)Writing the Genetic Body-Text."

5. Speaking of *The Front Matter, Dead Souls*, Scalapino states: "My intention in that work was to overlay the short prose paragraph as being the condensation of poetry to make a vivid extremity . . . This is imagined as the text 'overlaying' itself, as if physically bled into the paper (related to their not being line breaks in the text) in the manner of a visual image. It is as if the writing (text as physical print) is only visual image per se, such as the words 'man flying in black air floating on his own ejaculation' (as if, by the writing being 'extreme' visually, it is pushed on its border as lines/passages of print —only—into being real)" (Scalapino & Frost 23).

6. Scalapino acknowledges this trapping of the character on a metaliterary level by turning the base runner into a political dissident attempting to escape from the ever-expanding diamond (96; 99).

7. Similarly, in a series of episodes involving the base runner and the "gelechild"—a kind of potato moth—the pun on "child" is reinforced by the inclusion of illustrations of women from Kiki Smith's *Spinster Series*.

8. See Jason Lagapa, "Something from Nothing: The Disontological Poetics of Leslie Scalapino." "Bad is good; good is bad," Lagapa quotes from *Suzuki's Zen Mind, Beginner's Mind*. "They are two sides of one coin. . . . So to find pleasure in suffering is the only way to accept the truth of transiency" (37).

9. This paradox is in a sense summed up in Scalapino's statement: "Writing not having any relation to event/being it—by being exactly its activity. It's the 'same thing' as life (syntactically)—it *is* life. It has to be or it's nothing." (cited in Camille Martin (no source) n.p.).

10. I borrow the term "vibrant matter" from Jane Bennett's *Vibrant Matter*. Scalapino was reading (perhaps re-reading) *A Thousand Plateaus* in 2004, when she makes extensive (mostly negative) use of the book in discussing Jalal Toufic's *Forthcoming* (see her essay "Fiction's Present Without Basis").

11. For instance, Scalapino's use of punctuation throughout the novel is neither logical, nor grammatical but rhetorical and expressive. In one passage she glosses the term "interrobang," explaining that the hybrid mark gets closer to the representation of event itself than does language: "that's interrobang, the girl with the beautiful arched eyebrows combining the question mark (?) and an exclamation point (!) indicating a mixture of query and interjection always separated the moment one's speaking reading thought is vision that's event" (20). Note that the girls' face appears literally to have this punctuating mark on it (her eyebrows).

WORKS CITED

Bennett, Jane. *Vibrant Matter: A Political Ecology of Things*. Durham: Duke UP, 2010.

Brewster, Anne. Interview with Leslie Scalapino. "'We're always at war': the Worlding of Writing/Reading" (1997). *How2* 2:2 (2004).

Campbell, Bruce. "Neither In Nor Out: The Poetry of Leslie Scalapino." *Talisman* 8 (Spr 1992). 53-60.

Cohen, Alicia. "'I'm Seeing What We Call Normal Life as Being a Vision': Visionary Scrutiny in the Work of Leslie Scalapino." *How2* 2:2 (2004). np.

Coolidge, Clark. *The Maintains*. Oakland: This Press, 1974.

Deleuze, Gilles and Felix Guattari. *A Thousand Plateaus: Capitalism and Schizophrenia*. Trans. Brian Massumi. Mineapolis: University of Minnesota Press, 1987.

Dworkin, Craig. "The Imaginary Solution." *Contemporary Literature* 48:1 (2007). 29-60.

Frost, Elizabeth. Interview with Leslie Scalapino. (1993-5) *Contemporary Literature* 37:1 (1996). 1-23.

Golston, Michael. "At Clark Coolidge: Allegory and the Early Works." *American Literary History* 13:1 (Sum 2001). 295-316.

Hejinian, Lyn. "The Rejection of Closure." *The Language of Inquiry*. Berkeley: University of California Press, 2000. 40-58.

Keller, Evelyn Fox. "Master Molecules." *Are Genes Us? The Social Consequences of the New Genetics*. Ed. Carl F. Cranor. New Brunswick: Rutgers University Press, 1994. 89-98.

Lagapa, Jason. "Something from Nothing: The Disontological Poetics of Leslie Scalapino." *Contemporary Literature* 47:1 (Spr 2006). 30-61.

Lazzarato, Maurizio. "From Biopower to Biopolitics." Trans. Ivan A. Ramirez. *Pli* 13 (2002). 99-110.

Marcus, Gary F. and Simon E. Fisher. "*FOXP2* in focus: what can genes tell us about speech and language?" unpublished paper.

Martin, Camille. "Reading the Mind of Events: Leslie Scalapino's Plural Time." *How2* 2:2 (2004). np.

McCaffery, Steve. *Prior to Meaning: The Protosemantic and Poetics*. Evanston: Northwestern University Press, 2001.

Nancy, Jean-Luc. *Being Singular Plural*. Trans. Robert D. Richardson and Anne E. O'Byrne. Stanford: Stanford University Press, 2000.

Petrarca, Francesco. "The Ascent of Mount Ventoux: To Dionisio da Borgo San Sepolcro." *Petrarch: The First Modern Scholar and Man of Letters*.

Trans. and Ed. James Harvey Robinson. 1898. 307-320. In *Hanover Historical Texts Collection*. 2001. *https://history.hanover.edu/texts/petrarch/pet17.html*

Rosenthal, Sarah. Interview with Leslie Scalapino. (2001) *Jacket* 23 (Aug 2003). np.

Rubenstein, Raphael. "Gathered, Not Made: A Brief History of Appropriative Writing." *American Poetry Review* 28:2 (Mar/Apr 1999). 31-34.

The Tattered Labyrinth
On W. G. Sebald's *The Rings of Saturn*

DAN BEACHY-QUICK

Let me suggest that one marker of the poet's novel is a willingness to trust distraction, to follow digression, and that an essay about such a novel may need to follow a curiously divergent path to pay attention to the book that is its concern. Such diversions shouldn't be considered mere whimsy. The poet's novel, as with the poet's poem, must learn to undercut the circuit of its own intent if it is to discover those unwilled patterns—perhaps cosmic, perhaps universal—it seeks. The book of my concern is W.G. Sebald's masterpiece *The Rings of Saturn*, a book I think of not simply as poetic, but as a poem. I want to begin in two ways, almost simultaneously. First, I want to think about the title—those words that exist before a page has been turned, and that sets up in us a certain kind of anticipation. And I want to open the cover and read those first pages; I want to consider how this book opens us to the work it not only is doing, but the work that seems to be done against it—these pages that not only record history, but seem (like us) to suffer it. But let me, briefly, digress. By "poet's novel" we typically refer to a kind of sensibility that permeates the writing, a preponderance of imagery in place of plot, narrative governed by symbol more than character; and of the characters, our entrance into them is often according to their access to themselves, that is, through their own eyes and the thoughts that there bloom into consciousness. The sensibility of the poet's novel begins not as an atmosphere, but in the nerves, in the sensory life of the characters embodied in the prose, and that prose is nervous, visceral, embodied in such a way that it refuses, continually, the division between mind and body, and does so as severely as it denies the division between word and world.

But the novel that is a poem includes a deeper work than this poetic sense of sensibility. Such a book operates in its deep formal life along poetic principles. An image isn't simply some kind of flourish, almost musical. An image has in it a depth that resonates symbolically, and that symbol holds within it some ever-shifting meaning, one surface coming to light even as every other surface descends back into darkness. Revelation's cost is another form of concealment. Such a book has in its very core some spinning thing, some spherical jewel of countless facets, though the light of the reader's mind can brighten but one facet at a time; and so too the light of the writer's mind. For the poet's novel seems resistant to the kind of planning an outline offers. We feel as if it discovers within itself the law of its own inevitability, the gravitational core it cannot turn away from, but which can only be discovered by being within the world of the work itself—as if some *terra incognita* could only be discovered *as* the map of it was being drawn. World and word in such a book feel like simultaneous discoveries; world and word feel mutually dependant.

Once, in an Astronomy class, I was told that some scientists thought that at Jupiter's core, so massive was the planet (actually a proto-star), that what carbon it contains had been pressed into a diamond—a single jewel larger than the earth. I did not know then that the theoretical fact was teaching me more about the nature of the poetic novel than about planetary science. Jupiter also has a thin ring about it, so delicate it was discovered only in the late 20th century, photographed as Voyager I flew by in 1979. But the rings of Sebald's vision are those around Saturn. Most of us consider Saturn the most beautiful object in the solar system. There is a majesty to the rings that even seen through a small telescope seems almost impossible to believe, as if a joke is being played, and someone has put a tiny sticker on the lens of the scope just after you bent down to peer through the eye-piece. It hovers there in its perfection. Pale Venus pales in comparison. These rings were created by a moon, maybe many moons, being pulled too close to the massive planet, whose gravity broke them apart. The rings aren't solid. They're made of dust, of debris. They are a remnant of complete destruction, and the very force that caused that destruction has also created these rings—not only created them, but did so in such a way that one cannot help but see a picture of the planet and say: it's beautiful. Beauty made from debris. Beauty that is memorial to the ruin of its own creation. It's beautiful, yes—but Saturn wears a shroud. Just a thin line of countless rocks. From far enough away they look solid, delicate, as if strands of mourning silk had circled the planet. It wove its shroud out of what neared it, those helpless bodies in the tow of gravity, those bodies brought near disaster. Such is the symbol Sebald gives us before we've read one page of his book. It is the jewel-like symbol we must contemplate: how beauty is birthed from bitter force.

Sebald begins the novel under the spell of astronomical influence:

In August 1992, when the dog days were drawing to an end, I set off to walk the country of Suffolk, in the hope of dispelling the emptiness that takes hold of me whenever I have completed a long stint of work. And in fact my hope was realized, up to a point; for I have seldom felt so carefree as I did then, walking for hours in the day through the thinly populated countryside, which stretches inland from the coast. I wonder now, however, whether there might be something in the old superstition that certain ailments of the spirit and of the body are particularly likely to beset us under the sign of the Dog Star. At all events, in retrospect I became preoccupied not only with the unaccustomed sense of freedom but also with the paralyzing horror that had come over me at various times when confronted with the traces of destruction, reaching far back in the past, that were evident even in that remote place. Perhaps it was because of this that, a year to the day after I began my tour, I was taken into hospital in Norwich in a state of almost total immobility. It was then I began in my thoughts to write these pages.

Sebald, through his own awareness making us aware, opens *The Rings of Saturn* under the influence of two related, though different, realities This awareness draws us further into the unique qualities of the poet's novel. The Dog Star, trailing brilliantly the hunter Orion, brightest star in the sky, exerts in the late summer a malevolent influence that sickens both body and soul. Orion chases Scorpio, a cycle that repeats every year forever. Orion is trying in heaven to avenge his death on earth. The Dog Star casts down its blue intensity just as Orion begins to fail again, just as he fails forever, to inflict back on the creature that killed him that same mortal force. The story is etched in the sky, almost a celestial version of a child's Victorian toy, almost a zoetrope, playing eternally a story we see in the night sky only because it pleases the old gods, and they like their pleasure to be on infinite repeat. What greater powers take pleasure in our suffering so that they find ways to repeat it for their ongoing amusement? The earth's turning makes the tale spin, and in a few months, one could see Scorpio rising on the opposite horizon, just as Orion, for a season, will not be seen again.

Sebald brings us so subtly and so quickly into the very chasm of his concern that we hardly know we've arrived. Not only do we sense that the stories we tell ourselves, myths and poems, bear relation to various "traces of destruction," but we also are cast into an ancient mode of inquiry, suspicion almost, in which again we feel the stoic impulse that links macrocosm to microcosm, and then the "superstition" that the Dog Star's evil influence alters and becomes a poetical, philosophic, principle. Our lives are connected to the stars, he suggests. What forces pattern the universe also pattern us, and to study either is to learn of the other.

The second principle Sebald offers not only explains how the book in the reader's hands was written, but strengthens that bond that links modern life to ancient patterns. "A year to the day" after he completed his walking tour, Sebald is stricken by some debilitation that seems to have no medical explanation. He cannot move, but he begins to compose in his thoughts these words that make this book. A year marks one orbit of earth around the sun. It adds a year to the sum being counted, but more importantly in this context, returns us to a place of origin. We find within linear time symbolic time exerting its eternal influence, bringing us back to the same point that our common experience of time promises we've abandoned. But nothing in the poet's novel is abandoned. Everything remains resonant, tracing within itself evidence of those powers that create history without ever being subsumed into it. When history ceases to be merely historical, it puts back upon itself myth's ancient mantle. Then a year marks anything but linear progress through time. It draws instead a circle around that which is most real only outside of temporal change, the immutable fact of our mythic lives, deep-rooted in aversion and faith, seeking to name those cosmic patterns— in tales, in words—that remind us of how we are included in the world, comfort within, maybe against, devastation.

The poet's novel, like a poem, conducts an investigation that can only be accomplished through its own form. Telling a story may be a mere accident to the fundamental work the writing is trying to accomplish. It must seek an image, find a symbol, which can bear the intense need for belief the writer bears within himself. It must, I suspect, become a test for all that slips outside the empirical range, a test of faith, with faith itself being the cost of conducting the experiment.

> I can remember precisely how, upon being admitted to that room on the eighth floor, I became overwhelmed by the feeling that the Suffolk expanses I had walked the previous summer had now shrunk once and for all to a single, blind, insensate spot. Indeed, all that could be seen of the world from my bed was the colourless patch of sky framed in the window. Several times during the day I felt a desire to assure myself of a reality I feared had vanished forever by looking out the window, which, for some strange reason, was draped with black netting, and as dusk fell the wish became so strong that, contriving to slip over the edge of the bed to the floor, half on my belly and half sideways, and then to reach the wall on all fours, I dragged myself, despite the pain, up the window sill.

What this quote here excludes is the picture Sebald includes in the text: a window seen from a lower angle, cloud barely discernable against the light in the window so overexposed, and faintly, almost as if on a page of graph paper, a grid-like netting one could almost mistake for those graph-lines Renaissance painters used to perfect the trick of perspective.

It was in this same hospital, so Sebald learns from "the 1911 edition of the *Encyclopedia Brittanica*," that Sir Thomas Browne's skull was kept.

Thomas Browne, so Batty Shaw wrote in an article he sent me which had just been published in the *Journal of Medical Biography*, died in 1682 on his seventy-seventh birthday and was buried in the parish church of St Peter Mancroft in Norwich. There his mortal remains lay undisturbed until 1840, when the coffin was damaged during preparations for another burial in the chancel, and its contents partially exposed. As a result, Browne's skull and a lock of his hair passed into the possession of one Dr Lubbock, a parish councilor, who in turn left the relics in his will to the hospital museum, where they were put on display amidst various anatomical curiosities until 1921 under a bell jar. It was not until then that St Peter Mancroft's repeated request for the return of Browne's skull was acceded to, and, almost a quarter of a millennium after the first burial, a second internment was performed with all due ceremony.

Browne was himself uniquely concerned with death and burial rites, author of *Urn Burial*. A man of the Renaissance, though trained as a doctor, he wrote extensively on varied topics: medicine, natural history, history, religion, and all manners of esoterica. One could say of Sebald's own head, alive and immobile in the same hospital in which Browne's head once resided, that it fills itself with curiosities it is helpless not to follow. One's head seems to get away from oneself even when it is still attached. But there is a slow horror building in the image of Browne's skull in the hospital museum. Not only did he fear what might happen to one's body in the centuries after burial, but the curiosity of the relic involves only those things which can be imagined and not seen. There is the macabre gravity of the skull itself, but the draw is the thoughts that occurred within it, of which evidence we only have those books Browne wrote, a fact which makes of those books—might make of any given book—the discomforting sense that in reading one holds a skull in one's hands, and the lines are the brain's out-spooling thoughts. Quick in the reader's mind is the knowledge earlier imparted, that this book, *The Rings of Saturn*, began its life in Sebald's own head in the very same hospital, not as written words but as thoughts he then began composing. Quietly, never calling attention to itself, a connection has been drawn. Sebald's narrator, which seems always an aspect of himself if not himself entirely—so thin here is the ground between fiction and non-fiction, not to mention the ground between fictive work and poetic—discovers within himself a hidden sympathy, a word that in oldest sense maintains magical connotation, that links his current life to the life of Sir Thomas Browne. Sebald gives an image even as he denies it; we see Browne's skull in the glass-jar even as you know it is buried again with his body. Beyond the story's curious, almost humorous, affect, we are—as with the title of the book itself—drawn into an image whose meaning radiates throughout the entirety of the book. The skull that within it thought wonders and thought errors, asserted truths and strew misconceptions, that object is the object of our curiosity. In the name of science we exhibit in the bowels of the hospital the skull or the brain of those who interest us. We think about those heads that thought what they thought. Our thinking seems to justify our curiosity. So much so, that of a man whose last fears involved the possible disturbance of his mortal remains, we find the chance to display his skull—an object for our own education, for our own contemplation, an object of horror but within its horror also one of strange beauty—an opportunity worth taking.

Poems, and I'd argue, the poetic novel, bear within themselves the need to discover these kinds of linkages, as if in writing a chapter one simultaneously creates a kind of gathering place, the choral ground, the orchestra of old, where one discovers exactly who it is one is singing with. In unexpected ways, Sebald—in this poet's novel, this novel that is a poem—conducts a deeply, radically, traditional work. It is atavistic, not only because history gathers within it, but because it turns back to history, to writers long dead (though their work, obscure as it may be, lives on), to myths whose permanence now lives in periphery, in order to stitch together a thinking that can only be composed of multiple voices, even if the discovery is that each voice says the same thing. The very title of the book gives us our hint. Of all the millions of pages scattered through history, leaves of books and (to steal from Homer) those leaves that are the passing lives of men and women, what planet-sized diamond, what jewel, what force, aligns them into a ring? Of course, as with being a single tile in a vast mosaic, we might see those pieces next to our own, but we have no privilege to see the picture whole. We want to, though. We want to see the whole.

It is from such desire that Sebald, nearly paralyzed and despite the pain, pulls himself off his bed to look through the hospital window. What he looks through when he does so is the netting that covers it. Three-hundred years earlier Sir Thomas Browne wrote about similar desires, the *want* to see so as to *know*:

The greater the distance, the clearer the view: one sees the tiniest of details with the utmost clarity. It is as if one were looking through a reversed opera glass and through a microscope at the same time. And yet, says Browne, all knowledge is enveloped in darkness. What we perceive are no more than isolated lights in the abyss of ignorance, in the shadow-filled edifice of the world. We study the order of things, says Browne, but we cannot grasp their innermost essence. And because it is so, it befits our philosophy to be writ small, using the shorthand and contracted forms of transient nature, which alone are a reflection of eternity. True to his own prescription, Browne records the patterns which recur in the seemingly infinite diversity of forms; in the *Garden of Cyrus*, for instance, he draws the quincunx, which is composed by using the corners of a regular quadrilateral and the point at which its diagonals intersect. Browne identifies this structure everywhere, in animate and inanimate matter: in certain crystalline forms, in starfish and sea urchins, in the vertebrae of mammals and the backbones of birds and fish, in the skin of various species of snake, in the crosswise prints of quadrupeds, in the physical shapes of caterpillars, butterflies, silkworms and moths . . . Examples might be multiplied without end, says Browne, and one might demonstrate *ad infinitum* the elegant geometrical designs of Nature . . .

One might add, for instance, the netting of the window Sebald looks through in the very hospital where the head that saw such elegant patterning to the world once resided, the chamber of those thoughts unable ever to think them again. But Sebald thinks them again. He does more than think them. He gathers Browne's thinking into his own, invites the voice in—that most dear and ancient of lyric gestures—and lets another voice speak within his own.

That lyric capacity of Sebald's voice fuses together a deeper work with which the poet's novel is concerned—and that concern undergirds the necessity of this lengthy consideration of title and first pages above. The poet's novel, like a poem, asks a question about the world—one that is separate from character, from person, and yet cannot be asked save through the same. A poem, at least in the ways I consider a poem *a poem*, embroils itself in ontological crisis. It wants to know how it is we know what we think we know. It seeks origins it knows it cannot find. There is a violence in such searching, as if a flower would pull itself up to investigate its own roots. But can such violence be generous? Be creative? Can the rubble falling from the

roots reassemble into rings? A halo around the head, let's say. Sebald begins by looking through the window's quincunx. He sees that vision, and the
knowledge vision brings, comes to us from some ordering force we can only
sense when we give ourselves over to that unaccustomed freedom that lets
destruction's traces mark themselves upon us. Will the pattern hold against
atrocity? Is atrocity the pattern?

I hear very quietly in my head the end of Keats's "Ode to Psyche":

> And there shall be for thee all soft thought can win,
> A bright torch, and a casement ope at night,
> To let the warm Love in!

Sebald in his hospital bed seems himself some version of Psyche, reduced
as he is to a life of mind and soul alone. His window won't open, won't let
Cupid in—and so denies that consummation lyric potency depends upon.
And if it did, if the casement could be opened, Cupid would fly into the net
and be caught, a curio for examination, whose arrows would make a fine
display beneath a bell jar.

• • •

I'd like to make another claim, one that sifts down from the debris of the
thinking above. The poet's novel takes seriously—so seriously it may well
be considered deep within the fomenting crisis that leads the book to be
written—something akin to what Wittgenstein suggests when he says, in the
Tractatus Logico-Philosophicus, that "ethics and aesthetics are one." It is an
agonizing principle, forcing concerns that seem oppositional into mutual
embrace. The book, the poet's novel, offers itself as the very *agon* in which
that embrace occurs. Whereas a more typical novel might use plot as a device that shepherds the book through itself, words relating to content much
as time relates to event, simply the place where occurrence manifests for its
moment, and then is moved past, abandoned, and what force it contained
continues to exist only as a form of momentum, of consequence, and we
find ourselves not in the depths of inevitability, but in its shallows. The poet's novel differs. Even as plot moves forward, marching in lock-step with
time, it creates within itself another motion. I might call it mind's little loop,
some cache of consciousness that resists the forward motion of the book
in order to do what it is consciousness does: to think within itself, and by

such thinking, to question the nature and necessity of its own existence. Its aesthetic reach must grapple with its ethical limit, and the poet's novel opens up within itself a space for that grappling to occur. As does a mind, as does a soul, this novel thinks about its own thinking, considers vision even as it looks, doubts the music it hears even as it sings. It gives us a curious mirror. In demonstrating its relationship to itself it brings us into self-recognition—not the self a mirror shows, not the image of reflection, but the work of reflection, all of which occurs beneath the face, within it, and makes of identity a choral work, not self same, but an I that is filled with others.

Many times we witness Sebald lose hold of his own boundary. Such is the work of wandering so as to be awry. Planning to visit the poet and translator Michael Hamburger in the village of Middleton, Sebald finds himself as he walks lost in a labyrinth beneath a villa most notable for its tall observation tower. Sebald feels this maze has been "created solely for me," and in dreams years later he would find himself in the same predicament, lost in the maze, a maze solely his own, until finally escaping and coming to a rise, he could look down on the whole and see "a pattern simple in comparison with the tortuous trail I had behind me, but one which I knew in my dream, with absolute certainty, represented a cross-section of my brain." Sebald becomes uniquely aware of the very condition the poet's novel demands of its writer and its readers: that is itself the cross-section of the brain that creates it. Some writers create complexity so as to convince themselves this made-up world is real. Others know they must write so as to realize they're in the maze they're trying to escape. "Perhaps we all lose our sense of reality to the precise degree to which we are engrossed in our own work, and perhaps that is why we see in the increasing complexity of our mental constructs a means for greater understanding, even while intuitively we know that we shall never be able to fathom the imponderables that govern our course through life."

Poems tend to ask us who read them to suffer their own bewilderment, that *aporia* so dizzied by its own circuitous path that we find a threshold where before we assumed a wall—or we find ourselves saying "we" where we meant to say "I." Dizzied by the entrance into his own mind, and bewildered by his release from the same, Sebald arrives at Michael Hamburger's home vulnerable in a particularly poetic way:

But why it was that on my first visit to Michael's house I felt as if I lived or had once lived there, in every respect precisely as he does, I cannot explain. All I know is that I stood spellbound in his high-ceilinged studio room with its north-facing windows in front of the heavy mahogany bureau at which Michael said he no longer worked because the room was so cold, even in midsummer; and that, while we talked of the difficulty of heating old houses, a strange feeling came upon me, as if it were not he who had abandoned that place of work but I, as if the spectacle cases, letters and writing materials that had evidently lain untouched for months in the soft north light had once been my spectacle cases, my letters and my writing materials.

Such a moment, bewildering as it is, also redefines the mind, and that work the mind does. The place of work, the mahogany desk, the spectacles that bring letters on a page into clear focus, all of these gain a symbolic reality that supersedes their material one, so much so that consciousness ceases to be a figure of the individual, and instead becomes a strand, a silken thread, winding its way through the labyrinth of any given mind, graspable by all, and once grasped, leads us away from that minotaur, the hybrid-monster that sits at the center of our own complexity, and allows us to escape by becoming more than any sole self.

Against the horror of history and its countless destructions, amid the will toward knowing that offers excuse for atrocity in the name of discovering truth—as the killing of cod for their own benefit, so threatening was the sheer immensity of their numbers—Sebald seeks a form of art that links us back to the anonymous fertility of our mythic lives. He sees everywhere examples of art that align themselves with the atrocity they're trying to depict: the monuments to battles, paintings thereof that depict the scene from a vantage no one could climb up to, an impossible eye witnessing from the improbable air, or canvases of sea battles that still forever a scene that never occurred, and which captures nothing of the suffering it merely valorizes. Sebald, inveterate visitor to museums, knows that such paintings were often paid for by the very industries that so destabilized the world as to cause these wars—the sugar trade for example—and should one, when the guard isn't looking, lick the surface of the painting, it would taste sweet, as of sugar. Opposed to such uneasy alliances, Sebald seeks—I'd say poetically, bewilderingly—other experiences art might offer, so that the page of the book tastes of something other than economy's brute force. A page, perhaps, that tastes of the seeds of the field; or a thread of silk that holds within it the slightest pungency of the mulberry leaf.

He finds such work in a place that, akin to his experience with Michael Hamburger, feels as if it should be his home. He stays in a dilapidated house, pays for a guest room. It's owned by a mother and her three daughters. The daughters spend their days in a room that contains "great quantities of remnant fabrics."

> Like giant children under an evil spell, the three unmarried daughters, much of an age, sat on the floor amidst these mountains of material, working away and only rarely breathing a word to each other. The movement they made as they drew the thread sideways and upwards with every stitch reminded me of things that were so far back in the past that I felt my heart sink at the thought of how little time now remained.

It seems the part of the evil spell is that the daughters take apart all they put together, each a Penelope, but with no houseful of suitors, and worse, no Odysseus. Mrs. Ashbury, the mother, spends her days colleting the seeds from the flowers and plants in the field. Placing a paper bag over a flower, she shakes the seeds in, goes home and hangs the bags from the ceiling. Sebald feels he could spend eternity in the house; he feels so because the house is filled with eternal forms of work, that old labor art offers, a mimicking that is also a making. The daughters in their secret way become the three Fates, measuring out a life each day but undoing the cut that would end it. And their mother, wanders as Psyche wandered, figure of Soul and Eros's wife, caught forever in one of her tests, separating the many seeds from one another, each according to their type.

The daughters have kept one garment: "a bridal gown made of hundreds of scraps of silk embroidered with silken thread, or rather woven over cobweb-fashion, which hung on a headless tailor's dummy, was a work of art so colourful and of such intricacy and perfection that it seems almost to have come to life . . ." The Fates have woven Psyche's wedding gown, and all that we wait for is the appearance of that god through the open window, not to be captured, not even to be seen, but to commence again that endless cycle of Love conjoining with Mind that marks for us the deepest limit if what any given poem hopes to achieve. So secretly are we ushered into the mythic pattern of our lives we hardly know the shift has occurred.

Perhaps we sense it only when we let that most profound of metaphors do its work upon us, that symbol with which Sebald is most concerned, the silkworm in its cocoon. If we let writing become no more than one long dark thread, winding from margin to margin as it must; if we imagine that line is time's own line, marked by the "traces of destruction" that seem to fetter it, and we let the line spiral around us, so that unlike moments touch; if we wind around us that single silken thread we might ask of ourselves what the poet's novel asks of itself: what life is it I am, and what life is it I am becoming?

WORKS CITED

Sebald, W.G. *Rings of Saturn*. Translated by Michael Hulse. New York. New Directions. 1998.

"The Terrible I"
On Peter Waterhouse's Poem Novel:
Language Death Night Outside

DONNA STONECIPHER

Peter Waterhouse's *Language Death Night Outside* is a hybrid text whose tensions are announced in its subtitle, "Poem Novel," where two genres uneasily share space usually occupied by only one. This tension and transgression is reflected in a series of tensions and transgressions in the book which cumulatively amount to a desire for the transgression of boundaries in general, and particularly of the boundaries of the self: "the terrible I," in Waterhouse's words.

At the center of the poem novel is an expression of grief that both does and does not want to be expressed: for grief requires identity, and it is against the strictures of identity that the writing restlessly agitates. There is grief for a dead grandfather, for Austria's dubious and largely unacknowledged past in World War II, for loves that come and go and merit only brief mention. But the greatest grief is reserved for having to inhabit a self at all ("Being-me was a killing experience," the speaker says), and he dreams of escaping identity and historicity through various means, all of them beginning with trans-: translation, transmutation, transformation, transcendence, transgression, transition, transparency, transfiguration.

Originally published in German in 1989, *Language Death Night Outside* falls loosely into the tradition of Waterhouse's fellow Austrian Thomas Bernhard's monologic novels filled with disgust and fury at Austria and its wartime complicity, and also, in its melancholy, bears a resemblance to the novels of W. G. Sebald, who shared with Waterhouse an Anglo-German world. (Waterhouse was born of an Austrian mother and an English father, and grew up bilingual.) The doubleness of such a linguistic existence is reflected in the fact that translation is a major theme in the book (masterfully translated, not incidentally, by Rosmarie Waldrop): three substantial poems—by Andrea Zanzotto, Paul Celan, and Carl Rakosi— are placed in the text in their original languages, followed by translations and brief exegeses. Translation is one of the speaker's recurring activities (along with going to listen to lectures, driving out of the city, and researching in libraries and archives—all means of procuring knowledge to effect transformation). In the mini-exegesis of the Zanzotto poem, Waterhouse writes: "Everything in the poem was in transition. Nothing in the poem rested in itself," and that feels like both a cri de coeur and an ars poetica for Waterhouse's book.

The wish for the liquefaction of the self is in contention, however, with the constant actualization of the self through the book's sentences, fully half of which begin with "I," and many of which record the speaker's movements in the world, including the most banal ("I went to bed"):

> I bought everything promised in the advertisements. I traveled in all trains. I looked with interest at the newspapers. I left the clothing store, uncorrupted. I leaned against banks. I protected myself as one who gives the country a memory. I danced to all records. I passed under all bridges.

The form of the text resembles a diary more than it does a novel or a poem, though the distilled language is far more carefully constructed than dashed-off diary entries. As in any diary, the speaker is attempting to write himself into existence via language, even as he expresses the desire to be rid of the specificity of existence. But this "I," of course, is a kind of über-I—enacting a fantasy of being everywhere at once. The "I" is and is not the speaker; often it is as though he were commenting on the activities of another, and indeed he himself is aware of this detachment, as when he writes "I observed my feelings." Waterhouse is acutely aware that the "I" is a construction as much as any character in a novel is. At one point, the speaker's detachment from himself is so extreme that he reports himself as a missing person: "I stood in the police station. I had them take down a report that I was missing. The officer misspelled my name."

The often short, declarative sentences proceeding relentlessly from flat statement to flat statement are packed uneasily into long, dense, at times claustrophobic sections barely broken up, and the resulting speed and density turn the sentences into molten syntax, their components made available for reuse and transformation in subsequent appearances. This claustrophobia is the claustrophobia of the mind itself, crowded with perceptions, with the self constructing itself through language. The thoughts connect to each other associatively, so that a kind of linguistic map of the associating mind comes into being, with thoughts darting off into a dazzling variety of directions:

I talked to the city. I told it very little. I did not trust it. I loved it. The futile, tender city, assembled in stone, lit as if one incandescent bulb, lighting a cigarette along a match. At midday the city split into two cities.

In the book, a world results in which objects are freed of their usual physical properties: a city can touch the speaker's hair, and a tree can turn into "a staircase, an escalator, a pyramid, a sultan's palace." It is this state—the state, in translation, between two languages, where the original and target languages melt and intermingle before freezing again into a new text—that the self wants to inhabit, even while its sentences are building a linguistic structure the self will become caught in. Language is a double-edged sword—like the word "cleave," which means its opposite, the self both cleaves to language and cleaves it, is cleaved by it. In the speaker's exuberant moments, though, the self manages to achieve this desired state: "I heard the word I as the utmost in transitions . . . I saw the word I as a move toward breaking out, an unstoppable move toward transition." These sentences come out of a discussion about translating Zanzotto's poem, so it is as if the act of translating a text carries over to the reified self, and the "I" may also be subject to the process of translation (in this, Waterhouse prefigured the boom in Translation Studies, in which the poetics of translation is often applied to people as much as texts).

Long blocks of interpolated text, inserted whole as if in a form of collage—such as a discourse on ceiling paintings—turn the work into a perceptual space that can be penetrated by heterogeneity. This openness is counteracted by regular outbreaks of deep, repetitive structure: for example, three and a half pages of the book are covered with the repeated words "Consensus" and "Reconciliation," in an oblique reference to Austria's political past. It is often in these moments of repetition and variation that the most beautiful writing in the book occurs. For instance, at a funeral, the speaker engages in a lavish exercise in taxonomy that is revealed in all its vainglory at the end:

The grave stood open. I stood aside. I heard the voices of the birds. I identified the voice of the blackbird. I identified the voice of the thrush. I identified the voice of the swallow. I identified the voice of the starling. I identified the voice of the waxwing. I identified the voice of the warbler. I identified the voice of the brown creeper. I identified the voice of the wren. I identified the voice of the oriole. There was no resurrection of the soul as the priest promised.

As with the paradox of the restless writing self building a text that will ultimately become static, the desire for total fluidity is counterpointed by the rigidity of architecture, which is a recurring theme: the speaker befriends an architect, takes trips to visit buildings as an architecture tourist, and meditates on architectural details such as the doorknob (the door: the classic site of transition). Like the poem and the novel in the subtitle, the speaker wants both constant motion *and* stasis (and therefore, also, neither); he is often driving in a car (mobile architecture) or taking a train, on the move—but there are many moments when he simply lies down, on the ground or the street or a roof, suggesting a rejection of mobility, a succumbing to the stasis of the earth: which, of course, is nevertheless always moving. (This dialectic of horizontal and vertical echoes the dialectic of "novel" and "poem"— linguists throughout the twentieth century figured prose as horizontal and poetry as vertical and, by calling his book "poem novel," Waterhouse insists on not giving up either.)

The self feels most at home when it is not at home: A trip to Zagreb results in exultation: "I was happy about not-speaking-Croatian, not-knowing-the-city, not-knowing-the-looks, being-about-to-leave, being-a-foreigner, having-no-answer. . ." This not-speaking-Croatian liberates the speaker: "We did not know what was talked about. I was set free." It is significant that it is an ignorance of language that frees the speaker best from the burdens of belonging, from the responsibilities that result from being a participatory, named inhabitant of a named place, a speaking-and-comprehending subject, because in the book's worldview, language and its powers are deeply ambivalent, as seen in a steady stream of multifaceted ruminations on the subject. In a cemetery with Italian friends, the speaker meditates on the capabilities of the language he knows and the one he doesn't:

> I heard my native word reach the unreachable. I heard my native word reach the unreachable within me. I heard speech reaching. I heard the foreign word not reach the unreachable. I heard the foreign word show the unreachable as unreachable, pushing it farther into the distance.

Language can exist as "open-sesame words," creating the world as it is spoken ("I said the word brook-bed. The word brook-bed was, like any word, a sudden opening"), but it is also the essential component of identity formation: "I saw the poem loosen language from the compulsion to identity, the compulsion to death." Words must be animated by human care: "Without my affection, the river was not possible in the word river," but, of course, human intention can abuse language: "I saw the name of the bank made of large free-standing letters. I did not understand the difference between *Commerzbank* and *Deutsche Bank*: I considered the commerce bank a German bank" (in one of the book's rare moments of humor).

Ambivalence about language, about identity, about form crystallize in the ambivalence about genre, which is more pointed for Waterhouse than it would be for an American writer, since the prose poem, widely accepted in American literature, for reasons that remain obscure, has not gained widespread acceptance in the German-speaking world. Though there are many moments of seeming autobiography in the book, little resembling a traditional narrative makes itself felt; there is, however, a great deal of poetry in it. The insistence on calling the work a novel does achieve the assumption of a multifarious imaginary world that counteracts the lyric *I*'s hyperreality. If one thinks of Mikhail Bakhtin's classification of poetry as monologic and the novel as dialogic, then Waterhouse's designation points to a desire to cast the monolith of the self (the "terrible I") into a structural plurality. Because in fact the text does not exhibit many of the actual characteristics of the novel genre as we know it, the "novel" designation seems to become aspirational—the self *wants* to feel itself part of a novel, to be just one part of a multiplicitous world, but because no other characters really manifest and no plot emerges, because the "I," however complicated it might be, dominates, the speaker remains trapped in his own self—and the (unsuccessful) agitation against it becomes the book's magnificent gesture.

Despite the designation "poem novel," one cannot help but think of the book as an entry into Baudelaire's ambitions for the prose poem: that it be "musical but without rhythm or rhyme, both supple and staccato enough to adapt itself to the lyrical movements of our souls, the undulating movements of our reveries, and the convulsive movement of our consciences." The prose poem "genre that is not a genre" comes with its own historical baggage, and labeling the book as "prose poetry" would necessarily point to French and American models. By choosing "poem novel," Waterhouse ratchets up the contrast, and stakes out his own formal territory. One can imagine others writing "poem novels," but there will never be another quite like this haunting book.

WORKS CITED

Waterhouse, Peter. *Language Death Night Outside*, translated by Rosmarie Waldrop. Providence, RI. Burning Deck Press, 2009.

VII

Identification /
Dissolution /
Polemic /
Bildungsroman

She says to herself if she were able to write she could continue to live.
—THERESA HAK KYUNG CHA, *Dictee*

"I Got This Under the Bridge"
Notes on Audre Lorde's *Zami*

BY C.S. GISCOMBE

Audre Lorde's book *Zami* is a work of accumulating voice that becomes not more clear but more dense (if clarity implies singularity or synthesis or resolution, if density means overlay and complication) as the text progresses toward its end. It's forward-moving in spite of or because of its very nature as an almost unceasing account of specificities; its brilliance as a work of writing is necessarily tied to or, better, merges with Lorde's ability and will to present and examine situations and read them deeply and without particular adornment or gesture or ornamentation or *reach* in terms of race, gender, orientation, and class. (This is simply to say that the book is not easily didactic—it rarely builds toward moments or gifts to the reader of recognizable transcendence.) And one would be remiss to not give notice, in any discussion of *Zami*, to the presence of the fact(s) of migration. That is, Lorde is interested as well in the circumstances of origins—which are, she indicates, defining. But there's a codicil to this—the circumstances may well be defining but both the circumstances and the definitions must be *read*, the book suggests, by the subject who would name and/or claim them—that is, she must bring her intellect to them. In relation to origins, it's also necessary (as well as interesting) to note that *Zami* has three—arguably four—beginnings clustered more or less on top of one another in its first several pages. From that series of starts it proceeds through evocations of childhood, lucid fantasies, picaresque accounts, examinations and pickings apart of several cultures, occasional tediousness, and an unforgiving ability to, as Ralph Ellison said, "never lose sight of the chaos." But this is not some female and/ or Lesbian version of *Invisible Man*.

The book itself, subtitled "A New Spelling of My Name" (and then subtitled, further, "Biomythography"), is an accounting of the first two and a half decades of Lorde's life. Born in 1934 in New York and named Audrey Geraldine Lorde by her parents, Linda Gertrude Belmar Lorde and Frederic Byron Lorde, both immigrants from Grenada, she was the youngest—meaning the last—of three daughters and near-sighted enough to be counted as blind. Quoting *Zami*, Ann Trapasso gives a précis of her early schooling: "Educated at Catholic grammar schools, she faced 'patronizing' racism at

St. Mark's School and 'downright hostile' racism at St. Catherine's School [but at] Hunter High School she found a 'lifeline' in a 'sisterhood of rebels' who were also poets." She left home at eighteen and moved to Connecticut where she found employment in a ribbon factory and, later, at an electronics plant. Here, in Connecticut and living on her own, she took her first lover, a woman with whom she worked at the electronics plant, this in the late 1940s. From Connecticut, following the death of her father, she traveled to Mexico City and enrolled in courses—history and ethnology, folklore—at the university there, spending a year in Mexico, largely in the company of expatriate women, before returning to New York. In the pages recounting her life in Mexico she announces the censure of Joe McCarthy and describes reading the news about Brown vs. Board of Education; this conjunction of events, she seems to imply, permits her return to the United States. (I recalled, reading this, that many of the black refugees to Vancouver Island— the 1858 San Francisco exodus—had returned, hopeful, to the U.S. after the Civil War.) She gives accounts of library work situations, love affairs with women, and comments on the presences on the jukeboxes in the gay bars of the 1950s of Ruth Brown and Frank Sinatra; she discusses the incredible music of Fats Domino, who is still living as I type this in 2016. Toward the end of the book she narrates a long love affair which includes she and her lover enrolling in a contemporary poetry course at the New School; she describes going into therapy and—as the book ends—she describes in some detail the gay girl scene in New York in the 1950s. (More on that below.)

It's in the beginning though, in the first half or so of the book, that she details her relationship with her mother—she begins the first long paragraph in the first numbered chapter with this observation: "When I visited Grenada I saw the root of my mother's powers walking through the streets." Those powers were transformative—"She knew how to make virtues out of necessities," Lorde writes. And her mother also knew where and how to find the essential materials of life: tropical fruits for the family table and unbleached muslin for sheets and pillow-cases came from sources "under the bridge."

All this—from what Sherley Anne Williams called "the iconography of childhood" up through the femmes, butches, and "sistah outsiders" of Lorde's twenties—is the material covered in *Zami*; the timeline extends only as far as the late 1950s. *Zami* seems to have been written in the late 1970s as Lorde struggled with cancer. Her first poetry book, *The First Cities*, was published in 1968, ten years after the time accounted for here.

And *Zami* is also, somewhat curiously and formally, "about" Lorde becoming a poet. I use the quotation marks to suggest how uncomfortably that odd preposition, *about*, fits the arc—or the wave—of the book, *Zami*.

She tells her readers that she is becoming a poet or that she is a poet and though the book provides some examples of her poems from the forties and fifties and though the text abounds with other examples—notably from childhood—of serious wordplay the book more seriously *does* something else. "Poetry" is a thing that the book refers to but the poetry of the book is in the ungainly shape of the *journeying* (not "the journey"—that's finite and about destination) that the book follows as one might follow a river *away* from its source.

That is, *Zami* accomplishes or engages the state that Thoreau spoke of when he said, "A true account of the actual is the rarest poetry." In a 1986 interview with Karen Nolle-Fisher, Lorde comments on the text: "It is also an attempt to tell a few stories that are normally not told: what it's like to grow up as a black woman in the New York of the forties and become a lesbian woman. It is an attempt to consider how black women out there in the diaspora raise their children, and it has to do with how we articulate our strength." She goes on—"In addition, it is the opportunity to gather some of my ideas on how real fiction or types of fiction that are not novels can be created. If I call it a biomythography and not a novel, although it is for me fiction—narrative prose—that's because it embraces so many genres, certainly autobiography, but also history, mythology, psychology, all the different channels through which we, in my opinion, absorb information, process it, and *create something new*. [My italics.] Though much in *Zami* is autobiographical, it is not an autobiography . . . " At this point in the interview, at least as it is recorded, Nolle-Fisher seems to interrupt Lorde's differentiation with a new question: "What does the language in the book have to do with what you express in your poems?" Lorde replies: "Oh, I love words—and I believe that what makes *Zami* so appealing to many people who might even say, 'Oh, I don't like poems,' is in fact its lyrical quality. It is a quality that permits feelings to be expressed in words. And that is of course exactly what poems do and what we poets always try to do."

My thought here is that there are other truths alongside these. My thought is that *Zami*, in spite of the prominence of "biomythography" on the cover of all editions, is *apparently* a memoir, a work of autobiography; again, please note my italics. And my observation is that *Zami* is often referred to, in the popular press and elsewhere, as a novel. Wikipedia's category, "Novels by Audre Lorde," lists it, along with *The Cancer Journals*. An Amazon customer writes, "I often have my students read it because regardless of their backgrounds they find some level of connection to the text. This is a novel that is so multifacted [*sic*] that everyone can enjoy it." And Stefanie K. Dunning's *Queer in Black and White (Interraciality, Same Sex Desire, and*

Contemporary African American Culture): "The term"—Afrekete—"alludes to a character in Audre Lorde's autobiographical novel, *Zami: A New Spelling of My Name* (1982)." Other examples abound and the obvious Internet search for "zami autobiography" yields a similar spate. My thought is that *Zami* destabilizes ideas of the novel *and* autobiography by being—even as it salutes them, which I'll discuss below, by genuflecting to synthesis and the idea of bildungsroman/ coming of age—*bigger*, in its accumulations, than the familiar forms of prose can easily contain. In this way—the unstable nature of the giant text walking forward as it were, or rolling down the hill like the familiar snowball—the book to my reading is its whole self a wild poem in the threadbare *clothing* of prose, of autobiography, of novel. It is riverine indeed. And indeed, perhaps the arguable openness of the prose form (vs. the conventional wisdom that in a poem every word is important) allows for the excesses—including the willingness to be tangential which is, at its best, the willingness to explore and including the willingness to regard coherency as a choice or series of choices and not a necessity—that I've come to associate with the best sorts of literary experiment.

In an earlier interview Karla Jay asked Lorde why she had written an autobiography "at this point in your life." Lorde answered that *Zami* was

> not only an autobiography, but mythology, psychology, all the ways in which I think we can see our environment. And this is what I think good fiction does. And it is fiction. I attempt to create a piece of art, not merely a retelling of things that happened to me and to other women with whom I shared close ties. I define it as biomythography because I've found no other word to really coin what I was trying to do.

Zami seems to have been written in the late 1970s as Lorde struggled with cancer; writing it—she says elsewhere—was "a lifeline through the cancer experience."

But amidst all that I'm struck by the verbs and qualifications and restatements present in Lorde's interviews quoted above—she mentions to Nolle-Fisher, "how we articulate our strength"—and to articulate, the O.E.D. reminds us, is to *particularize* and to *specify*. I don't think I'm over-reading when I understand the specifying here to be a fairly literal calling of names that begins at all three (or four) of the book's beginnings and continues all the way through to the end. Such an articulation of strength as is this book is a chant of saints. Such real-life chants—like the saints themselves—are often unruly, expansive, *excessive*. They lurch into shape.

Litanies are different. They're public prayers, prayers in series, says the O.E.D. One can find overlap in the dictionary's field of examples: in the Catholic Church, "The Litany of the Saints is chanted on the feast of St. Mark." And one learns that, more recently, a litany is "[a] succession or catalogue *of* phenomena, esp. unfortunate events." This is a poem from *The Black Unicorn* (1978):

a litany for survival

For those of us who live at the shoreline
standing upon the constant edges of decision
crucial and alone
for those of us who cannot indulge
the passing dreams of choice
who love in doorways coming and going
in the hours between dawns
looking inward and outward
at once before and after
seeking a now that can breed
futures
like bread in our children's mouths
so their dreams will not reflect
the death of ours:
For those of us
who were imprinted with fear
like a faint line in the center of
our foreheads
learning to be afraid with our mother's milk
for by this weapon
this illusion of some safety to be found
the heavy
-footed hoped to silence us
For all of us
this instant and this triumph
We were never meant to survive.
And when the sun rises
we are afraid
it might not remain
when the sun sets we are afraid
it might not rise in the morning

when our stomachs are full we are afraid
of indigestion
when our stomachs are empty we are afraid
we may never eat again
when we are loved we are afraid
love
will vanish
when we are alone we are afraid
love will never return
and when we speak we are afraid
our words will not be heard
nor welcomed
but when we are silent
we are still afraid
So it is better to speak
remembering
we were never meant to survive

The poem's power comes, in part, from its being a blanket offered to the ones outside history, to all the marginals. The poem's affirmation comes in its irony—we were never meant to survive yet here we are, daring to speak, to spit in the eye of the master narrative that describes us. One notes that the poem's a distillation, a calculation (and poetry is often calculated or, more to the point, a series of calculations, a route perhaps toward, once again, a particular destination), an address at once to and from within the ranks of the voiceless ones, the "we"; the end of the poem is powerful because in three lines—"So it is better to speak/ remembering/ we were never meant to survive"—it addresses the complexity of mind and body (the intellect of memory or remembering and the physical act of speech) and because it crystallizes and restates the energies.

Chant is different and the O.E.D. draws a reader's attention to the commonality of chant and rogues' cant, the secret slang of beggars and thieves. Chant is rough trade. Chant is the vehicle, the "short melody or phrase *to which the Psalms, Canticles, etc., are sung* in public worship." [My italics.] *Zami* is the vehicle, the superstructure, the all-weather demonstration of how survival sometimes unexpectedly goes. The women she sketches and describes and whose names she calls all through the book butt up against each other in ungainly ways. And a reader is drawn back, partway, to rogues' chant. Craig Dionne and Steve Mentz's introduction to their edited collection, *Rogues and Early Modern English Culture*, begins with these lines: "Under various names—rogues, molls, doxies, cony-catchers, masterless men, caterpillars of the commonwealth—an emerging class of displaced figures, poor men and women with no clear social place or identity, exploded onto the scene in sixteenth-century England." In that extraordinary list of marginals the females are, perhaps too easily, doxies and molls; but (deliberately) stepping over such gendered limitations I am drawn to the phrases "masterless men" and "no clear social place" and all that makes me mindful of Lorde's description of her mother. Lorde wrote, early in *Zami*—

> My mother was a very powerful woman. This was so in a time when that word-combination of woman and powerful was almost unexpressable in the white american common tongue, except or unless it was accompanied by some aberrant explaining adjective like blind, or hunchback, or crazy, or Black. Therefore when I was growing up, powerful woman equaled something else quite different from ordinary woman, from simply "woman." It certainly did not, on the other hand, equal "man." What then? What was the third designation?

Just as the received categories of gender are not adequate to contain the gender that Lorde addresses, so too is the category of novel or the category of memoir inadequate to contain or categorize the writing that occurs between the covers of *Zami*.

In a long and stunning riff, the penultimate moment in *Zami*, Lorde does not avert her eyes from the chaos. I locate the center of the book—the most clear and insistent place in the book at the level of the page, the formality of *Zami*'s field of concerns made manifest—late in the book, the chapter in which she describes life at the Bagatelle, a gay-girl bar in New York, where race, gender, orientation, and category collide. The lengthy section on the Bagatelle covers the whole of the 29th of the book's 31 chapters, and below are excerpts from it.

> All of us who survived those common years had to be a little strange. We spent so much of our young-womanhood trying to define ourselves as woman-identified women before we even knew the words existed, let alone that there were ears interested in trying to hear them beyond our immediate borders. All of us who survived those common years have to be a little proud. A lot proud. Keeping ourselves together and on our own tracks, however wobbly, was like trying to play the Dinizulu War Chant or a Beethoven sonata on a tin dog-whistle.
>
> . . .

> *Being women together was not enough. We were different. Being gay-*
> *girls together was not enough. We were different. Being Black together*
> *was not enough. We were different. Being Black women together was not*
> *enough. We were different. Being Black dykes together was not enough.*
> *We were different.* (Lorde's italics.)
>
> . . .
>
> It was a while before we came to realize that our place was the
> very house of difference rather the security of any one particular dif-
> ference. (And often, we were cowards in our learning.) It was years
> before we learned to use the strength that daily surviving can bring,
> years before we learned fear does not have to incapacitate, and that
> we could appreciate each other on terms not necessarily our own.

Here, it seems, the actual work that's behind the more calculated "litany" poem is shown. If that poem is a distillation this is the raw material
of survival itself, not an allusion to it or capture of it. This is the actual, the
unbeautiful, the unadorned—there is no shoreline (or even river), only the
facts of life. And she continues to call names, her own conspicuously among
them:

> The Black gay-girls in the Village gay bars of the fifties knew each oth-
> er's names, but we seldom looked into each other's Black eyes, lest we
> see our own aloneness and our own blunted power mirrored in the
> pursuit of darkness. Some of us died inside the gaps between the mir-
> rors and those turned-away eyes. Sistah outsiders. Didi and Tommy
> and Muff and Iris and Lion and Trip and Audre and Diane and Felicia
> and Bernie and Addie.

This laying out of the gay girl scene is the acknowledgement of divisive-
ness on which the book seems to end if a reader takes seriously the billow-
ingness of the text, if one embraces the contradictions of the text. The idea
here, finally, is that the book is unstable. The best books are. That is, the
parts that don't "fit" are in there as well, making the books "flawed." In
Zami the end—the long encounter with the woman Kitty who becomes,
at least on the page, Afrekete—recapitulates the beginning of the book and
this final moment is what strikes me as Lorde's genuflection to synthesis.
But even this is not uncomplicated.

In that beginning, an untitled series of questions precedes the book's
Prologue and its first chapter—"*To whom do I owe the power behind my*

voice, what strength I have become, yeasting up like sudden blood from under the bruised skin's blister?"; *"To whom do I owe the symbols of my survival?"*; and *"To whom do I owe the woman I have become?"* (Lorde's italics.) Each question is "spoken to" by a number of paragraphs detailing encounters with named people before Lorde, in apparent final response and apostrophe, writes,

> To the journey woman pieces of myself.
> Becoming.
> Afrekete.

A couple of hundred pages later Afrekete appears in the flesh as it were. Arguably Afrekete as spirit-presence occurs throughout the book—in Lorde's relationships with her mother and sisters, with her childhood friend Gennie, who died by her own hand before they were lovers and with her first lover Ginger; and others.

Kitty enters the book at the start of Chapter 31, the final chapter. She and Lorde had apparently met previously at a house party and then, later, meet again at one of the "second-string gay-girl bars" Lorde was frequenting. Kitty, she explains to Lorde, is short for Afrekete. Lorde is oddly effusive for some pages in describing her clothing and Max Factor cosmetics. They're together for a while, in a series of erotic encounters, and then Afrekete/Kitty leaves. At the very close of the chapter, Lorde writes,

> We had come together like elements erupting into an electric storm, exchanging energy, sharing charge, brief and drenching. Then we parted, passed, reformed, reshaping ourselves the better for the exchange.
>
> I never saw Afrekete again, but her print remains upon my life with the resonance and power of an emotional tattoo.

And she salutes Afrekete in the book's brief epilogue, as "the mischievous linguist, trickster, best-beloved, whom we must all become."

But before the end, halfway through the final chapter, she writes,

> *And I remember Afrekete, who came out of a dream to me always being hard and real as the fire hairs along the underedge of my navel. She brought me live things from the bush; and from her farm set out in co-coyams and cassava*—those magical fruits which Kitty bought in the

West Indian markets along Lenox Avenue in the 140s or in the Puerto Rican bodegas within the bustling market over on Park Avenue and 116th Street under the Central Railroad structures.

"I got this under the bridge" was a saying from time immemorial, giving an adequate explanation that whatever it was had come from as far back and as close to home—that is to say, was as authentic—as was possible.

I would argue that the whole book is an "adequate explanation" for "the woman I became." Within that *adequate* are gestures beyond the adequate. The adequate is itself a good-enough gloss or covering or rubric for something ineffably huge, something that does not contain but that acknowledges and honors both past and not present as much as present *location*. Adequate here is the guise, a thing to satisfy the pedestrian. Adequate is an understatement, a garment that I read as deliberately barely covering—also, that is, adequate says, *Shut up.*

There's a brilliant ambiguity to Lorde's "adequate explanation." It's all you or any child of a powerful parent needs to know—*under the bridge*. It's a good-enough thing to say. It's a good-enough guise. In the same way the mantles of "novel," "autobiography," or "memoir" are adequate, but *only* adequate and only adequate for the ones who need a label. The subtitle—"A New Spelling of My Name"—and Lorde's genre invention—"biomythography"—talk back to the adequate that she claims at the end of the book, in the pages that seem to synthesize the complex experiences of the book into a single figure, Afrekete. Afrekete is adequate for those who want synthesis and teachability. The strain and unruliness of contradiction, the unfixable division, the *masterlessness* of poetry itself—these are different, these constitute the lived life of the book, *Zami*. These are part and parcel of its chant.

Zami begins—in part—with the question, "*To whom do I owe the woman I have become?*" This obligates one who would write in response to it to reveal one's own starting points or sets of relation, provisional or not. From where do I speak of Audre Lorde's work? I speak (with some degree of self-awareness) from the black bourgeoise and (with some degree of self-awareness) as a man born in the 1950s and more heterosexual than not. I'm in the generation that remembers the American South as a place or origin, a place from which my parents emigrated; and, like Lorde, I'm of West Indian descent and have made the pilgrimages to family sites in the Caribbean. The family speaks not through me but in me; the West Indian trope, Kamau Brathwaite says, is migration—"I want to submit that the desire (even the need) to migrate is at the heart of West Indian sensibility, whether that migration is in fact or by metaphor." I write as a pro-feminist man, a pro-womanist man, and as a black child of black emigrants; as a heterosexual I do what I can to advance the Homosexual Agenda.

And I'm a poet. As such my interest is particularly in the text of *Zami*—my interest is in Lorde's layerings, in what the text itself becomes and claims. And I claim for it, if I may, the peculiar and insufficient public mantle of the *difficult*. Yet I am aware of how contested *difficulty* is in the literary battles of the twenty-first century and note our most obvious commonality—blackness—and would suggest, out of my sense of respect for the singularity and expansiveness of Lorde's work in *Zami* and elsewhere, that together her writing and my own written responses to it complete no project.

WORK CITED

Lorde, Audre. *Zami: A New Spelling of my Name-A Biomythography*. Watertown, Mass. Persephone Press. 1982.

On Amiri Baraka's Six Plus One Persons
"a longish poem about a dude"

ALDON LYNN NIELSEN

The dude talking wasn't the dude I'm talking about, but then who am I?

AMIRI BARAKA

"Who he, wd be more like it" (Baraka, *Fiction* 273). In the space of nineteen years, in the movement from "LeRoi Jones" to "Amiri Baraka," a time period that encompasses Baraka's evolution from the New American Poetry via the Black Arts Movement and into "Marxism-Leninism-Mao Tse Tung Thought," Baraka spun through the materials of his own life in the production of three major innovative works in prose: *The System of Dante's Hell*, *Six Persons* and the curiously titled *Autobiography of LeRoi Jones / Amiri Baraka*. In *The System of Dante's Hell* and *Six Persons*, Baraka created astonishingly varied fictional structures out of the stuff of his own life, though the latter novel was largely unknown from the time of its composition in 1974, not quite a decade after his first autobiographical novel, to the time of its eventual publication in 2000. Not only did the *Autobiography*, which encompasses the time of *Six Persons*'s composition, appear before *Six Persons* was finally published, but the *Autobiography* itself did not appear in its entirety until thirteen years had passed from its initial publication in a truncated version. In each instance, the poet's life, though unfolded roughly in chronological ordering, emerges structured within a poet's framework. *The System of Dante's Hell* arranges its chapters following an altered charting of Dante's circles, rather the way Theresa Hak Kyung Cha would later rework the naming and structuring of the classic muses. In a chart accompanying the novel, Baraka explains his adaptations of the schema of Dante's epic, which he had first encountered as a student at Howard University. The novel opens appropriately enough in a vestibule, wherein Baraka confronts the breakup of his sensibility. But where Dante's *Divine Comedy* opens halfway through that journey of life in a dark wood, Baraka's version of *in medias res* offers a contrastive argument: "But Dante's hell is heaven" (*Fiction* 19). Once emerged from this vestibule, readers are greeted by the heathen, prefiguring Baraka's much later poetic sequence "Heathens," while at the same time hinting at the technique adopted in Baraka's second novel, beginning the chapter addressing himself in the second person: "You've done every-thing you said you wdn't" (23). Appended to Baraka's organizational chart is an explanatory note offering his reason for moving his heretics from Dan-te's sixth circle to Baraka's own deepest part of hell, though coincidentally enough they are moved from Dante's sixth circle to Baraka's sixth chapter.. The young Baraka writes that "it is heresy, against one's own sources, run-ning in terror, from one's deepest responses and insights . . . the denial of feeling . . . that" he sees "as basest evil" (17).

Baraka's *Autobiography* describes its chronology thematically, with chap-ters under the rubrics of "Error Farce," "Black Brown Yellow White," "The Village," etc. As we follow the poet's life, we move through the geography of his experience and through the history that is the major source material for the two novels. *Six Persons* stands as perhaps the most audaciously con-structed of these life narratives, with each chapter given over to narration from a different point of view, hence the *Six Persons* of the book's title, be-ginning with the singular: "I," "You." He." The latter half of the book is told from the point of view of the plurals: "They," "You, Yall, Ya," and "We." If, as Rachel Blau DuPlessis insists, poetry is at the very least segmented and sat-urated language [and, by the way, her reference to saturated language will put scholars of African American poetics much in mind of Stephen Hender-son's explorations of "saturation" as a feature of the new Black poetry] (5), then *Six Persons* is more than a poet's prose, it is, as the novel's self descrip-tion has it, "a longish poem about a dude."

I have written elsewhere of *Six Persons*'s tangled history of non-publi-cation, of its commissioning and then rejection by a chief editor from Put-nam's. But that debacle was largely related to the aesthetics of Baraka's second novel. The publisher had hoped for another *Godfather*; what he got instead was exactly the surreal, syntactically adventurous collage he had insisted he did not want (*Integral Music*). The years during which Baraka composed *Six Persons* bridge the period of his movement from Cultural Nationalism to Marxism, a movement in which he was joined by much of the leadership of the Congress of African People. This is a history and an ideological evolution that has yet to be detailed in its entirety, though Bara-ka's own *Autobiography* has been supplemented by Komosi Woodard's *A Nation within a Nation: Amiri Baraka and Black Power Politics,* and Michael Simanga's volume *Amiri Baraka and the Congress of African People,* books written by participant observers who had the advantage of having directly witnessed much of the central debates. And yet, *Six Persons* is not the work of agit-prop that mainstream critics have often accused Baraka of writing. The Baraka who had studied so closely the works of Brecht and Lu Hsun during these years did have an ideology to advance (he would later title a collection of poetry *Poems for the Advanced*), but he remained as revolutionary in his approach to form and language as he was in his politics, and this poem/novel is ample evidence of that adherence to linguistic and structural innovation.

Beginning at his beginning; autobiographical beginnings are sufficiently standard forms that they were already being parodied by Sterne early in the genre's history. If Tristram Shandy had a hard time getting himself born in the early passages of his autobiographical narrative, Baraka troubles the passage of birthing itself. This first person singular chapter commences with a challenge to the singularity of that very first person. "Who can speak of their birth?" (233) The novel poses this as its initial gesture. Clearly any and all of us can and do speak of our births, and yet we can never escape the second hand nature of our accounts of our own borning. Despite claiming at points that he could not remember his own age, Salvador Dalí also claimed to recall with great precision his earliest intrauterine existence. Most, though, recognize that their earliest memories tend to erupt around the time of their accession to language, and what little they know of the times before that linguistic big bang is, at very best, hearsay. But in Baraka's novel there is legible an additional layer of signifying in this generative first person's first sentence. If it is generally the case that autobiography begins with birth, African American autobiography in its beginnings is often cloudy on just this point. How many slave narratives, that of Douglass perhaps most famously, open and leave open the question of birth, the question of paternal parentage, the question of age, all questions troubled by the horrors of slavery? Who among Africans in bondage could speak of their birth? More than we might have thought, given the evidence of the narratives, and yet that straightforward first question of birther epistemology cannot be denied, and is redoubled in African American tradition. Autobiography is a genre marked by that fold at its ending. The story of how I came to be who I am begins at the beginning, but the person I am to become is already evident on page one in the person of the writing subject, the narrator contriving a beginning out of hearsay.

And if the writing subject of autobiography is necessarily a tenuous reconstruction, then Baraka's novel worries even the familiar lines of personal narrative, for the final chapter, the final evidence of the writing subject, is an address to and from "We and all." Baraka as writing subject alerts us to this development while writing as "I." "I am not who was born," he writes, "nor even less who was thought up. We are all projections of someone" (233). If it is always the case that the subject encountered in the first lines of autobiography is already the person we will read at the end, then that plural "we" in this instance and, Baraka hints, in all instances, is a projection out of the one. "So," he continues, "I is a process, a be-ing" (233). And if this opening gambit puts readers in mind of any number of poststructuralists upsetting our notions of the self at the very moment Baraka was first writing these first sentences, we should bear in mind that Baraka had been critiquing the Cartesian subject as early as his first novel. For many of us who came of age reading the evolving Baraka, our first questioning of Western views of subjectivity came in the reading of Baraka, our first lessons in the unsettling of the Cartesian subject came in our readings of Fanon. For many of us, it was Black writing that confirmed what we were to encounter later in critical theory and philosophy, not the other way around.

But the Baraka of 1974 was also by that time a close student of Marxism, and so that deep questioning of the Humanist legacies of the West (which he shared with Charles Olson as well as Fanon), had come to take an increasingly dialectical and political form. By the time he composes the first page of *Six Persons* he has come to understand the process of be-ing, what he terms "a verbal process ongoing even today" (meaning the today of his writing) [233], as an explicable abstracting, "simple capitalism. Imperialism" (233). What might earlier have been seen as a fashionable existential alienation is now viewed as having its roots in material processes and effects (which, we should remember, was how existentialism saw it too), "the greed of the 'I,' so removed, totally, from every other be-ing that its process allegedly goes on singularly, unrelatedly, totally in isolation . . ."233). This direction might well have come as a surprise to Baraka's readers in the early 1970s, had not his publisher's surprise been so great that the manuscript and its author were decommissioned upon first reading.

And a part of the apartness of the singular "I" is, as the opening sentences have suggested, a process of being beheld, and thus beholding to, the multitude of others. Baraka sees the self, sees himself, "Awash in a see of others" (240). He promises parenthetically to address that plurality later. "I will talk about those eyes as I's as others as theys after . . . " (240), he proposes, describing in essence the plural persons of the book's later half while seemingly alluding as well to Louis Zukovsky's volume *I's (pronounced eyes)*. Zukofsky had a fascination with the differential relationships of eye and tongue, no doubt in part the result of his learning English as a second language, but equally clearly a shared modernist aesthetic among the Objectivist poets of his circles, an aesthetic that insisted upon the simultaneity of the poem's objective existence as material print on the page and as material sounding in aural space. Baraka found this same insistence in the works of a Langston

Hughes and the out jazz of an Ornette Coleman. Baraka writes "An I," seeing in that "I" "A presence, an ego, put together in stone and steel. In charter and theory" (240), but visible and actionable only in that "see of others.

Second person narrative has the uncanny effect of mirroring all those questions of identity and singularity Baraka raises in his first chapter. Italo Calvino's *If on a Winter's Night a Traveler . . .* begins: "You are about to begin reading Italo Calvino's new novel, *If on a Winter's Night a Traveler*." The danger in this approach is that readers may find it precious, though in Calvino's case that opening sentence is a simple statement of fact, not withstanding the equal fact that some readers may decide not to read Italo Calvino's novel after all. Baraka's second person places stringent demands upon us, first of all the demand that we, as readers, become that first person process of be-ing that has written the chapter we have just read. "What is demanded is that you reveal yourself, "1st to yourself, and then to the other yous" (271). How am I, how are we, to reveal ourselves to ourselves if not by reading, by becoming the writer? We anticipate revelation when we read autobiography, even if, especially if, it is fictive memoir. We learn something of ourselves in reading, in being in a see of others.

What do you learn from reading Baraka's "you"? One thing you learn is that the fictionalized past keeps intruding on the present of the writing. That is not, thanks to the publisher's rejection of the novel, the present of the reading, however. By the time we, or you, were able to read this text, the present out of which Baraka observed its past has itself become another past. In the time of Baraka's writing, jazz trumpeter Donald Byrd has joined the faculty of Howard University and created among his students the hit jazz/pop assembly The Blackbyrds, events Baraka contrasts to Howard's seeming allergy to jazz in the days of his own attendance at the university, which forms the subject of much of the "You" chapter. As a Howard student, Baraka studied jazz with poet Sterling Brown, but those lessons took place off the books in the men's dormitory (and occasionally at Brown's home), because jazz was practically anathema to Howard President Mordecai Johnson, who each year had to assure the United States Congress that his African American student body remained a good investment for the nation. Baraka's second person remembers the Howard University brain trust that included E. Franklin Frazier, Alain Locke and Chancellor Williams, all kept, as the narration reports, "under wraps" (263) by Howard's Cold War era color struck administration, intent upon the mass production of ideologically appropriate middle class young, brown men and women acceptable to white America. In Baraka's radical retrospect, Frank Snowden, author of *Blacks in Antiquity*, comes off badly, primarily because of his speciality,

Classics, though Snowden proved one of the most popular instructors on campus, the only Classicist I've ever known to have standing room only crowds at his classroom door.

The past of Baraka's second person returns in the political present of his writing. Among Baraka's campus running buddies was a young man, here identified only as "Phil," who subsequently went on to a job in the Secret Service, whose duties came to include guarding the person of Vice President Spiro Agnew. "Agnew about to get busted (will he guard his body in slam?)" (259) Baraka writes shortly before Agnew in real life pleads *nolo contendere* to avoid that looming prison sentence. In later years, Baraka's campus friend was to be detailed to interview Baraka on the occasion of presidential visits near Newark, to assure that the increasingly politicized poet was no danger to the leaders of the free world. But the dangers represented by Baraka's writing, the dangers posed by thinking while Black, were of a different order, and second person makes any reader a part of that ideological threat: "You came from that, you still in that, you are all that, you are love and the final revenge of the Afrikan upon the colonizer" (252).

If Baraka's third person singular chapter sounds like he is talking about someone else, he is; not simply because he is writing fiction, but because this is the chapter in which his name begins its journey from Leroy to Amiri: "That's when he changed his name that first year in Colored School, from English to French. Why? It seemed cooler" (281). Here we watch as Amiri Baraka watches himself as other in the act of becoming the putatively cooler "LeRoi." But here, too, is another fascinating rhetorical effect. Neither the protagonist's given name nor his Frechified version of it is given in the text. Soon enough, the narrative is referring to this chapter's "he" as "L." "L actually wanted to be and was the hero of *No More Parades*, the swishy genius in *Brideshead Revisited* . . . " *(290)*; or "LJ, head down, hands jammed in pockets . . ." (291). Thanks to the title page, we know that the author of this book, Amiri Baraka, is the former LeRoi Jones, who was the former Everett Leroy Jones, son of Coyette Leroy Jones. Readers of the *Autobiography* have read of these name changes before, though they read that in a book written after *Six Persons*. Who reading here would not assume that "he" is "LeRoi Jones," though there is no internal motivation for that reading? "Is that you goin' for the ghos' narrator?" (291) That's a question posed by the narrating voice to the narrator. There is a first person plural lurking here, too, as this ghost of a narrator identifies himself simultaneously with his former friends and with his belated readers, he sees "L" "kicked back into reality, with all the rest of us" (300). But that comes fast on the heels of the novel poet's worst, and perhaps most revealing, pun. L, as a young man who had grown up with the funny papers and radio serials, had "developed a fantasy jones" (300). So "he," L, was addicted to fantasy, both fantasy as escape from the realities of American life at mid-century and fantasy as the social mapping induced in him by bourgeois ideology filtered through "colored school," and as a result had created of himself, for himself, *as* himself a fantasy Jones. The L who had altered the orthography of his name had created a fantasy representation of himself to the world, so that in that "see of others" he might be seen as other than what he had come to be. But it was for naught. Life "kicked him into" that same reality in which the rest of "us" abide.

That multiplying of selves in the "He" chapter leads naturally, if precariously, into the third person plural chapter, which largely coincides with the Village passages of Baraka's *Autobiography*. "All he's change" (307), he observes "and become they, a warm abstract." Race in America, in Baraka's life, seemingly stands as an "us versus them" affair, and yet inevitably "he" becomes "them." The chapter title is properly "They (Them Theirs Theyres &c)." As L enters New York, he becomes a multiple I/eye: "A huge I again, like a rolling me" (304). Racial representations get re-presented otherwise. "Even Kenyatta died his hair blonde" (309), a reference to alto saxophonist Robin Kenyatta. Like Baraka, a man of many loud changes, Kenyatta was not born "Kenyatta" and was not from Kenya. Born in North Carolina, he did at birth bear a royal moniker, Robert Prince Haynes. He was well known to Baraka in those Village days, and performed in the landmark October Revolution in Jazz alongside trumpet great Bill Dixon. On later albums such as his *Gypsy Man*, Kenyatta can indeed be seen sporting bleached hair. Baraka portrays this as an effect of the dis-integration of post World War II racial consciousness. "Like everybody else, they looked up, ca early 60s, & they were covered from head to toe w/ white folks" (315). The us and the them had gotten all wrapped up in each other, without dissolving the larger racialist apparatus.

The signs of Baraka's own life are also multiplied here. We meet "Lula Dutchman" (319) even as "they" get in touch with Allen Ginsberg, meet a series of "straightout aesthetes from BlkMountain College" (320) and even meet Jones himself (322). In the plural, we enter grammar's hall of mirrors. "He," become "they" is part of the revolution in writing that includes L's alter ego Jones. And as for the Back artists:

> They were spicier Creeleys and spicier Ginsbergs, Olsons with Negro myths to add to the pot. DeKoonings with a different cover story. Cages with a ghetto rationale. (342)

I want to read a pun here on the name of Jack Spicer, knowing that Baraka knew of Spicer and his work, but I have to admit there is nothing in the text to suggest that connection. On the other hand, "they" are soon enough seen publishing, within this narrative, the very magazines and newsletters that Baraka did in fact publish outside the narrative, which included contributions from Spicer.

The novel takes note, too, of a Washington, D.C., jazz phenomenon, one celebrated by the Howard/Dasein poets, though by the time of the writing of *Six Persons* Baraka is more focused on the politics of that group's naming than on their music. "There were niggers who called themselves the JFK Quartet" (343). Just here a reader has to ask if Baraka is mis-remembering or if he is making fiction of fact, for the actual group was the "JFK Quintet," a group discovered by Cannonball Adderly and recorded by Atlantic Records. What matters to the now older and Marxist Baraka as he writes is not so much how many members were in the group, but a recollection of what the Kennedy "New Frontier" meant to Black Americans in those days just before the assassination transformed the fact of a presidency into the myth of a Camelot. Baraka was himself swept up in controversies after the Kennedy assassination, disagreements swirling around a poem he wrote for the journal *Kulchur*. In this narrative he recalls the painter Bob Thompson, here simply "BT," crying in the streets. But in the wake of that mad act, the seeds of the New Black can be seen emerging. Recollecting a grouping of young artists he brought together in real life, Baraka re-imagines them as "The New Dudes" arguing "abt reality an un—its popular relative" (355). The Umbra group of writers reappears among "them" as well, but Baraka casts them as the "Eclipse" group, perhaps foreshadowing their breakup in the period after Kennedy's death.

There is an odd moment just here as Baraka describes "their" sliding in and out of Whiteness. He writes that Miles Davis's drummer (probably a reference to Tony Williams), "a yng whiz kid, got a set of complete works of Shakespeare (excluding this volume) to put beside his drums and signify that he went with a white woman" (366). "Excluding *this* volume" — is this an allusion to *Othello*, or a yet more audacious reference to the book in which we are reading? (Oddly enough, in the years we were waiting to read this book, another African American, Tony Williams, born in 1972, would come of age as an actor, eventually to play Othello in *Shakespeare in the Sphere*.)

Upon entering the second person plural chapter, we come to realize that this poet's novel is structured around a fold in its middle, rather like William Carlos Williams's poem about the red wheel barrow. The first half of the novel goes from first to second to third person; the book's second half reverses in the plural, running from third to second to first persons. English, unlike so many other European languages, uses the same form for singular and plural in the second person, and yet clearly American brains strain for some other path, as seen in the "Yall" squeezed into the middle of the next chapter's title. In parts of New York state we hear "yez"; older West Virginian might say "you 'uns"; young folk still say "you guys"; and the South's Y'all followed the great migration to the rest of the country, and to this chapter. This also means that we have another chapter in which the narrator is addressing himself and us at the same time; we are both the second person, and we are many.

And as happens in the second person singular chapter, this direct address implicates readers in the narration, with the added complications of racial address. The chapter opens on the 1964 Harlem riots, which some of us might remember, according to the text, though some of us were off teaching at some college "or at a writer's conference on the coast, down by the water at Monterey" (369), seemingly references to Baraka's time at Buffalo and at the Asilomar conference on African American literature, or "Negro" literature as the program at the time had it. Some of us were also at the night club panel on art where the increasingly militant Baraka shouted down sympathetic, if confused, whites. Were "we" there. "Yall" were, or some of "yall." For some of us, reading these lines will be the first we have heard of these events. For some of us, disentangling white from black will prove impossible. "That's what it was yall came to reject. White!" (369). How does a white person read this rejection of white? How does any white reader process the later address, "You were whitey haters" (387). I don't mean by this to invoke those largely mythological self hating white liberals of the era, but rather to ask a sort of phenomenological reader response question about how this text constructs a reader, any reader. How does any black reader who wasn't around for those moments fit themselves into this second person? When "They" make a reappearance, they are white. "They were white because you cd see they ran it" (370), but the white "you" can see that as well, even if they cannot simply volunteer to be not white while reading.

Then, too, this is the now Marxist Baraka writing, the Baraka who has rejected the cultural nationalism of his own then very recent past. "It rolled up 'white.' Because there was no clear analysis or understanding. The principle contradiction was white" (371). Baraka doesn't let himself off this hook, and he wonders aloud about the direction of poetics in these times. "Olson died! What the hell was one-eyed Bob Creeley doin' or 4-eyed Allen Ginsberg?" (371). Baraka recollects the folk poetry of the day as well, summoning the voice of a young man on the make in the Village who, with his girlfriend, attended a performance of Baraka's *Dutchman.* "Blowin' in the wind is a form—who's to do it was our first question. Is there a change can come?" (373). Sam Cooke is known to have asked a version of these questions when he heard Dylan's hit song, assumed into the radio heavens by Peter, Paul and Mary. He felt that "one of us" should have written that song, and proceeded to write one of his own. "I was born by the river in a little tent." Baraka, with a poet's eye to grammar, shifts Sam Cooke's question slightly. Where the hit record had expressed belief that "a change is gonna come," for Baraka it's an open question. "Is there a change can come?" Not simply can a change come at all, but is there *a* change that can make its way through to us, to yall. That, Baraka represents, is first question. As Olson, in *Call Me Ishmael,* takes space to be the central fact to man born in America, Baraka poses as primary, as first question, the availability of change, its ability to come among us.

Strangely, in addition to offering himself as the addressee of the plural "you" in this chapter, Baraka also presents himself as yet another persona with yet another name, "Nutty Jergen." NJ won the "Galahad" [Obie] award for his play when it ran downtown, only to be decried as a merchant of "hate whitey" when he produced the play in Harlem (388-89). The "I" of chapter one, having become the L and LJ of earlier chapters, appears, once he has moved uptown and changed his name again, as this "Nutty Jergen." Nutty is/was "you." "You left the Village & went to Harlem. You thought less about Ezra Pound & more about black people. That's interesting!" (397). Baraka, by the time he is writing this book, has come to recognize the problems with the nationalism of the mid-sixties. "Why wasn't it finally right?" (398) he asks himself, and us. He recognizes the necessities of the moment, the pressing need to overthrow the dominance of white culture and economic power. But he wonders about this "campaign to kill off the cracker in us" (399). In the end, "did you succeed?" (399). Well, did you? Did we? Has America killed off the cracker in itself? Has any reader, of any color? If, as Baraka portrays the more militant of his times, including himself, as naive children with America's guns pointed at them (399), what does this say about the America of that time, about the America of the time when he wrote this novel, about the America of our reading moment now?

There is a structural surprise awaiting readers at the close of the book, a sort of sixth-and-a-half person, a seventh chapter. The fifth person section closes with a rhetorical question. Describing that moment after the collapse of the Black Arts Repertory Theater School, pointing in the differing directions various sixties nationalists pursued, Baraka addresses the corporate him and us: "Where are yall rat now?" (402) This again raises the curious workings of temporality in our experience of the text. The "rat now" of his question is simultaneously the late 1960s when the dispersal occurred, the early 1970s as Baraka is writing the question, and the now of the reader, implied or embodied. The first person plural chapter, which at first readers think the final chapter, unfolds from that question: "In the middle of the night we show up" (403). The biographical reference is to Baraka's return to Newark and to his parents on the heels of the BARTS catastrophe, but the first person again enfolds us. "We together. Our love binds us" (403). The text speaks of the protagonist and his girlfriend, except that with the swirling perspective of the chapters and their points of identification, we as readers are a part of that loving "we." It is also in this penultimate chapter that Baraka, and his readers, come to the Marxism that he and his protagonist arrive at in the 70's, and that has been on view as a narratological backdrop from the first page. The title of Lenin's "WHAT IS TO BE DONE" becomes a repeated riff, with Baraka asking "us" that question and reflecting on his own change. "You sd you hated whitey, ain't Lenin whitey" (406) we are asked parenthetically, the second and first persons coming into political and rhetorical conflict. If we hated whitey, and now find ourselves compelled by white Lenin's socialism, then what is to be done?

One problem vexing Baraka scholarship for decades has been a too frequent failure to note the continuities in his thought and form stretching across the ideological shifts. *Six Persons* is clear about what has been at the heart of his searching from the outset: "We wanted reality. We still want it. We wanted to attack our enemies. We still want it" (407) Now a dialectician, Baraka recognizes how that search sometimes led him astray. He had fled white for black (408), and yet the demons of oppression were still at his heels. Now he rejects the metaphysics of color, without ever fooling himself that color doesn't matter. "Reality is more beautiful than fantasy" (408) he comes to recognize, and will make that the theme of a contemporaneous poem in his collection *Hard Facts*, "A New Reality Is Better Than a New Movie!"

There is the recognizable Baraka satire throughout this section (one militant organization is identified as the "Primitive Nationalists Chauvinist Atavists" [412]), characters have names like "Neddy Pikett" and "Ronald Pucker," and for a good stretch of the narration "we" are also named "Mickey.' "Mickey" as in Mickey Mouse? As in Mickey Fickey (or alternate spellings that add up to "MF")? Who can say? There are passages when "We Mickey" is the same Baraka projection known as "L" earlier in the book, but then the narrator professes confusion over the matter himself: "But wait that wasn't Mickey. That was Barney.... The two of 'em mash together in we head" (419). Soon enough, we see "Barney" where we might expect to meet "Mickey." "Barney sat in a meeting talking about meetings" (422). Yet more oddly, or satirically depending on your view, a character who shares the life story of Eldridge Cleaver shows up bearing Baraka's birth name, "Everett," but this is "Everett Hatchet," still an instrument for chopping, and his course from prison to nationalism to New Left leads to our, the narrator's, sense of the pressing need for yet more meetings. "All agrees we need a new Communist Party. We needed one for a while ago" (425). Even Leroi Jones makes an appearance in the first person plural chapter, but notably, even though the name ends in "i," he appears with his pre-college small "r" (426), something that could not be an accident given Baraka's naming history. "Jones" appears also in his real life role as one of the central figures of the Black Power conference held in Newark in 1967. But the ongoing sharing out of Baraka's life among the proliferation of characters continues as "we" are convicted in court of charges stemming from the Newark riots, and the judge in "our" case reads, as explanation for the sentence, from "a book Mickey wrote" (431).

Having come to the close of that sixth person, the first person plural chapter, readers turn the page to find, not a clearly labeled "afterward," but a further chapter titled "we & all." This further complicates the rhetoric of the book's chief organizing principles. While we might feel the separation normally attendant upon reading a first person singular account, no matter how much we might identify with a narrator, the second person chapters have deeply implicated us in the book's thought. Second person is considerably less common in fiction, more often encountered in poetry, though it is not unheard of. Contemporary writers have sometimes followed Italo Calvino's example in this, if not in the inventiveness of his prose, including Jay McInerney, Kwame Alexander and Tom Robbins. A reader might join in Baraka's narration in the third person chapters, but as we proceed through the text it is increasingly difficult to separate ourselves from "them." No matter the distancing effect of the third person, we have just passed through a chapter addressing us directly *as* protagonist, so that it is nearly impossible not to be the agonist of Baraka's third person. But weren't we the "we" of the penultimate chapter, no matter how much it was rooted clearly in the life of Baraka himself? In the scattering of Baraka's life among the several names of his narrative, as in the renaming of himself in life, that first person plural conjoins us inevitably to the thinking, writing subject. This is an inherently poetic effect, in my reading, a textual force demanding that we enact and interact with the grammatical functioning of these shifters in the world. These pronouns are deictic, but in the poet's use, in *Six Persons*, you can never find a resting place in indexicality. The pointing doesn't come to rest easily, no matter how much finger pointing goes on in the action of the book.

And so we end in "We & All," which is also the chapter corresponding to Baraka's coming to rest firmly in Marxist ideology, as a result of his, and our, material experience of the times. This book was written, and ends in, that moment when many were feeling the heat death of the sixties. What the seventies were to become was not yet evident, and many felt a slackening of pace, even as history proceeded with its usual pell mell hurtling from one dread to another. In this final chapter, we witness and feel the profound disappointment of nationalists who saw their newly acquired electoral powers resulting only in changing the color of the color guard. Baraka and his comrades organized a political revolution in Newark, bringing Kenneth Gibson (here embodied as "Gip Fatson") to the Mayor's office. But in the end, as *Six Persons*'s seventh chapter admits, "we was used" (439). "Subjective egotism," Baraka recognizes in a book that directly challenges all notions of self and ego, "is not struggle" (440). Then, sounding a bit like a fifth Musketeer, "You can't Hate Whitey. We isn't all black. We for white. We for all" (440). In Trinidad at carnival time, they say "all of we is one," and no matter how distant that may be from absolute truth, that is the ideal. "We & All" is Baraka's way of concluding that we must in fact as well as in dreams and novels and poems be *for* all.

In approaching that closing, Baraka admits of his own lingering resistance to the inevitability of that conclusion. And there are still scores to settle. There are the "Wabenzi" to be denounced ("tribe of Mercedes Benz drivers") [458]. There is the seeming apostasy of Black Arts era poets such as Nikki Giovanni (here portrayed as "Niggy Johnsonetta" [461], (also satirized vehemently in *Hard Facts*, though by the 1990s the two poets were again on affectionate terms). But the key, as suggested throughout the book, is the seeking, the continued searching after answers, answers that may not arrive in time. By the last pages "we" have begun to read Lenin, Marx, Touré, Boggs (that would be James Boggs, former associate of C.L.R. James, husband of Grace Lee Boggs and contributor to Baraka and Neal's *Black Fire* anthology), and, sad to see, Stalin, though yes, I suppose we should read Stalin, as a prophylactic measure if nothing else. At the end, when we meet "our raggedy-headed brothers" still "raging at the devil," "we" want to remind them the sixties are over (462). But then, what is left to us as we face the unraveling seventies, or the post-millennial era of the book's final publication? We, and all, are left with two encouraging lessons from *Six Persons*; first, that our social lives determine our ideology. Baraka has left the spirted metaphysics of Kawaida behind and replaces it with a materialist's hope for a scientific mode of encountering our world. The life sciences, however, have not given us a science of life. In the end, Baraka has learned one lesson even above that one, that organizing is the only tool "we" have. His book ends in a deeply personal hope for victory "to all peoples" (462). In this he is returning to something read long before he had become a Marxist, before even he had become a cultural nationalist. He is returning, as it were, to the native land of his, and our, reading, to that moment in Aimé Césaire's *Notebook* where that predecessor poet envisioned a place for all at the rendezvous of victory. Marxist philosopher C.L.R. James borrowed that line for the title of a volume of his collected writings. Baraka, too, comes back to that ennobling vision, though he has come back to it now as a material necessity, not just an enticing belief. *Six Person's* final page is the necessary but natural conclusion that had been in evidence in our reading from the first person to the last. "In our struggles, is part of all our struggle. Our roads to get here" (462).

WORKS CITED

Baraka, Amiri. *The Fiction of LeRoi Jones / Amiri Baraka*. Chicago: Lawrence Hill Books, 2000.

———. *Hard Facts*. Newark, NJ: People's War, 1975.

DuPlessis, Rachel Blau. *Blue Studios: Poetry and Its Cultural Work*. Athens, GA: U of Alabama P, 2006.

Nielsen, Aldon Lynn. *Black Chant: Languages of African American Postmodernism*. Cambridge: Cambridge UK, 1997.

———. *Writing between the Lines: Race and Intertextuality*. Athens, GA: U of Georgia P, 1994.

Theresa Hak Kyung Cha's Eroticism

JEANNE HEUVING

Theresa Cha was born in 1951 and was murdered in 1982, shortly after *Dictee* was published. Her continuance in *Dictee* contrasts radically with her premature death and underlines the generative relations between continuity and discontinuity in this collage text. It is ultimately in the ways that Cha pursues continuities amidst discontinuities that the poetic and erotic dimensions of her work are most pronounced.

Georges Bataille in *Erotism* explores three eroticisms: emotional, physical, and religious. For Bataille all eroticism has a sacramental character and aims to "substitute for the individual isolated discontinuity a feeling of profound continuity." Bataille writes, "The whole business of eroticism is to destroy the self-contained character of the participants as they are in their normal lives." Bataille emphasizes the "random" nature of our "individuality" and the erotic need to link with "everything that is . . . . What we desire is to bring into a world founded on discontinuity all the continuity such a world can sustain" (15, 19). Whereas emotional and physical eroticism seek continuity of existence within everyday worlds; religious eroticisim pursues this continuity beyond the immediate graspable world. All three eroticisms are present in *Dictee,* and merged.

Much has been made of *Dictee's* discontinuous collage formation as constituted through multiple genres and media. The "missing" or incommensurate elements of *Dictee* have been connected to the ways that emigrant populations in the United States, particularly female populations, are unaccounted for, unrepresented and unrepresentable.[1] Yet, what has gone unexplored is how *Dictee* radically breaks with the contract of classical realist fiction and the self-contained, distinguishable elements of its fictional apparatus. It is in *Dictee's* refusal of this contract—in its continuities—that its poet's novel exists. Let me count the ways, "beginning wherever I wish."

CHARACTERS / PERSONAGES
Classical realist fiction depends on individuated characters, and often on one main character or protagonist, such that its readers will engage with this existence through "a willing suspension of disbelief." This fiction is often realized through third person perspectives, such that the narrative can move seamlessly

without and within a character's point of view. In this way the fiction subor-dinates the worlds in which a character exists to character motivation itself, keeping readers' attention foremost on individual characters.

Theresa Cha's *Dictee* does not concentrate on individual characters, but rather multiple personages. Their identities merge through shared histories and responses and are "exceptional" not because of their uniqueness, but because of the intensity of their responses. They are culled from real life persons and depicted in photographs. The inclusion of their photographs disrupts the readers's willing suspension of disbelief, as we study their faces to find what Cha's elusive descriptions intimate and more.

There is Ya Guan Soon, a young woman revolutionary born in 1908 who was killed at the age of seventeen for leading a demonstration protesting the Japanese occupation of Korea: "History records the biography of her short and intensely-lived existence. Actions prescribed separate her path from the others. The identity of such a path is exchangeable with any other heroine in history, their names, dates, actions which require not definition in their devotion to generosity and self-sacrifice" (30). There is Cha's mother forced to live in China at an early age because of the Japanese occupation of Korea:

> Mother, you are eighteen years old. You were born in Yong Jung, Man-churia, and this is where you now live. You are not Chinese. You are Korean. But your family moved here to escape the Japanese occupa-tion . . . . [Y]our MAH-UHM, spirit has not left. . . . Because it is not in the past . . . . You are Tri-lingual. The tongue that is forbidden is your own mother tongue. You speak in the dark. In the secret. The one that is yours. (45).

There is Jeanne D'Arc and of St. Therese of Liseaux—all heroes, all self-sac-rificing. None of the photographs of these heroes and saints are captioned but placed in proximity to the texts which mention them. They could be anyone.

Dictee reminds in some ways of H.D.'s *Helen In Egypt*, but instead of a work about a Western iconic presence, it is about Asian presences. As Ra-chel DuPlessis remarks about H.D., the same could be said of Cha. Cha in serving as "writer, reader, and main character . . . has at least one theoretical effect—of collapsing subject-object distinctions between the thing scruti-nized and the viewer." (106).

SENTENCES / INVOCATIONS

Classical realistic fiction is constructed from well-crafted sentences written in the past tense and made up of clearly identified subject, verb, and predicate relations. Camille Roy in "Experimentalism" describes, "Mainstream fiction assumes a position not too close, not too far away. A situation is implied, an entire social horizon, which is speckled with individuals who maintain distance from one another and from social 'problems'" (174). Mainstream works maintain a "controlled" and "modulated" "distance": "a system that contains and represses social conflict" (175). Roy contends that there are any of a number of real life events that cannot be contained in mainstream fiction without disrupting representation itself.

In *Dictee* much of the seeing, even of distanced events, is up close. Past tense is replaced with present tense in a writing that Gertrude Stein designated as "continuous present." Description becomes invocation as Cha closes down the separation between writer and her others. Complete sentences give way to incomplete sentences, phrases, single words. Words replicate; pun, sound and mean differently.

In the section called, "Epic Poetry," Cha not only invokes her mother but she presents her through an action that persists in her:

> You suffer the knowledge of having to leave. Of having left [. . .]. You are moving accordingly never ahead of the movement never behind the movement you are carrying the weight from outside being the weight inside. You move. You are being moved. You are movement. Inseparably. Indefinably. Not isolatable terms. None. Nothing." (51)

Cha describes the moment she and her mother must leave one country for another, as the scene of embarkation fuses with the stations of the holy cross and with a grammar of inquisition: "Not a single word allowed to utter until the last station, they ask to check the baggage. You open your mouth half way. Near tears, nearly saying, I know you I know you, I have waited to see you for long this long. They check each article, question you on foreign articles, then dismiss you" (58). The "I know you" contrasts with the alienating scenes of embarkation and language inquisition, a knowledge that is intensified through this shared, alienating experience.

Throughout *Dictee,* the word "missing" forges connections between that which does not connect, that which is absent, and that which longs: "Face to face with the memory, it misses. It's missing. Still. What of time. Does not move. Remains there. Misses nothing . . . . The memory is the entire. The longing in the face of the lost. Maintains the missing . . . ". (37, 38). While this passage on one level emphasizes disconnection and the missing, it also propounds memory and longing without end. It "Maintains the missing."

SETTINGS / SPACES
In classical realistic fiction, historical, cultural, and geographical realities are engaged as settings for one or more characters. Classical realistic fiction

limits spatial and temporal relations through creating them as backgrounds for the development of individual characters.

Cha presents historical and cultural scenarios such that they extend beyond their potential to frame or be framed, or to be employed in single cause and effect relations. In the section called "History," Cha quotes from a historical account without attribution, providing a pervading cause for the numbed silences in her work:

> There were soon no less than fifty Japanese advisers at work in Seoul. They were men of little experience and less responsibility, and they apparently thought that they were going to transform the land between the rising and setting of the sun. They produced endless ordinances, and scarce a day went by save that a number of new regulations were issued, some trivial, some striking at the oldest and most cherished institutions in the country .... One ordinance created a constitution, and the next dealt with the status of the ladies of the royal seraglio. At one hour a proclamation went forth that all men were to cut their hair, and the wearied runners on their return were again dispatched in hot haste with an edict altering the official language. (28–29)

In the section, "Love Poetry," the spaces within a theater and within a film become interchangeable. "Love Poetry" begins with the entrance of a woman who could be an anonymous viewer, Cha's mother, or Joan D'Arc as presented in Carl Dreyer's film and portrayed in a photograph at the end of this section: "She is entering now. Between the two white columns. White and stone. Abrasive to the touch. Abrasive. Worn. With the right hand she pulls the two doors, brass bars that open towards her" (94). The movement within this woman's mind and on a whitened screen are conflated: "Drawn to the white, then the black. The shadows moving across the whiteness, dark shapes and dark light" (95). Conveying at times painful social scripts, modern cinema provides painless touch that is pure sensation: "The touching made so easy, the space filled full with touch. The entire screen" (106). The unidentified woman, just as she absents the screen, is named: "She moves

488 • IDENTIFICATION / DISSOLUTION / POLEMIC / BILDUNGSROMAN

now. Quickly. You trace her steps, just after, as soon as she leaves the frame. She leaves them empty. You are following her. Inside the mist. Close. She is buried there. You lose her. It occurs to you, her name. Suddenly. Snow." (114). Snow could refer to the poor quality of the filmic medium itself, or the purity of this woman's affections. On the following page, by itself, as if it is a slogan or even a billboard announcing a Korean Christian church, present- ed in quotation marks: "'The smallest act of PURE LOVE is of more value to her than all other works together'" (115).

NARRATIVES / TIMES

Time in classical realistic fiction is segmented and clarified in relationship to other times. While there are back stories and flashbacks as well as phantasma- goric presentations of dreams and memories, these are identified as such and do not confuse the linear time of the advance of the novel. Provided with an orderly time scheme, the reader can presume a fixed vantage with respect to the unfolding events.

For Cha, the concept of duration and a concern for the quality of that duration is far more important than measured time. Shelley Sunn Wong in "Unnaming the Same: Theresa Hak Kyung Cha's Dictee" analyzes Cha's presentation of time as a "poetics of cleaving." This "cleaving" constitutes an adherence to and separation from events, a being inside and outside of them. As such Cha makes herself continuous with diverse historical times, rather than specifying her relationship to these. Cha writes, "Total duration without need for verification of time" (50). "Heavy, inert is duration with- out the knowledge of its enduring" (156). "She knows during. While she says to herself she does not account for the sake of history. Simulated pasts resurrected in memoriam. She hears herself uttering again re-uttering to re- vive. The forgotten. To survive the forgotten supercede the forgotten." (150)

Secular and sacred, monumental and cyclical times coincide, as repeat- ed references to ritual, including references to the Eleusianian mysteries, are engaged, associated by Cha with the growth of a dandelion: "You wait when you think it is conceiving you wait it to seed you think you can see through the dark earth the beginning of a root, the air entering with the wa- ter being poured dark earth harbouring dark taken for granted the silence and the dark the conception seedling. Chaste the silence and the dark the conception seedling. Chaste you wait you are supposed to you are to wait for the silence to break you wait for the implanting of some dark silence some constant as a field distant and close at the same time all around sound far and near at the same time you shiver some place in between one of the dandelion seedling vague air shivering just before the entire flower to burst and scatter without designated time, even before its own realization of the act, no premonition not preparation" (156).

OBJECTS / THINGS

Classical realistic fiction hierarchizes existence, almost always making things in the world objects for character definition or use. While the narrative may pause, belabor or study some small piece of existence, a stone, for example; the stone is ultimately located somewhere, on a beach, whereon gazes or walks the protagonist. Cha in Dictee presents the singularity and presence of things apart from their use, augmenting the materiality of actual things, the thingness of things.

In Cha, speech itself is a thing, which haunts her in the expectation of its delivery: "She mimicks the speaking. That might resemble speech . . . . Bared noise, groan, bits torn from words." And then in italics: *"She would take on their punctuation. She waits to service this. Theirs. Punctuation. She would become, herself, demarcations. Absorb it. Spill it. Seize upon the punctuation. Last air. Give her. Her. The relay. Voice. Assign, Hand it. Deliver it. Deliver"* (34).

One of the documents collaged into *Dictee* is a copy of a handwritten letter dated August 16, 1920 from an unknown sendee to one Laura Claxton. Cha never explains by how she came by this letter, with its respectful, stilted, and agrammatical writing: "Dear Madam I will write in regards to your sister. She in an awful shape. She threatens to kill her self and her children and husband has done all they can possibly do and spend every sent to dr. her they can get and they are having a time. She is afraid of going crazy. No dr can do her any good she has been to them and none do any good at all but she wont give up goes all the time to them she spends all the money to dr instead of to get her something to eat. And she is afraid to eat. The Drs say it will just take time. All she wants to do is ride the roads and these horses are all old and wore out and very near dead from hawling her on the road . . ." (146-147). Although this document does not attach to the main historical and political situations portrayed in *Dictee,* given the Anglo identified name of Laura Claxton, it provides evidence of unaccounted for trauma and desertion. As such, it holds its own space, its own materiality and eloquence, apart from the dictation of *Dictee* itself.

CODA

If Theresa Cha had continued to live past her thirty-first year and gone on to create additional art and literary works, *Dictee* might have been an exceptional work in her evolving *opus,* but one work among others. *Dictee* has acquired an unusual status in the study of experimental works because of its biographical containment, created through Cha's premature death. If there is an illusion that is created through and that hovers over this work, it is that of "immaculate conception."[2] While this is attributable to the text's preoccupation with silence and its deliberateness in inscribing a blank page, it also has to do with the surprising qualities of this work and the short-lived aspect of Cha's life. The discontinuity of Cha's own life cuts into the eros of Dictee with a violence that has created amongst its readers a devotion to its continuance. This erotic continuance marks the poet's novel.

NOTES

1. See in particular Lowe and Wong.
2. This work, which has been taken up largely by literary commentators, is less singular when contextualized in relationship to Cha's engagements with multiple arts, including film, visual arts, and performance. See Lewallen.

WORKS CITED

Bataille, Georges. *Erotism.* San Francisco: City Lights Press, 1986.
Cha, Theresa. *Dictee.* Berkeley, CA: Third Woman Press, 1995.
DuPlessis, Rachel. H.D.: *The Career of that Struggle.* Bloomington, Indiana UP, 1986.
Lewallen, Contance M., ed. *The Dream of the Audience: Theresa Hak Kyung Cha* (1951-1982). Berkeley: U California P, 2001.
Lowe, Lisa. "Unfaithful to the Original: The Subject of Dictee." *Immigrant Acts: On Asian American Cultural Politics.* Durham, NC: Duke U P, 1996. 128-153.
Roy, Camille. "Experimentalism." *Biting the Error: Writers Explore Narrative.* Ed. Mary Burger, Robert Gluck, Camille Roy, Gail Scott. Toronto: Coach House Books, 2003. 174-179.
Wong, Shelley Sunn. "Unnaming the Same: Theresa Hak Kyung's Cha's *Dictee.*" Writing Self, Writing Nation: *A Collection of Essays on Theresa Hak Kyung's Cha's* Dictee. Berkeley, CA: Third Woman Press, 1994. 103-140.

A Fragmented Whole for Renee Gladman's *Toaf*

DANIELLE VOGEL

The book that would have a chance to survive, I think, is the book that destroys itself, that destroys itself in favor of another book that will prolong it.

—EDMOND JABÈS

Out of this bewilderment, I thought, one could attempt to make a project: a house, for example.

—ALDO ROSSI

Many arrive at the threshold of a book already assuming its parameters. We've learned to name a thing—before we even enter—*fiction* or *poetry*, *memoir* or *essay*, *literature* or *philosophical text*. Somewhere along the way, I began to unlearn this. I found myself drawn to books that slipped between and among these lineations. As they bewildered me with their unexpectedness, they called my body and thinking into focus: I experienced a new kind of correspondence occurring at the level of the language.

Within this conversation, I recognized language as a living organism inhabiting the place of the page, inviting me to take part in its transference. Without rigid delineations, these books more accurately represented what it was like to be in the world—this place that is at once physical and contemplative, a place constantly reshaped by our thoughts and desires.

These texts[1] have taught me that in language as in experience there is a profound and incredibly active connection between linearity and fragmentation, between progression and displacement, and that it is within these assumed dichotomies that a kind of entirety exists.

• • •

In Renee Gladman's *To After That (Toaf)*, a slim book of prose in which a (possibly fictional) memoir bisects a novella, we experience this sense of entirety through fragment. *Toaf* is a story of books converging, a past displacing a present, and one city interrupting another. In its unfolding, it demonstrates how language acts as an apparitional architecture capable of conveying the complexities of experience and memory. As Gladman builds its world for us, *Toaf* interrupts us with its composition revealing a fragmented totality, a completeness that we are very much a part of. In this essay, I would like to write through what *Toaf*'s accumulation and its conflation of genres reveal about the correspondences between linearity (i.e. any trajectory of time), experience, and language.

In its memoir state, *Toaf* performs a eulogy for the "failed" novella *After That*. As it eulogizes this failed manuscript, it also eulogizes the passing of time—its accretion, its confusions—as it becomes a kind of fiction. While Toaf acts as an archive of excerpts from the never-to-be-released novella *After That* it also serves as an account of the book's having been written: "I finished the final version of the novella *After That* sometime late summer 2003, after two extensive re-writings and probably two (less intense) re-workings and countless line and paragraph edits, plus two shelvings and one almost-utter shredding, and then I ran outside" (27).

As described in *To After That*, the novella *After That* carries the subtitle, "When I was a poet" (9). *Toaf*, then, becomes the caretaker of that "when I was," acting as a tensile structure laid across points in time: the time of the writing of *After That*, the multiple times of its revision, the time of not-writing *After That*, and the time of *Toaf*, which also encompasses periods of writing and not-writing. The memorial opens a new, genre-less space. A space that is at once whole and interrupted, wherein, through the fragmentation of books and times, a complete body comes into focus: the combined body of author and book bridged through the body of the reader.

•   •   •

In language, as in architecture, we are inhabitants. In every aspect of our living, we find ourselves within structures—a grammar, a home, a body. As we inhabit these structures, trajectories are formed creating an invisible, constantly shifting, geometry. Interrupting or fragmenting their infrastructures without completely altering them, we create a more complete version of each through our having interacted with it. We extend their architectures.

Wanting to learn more about built structures, I looked to architect Aldo Rossi's *A Scientific Autobiography*. Rossi's book, like Gladman's, writes through the history of his architectural projects as "a succession of unfinished or abandoned undertakings, or a pursuit of the unexpected appearance of some new event" (54). This *new event* resulting from some unfinished project interests me. It suggests that innovation appears through a succession of failures, showing up, unexpectedly, when we think we are headed somewhere else. Both Gladman and Rossi might agree that failure is productive, that whether or not one arrives, there is much to be gained in the unfolding.

To that end, Gladman tells us, "You risked the syntax when you wanted to make a place for the gaps. In writing [*After That*], I needed to say, 'I left the house,' plainly, in orchestration with other plain sentences, such that their combining would produce a newer, deeper effect. All plain would somehow become all cloudy" (41). The suggestion is that within a novella that privileges very direct, simple sentences there exists a silence or clearing that allows for the appearance of some "new event" to haunt the text. These gaps Gladman speaks of act as generative narrative spaces, interrupting the reader, where, within that interruption, a space separate but connected to the book emerges (the "new event" I discuss above). Toaf, on the other hand, reveals gaps of another kind—gaps that, rather than happening at the level of the sentence, exist between the excerpts (of After That) and the explanation of the excerpts. These gaps occur in the intervals between writing and not writing, between memoir and fiction. Toaf explores what happens in those translational spaces and finds something that can never completely be revealed but that will always haunt the infrastructure of the book.

In *A Scientific Autobiography*, Rossi explains, "the fragment in architecture is very important since it may be that only ruins express a fact completely" (8). Rossi is suggesting that a building fragmented, in its debris-state, may more accurately represent the full potentiality of what a building can and has contained—it reveals the "dimension of what we did not intend to see" (*Aldo Rossi Drawings* 253). Rossi seems to be implying that in ruins, a thing more accurately portrays its inner sense of completion. The gaps created by fragmentation produce an unexpected totality, immeasurably translatable. Through rubble, we can aggregate an animated whole. But, in a sanitary, uninterrupted space, there is no debris to jar us into reading. Placing these architectural ideas beside the conventional infrastructures of genre and narrative trajectory, we can see that Gladman's *Toaf,* as it choreographs a series of failed spaces, reflections on those failures, and gaps, creates within that dynamic a space capable of being infinitely extended by the reader.

• • •

Early on in *Toaf,* we are told that the problem of the novella *After That* was its failure to feel completed as a manuscript, that no matter how many times it was edited, it never appeared composed enough to send off for publication, and as the book sat, time went, taking the author with it, leaving the novella and its concerns behind.

Toaf became a way to have *After That* through the "story of its failure" (71). In moving between fragments of the failed book and reflections of that failing, we not only get to experience that lost book and this new book taking shape around it but also we get a glimpse of another book—a book below these readable ones, one whose bounds are hard to define but whose presence we recognize. *Toaf* lets us see a fraction of that extended space through its meditations on having written, and in doing so calls our focus to all the times an author is outside of her book, in the world, and how when the author returns to her pages, she brings the world with her. Gladman teaches us about the interruptive, yet reciprocal relationship between the body and its language. She tells us, "Writing was about coming home 'half the person' and looking into the space of language for a refill. But not just to put back what the outside had taken, also to add some new information. To graft the day's terrain onto the previously accumulated—so to make a great big map" (14). Gladman describes for us language's ability to pleat, to backstitch a person into place, its ability to inform as it creates a complex, sympathetic map of presence.

· · ·

In the opening pages of *Toaf* an exceptional thing happens: Luswage Amini,[2] a fictional character from a series of novels that seem to post-date *Toaf*, is brought into this reflective space. Gladman tells us, "Luswage Amini, the great Ravickian novelist, once conferred to an interviewer: the first novel will be given to you from the remains of some other's long lost project" (9). Though, seemingly added to justify why one might not know where a book is going, the quote more interestingly, acts as an oracle foreshadowing not *After That*, but its future, memorialized state. And thus the complex map of *Toaf* is revealed. Novella bisecting memoir to create something beyond the immediate dialectic of each, a third book, a new novel, which will appear out of the remains. But what are these remains? Most obviously, the excerpts from *After That*, but maybe also the traces that language cannot always convey, those gaps that belong to the author but also to the reader.

After That began as an intimate translation, "That is," Gladman tells us, "I put my ear to the left side of the journal and transcribed on the right" (10). The page speaking its sequence. The narrator (not exactly Gladman) gathers what she calls "apparition" into story. And here, time elapses in three separate but communal spaces: the space of the page/story, the space of the narrator's physicality (the city that holds her), and the eventual space of the reader. Right away, we know that the book *After That* is concerned with more than its narrative, it is a book whose secret is the strangeness of succession and language as they relate and interrupt time and presence.

Writing, Gladman tells us, takes place "somewhere in between" (14). I think reading, too, occurs in that *between* space. Language, as it accumulates, confuses life and fiction, the body and its etherealities (15). Language and its resulting books are "partial, a shaving from some whole, somewhere else" (19). And while reading interestingly continues this fragmentation, within this activity is this hidden writing that I've been talking about, whereby the reader senses the "immeasurable totality," the story that exists somewhere between language, failure, and time lapse.

As a fragmentary work, *Toaf* reveals a communal body that striates an innumerable series of spaces—through its past and its desire for the future, through thought and through language. The writer tells us in *Toaf* that her "challenge was to build, out of a series of empty spaces, a cohesive narrative long enough to be called a novella, but not so long nor so cohesive that it suffered from chronology" (42). This confession is told to us about *After That*, but it also reveals something vital about *Toaf*'s accumulation. Gladman is building, through language, a cohesive structure that invites inhabitation. Her sentences, her failed book leaning through another, and even her displacement as author in time, perform a fragmented but communal logic, one that calls us into a collaborative presence. Gladman does this through calling attention to the shifting presences that are held not only within this book but also in ourselves. So this leaning that occurs between books (*Toaf* and *After That*), author and the fictive character of herself, present and past, extends further into the reader. We become a street or bridge through which the text completes itself. We become a fragment dovetailed into the book, our ear pressed against the sentence. Gladman's aim to create through *After That* a book which calls attention to the strangeness of being a person in time, alongside language, alongside the passage of both is further realized through our displacement as we read. Slowly accumulating over the course of *Toaf*, we can see the concerns of the novella grafted and complexly realized as they are revealed. There are things *After That* wanted to say through story that only became possible through its fissure.

• • •

Toaf is a meditation on our poly-presences both within and without language—how we come into grand focus through our capaciousness. The architecture of language can hold all of this. Our bodies hold all of this.

After That and *Toaf* and the third gap-space created as we read them serve as substratums of one another upon which a new plane of trajectory and understanding is able to exist. As they interrupt one another, they make room for questions of language and experience to arise. Through *Toaf*, Gladman reveals an immeasurable whole. As she allows seepage between genres and books, between author and reader, between times, she offers us a map of a new narrative space, one that privileges language above genre, one that invites us to take part in a conversation, an interrupted unity, that is ever ongoing.

NOTES

1. Just some of which are Clarice Lispector's *The Hour of the Star*, Marguerite Duras' *Yann Andréa Steiner*, Hélène Cixous' *Promethea*, and more recently, Richard Froude's *Fabric*.

2. Luswage Amini is "the great Ravickian novelist"—a character from Gladman's cycle of novels, *Event Factory* (2010), *The Ravickians* (2011), *Ana Patova Crosses a Bridge* (2013), and *Houses of Ravicka* (2017).

WORKS CITED

Adjmi, Morris and Giovanni Bertolotto. *Aldo Rossi Drawings and Paintings.* New York: Princeton Architectural Press, 1993. Print.

Gladman, Renee. *To After That (Toaf)*. California: Atelos, 2008. Print.

Rossi, Aldo. *A Scientific Autobiography.* Massachusetts: The MIT Press, 1984. Print.

Three Ways to Sunday
The Mandarin by Aaron Kunin

BRIAN BLANCHFIELD

While Virginia Woolf was revising *Orlando* and then fielding its reception, she was making notes on and fleshing out a new idea for a novel she felt would be her most artful and most experimental, a return to form after lighter fare. She wanted in this novel, her seventh, which she thought first to call *The Moths*, a new sort of narration unrooted to a single person, one that would nonetheless offer "a mind thinking," a perspective that would be distributed among and patterned across the characters and entities in the novel's world: not only the several characters there whose lives would develop and intertwine from childhood on, but also the boats and night sky and nightingales and moths and waves of that world, which would together speak to a different understanding of time. "Life itself going on" would tell the story of *The Waves* (Woolf, *A Writer's Diary*, 140).

By design, narrative control seems in *The Waves* to inhere only in the sound room, so to speak, cueing and turning up certain live microphones, numerous and ready for selection to mix in. In shorthand references to the book and its methodology in her own notebooks, she referred to it as "a poem-play," "a play-poem." It was a revelation to her when she hit upon the idea of beginning the novel at a long table outdoors, overhearing six children at their morning lessons, under the guidance of a person who could seem to call upon each—young Bernard and Neville and Jinny, et cetera—to produce or import a parcel of speech that would demonstrate a grammatical principle or usage "and build up by that person the mood, tell a story . . . and so on . . . , and boats on the pond; the sense of childhood; unreality, things oddly proportioned. Then another person or figure must be selected" (141).

"I see a ring," said Bernard, "hanging above me. It quivers and hangs in a loop of light."

"I see a slab of pale yellow," said Susan, "spreading away until it meets a purple stripe."

"I hear a sound, "said Rhoda, "cheep, chirp; cheep, chirp; going up and down." (*Waves*, 4)

It is a kind of game we overhear as Woolf's novel begins, and a template in miniature for the book's method. Alternation among speakers—primarily in monologue—carries the entire novel, is a vehicle for its developments. There is no exposition outside of quotation marks, and all action is inferred or reported rather incidentally in the characters' monologues of midstream consciousness, never narrated. Alternation among speakers—even as the characters themselves come to occupy different cities and countries and reconvene variously, even as time seems to advance and recollect, retread and advance again, across a lifetime—proves durable as a formal vehicle. You read the novel *by* it, and you read the novel *across* it. Which is the quality of poetic form, as such, and the central indentifying characteristic of Aaron Kunin's 2008 novel, *The Mandarin*, very much influenced by Woolf's innovation, and regulated by the methodology she discovered for *The Waves* eighty years prior.

Keeping the novel in play.
The three central characters in *The Mandarin* are likewise busy upholding a book-length conversation, (there is a fourth primary character, Natasha, but she is asleep for the great majority of the novel and participates only in somniloquy, toward the end), busy working into circulation anything that is introduced into it, including the notion of the novel itself.

"Novel," said Hallamore. "An object of pleasure."
"Novelism," said Mercy. "A discredited ideology."
"Novelist," said Hallamore. "One who subscribes to it."
"Novelization," I said. "Becoming a novel."
"Take this menu," said Mercy. "Turn it into a novel."
"For that I need a pencil," I said.
"Use whatever you normally use," said Mercy. "Whatever you normally do, do. Show us how happy it makes you."
"But I don't write novels in order to obtain happiness," I said.
"What are you going to put in your novel?" said Hallamore. "Try to put everything you know about candy bar machines in it. You could write it with a candy bar . . . and the words might come out coated in chocolate."
"There are lots of things you could put in it," said Mercy. "There are trees. There are people. The chalk is white. The sun is shining. None of these things is true."
"The big boy," said Hallamore. "The dark boy. The boy with the hat. A cut lip. Funny. Huh. Kind of a funny boy. Very dark. A little dark.

Not a very nice boy. Talk this way all the time, and you won't have problems." (Kunin, 57)

This representative passage that opens the three-page Chapter 19 (of 57), "Novelization," demonstrates the method of Kunin's poem-play novel. A new or recovered idea or material object is remarked, and the remark is immediately countered or modified; indeed it produces new speech, and thereby instantiates and propels the book's system, and the dynamic of this disputatious and mercurial late-adolescent three-way relationship, which subsists on it and other unlikely food for thought: the newspaper, the telephone, a loaf of bread, a public appearance in Minneapolis by Saul Bellow, tea (or masturbation), a lost umbrella, or a plan to visit an ex-boyfriend. Any element introduced is fuel, input, for the pulsing circulation that accommodates and treats it, and is not especially significant of itself. Once bandied and exchanged in the turns at speech, the element has entered the system and may be manifested later. As the element is circulated, a scene develops, and when the element has been fully treated, metabolized and converted to other energy, the chapter can conclude. Indeed, the formula is simple, as Hallamore advises Willy, the narrator and writer (whose novel put Natasha to sleep before this one started), "Talk this way and you won't have problems."

He lays out one of the rules of the game of "becoming a novel" in this tradition. Once something is put into currency, any play is a play off the preceding play. As in a strategy game, in cards, when one play is over, the next has begun, by definition. Or in hackeysack (a better comparison: no one wins), a pass is the beginning of your own performance with the bag. And—as in good conversation—your play can add value to the prior play by arising from it, relative to it, extrapolating, mirroring, tailoring. Poetry likewise; a line turned well and fluidly from the line break before, and perhaps borrowing or countering a cadence or shape from above, improves the prior line by springing from it. These systems of contingency, performance, discovery, and recursion are not usually associated with the novel.

A few lines later in "Novelization," Hallamore is still regarding Willy and the menu Mercy has given him with her challenge. "He has written five sentences," said Hallamore, "with just one word." The word is indeed the one he himself has spoken to begin the chapter, the one on which the five opening variations pivot. A page later, as happens throughout *The Waves* as well, an opportunity is found to reinstate and vary the remark, now with the nominated word in a new position, "He wrote five novels," said Hallamore, "with one wolf" (62).

Talk is itself creative in this mechanism—and determinative. Early on in Chapter 5, because Mercy continually reintroduces as a topic her former place of employment, Gelpe's Old World Bakery, her testy former employer is herself produced for the scene ("'Are you still talking out there?' said Leah Gelpe") and the conversation continues unbroken but wholly transported to the bakery several years earlier, when it was still open. Leah joins the ongoing council. She is soon maestro of the same interlocutory magic that manifested her and brought her some business. "'Describe your umbrella,' said Leah Gelpe. 'The lost article goes to the one who can describe it best, as though you could make an umbrella appear by just talking about it.'"

In the central dinner scene in *The Waves*, when the six friends gather again in young adulthood to bid adieu to their heroic and tragic friend and beloved Percival (who like Natasha does not speak) and Bernard notes about the table's centerpiece that it is "now a seven-sided flower," comprising the seven perspectives on it (Woolf, 74). Mercy and Willy and Hallamore build the umbrella by offering competing accounts of what it must be like and what it may have suffered. Hallamore wins the description contest; his umbrella provides the most coverage. "My umbrella is a perfect novel," said Hallamore [whose first name we learn at the end of the book is Bernard], "because it gives everyone a chance to talk and no one can read the entire thing" (Kunin, 43).

Leah Gelpe, ever the rule-monger, plays another vital service to *The Mandarin*. It is she who notes the first violation of form. When Hallamore wishes to buy something in order to stay at Gelpe's with the others, he grows desperate when they're out of day-old bread even.

> "I do want to buy something," said Hallamore. "Here, look, I'll take—one of these." A pack of gum.
> "A pack of gum!" said Leah Gelpe. "You have got to be kidding! We don't even sell that; you brought that in here; I'm not going to sell you that." (43)

A pack of gum.

"A pack of gum," in Chapter 5, is a rare instance—beyond dialogue tags—of language outside of speech in *The Mandarin*. Outside of quote marks, the phrase can only be narration, and narration has been a prohibited play in this novel, since the long dialogue began. "You brought that in here; I'm not going to sell you that," Leah Gelpe announces (23). A pack of gum imported via narration cannot be inventoried, however much a player wishes to gain purchase for it: unattributed, it cannot be accounted and is outside of established trade. After all, without a narrator, whose would it be to offer?

Aaron Kunin is in *The Mandarin* as well. The author has provided, in addition to a prefatory synopsis, an index; so it is simple to verify. "Aaron Kunin" may be found on pages 29 and 118 of the book, in the latter instance indirectly in a remark by Willy: "'I'm not a very literary outcast at all' I said, "'but I do have the same initials as Alfred Kazin.'" He actually frequents the novel a bit more than the index allows, usually shadowing a determination that Willy is a failed novelist. A couple pages earlier we hear Willy trading "outsider" credentials with Mercy and Hallamore: "I don't consider myself an outcast from literature, but Reynolds Price says that I'm uncommercial." (Kunin received his Ph.D from Duke, where Price was a legendary professor.) Another chapter ends with a kind of complaint, this time in Hallamore's voice, while he and Mercy sort through and put away Willy's prize essays and fellowships, which he reviewed too often and which therefore turn to ash in the grapefruit box they find for storage: "'The spirit wants to award money,' said Hallamore, 'to Renee Gladman'" (41).

Purchasing the pack of gum you brought into the store is like beginning a novel you just elaborately synopsized in your preface. Currency itself, or commerce, is desirable, but only once value is canceled out.

Of course it is one sense Aaron Kunin who puts the illicit pack of gum in Hallamore's hand. In one of two other unattributed first-person sentences proliferating in that chapter, the novelist is apprehended by Leah Gelpe, who demands the pastry bag which had become a writing implement. "So I had to leave my work in progress, *The Busman's Holiday, a novel,* in icing on yellow cake, in a state of incompletion." It is then Willy, properly within quotation marks, who accepts the blame, restoring order to end the chapter. "'I'm sorry I ruined your cake,' I said" (23).

It isn't that the hand of Aaron Kunin is unwelcome in his own novel (questions of the infelicitous autobiographical novel are not of concern here) or that his world (ours) proves the constructed artifice of the one in *The Mandarin*. Quite the contrary, the characters agree that the "outside" world is marked by no seam in a novel's fabric. We watch them arrive at this conclusion when, at one point, answering an accusation of Mercy's about treatment of women in his novels, Willy equivocates:

> "Rape is a problem in the novel," I said, "as it is in Minneapolis (but not a social problem)."

"But, I mean," said Hallamore, "if crime is on the rise in the novel and not in Minneapolis . . . "

"Doesn't Minneapolis include the novel?" said Mercy. (61)

There is no reason indeed, the three concur, that the crime rate in Minneapolis should exclude crime that happens in novels set or written in Minneapolis. Of course it is a bit self-serving for them to so reason. The characters are likewise undeceived by the presence of Aaron Kunin, and unperturbed by it, since it seems he may not speak, and may not therefore operate its equipment as they can. Indeed the primary characters seem to have agreed on a reasonable world view that explains his existence and their own contestable agency.

"We all have an Aaron." says Mercy (29),

Our better angels.

"We all use puppets," said Hallamore, absently arranging his hair in a way that made him look inhuman. "We call them Aarons, because Aaron was Moses's puppet in ancient myth. I am the Aaron of Leah Gelpe: I speak for her to the people."

"We all use spokespersons," said Mercy, backing into a wall.

"We are all mouthpieces," said Hallamore, without opening his mouth.

"You are all bullshit artists," said Leah Gelpe, rolling up her sleeves, "and brilliant young things pontificating."

"We all have an Aaron," said Mercy, ripping pages out of a book and scattering them on the floor. "I am the Aaron of Hallamore, because no one else will believe him or listen to his voice."

"I feel ridiculous in this sweater," said Hallamore, and started to pull it over his head.

"I am the Aaron of Natasha," I said. "Is that right?" (29)

Hallamore's comical addition to the collaborative explanation ("we are all mouthpieces") is not as contradictory as it first appears. Puppet can be said to speak for puppeteer (is used to speak), but it is equally true that puppeteer speaks for puppet (voicing him).

It is in interesting that although their elaboration for Leah Gelpe indicates that each has an aaron, the assertion is that "we *all* have an aaron." The misstatement on further inspection is demonstrably true, even in the interstices of this very dialogue. Again a touch of sacrosanct narrative infiltrates. The unseen hand is dollplaying here, in the puppet discourse, as in none other. Mercy is shown "backing into a wall" and Hallamore "absently arranging his hair."

The respective aaron that *each* has, the several aaron, each has *in one another*, according to the discussion. And the pairings the characters nominate here indicate that the aaron relationship is one of power and fidelity. It is an additional peculiarity of their world that each character also has, at times when guidance is needed, "a biology teacher." He can be called upon to remind him or her of best practices in his or her physical life.

In this novel without plot, without action or standard exposition, a novel nearly all talk, in which turns at speech produce other turns at speech—a game of plays—in which speech is heard or overheard across divisions in time or space or consciousness, concentration falls on who the characters are respective to one another, in relationship. As Kunin writes in the synopsis:

> Relations between characters are predominantly fraternal-sororal. The characters don't seem to have parents (although in Chapter 8 Willy addresses Mercy and Hallamore as "Mother" and "Father"), and they don't seem to be capable of producing children . . . Occasionally one of the characters conceives a kind of infatuation for one of the others, but this feeling is consistently one-directional: if Willy has it, Mercy and Hallamore don't have it; if Mercy has it, Willy and Hallamore don't; and so on. And if Natasha has it, no one knows about it. (iii)

They are a rather fluid resource for one another. They seem to answer any interpellation. When Hallamore expresses the desire to sleep with Willy ("'Willy, I want to fall asleep in your bed,' said Hallamore, 'I want to wear your clothes, I want to eat the food out of your mouth'"), Willy becomes the reluctant beloved the situation demands. When Mercy circulates the notion further ("If Willy and Hallamore fall asleep next to each other") doing so seems to enact the occurrence: the next three chapters each begin "'They awaken in the same bed,' said Mercy, 'and their memories are momentarily confused'" (35, 37).

When identities can be upset or even transposed easily, when agency is subject to suggestion, there is nothing essential about a person, beyond the familiar or genius of his biology teacher. At least in this world, a person's existence is instantiated only in relation to another. There is some liberty in it. If, speaking in the same room with her counterpart, a person decides to telephone him instead, he answers the call and the relations adjust.

"You've become a Board of Welfare for me," I said. "You control my thoughts by making it impossible for me to think of anything else."

"I must learn to content myself with proximity," said Mercy. "To become indispensable . . . until there's no difference between the contents of our heads, yours and mine."

"Being inside a person's head is not the same as knowing a person," said Hallamore. "It's not even a way of knowing."

"I hate the way you behave in restaurants," I said. "And on the phone. You stand in front of everything I want to look at, and your voice intrudes in every conversation, until I start to answer you in your own voice and wonder who is speaking when I speak."

"Who is speaking?" said Mercy. "What voice do I hear? When you open your mouth, who speaks?"

"The telephone is speaking to you," I said. "The novel is speaking to you. Literature is speaking to you—through the telephone. I feel about you the same way I feel about the police or the FBI or a collection agency. It seems that your feelings about me are strictly juridical, which means that they aren't exactly feelings anymore."

"I'm sorry, you're breaking up," said Mercy. "You say you want to talk to Hallamore?" (125)

Of course Mercy may pass the phone to Hallamore; she is his Aaron.

• • •

Virginia Woolf was, as early as 1918, sure about what she wanted to borrow from poetry for her prose. She regretted that books proper to her chosen genre "respect illusion devoutly all the time." She admires about Byron's *Don Juan* that it is the "most readable poem of its length ever written":

> a quality which it owes in part to the springy random haphazard galloping nature of its method. This method is a discovery by itself. It's what one has looked for in vain—an elastic shape which will hold whatever you choose to put into it. Thus he could write out his mood as it came to him; he could say whatever came into his head. He wasn't committed to be poetical; and thus escaped his evil genius of the false romantic and imaginative. (*Writer's Diary*, 3)

The distributive and recursive methodology Woolf uncovers by telling a novel entirely and continuously in voices attuned to one another, in and out of one another's company, achieves the elastic fabric she admired in Byron. After the example of *The Waves*—for anyone testing its ability to accommodate and shape what comes to mind—the novel is no longer opposed to sharing authorship with "life itself going on." "Talk this way all the time, and you won't have problems."

WORKS CITED

Kunin, Aaron. *The Mandarin*. Hudson, New York. Fence Books. 2008.

Woolf, Virginia. *The Waves*. Oxford University Press, 2014.

Woolf, Virginia. *A Writer's Diary*, ed. Leonard Woolf. Mariner Books, 2003.

Romantic Substance
Reading *Leaving the Atocha Station* with the Künstlerroman

LYNN XU

Hypothesis: Intoxicated by the intricacies of its own making, the poet's novel makes psychic operation itself the spectacle. This is what Valéry observes in Descartes' philosophical writings, and perhaps the source of pleasure he derived from reading them. "I will say that the true method of Descartes should be called egoism," he writes, "the very workings of thought . . . the vicissitudes of lucidity and will, the interventions and interferences [that] enchant the amateur of the life of the mind."[1] For Valéry, the power of the Cartesian Cogito lies not in thinking per se, but in the moment of its enunciation. The phatic force of an old world power, as Rosmarie Waldrop reminds us: "I have no thoughts, I only have methods to make language think."[2] It is this felt-movement of thought that is on display in Lerner's *Leaving the Atocha Station* which, by making aesthetic life itself the drama, returns us to the Künstlerroman, a family of artist-novels, of which Goethe's Werther was its herald and fated harbinger.

The Künstlerroman, a sub-species of the German Bildungsroman, takes the artist as its hero and protagonist. The presumption of the Künstlerroman, writes Herbert Marcuse in his 1922 habilitation thesis, is "the opposition of art and life."[3] The ensuing struggle to overcome this debilitating dualism, therefore, assumes that a primordial unity exists, between subject and object, idea and reality, art and life. As a specific social type, the artist is thus himself an "embodiment of negation . . . 'he stands alone, over and against reality'."[4] How the Künstlerroman resolves these struggles will divide the genre into early and late periods, Marcuse insists: the early Romantics (citing here Tieck, F. Schlegel and Novalis) create a "dream-like world which in the final sense [is] no longer problematic to the artist," while the later (Brentano, E.T.A. Hoffman and Eichendorff) are forced to find more practical transformations, in order to meet the demands of social or political reform.[5] But both trajectories take us right to the heart of the Künstlerroman: the critique of *Bürgerlichkeit*, the bourgeois mode of life. Regarding *Die Leiden des jungen Werthers*, Benjamin writes: "Goethe provided the bourgeoisie of his day with a perceptive and flattering picture of its own pathology, comparable to the one supplied by Freud for the benefit of the modern bourgeoisie."[6] What Freud gave us—more than the tools to administer our own diagnosis, more than this new method of reading—was the permission to be pathological, to greet our pathologies as existential qualities of the modern man.

To read *Leaving the Atocha Station* in the company of the Künstlerroman is, therefore, to read Adam Gordon's infatuation with his own fraudulence as a species of romantic thinking and, in turn, to recognize the limits of this reading by observing where the stakes have shifted to find footing in our contemporary world. The apprized dualisms between subject and object, idea and reality, art and life, can no longer be delineated as such. Fractured beyond recognition, we can seek no holistic comfort. For Adam, romantic striving is available only as an artificial hum:

> Night-blooming flowers refused to open near the stadium lights. Freedom was on the march. Aircraft noise was having strange effects on finches. Some species synchronized their flashes, sometimes across thousands of insects, exacerbating contradiction. Why was I born between mirrors?[7]

For a moment the world acquires symphonic shape. Taken from the penultimate paragraph of Lerner's novel, these sentences seem to take inventory of a slew of news headlines, declarative insofar as they admit a strident lyricism, which I find extremely beautiful—but only because it (this lyrical voice) so clearly understands itself to be a stage—a petrifying, atmospheric, sentience seeking purchase for the final question. "Why was I born between mirrors?" But lamentation can no longer make mimic cry—or, does so only to consign itself to fact, a statement which fails the reach of pathos. Our sympathies, what pains I feel or take share in, are somehow erased, made less, by lucidity—as if not fraudulence, but *eloquence*, was the sickness, the addiction, letting no thought or feeling escape the clarity of its discursive script.

This eloquence, I will say, is the signature of the autopoiesis we find in the Künstlerroman: "the self-reflexive, self-critical, self-production of the subject (das Ich) [whose] goal is the representation of the unrepresentable, the pure ego."[8] In Novalis' *Heinrich von Ofterdingen*, for example, the famous Blue Flower leads to a vision of self-generation. And in E.T.A. Hoffmann's *Der goldne Topf*, Anselmus is a copyist who learns to write poems by reproducing texts. Poetic creation and the creation of the subject become one. Inscribing himself onto the larger narrative of literary production and discursive thought, onto the poetic-philosophical system in and through which he is, in turn, produced, Adam is designed to be a foil onto himself. His self-effacing logic rehearses a metabolism which contaminates our senses, so much so that we begin to hallucinate its waking voice. Self-reflection takes on punishing form. We are trapped by it, as by a system of absolutes, which is nothing but the ease of Adam's rhetorical flourishing, his sleights of hand. A system of poetics, we discover, the program of Ashberian verse.

> It is as though the actual Ashbery poem were concealed from you, written on the other side of a mirrored surface, and you saw only the reflection of your reading. But by reflecting your reading, Ashbery's poems allow you to attend to your attention, to experience your experience, thereby enabling a strange kind of presence.[9]

This is the sign under which *Atocha* is narrated. Adam's own strange narrative presence is the result of Lerner offering us just that: a second-order experience, mediated by pills, hash, the internet, various news sources, the form of online chat, art, poetry, the Spanish language, the act of translation, History, other people, himself, etc. . . . technologies which condemn us only to mind's shadow; as seen from the backside of a mirror, unable to face ourselves, we face a self-denial which in praise of its own virtual life deprives the original of any reason for being.

Divided into "phases" of fellowship research, *Atocha* operates more with the movements of a Beckettian score than any stringent sense of plot. As if the practice of writing could thus be staged, a coming-of-age as a coming-into-reading, the narrator trundles on, through various acts of looking and of reading and increasingly we find his actions and logical leanings falling under the formal appetencies of an Ashbery poem.

> *Phase one*: The first phase of my research involved waking up weekday mornings in a barely furnished attic apartment . . . then putting on the rusty stovetop espresso machine and rolling a spliff while I waited for the coffee . . . I would open the skylight . . . and drink my espresso and smoke on the roof overlooking the plaza . . . .[10]
>
> *Transitional phase*: The ability to dwell among possible referents, to let them interfere and separate like waves, to abandon the law of excluded middle while listening to Spanish—this was a breakthrough in my project, a change of phase.[11]
>
> *Phase two*: In this, my project's second phase, Isabel assigned profound meaning, assigned plurality of possible profound meanings, to

my insight and latent eloquence and because she projected what she thought she discovered, she experienced, I liked to think, an intense affinity for the workings of my mind.[12]

This self-possession we attribute to routine, the way the novel opens (waking up, making coffee, smoking on the roof... and so on), this sense of the concreteness of life, quickly dissolves, until indeterminacy (as a poetic principle) becomes a value Adam internalizes in his person. "The ability to dwell among possible referents," as well as the pride he takes in his "latent eloquence," are discoveries which elides a method of writing with ways of behaving in the world.

In phase three, Adam claims that the impossibility of representing certain experiences forecloses the possibility of inhabiting them. And yet, precisely by denying their existences as such, as moments which can be actualized and thus felt, they retain their "negative power"[13] and become available to us as a kind of texture:

> *Phase three*: These periods of rain or periods between rain in which I was smoking and reading Tolstoy would be, I knew, impossible to narrate, and that impossibility of experience: the particular texture of my loneliness derived in part from my sense that I could only share it, could only describe it, as pure transition, as slow dissolve between scenes, as boredom, my project's uneventful third phase, possessed no intrinsic content ... During this period like all periods of my life were called forth to form a continuum, or at least a constellation, and so, far from forming the bland connective tissue between more eventful times, those times themselves became mere ligaments. Not the little lyric miracles and luminous branching injuries, but the other thing, whatever it was, was life, and was falsified by any way of talking or writing or thinking that emphasizes sharply localized occurrences in time. But this was true only for the duration of one of these seemingly durationless periods; figure and ground could be reversed, and when one was in the midst of some new intensity, kiss or conclusion, one was suddenly composed exclusively of such moments, burning always with this hard, gemlike flame. But such moments were equally impossible to represent precisely because they were ready-made literature, because the ease with which they could be represented entered and cancelled the experience: where life was supposed to be its most immediate, when the present managed to differentiate itself with violence, life was at its most generic, following the rules of Aristotle, and

one did not make contact with the real, but performed such contact for an imagined audience.[14]

The "texture of the contemporary,"[15] a phrase Lerner uses in an interview, refers necessarily to the larger poetic, philosophical, cultural and historical systems in and through which such a subject (like Adam) can be produced and likewise sustained. As is the problem with "lyric miracles," the (lyric) "I" can no longer convince itself that there is a position to speak from which has not already been dissolved by the coordinates of its speaking voice. "I came to realize that far more important to me than any plot or conventional sense was the sheer directionality I felt while reading prose, the texture of time as it passed, life's white machine."[16] Both a body and the technological hum through which it passes, "life's white machine" permits a dissolution against which it can no longer defend. What is "texture" but the authenticating power of mediation itself?

As such, given purview into Adam's interior life does not grant the character interiority in the traditional sense, but contributes to the production of a kind of surface akin to the palimpsestic consciousness we find in Woolf's *The Waves*, an aquatic clarity we can skate on. Equally entranced by his mirror-like quality, Adam indulges in himself as a carrier of experience rather than the bearer of certain pains or pains of uncertainty.

> *Phase four*: I believed I saw she saw right through me. Or I saw her see herself reflected in my eyes, saw that she knew, or was coming to know, that was interest I held for her, all of it, was virtual, that my appeal for her had little to do with my actual writing or speech, and while she was happy to let me believe she believed in my profundity, on some level she was aware that she was merely encountering herself. This anxiety was characteristic of my project's fourth phase.[17]

What begins as a singular angle of perception ("I believe") soon refracts ("I believed I saw she saw") and snowballs into a line of self-alienating vision ("Or I saw her see herself reflected in my eyes")—forcing Adam to face himself as a form of mediation. Likewise, anxiety takes on a formal power because it requires that temporality itself be the alterity of experience. Anxiety, spiraling inward with dream-like lucidity, divides him against himself, such that every encounter acquires the ludic face of an involution whose deictics lie elsewhere.

Entering his final phase, we find Adam shade increasingly into the apprized realm of the virtual. In this passage in particular, time seems protracted, one big mass or current, in which one shifted merely from waking to fatigue to further sleep.

> *Phase five*: I woke up in the fifth phase of my project as if in response to a loud noise . . . I went back to my apartment and refreshed the *Times* . . . I could feel the newspaper accounts modifying or replacing my memory of what I'd seen: was there a word for that feeling? The only other feeling I registered was fatigue. I fell asleep and when I woke it was dark.[18]

Amidst this we learn that civilians are injured from a bomb at Atocha Station. Adam watches a video online showing footage from security cameras of commuters "leaving the platform littered with bodies and stained with blood."[19] For a while he stands in line to give blood but is turned away for feeling sick. He tells himself that the donation trucks were "probably still there only so people could feel like they were contributing. They probably don't even need any more blood, he reasons; and are there only to offer consolation to those who, like himself, wish to be included by History, taking contributions in exchange for the symbolic currency of individual worth, in the face of something as abstract and faceless as History with a capital H. "I thought about how blood from my body might have been put into the body of someone injured by History."[20] This thought reads like a totem borrowed from dream logic, calling upon the active boundaries of the surreal to reestablish contours of the banal.

To reason through the quandaries of political action under the aegis of a literary logic returns us to the problem of thinking morality with aesthetics. If Schiller recommended that the cultivation of our senses provide training wheels for how we should behave in public life, then has this apprenticeship in the Lerner gone terribly awry? By turning into a poem (or, more precisely, by treating himself as something that can be read and is, at best, a poem) Adam fulfills his narrative contract in the Künstlerroman tradition. But tarrying in the antechambers of Romanticism does not diminish his vitality in our contemporary world.[21] Rather, amid the debris of old forms, the nature of his character is further illuminated:

> But my research had taught me that the tissue of contradictions that was my personality was itself, at best, a poem, where "poem" is understood as referring to a failure of language to be equal to the possibilities it figures; only then could my fraudulence be a project and not merely a pathology; only then could my distance from myself be rede-

scribed as critical, aesthetic, as opposed to the side effects of what experts might call my substance problem, felicitous phrase, the origins of which lay not in my desire to evade reality, but in my desire to have a chemical excuse for reality's unavailability. But wasn't my relationship with substance also fake? . . . Or was that the lie, the claim that my excessive self-medication was simulated . . . had I stepped into the identity I had projected . . . had mythomania become methomania? I less thought than felt these things on my skin as I wandered the city.[22]

Restlessness of the eighteenth-century subject for self-improvement seeks aesthetic repair. But our contemporary subject seeks only reparation for "reality's unavailability." Aesthetic education, rather than providing us with the trusting compass of idealism, further embroils us in our disillusionment. Only fraudulence can make claims for truth. And reality, whatever it is in *Leaving the Atocha Station*, is caught in the fractal flowering of its ever-dividing face.

NOTES

1. Valéry qtd. in Suzanne Guerlac's chapter titled *Valéry* in *Literary Polemics: Bataille, Sartre, Valéry, Breton*. Stanford: Stanford University Press, 1997. Pg. 108-9.
2. Dissonance. Tuscaloosa: The University of Alabama Press, 2005. Pg. 209.
3. Herbert Marcuse qtd. in Barry M. Kätz. "New Sources of Marcuse's Aesthetics: Schriften 1. Der deutsche Künstlerroman, Frühe Aufsätze by Herbert Marcuse." *New German Critique*, Spring 1979, 176-188. Pg. 177.
4. Ibid. Pg. 180.
5. Ibid. Pg. 181.
6. *Selected Writings*. Vol. II, Part I. Trans. Rodney Livingstone. Ed. Michael W. Jennings, Howard Eiland and Gary Smith. Cambridge: Harvard University Press, 1999. Pg. 164.
7. Lerner, Ben. *Leaving the Atocha Station*. Minneapolis: Coffee House Press, 2011. Pg. 181.
8. Helfer, Martha B. "The Male Muses of Romanticism: The Poetics of Gender in Novalis, E.T.A. Hoffmann, and Eichendorff." Germany Quarterly, Vol. 78, 299-319. Pg. 301.
9. Pg. 91.
10. Pg. 7.
11. Pg. 14.
12. Pg. 46.
13. This phrase recurs in the novel. For example, on pg. 39: "And translation

would further keep my poems in contact with the virtual, as everyone must wonder what Arturo or Spanish was incapable of carrying over from the English, and so their failure, their negative power, was assured."

14. Pg. 64.

15. In his interview with Jason Rehel at the *National Post*, Lerner says: "I'd like to think [Adam] reveals—as characters in any serious novel reveal— something about the texture of the contemporary."

16. Lerner, pg. 19.

17. Pg. 84.

18. Pg. 117-9.

19. Pg. 210.

20. Ibid.

21. In Benjamin's essay on Goethe, he uses the phrase "tarrying in the ante-chambers of idealism" to describe the German author's work, *Wilhelm Meister. Selected Writings.* Pg. 179.

22. Pg. 164.

WORKS CITED

Lerner, Ben. *Leaving the Atocha Station.* Minneapolis: Coffee House Press, 2011.

Stupendous Lore
Poet's Novels by Tan Lin and Pamela Lu

PATRICK DURGIN

The work of Chinese-American writers Tan Lin and Pamela Lu is involved with at least three problems. The first is identity. The second is the novel, from the point of view of poetry. The third is facticity, that condition of truth that modulates what fiction can or ought to do. These problems coalesce in the motif of "ambience," and ambient music in particular. I will survey some of the ways these problems are articulated and propose a way of thinking about ambience that amplifies the commonality of several works by these otherwise often very distinct literary stylists; ambience is not a style. Ambience is anything remaining available beneath a certain threshold of attention—a kind of lore whose superficiality is matched only by its ephemerality. It is not unreal, but it is really stupefying.

Identity

Pamela: A Novel, Lu's first book, described as "the last masterpiece of the twentieth century" (Wilson 9), uses experimental narrative techniques to question the relevance of avant-garde ideology to negotiate the more precarious facts of hyphenated identity. *Pamela* chronicles the artistic and amorous quasi-liaisons of a group of ethnically marked and/or queer student-artists, writers and philosophers in their formative years, mainly their hilariously confounded conversations—not much actually *happens* in the book. Proper names are jettisoned and replaced by pronominal initials (L, R, P), most significantly "I." As "I" lapses gradually into a putative "we," what was at first a question of belonging becomes a polished monument to myopia. In the first published review of the book, poet and novelist Aaron Kunin describes beholding this monument as a "mystical experience." Her second novel is possibly the first masterpiece of the 21st century; *Ambient Parking Lot* is written from the point of view of a "we," a band of musicians/field-recordists whose self-image is crowd-sourced to the fickle singularities of personal taste, reluctant mentors, and mutinous collaborators. Here the group is a musical collective negotiating the stipulative confines of cutting-edge pop sub-culture, enamored with received notions and rote tokens of infamy, sold on the idea of never selling out. Both novels temper the wry detachment and monumentality of avant-garde ambition by using liminal subject positions as an engine, taking risks formally where substantiation is elusive. Lu has even described herself as a sort of neo-avant-garde everyman:

> I never in my life thought of the avant-garde as being an elitist aesthetic (its social/historical exclusivity, of course, is another matter); rather, I saw it as a natural transliteration of an identity and an existence that could not possibly be satisfied with neat, one-to-one correspondences between language and lived experience. So-called experimental writing, therefore, became a sort of ESL, an unpretentious vehicle for representing and inhabiting the still not fully explored reality of living in a cultural, political, and linguistic diaspora. ("Some Thoughts on Ethnicity and Language")

Also straddling the turn of the century is Lin's "ambient stylistics" series, beginning with his *BlipSoak01* and *Seven Controlled Vocabularies*, both marketed as poetry, through very recent "ambient" novels such as *Insomnia and the Aunt* and *The Patio and the Index*, installments in a larger project he calls *Our Feelings Were Made by Hand* (the title is derived from a sentence late in *Patio*). Lin's elective affinities (not least in his capacity as an art critic) ground ambient stylistics in the historical avant-garde. Like Duchamp's predictions of primary structures and specific objects, or really any old saw of post-minimalist aesthetic theory, Lin's point about style is relative to mediation rather than intention, stylistics rather than style per se. In *Patio*, Lin writes,

> For my father, all the things that were broken in America (and all the parts of things that were broken) could talk, and what they said was "America" ... but from my point of view, things looked diffident and mostly delusional, like a watery hologram of the all-American object—in the same way that Marcel Duchamp once took a used bicycle wheel and made it into something that it wasn't but in fact was. ... [T]he Immigrant Experience ... is basically when the words for the things of the world die before they get to the things they are supposed to take care of, except that the words for those things never die, they just become lies, a kind of handicapping system for the imaginary dictionaries and the crimes of the world. (unpaginated)

So much for "one-to-one correspondences," like "imaginary dictionaries," with postcards and family photos purchased at flea markets, the illustrations in Lin's novels offer an image of what "wasn't but in fact was" described in the language like a hallucination. In *Seven Controlled Vocabularies*, brackets, often empty, punctuate statements with potential meanings, "a kind of handicapping system" for the readerly imagination's inevitable interjections. In an earlier installment of *Our Feelings*, Lin corroborates his father's claim that "it's a lot easier to lie with photographs than without them" (*Ambience Is a Novel with a Logo*, unpaginated). But it's that much easier to lay broadly corresponding paths through the narrative, also. *Insomnia* and *Patio* are footnoted with Google reverse-search results that masquerade as hypertext but are inert. A reverse search reads the relevance of images or tracks a digital inlet back to an IP number. Using an image as a "search term" hoists upon that image the burden of fact, treating it as prose, while tracing how a site visitor managed to "hit" upon a page involves a metric of sense, like verse and its associations of statement and sonority. While lending these works the "ambience" of extensity, what reader-response critics used to call "intension" prevails. "[A] novel becomes the place where the eye stops reading the words that are there" (*Seven Controlled Vocabularies* 144). Lin calls this form of reading "sequencing" in light of the belatedness of the search results, and their obvious impertinence (they resoundingly fail to inform, so as footnotes they fail as well). But that doesn't make them mere elements of style. They are there to remind us of that other application of "ambience," as when an effects filter is applied to a dry recording to evoke "live" sound by degrading or designing its resonance. Tempering the burden of fact with a measured dose of fiction this way is a way of saying that "Writing a novel is a variant of writing a poem" (132).

Just as the Ambient Parkers, Lu's protagonists, rely upon others to justify their existence—to put the (plural) there there—in the form of the Station Master, a reluctant mentor, and the Automotive Dancer, a mutinous collaborator, Lin's best known work of ambient stylistics (also a generic hinge between poetry and prose), *Seven Controlled Vocabularies* flaunts its "voice and data holes: most notably, where is the 'China—Poetry' of the first L[ibrary of] C[ongress] subject heading? To get some of this book you have to go outside it," to its ambient content ("Writing as Metadata Container"). "Subject headings," he explains, "are conflict-prone near ethnicity/identity issues." What makes the Station Master of the local underground radio program reluctant is that, to mean what he is poised to mean for their career profile, he must engage in lore, assume, that is, the mantle of advisor about matters that are only fodder for superstition. "What you've created here isn't music," he complains at first. "At best, it's a representation of music, a conceptual trick, a pathetic substitute for the real thing," finally admitting, "we are united...in this campaign of daily toil and invisible striving, fueled solely by our faith in a listenership" (69, 70). Similarly, *Pamela: A Novel* begins by "Returning to the subject," which we quickly learn is a question of the adequacy of "a series of gestures" to "real life," a question of "manners": "I was a very poor impersonator of myself in public" (13). The axes of nationalism and heterogeneity that have characterized the debate of Asian-American identity since mid-20th century[1] and that debate itself are axiomatically and opportunely vacuous, according to the filial functions that stand in for characters in these works—like integers in an equation[2], which is of course the logical form of identity.

> [I]t was never simply being sexual or being a minority or being a sexual minority that mattered in itself, but the various combinations thereof that produced confusion and triggered those politicized art-forms that repeated clichés of "displacement"... "[I]dentity-related" experiences...ultimately affirmed everyone's masochistic desire to be conflicted and to stay that way. ...[W]e could only be real, really real, when we mimicked the representations of ourselves as they appeared in theory, commercials, and general conversation... [W]e were always expiring before ourselves... "[L]iving" post-structuralism...made us feel both immensely important, for having the ironic self-consciousness that we were fictional, and immensely unimportant, for being fictional in the first place. (*Pamela: A Novel* 20)

I recently asked Lin about the mixed authenticity of the scrapbook-like items illustrating the ambient novels, to which he replied, "I think there is a desire, in fiction, to make something real and in real life there is always the wish to transform something, to make it into a version of itself. So I was interested in this double (blind) operation, and seeing it occupy the same place so that there is no meaningful distinction between making something real and making something fictive" (email). Yes, the author constitutes the "I" who narrates *Pamela* and the "I" whose father is the subject of *Patio* and whose aunt is the subject of *Insomnia*, but only as a constituent of a living irreality prone to what we want from the real. The "us" in Pamela may be "forever amateurs in the art of self-representation," for example (18). But this labor of love was determined by "the only available world in which we could choose not to believe" (49). "Love was always part of our story, or we were part of its story, for if we were lucky enough to escape from love, then there still remained the problem of the love story, which persisted in hounding us in the form of cowboy westerns, therapeutic pep-

518 • IDENTIFICATION / DISSOLUTION / POLEMIC / BILDUNGSROMAN

talks, and episodic contemporary coffee commercials" (49, 51). If the amity at the etymological root of the term *amateur* siphons passion to circumvent expertise, the dis-fluency indirectly apparent to these first- and second-generation protagonists is only directly audible in its ambient aspect. Lin's "father" "had a pronounced Chinese accent which I could not hear but which produced endless grammatical errors that I was extremely sensitive to"—"the only part of [the aunt] that I *can* recollect" produces a "linguistic biography," the "understanding" of which causes "a delay in the speed of an understanding... In other words, the proper study of an aunt is a delayed aunt, like a father who has passed away" (unpaginated). The Ambient Parkers look to the Station Master for validation but receive only inspiration. They look to the Automotive Dancer for illustration of their own ideals, but they finally become a catalyst for her more singular, mature practice and, in a disquieting irony that pervades the penultimate chapter of the novel, overhear *her* being interviewed about *them* on the airwaves, rather than the music they provided as a platform "to personally undergo the torture [they had] in mind"—the Ambient Parkers are depicted "cross-legged on a shabby oriental carpet with a repeating floral pattern" that rhymes with the "circle of nodding heads" that meets the dancer's every suggestion (153-4). Patterning, sequencing, semi-voluntary swarms of attention are motifs of the ambient stylistics series perhaps largely because identity is expressible only at the threshold of experience, being, like music, its natural platform, a creature not unlike poetry. Ambient music may be a genre, but its mode presents to listening something like the experience of being dimly read on the surface of events, intensely real but immaterial.

In a recent essay, Yunte Huang compares the "telephone game" otherwise known as Chinese Whispers to "all instances of textual reproduction that direct attention to the acoustic dimensions of language" (54-6). The sound relation is, pace C.S. Pierce, a "real" relation of "contiguity" (rather than similarity), just as homophonic translation renders any sign a proper name, indices "foreign to any language, because they are not semantically constrained," being instead "presentable in any language but belonging to none" (56-7). Hence "what's specifically Chinese in the Chinese Whispers is the very word 'Chinese' itself, which is derived homophonically, through hearsay" (54). Huang here refers to the "poetic conflation[s]" of Marco Polo which reveal "the sound origin of currency...increasingly important when we move into the twenty-first century economy of the intangible...ethereal streams of data, images, and symbols" as it brushes against the "localness of monetary imagination," themselves pervasive themes of *Seven Controlled Vocabularies* and *Ambient Parking Lot* (58-9). Gilles Deleuze famously calls the "proper name" that which is non-identical in an encounter, the nonce of ethnic marking (*Negotiations* 6-7). Sianne Ngai develops the term "stuplimity" to describe the "aesthetic uses of tedium" quoting Deleuze's *Difference and Repitition*: "we define a word by only a finite number of words. Nevertheless, speech and writing, from which words are inseparable, give them an existence hic et nunc; a genus thereby passes into existence as such; and here again extension is made up for in dispersion" (para. 17). Though another touchstone (as one works through the Kantian concept of the sublime) would be Derrida's *The Truth in Painting*, where the notion of the par-ergon is deconstructed as the "*almost* too large," a tepid average rather than the quivering and finally earth-shattering experience of intelligent design that is, for the transcendental critique, the exception that proves the rule of the categorical imperative. I would argue that *lore* is "hearsay" honed to the pitch of legend; lore is to advice what jargon is to definition—or "terminology" (Agamben 207-9). And this is how identity appears, only to dissolve, in Lin and Lu's poet's novels.

Sickbed scenes are pivotal in *Ambient Parking Lot*; the Station Master, Automotive Dancer and the Ambient Parkers alike undergo transformations, though the latter is anti-heroic—"We awoke...to the sounds of our unspectacular existence" and hear only "commuters off-boarding...as they headed to work" (187). Disabused once more and for all, they believe now in what they have heard about their mission, rather than authorizing it on their own. In his review of the novel, poet Devin King recounts the legend of the birth of ambient music as, according to Brian Eno, an accident, and according to Judy Nylon, a collaborative experiment. Nylon brought Eno a tape of 18th century harp music. He had been hit by a taxi and was laid up, recovering. Nylon presses play and leaves the room, and left to his own devices, Eno struggles to attend to the music:

> the amplifier was set at an extremely low level, and ... one channel of the stereo had failed completely. Since I hadn't the energy to get up and improve matters, the record played on almost inaudibly. This presented what was for me a new way of hearing music—as part of the ambience of the environment just as the color of the light and the sound of the rain were parts of that ambience.

Ambient music tests plausibility at the cusp of inaudibility, and the choice it presents to the listener becomes an aleatory organizing principle of the composition. The truth value of the coining of a sub-popular musical genre in 1975 captures only so much, *almost* too much to be plausible, hence the hint of disingenuousness in Eno's "heroic" account; Nylon claims they worked together to balance the music with the environmental noise, like unwitting ensemble players in an ad hoc studio or experimental clinic. Like Beckett (in Ngai's analysis), Lin and Lu demonstrate how "the gradual accumulation of error often leads to the repetition of a refrain" (para 19). According to Ngai, "stuplimity" is the characteristic affect effected by works whose "simultaneous layering of elements in place of linear sequencing" forces a degree of "utter receptivity" to differences that are "modal" rather than "formal" (para. 9). Astonishment and fatigue are combined. "The stuplime [of anti-euphoric tedium] resides in the synecdochal relationship between these minute materials [proper names, the index] and a vast ecology of repetition and agglutination" much like the novelistic elaboration of Lu collapses into its own disfluent effects, and automotive culture thrums through the modular spaces of a parking structure (para 21).

Lu and Lin traffic in stupendous lore, but in markedly different, if equally ambient ways. *Pamela: A Novel* opens with the routine description of a curious character, charming the reader with the narrator's interest and interesting the narrator in the events this character's circle of friends and foes will develop. But instead of unfolding, the events are deferred by more and more description, producing a sense of unending self-discovery. Selfhood turns out to be a feckless achievement, though. With very little left to do, discourse takes the place of events, and philosophical dialogue overtakes plot. In email, Lu mentions the influence here of Dostoevsky, Kleist, and "Kirkegaard, whom I love because he basically wrote philosophy & theology in the form of fiction, and the collected pantheon of his various pseudonyms and fictional alter egos reads like a meta-fiction in itself, a meta-novel of the life of Kierkegaard." *Ambient Parking Lot*, rather, takes cues from the encyclopedic mode of Flaubert's *Bouvard and Pecuchet* or Melville's *Moby Dick*; the Ambient Parkers are exhaustive "speed-readers" of the geological blip that is urban-planning, automotive culture, geopolitical precarity (13). Lin, on the other hand, celebrates the transmissive spew of reproductive technology, comparing the aunt to her beloved television, "so minor, beautiful and post-colonial...She feels like the weakest of descriptions of things I can no longer see," such that in her actual absence "the world can finally be made to unfurl without the violence of the feelings that normally attaches to them." In the digital era, "forgetting isn't over, it just needs to be reinvented by databases." Hyphenated identity is the statist sanction of an ambient lore, avowals floated on a slipstream as much hereditary as digital. In any case, narratological givens are transformed from formal to modal elements of the stuplime—"what" finally *is* the only difference between prose and poetry[3]—but a stuplime production whose novelistic delays rehearse the impossibility of moderation in relation. They emit ambient advices that flit through what's said, playing a game of "Chinese Whispers." Early in the novel, the Ambient Parkers swap stories in an effort to "recognize the difference between ambient narrative and lyric," a difference that mirrors the nature/culture dichotomy in a quasi-Darwinian assembly line of obsolescence and neo-Pleistocene grandeur (31, 14). "In the vast determination of this landscape novel, living things were consigned to the backdrop," a "backdrop of synthetic particles" they ever record but never perform, hic et nunc (32, 14). Civic planners replace authors: post-war highway expansion policies, late-capitalist information super highways, the spit and polish and "lazy drawl" that "crept into [the Ambient Parkers'] speech as we read nature guides and chewed on leaves of grass" (129).

The (Poet's) Novel

Insomnia is advertized as an "ambient novel" containing, among other things, "an index to an imaginary novel." Removing the bright yellow dust jacket reveals a white paperback whose cover reads simply "JACKET HAS BEEN REMOVED." *Seven Controlled Vocabularies* distinguishes "books [that] fuction as labels rather than mirrors," the former being "generic" such that "removing the jacket...is the best way to create a kind of empty enclosure... or closed parking garage without it...[T]here is no plot and/or character" to be indexed or with whom to identify, as one stands before their own (self-) image in a looking glass (78). Beside the "less than visible things beyond the book" which are infinitely available to indexical marks—the mirror is "manual" and the label is "digital" ("Index and the Expanded Preface"). "One never really knows what is beside a parking lot or a book" (*Seven Controlled Vocabularies* 78). Referral-cum-deferral, the lives depicted form a "'living' post-structuralism," to cite "I." The Ambient Parkers, meanwhile, sample and play the pavement whose anonymous parking spaces recombine work and leisure as modular points between a story's very stuff. "[S]et out in pursuit of the ideal mobile community," enjoying the "convincing yet ineffective theater of privacy" that "only the automobile could offer," they negotiate a "love-hate relationship with [their] source materials" (13, 12, 154). The Station Master prophesies the extinction of the automobile, the "melting, liquefying into primordial asphalt" of a "byproduct of geology that never quite reached the spark and drive of refined petroleum . . .

[W]ith this crude substance," he advises the fledgling musicians, "let us pave the globe" (119). But their music is always-already "indelibly" reminiscent of this essential obsolescence.

The book, like a parking lot, shares the dilemma of the novel, which may in fact function like a mirror for that labeling function we call poetry. The novel is less a fact than a coping mechanism for the stupefying fictions of culture; stories are our way of escaping the narratives that actually fate us. The relationship of stupefaction to facticity is the problem poetry wants to be; the dubious ontological status of that artwork called *literature* can be considered the burden motivating poetry's self-styled exceptionality, whereas prose of most kinds enjoys a vigorous cogito.

Reading Lin and Lu's poet's novels reminds me of Robert Creeley's introduction to Objectivist poet Charles Reznikoff's 1977 novel *The Manner Music* (a title that is hard to write, since the word music is italicized—I have even seen it written with a comma inserted after manner, to *inflect* the word "music"). The novel is, he says, semi-autobiographical. The protagonist, Jude Dalsimer is a musician forced to find a livelihood elsewhere, whatever his talents (on the hammered dulcimer, setting his words to sonorous meter—this the same Reznikoff of *Holocaust* and *Testimony*, proto-conceptualist prose poems whose praises were sung by the Bach aficionado Louis Zukofsky). The blissful stupor of music as novelistic fodder dramatizes poetry's existential crisis, both traditionally forced to swap extensity for utter intensity. Creeley describes "Reznikoff's power as a poet, always, and now in this novel, without exception, is his singular ability to state the case—not the right answer, or the wrong one—but the *case*" (8). Decidedly not heroic, fantastic, or even compelling, Reznikoff's manner is like an exercise in forensics: evacuating discourse and pragmatics, leaving behind only obstinate, unique and indifferent matters of fact. To this end, Creeley gives him the last word: "With respect to the treatment of subject matter in verse [or in this novel] and the use of the term 'objectivist' and 'objectivism,' let me again refer to the rules with respect to testimony in a court of law...The conclusions of fact are for the jury and let us add, in our case, for the reader" (8-9). Those brackets contain Creeley's interjection.

This has everything to do with how the poet's novel is claimed or disavowed by its author. Rezknikoff abdicates conviction to a reader from whom fantasy and heroism are summarily withheld, yet the identification of his manner-music with poetry sharply contrasts with Lin's gnomic pronouncements regarding the state of poetry—usually in prose—under conditions of readership resembling less a book than "perfume," ambient music, RSS feeds and other virtual tickers. It makes him especially unlike Lu, who to my knowledge has never written a book of poetry. Yet the poet's novel might be just the kind of novel that withholds routine cues for the deduction of morals, sentiments and approbation, while calling attention to the facts that are too near to notice, and keeping them excessively *there*. In this sense, she writes "as a poet," while Lin is a poet with much to say about the state of the novel.

The novelist pays attention to fact, but more so to plot, which Aristotle theorized as the medium of plausibility. And the novelist pays attention to language, in its literal or denotative features (what linguistics call its substance) as well as its literary effects (poetics). Yet the implausibility of what the *Tel Quel* authors called *signifiance* means another type of attention is due. In the poet's novels of Lin and Lu, acts both literal and literary have effectively identical conditions of plausibility. This has everything to do with how authors identify with respect to the isomorphic purport of the poet's novel as genre, a snug fit between the fact of being a music and a message. Quoting Francois Chatelet, Deleuze affirms post-structuralism's optimistic recourse to music: "It has this virtue: to act through a subtle matter, to render sensible the materiality of movements that are ordinarily attributed to the soul" (*Dialogues II* 165). This plays into the Deleuzian post-identity program, as well as his ambition to produce a hybrid-genre of "pop philosophy": "[B]eyond a minority-becoming, there is the final enterprise of the becoming-imperceptible" (*Dialogues II* 45). Ambient music is non-identical. It is wallpaper, in the air, dispersed and pneumatic. It is cool, subtle material immateralized or immolated—the materiality of movements, becoming-imperceptible.

It is like what Walter Benjamin called an "aura," the "new beauty" that picks up where the storyteller left off. With the increasing incommunicability of experience, the novelist's "counsel is less an answer to a question than a proposal concerning the continuation of a story" (86-87). Unable to counsel, the novelist can merely inform; "information" is the new currency, and rather than the miraculous consistency of lore, data is only as good as it is plausible, and so "it is no more exact than the intelligence of earlier centuries was" (89). "Boredom is the dream bird that hatches the egg of experience"; its operative value is "unraveled" by the novelist "after being woven thousands of years ago in the ambience of the oldest forms of craftsmanship" (91). What survives this proto-cybernetic paradigm shift is a kind of "storytelling that thrives...in the milieu of work" (ibid.). The storyteller reminisces and the novelist remembers, according to Benjamin, and citing György Lukács, he furthers the distinction by substituting the novel's morbid "meaning of life" for the "moral of the story" (98-99). With all of this, I want to argue that this description is even more relevant to poetry. *All* poetry is lore, insofar as it is self-perpetuating—a kind of work song or reflexive goad to sing, like the muses invoked at the cusp of an epic recitation, but one which never quits, ceaselessly deferring the narrative in order to subsist. Poetry is obsessed with milieu because it has no place to be. Hinging itself to the novel substantially transforms poetry's lack of "*cis*-Apocalypse," to cite a modern epic poem, i.e. its lack of standing this way or that (Tolson 249). Ambient music works as counsel, in its self-perpetuating diminution, just as poetry sings *of* its continuation *for* its own sake, having nothing else plausible about it, not even its medium. As Lin puts it,

> Fiction or non-fiction, conscious or unconscious, language is the ephemera of daily spoken life, or maybe we should reverse that saw: daily life is the ephemera left behind by the language we spoke. If Language is infinite and endlessly self-generating, like some organic cell that spontaneously divides and mutates a structure, it is also a series of dead formulas, stale jokes, archetypes, unmemorable ads, clichés which are rigidly scripted by the rhymes that stick in our head, by the country and city we live in, the social world we hang out in, the Nissans and Fords we drive, the soap we shower with, the friends and lovers we have, the t.v. shows we half-listen to, the dog we talk to— and this world, far from being infinite, is also empirically quantifiable. Language is a census or counting device. We all have various transparent selves, each of which we inhabit in language. How might we make its transparence in our everyday world known? By allowing it to count and reference the things we know. ("Information Archives" unpaginated)

Similarly, in his introduction to the Alice novels of Lewis Carroll, Lin points out that both "begin with dullness, pass through fantasy and end with talking (back to dullness)," an uncannily pertinent description of both of Lu's novels, not to mention the published installments of his own *Our Feelings Were Made by Hand* (xxix). Somewhere between Dadaist chant, *bildungsroman*, and aesthetic-political polemic, every text I have mentioned here does what *Alice's Adventures in Wonderland* does— according to Lin, "It teaches the adult (Alice is an adult before her time) that nonsense is both possible and necessary; it also teaches the adult that nonsense is a regressive fiction that one wakes from and waking from, then mourns" (xxxi). Contemplating their "silence and invisibility" as transparently "important," the character-functions of *Pamela: A Novel* cite the opening sequence of *Sesame Street*, that proto-hybrid-genre series offering itself up as "a harmonic, multicultural neighborhood" that is "less a place than a time of day,"

> [T]his was one of those rare good scenarios of "there" coming here to us, since television was the perpetual "here" that managed to go everywhere with hardly any effort at all . . . all this gave us the sensation of movement even when we were sitting absolutely still, and the impatient pitter-patter in our chests was like a shift in our core awareness, the first stirrings of emotion. It was as if television had trained us to be nostalgic from the start, so that we yearned for childhood while we were still children and continued to be nostalgic for the present moment before we had finished living it. (29-31)

In *Insomnia and the Aunt*, a similar time warp stems from the aunt's dislike of live broadcasts, which make too readily apparent how she seems to be "a part of the anthropology of somebody else's TV set," the set itself being "furniture that moves like a glacier through American life...[F]or an immigrant...America is not the images on a TV, it basically is the TV." Being the audience to the aunt's viewing is "deeply optimistic and romantic" for the narrator, while the non-reciprocity between the audiences for a simulcast Boston Pops performance presents "an unwatchable void" to the aunt, whose motel office, where she works the night shift, and the New England lawnchairs on screen proffer a mere family resemblance, "rehearsed once in real life and once on television." Lin is probably thinking of Erik Satie's concept of "furniture music," a first stab at ambient music; just like it sounds, furniture music was meant as decor and unnoticeably played during intermissions between traditional musical performances.

Lin left poetry to pursue "a generic story, Chinese-American Mirror [that] would have...an anti-gravitational, pro-immigration effect," and so "A novel...should be a release from emotions that are distracting us from feeling the things we are waiting to feel (the awkward infusions of the political)" (*Ambience is a Novel with a Logo*). Politics are plagiarized "events" and the awkward realization of such lazy artifice interrupts the soothing "blandness"[4] of the real with language's obtuse and genre-defying singularities. Likewise, "aesthetic judgments" would only "mar" one's desire to "merely think novelistically." The "language" of such a novel "would be subject to the most generic and formless reading spaces" (ibid.). Lin's novels follow from his poetry. His first book, *Lotion Bullwhip Giraffe* is in the mode of verse and period style of post-language poetry. But with *Blip-*

526 • IDENTIFICATION / DISSOLUTION / POLEMIC / BILDUNGSROMAN

Soako1 and *Seven Controlled Vocabularies*, prose intrudes and eventually takes over, as do sacrilegious assertions of what poetry *should* do, what it ought to be once its reading platforms are exhausted[5]. In the novels, "should" shifts to "would," shifting from an aesthetic imperative to a textual condition. *Insomnia* closes with a rumination on the motel vending machine the aunt curates like the "inventory of the life of a town that the town itself did not know it was compiling," "local and unlocal" like her amalgamation of dialects, accents, languages, and temporal frameworks (she is "half-English" mostly by virtue of studying a British-Mandarin instructional cassette in reverse). What *should* be art would *be*, *were* it true. Poetry may be fodder for listeners and etymologically poetic nomenclature stems from all things sonorous: sonnet, lyric, etc. What could it mean to listen live, to a novel? The place of language as between the two formless banks of thought and speech-image is an ambient moment, no *where* at all. You can choose to listen to ambience, but its style consists in being heard regardless.

Music and reading are alike because they are temporal phenomena, though they feature distinct investments in narratological time. Are hearing and listening practically distinct? Is listening a practice on par with writing, hearing with looking/viewing? "I hear you": I know what you mean. Can you listen to meaning or does listening produce the hearing of meaning, give one "a hearing"? But meaning is not something you work up to; it is primary. If anything, we work down. According to Deleuze and Guattari "the elementary unit of language" is already "the statement," and the statement functions as an "order-word" ("mot d'ordre" is French for slogan), until distilled at last, all the way from a meaningful performance to the possibility of language (*A Thousand Plateaus* 76). Jean-Luc Nancy offers this distinction: "The visual persists until its disappearance; the sonorous appears and fades away into its permanence" (*Listening* 2). "In terms of the gaze, the subject is referred back to itself as object. In terms of listening it is, in a way, to itself that the subject refers or refers back...the visual is tendentially mimetic, and the sonorous tendentially methexic (that is, having to do with participation, sharing, or contagion)" (10). "[L]istening takes place *at the same time* as the sonorous event, an arrangement that is clearly distinct from that of vision... visual presence is already there, available, before I see it, whereas sonorous presence arrives—it entails an *attack*" (14). "Moreover, sound...propagates throughout the entire body something of its effects, which could not be said to occur in the same way with the visual signal" (ibid.) The "attack" is like a wave, says Nancy, and "as soon as it is present, the sonorous is omnipresent" (15). "So the sonorous place...is a place that becomes a subject...as the architectural configuration of a concert hall or a studio is engendered by the necessities and expectations of an acoustic aim" (17). In the opening scene of *Ambient Parking Lot*, the initiative is taken by the parking lot itself, which, anticipating the group's unconventional use of its sumptuous surface, is both concert hall (or amphitheater) and studio. Nancy rightly wonders if "musical instruments" are "not really amplified bodies...before any distinction of places" (78 n.10, 31). "We watched in rapture as the parking lot cooperated with our long-arm mike and seemed to relax into the session" (*Ambient Parking Lot* 3).

Because readers are anticipated, novelists know what to say to us. Because we anticipate what we know, we can forget it, and do. Of the precipitating incident, really a paving project, that organizes *The Patio and the Index*, Lin's narrator writes,

> People think that time, or perhaps language, makes a patio, but it is really the other way around, and what a patio reinstates inside a life is a kind of vagueness of life itself, or perhaps its future, like a person writing him- or herself notes to be read at a later time. What you are reading is really a patio that is vaguely like me, or maybe like my death.... As the philosopher Henri Bergson noted, "I never pretended that one can insert reality into the past and thus work backward in time." A patio built one summer next to Pabst Blue Ribbon beer is now mainly a side effect or maybe a symbol of a feeling that is no longer expected, which the Chinese as a whole and my father in particular tried to avoid.

Facticity

Facticity stupefies because it demands devotion to a partial vision of events, their subjects and objects. Any juridical and journalistic notion of impartiality is revealed as its opposite by a *literature* that matter of factly resigns itself to giving information or administering evidence.

Lore is the superstitious cousin of advice. The latter descends from use-value in the Socratic sense of apprenticeship (read: work experience). The former is like a command issued from the beyond, hence its veracity is incontestable. Lore is legend reconciled with the real thing to structure a topos (index), a map's legend or key code. As all that is solid melts into air, ambient pop music becomes an ideal figure of the real relations that constitute poetics: author/reader, signifier/signified, narratological elements to one another and/or to sonorous, "poetic" quality, time/space, contiguity/similarity. Having (for the purposes of forgetting) desires, and forgetting them for the sake of kinship (nonce fate) marks the community of knowledge once forged by irony, but now affirmed in/as ambience. You can't *have* what saturates you. Neither can you have what you want. The final words of *Insomnia and the Aunt* evoke "versions of happiness I thought a family *would* have" (emphasis added). In *The Patio and the Index* Lin writes, "Unhappiness can be designed, as history and many world leaders have shown; happiness cannot." He is contemplating the identical "diagram" of a pair of plans for a novel: Plan A concerns his parents' separation just prior to the death of his father and Plan B involves the project his father devised to build with his son a patio, upon the latter's return home from college, perhaps something like a monument to a proverbial empty nest. But also "some lost history that had washed up in Appalachia [the novel is set in southeastern Ohio] and was stamped MADE IN CHINA."

Ambience is a precarious fact. The fact that you are soaking in it has to be pointed out to you, like the old dishwashing liquid commercial. The facts are so much computationally tractable data, and the repository of such facts is the there that was waiting to be there when Stein's Fordist optimism returned to an immemorial America, a landscape already virtually paved but utterly irretrievable, even on foot. The world's facts are well beyond the capacity of human processing. This precarity presents an impasse for Lu's would-be artists. For Lin it is the option, without alternative. In the neighborhood where I live, gentrification is rife. A block from my home, a city mental health clinic was recently closed due to budget cuts, and for a month or so a highly visible protest was conducted by its primary beneficiaries: the building painted with slogans and colorful displays. Days after the protest was squelched and all traces removed, a sign in the window advertized subsidized studio space for local artists, and hipsters by the dozen now file into and out of the building. This reminds me a bit of the father paving the way for a barbeque. Like a cookout, which transfers work for which indoor facilities are imminently available to a context that can only complicate matters, the building of a platform for vacancy is unhappy by design. Only anything or nothing can happen upon such a readied surface. Across the street, a coffee shop stamps its paper cups, "Life is rubbing elbows at the community table." This puts me in mind of the Station Master's advice to the Ambient Parkers, which is not actionable at all, but more like those deflating fortune cookie messages that simply tell us what is, was, or ought to be, rather than telling our fortune: "The inevitability of nature is stalled through human mechanization. Then artifice takes over and the scene is duly reset" (120).

NOTES

1. Timothy Yu's assessment of how this debate shaped the formation of Asian-American poetry as a critical category, in his chapter on the work of Theresa Hak Kyung Cha in *Race and the Avant-Garde*, is an excellent and concise guide here.

2. Lu's "I" becomes a differential equation between "P" and "Pamela" while perpetually contrasted to "R" whose file cabinets are organized by "complete statements of fact, as in 'R goes to school'" rather than ciphers like "school" or pronouns like "she," the latter representing, in conversation "none other than R herself being discussed...by a pair of first and second persons," among which is an "I" who "attempted to build my foundation on a proof by contradiction" (66). But having "failed mathematics and fallen to the level of a mere mortal, or 'sub-mathematician,'" "I" becomes "bored with my own identity crisis" and involves herself with "someone else's" instead (67). The novel's anti-climax involves an epiphany in the form of a fraction, "a vertical ratio, and I, as the lower half of an undefined term" leaving her "more than willing to let the whole subject drop, in the midst of a moment that technically never existed" (97-8). Lin's daunting use of acronyms behaves similarly: "MOSS" is my favorite, "any Mobile Optical Semiotic Surface" that "substitutes for a sense of place" (*Seven Controlled Vocabularies* 135).

3. Ngai's essay opens with a hilariously literal interpretation of Gertrude Stein's question, "What is the difference between words and a sentence and a sentence and sentences." The declarative format is used to "ask" about the difference between poetry and prose in "Poetry and Grammar."

4. In the "Editorial Note" to *Seven Controlled Vocabularies*, Lin writes, "There are numerous errors of omission because blandness has no boundaries. Plagiarism is another manner. It was one of the necessary aims of revision" (10).

5. "As we all know, poetry and the novel should aspire not to the condition of music but to the condition of relaxation" (*Seven Controlled Vocabularies* 22). "The page should turn before you got there" (40).

WORKS CITED

Agamben, Giorgio. "Pardes: The Writing of Potentiality." *Potentialities: Collected Essays in Philosophy.* Stanford University Press, 1999: 205-219.

Benjamin, Walter. *Illuminations.* New York: Schocken Books, 2007.

Deleuze, Gilles. *Dialogues II.* New York: Columbia University Press, 2002.

——. *Negotiations.* New York: Columbia University Press, 1995.

Deleuze, Gilles and Felix Guattari. *A Thousand Plateaus*. Minneapolis: University of Minnesota Press, 1987.

Derrida, Jacques. *The Truth in Painting*. Chicago University Press, 1987.

Huang, Yunte. "Chinese Whispers." *The Sound of Poetry / The Poetry of Sound*. Marjorie Perloff and Craig Dworkin eds. University of Chicago Press, 2009: 53-59.

King, Devin. *Review of Ambient Parking Lot* by Pamela Lu. *Make Magazine*

Kunin, Aaron. *Review of Pamela: A Novel* by Pamela Lu. *Rain Taxi*

Lin, Tan. *Ambience Is a Novel with a Logo*. Cambridge, MA: Katalanche Press, 2007.

——. *BlipSoak01*. Berkeley: Atelos, 2003.

——. "Boredom and Nonsense in Wonderland." In *Lewis Carroll Alice's Adventures in Wonderland and Through the Looking Glass*. Barnes and Noble Classics, 2004.

——. Email to author, April 2013.

——. "Index and the Expanded Preface." *Dear Navigator* (Fall 2010)

——. "Information Archives"

——. *Insomnia and the Aunt*. Chicago: Kenning Editions, 2011.

——. *The Patio and the Index. Triple Canopy* 14 (2011)

——. *Seven Controlled Vocabularies*. Wesleyan University Press, 2010.

Lin, Tan and Chris Alexander, Kristen Gallagher, Danny Snelson, Gordon Tapper. "Writing as Metadata Container." *Jacket2* (2012)

Lu, Pamela. *Ambient Parking Lot*. Chicago: Kenning Editions, 2011.

——. Email to author, March 2013.

——. *Pamela: A Novel*. Berkeley: Atelos, 1998.

——. "Some Thoughts on Ethnicity and Language." *Aufgabe* 1 (1999)

Nancy, Jean-Luc. *Listening*. New York: Fordham University Press, 2007.

Ngai, Sianne. "Stuplimity: Shock and Boredom in Twentieth-Century Aesthetics." *Postmodern Culture10.2* (2000)

Reznikoff, Charles. *The Manner* Music. Santa Barbara, CA: Black Sparrow Press, 1977.

Tolson, Melvin. *Harlem Gallery and other Poems*. Charlottesville: University of Virginia Press, 1999.

Wilson, Rob. "Tracking Un/American Poetics in Asia/Pacific Experimental Writing: Pamela Lu and Catalina Cariaga" *boundary 2* 28.2 (2001): 9-12.

Yu, Timothy. *Race and the Avant-Garde*. Stanford University Press, 2009.

The Doors of Perception in Eileen Myles's *Inferno*

CEDAR SIGO

I had first read the prose of Eileen Myles in a book of stories, *Chelsea Girls* and in the tiny one story Hanuman volume, *Bread and Water*. Because both of these use Eileen's youth and apprenticeship as a poet as its main material it seemed the perfect (years old) introduction to their novel *Inferno*. The stories in *Chelsea Girls* actually read to me as a loosely girded novel. There seem to be lapses of time in between the stories that didn't ultimately interfere with a total and lasting vision when the book ended. I had often thought back on the stories and how easy it was to believe in the feelings and reactions as they arise in voice of the narrator. *Inferno* deals in the same arena but with finer tailoring. It's a much longer gown. The voice knows the tricks it can land, practically anything because of its custom frame, a relentless sense of containment someone else might consider warped but is in fact (when up and running), inexhaustible. The signature warp would be the absolute and totally biased truth. All utterances are created equal in Myles's voice, the asides are as important as any rise or fall in the action, often they move the book forward, using the same sudden turns their poetry takes, the inner and outer life are both rendered in equal measure. The breathing in and out of the poet. How the poet takes in the phenomenal world spits it back out and gets led around by it.

The book is broken into three parts. The first begins with their home life in Boston and dying to get away and early inklings of thinking in poetic form. When their class is assigned to write their own *Inferno* Eileen is the only one to think to write a poem. It's easy of course for any poet reading this to transpose themselves into the narrative. And if a non poet is reading it its as close to an inside track as one can hope to get. It's the life of the mind on display through short little affirmations or closures within the voice.

We all took our look from Art Carney. Walking around in our undershirts and vests and soft hats. I was one of them. But I'm female so there was an added bit of danger people always attacked me with. Like I would find myself alone and something bad would happen. Nothing did, of course, but, economically I was pretty naked. Once people saw how broke I was they decided I was for sale. (Myles 21).

Part one centers on Eileen meeting with a young woman named Rita who enters under the guise of wanting to know about poets. She eventually coaxes Eileen into meeting two older Italian men with her. Part one begins with the two women meeting at a bar and closes with the actual date with the two men. In between Eileen mixes up getting an apartment in New York, becoming curious about the poetic landscape and eventually meeting some poets. Memory is definitive in Myles's hands, the perfect sleight of hand for any and all embellishment. This is a self proclaimed poet's novel whose main character has the same first name as the author. Whether or not the reader is at all familiar with *Chelsea Girls* or *Cool for You* (Myles's first novel) they are free to invent. It's like stumbling onto a strip of color film that can't help but define their era, a thread through your life that you thought only existed in the xeroxed rushes of poems or stories, but *Inferno* is willing to turn us on at such length. The linking of the several narratives is contingent on our willingness to go anywhere with them through the strength of their continually talking back to us. We get to be near them for the duration of this reading experience. It's similar to hearing Myles read in person. Regardless of if they are reading prose or poetry. There is very little veneer between them reading onstage and being introduced to them afterward. There are some writers that you go and hear read only to find that they seem to enjoy fielding questions and answers more than actually reading their work. I'm thinking of Fran Leibowitz, even Gary Snyder. Eileen goes them one better by increasing their technical skill, the book never rests entirely on their speaking voice. Eileen seems to recognize poetry as a broad element at play in the world and holding it up as they do the remains fall back to us as charm. They can finesse behavior we might consider shocking by placing us near their heart in the moment of anticipation or glory.

The poet's life is just so much crenelated waste, nights and days whipping swiftly or laboriously past the cinematic window. We're hunched and weaving over the keys of our green our grey or pink blue manual typewriter maybe a darker stone cold authoritative Selectric with its orgasmic expectant hum and us popping pills and laughing over what you or I just wrote, wondering if that line means insult or sex. Or both. Usually both. (Myles, 65).

The considerations of being a poet are given a lot of place in part one. Only time can reveal your place within poetry so often "real poets" stay in the complete present, but then all along you are unconsciously moving away from the picture and gaining a larger view. This makes the sort of camera like retelling of *Inferno* possible. A camera that also remembers how it felt within each instance of recording. Myles describes attending their first poetry readings in New York. What they often hear first are the poets limitations. The way you might appraise a musician by the end of their first song. Any veil between the life and the words being read that is not a component of the rhythm feels phony.

> I understood community. Going to the place and standing around. Aiming for connection to bodies, language and the future. I could be an artist. I had the tools. It wasn't politics. Not that I knew. It was nothing. It was boredom turned electric. Music from cars. It was watching. Watching the scene.
> I was going to look into the St. Mark's poetry scene for sure but now I was outside rambling. I was in school. (Myles 41)

> The science of existence was completely out there for me to explore. Me, a twenty-five year old female. There's no mystery why poetry is so elaborately practiced by the young. The material of poems is energy itself, not even language. Words come later. Eventually I stood, a big human, the day spinning all around me. I pushed the pies into the refrigerator where they sat for a month. I tugged on one when I was hungry. I pulled on some cut off jeans. (Myles 44)

Inferno begins with a quote by Walter Benjamin, "A distracted person, too, can form habits." This prepares the reader in some way for how much of the narrative is taken up with the habits of the poet. Being outside yourself so seamlessly as when a great poet can read and walk you through a "things to do poem." The life of Myles's prose and poetry seem dependent on the containment of split second spasms of thought. These all take place within a bereft or totally decadent hell. Selling their old sentimentally worn poetry anthologies for beer, or explaining what they love about their pack of Gauloises. I remember the covers of Myles's first book of poetry, *A Fresh Young Voice from the Plains*. The back cover showed a poet's dream of weapons set out on a desk. A pepsi, cigarettes and typewriter. (It's been years since I have seen the book actually.) They are small charms and pleasures that keep the poets kingdom in tact even as the rent is yet to be paid. There is some excellent cutting between scenes in part one. From sitting around a massage parlor being prematurely chosen by a group of men to sneaking into opening night at The Met and back to a nervous training segment that closes out the massage parlor scene. These are not risky jumps they are like the thinnest veils piled up. No scene is left long enough for the reader to forget anything, it is a series of rooms kept warm for the wandering guest. Eileen is actually sort of herded into the Met by the rushing of the large crowd, and feels like they are on the same sort of rails while on the date with Rita and the Italians.

> I would be a man if I wrote. And being a man would render these steps I'm taking toward a place called Tuesday's- Tuesdays in my masculine hands would be literature. Each step was a coin. Ting, the door flew open. It was art. (Myles 80).

Part two or the purgatory of this book is titled *Drops*. It takes the form of a grant application to The Ferdinand Foundation. Eileen cordons off certain periods of their life as a writer under headings like *Solo Performance* and *The Upper Meadow*. They are breaking the early nineties into chapters essentially. Returning to some topics they have covered and dealing with others out of sequence the reader is given a lovely sense of refraction. It's sort of a witty case file, a joke on how one goes about editing a book like this and bearing out the evidence of having survived as a working writer. They chart the periods of not knowing where the next network of support will spring from. The form of the grant application doesn't get in the way as it isn't overplayed. Once in a while Eileen reminds you that they're asking for support but most often when we are completely inside the various stories. Money and support regardless of its source are necessary forms of protection in Myles's purgatory. *Drops* works well as a vortex whose events overlap, like a well wrought fountain going full blast in the exact middle of the book. They are cataloguing different strategies of escape, mainly killing time with money. One of the longer sections here deals with living in the unused country house of two well known artist friends. Being a pet poet to rich painters that can't help but be described as paradise but even within that exhilaration awkwardness abounds with the grounds keepers. They can never quite grasp why Myles is living in the house.

> I called Todd each time I was coming and then had to march over to apologetically pry the O'Malley's VCR away from them.

Thanks Todd I grinned backing out the door with the warm console. I'm sorry Eileen I keep forgetting that you like to watch movies when you're here. No problem I grunted the cord bouncing by my side as I wound my way along the darkening path to the house.

Todd was keeping a museum. And I upset his idea. I used every pan in the kitchen cabinets and one by one I discovered they were not pans at all. The kettle dispensed years of soap when I hit the faucet to fill. He scrubbed it with Clorox or something really harsh. Everything looked clean but noting was meant to be used cause the real people were gone. They hadn't lived there for ten years. (Myles, 164)

The form of grant application has a reflexive and condensed influence on Myles's style. Almost more like a lecture, the interjections can contain whole other worlds, then become just as easily closed off with a stack of rubble, a joke in their voice. There are also a few of their own favorite poems from the 90's on display.

Shhh

I don't think
I can afford the time to not sit right down &
write a poem about the heavy lidded
white rose I hold in my hand
I think of snow
a winter night in Boston, drunken waitress
stumble on a bus that careens through
Somerville the end of the line
where I was born, an old man
shaking me. He could've been my dad.
You need a ride? Wait he said.
This flower is so heavy in my hand.
He drove me home in his old blue
Dodge, a thermos next to me,
cigarette packs on the dash
so quiet like Boston is quiet
Boston in the snow. It's New York
plates are clattering on St. Marks
Place. Should I call you?
Can I go home now
& work with this undelivered
message in my fingertips

> It's summer
>
> I love you
> I'm surrounded by snow. (Myles 121)

Eileen Myles once said to me that they had a lot of "handles" in their poems. I took that to mean places to make strategic crash landings every now and again. The traction of the poem is rewound when they stop to take a breath. Like if Robert Creeley only hit his line breaks so hard a quarter of the time. In between the voice feels thrown down concurrent flights of stairs. You need to hit the words correctly when reading aloud. The prose of *Inferno* works a little differently. There is more time allowed here than in the flashing tumult of Myles's poetry. You get all wrapped up in the narrative that *Inferno* offers and they are forced to place themselves within the memories, or to dredge up a few more details to hold us as a film does.

The closing of *Drops* deals with a reading trip to Hawaii and Eileen getting lost after starting off too late toward an active volcano. On their way back from the glorious view they succumb to sheer exhaustion in the dark and sleep the night at the edge of a cliff. I found this section to be the most traditionally Dante inspired, as I had always imagined Dante and Virgil as action figures with the screen changing behind them as they muscle onward. Eileen in peril is absolutely fascinating as in every previous instance of the book they seem to always have an instantaneous cerebral response. There is something so endearing in their surrender to sleep here. Myles's Purgatory manages to hold the whole heart of the book in its hands. The funding of a poet who has survived under such conditions is really the least any foundation can do.

> I turned to the horizon. I headed that way. I saw a small house and those telltale piles of stones they call helau. Those little piles are holy. The house was the beginning of the road; there was my dark green rental car and my water and I drove out of the park and I had to get some caffeine, lots of it because I was falling asleep at the wheel. Everything was good after that, all three planes and especially now giving this account to you. (Myles 179)

Heaven feels different than hell but the actual backdrop is somewhat similar. The final section of *Inferno* has less of the desperation and unknowing of the first. Eileen has met poets they can speak with about the process of writing and they begin to perform their work. They also begin meeting women they want to sleep with bad enough to speak up. They are being given so much more attention. The rhythms of their life begin to fit effortlessly in sync with the rhythms of other poets and a new constellation of community begins to move on its own. Community is heaven and the way in which it drives you. Eileen is still being lead around to a degree but within the marked path of poetry. It has become a practice they can begin to believe in. These are fragments that sit and glow next to each other. They give off enough light to make us feel that these must have been joined at some point. It's important to play with that edge during a reading of your work.

> The walk to Roses was a flood of details. Car coming towards me as I crossed Houston. Put a cigarette between my lips. My lungs, this very good burn going down. I rub it. Flooding my chest like a flower. Go into the bodega and pick up a couple beers. The possibility that I should keep living in this particular time in which I had been born.,.not bleeding into all the other times, hear this footstep, not that. Feel that possibility and let it leak. Bump into a friend. Even if he was talking and talking I can jump in and stop him. People were hearing me now. A little bit. I liked standing up in front of a room full of people giving the torrent of words I chose. But each poem was a tiny torrent. A hole. Each person was a monad. A jot. (Myles 221)

Heaven is sleeping with Rose and the particulars of that experience. In an incredible chapter titled *My Revolution* these details bleed into remembering a host of past lovers, portraits of their vaginas really, one after the next.

> But she was in there for fucking. I mean that's pretty good. There was a small woman who had a lacy looking pussy that she hated. There was like this frottage over her clit. Instead of a hood it had a large mantilla. She wasn't the kind of woman that could laugh at her puss. It made her sick what she considered her irregularity, the wave of skin that dangled between her legs. I would have told her it was pretty if she had let me. It was unique. (Myles 234)

It almost has that light sweep of humor and remembrance that one associates with the work of Kenneth Koch. Eileen finds the perfect opening to let the list march right through the novel. They really do tackle the form of heaven, the ultimate release of the form of their novel. One section entitled *Friday* is a dialogue between women at a table and a meditation on fish. The last sentence is,

"Yeah I'm definitely feeling a bit weak. The light looks weird. Yup, this is definitely going in."

They have earned our attention and faith to the degree that there is even space for Myles's to share fugitive pieces of writing that make the closing of *Inferno* possible. An instance of poetry absolutely infecting the prose, pieces like *Friday* usually function more like catalogues of parts, essential maps that often go unpublished. In the poet's novel it is their prerogative to throw that kind of thing in especially as they have held us so long within the narrative.

Inferno has none of the pitfalls one associates with poetic prose, being underdeveloped or writhing within the surface and never getting past that or never getting off the ground enough to take the reader into another life. Myles's does well to recognize that the public is more interested in poets than in poetry. They have probably helped to reinvent that fact. I think of Myles's within the tradition of Jack Kerouac or Amiri Baraka, such fine all around writers that the designation of the poet's novel is not so much needed. In their hands a poet's novel just becomes a form that presents itself in order to continue writing. The material springs from the same mine field.

There is less scaling the gaps of their life as in *Chelsea Girls*. This is the time afforded them to tell the story straight through then cut it all like film. The editing of this work must have been such a pleasure. It mixes past and further past but remains just episodic enough that it never loses you. It sometimes takes a lovely kind of break into pure portraiture sketching their friendships with Ted Berrigan, Alice Notley and (more surprisingly) the great poet and art critic Rene Ricard. His is among the most unapologetically queer voices ever committed to paper. A true architect of queer and drag damaged vernaculars. Myles's does a similar thing always talking right to you or taking you aside. They move the way they want within the text. During the reading of this book I would walk the streets and catch myself staring into the landscapes. I could begin to hear how I might wrangle my voice into blocking the stage of my past. It's like seeing your life through a lens, exhaling and beginning to record. Throwing the subway platform up there and putting us on so we can get to the bar where the heavy curtain cuts the room in two. We are still nestled within Eileen's mind and all the while it's popping off.

Heaven is also where people die. Myles remembers in 1990 the uncountable deaths in the circle of AIDS. They mention the great poet Tim Dlugos as one of the first to die, as well as a friend from Provincetown named Paul Johnson. They first hear of his death at the Whitney, watching a video by Nan Goldin. Provincetown is a queer heaven that Eileen now feels equipped to actually enjoy. They love women and begin to hear in their poetry the possibility of transformation.

> It was the only way to produce the kind of glancing and wincing and exclaiming-to depict a world of so many surfaces, wider than a book, the world's pouring would have to be a curve, the line would be running, cursive, infinity a fight. The words needed to splinter off in some way just to describe it, so that any one poem would be a surge and nothing more, an intrepid break in time. (Myles 245)

Inferno would be an excellent book to hand to one's parent, after years of their sneering at your unabashed involvement with poetry. We have a hero on our hands who has survived the depths of someone else's famous epic and is writing their best sentences yet. How do you turn such a machine off? How do you disappear from a party in which you have told a major piece of your life story? This book went by so quickly.

WORKS CITED

Myles, Eileen. *Inferno: A Poet's Novel*. New York: OR Books, 2010. Print.

Jacques Roubaud's poet's prose

ABIGAIL LANG

Jacques Roubaud is first and foremost a poet though, quantitatively, he has published more prose[1]. He is the author of a prose cycle entitled '*le grand incendie de Londres*'[2] (lowercase, single quotes) composed of 6 branches, published from 1989 to 2002, republished as a single 2000 page volume in 2009. It presents itself as a "story with interpolations and bifurcations." He is the author of three self-conscious detective novels *à clef* patterned on the sestina: *La belle Hortense* (1985), *L'enlèvement d'Hortense* (1987), *L'exil d'Hortense* (1990)[3]. With Florence Delay, he dramatized the Grail cycle as *Graal Théâtre* (1977-1981; 2005). He has written tales (*La Princesse Hoppy ou le conte du Labrador*[4], 1972-2008) and children's stories (*Le chevalier Silence*, 1997). Two collections of prose pieces claim distinctive genres for themselves: *Nous, les moins-que-rien, fils aînés de personne* (2006) is designated as a "multinovel" and subtitled "12 (+1) autobiographies," and *L'abominable tisonnier de John McTaggart Ellis McTaggart* is a collection of "more or less brief lives." And some of his books of poems are composed, partly or entirely, in prose.

Jacques Roubaud is also a scholar. He has written a great deal about poetry, making decisive contributions to the understanding of the troubadour lyric (*La Fleur inverse*), of modern French verse (*La Vieillesse d'Alexandre*) and of the sonnet (*Quasi-Cristaux*). His comprehensive investigation of verse required he think its other, prose, which he did by privileging a readerly approach (see "Roman du lecteur") and what he has called the "infancies of prose," the emergence of literary prose in the thirteenth century.

> Here I begin to reflect on the distinctions between poetry and prose; on the possible definitions of narration, narrative (*le récit*), and the tale (*le conte*); the texts of the *Matter of Brittany* occurring in French literature at the hinge between versified romance and its prosified version, an extremely privileged moment of the "infancies of prose[5]." (DescPro, # 126)

There are many excellent studies, in French and in English, of Roubaud's works in verse and in prose[6]. My aim is not to propose a new interpretation but simply to synthesize, for the hurried reader, Roubaud's view and use of prose[7]. While the question of the novel is raised as such, it gains from being addressed from the larger perspective of prose.

Why write in prose? Because of the failure to write a novel.

In the beginning, there was only poetry: "And as I had willed myself a poet, I did not consider prose as a third way. Nor silence." (DescPro, #23) But in 1961, Roubaud dreams a dream, makes a decision and conceives the Project. On awakening from the dream, Roubaud knows he will write a novel entitled *The Great Fire of London* (upper-case) and that he will preserve this dream intact for as long as possible.

Roubaud is first and foremost a poet. His works in prose are subordinated to a project that is essentially "a *project of poetry*" (DescPro, #6). It is presented at length in *Description du Projet* and '*le grand incendie de Londres.*' In the Preface to the first branch of the latter, Roubaud tells how the Project, initially conceived in 1961, and its concomitant dream in particular, demanded a novel:

> *The Great Fire of London* (such was the title a dream imposed upon me after the crucial decision leading to the *Project*'s conception) would have held a singular place in the construction of the whole, distinct from the *Project* itself, although fitting into it, telling the story of the Project, which would be real, as though it were fictional; furnishing the *Project*'s edifice at last with a roof that—in the manner of Japanese dwellings, whose roofs project far beyond their walls and curve down almost to the ground—would have ensured the shade necessary for its aesthetic protection.
> This did not turn out to be the case. (GFL, vii)

Roubaud finds himself unable to write his novel. He cannot appropriate any of "the lofty conceptions of the novel" that "could accommodate the irreducible originality of [his] Project" in spite of the breadth of his readings, ranging from medieval France and Japan to the postmodern present; he realizes that he will never "approximate either Sterne or Malory or Murasaki or Henry James or Trollope or Szenkuthy or Melville or Queneau or Nabokov;" finally "*The Great Fire of London* has not been written because the *Project* failed, because it was destined to fail." (viii) '*the great fire of London*' (lower-case) recounts this failure and what *The Great Fire of London* (upper-case) "might have been" (GFL, viii). Having, from his point of view, failed as a novelist, Roubaud must settle for being "a Saturday novelist"[8]—as one says a Sunday painter: a writer of prose.

Why write in prose? Because grief made poetry impossible.
In 1983, Roubaud's young wife dies. After the death of the loved one, poetry becomes impossible.

> Now what has actually become nonexistent for me since January 1983, what I can't even entertain in thought, is *poetry*. Prose, at least the sort I am practicing here, strikes me quite to the contrary as an absolutely neutral zone, free of any pressing need for a reader's eyes or an audience's ears. Poetry, due to my acquired habit of reciting it aloud, of giving public readings, as well as for her, the woman I lived with, has ground to a halt. I open my eyes in the darkness. It is three or four o'clock in the morning. I find my place under the black lamp, with paper, notebook, four colors of felt-tips. I move forward line by line, devoid of hope, and when the light drives me away, a little later each day, I once again return to the semblances of life. (GFL, 36)

Poetry requires an audience while prose adjusts to solitude. When poetry has failed to conquer time, there remains only prose to while it away and destroy memories.

Prose is the opposite of poetry.
Roubaud's conception of prose derives, often antinomically, from his idea of poetry[9]. Roubaud's idea of poetry derives from Mallarmean premises and is rooted in his thorough reading of the troubadours, later perfected by his study of the arts of memory.

> The troubadours, as is known, invented, "found," the first great modern poetic tradition from which directly or indirectly proceeded almost the whole history of poetry in almost all European languages for the past nine centuries. They also invented, and reinvented, an idea of poetry as first of all poetry, as above all poetry, [...] they gave it a name, a double name which is Love and Song. Love (without Song), is their invention (at least love as we conceive of it today): this is a known fact. But Love, inseparable from Song, which is their idea and designation for poetry, is more than Love on its own and more than Song on its own. It is the proper name of poetry, of what links the beings who share a language, through this language, through the love of language, through the memory of language.[10]

Through rhymes and rhythm, through what Roubaud quoting the trouba-dours calls *entrebescar*, love and language become intertwined in poetry like the tongues of lovers kissing in Bernard Marti's poem: "and thus I en-twine   words and purify sounds   like the tongue entwines   with the tongue in a kiss."[11]

Poetry is the memory of language.

Rhythm aids recall; poems are (were, anyway) learnt by heart from child-hood, committed to memory where they live on, making a store of language, sometimes a portable library; verse memorizes language in its present state; poetry moves the reader/listener's memory of language and activates per-sonal recollection.

In *La Fleur inverse*, Roubaud explicitly links the birth of the novel to the provençal lyric:

> One can posit, and that is my hypothesis, that the first novelistic prose, that of the *Lancelot en prose*, following the octosyllabic verse novel by Chrétien de Troyes, is an immense and polemic illustration of *amors*. The theory of *amors* cannot be explained, cannot be said in any other way than in the very poems where it appears, but it can, indirectly be shown. The medieval love novel is, to a large extent, the enactment of this "monstration," the *novelistic manifestation* of *amors*. (13)

Poetry says. Prose shows.

Here Roubaud borrows Wittgenstein's vocabulary. Poetry preserves and fosters *images*, memory-images. "The image is the change induced in me by an object, by something in the world." (see *The Loop*, interpolations from chapter 2, pp. 234 ff). Prose produces *pictions*, mere reproductions or de-scriptions.

Prose destroys memories.

The thesis at the heart of "the great fire of London" posits that "narrating a project (a dream, a memory) annuls it." (GFL 32) Writing is "a power of destruction more radical than forgetfulness." (GFL 199)

> Once set down on paper, each fragment of memory [...] becomes, in fact, inaccessible to me. No doubt this doesn't mean that the record of memory, located under my skull, in the neurons, has disappeared, but everything happens as if a transference had been made, something in

the nature of a translation, with the result that ever since, the words composing the black lines of my transcription interpose themselves between memory and myself, and in the long run completely supplant it. (GFL 197)

For all practical purposes this process involves, in fact, a destruction. I've devoted myself to the enterprise of destroying my memory [...]. I set fire to it, and with the debris I charcoal-scrawl the paper (another image). [...] Henceforth my recollection is at a standstill [...] now it's my recollection that comes second, turning it to a ghost, a simulacrum. I've lost it without even forgetting it; because, of course, it simultaneously became impossible to forget: I can have access to it anytime I want, like some piece of trivia I command. It is here, somewhere in the prose. It is here, it exists, and is dead. [...] The prose, this prose, becomes the source of my recollections. One by one it replaces them. It aspires to being my only memory. In the end, it will be my only memory. (GFL 198)

'the great fire of London' is a controlled destruction of memory: "I assure my destruction through memory, which parallels time's aging me body and mind. I strive to put order in this destruction—in the construction of its destruction." (GFL 211)

Further antinomies: Poetry is absorbed; prose is read.

I read [prose] quickly. The question of pace, of speed is important [...] For the longest time I only read poetry slowly, which moreover meant one and the same thing as learning it by heart [...] I absorb rather than read poetry [...]; I absorb it in order to transform it into my own poetry. (GFL 238)

Poetry is composed; prose is written.

Roubaud says he composes poetry in his head, typically walking, and only transcribes it once it is committed to memory. Prose and mathematics cannot be composed thus; they require the drudgery of writing and tie one to a table and chair. To compose walking and to write at a desk say something of the respective relation of poetry and prose to time.

When at rest, I don't possess time, time possesses me. [...] Seated at my table, or lying down, I feel once again like an object being transported : I am being transported by the earth ; the earth is time carrying me away. [...] walking is a conversation with time [...] By walking, I imprint my trace of time on this earth, I mark the time of my attention, I touch it. (GFL 220)

When out walking, time more or less comes into my possession; ambulation converts time into space through the medium of footsteps more directly and sensitively than through the commonplace use of time-measuring instruments. (GFL 96)

Poetry conquers time; prose whiles it away.

In 'the great fire of London', the real life of the author is declared empty after the death of the loved one. Life is converted into prose (read or written) as much as possible—"as if the only life I had was there" (GFL 280): "Henceforth I will do my best to see that my solitude, the period of my solitude, is entirely occupied with the prose, and converting into lines its colorless passion, which has no homeland." (GFL 237)

Fiction—possible world.

Reading and writing prose furnish the fiction of another possible world, "as if the only life I had was there—which by the way is not unrelated to this novelistic enterprise." (GFL 280)

In *Quelque chose noir*, coming to terms with the death of Alix Cléo Roubaud proceeds through meditations, notably on modality and detours through possible worlds: "'She is alive.' I imagine that this proposition, false in my universe, is true in that other, the (fictive) universe of her truth."[12]

Prose and time: "the arrow of reading."

Prose is read and written head first[13], straightforwardly, continuously along the irreversible arrow of time, as Roubaud insists in his "Le Roman du Lecteur?" essay.

> Our world [...] obeys the irreversible arrow of time. There is, of course, more temporal freedom in narrative; it is a branching time so to speak, a non-irreversible time; one can pull the drawers of verbal tenses with enthusiasm, with elegance, with ruse, with finesse (the future perfect has its charm). But novels are read, I think, in a time that is severely ordinary, sequential, linear [...] from the first to the last page. I see no weakness in the form of this constraint. [...] it's in the perception of ratios, antagonist or not, between the time of the story and the time, unique and universal, of the reading, that the novelistic time is in play.[14]

The curse of the novel is that it ends and can never be read for the first time again—"contrary to poems whose *raison d'être* is to exist for memory and therefore only exist from being reread" (P&M, 237). In that sense, Roubaud claims, *The Murder of Roger Ackroyd* is the archetypical novel. "The fate of the novel-form is that it comes to an end. And that is its catastrophe. All novels disappoint at the end; *because* they end."[15]

"Avoidism" or how not to end.

As Florence Marsal has shown at length, the earliest prose romances provide Roubaud with a dual strategy to postpone the ending: incompletion and interweaving. Each installment, each branch, offers a "provisory ending." The incompletion of the Grail is a strategy to allow for sequels—and prequels. So too, in 'the great fire of London,' "the end of each branch marks a provisory ending, or a possible ending of the ordered set of branches.' (GFL 9) The unremittingly forward thrust of the narrative is concealed and complicated by surface twists and turns, digressions and interruptions, "to give varied twists to the straight thread of prose."[16] Where the prime mover of the troubadours' *grand chant* is Eros, desire reined in by continence, prose is fueled by adventure. Like the Arthurian knight, the narrator must be both persevering and available for adventures and digressions.

Improvisation

In *La Dissolution*, the first part of the sixth branch, Roubaud writes he regrets that he never attempted to compose poetry in an improvisatory manner, even after he discovered Parry and Lord's hypotheses on the composition of the Homeric poems. Although the first branch of 'the great fire of London' was composed in longhand and the following branches on several Macintosh computers, the set of strict rules presiding over its composition confer on it some of the characteristics of orality and even of improvisation.

> - no preliminary plan(s);
> - no turning back, no corrections, no second thoughts,...; progression of prose in the present tense of narration with my mind set only on the horizon (possibly changing, but consistently clear) of my initial aim left unsaid;
> - principle of a completion criteria exterior to the narrative [text]; [...]
> - refusal of any intervention contradicting the interior truth of memories. (*gil*, 1794)

'the great fire of London' is composed of a series of *moments* or *moments-proses* written daily at daybreak. Roubaud proscribes any turning back to emend, correct or rewrite, thereby relinquishing one of the greatest assets of writing, what Jack Goody has called "backward scanning," and abiding by the etymology of prose: straight-ahead, indeed headlong. And as the project progresses, Roubaud decides to accept glaring inconsistencies which testify to his unstable memories. Where Proust had glorified the powers of memory, Roubaud exposes its failures; and where Proust had elevated the novel to the grandest poetic prose, Roubaud shuns any trace of a belletristic style. Roubaud's œuvre spans an exceptionally wide range of tones but in his prose cycle he always keeps to a willfully prosaic style.

Orality

Roubaud's prose captures something of speech, of what Walter Ong has called "oral-style thinking." Revealingly, he named his successive typewriters Miss Bosanquet, after Henry James' last secretary to whom where dictated

> those immense astonishing sentences, precariously teetering but always at the last moment recapturing their miraculous equilibrium, their "balance." These sentences, such as we read them in *The Golden Bowl* or "The Jolly Corner," have not, in fact, ever been written, in the strict sense, by their author, but rather were transmitted to paper by half-human, half-mechanical intermediaries, like the faithful Miss Bosanquet. (GFL 26)

Moreover, Roubaud's prose increasingly resists the perfection and completion that print conveys and demands. "Print is comfortable only with finality" and "encourages a sense of closure" writes Walter Ong[17]. One of the great practical advantages of printed prose is its allographic quality, its perfect reproducibility. With their idiosyncratic use of fonts, numbered and multicolored indents, *La Dissolution* and *Tokyô infra-ordinaire* are frankly autographic. Roubaud theorizes this new layout in the third chapter of *La Dissolution* as "netscrit" and writes:

> 3 3 8 1 1 17 2 10 of course, the attraction I feel for medieval literature in manuscripts is not unrelated to my desire to "upset" print (*La Dissolution*, 51; this remark printed in pink ink and set at the seventh level of indentation)

This prickling of print is a surface manifestation of a more radical challenge to prose. Prose is always defined negatively, as not-verse and as a fall from the novel. "In 'the great fire of London,' the fall is a downfall" (GFL 148); "The prose of memory was to be disharmonious, 'poetry fragments[18]', a fallen poetry" (GFL 153). In grief, it is embraced for its mediocrity, its absence of positive characteristics. Roubaud's diffuse hostility towards prose may be explained by the fact that prose is not just the opposite of poetry.

Prose is the antagonist of poetry.

And Roubaud is the champion of poetry in an age when poetry's domain is again threatened (see *Poetry, Etc: Cleaning House*). In the Western world, upstart genres have been keen to gain ground at the expense of poetry, by giving it a bad name, by accusing it of being untrustworthy. This begins with Plato banning the poet from the City and continues in the Middle Ages when literary prose emerges and establishes itself at the expense of poetry, launching a great wave of *dérimage*, the translation of works in verse into prose. In a mischievous gesture, Roubaud appropriates prose's claim to truthfulness for his own project, in the hope to gain "the glamour of novelistic attire."

At the outset of my exploration of old French prose, when I was endeavoring to understand the architecture of the Grail romances, the *Prose Lancelot* and *Tristan*, the *Guiron*... I had been struck by a polemical affirmation, on the part of the first French translator of the Chronicle of the Pseudo-Turpin, produced from a Latin manuscript in the possession of Yolande and Hugues de Saint-Pol, around 1195, and reproduced by Brian Woledge in the introduction of his *Répertoire des plus anciens textes en prose française depuis 842 jusqu'aux premières années du XIIè siècle* [...] *Nul conte rimé n'est vrai*: no tale in rhyme is true. French art prose (and I extrapolate beyond what Woledge allows, but I'll take liberties here, unscrupulously, since this too is a place for fiction) is spawned by a translation occasioned by the express intention of telling the truth, something verse, and therefore poetry, is by nature incapable of doing. From this mistrust of poetry that has so long a posterity, I draw a few personal conclusions: in the first place, since the prose novel I was going to undertake was to be above all nonpoetry, antonymous and complementary to a poetry Project, it would certainly be to my advantage to adopt this criteria, and to invest it with a constraint of truth as its driving force, as impetus; and by doing so, I would have help in creating an at least fictional tie with the *infancies of prose*; and I would investigate how novel-prose (which lays claim to truth) functions, develops, and becomes intertwined, so as to lend a banal and merely truthful story the glamour of novelistic attire. (GFL 199)

Not only does prose become the preeminent and increasingly hegemonic signifying practice, relegating verse to an ever-shrinking domain, but prose also threatens to corrupt the essence of verse as *entrebescar*[19], the intertwining of words and love. As Jean-François Puff has shown, Roubaud conceives of prose as the negation of the troubadours' *entrebescar*. In *La Fleur inverse*, his study of troubadour lyric, Roubaud translates and comments Raimbaut d'Orange's curious canso "no sai que s'es" which begins:

> Escotaz mas no say que s'es . senhor so que vuelh comensar . vesr estribot ni sirventes . non es ni nom no-l sai trobar . ni ges no say co-l mi fezes . s'aytal no-l podi acabar . que ja hom mays non vis fag aytal ad home ni a femna en est segle ni en l'autre qu'es passatz
>
> Listen but I don't know what it is   lords what I am beginning *estribot* verse or *sirventes*   no I cannot find a name   and yet I cannot make it   if I cannot end it in such a way that nobody has seen the like of made by man or woman in this century or in the one that passed. (41)

What Raimbaut d'Orange cannot name is what arises at the end of each *cobla* (stanza) because no one before him has done it: *prose*. "Because of this prose, the poem loses its name as poem, becomes an "I don't know what," comes close to "nothingness," to "*nien*" and "*non re*." This is a second indication of *the extreme fragility of trobar*. [...] any irruption of an outside in the *trobar*, such as prose in this instance, is a scandal and threatens its balance." (*La Fleur inverse* 44) Roubaud retains the layout used in the manuscript: there are no line breaks, only stanza breaks; the lines are separated by a full stop—a blank space in the translation—and do not begin with a capital letter. Transcribing manuscripts reminds one that verse did not always abide in layout but more importantly in a metrical pause.

More recently, a third major assault on poetry began with the *Crise de vers* and the advent of free verse, supported by successive avant-garde movements. In a major critical essay entitled *La Vieillesse d'Alexandre*, Roubaud exposes the ongoing blind spots of free verse, and the naiveté of the surrealists in particular. Roubaud embraces Mallarmé's idea according to which « in truth, there is no prose »[20]: as soon as attention is paid to diction, rhythm and style, prose tends to verse. Roubaud espouses Mallarmé's poetic imperialism and denies rhythm to prose.

> - There is no rhythm in prose. There is no rhythm without metre and there is no metre in prose. [...]
> Prose is as good as confused verse.
> What separates a verse from a sentence is silence. Silence, the blank that separates one verse from another is missing in prose. The period has taken its place.
> What separates verse from prose is the period.
> Prose has no rhythm.
> As soon as rhythm is found we are outside prose, in pre-poetry.
> (*Poésie, etcetera: ménage*, 223-228)

At a time when much contemporary poetry is written in prose, when some of the foremost French poets refuse to call themselves poets and introduce themselves as writers, when in the wake of *Tel Quel* and in the words of Denis Roche's indictment "Poetry is [deemed] inadmissible; besides it doesn't exist" and should loose itself in the super-genre of 'the text', Roubaud insists on keeping poetry separate from prose. This does not mean that nothing happens at the border, but precisely, this border needs to stay in place to remain productive. Unsurprisingly, Roubaud's position is frequently misunderstood, sometimes no doubt willfully so, as a reactionary posture. If prose threatens the characteristic *entrebescar* of poetry, poetry threatens prose in return:

> - What if prose, today, annexes poetry, makes the distinction, the separation useless, obsolete?
> - Then prose falls ill. Poetry's illness (the modernist crisis, the *crise de vers*, the poetry crisis) contaminates prose.
> Always poetry rules prose, violates it, troubles it.

It has been said that poets are verse-eaten. Quite possibly. But from the *crise de vers*, this arises: Contemporary prose is poetry-eaten. (P&M, 230)

This contamination not only threatens prose poems and poetic prose, which by right belong to the realm of poetry, but also the prose of novels. After World War II, the French novel has indeed been poeticized in all sorts of experiments, most famously in the Nouveau Roman. For Roubaud, "There is nothing worse (in my opinion) than the presence of "the poetic" in the novel." (P&M, 231) When it comes to novels, Roubaud favors "silent English prose" (DescPro #343), ranging from Austen to Woolf through Trollope and James, with a preference for "the invisible prose of Jane Austen." Beyond a personal inclination, it represents a "harmless prose," harmless in the sense that it does not compete with poetry. (Puff 370)

Conversations of poetry and prose.

If poetry and prose are maintained as distinct, they can enter into a productive conversation of which a few examples follow by way of conclusion.

Rest in prose. *Autobiography chapitre X*[21] is what Roubaud has called a "'formal novel,' a poetry book 'reciting' the formal: a metre, a formal concept, a form" (DescPro #143). It is presented as "poems with *moments de repos en prose*": moments of rest in prose or, anagrammatically, moments of prose in prose. Jean-François Puff likens these to the provençal *vidas* which distilled the lives of the troubadours from their poems.

Poetry in prose, and more specifically the prose-sonnet[22] as used in Roubaud's first book ∈, inspired from Pierre-Jean Jouve's prose rendition of Shakespeare's sonnets which Roubaud comments upon as follows:

And yet, they remained, irrefutably, sonnets by "transport of the structure," by translation of the model's sonnet nature. The "axiomatic method" suggested to me the "prose sonnet:" unstressed, unrhymed, divided in units analogous for the mind (interior eye-ear) to the traditional varieties, destined to play the same role (but abstract, and virtual) as the English original by (translated from) Shakespeare, in Jouve's examples. (DescPro #38)

Prose in poetry, or the "annexation of prose to poetry."

If the prose poem can, without any damage, borrow scraps and cadences from the surrounding metric, prose in poetry, however, must repudiate any regular scansion; which can only be attained by submitting to a constraint. (Desc Pro #142)

The two most striking examples of prose in poetry, as interpreted by Jean-François Puff, are *Quelque chose noir* and *La Pluralité des mondes de Lewis*, the two books of meditation written in time of mourning, two books of poetry laid out as prose, most poems consisting in 9 paragraphs. The death of the loved one makes both poetry and the novel impossible. All that remains is a prose of memory and a poetry "refracted" by prose (Puff, 390). Death dissolves form.

> For form cannot declare itself without also declaring the formless, although the latter is not apart from it or located elsewhere: on the contrary, form can only give rise to the formless, can only expose, secretive, interior, its impropriety.[23]

The arc of Roubaud's œuvre is, among other things, a coming to terms with mortality which parallels the twentieth century's relinquishing of a certain ideal of form and its embrace of process.

Coda: the novel on the quiet and after all.

In a text written for Roubaud's eightieth birthday, fellow Oulipian Jacques Jouet points out some of Roubaud's undeclared almost-novels and muses on the possibility of a novel to come.

> Supposing I am then asked if the absence of a novel (I mean a novel that isn't a novel by Raymond Queneau, such as the *Hortense* novels are) in Roubaud's œuvre pains me, I would of course answer yes— Perec, Mathews or Calvino did not suffer from such inhibitions—, *Dernière Balle perdue* and *Parc Sauvage*[24] suggesting that an octogenarian Roubaldian novel is in no way impossible, maybe a great Bildungsroman of a Churchillian adolescence in the forties (but I should evidently mind my own business when poetry, mathematics, prose and memory already amount to a quite solid production) which would become conceivable only if the character could once more be trusted in spite of a number of typically twenty-century proscriptions.[25]

NOTES

1. A comprehensive bibliography for the years 1967-2006 can be found on oulipo.net.

2. Abbreviated as gil. Three branches so far have been published by Dalkey Archive in English : *The Great Fire of London: A Story with Interpolations and Bifurcations*. Trans. Dominic Di Bernardi. Elmwood Park, IL, USA: Dalkey Archive Press, 1991 [Hereafter referred to as GFL]; *The Loop*. Trans. Jeff Fort. Champaign, IL: Dalkey Archive Press, 2009 ; *Mathematics:* Trans. Ian Monk. Champaign, IL: Dalkey Archive Press, 2012.

3. Translated into English as *Our Beautiful Heroine*. Trans. David Kornacker. Woodstock, NY: Overlook Press, 1987 ; *Hortense is Abducted*. Trans. Dominic Di Bernardi. Elmwood Park, IL : Dalkey Archive Press, 1989 ; *Hortense in Exile*. Trans. Dominic Di Bernardi. Normal, IL: Dalkey Archive Press, 1992.

4. *The Princess Hoppy, or The Tale of Labrador*. Trans. Bernard Hœpffner. Normal, IL: Dalkey Archive Press, 1993.

5. Jacques Roubaud, *Description du projet*, préface de Jean-Jacques Poucel. Paris, Nous, 2013. Hereafter DescPro. I refer to the numbered paragraphs.

6. In English: Jean-Jacques Poucel, *Jacques Roubaud and the Invention of Memory*, The University of North Carolina Press, 2006 ; *The Great Fire of London* by Jacques Roubaud. *A Casebook*, ed. Peter Consenstein, accessible online on the Dalkey Archive website. In French: Agnès Disson et Véronique Montémont (dir.), *Jacques Roubaud, compositeur de mathématique et de poésie*, Éditions Absalon, 2011; Florence Marsal, *Jacques Roubaud: Prose de la mémoire et errance chevaleresque*. Presses Universitaires de Rennes, coll. "Interférences," 2010; Véronique Montémont, *Jacques Roubaud: l'amour du nombre*, Presses Universitaires du Septentrion, coll. Perspectives, 2004 ; Jean-François Puff, *Mémoire de la mémoire. Jacques Roubaud et la lyrique médiévale*, Editions Classiques Garnier, coll. "Etudes de littérature des XXe et XXIe siècles," 2009; Christophe Reig, *Mimer, Miner, Rimer: le cycle romanesque de Jacques Roubaud* - préface de Bernard Magné, New-York/Amsterdam, Rodopi, coll. "Faux-Titre" no 275, 2006.

7. I am very grateful to Jean-Jacques Poucel for his generous suggestions and for our ongoing conversation.

8. Michel Chaillou, Michel Deguy, Florence Delay, Natacha Michel, Denis Roche, Jacques Roubaud, *L'Hexaméron*, Seuil, p. 114. Roubaud's "failure as a novelist" needs to be qualified. The three existing installments of the six-volume projected *Hortense* cycle are novels, even if pertaining to the popular sub-genre of the detective novel, here at once constrained by the

rigors of formal composition encouraged by Raymond Queneau, and indulging itself as a humorous and metafictional *roman à clef*. Jean-Jacques Poucel devotes a chapter to the Hortense cycle and has also much to say on Roubaud's "rhetoric of failure" (p. 220 ff).

9. This polar opposition is complexified and mediated by a third "transversal" genre of great importance in Roubaud's work, the tale (*le conte*). The tale is prose narrative that demands to be regarded rhythmically (DescPro # 349 and 127).

10. *L'invention du fils de Leoprepes. Poésie et mémoire*, Circé, 1993, pp. 147-148. The bold type is in the original.

11. *Les Troubadours. Anthologie bilingue*, Seghers, 1971, pp. 106-107

12. *Quelque chose noir, Gallimard, 1986, p. 128. Some Thing Black*. Trans. Rosmarie Waldrop. Photographs by Alix Cleo Roubaud. Elmwood Park, IL: Dalkey Archive Press, 1990; *The Plurality of Worlds of Lewis*. Trans. Rosmarie Waldrop. Normal, IL: Dalkey Archive Press, 1995.

13. In their introduction to *The Emergence of Prose, An Essay in Prosaics*, Wlad Godzich and Jeffrey Kittay remind us that "*Prorsa* is the name of the Roman goddess who presides over births in which the head of the infant is presented first. Her name comes from the Latin adjective *prorsus* meaning "straightforward." (University of Minnesota Press, 1987)

14. « Le roman du lecteur ? », *Le Débat*, 1996/3 n° 90, p. 52-61. This essay begins with a list of 61 novels that, understatedly, Roubaud would encourage one to read.

15. *Poésie, etcetera, ménage*, Stock, Paris, 1995, p. 237. Now abbreviated as P&M. *Poetry, etcetera: Cleaning House*. Trans. Guy Bennett. Los Angeles, Green Integer, 2006.

16. Emmanuèle Baumgartner quoted in Marsal, p. 3.

17. Walter J. Ong, *Orality and Literacy: the Technologizing Of The Word*, London & New York, Routledge, 1982, p. 129.

18. More literally "broken poetry." The original says "poésie rompue," an allusion to Mallarmé's definition of literary prose as "vers rompu" (broken verse) in "Crise de vers."

19. For a more complete and critical presentation of this concept see Poucel p. 46 ff.

20. In "La musique et les lettres."

21. *Autobiographie, chapitre dix, poèmes avec des moments de repos en prose*, Gallimard, Paris, 1977.

22. Gallimard, Paris, 1967.

23. *La pluralité des mondes de Lewis*, Gallimard, 1991, p. 69; *The Plurality of Worlds of Lewis*. Trans. Rosmarie Waldrop, Normal, IL: Dalkey Archive Press, 1995.

24. *La Dernière balle perdue*, Fayard, Paris, 1997; *Parc Sauvage*, récit, Seuil (coll. *Fiction & Cie*), Paris, 2008. *Eros mélancolique* (written with Anne F. Garréta), Grasset, Paris, 2009 also rightly belongs to that list.

25. Jacques Jouet, "À supposer Roubaud," *J.R.*, unpaginated leaflet handed out at the Centre Georges Pompidou on 5 December 2012.

Juliana Spahr's *The Transformation* thinks wit(h)ness

RACHEL ZOLF

Thinking thought usually amounts to withdrawing into a dimensionless place in which the idea of thought alone persists. But thought in reality spaces itself out into the world. It informs the imaginary of peoples, their varied poetics, which it then transforms, meaning in them its risk becomes realized.

—ÉDOUARD GLISSANT, *POETICS OF RELATION*

Both my grandfather and father published books paradoxically deemed "autobiographical novel" and "fictional biography." I became quite certain of the fictional part when I read the same unlikely passage in my father's "memoir" as I did in his book of "stories." It was a suicide note penned by a woman scorned by my father's brother (or the thinly veiled representation of my father's brother): "I love you, Meyer [or Saul], the way your body moves in bed, the way you laugh, the way you listen, and the way you talk. Without you life is shit, so fuck it. See you upstairs. Monique [or Eve]." Now, I doubt the first thing that comes to mind after reading that passage is that the letter "rings true" in that well-wrung verisimilitude fiction tends to vaunt. I doubt the reader can easily picture Monique (or Eve) feverishly writing these barked-out words during her last rapturous gasps in Winnipeg, Canada, in 1950. In fact, I doubt the reader thinks much about Monique (or Eve) at all, because she is simply a badly composed stick/stock figure in whatever generic setting, fiction or non-fiction. To coin a trite bumper sticker, it's not the genre that matters; it's the writing.

Why this preamble to an essay on Juliana Spahr's *The Transformation* as a poet's novel?[1] Partly because I'm not sure if *The Transformation* fits into the genre contours of the novel form, even a semi-autobiographical novel written by a poet; and I'm not sure it matters. I am certainly bored of the genre debates and am happy to call this book writing or prose or even sentences, an experiment fitting with the aim of the book's publisher, Atelos, to publish "under the sign of poetry, writing that challenges conventional, limiting definitions of poetry."[2] The plural "they" protagonist of *The Transformation* even states, "Because they were poets, they thought a lot about how they were glad they did not write novels" (104). In her Afterword to the book, Spahr writes that she produced *The Transformation* "under the spell of" Renee Gladman's and Pamela Lu's sentences (217), both writers who have produced innovative prose that is not "New Narrative" and not "New Sentence," but something else entirely. Spahr's note also states that *The Transformation* "tells a barely truthful story" (217), which could give the book status as fiction (or, from another angle, non-fiction).

And yet, even though the book enacts certain conventions of the novel or memoir, such as a (sort of) linear narrative in chapters, and a central figure (or figures) going through a process of, uh, transformation, I don't think it's the genre itself that makes this writing *matter* in the material sense. It seems to me that Spahr wrote *The Transformation* as a long-form prose narrative because she needed a broad, fictionalized canvas to explore a set of complex issues related to ongoing U.S. colonization, exceptionalism, and hegemonic practices that couldn't be encapsulated in a book of poems, even a book-length long poem. In fact, she had already addressed some of the issues she takes up in *The Transformation* in earlier books of poems. In broad strokes, *Fuck You–Aloha–I Love You* (2001) is a response to her experience as a settler in Hawai'i, which is also the experience outlined in the first half of *The Transformation*. *This Connection of Everyone with Lungs* (2005) explores feeling like a cog in the post-9/11 American "military-industrial complex" (*The Transformation* 56), which is also the experience outlined in the second half of *The Transformation*. Spahr has even published a book of non-fiction (well, academic essays) called *Everybody's Autonomy: Connective Reading and Collective Identity* (2001) that focuses on some similar themes as *The Transformation*: questions of the *we* and the *they* and the *you*—key pronouns in all of Spahr's work—and writer and reader responsibility and complicity, and the wedge between ethics and politics. But Spahr employs *The Transformation*'s barely truthful long-form prose frame as a laboratory to exhaustively experiment with form and "think with" (21, first instance of many) colonization and complicity on a much more expansive level than the earlier poetry books. In the language lab, she subjects her characters to vulnerable intrusions, revealing the sometimes monstrous face of the self and neighbor, alongside the intensities of what she calls, citing Anne Carson, the "third Sapphic point" (206), a point of desire in encounter that Carson claims (via Sappho's poetry), "plays a paradoxical role for it both connects and separates, marking that two are not one, irradiating the absence whose presence is demanded by eros" (16).[3] One could claim, via psychoanalyst Jessica Benjamin, that in *The Transformation*, "the third point creates a space rather than a line," a space of and for shifts in thought and action (Benjamin 123). As Benjamin suggests, the intersubjective third is a mental space where responsibility begins.

The Transformation doesn't try to be everybody's autobiography, but it does show its debt to Gertrude Stein through paragraphs that take emotional form. These paragraphs enact a process of deeply felt inquiry, in the sense that Lyn Hejinian has called on in her essays (and, not incidentally, Hejinian is the co-publisher of *The Transformation*). The text's (because *The Transformation* is not simply non-fiction, just as much as it is not simply fiction or poetry) recursive, spiraling "long sentences and lists of connections, both paranoid and optimistic" (213), its indeterminate characters, its reiterative questioning and worrying at/of the same wounds, its raw honesty, its open beginning, its open middle, its open ending, enact processes of transformation in thinking—and being:

> So this is a story of three who moved to an island in the middle of the Pacific and how it changed them. And a story of how they became aware that they were a they in the cruel inquisitive sense, in the sense of not being a part of us or we, in the sense of accusation, whether they wanted to be or not. It is a story about realizing that they cannot shrug off this they and so a story of trying to think with it. A story of how much this realization of being a they changed them and a story of embracing this change [...] And so perhaps it is a story of coming to an identity, coming to realize that they not only had a gender that was decided for them without their consent and by historical events that they had not even been alive to witness, but they also had a race and a sexuality that was decided for them without their consent and by historical events that they had not even been alive to witness and they just had to deal with this. So it is also a story of finding an ease in discomfort. And a catalogue of discomfort. (21–22)

One could say that the form of *The Transformation* embodies the content, and both are indeterminate, and a label isn't necessary after that; perhaps this helps define the perhaps indefinable poet's novel.

What is clear to me is that it is an infectious transformation that Spahr releases into the world, akin to the "prickly new cells" (39, first instance) of awakening that become activated in the body of the text's speaker. Rarely has a book resonated with me as much as *The Transformation* did when I first read it in 2008. I was in the middle of writing a book of poetry on settler-colonialism in Palestine-Israel when reading Spahr's book led me to a deeper awareness of my own complicity with ongoing settler-colonialism in Canada. It was much easier to offer a critique of imperialism "over there" than examine my role in the "history of arrival by people from afar who came and acted as if the place was theirs" in Canada (*The Transformation* 41). Reading *The Transformation*, I felt the "tiny muscles at the base of each hair [...] contract and thus pull the hair erect" (33) when the book's speaker—the "they" who can be read as singular and plural—recognizes their role as a "stupid fucking haole" (foreign, white) colonizer in Hawai'i (40, first instance). I felt a similar shameful "cringe of recognition" (41) of my own role as a "mediocre colonizer" when Spahr alluded to Albert Memmi's term for the left-wing colonizer who rejects the colony but can't help but benefit from it.[4] I became a "colonization groupie" like the figures in *The Transformation* (32), and started working on a book in response to these issues in Canada.[5] And when "they" moved from Hawai'i back to the "continent" (New York) in the second half of *The Transformation* I found myself wishing that they could have continued their reflection on ongoing colonization of Indigenous peoples on the continent. I resisted thinking it was because the "Indians" had "vanished" there. This is just some of what came to mind as I did my own "thinking with," and feeling with, Spahr as she states in an interview, "use[d] the genre of individual exploration to think about how that shapes ... cultural issues" (Rosenthal 311). She continues, in reference to U.S. practices at "home" and as occupier in Iraq and elsewhere, "I was interested in thinking about what I'm complicit with. ... In order to bomb someone you have to make them into a 'they.'... Can one think ethically from a position of 'they'? Maybe the beginning of doing that work is to see yourself as part of that 'they'" (Rosenthal 311).

Considering this proposition of changing perspective in order to understand complicity and responsibility, I'd like to suggest that part of the transformation that Spahr enacts in *The Transformation* is related to reading. In her essay on Theresa Hak Kyung Cha's *DICTEE* in *Everybody's Autonomy*, Spahr cites Cha on the reader-text relationship: "You read, you mouth the transformed object across from you in its new state, other than what it had been" (125). Spahr then claims, "Cha wants readers who, as they read, as they mouth the words, transform" (125). Perhaps Spahr desires a similar response out of her readers (however much we're not supposed to talk about authorial intention). Spahr argues that *DICTEE* is not only a critique of colonialism in content but that reading *DICTEE* calls for "decolonizing" "politicized" reading practices, whereby the reader engages self-reflexively with the text and is changed by it (125). Interestingly, Spahr had previously called for similar reading strategies in an essay on Hejinian's *My Life* as a "postmodern autobiography."[6] Spahr describes *My Life* as a "reader-centered" work, "in that it requires its readers to bring multiple interpretations to the work

[...] with its dual resignifying of subjectivity and readerly agency" (142; 155). She also applies Judith Butler's theories on the political subject (and hence the reading subject) as a constant site of resignification, highlighting the constructed nature of the subject in/of language, and deeming *My Life* "a mutating product centered around the way life and practices of representing subjectivity change from moment to moment" (142). The repeated "one" in *My Life* is "a pronoun that *anyone* can inhabit" (146, Spahr's emphasis), like the singular neuter pronoun "it" that Hejinian also employs. This gesture is echoed in Spahr's use of the singular/plural neuter and gender-neutral pronoun "they" in *The Transformation* as a stance of textual encounter that the reader can actively inhabit and question rather than passively absorbing the colonizing "author who conquers and claims dominion over readers" (152). Reading is configured in these early essays of Spahr's as not simply appropriating knowledge, but as taking response-ability, resistantly; reading as an active witnessing and interpretation that is a kind of trans-lation and trans-formation. "After crossing the boundary which distinguished the work from the rest of the universe, the reader is expected to recross the boundary with something in mind" (*My Life* 77).

Rosi Braidotti's "radical ethics of transformation" is applicable here, a post-Deleuzian an ethical stance that:

> rejects individualism, but also asserts an equally strong distance from relativism or nihilistic defeatism. A sustainable ethics for a non-unitary subject proposes an enlarged sense of interconnection between self and others, including the non-human or 'earth' others, by removing the obstacle of self-centred individualism. [...] This is an ethical bond of an altogether different sort from the self-interests of an individual subject, as defined along the canonical lines of classical humanism. It is a nomadic eco-philosophy of multiple belongings. (*Transpositions* 35).[7]

Spahr displays a similar type of eco-philosophy in *The Transformation* and *This Connection of Everyone with Lungs*, with the ecological aspect developed further in a subsequent poetic text also focusing on Hawai'i, *Well Then There Now* (2011). It is a philosophy indebted to Indigenous knowledges and based on the interrelationality of all things plant, animal and human. Indeed, Spahr's writing repeatedly features the kind of posthumanist, plural, embodied and embedded subjects that Braidotti promotes, and this complex subject position seems to be one Spahr would like her readers to inhabit.

My own thinking on reading, writing and witnessing follows some similar trajectories to Braidotti and Spahr. I have been using the final lines in Paul Celan's poem "Ashglory," "Noone / bears witness for / the witness" to rethink received notions of the "poetics of witness" as being limited to poets who have experienced trauma firsthand, and to writing from a confessional stance. Some may interpret Celan's "Noone" as the oft-withdrawn Hebrew god, just as many read Emmanuel Levinas's ethical figure of the face as the uncaressable visage of a similar god. Yet, in my own readerly license, I prefer to read Noone as a multiple figure, not one but many partial subjects, beyond the overdetermined ethical two to the political three or more, something like a "they," with the distorted face of a human or not quite human. Or a zombie, the always-already-dead figure Spahr employs in *The Transformation* to represent the "they" flailing for a job in the "national education complex" (55). Or perhaps a Thing, in the psychoanalytic sense (*Das Ding*), the unassimilable, monstrous part of the human within us and beside us that some of us still feel drawn to attempt to communicate with, even if that communication is via "mad" or ungovernable affects.[8] "They needed to become monstrous in their heart [...] That singular organ needed to be made bigger. They need to bring things inside them that shouldn't be inside them" (*The Transformation* 209). To bear witness to and with contiguously, "to think with others, to think with the traditions of the island, to think beside them and near them but not as part of them" (115). Not multiple essential subjectivities, but several partial becomings, constantly forming and unforming, never stable—"splintered," as Spahr describes the subject in *My Life*. And yet, always already connected to others. "This thing that entered their bloodstream changed them" (39). Such is the process of reading, and also becoming.

Spahr's ideas on identity and poetry also shift in *The Transformation*. Her earlier thinking on *My Life*'s nonessentialist relation to multiple subjectivity shifts into a focus in *The Transformation* on identity as politically constructed, on identity formations being central to organizing among colonized peoples. Language isn't innocent in *The Transformation*, as Spahr demonstrates. Modernist notions of writing as a "foreigner in their own language" (99) and moving between borders of language have radically different connotations and realities in contemporary colonized spaces, especially given that English is now the primary "expansionist" language of western imperialism: "they were finally not all that sure that using fragmentation, quotation, disruption, disjunction, agrammatical syntax, and so on escaped any of the expansionism" (99). This story of "coming to an identity" as a white settler complicit in ongoing colonization, this "catalogue of discomfort," transforms the speaker's perspective on identity, while still avowing primary connections among partial, multiple/hybrid subjects (22).

Spahr has written continuously on the themes of connectivity and co-poesis (co-*making* of meaning) in reading and other human interactions, as simply evidenced in the title of her book of poetry, *This Connection of Everyone with Lungs,* and her book of criticism, *Everybody's Autonomy: Connective Reading and Collective Identity.* Psychoanalyst and artist Bracha L. Ettinger's work has interesting affinities to Spahr's thinking on connectivity, co-poesis and the process of transformation. Not throwing out the Oedipal triad with the bathwater, Ettinger proposes an-other primary formation centered in the common experience we all go through of coming to being in the body of a person we haven't yet faced, a person who is also being changed by the process. Ettinger theorizes spaces of "co-poesis" and "differentiation in co-emergence" that occur in later-term pregnancy to think through and *work through* (in the Freudian sense) the threads of connection that she deems primary to human existence, beside and against notions of lack, castration and separateness that dominate Oedipal modes of thinking. Ettinger attempts not to essentialize pregnancy, but misses the fact that trans people who don't identify as women can still birth babies and adopted children may not have a connection to the person who gave birth to them. She employs neologisms such as "transjective," "severality" and "wit(h)nessing" to develop notions of subject formation that insist that we are always already connected to one another, partly through our common experience of connection in the womb. Within what she calls the "matrixial borderspace," several partial identities (what she calls *I's* and *non-I's,* channelling Lacan) interweave, forming and unforming, consciously and unconsciously; never fixed, yet always straining towards the possibility of threshold. As Judith Butler notes, "The matrixial is what we guard against when we shore up the claims of identity, when we presume that to recognize each other is to know, to name, to distinguish according to the logic of identity" (Butler, "Bracha's" x—xi).

In Ettinger's idea of "severality," she again takes pains not to essentialize this notion as multiple fixed identities. Similarly, Spahr focuses her analysis of *My Life* as enacting a space beyond essentialist notions of multiple identity, presenting a "shardlike autobiographical subject" (146) that the reader is actively involved in co-forming. Perhaps this decentered subject is also the subject of the poet's novel, a forever refracted "they" witnessing themselves telling/reading a barely truthful, non-Fichtean story, but a story nonetheless, one that travails the expansive canvas of novelistic space as it enacts its working-through in relation:

They agreed to let the story they told about themselves as individuals be interrupted by others. They agreed to let their speech be filled with signs of each other and their enthrallment and their undoing. They agreed to falter over pronouns. They agreed to let them undo their speech and language. They pressed themselves upon them and impinged upon them and were impinged upon in ways that were not in their control. (206)

The echoes of Butler's extensions of Hegel and Levinas are strong here, how subjectivity is always already constituted in relation and interrupted by relation, how "[l]oss makes a tenuous 'we' of us all," how I and you and we and they are impinged upon and undone and dispossessed of our self-identity by the other—and others (*Precarious Life* 20). Just as Spahr deems *My Life* "a process-centered work that calls attention to the method by which the autobiographical subject is constructed by both author and reader" (147), so does Spahr call attention to the construction of the subject in much of her poetic work, not just the "they" in *The Transformation* but also her interrogation of the indeterminate "we" in *Fuck You-Aloha-I Love You* and the doubled apostrophic "yous" in *This Connection of Everyone with Lungs*. In all cases, the reader must confront and question their own relation to the construction of subjectivity in the process of reading. "What they meant was that they were other than completely autonomous but that they were not one thing with no edges, with no boundary lines" (*The Transformation* 207).

As an artist, Ettinger works in series (the paintings "come in crowds"), photocopying archival photos and other images from the Nazi holocaust and other traumatic events, but stopping the photocopier partway through the machinic process, so that the photocopic dust forms aleatory blurred interpretations of the image, "between ash and pastel." She repeats this process a number of times with the same image, then paints from "scan[ning]" the photocopied images, in series that "fade out what the image should have become." The viewer is also meant to scan across the images, seeing mutual implications within and across the series, feeling the intensities of partial objects, accumulated meanings in and out of time, just as the interrupted copy "stop[s] time."[9] This process relates to my experience of reading *The Transformation* (and *My Life,* and Gertrude Stein's work, for that matter). Repeating phrases draw out emotion and subtle difference, while also drawing attention to time's slips. As Hejinian notes in her classic essay, "Rejection of Closure" (and Spahr also highlights in her essay on Hejinian), "meaning is set in motion, emended and extended, and the rewriting that repetition becomes postpones completion of the thought indefinitely"

(44). Yet, do I read every instance that Spahr repeats, mechanically, "avant-garde techniques of fragmentation, quotation, disruption, disjunction, agrammatical syntax, and so on," or do I register the line as specific and cumulative as I scan by? This goes back to Butler's resignifying that Spahr draws on to theorize the postmodern autobiography, how the subject and agency are deconstructed, yet we can "continue to use them, repeat them, to repeat them subversively, and to displace them from the contexts in which they have been deployed as instruments of oppressive power" (Butler, "Contingent" 14).

This process of resignifying can also apply to how affect is generated and processed in the viewer or reader. According to theorist Brian Massumi, "Ettinger considers it the goal of her art to 'make affect transmissible.' Her series are affective carriers of traumatic renewal" (213). In front of Ettinger's "Eurydice" series of paintings, the viewer "looks back" down the lens of the unnamed Nazi photographer who captured naked Jewish women and children standing in line to be shot on October 14, 1942, at Mizocz, Rovno, Ukraine. We are implicated "in a gaze that cannot but kill again" (Pollock, "Aesthetic" 857). Similarly, in the face of *The Transformation*, the North American reader must confront the "difficult feelings" (220) coextensive with their always-implicated role in the ongoing colonization on Turtle Island. One could say that Spahr's they turns the phallic gaze into a "matrixial" gaze that, rather than possess and cut us off from the witnessing event, "fragilizes" our relation to the trauma of history, so that the traces of connection thread into a constantly changing web, "metramorphose," to use another Ettinger neologism, into the monstrous heart bloated by severality at the end of *The Transformation*. We are complicit in atrocities done "in our name" every day, but this doesn't cut us off from our obligations; instead, our being impinged upon by others, the they, opens us to our response-ability, transjectively, as part of they. Ettinger writes, "We are carrying, at the beginning of the twenty-first century, enormous traumatic weight, and aesthetic wit(h)nessing in art brings it to culture's surface. Certain contemporary art practices bring to light matrixial alliances by confronting the limits of trauma's shareability and the *jouissance* of the Other. ...[A]esthetics converges with ethics even beyond the artist's intentions or conscious control" (*Matrixial Borderspace* 147).

It could be that what makes *The Transformation* a poet's novel is its constant pressure on the reader to be involved in the content in a non-possessive manner. To be fragilized by the content and transformed by the affects it generates, "tak[ing] the accusative they into their bodies and let[ting] it change them," rather than simply consume or be consumed (*The Transfor-*

mation, 47-48). Transformed through thinking with, wit(h)nessing, into a different consciousness. As Spahr notes, "It didn't end up as an autobiography because it isn't a life story really, but it might be a [...] somewhat true somewhat false [...] memoir of an attempt to come to a political consciousness" (Rosenthal, 313). A fictional autobiography, perhaps.

In an article on Ettinger's process "from grain to screen to series," Massumi writes:

> The process starts with a machinic technique for the grain to self-express in collaboration with the artist's hand. It ends with an expanded indistinction between activity and passivity, subject and object, intensively distributed across a plurality of elements, levels, and matters. This makes it impossible to assign a self-enclosed subject of the process that would be separate from it. There is no-one behind the process, no One, only "severality," self-organizing between material-abstract surfaces. (210)

Noone bears witness as a "wit(h)ness with-out event," in Ettinger's inversion of Shoshana Felman and Dori Laub's famous iteration of the Shoah as an "event without a witness."[10] Via the matrixial gaze, the viewer/reader/witness scans the iterations of the degraded, ghosted image and constructs meaning that is always just out of reach. Working through. Traumatic repetition sieved through the grain. Like the process of reading a poet's novel. "They agreed to no longer see relationship as a feedback loop of face-to-face desire. Instead they had to deal with a sort of shimmering, a fracturing of all their looks and glances. And it was because of this third Sapphic point that they implicated themselves in they" (*The Transformation* 206). We enter the image of women and children in line for the open pit through the grained-out but still palpable gaze of the perpetrator. Our complicity, our folded togetherness, accompanies us. "They are three points of transformation on a circuit of possible relationship, electrified by desire so that they touch not touching" (Carson 16).

NOTES

1. Expanded thoughts on this topic are in my book *No One's Witness: A Monstrous Poetics* (Duke University Press, 2021).

2. Publisher's note to *The Transformation*, 226.

3. Spahr points to Carson's *Eros the Bittersweet* in her Afterword to *The Transformation*, 223.

4. Spahr's Afterword to *The Transformation* attributes the term "mediocre colonizer" to Aimé Césaire, but it is actually discussed in Memmi's *The Col-*

onizer and the Colonized.

5. *Janey's Arcadia* was published by Coach House Books in 2014. The book on Israel-Palestine is *Neighbour Procedure.*

6. "Resignifyng Autobiography: Lyn Hejinian's My Life."

7. I am indebted to Heather Milne's critical work on Spahr for the reference to Braidotti. See "Dearly Beloveds."

8. I discuss the poetics of witness and "mad affects" in the essay "Noone Bears Witness."

9. The parts in quotes come from an interview between Ettinger and Brian Massumi. See Massumi in Works Cited.

10. Ettinger discusses "wit(h)nesses with-out events" vis-à-vis Felman and Laub in her essay "Wit(h)nessing Trauma...," 109.

WORKS CITED

Benjamin, Jessica. "Two-Way Streets: Recognition of Difference and the Intersubjective Third." *differences,* Vol. 17, No. 1 (2006): 116-146. Print.

Braidotti, Rosi. *Transpositions: On Nomadic Ethics.* London: Polity, 2006. Print.

Butler, Judith. "Bracha's Eurydice." Foreword to *The Matrixial Borderspace.* Ed. Brian Massumi. Minneapolis: U Minnesota P, 2006. vii—xii. Print.

——. "Contingent Foundations: Feminism and the Question of 'Postmodernism.'" *Feminists Theorize the Political.* New York: Routledge, 1992. 3-21. Print.

——. *Precarious Life: The Powers of Mourning and Violence.* London: Verso, 2004. Print.

Carson, Anne. *Eros the Bittersweet.* Champaign: Dalkey Archive, 1998. Print.

Celan, Paul. "Ashglory." *Breathturn.* Trans. Pierre Joris. Los Angeles: Green Integer, 2006. 190-193. Print.

Cha, Theresa Hak Kyung Cha. *DICTEE.* Berkeley: U California Press, 2001. Print.

Ettinger, Bracha L. *The Matrixial Borderspace.* Ed. Brian Massumi. Minneapolis: U Minnesota P, 2006. Print.

——. "Wit(h)nessing Trauma and the Matrixial Gaze: From Phantasm to Trauma, from Phallic Structure to Matrixial Sphere" *parallax,* Vol. 7, No. 4 (2001): 89–114. Print.

Felman, Shoshana and Dori Laub. *Testimony: Crises of Witnessing in Literature, Psychoanalysis, and History.* London and New York: Routledge, 1992. Print.

Forché, Carolyn, ed. *Against Forgetting: Twentieth-Century Poetry of Witness*. New York and London: Norton, 1993. Print.

Glissant, Edouard. *Poetics of Relation*. Trans. Betsy Wing. Ann Arbor: U Michigan P, 1997. Print.

Hejinian, Lyn. *My Life*. Los Angeles: Green Integer, 2002.

——. "The Rejection of Closure." *The Language of Inquiry*. Berkeley: U California P, 2000. 40–58. Print.

Massumi, Brian. "Painting: The Voice of the Grain." Afterword to Ettinger, *The Matrixial Borderspace*. 201–214. Print.

Memmi, Albert. *The Colonizer and the Colonized*. Trans. Howard Greenfeld. Boston: Beacon Press, 1965.

Milne, Heather. "Dearly Beloveds: The Politics of Intimacy in Juliana Spahr's *This Connection of Everyone with Lungs*." *Mosaic: A Journal for the Interdisciplinary Study of Literature*, Vol. 47, No. 2 (June 2014): 203–218. Print.

Pollock, Griselda. "Aesthetic Wit(h)nessing in the Era of Trauma." *EurAmerica*, Vol. 40, No. 4 (December 2010): 1–40. Print.

——. "Feminity: Aporia or Sexual Difference?" Introduction to Ettinger, *The Matrixial Borderspace*. 201–214. Print.

Rosenthal, Sarah, ed. "Juliana Spahr: How Does The Work Get Used." *A Community Writing Itself: Conversations with Vanguard Writers of the Bay Area*. Champaign: Dalkey Archive, 2010. 298–320. Print.

Spahr, Juliana. *Everybody's Autonomy: Connective Reading and Collective Identity*. Tuscaloosa: U Alabama P, 2001. Print.

——. *Fuck You-Aloha-I Love You*. Middletown: Wesleyan UP, 2001. Print.

——. "Resignifying Autobiography: Lyn Hejinian's *My Life*." *American Literature*, Vol. 68, No. 1 (March, 1996). 139–159. Print.

——. *The Transformation*. Berkeley: Atelos, 2007. Print.

——. *This Connection of Everyone with Lungs*. Berkeley: U California P, 2005. Print.

——. *Well Then There Now*. Boston: Black Sparrow Books, 2011. Print.

Zolf, Falk. *On Foreign Soil: An Autobiographical Novel by Falk Zolf*, trans. Martin Green. Winnipeg: Self-published, 2001. Print.

Zolf, Larry. *The Dialectical Dancer: A Simple Tale*. Toronto: Exile Editions, 2010. Print.

——. *Scorpions for Sale: A Fictional Biography*. Toronto: Stoddart, 1989. Print.

Zolf, Rachel. *Janey's Arcadia*. Toronto: Coach House, 2014. Print.

——. *Neighbour Procedure*. Toronto: Coach House, 2010. Print.

——. "Noone Bears Witness." *Canadian Literature* 210/211 (Autumn/ Winter 2011), 260—264. Print. Reprinted in *Jacket2* (December, 2012).

ACKNOWLEDGEMENTS

The editor would like to thank all of the contributors, authors of texts discussed, publishers, and editors without whose terrific work, patience, and support this book would not be possible. Thank you to my contemporaries, my poet companions engaged in the long and ongoing conversation, which makes this work possible. Above and beyond everyone included in this volume, whose work is invaluable, thank you for engaging in dialogue, agreeing to interviews, reading drafts of the introduction, supporting my work along the way and so much more: Julia Bloch, Lee Ann Brown, Julie Carr, Joe Donahue, Pattie McCarthy, Dan Beachy-Quick, Al Filreis, Patricio Ferrari, Norman Fischer, Lyn Hejinian, Jeanne Heuving, Bhanu Kapil, Aaron Kunin, Lisa Jarnot, Erín Moure, Alice Notley, Jena Osman, Julie Patton, Sarah Riggs, Lisa Robertson, Ron Silliman, Sasha Steensen, Molly Sutten-Kiefer, Rosmarie Waldrop & Elizabeth Willis. Tremendous thanks for your ongoing presence—you are greatly missed: Robert Creeley, Stacy Doris, Kevin Killian, Leslie Scalapino, and C.D. Wright. Thank you to Jessica Lowenthal for inviting me to write a commentary for *Jacket2* when I was first considering this project. Thank you to Stephen Motika for inviting me to write a talk on the Poet's Novel to present at Poets House, and for his belief and collaboration on the project. Thank you to Noah Saterstrom, for his illustrations to my talk and ongoing collaboration. Thank you to Lindsey Boldt at Nightboat, for all of your work on the project. Thank you to Kit Schluter for your patience and close attention during the final stages of production.

PERMISSIONS

ABOUT THE CONTRIBUTORS

Kazim Ali's most recent books are a volume of poetry, *The Voice of Shei-la Chandra*, and a nonfiction book, *Northern Light: Power, Land, and the Memory of Water*. He teaches in the Department of Literature at the University of California, San Diego.

Dan Beachy-Quick is a poet, essayist, and translator. He teaches at Colorado State University where he is a University Distinguished Teaching Scholar.

Edmund Berrigan is the author of *Disarming Matter, Glad Stone Children,* and *Can It!* He edited *Selected Poems of Steve Carey* (2009), and co-edited with Anselm Berrigan and Alice Notley *The Collected Poems of Ted Berrigan* (2005) and *Selected Poems of Ted Berrigan* (2010).

Brian Blanchfield's two most recent books, *Proxies: Essays Near Knowing* and *A Several World*, received a 2016 Whiting Award in Nonfiction and the Academy of American Poets' 2014 James Laughlin Award. He lives in Moscow, Idaho, where he teaches literary nonfiction and poetry at the University of Idaho.

Julia Bloch's most recent book of poetry is *The Sacramento of Desire*. She is co-editor of *Jacket2*; director of creative writing at the University of Pennsylvania; and a Pew Fellow. Her current critical book project investigates genre, gender, and lyric in the postwar long poem.

Anne Boyer is the author of *Garments Against Women*. She lives in Kansas City.

Traci Brimhall is the author of four collections of poetry: *Come the Slumber-less to the Land of Nod, Saudade, Our Lady of the Ruins,* and *Rookery*. She teaches at Kansas State University and lives in Manhattan, KS.

Vincent Broqua is a writer, translator and Professor of North American arts and literature (University Paris 8). Among his books: *A partir de rien* (2013), *même=same* (2014), *Récupérer* (2015). He is the co-founder of Double Change and *Quaderna*. Among other translated poets: Antin, Bergvall, Berkson, Bernstein, Field, Notley, Waldrop, Waldman.

Brandon Brown is the author of five books of poetry. He is a regular contributor to *Art in America,* and a co-editor at *Krupskaya.* His newest full-length book is *The Four Seasons (Wonder,* 2018.) He lives in El Cerrito, California.

Lee Ann Brown is the author of five books of poetry, edits *Tender Buttons Press* and teaches at St. John's University. She has held fellowships from NYFA, the Fund for Poetry, the Howard Foundation and was Judith E. Wilson Poetry Fellow at Cambridge University.

Angela Carr's poetry titles include *Ropewalk, The Rose Concordance, Here in There* and *Without Ceremony.* Her most recent book-length translation is *Ardour* by Nicole Brossard. Originally from Montreal, she lives in New York City and teaches poetry and poetics at The New School.

Julie Carr's most recent books are *Real Life: An Installation, Objects from a Borrowed Confession,* and *Someone Shot My Book.* She teaches at the University of Colorado in Boulder and lives in Denver where with Tim Roberts she runs Counterpath.

Norma Cole's most recent book of poetry is *Fate News.* Other books include *Win These Posters, Where Shadows Will, Actualities* (collaboration with painter Marina Adams) and *TO BE AT MUSIC.* Her translations from French include Danielle Collobert's *It Then* and Jean Daive's *White Decimal.* Cole lives in the sanctuary city of San Francisco.

Brent Cunningham is the author of two poetry books, *Bird & Forest* (2005) and *Journey to the Sun* (2012), as well as a chapbook of fake Rimbaud translations titled *The Sad Songs of Hell* (2017). He has been working on a novel for a disconcertingly long time.

Mónica de la Torre is the author of six books of poetry, including *Repetition Nineteen.* She translates poetry, writes about art, and is a contributing editor to BOMB Magazine. She teaches at Brooklyn College.

Rachel Blau DuPlessis, poet, critic, collagist is the author of the multi-volume long poem *Drafts,* from Salt Publishing and Wesleyan. Recent books are *Graphic Novella* (2015), *Days and Works* (2017), *Around the Day in 80 Worlds* (2018), *NUMBERS* (2018), and numerous critical essays on gender, poetry, and poetics.

Marcella Durand's latest books include *The Prospect* (2019), *Rays of the Shadow* (2017) and *Le Jardin de M. (The Garden of M.)*, with translations by Olivier Brossard. Her translation of Michèle Métail's poem, *Earth's Horizons/Les Horizons du sol*, was published by *Black Square Editions* in 2019.

Patrick Durgin is the author of *PQRS: A Poets Theater Script* and, with Jen Hofer, *The Route*. His artist's books include *Singles, Daughter*, and *Zenith*. He edited *Hannah Weiner's Open House* and the *Ordinance* series, and he teaches at the School of the Art Institute of Chicago.

Norman Fischer is a poet, essayist, and Zen Buddhist priest. Recent books include *Untitled Series: Life As It Is* (2018), *On A Train At Night* (2018), *any would be if* (2016), poetry; and *Experience: Thinking, Writing, Language and Religion* (2015), essays.

C.S. Giscombe teaches English at the University of California, Berkeley. His recognitions include the 2010 Stephen Henderson Award, an American Book Award, and the Carl Sandburg Prize. His recent books include *Prairie Style*, *Ohio Railroads*, and *Border Towns*.

Judith Goldman is most recently author of *agon*. She teaches in and directs the Poetics Program at SUNY, Buffalo and is Poetry Features Editor for *Postmodern Culture*.

Rob Halpern lives between San Francisco and Ypsilanti, Michigan, where he teaches at Eastern Michigan University and Huron Valley Women's Prison. His books include *Weak Link, Common Place,* and *Music for Porn*. Recent essays appear in *Communism and Poetry* and *Ecopoetics: Essays in the Field*.

Carla Harryman is a poet, prose writer, essayist, and performance writer. Her books include *Adorno's Noise (2008), Sue in Berlin(2018)*, and the forthcoming collection of performance writing *A Voice to Perform,* which features an adaptation for opera of her poet's novel, *Gardener of Stars*.

Laura Hinton's scholarly books include *The Perverse Gaze of Sympathy: Sadomasochistic Sentiments from* Clarissa *to* Rescue 911 and her poetry books include *Sisyphus My Love (To Record a Dream in a Bathtub)*. She is a Professor of English at the City College of New York (CUNY).

Jeanne Heuving is the author of *The Transmutation of Love and Avant-Garde Poetics* and co-editor of *Inciting Poetics: Thinking and Writing Poetry*. Her cross genre book *Incapacity* won a Small Press Traffic Book of the Year Award. She was the founding director of the MFA in Creative Writing & Poetics at the University of Washington Bothell.

Daniel Katz is Professor of English and Comparative Literary Studies at the University of Warwick, and the author of many articles and three books on 20th and 21st century literature, including *The Poetry of Jack Spicer* (2013). He is currently editing an edition of Jack Spicer's *Uncollected Poetry and Plays*, which will be published by *Wesleyan UP* in 2021.

John Keene's most recent short fiction collection *Counternarratives* (2015) received a range of honors, including a 2018 Windham-Campbell Prize. The recipient of a 2018 MacArthur Foundation Fellowship and the translator of Brazilian author Hilda Hilst's novel *Letters from a Seducer* (Nightboat Books), he teaches at Rutgers University-Newark.

Karla Kelsey is author of four books of poetry, most recently *Blood Feather*, and *Of Sphere*, a book of experimental essays. With Aaron McCollough she co-publishes *SplitLevel Texts*, a press specializing in hybrid genre projects.

Mark Kline is an American writer and a literary translator of works ranging from children's books to avant-garde poetry, from crime novels to essays on art and philosophy. He lives with his wife in Copenhagen, Denmark.

Aaron Kunin is the author of *Cold Genius* and six other books of poetry and prose. He teaches at Pomona College in California.

Abigail Lang is associate professor at Université de Paris, a translator of American poetry into French, and a member of Double Change. She is the author of *La conversation transatlantique* (2021) and of two books written in collaboration with Thalia Field.

Sonnet L'Abbé, Ph.D. is the author of *A Strange Relief, Killarnoe,* and *Anima Canadensis* and was the 2014 guest editor of *Best Canadian Poetry*. In their most recent collection, *Sonnet's Shakespeare* (2018), L'Abbé "writes over" all 154 of Shakespeare's sonnets. L'Abbé is a professor at Vancouver Island University.

Kimberly Lyons is the author of books of poetry including *Calcinatio, Approximately Near,* and *Capella.* Essays by her may be found at the *Jacket2, Talisman,* and *Dispatches From the Poetry Wars* websites and in *Aufgabe* Magazine. She publishes *Lunar Chandelier Press.*

W. Jason Miller is a Professor of American Literature in the English Department at NC State University. He is author of *Langston Hughes: Critical Lives* (2020), *Origins of the Dream: Hughes's Poetry and King's Rhetoric* (2015) and *Langston Hughes and American Lynching Culture* (2011).

Mette Moestrup is a Danish poet, literary critic, and feminist, born in 1969. Her latest book *To the Most Beautiful. 117 poems* was published in 2019, and her award-winning poetry is translated into German, Swedish, and English (*kingsize,* subpress). She also works collectively and cross-aesthetics. She lives in Copenhagen.

Laura Moriarty's most recent book is *Personal Volcano* (2019). Other recent books are *Verne & Lemurian Objects* (2017), *The Fugitive Notebook* (2014), *Who That Divines* (2014), *A Tonalist* (2010), *A Semblance: Selected and New Poems* (1975-2007), and the novel *Ultravioleta* (2006). She was Deputy Director of Small Press Distribution for two decades and is now on the SPD board. She lives in Richmond, California.

Laura Mullen is the author of eight books: *Complicated Grief* is the most recent; recognitions for her poetry include a National Endowment for the Arts Fellowship and a Rona Jaffe Award. She collaborates with musicians and artists and she is the translator of Véronique Pittolo's *HERO.*

Denise Newman's fourth poetry collection is *Future People.* She is the translator of *Azorno* and *The Painted Room,* both by the late Danish poet, Inger Christensen, and *Baboon* by Naja Marie Aidt, which won the PEN Translation Award. She has received a Creative Work Fund grant and an NEA Fellowship.

A.L. Nielsen's works of poetry include *Heat Strings, Evacuation Routes, VEXT, Mixage, Mantic Semantic, A Brand New Beggar* and *Tray.* His works of scholarship include *Reading Race, Writing between the Lines, Black Chant, C.L.R. James: An Introduction* and *Integral Music.* He is the Kelly Professor at Penn State University.

Geoffrey G. O'Brien's latest book is *Experience in Groups* (Wave). O'Brien is a Professor of English at UC Berkeley and teaches for the Prison University Project at San Quentin State Prison.

Jena Osman's books of poems include *Motion Studies, Corporate Relations, Public Figures, The Network, An Essay in Asterisks,* and *The Character.* She co-founded and co-edited the literary magazine *Chain* with Juliana Spahr from 1994-2005. She is a Professor of English at Temple University in Philadelphia.

Julie Ezelle Patton considers herself a poet *of* paper as a form of connecting infinite thought planes & inner pulpiness. The recent *Best American Experimental Writing* (2016) & *What I Say: Innovative Poetry by Black Writers in America* (*University of Alabama Press*) show her at her inky best.

Elizabeth Robinson has been the recipient of grants from the Foundation for Contemporary Arts and the Fund for Poetry, a winner of the National Poetry Series (for *Pure Descent)* and the Fence Modern Poets Prize (for *Apprehend*). Robinson is a co-editor of the critical anthology *Quo Anima.*

Jennifer Scappettone is the author of *The Republic of Exit 43: Outtakes & Scores from an Archaeology and Pop-Up Opera of the Corporate Dump, Locomotrix: Selected Poetry and Prose of Amelia Rosselli, From Dame Quickly,* and *Killing the Moonlight: Modernism in Venice.* She is Associate Professor at the University of Chicago.

Susan Scarlata lived among the skyscrapers of Hong Kong and now lives in the mountains in Jackson, Wyoming. Scarlata's book is *It Might Turn Out We Are Real,* and her recent work is forthcoming in the anthology *Certain Stars Shoot Madly.* Scarlata is the Editor of *Lost Roads Press.*

Brandon Shimoda's books include *The Grave on the Wall, The Desert,* and *Evening Oracle,* which received the William Carlos Williams Award from the Poetry Society of America. He co-edited, with Thom Donovan, *To look at the sea is to become what one is: An Etel Adnan Reader.* He lives in the desert.

Cedar Sigo was raised on the Suquamish Reservation in the Pacific Northwest and studied at The Jack Kerouac School of Disembodied Poetics at the Naropa Institute. He is the editor of *There You Are: Interviews, Journals, and*

Ephemera, on Joanne Kyger, and author of eight books and pamphlets of poetry, including, *Royals, Language Arts, Stranger in Town, Expensive Magic* and two editions of *Selected Writings*.

Sasha Steensen is the author of four books of poems: *House of Deer, The Method, A Magic Book,* and *Gatherest*. She teaches Creative Writing and Literature at Colorado State University, where she also serves as a poetry editor for *Colorado Review*.

Donna Stonecipher is the author of five books of poetry, most recently *Transaction Histories* (2018), and one book of criticism, *Prose Poetry and the City* (2018). She lives in Berlin.

Brian Teare is the author of six critically acclaimed books, most recently *The Empty Form Goes All the Way to Heaven* and *Doomstead Days*. An Associate Professor at the University of Virginia, he lives in Charlottesville, where he makes books by hand for his micropress, Albion Books.

Sarah Vap is the author of seven books of poetry, poetics, and creative non-fiction, including her most recent *Winter: Effulgences and Devotions*. She is faculty in the MFA program in Poetry and Poetry in Translation at Drew University.

Danielle Vogel is a long-form poet, lyric essayist, and interdisciplinary artist working at the intersections of poetry, ecology, somatics and ceremony. She is the author of *Edges & Fray, The Way a Line Hallucinates Its Own Linearity,* and *Between Grammars*. Vogel teaches at Wesleyan University, where she leads workshops in poetry, creative nonfiction, and composing across the arts.

Joshua Marie Wilkinson lives in Seattle, where he's at work on his first novel.

Tyrone Williams is the author of six books of poetry and, with Jeanne Heuving, the co-editor of *Inciting Poetics* (2010). He teaches literature and literary theory at Xavier University in Cincinnati Ohio.

C.D. Wright published over a dozen books, including *Shall Cross* and *One With Others*. She was recipient of numerous awards including a MacArthur Fellowship, a Lannan Literary Award, a Robert Creeley Award.

Lynn Xu is the author of *Debts & Lessons*, which was a finalist for the L. A. Times Book Prize. She lives with her husband and daughter in Marfa, Texas.

Rachel Zolf has published five books of poetry, with a collection of selected poetry, *Social Poesis*, released in 2019. *No One's Witness: A Monstrous Poetics*, is forthcoming from Duke University Press in 2021. Zolf lives in Philadelphia and teaches writing and art at the University of Pennsylvania.

ABOUT THE EDITOR

Laynie Browne is a poet, prose writer, teacher and editor. She is author of fourteen collections of poems and four books of fiction. Recent publications include: a book of poems, *In Garments Worn by Lindens*, a novel, *Periodic Companions*, and a book of short fiction, *The Book of Moments*. Her work has appeared in journals such as *Conjunctions*, *A Public Space*, *New American Writing*, *The Brooklyn Rail*, and in anthologies including: *The Ecopoetry Anthology*, *The Reality Street Book of Sonnets*, and *Postmodern American Poetry: A Norton Anthology*. Her poetry has been translated into French, Spanish, Chinese and Catalan. She co-edited the anthology *I'll Drown My Book: Conceptual Writing by Women*. Honors and awards include a Pew Fellowship, the National Poetry Series Award for her collection *The Scented Fox*, and the Contemporary Poetry Series Award for her collection *Drawing of a Swan Before Memory*. She teaches at University of Pennsylvania and at Swarthmore College.

NIGHTBOAT BOOKS

Nightboat Books, a nonprofit organization, seeks to develop audiences for writers whose work resists convention and transcends boundaries. We publish books rich with poignancy, intelligence, and risk. Please visit Nightboat.org to learn about our titles and how you can support our future publications.

The following individuals have supported the publication of this book. We thank them for their generosity and commitment to the mission of Nightboat Books:

Kazim Ali
Anonymous
Jean C. Ballantyne
Photios Giovanis
Amanda Greenberger
Elizabeth Motika
Benjamin Taylor
Peter Waldor
Jerrie Whitfield & Richard Motika

In addition, this book has been made possible, in part, by a grants from the New York State Council on the Arts Literature Program.

NEW YORK
STATE OF
OPPORTUNITY. | Council on
the Arts